Alice R. Gaby
A Grammar of Kuuk Thaayorre

Mouton Grammar Library

Edited by
Georg Bossong
Bernard Comrie
Patience L. Epps
Irina Nikolaeva

Volume 74

Alice R. Gaby

A Grammar of Kuuk Thaayorre

In collaboration with
Kuuk Thaayorre language experts

DE GRUYTER
MOUTON

ISBN 978-3-11-065330-4
ISSN 0933-7636

Library of Congress Cataloging-in-Publication Data
A CIP catalog record for this book has been applied for at the Library of Congress.

Bibliographic information published by the Deutsche Nationalbibliothek
The Deutsche Nationalbibliothek lists this publication in the Deutsche Nationalbibliografie; detailed bibliographic data are available on the Internet at http://dnb.dnb.de.

© 2019 Walter de Gruyter GmbH, Berlin/Boston
This volume is text- and page-identical with the hardback published in 2017.
Typesetting: Frank Benno Junghanns, Berlin
Printing and binding: CPI books GmbH, Leck
♾ Printed on acid-free paper
Printed in Germany

www.degruyter.com

For the Thaayorre people.
May your language, your culture and you
continue to keep one another strong.

Acknowledgements

That this grammar is published under my name reflects the fact that the following analysis of Kuuk Thaayorre grammar is written in my words. However, this should in no way be taken to assert authority over the Kuuk Thaayorre language itself. The language, the examples of its use quoted here, and the knowledge expressed therein must always remain the intellectual property of the Thaayorre people. The language experts I worked with also made a crucial contribution to the analysis, as detailed in the first chapter.

I wish to express my deepest gratitude to all the Kuuk Thaayorre language experts I worked with, who invested vast quantities of their time and energy into teaching me Kuuk Thaayorre language and culture. Many other, unnamed Kuuk Thaayorre speakers also welcomed me into their homes, dance ceremonies, funerals, house openings, fishing expeditions, bushwalks, trips to outstations, movie nights, fireside ruminations and quick chats over cups of tea. These relationships – though too numerous and too personal to detail here – contributed immensely to both my understanding of Kuuk Thaayorre language and culture and my enjoyment of life in Pormpuraaw. This grammar is a much impoverished representation of all that they shared with me.

John Taylor first introduced me to the Pormpuraaw community, and generously shared with me his extensive local knowledge, unpublished materials, and many wonderful meals. Both Allen Hall and Tom Foote have contributed much to this grammar posthumously. I thank them and their families for the linguistic legacy they have left future generations of Kuuk Thaayorre speakers and linguists, including myself.

My fieldwork was funded by the Pormpuraaw Aboriginal Shire Council, the Australian Research Council, the University of Melbourne, the Max Planck Institute for Psycholinguistics, the University of California (Berkeley), the Endangered Languages Documentation Programme, and the Department of Communications, Information Technology and the Arts (DCITA). The Pormpuraaw State School, Pormpuraaw Aboriginal Shire Council, Pormpur Paanth and BRACS provided work spaces and other practical support.

The first version of this grammar was written as a doctoral thesis. I feel so fortunate to have benefitted from the supervision of Nick Evans and Rachel Nordlinger (at the University of Melbourne), as well as Nick Enfield and Steve Levinson (at the Max Planck Institute for Psycholinguistics, Nijmegen), each of whom played a formative role in my understanding of both the language and how it should best be described. This grammar could not hope for more brilliant academic grandparents. Many further improvements and refinements were made on the basis of feedback and advice from, in alphabetical order: Sasha Aikhenvald, Jeanie Bell, Sarah Cutfield, Bob Dixon, Rosanne Gaby, Dan Hirst, Sharon Inkelas, Debbie Loakes, Anna Margetts, Felicity Meakins, Lev Michael, Elizabeth Norman, Alan Ray, Erich Round, Ruth Singer, Mary Stevens, Hywel Stoakes, Peter Sutton, and Jean-Christophe Verstraete. Barry Alpher and Barry Blake, in particular, gave me enormously valuable feedback on every aspect of the original manuscript. I am also grateful to all my colleagues at the UC Berkeley and Monash University for their moral support, inspiration and discussions during the long gestation of this book. In its final stages, Bernard Comrie's thorough reading of this manuscript produced numerous helpful suggestions and eradicated just as many errors and infelicities. I am so grateful to have had such an assiduous and wise editor. At Mouton De Gruyter, Julie Miess and Birgit Sievert provided editorial assistance and advice. I also thank Frank Benno Junghanns for typesetting the manuscript and compiling the index.

I, let alone this book, would not be possible without the enormous investment of love, time and attention of Rosanne Gaby, the wisest, kindest and silliest person I know. She, as well as Ralph and June Mottram, Andrew Gaby, Phoebe Palmieri, Santo Palmieri, Kate Mottram and Brian Greer, has nurtured both me and my love of language(s) since the very beginning. I hope to have many opportunities to demonstrate my gratitude and love over the decades to come.

My love for Dan Hirst likewise predates my love of linguistics and Kuuk Thaayorre. He may not have typed this manuscript, but it would not have been written without his unwavering support for me and my research. His wholehearted embrace of life in Pormpuraaw provided me with countless insights into the language and culture, as well as fish and fodder for example sentences. Most wonderful of all are our recent collaborations, Leonard Charlie and Alfreda Jane, whose adventures in grammar are only just beginning.

Contents

Acknowledgements —— vii
Glosses and abbreviations —— xix

1	Introduction —— 1	
1.1	Linguistic profile of Kuuk Thaayorre —— 1	
1.1.1	Kuuk Thaayorre in typological context —— 1	
1.1.2	Kuuk Thaayorre varieties and relatives —— 3	
1.1.2.1	Names and dialects —— 3	
1.1.2.2	Genetic relationships —— 4	
1.1.3	Previous work —— 5	
1.2	Physical environment —— 6	
1.2.1	Local topography —— 6	
1.2.2	Climate —— 7	
1.3	Kuuk Thaayorre in social and historical context —— 8	
1.3.1	History of contact with Europeans —— 8	
1.3.2	Linguistic ecology —— 10	
1.3.2.1	Hand signs —— 11	
1.3.2.2	Respect register —— 12	
1.3.2.3	Multilingualism and inter-group relationships —— 13	
1.3.3	Kinship and speech etiquette —— 15	
1.3.3.1	Kinship and kin terms —— 16	
1.3.3.2	Speech etiquette —— 18	
1.4	This grammar —— 19	
1.4.1	Origin —— 19	
1.4.2	Theoretical background —— 21	
1.4.3	Sources and methodology —— 23	
1.4.3.1	Hall and colleagues —— 24	
1.4.3.2	Conversation —— 25	
1.4.3.3	Narrative —— 25	
1.4.3.4	Elicited data —— 26	
1.4.3.5	Re-speakings —— 26	
1.4.3.6	On-record and off-record communicative contexts —— 27	
1.4.4	Language experts and collaborators —— 28	
1.4.5	Example sentences —— 31	
1.4.6	Overview of topics —— 33	
2	Phonology —— 37	
2.1	Phonemic inventory —— 37	
2.1.1	Consonant inventory —— 37	
2.1.2	Vowel inventory —— 38	

2.2	Phonological processes —— 39	
2.2.1	Obstruent allophones —— 40	
2.2.1.1	Bilabial obstruent /p/ —— 40	
2.2.1.2	Velar obstruent /k/ —— 40	
2.2.1.3	Lamino-dental /t̪/ —— 41	
2.2.1.4	Apico-alveolar /t/ —— 41	
2.2.1.5	Lamino-palatal /c/ —— 42	
2.2.1.6	Glottal stop /ʔ/ —— 42	
2.2.2	Nasal allophones —— 43	
2.2.3	Rhotic allophones —— 44	
2.2.4	Lateral allophones —— 44	
2.2.5	Semivowels —— 44	
2.2.6	Vowel allophones —— 44	
2.2.7	Morphophonological processes —— 45	
2.2.7.1	Lenition at affix boundaries —— 46	
2.2.7.2	Lenition at clitic boundaries —— 46	
2.2.7.3	Lenition at compound boundaries —— 46	
2.3	Minimal pairs —— 46	
2.4	Phonotactics —— 51	
2.4.1	Epenthetic, reduced or absent vowels —— 51	
2.4.2	Syllable types —— 53	
2.4.2.1	Syllabification —— 53	
2.4.2.2	Permissible monosyllables —— 55	
2.4.2.3	Syllable types in polysyllabic words —— 56	
2.4.3	Phonotactic constraints within the syllable —— 58	
2.4.3.1	Onset —— 58	
2.4.3.2	Nucleus —— 59	
2.4.3.3	Coda —— 59	
2.5	The word —— 62	
2.5.1	Phonotactic constraints at the word level —— 62	
2.5.2	Fluid speech and contractions —— 64	
2.5.3	Phonetic effects of syllable structure —— 64	
2.6	Reduplication —— 65	
2.6.1	Reduplication by vowel lengthening —— 65	
2.6.2	Rhyme reduplication —— 66	
2.6.3	Onset-nucleus reduplication —— 67	
2.6.4	First syllable reduplication —— 68	
2.7	Stress —— 68	
2.8	Orthographic conventions —— 70	
2.8.1	History of Kuuk Thaayorre practical orthographies —— 70	
2.8.2	Pormpuraaw Orthography and conventions —— 71	

3	**Word classes** —— 73
3.1	Nominals —— 73
3.1.1	Nomina —— 75
3.1.1.1	Generics —— 75
3.1.1.2	Specifics —— 77
3.1.1.2.1	Referential kin terms —— 78
3.1.1.2.2	Body part terms —— 78
3.1.1.2.3	Proper nouns —— 79
3.1.1.3	Adjectives —— 79
3.1.1.4	Quantifiers —— 79
3.1.2	Pronouns —— 80
3.1.2.1	(Free) personal pronouns —— 80
3.1.2.2	Enclitic pronouns —— 81
3.1.2.3	Reflexive pronouns —— 81
3.1.2.4	Reciprocal subject marker, -*nharr* —— 82
3.1.2.5	Emphatic pronouns —— 83
3.1.2.6	Inclusory pronouns —— 83
3.1.2.7	Ignorative pronouns —— 84
3.1.3	Demonstratives —— 86
3.1.3.1	Demonstrative pronouns —— 86
3.1.3.2	Adnominal demonstratives —— 86
3.1.4	Predicate adjectives —— 87
3.2	Verbs —— 88
3.3	Adverbs —— 93
3.3.1	Spatial Adverbs —— 94
3.3.1.1	Deictic adverbs —— 94
3.3.1.2	Directional adverbs —— 96
3.3.1.3	Topological relation markers (TRMs) —— 97
3.3.2	Temporal adverbs —— 98
3.3.3	Iterative adverbs —— 98
3.3.4	Manner adverbs —— 98
3.3.5	Degree adverb —— 98
3.4	Ideophones —— 99
3.5	Particles —— 100
3.5.1	Interjective particles —— 100
3.5.2	Connective particles —— 101
3.5.3	Negative particles —— 102
3.5.4	Modal particles —— 102
3.6	Other enclitics —— 102
3.6.1	=*Nhurr* 'only' —— 103
3.6.2	Pragmatic/emphatic enclitics —— 103

4 Morphology of nomina (nouns, adjectives and numerals) —— 104
4.1 Case —— 104
4.1.1 Case marking of nomina —— 106
4.1.2 Genitive pronouns inflected for relational case —— 110
4.2 Case categories —— 113
4.2.1 Ergative —— 113
4.2.1.1 Ergative – Transitive subject —— 117
4.2.1.2 Ergative – Instrument —— 117
4.2.1.3 Ergative – Unexpected Actor —— 119
4.2.2 Nominative —— 120
4.2.3 Accusative —— 121
4.2.4 Genitive —— 122
4.2.5 Dative —— 125
4.2.5.1 Dative – Recipient —— 125
4.2.5.2 Dative – Affected party —— 126
4.2.5.3 Dative – Goal —— 128
4.2.5.4 Dative – Location —— 128
4.2.5.5 Dative – Path (goal-focus) —— 129
4.2.5.6 Dative – Duration —— 130
4.2.5.7 Dative – Purpose —— 130
4.2.5.8 Dative – Stimulus —— 131
4.2.5.9 Dative – Experiencer —— 132
4.2.5.10 Dative – Accompaniment —— 132
4.2.6 Ablative —— 133
4.2.6.1 Ablative – Source —— 134
4.2.6.2 Ablative – Path (origin-focus) —— 136
4.2.6.3 Ablative – Attribution —— 137
4.2.6.4 Ablative – Conversation topic —— 138
4.2.6.5 Ablative – Portmanteau case —— 138
4.2.7 Comitative suffix -*kak* —— 140
4.2.7.1 Incipient dyadic uses of comitative NPs —— 142
4.2.8 Proprietive =*aak*, =*kaak* —— 143
4.2.9 Privative =*aar*, =*kaar* —— 144
4.3 Nomen derivation —— 146
4.3.1 Reduplication —— 146
4.3.2 Compounding —— 146
4.3.3 Verbalization and nominalization —— 149
4.4 Other nomen suffixes —— 150
4.4.1 -*tharr* —— 150
4.4.2 Loan numeral marker -*nharr* —— 150
4.4.3 =*Yuk* 'stuff' —— 151

5	**Pronouns, ignoratives and demonstratives —— 152**	
5.1	Pronouns —— 152	
5.1.1	Personal pronouns —— 152	
5.1.1.1	Morphology of free personal pronouns —— 152	
5.1.1.2	Functions of personal pronouns —— 154	
5.1.1.3	Morphosyntax of pronominal enclitics —— 154	
5.1.2	Reflexive pronouns —— 156	
5.1.2.1	Morphology of reflexive pronouns —— 156	
5.1.2.2	Functions of reflexive pronouns —— 157	
5.1.3	Emphatic pronouns —— 158	
5.1.3.1	Morphology of emphatic pronouns —— 158	
5.1.3.2	Functions of emphatic pronouns —— 159	
5.1.4	Inclusory pronouns —— 160	
5.2	Ignoratives —— 161	
5.2.1	Morphological structure of ignoratives —— 162	
5.2.2	Ignorative categories —— 164	
5.2.3	Functions of ignoratives —— 170	
5.2.3.1	Interrogative —— 170	
5.2.3.2	Indefinite pronoun —— 171	
5.2.3.3	Free choice pronoun —— 172	
5.2.3.4	Relative pronoun: *ngan* 'which' —— 172	
5.2.3.5	Rhetorical emphasis: *ngan* 'what' —— 173	
5.2.3.6	Imprecision: *ngan* 'what' —— 173	
5.2.3.7	Apprehensive counterfactual *ngene* 'why' —— 174	
5.2.3.8	Negative indefinite pronouns – not attested —— 174	
5.2.4	Ignorative morphosyntax —— 175	
5.3	Demonstratives —— 178	
5.3.1	Demonstrative pronouns —— 180	
5.3.1.1	Morphology of demonstrative pronouns —— 180	
5.3.1.2	Syntax of demonstrative pronouns —— 182	
5.3.2	Adnominal demonstratives —— 183	
5.3.2.1	Adnominal demonstrative categories —— 183	
5.3.2.2	Morphosyntax of adnominal demonstratives —— 186	
5.3.3	Functions of demonstratives —— 188	
6	**Noun phrase syntax —— 195**	
6.1	Arguments for the existence of a NP —— 195	
6.2	N – The classifying construction —— 197	
6.2.1	Semantics of the classifying construction —— 197	
6.2.2	Syntax of the classifying construction —— 198	
6.3	N_{GN}, N_{SP}, Adj: Word classes or syntactic slots? —— 200	

6.4	AdjP – The adjective phrase —— 204
6.5	N' – Head noun and modifiers —— 205
6.5.1	Overview of N' —— 205
6.5.2	Order of nominal modifiers —— 206
6.5.3	Ignorative and demonstrative pronouns in N' —— 207
6.6	Determination, determiners and specifiers —— 209
6.6.1	Determination —— 210
6.6.2	Adnominal demonstrative determiners —— 211
6.6.3	Pronominal determiners —— 212
6.6.4	Over-determination: pronoun + demonstrative —— 213
6.6.5	Determiner phrase —— 215
6.7	Wholly coreferential NPs —— 217
6.7.1	Apposition via referential case —— 217
6.7.2	Peripheral phrases —— 217
6.8	The inclusory construction —— 219
6.8.1	The simple inclusory construction —— 220
6.8.2	The comitative inclusory construction —— 222
6.8.3	The dative inclusory construction —— 224
6.8.4	The ergative inclusory construction —— 225
6.8.5	Inclusory pronouns —— 227
6.9	Nominal coordination —— 230
6.9.1	Conjunction by coordinator —— 230
6.9.2	Asyndetic conjunction (referential case linkage) —— 232
6.9.3	Conjunction by adnominal case linkage —— 233
6.9.3.1	Comitative conjunction —— 233
6.9.3.2	Dative conjunction —— 234
6.9.4	Concessive conjunction —— 235
6.9.5	Disjunction —— 235
6.10	Possession —— 237
6.10.1	Part-whole apposition (referential case linkage) —— 237
6.10.2	Possessum-head (adnominal case linkage) —— 240
6.11	Noun phrases and discourse structure —— 242
6.11.1	Anaphora and cataphora —— 242
6.11.1.1	Demonstrative pronouns —— 242
6.11.1.2	Generic nouns and the classifying construction —— 242
6.11.2	Focus markers —— 244
6.11.2.1	*thono* 'one' —— 244
6.11.2.2	*=thurr* 'focus' —— 246
6.11.2.3	Other focal enclitics —— 248
6.11.3	Other discourse pragmatic enclitics —— 250
6.11.4	'Filler' (*whatchamacallit*) terms —— 251

7	**Verbal inflection — 255**
7.1	The verbal word — 255
7.1.1	Overview of inflectional categories — 255
7.1.2	Verbal conjugations — 256
7.2	Tense and aspect — 263
7.2.1	Nonpast — 263
7.2.2	Past perfective — 268
7.2.3	Past imperfective — 270
7.2.4	Reduplication — 276
7.2.4.1	Iterative reduplication — 276
7.2.4.2	Durative reduplication — 278
7.2.4.3	Contrast between alternative reduplicative forms — 278
7.2.4.4	Alternatives to reduplication — 281
7.3	Mood — 283
7.3.1	Imperative — 283
7.3.2	Subjunctive — 284
7.3.3	Counterfactual — 286
7.3.4	Purposive — 287
7.3.5	Imminence — 288
7.3.6	Semantic overview of the modal affixes — 289
7.4	Infinitive — 291

8	**Verbal derivation — 292**
8.1	Derivational suffixes — 292
8.1.1	Valence increaser — 293
8.1.2	Reflexive — 299
8.1.3	Reciprocal — 299
8.1.4	Associated motion — 300
8.1.4.1	*-nha-* 'go&' — 301
8.1.4.2	*-(nh)ic* 'run&' — 304
8.1.5	Subordinate — 305
8.1.6	Verbalization and nominalization — 306
8.2	Complex predicates — 309
8.3	Body part noun + verb compounds — 313
8.3.1	Body part = instrument or theme — 314
8.3.2	Feature of body part = feature of event / result state — 315
8.3.4	Meaning non-compositional — 317
8.3.5	Related functions of body part terms — 317

9	**Particles and adverbs — 319**
9.1	Particles — 319
9.1.1	*Kana* 'well' — 319

9.1.2	*Yarriy* 'thus' —— 325
9.1.2.1	Illustration: quoted speech —— 326
9.1.2.2	Illustration: quoted thought —— 327
9.1.2.3	Illustration: verbal description —— 327
9.1.2.4	Illustration: pantomimic gesture —— 327
9.1.2.5	Illustration: live action/event —— 328
9.1.2.6	Morphosyntax of *yarriy* 'thus' —— 328
9.1.3	Analogical *kar* 'like' —— 328
9.1.4	Contrastive *wuump* —— 332
9.1.5	Dubitative *=okun* —— 334
9.1.6	*Minc* 'against expectations' —— 337
9.2	Adverbs —— 338
9.2.1	Spatial adverbs —— 338
9.2.1.1	*Pal* 'towards' —— 338
9.2.1.2	Other spatial deictic adverbs —— 342
9.2.1.3	Directionals —— 344
9.2.1.4	Topological relation markers (TRMs) —— 351
9.2.2	Temporal adverbs —— 356
9.2.2.1	Deictic temporal adverbs —— 356
9.2.2.2	Non-deictic temporal adverbs —— 357
9.2.3	Iterative adverbs —— 358
9.2.4	Manner adverbs —— 359
9.2.5	Degree adverbs —— 361
9.2.6	Body part prefixes to adverbs —— 363
9.3	Ideophones —— 364
9.4	Interjections —— 365
10	**Syntax of the simple clause —— 368**
10.1	Verb-headed clauses —— 368
10.1.1	Intransitive clauses —— 372
10.1.2	Intransitive copula clauses —— 373
10.1.3	Semitransitive clauses —— 373
10.1.4	Quasitransitive clauses —— 376
10.1.4.1	Bivalent predicate adjectives —— 377
10.1.5	Transitive clauses —— 379
10.1.6	Transitive copula clauses —— 379
10.1.7	Semiditransitive clauses —— 380
10.1.8	Ditransitive clauses —— 381
10.2	Locative, copula and existential constructions —— 382
10.2.1	Background —— 382
10.2.2	The set of postural verbs —— 383
10.2.2.1	Secondary senses of *nhiin* 'sit' and *wun* 'lie' —— 384

10.2.3	The postural construction —— 385
10.2.4	The copula construction —— 385
10.2.4.1	Additional copula clauses —— 391
10.2.5	The locative construction —— 392
10.2.6	Existential construction —— 395

11 Non-basic, non-complex clauses —— 397
11.1	Interrogative constructions —— 397
11.2	Imperative, prohibitive, hortative and jussive constructions —— 398
11.2.1	Imperative (and prohibitive) constructions —— 398
11.2.2	Jussive and hortative —— 400
11.3	Negation —— 403
11.3.1	Negative interjections —— 403
11.3.2	Clausal negation —— 405
11.3.2.1	Impossibility construction —— 406
11.3.3	Constituent negation —— 407
11.3.4	Prohibition —— 410
11.3.5	Negative constructions as a politeness strategy —— 410
11.4	Apprehensive constructions —— 411
11.4.1	*Pam* and 'potential detriment' —— 411
11.4.2	Counterfactual apprehensive construction —— 413
11.5	Reflexive constructions —— 414
11.5.1	The pronominal reflexive construction —— 414
11.5.2	Morphosyntax of the verbal reflexive construction —— 415
11.5.3	Core reflexive —— 418
11.5.4	Partitive object —— 419
11.5.5	Collective reflexive —— 419
11.5.6	Medio-passive —— 421
11.5.7	Deagentive —— 421
11.5.8	Further extended uses of the verbal reflexive construction —— 421
11.5.9	Lexical reflexives —— 424
11.6	The reciprocal construction —— 425
11.6.1	Morphosyntax of the reciprocal construction —— 425
11.6.2	Core reciprocal —— 426
11.6.3	Co-participation —— 426
11.6.4	Asymmetric-converse —— 427
11.6.5	Distributive —— 428
11.6.6	Extended uses of the reciprocal suffix —— 429
11.6.7	Lexical reciprocals —— 430
11.6.8	Reciprocal by implicature —— 430
11.7	Desiderative constructions —— 432
11.7.1	Subjunctive desiderative constructions —— 432

11.7.1.1	Simple subjunctive —— **432**
11.7.1.2	Subjunctive + *angarr* —— **433**
11.7.1.3	Subjunctive + *waarr* —— **434**
11.7.1.4	Subjunctive + *wanthan* —— **435**
11.7.2	Nonpast desiderative constructions —— **435**
11.7.2.1	Simple nonpast —— **435**
11.7.2.2	Nonpast + *angarr* —— **436**
11.7.2.3	Nonpast + *ak* —— **436**
11.7.3	Associated motion desiderative constructions —— **437**
11.7.3.1	Simple associated motion (nonpast) —— **437**
11.7.3.2	Associated motion (nonpast) + *waarr* —— **437**
11.7.4	Purposive desiderative construction —— **438**
11.7.5	Verbless desiderative constructions —— **438**
11.7.5.1	Simple verbless clauses —— **438**
11.7.5.2	Verbless + *kaar* —— **439**
11.8	Secondary predication —— **440**
11.8.1	Depictive construction —— **440**
11.8.2	Resultative construction —— **441**

12 Complex clauses —— 444
12.1	Subordination —— **444**
12.1.1	Non-finite subordinate clauses —— **445**
12.1.1.1	Infinitive subordinate clauses —— **445**
12.1.1.2	Subordinate verbs marked by *-marr* —— **446**
12.1.2	Finite subordinate clauses —— **448**
12.1.2.1	Unmarked finite subordinate clauses —— **448**
12.1.2.2	Purposive-marked subordinate clauses —— **456**
12.1.2.3	Subjunctive-marked subordinate clauses —— **457**
12.2	Coordination —— **458**
12.2.1	Conjunction —— **458**
12.2.1.1	Asyndetic conjunction —— **458**
12.2.1.2	Ngul-marked conjunction —— **460**
12.2.2	Disjunction —— **462**
12.2.3	Concessive conjunction —— **463**

References —— **465**
Appendix 1: Index of tasks and narrative texts —— **480**
Appendix 2: Narrative texts —— **482**
Index of subjects —— **494**

Glosses and abbreviations

+/−	older / younger sibling	incl	inclusive
♀/♂	female / male ego (for calculating kin relationship)	INF	infinitive
		M	mother
1	first person	NEG	negative particle
2	second person	NO	constituent negator
3	third person	NMLZ	nominalizer
ABL	ablative case	NOM	nominative case
ACC	accusative case	NP	noun phrase
ADN.PRIV	adnominal privative case	NPST	nonpast tense
ATTN	attention-drawing prefix (to adnominal demonstratives)	NUM	loan numeral marker
		OPT	optative particle
B	brother	P.IPFV	past imperfective
CDICT	contradictory particle	P.PFV	past perfective
CMP	completive particle	PERM	permissive particle
COM	comitative case	pl	plural number
CONTR	contrastive particle	PRAG	pragmatic enclitic
CTF	counterfactual mood	PRIV	privative enclitic
D	daughter	PROHIB	prohibitive particle
DAT	dative case	PURP	purposive
DETR	potential detriment particle	RCPCANT	marker of reciprocant subject argument
DIRECTED	directed verbal prefix		
DP	determiner phrase	RDP	reduplication
du	dual number	REL.PRIV	relational privative enclitic
DUB	dubitative enclitic	REL.PROP	relational proprietive enclitic
ERG	ergative case	RFL	reflexive (verbal suffix or pronoun)
#ERG	pragmatically conditioned omission of ergative morpheme	S	son
		SBD	subordinate
ERG^	pragmatically conditioned inclusion of ergative morpheme	SBJV	subjunctive
		TR	transitive verbalizer
F	father	TRM	topological relation marker
GEN	genitive case	UNXP	unexpected event particle
GO&	first associated motion morpheme	V^	valence increasing derivational suffix
IDPH	ideophone		
IMM	imminence morpheme	VBLZ	verbalizer
IMP	imperative	WANT	desiderative/purposive particle

1 Introduction

1.1 Linguistic profile of Kuuk Thaayorre

Kuuk Thaayorre is a Pama-Nyungan language spoken on the west coast of Cape York Peninsula, Australia. Although it is threatened by the encroachment of English, Kuuk Thaayorre remains one of the very few Australian Aboriginal languages still being acquired as a first language, albeit by only a handful of children. Of approximately 350 ethnic Thaayorre, around 250 use the language in their daily interactions. Most of them reside in the community of Pormpuraaw, which sits on the traditional lands of the Thaayorre people. The Thaayorre still maintain close links to their traditional lands, many living for part or most of the year on outstations to the south and east of Pormpuraaw. Ceremonial and other activities relating to the maintenance and increase of the land's resources remain well known and practiced.

This introductory chapter begins with a summary of the typological profile of Kuuk Thaayorre (§1.1.1), the genetic relationships between Kuuk Thaayorre and other languages and varieties (§1.1.2), and previous work on the language (§1.1.3, see also §1.4.3). Following from that, §1.2 and §1.3 focus on the geographical and socio-historical contexts Kuuk Thaayorre is spoken within. Section 1.3.1 describes the history of contact with Europeans and the establishment of Pormpuraaw, §1.3.2 describes the linguistic ecology of the area, both traditionally and today, while §1.3.3 considers the relationship between kinship and the appropriate use of language.

Finally, section 1.4 provides a metadescription of this grammar. This includes a description of its inception (§1.4.1), theoretical framework (§1.4.2), the data it draws upon and the methodologies used to gather it (§1.4.3), the Kuuk Thaayorre speakers who contributed to the data and analysis (§1.4.3.5), and conventions employed in the presentation of examples (§1.4.5). This chapter concludes with an overview of the topics covered in this grammar and how they are divided between its chapters (§1.4.6).

1.1.1 Kuuk Thaayorre in typological context

Kuuk Thaayorre is a predominantly dependent-marking language (cf. Nichols 1986), with grammatical relations signalled by the case-marking of arguments. The Kuuk Thaayorre case system distinguishes the grammatical functions of intransitive subject, transitive subject and transitive object. In terms of morphological form, however, there is a split between the pronominal paradigm (among which the syncretism of nominative and ergative case forms results in a nominative-accusative marking pattern) and other nominals (in which nominative/accusative syncretism gives rise to an ergative-absolutive marking pattern).

Typically for a Pama-Nyungan language, Kuuk Thaayorre inflection is strictly suffixal. Closer to the analytic than the polysynthetic end of the spectrum, it is rare for a word to contain more than four morphemes. The verbal word *nhaathnhanrrnhanunt* in (1) represents an unusually morphologically complex example, containing six morphemes (two of which are realized by a portmanteau morph, a third being an enclitic).

(1) *pulnan   yup   nhaath-nhan-rr-nhan=unt*
    3du(ACC) soon   see-V^-RCP-GO&:NPST=2sg(ERG)
    'you'll soon be making them two see each other'
    [Hall 1972: 392]

Kuuk Thaayorre is one of a very few languages demonstrated to possess phrasal affixation (cf. Dench and Evans 1988, Anderson et al. 2006) and portmanteau case morphology (expressing two distinct cases at once, cf. Dench and Evans 1988).

There is an incipient system of pronominal enclitics to the verb, but these are optional and functionally equivalent to the free pronouns from which they are in the process of grammaticalizing. For instance, the enclitic form *=ay* in example 2 is equivalent to the second person singular free pronoun *ngay*. Because this system is still in its infancy, the enclitic forms are analyzed here as essentially pronominal, rather than verbal cross-referencing. As such, they are described as bearing case; this is congruent with the broader dependent-marking profile of the language.

(2) *angunp   therk-r=ay   ii-rr-korr   ii*
    at.that.place   return-P.PFV=1sg(NOM) there-towards-outside   there
    'I went back over there'
    [KTh_AC14Nov2002 Narrative LosingIrma]

Kuuk Thaayorre approaches the prototype of a non-configurational language (Hale 1983, Austin and Bresnan 1996), with extremely flexible ordering of constituents and free ellipsis of arguments and other constituents. Word order within the noun phrase is more fixed, although permutations motivated by pragmatic focus or speech style are possible. In general, the head noun is followed by all modifiers. Arguments take the form of one or more noun phrases (including pronouns) apposed in the same case, as in (3). The repetition of pronouns is common, in both full and reduced (encliticised) forms:

(3) *ngali   I. C.   ngali   yat   kuthirr*
    1du:excl(NOM) I. C.(NOM) 1du:excl(NOM) go:P.PFV   two(NOM)
    'I. C. and I went, the two of us'
    [KTh_GJ16Oct2002 Narrative MelbourneTrip]

Kuuk Thaayorre is unusual in possessing multiple distinct inclusory constructions, used to highlight a subset of individual(s) within a larger participant group. This includes a set of inclusory pronouns that express both the participant group as a whole and an individual member thereof distinctly within a single lexeme.

The Kuuk Thaayorre consonant inventory – comprising sixteen phonemes – is not unusual for an Australian language. Its vowel system, however, is rather rich by Australian terms, comprising five distinct vowel qualities and two contrastive lengths, producing ten vowel phonemes. It is in the phonotactic combination of sounds that Kuuk Thaayorre phonology is particularly noteworthy, however. Kuuk Thaayorre's tendency towards closed syllables (with codas containing up to three consonants) frequently leads to consonant clusters of as many as four segments. Kuuk Thaayorre is also cross-linguistically unusual in allowing sequences of its two rhotics (an alveolar tap/trill and retroflex continuant) within the syllable – either as a complex coda or as onset and nucleus (the latter being filled by a syllabic rhotic). Monosyllables are ubiquitous across all Kuuk Thaayorre word classes, despite being generally rare in Australian languages (Dixon 2002: 553).

Kuuk Thaayorre possesses many polyfunctional, homophonous or polysemous forms. Of particular interest here is the exploitation of morphosyntactic categories for pragmatic purposes (e.g. the use of spatial distinctions in demonstratives to express how easily the referent is retrievable, or the use of ergative case-marking to signal whether or not the subject's reference accords with the addressee's expectations, cf. Gaby 2008a, 2010). The fact that Kuuk Thaayorre is one of the very few traditional Australian Indigenous languages still being used by native speakers in daily interaction allows us a rare opportunity to explore such pragmatic concerns alongside the grammatical structures through which they are expressed.

1.1.2 Kuuk Thaayorre varieties and relatives

1.1.2.1 Names and dialects

Kuuk Thaayorre [kuːk ṯaːjor] is the name applied by the Thaayorre people to their own language. This bipartite term comprises the Thaayorre generic noun *kuuk* (meaning 'language') followed by the (specific) ethnonym *Thaayorre*.[1] Throughout this grammar, the binomial expression is used with reference to the language (e.g. *She is learning Kuuk Thaayorre*) and the specific noun alone with reference to the Thaayorre people, land and culture.

There are a range of alternative spellings for *Kuuk Thaayorre*. The one adopted here is also used by Hall (1968, 1972 and elsewhere) and has the widest currency in the Pormpuraaw community. The spelling *Koko Daiyuri* is used by Simmons et al. (1958), *Thayore* by Alpher (1972), *Taior* by Tindale (1974) and both *Koko Taiyor* and *Koko Daiyuri* in the notes of Donald Thomson. Other documented spellings vary in

---

[1] The term *Thaayorre* is most likely a compound in origin since the morpheme *thaa+* < *thaaw* 'mouth' commonly occurs as the first element of compounds (see §4.3.2). However, the etymology of the putative second element, *yorre*, is unknown.

their (non-)representation of vowel length, consonant voicing, the alveolar tap/trill (transcribed here as 'rr'), and final vowel (which marks ergative/instrumental case): *Kuuk Thaayoore, Thaayore, Thayorre, Taior, Tayore, Taiol, Da:jor, Gugudayor, Kuktayor, Koko-Daiyuri, Kokkotaijari, Kokotaiyari* and *Kukudayore*. Grimes (2000) also list the language name *Behran* as an alternative to *Kuuk Thaayorre*, but this is not a form I have encountered elsewhere.

Some of the Kuuk Thaayorre speakers I consulted were able to name three Kuuk Thaayorre dialects; Kuuk Thaayunth, Kuuk Thayem and Kuuk Thanon.[2] Although they were not able to provide specific examples of lexical or grammatical divergences from standard Kuuk Thaayorre, the way local language experts talk about these varieties left me confident of their dialectal status, confirming notes in AUSTLANG (AIATSIS 2014). Synchronically, Kuuk Thaayorre appears to comprise a single standard variety with only small idiolectal and family-lectal differences (mostly in vocabulary). Notwithstanding minor inter-speaker variances in allomorphy (notably in the forms of ergative case marking), I have found no dialectal differences in grammar proper. The few instances of grammatical variance between individuals and age groups seem better attributed to obsolescence than to enduring dialects.

1.1.2.2 Genetic relationships

Kuuk Thaayorre is a Pama-Nyungan language of the Paman subgroup, as suggested by its reflex of the eponymous **pama* 'man'; *pam* 'man'. The languages of Cape York are in many respects aberrant from the standard Pama-Nyungan typological profile. Cape York languages were therefore routinely excluded from this family (e.g. by Schmidt 1919) until Hale (1964) convincingly demonstrated their genetic relatedness.

In Alpher's (1972) analysis of the genetic relationships between the languages of the western Cape York area, Kuuk Thaayorre and Uw Oykangand form Upper Southwest Pama, which alongside the 'Coastal Southwest Pama' languages, Koko Bera, Yir Yoront and Yir Thangedl (these latter two forming the 'Yir' subgroup), forms Southwest Pama, as depicted in Figure 1. This classification differs significantly from those of Capell (1962, 1963), O'Grady and Voegelin (1966), and Hale (1964, 1966a, 1976a), who classify Kuuk Thaayorre as a member of the 'Western Pama' subgroup. Dixon (2002: xxxii) alternatively proffers an areal classification of Kuuk Thaayorre (Ea1; upper southwest Pama group of the Western Cape York Peninsula areal group) in lieu of committing to a broader genetic relationship. The genetic structure of Paman (and in particular Southwest Paman) is understudied, and should be considered subject to revision pending further research (cf. Bowern and Atkinson 2012)

---

[2] Note that Taylor (1984: 6) lists these along with Kuuk Yak as dialects of Kuuk Thaayorre. Hall (1972: 27) describes Thaayunth, yak (sic), and Thaawanchin as dialects of Kuuk Thaayorre, and says that "the Thaanhon language tradition [...] is probably identical with the Minchana language from Mitchell River". I infer that 'Minchana' here refers to Yir Yoront.

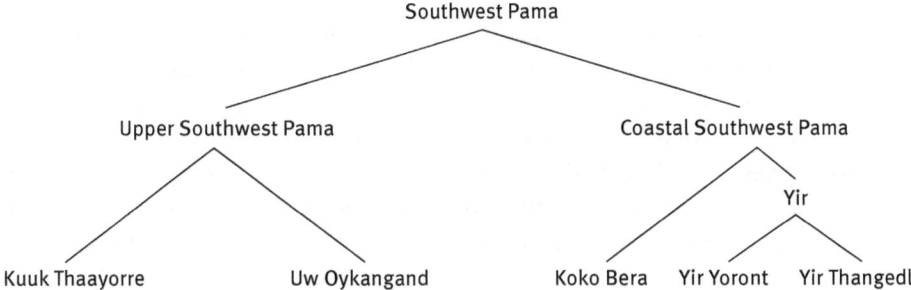

Figure 1. Southwest Paman languages (adapted from Alpher 1972).

The genetic status of a further, related variety – *Kuuk Yak* – remains unclear. From discussions with the handful of people in Pormpuraaw who remember this language I had the impression that it is closely related to Kuuk Thaayorre. Alpher (1972: 68), on the basis of personal communication with Allen Hall, similarly concludes that Kuku Yak is likely to be the most closely related language to Kuuk Thaayorre, or perhaps a 'sister dialect'. This impression should not be given too much weight, however, as mutual intelligibility is a problematic diagnostic in multilingual contexts. Barry Alpher (p.c.) continues to work on the somewhat meagre available documentation of Kuuk Yak lexicon and grammar. This may shed more light on the genetic status of Kuuk Yak, especially vis à vis Kuuk Thaayorre. It may be, though, that the obsolescence of Kuuk Yak is too far progressed to allow detailed reconstruction.

1.1.3 Previous work

By far the most extensive prior treatment of Kuuk Thaayorre grammar is the Reverend Allen Hall's 1972 PhD Thesis, "A study of the Thaayorre language of the Edward River tribe, Cape York Peninsula, Queensland: being a description of the grammar". This tagmemic grammar was preceded by Hall's (1968) "A depth-study of the Thaayorre language of the Edward River tribe, Cape York Peninsula: being a description of the phonology with a brief grammatical outline and samples of lexicon and oral literature", an unpublished M.A. thesis. I make extensive reference to these works throughout this grammar. Since our analyzes diverge more than they converge, I note points of similarity more often than difference. Hall additionally published two papers in Sutton (ed. 1976a), and produced three Kuuk Thaayorre – English dictionaries and numerous pedagogical materials in collaboration with †Tom Foote,[3] a native speaker

---

[3] Mr Foote was by all reports an extremely intelligent and diligent man with a natural talent for linguistics. Although he had sadly passed away by the time of my arrival in Pormpuraaw, I was fortunate enough to work with several members of his immediate family, who were keen to see his legacy augmented.

linguist. Many of these were kindly made available to me by the Pormpuraaw Aboriginal Shire Council and Mr Foote's family. Many further printed pamphlets, primers and readers were found in a dumpster outside the school. Their style, typography and orthographic conventions resemble those employed by Foote and Hall, so I attribute them to these two along with the other Kuuk Thaayorre speakers Allen Hall was known to have worked with (especially those who worked as teacher aides in the school, such as Jessally Coleman and Georgina Norman, and †Tom Foote's wife, Mrs Myrtle Foote).

In addition to the published and unpublished materials of Foote, Hall and their collaborators, a number of other linguists and anthropologists have collected Kuuk Thaayorre data (in the form of field notes, audio-recordings and video recordings), often in the course of their research on other languages and/or ethnographic topics. Barry Alpher has the most extensive field notes on Kuuk Thaayorre as far as I am aware, but other notable researchers in the area include: John Taylor, Ian Smith, Steve Johnson, John von Sturmer, Lauriston Sharp, William Oates, Lamont West, Donald Crim, Arthur Capell, Donald Thompson, Paul Black, Michael Martin, Ken Hale, Ursula McConnel, and Bruce Sommer. Aside from personal communication with Barry Alpher, I have not sighted any of these unpublished materials and am unable to comment on their contents.

John Taylor's (1984) PhD thesis represents the most detailed anthropological study of the Thaayorre people specifically (supplemented by a number of later articles – e.g. Taylor 1976, 1977 – and contributions to land claims). Studies of the neighbouring Yir Yoront and Wik peoples by Ursula McConnel (1953, reporting on research conducted in the 1920s and 1930s), Donald Thomson (1935, 1936, 1955, 1972), and Lauriston Sharp (1937) should also be understood largely to apply to the Thaayorre people.[4]

1.2 Physical environment

1.2.1 Local topography

The community of Pormpuraaw is located on the west coast of Cape York Peninsua, at latitude 14 degrees 54 minutes south, longitude 141 degrees, 37 minutes east. Pormpuraaw is situated between the mouths of the Chapman river (to the south) and Moonkan Creek (to the north), both of which are popular fishing spots.[5] Mangroves surround the river estuaries, and "melaleuca gallery forests" (Taylor 1984: 45) line the

---

4 In keeping with standard anthropological practice at the time, Sharp (1937, and elsewhere) intended explicit reference to the Yir Yoront to extend to their culturally similar neighbours the Thaayorre; cf. Sutton (1978: 30) and Taylor (1984: 4).
5 The Chapman River mouth is primarily frequented by Kuuk Thaayorre-speakers and Moonkan Creek by Wik-language-speaking groups.

watercourses further inland. A low sand ridge runs along the coastline, rising just a few metres above sea level and extending some kilometres inland. Pormpuraaw is situated upon this sand ridge, and at the time of this study the town's streets were sand.[6] Inland of this sand ridge, areas of black soil, clay and salt pans chase on one another's heels, their sequence being highly prominent due to the very different vegetation they support. This ranges from scrubby ridges and grassy flats to larger expanses of open woodland and more densely forested areas. As Taylor (1984: 41) observes, "the plains are extensively riven with distributary channels, levees, floodouts and clay-bottomed swamps. There are no rock outcrops and apart from river gravels, no hard stone is to be found in the area at all". Further inland from the beach ridges runs a parallel series of sand ridges. These are apparently a relic of what was the shoreline during the Pleistocene (Taylor 1984: 41, Rhodes 1980). In the wet season, the saltpan to Pormpuraaw's east becomes completely submerged and the road unpassable, rendering the town effectively an island. During these months, all food and fuel must be imported by either barge or plane, and trips to outstations cease. It is difficult to overstate the dramatic change in landscape, flora and fauna effected by the onset of the rainy season.

The local ecology of the area surrounding Pormpuraaw has been quite extensively described by Thomson (e.g. 1935), Pedley and Isbell (1971), von Sturmer (1978), Sutton (1978) and John Taylor (1984), though there remains much to learn about the local Indigenous ontologies. Taylor (1976) offers the most thorough description of pre- and post-settlement land usage and rights, including maps of named tracts.

1.2.2 Climate

Climate data has not been systematically gathered for Pormpuraaw. Closest are the Bureau of Meteorology's records from Kowanyama. Kowanyama lies approximately seventy kilometres south of Pormpuraaw and a little over 30km inland. Impressionistically, this accords with slightly higher maximum temperatures and colder nights in the dry season. The mean maximum temperatures in Kowanyama (over the period 1965–2010) range from 30.7 degrees celcius in June/July to 36.2°C in November, with overnight lows ranging from 15.4°C in July to 24.4°C in December (Australian Government Bureau of Meteorology [BOM] 2016). This temperature peak comes during the 'build up' to the first rains of the rainy season, which typically come in November (although the rain does not fall in earnest until December). Most of the rain falls through January and February, with these months averaging well over 300mm. By contrast, there is virtually no rainfall between May and October (BOM 2016).

---

6 Just inland of Pormpuraaw, there is a stretch of some kilometres of bitumen on the road connecting Pormpuraaw to Cairns via Laura. This road is otherwise sand and clay, and becomes deeply corrugated over the course of the dry season.

1.3 Kuuk Thaayorre in social and historical context

This section considers the contexts Kuuk Thaayorre is spoken within. Section 1.3.1 begins by describing the establishment of Pormpuraaw in the context of the broader history of contact between the Thaayorre and Europeans (and Australians of European descent).[7] In section 1.3.2, we turn our attention back to language, and specifically the range of other languages and varieties commanded by speakers of Kuuk Thaayorre. Section 1.3.2 outlines the distinct speech registers that together traditionally comprised Kuuk Thaayorre, including hand signs (§1.3.2.1) and a respect register (§1.3.2.2). Section 1.3.2.3 describes the multilingual repertoire of a typical Kuuk Thaayorre speaker. Finally, §1.3.3 briefly outlines the Kuuk Thaayorre kinship system and how it bears upon speech etiquette.

1.3.1 History of contact with Europeans

Anthropological studies describe the Thaayorre as having lived as semi-nomadic hunter-gatherers prior to settlement (e.g. Taylor 1984: 1, cf. Stanner 1937, Sutton 1978). It is possible, however, that some traditional practices of cultivation and harvesting have been overlooked (cf. Pascoe 2014). The earliest contact made between the Thaayorre and Europeans was with a number of Dutch seafarers throughout the 17th and first half of the 18th centuries, the Dutch abandoning their interest in the area in part due to hostile reception (Taylor 1984: 1). It was not until 1864 that Europeans first travelled through Thaayorre country. This group of stockmen (led by Francis and Alexander Jardine, then in their early 20s) were met with increasing resistance from the local groups they encountered as they travelled northwards up the Cape. This climaxed in what the Jardine brothers somewhat euphemistically refer to as the "Battle of the Mitchell", in which they massacred more than thirty people protesting the invasion of their land (none of the Jardine party were injured; Jardine et al. 1867).

The name Edward River was bestowed in 1884 by a government surveyor, J. T. Embley (Taylor 1984: 2, cf. Jack 1922: 632). This period saw a brief flurry of European settlement (primarily in the form of cattle stations and pastoral holdings), which was largely halted by the passing of "The Aboriginals Protection and Restriction of the Sale of Opium Act of 1897". European impact in the area was next felt in the establishment of the Edward River mission. Beginning in 1932, speakers of Kuuk Thaayorre and various Wik languages were "encouraged to draw together in one central situation"[8] by the Church of England (Hall 1968: 29). The Edward River Mission was officially

---

[7] In Pormpuraaw, Australians of European descent are referred to as *pam wang* (literally, MAN devil) in Kuuk Thaayorre, and either *whitefella* or, more euphemistically, *Europeans* in Pormpuraaw English. I follow this usage in the discussion here, even where the people described may not self-identify as 'European'.

[8] I have no information as to what form this "encouragement" took.

established by Joseph W. Chapman in 1938, under the supervision of the Bishop of Carpentaria. The history of the mission is discussed in great detail by Taylor (1984). Several of my friends and language teachers remember Superintendant Chapman, and tell stories of their hard life on the mission. These stories often reveal a certain ambivalence, however. The mission era replaced the Thaayorre's prior autonomy with hard labour under imposed rule, and yet in some respects this era compares favourably with today's lifestyle. As harsh as the conditions on the mission may have been, people still retained relatively active involvement in the stuff of life. As Alfred Charlie explains in the excerpt below, people grew their own fresh food on the mission rather than buying processed and packaged food from the Pormpuraaw store. There is thus a cline from the pre-contact era to the mission era to the present day in terms of control over and involvement in subsistence activities (primarily the sourcing of food, but also tending the land).

(4) 1. *Ngancn   yoorr kaar=p   nhiina-n-r.*[9]
        1pl:excl(ERG) now   NEG=PRAG   sit-v^-NPST
        'Nowadays we no longer make gardens'
    2. *Yoorr... government-thurr take.over rirk-r.   May   ulp-th*
        now   government-ERG   take.over DO-NPST   VEG   dem.fam=PRAG
        'Today the government takes over. That food, ...'
    3. *Yoorr ngancn   may   kaar=p   nhiina-n-r,   pokon!*
        now   1pl:excl(ERG)   VEG(ACC) NEG=PRAG   sit-v^-NPST   NO
        'Today we don't plant any of that food, not at all / none of it!'
    4. *Kanangkarr mong,   missiontime... plant-m   rirk-m,*
        long.ago   many(ACC)   mission.time   plant-TR DO-P.IPFV
        'Long ago we used to plant many [types of vegetables]'
    5. *may   potat,   sugarcane,   paw paw   and cassava, taro,   what's that,*
        VEG   potato,   sugarcane,   paw paw   and cassava, taro,   what's that
        '[we planted] potatoes, sugarcane, paw paw and cassava, taro, and whatsits...
    6. *nhiina-n-m   kanangkarr   may.*
        sit-v^- P.IPFV long.ago   VEG(ACC)
        'we used to plant food long ago.'
    7. *May   ngancn   mungk-m.*
        VEG(ACC) 1pl:excl(ERG)   eat-P.IPFV
        We used to eat that food.'
        [KTh_AC22Jul2002 Narrative ChapmanEra]

---

9 The combination of the verb root *nhiin* 'sit' and the valence increasing morpheme (glossed as 'v^') is lexicalized with the meaning 'plant (v.tr.)'

In 1967 the church handed administrative control of the settlement to the Department of Aboriginal and Islander Affairs (Taylor 1977: 150). Since then, the community generally referred to as Pormpuraaw has had a variety of official titles, currently 'Pormpuraaw Aboriginal Shire Council'.

1.3.2 Linguistic ecology

Pormpuraaw is situated on Thaayorre land, and Kuuk Thaayorre remains the most widely spoken Indigenous language in the community. As at 2006 (the endpoint of the main data collection phase, cf. §1.4.1), the Australian Census lists 644 residents of Pormpuraaw, of whom 90.1% were Indigenous and 58.7% reported speaking a language other than English at home (ABS 2010). This implies that 378 Pormpuraawans speak one or more Aboriginal languages at home,[10] of whom a little over half would likely speak Kuuk Thaayorre (see §1.3.2.3). These results largely concur with an informal survey I conducted in 2001, which found that of approximately 570 Indigenous residents of Pormpuraaw, around 350 identified as ethnically Thaayorre and 200–250[11] as fluent speakers of Kuuk Thaayorre. This number is somewhat lower than Hall's (1972: 26) estimate of "nearly 300 speakers", though there is no reason to believe that the pre-contact speaker numbers were much higher. Undoubtedly, however, English has since disrupted the intergenerational transmission of Kuuk Thaayorre. Only a very small number of children born this century (including just four that I have spoken to myself) are growing up with Kuuk Thaayorre as their first language.[12]

Before the establishment of the mission in 1938, adult speakers of Kuuk Thaayorre commanded a number of distinct 'registers', or context-sensitive varieties, in addition to dialects and neighbouring languages.[13] The following subsections describe in turn: (1) the manual register of hand signs (§1.3.2.1); (2) the respect register triggered by the presence of, or reference to, a *nganc* 'poison, sacred, taboo'[14] people and/or topics

---

10 To my knowledge, there was only one person in Pormpuraaw in 2006 who was a native speaker of a non-Aboriginal language other than English (German), and she did not appear to use that language at all while in Pormpuraaw.

11 The group of speakers is given as a range rather than a number because some individuals could not be contacted directly during the survey. In these cases, I relied on the evaluation of family members, who tended to agree in their judgements of ethnicity, but often disagreed in judging fluency.

12 Nevertheless, the situation seems to me somewhat less dire than reported by, e.g., the National Indigenous Languages Survey Report (AIATSIS 2005), which identified only twenty-six speakers for Kuuk Thaayorre. (Kuuk Thaayorre is not mentioned at all in NILS2 (Marmion et al. 2014)).

13 In addition to the sign and respect registers described here, there may once have been a distinct song language. The people whose traditional songs (*wuuc*) I recorded were either unable or unwilling to re-speak the language of the songs in order for me to transcribe them, nor was I able to identify any recognizable Kuuk Thaayorre words within them.

14 The word *nganc*, translated here by the Aboriginal English word 'poison', is difficult to translate into other varieties of English. Within the kinship system, one's *nganc* relations are those one is

(§1.3.2.2); (3) the multilingual ecology Kuuk Thaayorre is spoken within (§1.3.2.3). It should be acknowledged that Kuuk Thaayorre not only spans multiple dialects and registers, but is also inherently a multimodal system, with interlocutors drawing upon lip pointing, hand gestures, gaze, movements of the head and eyes and more, alongside the speech forms described here. I lack both the space and understanding to do these communicative resources justice here, though prosody and gesture will occasionally be noted where relevant throughout the grammar.

1.3.2.1 Hand signs

Before 1938, Kuuk Thaayorre speakers drew on a rather elaborate system of hand signs in order to communicate over large distances (out of earshot but within sight), while hunting (so as not to disturb the quarry), in parallel with singing, or in certain *nganc* 'poison, sacred, taboo' contexts (such as in the presence of one's mother in law, or while in seclusion following the death of one's husband). In an elicitation context, the people I consulted were only able to produce a very small subset of what I understand to be the earlier inventory of signs. Yet the same people often found themselves using others of the signs during performances of *wuuc* 'ceremonial dance' or while telling stories.[15] The most easily recollected signs included those denoting animals (e.g. Figure 2) and kin categories (Figure 3, see also §1.3.3).

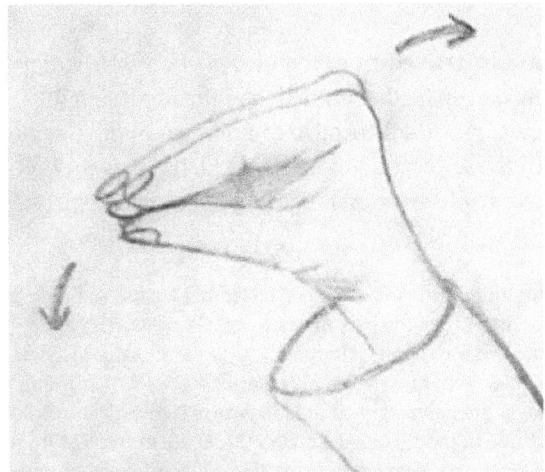
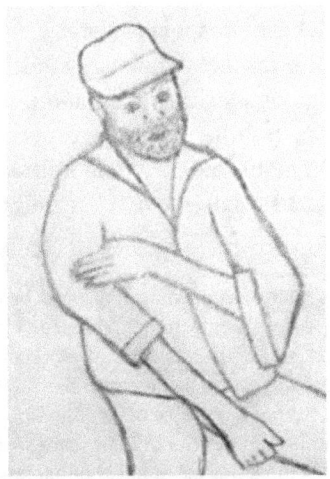

Figure 2. Hand sign 'emu' **Figure 3.** Hand sign 'father'

obliged to avoid. *Nganc* stories or places are powerful and potentially dangerous.
15 There is reason to believe that knowledge of the sign system might be highest among older women, who have experienced multiple bereavements (cf. Kendon 1988: 93). For a number of reasons, including reticence to be video-recorded, I did not collect signed data from women in this category. This remains a priority for future research.

The hand signs for kin categories each involve touching a different part of the body (e.g. the biceps, in the case of one's father, paternal uncles, brothers' children and/or a man's own children – see Figure 3). These signs are also deployed as a conventional response to a sneeze (analogous to *gesundheit*), such that a woman would touch her biceps if her father sneezed in her presence.[16] Also in common use is the question sign, which has the form of a rapidly upturned hand. This sign can either combine with other signs (in the manner of an interrogative particle) or appear on its own. Used in isolation, this form could variously mean 'where are you going?', 'what should we do now?', 'have you got any cigarettes' and more, depending on context. Another sign in common use euphemistically signals that the signer is going off to urinate. This sign is made by puffing one cheek out with air and tapping it with a hooked index finger.

It seems likely that the Kuuk Thaayorre hand signs would have originally fit Kendon's (1988: 3) definition of "a fully autonomous mode of discourse", given both its proximity to other Cape York languages with highly developed sign languages (Kendon 1988 : 45–46), and the fact that the Kuuk Thaayorre signs appear to be mostly one handed,[17] without much whole body action or face action, and involving high differentiation of hand shapes.[18]

Finally, it should be noted that while there is no record of a dedicated Thaayorre initiation register as such, Taylor (1984: 120) suggests that the sign register was traditionally "used by initiates during seclusion, [...] during ritual performances".

1.3.2.2 Respect register

The respect register of Kuuk Thaayorre is derived from the everyday spoken variety through lexical substitution. Though now even further eroded than the hand sign register, in earlier times the respect register was reportedly used to communicate with people in mourning, or while in proximity to those in a taboo (*nganc*) kinship category (cf. §1.3.3). Hall (1969: 312) makes the following observation regarding the respect register:

---

16 This custom may or may not be related to Bininj Gun-Wok speakers' belief that "to use someone's personal name in their absence, it is believed, can cause the person to sneeze" Garde (2002: 203).
17 One of the language experts I consulted did use both hands (alternately) to make the same kin sign. He was one of the less confident signers I worked with, however, so this may be an effect of attrition.
18 The best source of evidence for evaluating and analyzing the Kuuk Thaayorre sign register would appear to be a set of films made by Glen McBride in the 1960s. As Kendon (1988: 46) observes, "from his films it is clear, as it is from the films of West, that sign language in this region of Western Cape York was, or is, developed and in widespread use". However, the video viewed by Kendon (and deposited at AIATSIS) records sign communication between two deaf men. It is clearly possible that these men (and other Thaayorre deaf signers, past and present) elaborated on the sign register used by hearing Kuuk Thaayorre speakers. Kendon (1988: 46, 521) notes that McBride also made recordings of many hearing signers in films held at the University of Queensland. However, the libraries at the University of Queensland were not able to locate these films in 2015, and Glen McBride himself suggests that they were likely lost when the UQ Animal Behaviour Unit in which he worked was disbanded in 1990 (McBride, personal communication 23rd July 2015).

A phantom class of 'lexemes' parallels the normal vocabulary in so far as sensitive cultural concepts make the Aboriginal diffident in communication. This lexical set of alternatives comprises the 'secret words' used for ceremonial and mourning. They are the substitute lexemes when avoidance or prohibition compel an individual to forsake the usual term of reference.

There is clearly some overlap in the contexts triggering the use of the sign and respect registers, raising many (possibly unanswerable) questions about their distributions and potential combination. It is also unclear whether the set of 'bereavement' kin terms (described in §1.3.3) are part of the respect register, or are merely sensitive to some of the same contextual factors. Recent research shows the distinction between everyday speech and circumspection to be gradient (e.g. Garde 2014). This supports the notion that speakers may have enjoyed some flexibility in choosing between (some mixture of) the everyday, sign and respect registers in certain speech contexts.

1.3.2.3 Multilingualism and inter-group relationships

Pormpuraaw is home to a number of different ethnic groups, most of whom were drawn to the settlement from adjacent territories upon the establishment of the Edward River Mission. Because the Thaayorre are the most numerous and politically powerful group, on whose land Pormpuraaw is situated, most other Indigenous community members have at least a passive knowledge of the Thaayorre language, and many are fully fluent. As Hall (1968: 31) puts it, "This virile language is virtually a 'lingua franca' for nearly 300 inhabitants of the Edward River village". To my knowledge, there are no monolingual Kuuk Thaayorre speakers, nor were there likely to have been many in the past. This multilingualism stems from a range of social and familial structures discussed by Sharp (1934), Sutton (1978) and Taylor (1984), inter alia. This section very briefly outlines the multilingual ecology of Pormpuraaw today, relating this to the stable patterns of multilingualism obtaining in the area prior to European invasion.

Cape York Peninsula has long been an area of widespread and sustained multilingualism (cf., e.g., Sutton 1978, 1991 and Mülhäusler 2000 who characterizes Cape York as a 'balanced equitable ecology').[19] For generations, then, the Thaayorre would also have been proficient (to various degrees) in other languages of the area, in particular Yir Yoront,[20] Koko Bera, and Pakanh, as well as, potentially, Kugu Nganhcara, Ayapathu, Kunjen, Uw Oykangand and more. In general, the strongest ties, both in the past and today, bind the Yir Yoront and Kuuk Thaayorre. As Stanner (1937: 7) puts it, the Yir Yoront and Kuuk Thaayorre are "unified by common custom, beliefs, and

---

19 Indeed, humans have lived in multilingual, small-scale societies for all but our most recent history (Grosjean 1982: 1), and multilingualism was the norm in many – if not all – parts of Australia (Brandl & Walsh 1981, Singer & Harris 2016).
20 Both the Yir Yoront people and their language are referred to in Kuuk Thaayorre as Koko Mincena (pronounced with a very rare penultimate stress).

social organization, and by kinship inter-relationships through marriage across tribal lines. Between these four tribes [which between them speak Yir Yoront and Kuuk Thaayorre] and the Wik-speaking tribes north of the Edward River there is a distinct line of cleavage". The arrangement of domestic dwellings in Pormpuraaw today replicates this divide.[21] Most obviously, almost all of those living on the southern side of 'Pormpuraaw Street' (which becomes the road to Cairns, and on which is located the school, the shop, most council buildings, the garage and the canteen) are ethnically Thaayorre or Yir Yoront. Kuuk Thaayorre is the primary language of communication in and around these homes, Yir Yoront is spoken rarely if at all, and all those who remember it now use Kuuk Thaayorre or English in their daily interactions.[22] Nevertheless, the close genetic relationship and long history of contact between Kuuk Thaayorre and Yir Yoront (and their respective speakers) is evident in the many shared linguistic and cultural features.

The Wik peoples, reflecting their traditional territories to the north of the Thaayorre, live almost exclusively on the northern side of Pormpuraaw St. This northern area is known in the community as 'Munkan side',[23] and is populated mostly by ($\approx$250) Kugu Nganhcara people. Wik Mungkan is becoming a lingua franca among 'Munkan siders' due to its strength in Aurukun, where most of the Kugu Nganhcara have lived and/or have family, although there are few ethnically Wik Mungkan people living in Pormpuraaw. Of the six patrilects[24] collectively labelled Kugu Nganhcara – Kugu Muminh, Kugu Mu'inh, Kugu Uwanh, Kugu Ugbanh, Kugu Yi'anh and Wik Iyenh – Kugu Muminh and Kugu Mu'inh are the only two I have heard used regularly on the street. Even these patrilects, however, have fewer than forty speakers in Pormpuraaw, and the effects of contact with English and Wik Mungkan upon Kugu Muminh in particular have been well documented by Smith (1986). More clearly moribund, is the Kugu Yi'anh patrilect, of which I have been able to locate only a single speaker. Kugu Nganhcara is presently documented by a sketch grammar (Smith and Johnson 2000) and related papers, as well as some unpublished documentary materials archived at AIATSIS. Although we may infer a long history of contact between speakers of Kugu Nganhcara and Kuuk Thaayorre, the nature of this contact was dramatically altered

---

21 Alpher (1973: 2) notes the same correspondence between the arrangements of dwellings and the traditional territories of their occupants at the Mitchell River settlement (now 'Kowanyama').
22 The close relationship between speakers of Kuuk Thaayorre and the varieties spoken further south was observed by Hall during fieldwork in the 1960s, of which he notes: "almost everyone [in Pormpuraaw] is at least trilingual including English, with the Mungkan clans speaking their own dialects as well as Thaayorre, and the Thaayorre clans speaking their own dialects as well as some known in the Mitchell River community [now Kowanyama, to the south], but not necessarily Mungkan" (Hall 1972: 26).
23 This is somewhat of a misnomer, often leading to confusion with the Wik Mungkan people. While many people living on 'Munkan side' (and referred to as 'Munkan') do speak Wik Mungkan, few identify with this ethnicity.
24 'Patrilect' is used as shorthand for a dialect shared by people of a single line of patrilineal descent.

by the establishment of the Edward River mission. Prior to this, the two groups were isolated from one another for much of the year (Smith 1986: 513) despite their occupation of contiguous territories. Nowadays, they are in daily contact and there is occasional intermarriage, although there remains some hostility between the groups.

English is the official language of schooling and most administration in Pormpuraaw. Indigenous people in Pormpuraaw generally command multiple varieties within a spectrum that I shall refer to collectively as Pormpuraaw English. These varieties are deserving of further study in their own right. At one end of the spectrum, Pormpuraaw English shares much in common with the various English-lexified Creoles spoken in Aboriginal communities around Australia. At the other end of the spectrum, Pormpuraaw English falls within the range of the (broadly defined) Standard Australian English variety. Many of the hallmark features identified for 'Aboriginal English' (e.g. by Capell 1979, Black 1995, Arthur 1997 and Malcolm 2002, inter alia) are in evidence across all of these varieties. The introduction of English has effectively destroyed the multilingual balance of the western Cape York region. Although there is no reason to suppose that this ecology could not have absorbed one more language, the attendant political, technological and cultural changes have seen the death of many languages in the area and the obsolescence of many more. Sharp (1952, 1958, inter alia) and Taylor (1984) have documented the immediate and irrevocable impact of imported European cultural traditions and – in particular – technologies upon the traditional cosmology and social system, both of which are predicated upon a stable and unchanging social and physical context.

1.3.3 Kinship and speech etiquette

Anthropological descriptions of Thaayorre social structure emphasize the patrilineal clan as the most important social unit, particularly with respect to land tenure (Taylor 1984, Stanner 1937). Each patriline is affiliated with a number of totemic beings (*pulowar*, such as the *minh kothon* 'wallaby') and associated stories, songs, dances and 'story places' (*raak woocorrm*). The Thaayorre, like most groups of Cape York Peninsula, traditionally lived in local bands revolving around a 'focal male' (Sutton 1978, Sutton and Rigsby 1982), nowadays often identified as a (deceased) ancestor. Other members of the local band would be related to this man by descent, marriage or sometimes merely friendship (Smith 1986: 514). As Simmons, Graydon and Gajdusek (1958: 62) point out, the Thaayorre "have long been allied to the Yir-Yoront by intermarriage and common custom, although they are linguistically divergent. These two allied tribes have traditionally had little association with the Wik-speaking tribes to the north or the Koko-speaking tribes to south."

The following two subsections detail the Kuuk Thaayorre kinship system and set of kin terms (§1.3.3.1), and how kinship is inherently tied to speech etiquette in Pomrpuraaw (§1.3.3.2).

1.3.3.1 Kinship and kin terms

Kuuk Thaayorre kin terms may be divided into four sets: referential terms (used to talk about kin to a third party, as in *nganam nhangkn* 'your mother'); vocative terms (used to address someone by indexing the relationship between them and the speaker, as in *Kalin!* 'Mum!'); bereavement terms (used to refer to someone bereaved of kin in a particular category, as in *kuukum* 'one bereaved of their mother'); and hand signs (such as touching the breast to index one's mother, cf. §1.3.2.1). The Kuuk Thaayorre kinship system can be described as 'classificatory', inasmuch as a Thaayorre person may address anyone in the Thaayorre social world using a vocative kin term whether they are related through blood, marriage, or neither. The kin hand signs are likewise extended to all individuals. More unusually for an Australian language, other Kuuk Thaayorre kin terms are emphatically not classificatory. Referential terms are restricted to kindred; those related through blood, marriage or as 'surrogate' (Taylor 1984: 124). So the referential term *nganip* 'father' can describe a father's brother, father's mother's son, and so on, but not an unrelated man treated as 'equivalent' to a father in the classificatory system. Bereavement terms are even more limited in their denotation, being used only to refer to the 'focal member' of the relevant kin category. The focal member is defined by Taylor (1984: 127) as one who:

> [...] exercised the full panoply of duties involved in the status from the observance of pre-birth taboos through to special mourning duties [...] The primary or first incumbent of this status [for the category of nganhin 'father' – AG] was normally an individual's genitor. In ordinary circumstances it was usually impossible for a person's genitor to discharge every duty and obligation implied by the status of "blood" father, if only because the father usually died before the child. When a man's genitor died, rules of succession operated to ensure that another member of the kindred, also addressed as "nganhin" or "father" stepped in to occupy the status and assume the relevant duties. Thus an individual's kindred members classified by a single vocative term can be regarded not only as occupiers of a set of statuses defined primarily in terms of kin criteria, but also as a pool from which kindred members were elevated to focal statuses. By the same token, rules also operated to bring non-kindred members into a person's kindred permanently or temporarily in order to play key roles.

With regard to marriage, the Kuuk Thaayorre kinship system hinges upon an asymmetrical, 'matrilateral' ideal marriage whereby a man marries a woman he addresses as *rorko* 'mother's brother's daughter', and a woman addresses her husband as *maarn* 'father's sister's son'. This – paired with the differentiation of one's mother's mother's brother and father's father, but not father's mother's brother and mother's father – fits Radcliffe-Brown's (1951: 42) definition of the *Karadjeri* kinship system.

The inventory of Kuuk Thaayorre kin terms is presented in Table 1, which is adapted from Taylor (1984: 122) with minor modifications in accordance with my own data on the topic. The leftmost column specifies the focal member for each category.[25]

---

[25] The following abbreviations are used (often in concatenation) to represent kin relationships: M

Table 1. Inventory of Kuuk Thaayorre kin terms (adapted from Taylor 1984: 121, Table 3.2).

Relationship (X)	Referential (ego's X)	Vocative (X!)	Bereavement (one bereaved of X)	Hand sign (X)
B+	(pam) kanam	waanhn	piluump	shin
♂SS, ♀BSS	parr_r **punth**-waanha			
Z+	yapa	yapn		
♂SD, ♀BSD	parr_r **punth**-yapa			
B-	puumi	puumn	yangkar-kaar	
FF	**punth**-puumi			
Z-	wiila	wiiln	kumuniya	
FFZ	**punth**-wiila			
F	nganip	nganin	kaal-mangk	biceps
FZ	ngan pinhirr	pinharr		
♂S, ♀BS	pam nherngk	ngothon	thanakunm	
♂D, ♀BD	paanth nherngk			
MF, MFZ	paanth ngan-ngethe	ngethin	yuumanthaar	shoulder
FM, FMB	pam ngan-ngethe			
♀SS, ♂ZSS	pam nhemthinthin	ngethe	thaa-ngethe-kaar	
♀SD, ♂ZSD	paanth menthinthin			
M	(nha)nganam	kalin	kuukum	breast
MB-	ngan kaala, pam kaal-mele	kaaln	raprrm	
MB+	ngan mokr	mokr		
♀S, ♂ZS	pam rothom	thuuwn	ngamkaar	
♀D, ♂ZD	paanth rothom			
MBD, ♂W	rorko, paanth paathum	rorko	yuk-waarr-mungkm	thigh
MBS, ♂WB	ngan kuth, pam muth	kuthn	thaknham	
FZD, ♀HZ	paanth meer-mele	maarn	muthyurum	
FZS, ♀H	pam meer-mele			
MM	paanth kamthil-mele	kaman	thaa-keme-kaar	ribs
MMB	pam meer-mele			
♀DS, ♂ZDS	pam ngan-keme	kemeth		
♀DD, ♂ZDD	paanth ngan-keme			
MMBS	ngan thaam	thaaman	yencil	buttock
MMBD	ngan mayath	mayath		
FZDS	pam parr_r punth-wayump	paangun	yangan-waarra	
FZDD	paanth parr_r punth-wayump			

'mother', F 'father', S 'son', D 'daughter', B 'brother', Z 'sister', H 'husband', W 'wife', +/− 'elder/younger' (e.g. B- 'younger brother'), ♀/♂ 'female/male ego' (e.g. ♀FB+W 'a woman's father's elder brother's wife').

The next column provides the referential term used to talk about this focal member or another close ('kindred') relation in that category (see §3.1.1.2.1 and §6.3 for a discussion of the generic nouns found in some binomial referential kin terms). The third column provides the vocative term used to address anyone in that category (whether a kin relation or not). The fourth column provides the bereavement term applied when one is bereaved of a focal member of that category. Lastly, the rightmost column identifies the body part used to sign for members of that category.

Taylor (1984) provides a wealth of information about the Thaayorre kinship structure and the various roles and responsibilities assigned to members of each kin category. The kinship systems of the neighbouring Wik Mungkan and Yir-Yoront have also been extensively described by McConnell (e.g. 1940), Thomson (1955, 1972), and Sharp (1937, 1958). Gaby (2016, 2017), meanwhile, considers the semantics of Kuuk Thaayorre kin terms in much greater detail than space allows for here.

1.3.3.2 Speech etiquette

Many accounts of speech etiquette in Aboriginal societies have emphasized indirect forms of communication, often to the exclusion of more direct speech. To take a locally relevant example, von Sturmer (1981: 16) noted that people in Pormpuraaw "habitually have great difficulty in making requests, even for seemingly trivial items such as a box of matches". Yet examples of rude jokes (e.g. Thomson 1935), direct gaze, imperatives and forms of address (e.g. Garde 2008: 247) abound in both classic and recent research. Indeed, in the very same article quoted above, von Sturmer provides an anecdocte that suggests – without proving – very direct forms of request were very much in evidence in Pormpuraaw: "one day the wife approached me and said that her husband was down at Chapman Creek and that I should drive her down to pick him up" (von Sturmer 1981: 24). Indeed, von Sturmer himself provides the key to understanding when direct requests are appropriate and when they are not; "complex rules and normative behaviours are attached to all kin relationships" (von Sturmer 1981: 17). This recalls Thomson's earlier observation that "when a man swears, it is not a question of what he says so much as to whom he says it" (Thomson 1935: 465). An account of speech etiquette in Thaayorre society – past or present – thus cannot be divorced from a description of the kinship system. A perfectly polite way of speaking to one's *puumn* 'younger brother' or 'father's father', would be unspeakably rude in addressing one's *kaaln* 'mother's younger brother'. Indeed, a man couldn't initiate a conversation with anyone in the *kaaln* kin category, and had to act with great restraint around them (Taylor 1984: 164). These interactional norms traditionally extended to everyone classificatorily assigned to the relevant kin category, not just focal members or kindred. So women in the *mayath* 'wife's mother' category were interactionally equivalent to the mother of a man's actual spouse, and thus subject to the same avoidance behaviours (Taylor 1984: 169). Today, the system is somewhat more relaxed, though avoidance is still widely practiced. For example, certain people were keen to participate in linguistic work, but were markedly uncomfortable in my presence owing to our classificatory kin relationship. In certain cases, people will exploit the flexibility of the classificatory system by reckoning kin relationships by alternative routes (e.g. a man whose mother addresses me as 'brother's wife' might choose to calculate his relationship to me through his father, or some other family member, thereby arriving at an address term that better suits the desired mode of interaction). Indeed, the form of speech etiquette a person adopts might itself be indicative of such creative kin reckoning; Taylor (1984: 168) observes that a man can signal his intention of a 'wronghead' marriage by treating his prospective WM with restraint.[26]

While Kuuk Thaayorre speakers must take kinship into account in order to speak appropriately, this is not the only consideration. Sutton (1978: 192) rightly points out that interactions among Wik-speaking people (and likewise, I would add, speakers of Kuuk Thaayorre) are governed by a suite of factors including: (a) relations between speakers, addresses and referents (including sex, generation, age, seniority, marriage ties, genealogical distance, geographical/political ties, affective relations, wider ethnic relations); (b) personal state (including bereavement, initiation, illness, injury, agedness); (c) situational context (including hunting, arguing, joking); and (d) topic (including non-taboo topics such as fishing, somewhat taboo topics such as birth, or highly taboo topics such as ritual property or death).

1.4 This grammar

This grammar offers a linguistic description of the phonology, morphology, syntax and (grammatically-relevant) semantics of Kuuk Thaayorre. It employs the specialist terminology and concepts peculiar to the discipline, and as such assumes some prior linguistic training of its reader. There are, of course, many non-linguists who may have an interest in learning more about Kuuk Thaayorre grammar. They are recommended to the Kuuk Thaayorre Learners' Grammar (authorship under negotiation, in preparation). In it they will find a plain English description of the language's sound system, how to form words, how words combine words to form phrases and sentences, and the basics of everyday conversation.

1.4.1 Origin

Around the time I finished my undergraduate studies, the University of Melbourne's Linguistics Department received a fax from the Pormpuraaw Aboriginal Shire Council, which was seeking a linguist to conduct a survey of languages spoken in the community.

---

26 This accords with Garde's (2013: 25) observation that "attempts to capture the sense of a particular kin term through genealogical links will not always reflect the social realities of how Bininj Gun-wok speakers reckon kin relations. Context, speaker goals and intentions are integral aspects of Aboriginal kinship systems".

The timing was perfect, as I had a strong interest in conducting research on Australian Aboriginal languages but wanted any collaboration to be instigated by the speech community itself (cf. Wilkins 1992a, Land 2015, Carew 2016). I was duly engaged as a linguistic consultant to the community and made my first, two-week trip to Pormpuraaw in March of 2002. I spent that two-week trip knocking on every door – thereby breaching the rules of etiquette I was only later to learn – and inquiring, as sensitively as I could, about the language use of each community member. I also let it be known that I was looking for a community that might be interested in collaborating with a linguist in the long term, with a view to writing about language for my University studies. The response was less effusive than I had unreasonably hoped for, but at least I met with no objection, and several people expressed enthusiasm for the idea.

After posting them the survey report and a proposal for further linguistic research, the council invited me to return. So in the middle of 2002, I returned to Pormpuraaw as a PhD student ready to dedicate the next six months to learning Kuuk Thaayorre and collaborating with its speakers to produce materials of use to them. I announced as much to the council and put up a sign saying that I would wait under the big fig tree for anyone who was interested in working with me. And under that fig tree I sat for many an hour. Eventually, Uncle Alfred Charlie sat down beside me. After sitting in silence for some time, we began to talk in a very general way about language and language work. I reigned in every urge to beg him to record pronominal paradigms with me there and then, hiding my disappointment when he said he might find me again another day. But find me he did, and so he became my key language teacher, cultural mentor and friend. It was Alfred who first addressed me by a kin term, *Wiiln* 'younger sister'. As the days passed, I met many other Kuuk Thaayorre speakers with whom I would eventually work, and still further people would come by the fig tree to suggest other people who would make good language teachers. Prime among them was Aunty Myrtle Foote, widow of the famed †Tom Foote (who had worked with Allen Hall), who addressed me as *Thuuwn* '(woman's) daughter'. Myrtle not only worked with me herself, but also put me in touch with other language experts from her family. Uncle Gilbert Jack was my third major language teacher, and became my most frequent teacher and collaborator. Gilbert returned to Pormpuraaw some time after I had begun work there, and sought me out with an urgent enthusiasm. The various contributions of each of my key language teachers and collaborators are described in §1.4.4.

As my research progressed, I was keen to find ways to reciprocate the generosity of the many people sharing their language and knowledge with me. It was clear that they had no particular interest in the academic papers and grammar I was working on for my own benefit, although they were supportive of their production. It was less clear to me how my linguistic training and growing language knowledge could be of benefit to them. I made various suggestions – a dictionary, books of traditional stories and literacy primers to put in the school, collaborating with teachers to develop a modest Kuuk Thaayorre curriculum, developing Kuuk Thaayorre and Kugu Nganhcara content for the BRACS (local radio and TV broadcasting station), some of which were taken up (e.g. Tarpencha & Gaby 2003) – but there was no local ownership of or drive for such projects. Other projects that Daniel Hirst and I initiated were very well received. For example, a CD of traditional and modern songs in the community's languages was played at great volume on high rotation (Charlie et al. 2003), and set of literacy CD-ROMs used in the school were very popular among a generation of children (Hirst & Gaby 2004, 2005a, 2005b). But over time I came to realize that the people I was working with saw me as a conduit to whitefellas and institutions, rather than someone who might help produce materials for the Indigenous Pormpuraawans. Once I began to really listen, I got the message loud and clear: my job was to talk about Kuuk Thaayorre and Kugu Nganhcara to the whitefellas in Pormpuraaw, and to my family, friends, colleagues and students outside. I was to explain to people that these were real languages; as complex and important as English. Indeed, more important in the local context owing to their ties to country and their role in keeping country strong. Furthermore, the people I worked with wanted outsider service providers to learn the basics of communicating in language. Their expectations in this regard were exceedingly modest; just a few simple phrases were sufficient to indicate a respect for the language and its speakers on the part of a whitefella nurse, ranger, or police officer. Some collaborators also wanted individual help in filling out forms or dealing with bureaucracy in Brisbane or Cairns. Overall, we agreed that my primary role was to produce materials for an audience of whitefellas, designed to increase the understanding and respect for language in the broader Australian community, and to increase practical understanding / basic fluency in local languages among service providers in Pormpuraaw. I viewed my academic work as aligning with this goal, since it aimed to raise the profile of Australian languages (and Pormpuraaw languages in particular) among linguists and other researchers, as well as among the students I teach. I have not done so well in increasing language fluency among service providers, however, as I have spent little time in Pormpuraaw since graduating.

In 2006 I completed my PhD thesis; a grammar of Kuuk Thaayorre. Since then I have continued to revise this grammar in light of continued analysis as well as data from subsequent field trips, culminating in the present volume. I have no doubt that another ten years will reveal further errors and inadequacies of this account. I hope that members of the Thaayorre community and other experts will scrutinize, critique and build upon the starting point made here.

1.4.2 Theoretical background

Constant revision, redevelopment and replacement are the nature of most theories. A grammar too constrained by a particular theoretical framework therefore risks becoming unreadable or uninteresting to linguists of other theoretical orientations and generations. This has sadly been the fate of too many grammars already; for example the numerous very detailed grammars written within the tagmemic tradition, which rarely find their way into typological (or other) samples today. Yet, as

Dryer (2006) has convincingly argued, "there is no such thing as an atheoretical description". The present grammar can be broadly described as falling within the tradition of 'Basic Linguistic Theory' (Dixon 1997), inasmuch as it builds upon the descriptive theoretical framework that has evolved through grammatical descriptions (particularly of Australian languages) aiming to describe each language on its own terms. There is increasing recognition that even cross-linguistically common categories need to be identified – and the criteria for doing so be made explicit – for each language independently (Cristofaro 2006). To obstinately and blindly describe Kuuk Thaayorre on its own terms, however, would be to run the risk of obscuring the many ways in which Kuuk Thaayorre resembles other languages inside and outside Australia. This grammar attempts to avoid employing formalisms likely to date the grammar (cf. Evans and Dench 2006), while still linking into the relevant typological, theoretical and descriptive literature. This includes the use of widely recognized glosses, terminology and conventions (wherever these are not misleading) to allow future researchers to make still more connections. Where Kuuk Thaayorre exhibits a feature or structure of relevance to recent theoretical debates, or where particular theoretical models are helpful in explaining particular aspects of the language, I make reference to whichever theoretical framework appears most relevant to the case at hand.[27] There doubtless remain many points at which this balance is lacking, however.

In its attempt to describe the grammatical system of a single language variety, this grammar unfortunately reinforces the fiction of "an ideal speaker-listener, in a completely homogeneous speech-community" (Chomsky 1965: 3). Yet monolingual conversations in Pormpuraaw are vanishingly rare, with most conversations involving between two and four languages (cf. §1.3.2.3). Much as Kuuk Thaayorre speakers would draw on their multilingual repertoire in conversations with one another, the language experts I worked with wove English loanwords and rampant code-switching into their Kuuk Thaayorre narratives and conversations with me. Indeed, I believe at least one of my language teachers, Alfred Charlie, saw this as an effective pedagogical strategy when I was first learning the language.[28] And so I rarely recorded the purely monolingual texts for which documentary and descriptive linguists traditionally strive.

A full account of how multilingualism operates in the Pormpuraaw context, and how it affects and is affected by Kuuk Thaayorre grammar, is a topic for future research rather than the present work. This grammar does, however, make some spo-

---

27 It is true that the references to Lexical Functional Grammar herein outstrip references to any other theoretical framework, but this is due at least in part to the fact that LFG expressly attempts to be relevant to non-configurational languages like Kuuk Thaayorre.

28 In my naivety, I was at first frustrated by Alfred's insertions of English into his narratives, believing they muddied the otherwise pure language data he was creating. In retrospect, I see that he was in fact an excellent language teacher who knew what he was doing; I learned much faster during my sessions with him than those with language experts who more strictly conformed to my requests for word lists, paradigms and monolingual texts.

radic appeals to language contact as a potential explanation for puzzling facts about Kuuk Thaayorre grammar. Similarly, I make a number of references to grammaticalization and putative earlier linguistic forms and structures in lieu of a full and integrated account of the diachrony of Kuuk Thaayorre grammar. Advocating the latter approach, Martinet (1986: 248) observes:

> A dynamic approach to linguistic description has of late often been recommended even in the case of unilingual situations where we have to reckon with imbalance in every linguistic system, arising from tensions within the system itself, and the permanent conflict between the ease of the speakers, the needs of communication, and the pressure of tradition. The more so in the case of diglossia where, in addition to all these, we have the inevitable tensions between the languages in contact.

Finally, I have tried to emulate Hall's (1972) munificent provision of example sentences as far as space will allow. I believe this is important not only for the benefit of future linguists who may wish to form their own conclusions without their being mediated by my own analytical interpretation, but also to help the reader form an impression of the Kuuk Thaayorre language as it is used. But while Mithun (2001: 53) exhorts that grammars should let speakers "speak for themselves, creating a record of spontaneous speech in natural communicative settings", the reader should not assume that the example sentences herein accurately reflect the culture, interests, priorities or personalities of the speakers that uttered them. The descriptive imperatives to illustrate a particular linguistic form or structure have in many cases had to outrank the desire to provide sociologically representative or encyclopaedically informative example sentences.

1.4.3 Sources and methodology

Two broad corpora inform the analysis and supply the examples presented in this grammar. The first is drawn from the unpublished thesis and pedagogical materials of Allen Hall and his collaborators, as discussed in §1.4.3.1. The other comprises data collected during the six visits I made to Pormpuraaw between 2002 and 2008, totalling over nine months. The contexts in which data were elicited are outlined in the following subsections. The core of this second corpus is just over sixty-three hours of audio and /or video recordings of elicitated data, narratives and conversation, plus many further hours of elicitation sessions with language experts who were happy to have their language written down, but either did not want to be recorded or requested to have audio recordings destroyed following transcription.[29]

---

[29] It should be noted that the total number of hours given here includes some substantial periods of silence, English-language conversation and off-topic activity during recording sessions. It also includes several sessions spent transcribing previously recorded texts, since these sessions contained some informative discussions of grammar and meaning. Audio and video recordings of the same session are only counted once.

Video recordings were made either with a Sony DCR mini-DV tape camcorder (before 2007) or a JVC HD Everio camcorder (2007 and after). Audio recordings were made with either a Sony MZ-R900 minidisc recorder (before 2007), a DAT recorder (in 2007 and 2008), a Marantz PMD-660 solid state recorder (2007 and after), and/or a portable analogue cassette tape recorder (a backup option that was necessary on only a couple of occasions prior to 2006). A range of microphones were used, including two cardioid condenser microphones (set on the table or ground), a hand held directional microphone, lapel microphones, and/or the built-in microphone of the video/tape recorder. A small number of language experts did not wish to be audio- or video-recorded, in which case I simply took notes in one of five notebooks. Recordings have been deposited at the Endangered Languages Archive (ELAR; https://elar.soas.ac.uk/Collection/MPI542791) and/or the Australian Institute of Aboriginal and Torres Strait Islander Studies (these materials are being processed at time of print). Some portions of recordings were cut prior to archiving, where they involve sensitive topics, potentially libelous information, or participants who did not give explicit consent to be recorded.

A subset of recordings were transcribed using Transcriber (Barras et al. 1998; http://trans.sourceforge.net/), Toolbox (Summer Institute of Linguistics International; http://www.angelfire.com/planet/linguisticsisfun/) or ELAN (Wittenburg et al. 2006; http://tla.mpi.nl/tools/tla-tools/elan/). The process of transcription and translation is described further in §1.4.3.2–1.4.3.6.

The variety described in this grammar was selected by providence rather than by design. The three language experts with whom I spent most time (Alfred Charlie, Myrtle Foote and Gilbert Jack) are only distantly related and spend little social time together. Nevertheless, their speech converges to the point that it can confidently labeled a single dialect, with only a few minor differences in vocabulary and pronunciation.[30] That this variety is standard was confirmed by conversations with and observation of other Kuuk Thaayorre speakers in the community. Most divergences from the grammar set down here were found among younger speakers whose speech displays multiple effects of language attrition.

1.4.3.1 Hall and colleagues

The example sentences included in Hall (1968, 1972) and the unpublished works of Foote and Hall have made an enormously valuable contribution. Examples sourced from these works have been re-transcribed to reflect changes in the practical orthography and (in some cases) phonological analysis. I have also – except where otherwise noted – modified segmentation, glossing and translation in order to align these examples with the present grammatical analysis, which differs from Hall (1972) in

---

[30] For example, the adverb *angunp* 'in this place' is pronounced [aɲunp] by AC, [ŋamunp] by GJ, and [ajunp] by a third language expert (LN) and many other younger speakers.

numerous key respects. It should therefore be noted that where these works are cited as the source of an example sentence, this source represents the point of origin only. I take full responsibility for all errors in transcription and analysis of example sentences. Readers interested in any example sentences cited from these works are recommended to the original source materials.

The following sections describe the different classes of data collected by the author between 2002–2008, as well as the methodologies employed to this end.

1.4.3.2 Conversation

There are three main subtypes of conversational data in my corpus: (1) conversations that occurred in the context of elicitation; (2) elicited conversations between native speakers; (3) unrecorded, 'natural' conversations. The first of these, labelled 'Elicitation / Conversation' below the relevant example sentences, describes conversational exchanges between the language expert and me during the course of a recorded elicitation session. These conversations may be informal and off-topic (for example, the language expert requesting a cup of tea, or asking me why I didn't answer the door when he came by the day before), or related to the topic of elicitation (for example, my soliciting the Kuuk Thaayorre term for 'woomera' and asking about how one is used). The second class of conversational data was elicited by arranging a session with multiple native speakers of Kuuk Thaayorre, and asking them to talk together about a particular topic (for example, what life was like during the mission). Such 'conversations' were often rather unnatural in tone, and/or evolved into a co-constructed narrative genre rather than a conversation proper. In any case, they yielded much useful and interesting data, and often included more spontaneous and naturalistic conversations at their periphery. Examples sourced from such interactions are coded 'Narrative/Conversation'. Thirdly, I took the opportunity to converse with anyone who could bear so inept a conversational partner.

It goes without saying that none of these conversations should be considered fully representative of Kuuk Thaayorre conversational norms. Where I was among the interlocutors, my lack of cultural and linguistic fluency is certain to have influenced the flow of conversation. In other cases, the presence of recording equipment would have resulted in some level of self-consciousness. Mitigating this problem somewhat, I was able to compare the conversations I recorded with the hundreds of conversations I eavesdropped upon while living in Pormpuraaw. Overheard structures of particular interest were checked in formal elicitation sessions and thereby made their way into this grammar.

1.4.3.3 Narrative

The topics of narratives were generally selected by the language expert, though often in response to a rather vague prompt (such as 'what was Pormpuraaw like when you were a child?' or 'can you tell us a *wuuc* 'traditional song/story') upon which the language expert(s) would expound at length. I avoided any further prompting or intervention in the narrative where possible, though it usually felt most natural to provide backchannel responses. The line between conversation, elicitation and narrative often became blurred. Often we would begin a session with something akin to either a conversation or lexical elicitation in a particular semantic field, but the language expert's responses would become increasingly lengthy, often evolving into storytelling about what they had been doing that morning, or the last time a cyclone had passed through town, or the first time they had ever seen a plane. Example sentences sourced from such lengthy turns are classified 'Narrative' (or, in borderline cases, 'Conversation/Narrative') in the source code.

1.4.3.4 Elicited data

All the data I have access to must properly be considered 'elicited', simply by virtue of my presence as a 'language worker'. In the source codes below this grammar's example sentences, however, the classification 'Elicitation' indicates that the utterance was produced under one of the following circumstances: (1) I asked speakers to translate English words and clauses into Kuuk Thaayorre and vice versa; (2) I provided speakers with a context (e.g. 'imagine your son walked by us and you wanted to know if he had finished building the fishtrap'), asking them what they might say in that situation; or (3) I provided language experts with a Kuuk Thaayorre clause (usually one I had heard uttered by a native speaker on another occasion), asking them in what contexts they could imagine uttering it. A number of elicitation tasks (such as Dahl 1985, Wilkins 1999) drew on some variation of these methods. A further important source of data was the array of video stimuli developed by the Max Planck Institute for Psycholinguistics. These were played to language experts, who then described what had happened in the video just viewed. Other elicitation tasks involved pairs of language experts, one of whom would use verbal cues to direct the other to identify among a group of photos the correct match for the one held by the director. Every elicitation task yielding data that contributed to this grammar is listed in Appendix 1.

One well recognized drawback of grammatical elicitation is 'judgement hypercorrection'; where language experts reject sentences as ungrammatical because they are not provided with the discourse context in which they might be uttered. This was also sometimes in evidence when transcribing narrative texts (see §1.4.3.5). For this reason, elicitation was used only as a supplement to more naturally occurring data.

1.4.3.5 Re-speakings

It often happened that a language expert working with me on the transcription and translation of (their own, or another language expert's) narrative would suggest a slow-spoken version of the text that departed markedly from what I heard on the recording itself. In some cases, this involved correcting grammatical errors in the original, in other cases it seemed more a case of stylistic preference. These re-spoken versions of the original narrative provided a useful source of data in and of themselves. Where re-speakings are quoted in this grammar as example sentences, the source credit immediately below the example reflects the re-speaker rather than the original narrator. In the texts provided in Appendix 2, re-speakings are presented alongside my own transcription of the original wherever the language expert helping me to transcribe the text explicitly disagreed with my own interpretation of what the original speaker had said.

1.4.3.6 On-record and off-record communicative contexts

The vast majority of data in my corpus – and all the currently accessible archived data – is drawn from on-record communicative contexts. Such contexts occur within a designated work session, once we have turned on the audio/video recorder and explicitly agreed that we are ready to work. Most such work sessions began with me asking "are you ready to work now?". When the language expert signalled assent, I would turn on the recording device and one or both of us would say (with sharply falling intonation); *kana!* or 'alright!'. In certain other, off-record contexts, I would notice something worth recording (either a grammatical structure used in conversation, or a new species of bird I wanted to record the name of). In such cases I might say "can we work for a minute?" and, with the speaker's consent, jot down verbatim what they said, or turn on a recording device if one was available. Such data are also considered sourced from an on-record context.

Off-record contexts include everything that falls outside the definition above, from an informal and unrecorded chat over a cup of tea, to a video recording of singing and dancing at a house opening (made with participants' consent, but not explicitly framed as "work" contributing to my own studies). Moreover, off-record contexts may be embedded within an on-record macro-context. For example, in the middle of a recorded session, a family member might walk in and begin to chat, argue, or gossip. Or in the middle of a recorded narrative, the language expert might appear to forget that they are being recorded and disclose information they may not wish to be shared. A small number of example sentences in this grammar are excerpts from passages of off-record speech that do not contain any identifying or potentially sensitive information. On several occasions, snippets of conversation I happened to overhear (and later checked for grammaticality with a native speaker) have proven analytically interesting and have also found their way into this grammar as 'anonymous' examples. Although it would of course be preferable to be able to furnish audio recordings of all data referred to, I have endeavoured to strike a balance between the privacy of the speakers concerned and the inclusion of rich and natural language data. Opportunistic observations from informal interactions were frequently more interesting than those conducted in the rather sterile 'language work' context. As Sutton (1978: xvii) declares, "my main 'research tool', if it can be called that, was paying attention".

1.4.4 Language experts and collaborators

The example sentences quoted in this grammar were uttered by dozens of people in numerous speech contexts. Not all of the people who worked with me wanted their utterances to be attributed to them in this written document. Many others, however, were keen to be identified along with quotations of their speech. They are listed here in alphabetical order, along with a very brief summary of the kinds of data they contributed. The initials that follow their name in the subheading corresponds to the language expert reference in the source file names listed immediately below example sentences.

Alfred Charlie [AC]

Thaayorre elder Alfred Charlie primarily views himself as a storyteller, language expert and 'culture man'. He happily answered my questions, but was most comfortable producing narratives in a mixture of Kuuk Thaayorre and English (so to ensure I could follow the story). His narratives spanned the traditional *wuuc* origin songs and stories (such as *Minh Kothon* 'Wallaby', cf. Charlie et al. 2003) and personal history (both from his boyhood, such as the time his uncle was killed by a snake, and from the more recent past, such as the Losing Irma story in Appendix 2).

† Alice Chillagoe [ACh]

I had the privilege of working with Thaayorre elder Alice Chillagoe towards the end of her life. Her main interest was in providing – frequently hilarious – personal narratives about her family, as well as singing *wuuc* origin songs relating to the Rainbow Serpent / Cyclone down to the south (some of which were recorded in Charlie et al. 2003). Her almighty cursing was often heard ringing out from the air-conditioned school store room we liked to work in.

Albert Jack [AJ]

Thaayorre elder Albert Jack shared with me many entertaining personal narratives as well as providing conversational data from exchanges with me and / or his brother, Gilbert Jack, and their sister, Ivy Conrad. Albert also spent many hours providing descriptions of elicitation videos, always with great patience.

Celia Holroyd / Peter [CH]

Kugu Muminh elder Celia Holroyd was one of my key Kugu Muminh teachers. She is a passionate advocate for her language and retains deep knowledge of both language and culture. She teaches Kugu Muminh, basket-weaving, songs and dance to children in the community, both through the school and outside. Although my other Kugu Nganhcara language teachers do not figure in this grammar, Celia served as an interactant in several multilingual texts recorded with Alfred Charlie, including the Losing Irma story included in Appendix 2. Celia goes both by her original surname (Holroyd) and her married surname (Peter).

Cyril William

Though Thaayorre elder Cyril William did not work with me as a language teacher – and as such does not appear in the example sentences below – he recorded a number of *wuuc* traditional songs for the CD I co-produced (Charlie et al. 2003), and taught me a lot about the songs and stories of the country around Pormpuraaw. He sang the song of the Two Crocodiles with his brother Donald; the accompanying story (as told by Donald William) appears in Appendix 2.

Donald Joe [DJ]

Donald Joe participated in several elicitation tasks requiring a director and matcher (e.g. the Man & Tree task, see Appendix 1). He also worked with me on lexical and basic grammatical elicitation, including kinship hand signs.

Donald William [DW]

Thaayorre elder Donald William is a master storyteller and repository of a wealth of historical and cultural knowledge. He told the story of the Two Crocodiles, the transcription of which can be found in Appendix 2.

Edna Charlie [EC]

Over the course of her life, Thaayorre elder Edna Charlie has made a great contribution to linguistics and the documentation of Kuuk Thaayorre and Yir Yoront. I only had the opportunity to record a few words and sentences with her, but she took a keen interest in the work I was doing with other Kuuk Thaayorre speakers and offered me much valuable advice along the way.

Elizabeth Norman [EN]

Although she is extremely modest about her own language abilities, Elizabeth Norman is a fully fluent speaker of Kuuk Thaayorre who proved invaluable in helping me to understand the language. Though she did not claim the authority to provide narrative texts, our many long chats contributed to my corpus of conversation. Elizabeth also was an excellent collaborator in transcribing and translating recordings made with other language experts. Elizabeth now serves as Minister of the Anglican Church in Pormpuraaw.

Esther Foote [EF]

Esther Foote is one of the daughters of Tom and Myrtle Foote. She did not assume the cultural authority to author narratives or record conversations, but she answered many hundreds of elicitation questions and was an excellent language instructor during my first months in the community. She and her sisters have followed their parents' lead in supporting language use in the Pormpuraaw Primary School and other local institutions.

Freddy Tyore [FT]

Thaayorre elder Freddy Tyore is an invaluable source of historical, cultural and ethnobiological information. He opened my eyes to the culturally significant categories of local flora, fauna and land types. He contributed both conversational and elicited data to my corpus, though his political and other responsibilities limited the time he could devote to language work.

Gilbert Jack [GJ]

Thaayorre elder Gilbert Jack was one of the main contributors to this grammar. He provided numerous narrative and conversational texts, responded to elicitation prompts, and helped me to transcribe and translate his own and others' texts. This work was just part of Gilbert Jack's long history of support for language documentation and maintenance, following from his early work with Rev. Allen Hall. Gilbert is a profoundly religious man and committed to the Pormpuraaw church. Outside our work on grammatical topics, Gilbert enlisted my help in transcribing a number of religious songs he had variously composed or translated into Kuuk Thaayorre (some of which appear on Charlie et al. 2003).

Ivy Conrad [IC]

Thaayorre elder Ivy Conrad participated in a group discussion with her brothers, Albert Jack and Gilbert Jack, about what life was like in Pormpuraaw during their childhood.

John Coleman [JCo]

Thaayorre elder John Coleman held the office of Council Chairman when I first lived in Pormpuraaw. As such, he had limited time available to work with me, though the conversations I had with him were unfailingly entertaining and enlightening. He was also extremely supportive of the language work conducted by me and others in the community, insisting that the 'Munkan' languages should not be neglected.

Lawrence Foote [LF]

Thaayorre elder Lawrence Foote is the brother of †Tom Foote. He had remarkable patience for my sometimes tedious elicitation questions, and provided many beautifully enunciated word lists, paradigms and sentences. Owing to his many commitments in Pormpuraaw and elsewhere, our working time was limited though very productive.

Molly Edwards [ME]

Thaayorre elder Molly Edwards has an extremely deep knowledge of Kuuk Thaayorre language, culture and history. She contributed many word lists, narrative texts and conversational data to my corpus. Her husband, Thaayorre elder Ned Edwards, was a frequent foil in these conversational texts. On another occasion, she was interviewed by Gilbert Jack.

Myrtle Foote [MF]
Thaayorre elder Myrtle Foote has a long history of championing Aboriginal languages in Pormpuraaw, through the Pormpuraaw Primary School (where her husband †Tom Foote worked as a Teacher Aide), the health clinic, and through her work on the council and as a Director of the Pormpur Paanth Aboriginal Corporation Board. She generously made time in her busy schedule to teach me Kuuk Thaayorre, record texts, and answer elicitation questions.

I also worked more briefly with the following language experts, who helped me to compile word lists, check the grammar of basic sentences and/or practice my early conversational skills: **Florence Foote** [FF], **Alice Peter** [AP], **Georgina Norman** [GN], **Irene Charlie** [ICh], **Jocelyn Coleman** [JC], †**Bob Holroyd** [BH], **Ned Edwards** [NE]. Many other people contributed to this grammar indirectly through informal interactions (see §1.4.3.5) and other forms of support during my time in Pormpuraaw. Though they are not acknowledged by name here, their contribution is deeply appreciated.

1.4.5 Example sentences

Example sentences are numbered according to their sequence within the grammar. Where examples are repeated they bear the original example number followed by a prime, as in (124'). Standard Pormpuraaw Orthography is employed for all examples except where phonetic transcription is required (e.g. throughout Chapter 2, Phonology). This orthography (along with its alternatives) is introduced in §2.8. Examples are glossed in accordance with the *Leipzig Glossing Rules* (Comrie et al. 2003; cf. also Lehmann 1983) where practicable. The few necessary departures from this standard are justified where introduced.

Most example sentences are translated into English by me, though this has usually been informed by discussions with native speakers. Where a language expert's translation is provided verbatim, this is enclosed in double quotation marks ("..."). This translation is sometimes in the words of the speaker of the example sentence (often in the form of code-switch echoing), at other times it is in the words of another language expert who assisted in transcribing the passage (see §1.4.4). All example sentences taken from the work of Hall (1968, 1972) and Foote and Hall (1992, undated school materials) are segmented, glossed and translated by me except where otherwise indicated. Although Hall often provides segmentations, glosses and translations, for the sake of consistency all glosses and translations reflect the analysis presented here (cf. §1.4.3.1).

The source of each example sentence is given in square brackets below the translation line. Where the example has been extracted from my own corpus, this constitutes "KTh_" (for the Kuuk Thaayorre corpus) followed by the speaker's initials, date of recording and data classification code (cf. §1.4.3). Where a recording session included multiple speakers, each of the speakers' initials is listed separated by hyphens, with the quoted speaker in bold. Data classification may simply reference the genre (e.g. 'Narrative'), or may additionally include reference to the particular story, song or elicitation stimulus the example sentence relates to (e.g. 'Narrative LosingIrma'). The full list of data classification codes is given in Appendix 1.

The following example illustrates all of the typical characteristics of an example sentence:

(5) ngay   kuuk   Thaayorre   yiik   ← transcription
     1sg(NOM) WORD   Kuuk.Thaayorre(ACC) say:RDP:NPST   ← gloss
     'I'm speaking Kuuk Thaayorre'   ← my translation
     "Me, I'm talkin Kuuk Thaayorre language"   ← language expert's translation
     [KTh_AC22Jul2002 Elicitation]   ← example sentence uttered in Kuuk Thaayorre by AC on 22nd July 2002 in a standard elicitation context.

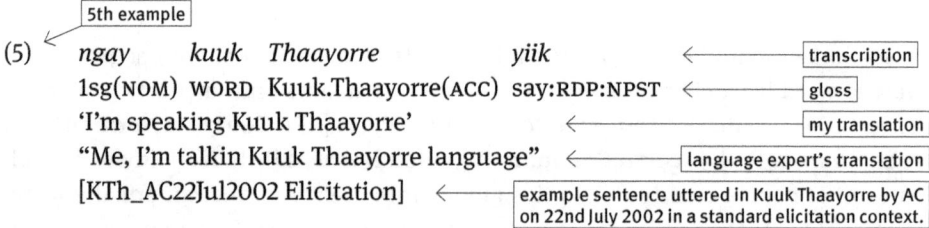 5th example

Example (5) also illustrates the use of small caps in the glossing of generic nouns (e.g. *kuuk* 'WORD').

Where an example comprises a sequence of clauses uttered in succession, each clause is marked by a sequence number as in example (6):

(6) 1. *werngr*   *ii-parr*   *thunp-m*
       boomerang(ACC) there-at:south   throw-P.IPFV
       '[they] were throwing a boomerang down in the south'
    2. *pam peln*   *mong, werngr*   *ulp*   *thunp-m*
       man 3pl(NOM)   many boomerang(ACC)   dem:ad.prx   throw-P.IPFV
       'there were a lot of men [who were] throwing that boomerang'
    3. *ulp*   *koo-pal=p*   *therk-m*
       dem:ad.prx   DIRECTED-towards=PRAG   return-P.IPFV
       'it kept coming back'
       [KTh_AC13Sep2002 Narrative Werngr]

Where an example presents an excerpt from a dialogue, each speaker is identified by their initials at the start of the transcription line, or the gloss line of the first turn, as in (7).

(7) [AJ] *brick house*   *inh*   *perpr*   *inh*
         [brick house(ACC)   dem:sp.prx   build-NPST   dem:sp.prx
         '[Nowadays they] build these brick houses'
    [IC] *bush-ak*   *wun-m*   *kanangkarr*
         bush-DAT   live-P.IPFV long.ago
         '[We] used to live in the bush long ago'
         [KTh_**AJ**-GJ-**IC**26Nov2002 Narrative/Conversation]

Where speakers have requested anonymity, or the example is drawn from an unofficial communicative context (cf. §1.4.3.5), the speaker's initials are replaced by, e.g., 'AA', 'BB' and 'CC' (in the case of a multi-person interaction). This convention is also followed for hypothetical exchanges (between imagined interactants) as constructed by language experts in the context of certain elicitation tasks, such as the 'Demonstrative Questionnaire' (Wilkins 1999).

As mentioned above, in many instances one language expert collaborated with me in transcribing and translating the texts produced by another language expert. In most cases, only the originator of the text is credited below the example sentence. However, where the transcription collaborator and I disagreed about what the original speaker had said, I might include the transcription collaborator's version of the text as an example sentence. In such cases, it is the transcription collaborator (and date of the transcription session) that is credited as the source of the example.

Some phrases or expressions are too common to be ascribed a single source; for instance I have heard the expression *ngay pamngoongkom* 'I don't know' so many times that I feel confident including it as an example (illustrating, for instance, the first person singular nominative pronoun *ngay*) without specifying a source. All example sentences presented without an explicitly named source are similarly commonplace expressions.

Non-standard (dialectal and idiolectal) forms in example sentences are dealt with in one of three ways. Where the difference is simply one of pronunciation (e.g. *waap ~ wa'ap* 'river'), the transcription reflects the standard form[31] rather than what may have been uttered in the particular context. Where the difference is more significant (e.g. *angunp ~ nhamunp* 'in this place'), the form is transcribed as uttered by the speaker and no comment is made except where relevant to the discussion at hand. Where the differences are considered to reflect a divergence from the standard Kuuk Thaayorre grammar described here (e.g. regularization of ergative morphology by younger speakers), this is noted in a footnote.

1.4.6 Overview of topics

A grammar is rarely read from cover to cover. This is fortunate since the structure of few – if any – languages is amenable to purely linear presentation. I have therefore attempted to organize this description in such a way as to allow typologists and linguists interested in either the languages of this region or particular topics in the grammar of Kuuk Thaayorre to find what they are looking for.

In standard grammars, it is usual for a phonology chapter to follow the introduction as 'Chapter 2'. There is less consensus as to the respective contents of subsequent

---

[31] The standard form is determined by token frequency in my corpus.

chapters, however. There is often a tension between organizing topics according to function (for instance grouping together the genitive nominal suffix, the comitative suffix, genitive pronouns, the associative particle *mangka*, noun phrase apposition, and attributive clauses, because each may code possession) and organizing topics according to form (e.g. discussing all verbal suffixes together, spanning reciprocity, reflexivity, causation, associated motion, various tense, aspectual and modal categories, and so on). As Cristofaro (2006: 141) points out:

> the function-to-form approach and the form-to-function approach reflect two distinct processes: the encoding process that takes place in the speaker's mind, on the one hand, and the decoding process that takes place in the hearer's mind, on the other. Both approaches are therefore essential to language description.

Confronted with a choice between the two, this grammar leans strongly towards a semasiological – form-first – structure. This approach means that related semantic or conceptual fields may be discussed in a number of different sections of this grammar, depending on the morphosyntax of their encoding. Abundant cross-reference and a detailed index are provided to help the reader find semantically linked topics that may be distributed over a number of different chapters and sections.

This chapter now concludes with a summary of the other eleven chapters of this grammar.

Chapter 2 will outline Kuuk Thaayorre phonetics and phonology. First, it details the inventory of phonemes and their allophones. This is followed by a consideration of the phonotactic structure of Kuuk Thaayorre words and syllables, and the various (morpho)phonological rules and processes in operation. It concludes with a description of the suprasegmental features of Kuuk Thaayorre speech and the practical orthographies that have been employed in the documentation of Kuuk Thaayorre.

Chapter 3 outlines the Kuuk Thaayorre word classes and their defining characteristics. This includes both major word classes (nomina, verbs, adverbs) and minor ones (ideophones and the many and various particles and enclitics). There is also detailed consideration of the internal subtypes of major word classes, including evidence for establishing generic nouns, specific nouns, adjectives, quantifiers and predicate adjectives as subclasses of the nominal class, along with various subclasses of demonstrative and pronoun.

Chapter 4 describes the morphology of nomina (a nominal subclass). Most importantly, it details the forms and functions of case categories, which are variously expressed through suffixation and encliticization. As part of this discussion, we review the evidence that case is marked by phrasal suffixation in Kuuk Thaayorre. This chapter also provides an overview of the derivational processes that derive new nomina and/or take nomen roots as input. The chapter concludes with a brief discussion of three miscellaneous morphemes that attach to nomina.

Chapter 5 begins with a description of the morphology, functions and morphosyntax of pronouns. Cardinal, reflexive, emphatic, inclusory, and ignorative pronouns are each discussed in turn. This is followed by a rather lengthy description of demonstratives, both pronominal and adnominal, revealing considerable commonalities between the demonstrative subclasses in terms of form, semantics and morphosyntax.

Chapter 6 examines how the various forms discussed in chapters 4 and 5 combine in the formation of the Kuuk Thaayorre noun phrase. Following a justification for positing a noun phrase structure in the first place, this chapter considers the internal structure of the NP (including the classifying construction and adjective phrase), the relationship between the head noun and its modifiers, and the role of pronouns and demonstratives as determiners (and whether there is evidence of a determiner phrase). We then move to consider the apposition of (partially) coreferential NPs, including five types of inclusory construction and the apposition of wholly coreferential NPs. This is followed by a description of nominal coordination and two means of expressing possessive relationships. The chapter concludes with a brief description of how reference tracking operates in larger stretches of discourse.

Chapter 7 turns to the verbal domain, exploring the range of inflectional categories coded on the Kuuk Thaayorre verb. These fall into two main types; mood and tense/aspect. The discussion of aspect includes quite extensive consideration of the semantic effects of reduplication (the morphophonology of which is described in Chapter 2). Chapter 7 also establishes the two major conjugation classes Kuuk Thaayorre verbs fall into, as well as the smaller set of irregular verbs.

Chapter 8 continues to focus on verbs, now considering the range of derivational morphemes that may attach to them. These include valence-decreasing suffixes (such as the reflexive and reciprocal) and a valence-increasing suffix. There are also two 'associated motion' morphemes – derived from the free motion verbs *ya-* 'go' and *riic* 'run' – and a suffix that derives a subordinate verb form. We also encounter a curious suffix that can derive both de-nominal verbs and de-verbal nouns. In addition to derivational suffixes, this chapter considers the formation of complex predicates and noun+verb compounds.

Chapter 9 presents a range of particles and adverbs used to enrich the clause. The adverbs discussed range from spatial, temporal and iterative adverbs to manner and degree adverbs. There is also a discussion of the body part nouns that may be compounded with adverbs. The description of Kuuk Thaayorre's many particles is distributed across several chapters. For example, the various particles used in negative clauses are discussed in Chapter 11. This chapter discusses only the high frequency and/or syntactically significant particles that do not fit thematically with the topics of other chapters. Other particles of less significance are listed in Chapter 3.

Chapter 10 describes various simple clause structures. First, it details eight different verb-headed clause types which differ in transitivity. Next, it considers a group of three constructions (existential, copula and locative) that share the characteristic of being optionally headed by a postural verb. This discussion includes consideration of the semantics of the postural verbs themselves, as well as the postural constructions that they head.

Chapter 11 moves on to consider more elaborated clauses, including: interrogative, negative, imperative, hortative, jussive, apprehensive, reflexive, reciprocal and desiderative constructions. The inflectional and derivational morphology associated with many of these functions was already introduced in Chapters 7 and 8, but these topics are revisited here owing to the important ways in which this verbal morphology combines with various particles, pronouns and other structures to form constructions greater than the sum of their parts.

Chapter 12 details the complex clause structures found in Kuuk Thaayorre. This includes a discussion of subordinate clause types as well as clausal conjunction, disjunction and concessive disjunction. The widespread use of asyndetic coordination (parataxis) is also explored.

2 Phonology

Chapter 2 provides an overview of Kuuk Thaayorre phonetics and phonology, including: the inventory of phonemes (§2.1); the range of allophones associated with each phoneme (§2.2.1 and 2.2.6); the morphophonological rules and processes that derive the various allophones (§2.2.7); minimal pairs illustrating phonemic contrasts (§2.3); the nature of Kuuk Thaayorre words and syllables, and phonotactic constraints on their internal structure (§2.4–2.52.6); reduplication (§2.6); suprasegmental features of Kuuk Thaayorre speech (§2.7); and the practical orthographies that have been employed in the documentation of Kuuk Thaayorre, in particular the 'Pormpuraaw Orthography' used in the following chapters (§2.8). Since Kuuk Thaayorre phonetics and phonology have received detailed treatment in Hall 1968, this chapter will be summary in form, focusing on the differences between the analysis followed herein and that of Hall.

Though not unusually complex, the Kuuk Thaayorre phonological system is typologically interesting in several respects. Phonetically, Kuuk Thaayorre stops are more frequently aspirated than one would expect of an Australian language. It is in its phonotactics, however, that Kuuk Thaayorre is particularly noteworthy. A tendency towards closed syllables – with codas containing up to three consonants – frequently leads to consonant clusters of as many as four segments (once one adds the onset of the subsequent syllable). Kuuk Thaayorre is also unusual in allowing sequences of rhotics (both /ɻr/ and /rɻ/) either as a complex coda, an onset plus syllabic rhotic, or a coda followed by an onsetless syllabic rhotic (see §2.4.1 and §2.4.3.3). Kuuk Thaayorre's plentiful monosyllables – found in all word classes – are also unusual in the Australian context (Dixon 2002: 553). Two further topics are given especial attention given their typological and theoretical interest: the morphophonology of reduplication (§2.6), and the tendency for stops to fricate word-initially but not morpheme-internally (§2.2.7).

Broad phonetic (IPA) transcriptions will be used throughout this chapter until the introduction of the practical Pormpuraaw Orthography in §2.8. Subsequent chapters employ a variant of the Pormpuraaw Orthography except where noted.

2.1 Phonemic inventory

2.1.1 Consonant inventory

Table 2 presents the sixteen Kuuk Thaayorre consonants. These comprise a single oral stop series with a corresponding nasal at each place of articulation but the glottal. Further to these, there are three glides (labio-velar, palatal and retroflex) and an alveolar lateral and tap/trill. No phonemic distinction is made between the alveolar and retroflex places of articulation; apical segments are generally articulated at the alveolar ridge, excepting the glide /ɻ/ which is undeniably retroflex.

Table 2. Kuuk Thaayorre consonants.

	bilabial	lamino-dental	apical	lamino-palatal	velar	glottal
Obstruent	p	t̪	t	c	k	ʔ
Nasal	m	n̪	n	ɲ	ŋ	
Lateral			l			
Tap/Trill			r			
Glide			ɻ	j	w	

Though the Kuuk Thaayorre consonant inventory is not unusual for an Australian language, it distinguishes fewer consonants than its nearest neighbours, Yir Yoront (Alpher 1973, 1991) and Kugu Nganhcara (Smith and Johnson 2000). The former distinguishes retroflex consonants (oral, nasal and lateral), while the latter contrasts voiced and voiceless obstruants.

2.1.2 Vowel inventory

Kuuk Thaayorre distinguishes five vowel qualities (/i/, /u/, /e/, /o/, and /a/), each of which has two phonemic lengths. Front and central vowels (/i/, /e/ and /a/) are unrounded while the back vowels (/u/ and /o/) are rounded.

Table 3. Kuuk Thaayorre vowels.

	front	central	back
high	i(ː)		u(ː)
mid	e(ː)		o(ː)
low		a(ː)	

This ten-vowel system is quite rich by Australian standards; Dixon (2002: 643) lists only twelve Australian languages (including Kuuk Thaayorre) that distinguish more than three vowels as well as a phonemic length contrast. Nevertheless, the phonetic distribution of the Kuuk Thaayorre vowels is not unusual, particularly in the local context. Kugu Nganhcara and Pakanh, for example, have (near-)identical vowel systems (Gaby, field notes), Uw Oykangand and Uw Olkola distinguish the same five vowel qualities though not length (Hamilton 1996), and Yir Yoront possesses the same five short vowels as well as a phonemic schwa (Alpher 1991: 7).

2.2 Phonological processes

Allophones of the Kuuk Thaayorre oral stops vary in voicing, aspiration, frication, length and release. Nasal stops vary in voicing. Dental and alveolar phones vary somewhat in their place of articulation. Although each of the allophones described in the sections below is associated with a particular phonetic environment, this relationship between allophone and environment is not exclusive. Exceptions are noted throughout the grammar as relevant.

The sections below detail the range of allophones attested for each phoneme. Some generalizations are possible across classes of phonemes, however. For example, aspirated allophones of obstruents tend to occur as the onset of a stressed, word-initially syllable (as in /pan/ [pʰan] 'bait' and /kaːl/ [kʰaːl] 'ear'). Unaspirated, released allophones may appear in a variety of positions, including word-finally (e.g. /waʔap/ [waʔap] 'river' and [pʰuŋk] 'knee'). All obstruents have an unreleased allophone that appears as the coda of a non-final syllable (especially where the onset of the following syllable is homorganic and/or bilabial), as in /katpir/ [kʰat̚pɪr].[32] The voiced stop is typically found word-initially following a word ending in a nasal or vowel (e.g. /miṉ kuːc/ [mɪṉ guːc]). The same environment may also condition frication, however (e.g. /miṉ koton/ [mɪṉ ɣot̪on]). Both the voiced fricative and glide allophones are found intervocalically at a morpheme boundary (usually as the initial segment of a reduplicative infix, e.g. /koːkope/ [kʰoːɣope] or [kʰoːjope] 'wait'). It seems likely that the glide allophone has arisen as a further lenited variant of the fricative allophone, and indeed speakers most often pronounce the obstruent as a fricative when asked to slowly repeat a word initially produced with a glide allophone. The palatal glide allophone of the velar stop in fact represents a range of phonetic realizations, from a palatalized velar fricative to a purely palatal glide.

Although Hall does not analyze obstruents as possessing glide allophones, he does (1968: 47) acknowledge that "an affinity exists between /p/ and /w/. These two phonemes fluctuate in morphs like /wal/ ~ /pal/".[33] The labiovelar glide has phonemic status in Kuuk Thaayorre (e.g. /waːt̪/ 'search' contrasts with /paːt̪/ 'fire', cf. §2.3) as well as being an allophone of the obstruent /p/; the neutralization of this contrast is unidirectional (i.e. /w/ is never realized as [p]). For instance, the onset of the second syllable in the reduplicated /paːpat̪/ 'hot' (from /paːt̪/ 'fire') may be realized either as a voiced bilabial fricative or as a labiovelar glide (i.e. [paːwat̪] ~ [paːβat̪]), but there is no variation in the production of the labio-velar glides in /waːwat̪/ 'search:RDP'.

---

[32] Such variation in release is commonplace and will not be remarked upon in the discussion of the following obstruent phonemes.
[33] Hall (1968: 61) also remarks: "/p/ has an alternative nasal release used by most speakers word-medially before /m/. It is a voiceless velic flap with the lips closed as in /tanp-m/ ~ [unreproducible] 'pushed'". No such pronunciation is attested in my data.

Similarly, while /pal/ 'towards' has allophones [pal]~[wal], this word form contrasts with /wal/ [wal] 'dilly bag', which is never pronounced [pal].

Along with the voicing noted above, there is often some leakage of nasality wherever an obstruent follows a nasal segment. This is not reflected in the listing of allophones below.

The following sections present the range of allophones associated with each phoneme. This is followed by a discussion of the morphophonological processes that condition the distribution of allophones in §2.2.7.

2.2.1 Obstruent allophones

2.2.1.1 Bilabial obstruent /p/

The bilabial obstruent phoneme be realized as: (1) a voiceless aspirated stop; (2) a voiceless unaspirated stop; (3) a voiceless unreleased stop; (4) a voiced stop; (5) a voiced fricative; and (6) a glide, as follows:

/p/ → [pʰ] / #_
 → [p̚] / _$
 → [b] / N#_ [34]
 → [β] ~ [w] / RDP [35]
 → [p] ~ [β] ~ [w] / -_ [36]
     +_
 → [p] / elsewhere

2.2.1.2 Velar obstruent /k/

The velar obstruent /k/ possesses a similar range of allophones to its non-coronal[37] counterpart (bilabial /p/), namely:

/k/ → [kʰ] / #_
 → [k̚] / _$ /p/ [38]
 → [g] ~ [ɣ] / N#_

---

[34] Unusually, the voicing of obstruents appears to be conditioned only across word boundaries, not within words.
[35] This is intended to represent the frication in the context of reduplication, as described in §2.6.
[36] This allophone is found following a morpheme boundary.
[37] It is conventional in Australianist phonologies to group the bilabial and velar places of articulation together as a 'peripheral' series (Hamilton 1996, Evans 1995c). There is little evidence of the psychological reality of such a grouping in Kuuk Thaayorre, though the realization of labio-dental fricatives as velar stops in some loan words (e.g. /kutpol/ 'football') is suggestive.
[38] This allophone is found in codas preceding a bilabial stop as onset of the following syllable.

→ [ɣ] / = _
   + _
→ [ɣ] ~ [j] / RDP
→ [k] / elsewhere

2.2.1.3 Lamino-dental /t̪/

As with the non-coronal obstrents, the lamino-dental stop has aspirated, unaspirated (released and unreleased), fricated and glide allophones:

/t̪/ → [t̪ʰ] / #_
   → [t̪˺] / _$
   → [d̪] / N#__
   → [d̪ᵒ] / -__
   → [ð̪], [j] / RDP
   → [t̪] / elsewhere

There is additional variation in the place of articulation, with some speakers tending to produce an interdental [t̪], while most produce it just behind the upper teeth. This appears to be an idiolectal difference between speakers rather than being conditioned by phonetic context.

The voiced stop allophone, commonly found word-initially following a nasal-final word (e.g. /pam t̪uːmp/ [pʰam d̪uːmpʰ]) is often slightly fricated. Full frication of the lamino-(inter)dental fricative is rare, unlike the relatively common fricative allophones of the peripheral stops. In the suffix-initial position, however, [t̪] has an audible fricative release (e.g. /kuta-t̪ak/ [kʰutad̪ᵒakʰ] 'dog-DAT'). In the process of reduplication the dental stop often lenites to a palatal glide, or a strongly palatalized dental approximant (as in / t̪uːt̪ut̪ɪ/ [t̪uːjut̪ɪ] ~ [t̪uːðut̪ɪ] 'crawl:RDP').

2.2.1.4 Apico-alveolar /t/

The apico-alveolar stop is the second rarest consonant in my data (behind the glottal stop), and no clearly fricated variants of it were found. This might be attributed to the fact that apico-alveolar stops are not found in root-initial position (the usual target of frication). This phoneme does, however, vary in aspiration, voicing, place of articulation and the presence or absence of release, as follows:

/t/ → [t̚] _$
   → [t̚] / [ɾ]_
   → [t] ~ [tʰ] / _#
   → [t] / elsewhere

Despite the absence of phonemic retroflex stops in Kuuk Thaayorre, apico-alveolar stops are realized as retroflex stop allophones following the retroflex glide.[39]

2.2.1.5 Lamino-palatal /c/

Hall (1968: 46) classifies the lamino-palatal stop /c/ as an affricate, whereas I consider it a simple palatal obstruent, although it usually does have a clearly fricated release. My data contains aspirated and unaspirated allophones, but no voiced fricative as Hall (1968: 67) found.

/c/ → [cʰ] / $_
→ [c] / elsewhere

2.2.1.6 Glottal stop /ʔ/

The final obstruent in the Kuuk Thaayorre phonemic inventory is the glottal stop. This has only two allophones, a glottal stop and suprasegmental creaky voice realized on adjacent segments:

/ʔ/ → [ʔ] ~ [+creaky voice] / [α] _ [α]
→ [ʔ] / elsewhere

The creaky voice allophone is found only between identical segments. Hence /iṉʔṉuŋun/ 'to this very one' is frequently pronounced [iṉ:uŋun], and /waʔap/ 'river' pronounced [wa̰:p]. It seems that the creaky voice realization of the glottal stop may lead to the eventual loss of this phoneme. There are few tokens of the glottal stop in any stretch of Kuuk Thaayorre discourse, but also notably fewer in the speech of the young than in that of elders. Further evidence that [ʔ] is being phased out is the fact that many younger speakers will give the – carefully pronounced – citation form [waːp] for /waʔap/ 'river'. Even some elders, whose speech is generally more conservative, occasionally give these latter pronunciations. The fact that the phonemic glottal stop appears to be a relatively recent innovation in Cape York languages (cf. Alpher 1972, Hale 1976a, Dixon 2002) may help explain why it might also be early to leave the Kuuk Thaayorre phonemic inventory (according to the 'last in, first out' principle). Nevertheless, there exist some minimal pairs (e.g. /koʔor/ 'speared each other' vs. /koːr/ 'outside') where the glottal stop contrasts with zero for all speakers.

---

[39] Osborne (1970) argues for an analysis of phonetic retroflex stops in Tiwi as underlying clusters (e.g. [ʈ] = /ɻt/). Cf. also Breen (1992) on Kukatj retroflex stops.

2.2.2 Nasal allophones

For each of the nasal allophones except /ɲ/ there is a voiceless variant found in a syllable onset following a syllable containing a voiceless coda (e.g. in *rintn̪an* 'cook:GO&:NPST').⁴⁰ The apico-alveolar nasal also has a retroflex allophone, conditioned by a preceding retroflex rhotic:

/m/ → [m̥] / C $ _
             [-voice]
       → [m] / elsewhere

/n̪/ → [n̪̥] / C $ _
             [-voice]
       → [n̪] / elsewhere

/n/ → [n̥] / C $ _
             [-voice]
       → [ɳ] / [ɽ] _
       → [n] / elsewhere

/ɲ/ → [ɲ]

/ŋ/ → [ŋ̥] / C $ _
             [-voice]
       → [ŋ] / elsewhere

The absence of voiceless allophone for the palatal nasal may be attributed to the fact that the palatal nasal is itself quite rare, and my corpus contains no lexemes in which this nasal follows a voiceless consonant (the conditioning environment for nasal devoicing).⁴¹

The lamino-dental nasal may be produced at either interdental or dental places of articulation. As with the corresponding obstruent, this is attributed to interspeaker variation.

---

40 In some cases, voicing of the nasal may be delayed but not altogether absent. This is not differentiated from the voiceless allophone here.
41 Hall (1968: 63) analyzes this phoneme as a single segment formed by compounding the alveolar nasal and palatal glide (as suggested by the digraph /ny/ in his working orthography), which he claims also has a "voiced apico-dental lamino-alveolar nasal" allophone.

2.2.3 Rhotic allophones

The alveolar rhotic may be realized as either a tap or a trill, with a voiceless allophone found where the preceding syllable ends in a voiceless consonant:

/r/ → [ɾ] / ɻ_
    → [ɾ̥] /   C $_
           [-voice]
    → [r] ~ [ɾ] / elsewhere

Throughout my data the retroflex rhotic seems to have only one phonetic form; /ɻ/ = [ɻ]). As Barry Alpher (personal communication) notes, the Kuuk Thaayorre retroflex glide is particularly extreme, articulated with a deeply depressed tongue root.[42]

2.2.4 Lateral allophones

There is a single lateral phoneme which is basically alveolar in articulation, though a retroflex allophone is conditioned by a preceding retroflex approximant.

/l/ → [ɭ] / [ɻ] _
    → [l] / elsewhere

The phonemes /ɻ/ and /l/ are phonetically similar, and in some words appear to be in free variation: e.g. /pork/ 'big' ~ /polk/.[43]

2.2.5 Semivowels

I found both the palatal and labiovelar glide phonemes to have only a single phonetic realization ([j] and [w] respectively), although Hall (1968: 72) finds the latter to also have a bilabial fricative allophone.

2.2.6 Vowel allophones

Each of the Kuuk Thaayorre vowels appears to undergo rhoticization preceding a retroflex rhotic. Further conditioned variation appears to mainly involve the central-

---

[42] This depressed tongue root sometimes gives rise to a preceding phonetic palatal glide (particularly following the reflexive morpheme, -e), which Alpher (personal communication) suggests may relate to the Arandic pre-palatalized stops, which themselves developed from original retroflex phonemes.
[43] Although all but two of the language experts I consulted give the citation form /poɻk/ 'big', this lexeme has cognates that support the reconstruction of /l/ (e.g. Dyirbal *bulgan* 'big' (Dixon 1972), Pitjantjatjara *pulka* 'big' (Goddard 1996)).

ization of vowels in unstressed syllables (see Hall 1968: 88 for a detailed account). Detailed acoustic analysis is required before firm conclusions can be drawn regarding the phonetic distribution of Kuuk Thaayorre vowels, but impressionistically they do not seem to vary in their production to the same degree as some other Australian languages (e.g. Gurindji, Jones et al. 2012).

Long vowels are found only in stressed syllables, which are usually word-initial. The difference between a long and short vowel is usually very clear in context, although actual vowel duration is relative to surrounding segments and pragmatic context. A short vowel may be significantly longer when emphasized than a long vowel in a pragmatically neutral context. Thus the short vowels in the first syllable of semantically gradable words like /ŋamal/ 'large', /toɻkor/ 'long, tall, far' and /kanaŋkar/ 'long ago', for example, are commonly lengthened to a duration of a second or more for emphasis (hence [ŋaːːːmal] 'really enormous').

2.2.7 Morphophonological processes

In Kuuk Thaayorre, the likelihood of lenition generally increases with the 'size' of the preceding morphological boundary. So frication across a compound juncture is extremely common, as is frication between clitic and host, but frication at suffix boundaries is less common, and intramorphemic frication rare. In the few cases I have found of frication within a morpheme, the morpheme is likely to have once been a compound (e.g. /meːɻkole/ [meːɻɣole] 'taipan', where /meːɻ/ 'eye' is frequently found as first element of a compound). Where frication occurs across word boundaries, however, this does not necessarily suggest that the words form a compound (contra Hall 1968). A compound analysis may be possible for some sequences of words (like /pam tuːmp/ [pʰam ðuːmp] 'old man' and /paːɲt kunjaŋkaɻ/ [pʰaːɲt ɣunjaŋkaɻ] 'sister'), but the frication evident between words such as *Ansett* and *katpirr* in the second line of example (8) could not possibly be attributed to morphophonological processes:

(8) 1. T.A. ngancn katpi-rr
   T.A.(ACC) 1pl:excl(ERG) grasp-P.PFV
   'we caught T.A. [airline]'
 2. T.A.=okun Ansett katpi-rr=okun
   [thiːjeːjokun ɛnsɛt ɣatpɪrokən]
   T.A.(ACC)=dub Ansett(ACC) grasp-P.PFV=DUB
   'either T.A. or Ansett [airline]'
   [KTh_GJ16Oct2002 Narrative MelbourneTrip]

This lenition of word-initial onsets is likely to be an effect of phrase-level prosody on word-level phonology. Although such a correlation between size of juncture and lenition is cross-linguistically rare, a parallel may exist in Japanese 'rendaku' voicing of consonants in compounds (Ito and Mester 1986).

2.2.7.1 Lenition at affix boundaries

Whether or not a suffix-initial stop lenites depends on the identity of the stop itself and of the preceding segment. So, for instance, the velar onset of /-kuw/ 'west' and /-kaw/ 'east' tends to fricate following stem-final /r/, but not following vowels or other consonants (e.g. /iː-r-kaw/ [ɪrɣaw] 'there-to-East' but /iː-kaw/ [iːkaw] 'there-East'[44]). The apical onset of the dative suffix /-ṯak/ seems always to lenite (e.g. in /kuta-ṯak/ [kʰutaḓᵒak] 'dog-DAT' and /mit-ṯak/ [mɪtʰðak] 'work-DAT'), whereas the apical onset if the ablative suffix rarely lenites (e.g. /kanpa-tam/ [kʰanpatam] 'first-ABL' and /ŋan-tam/ [ŋantam] 'what-ABL').

2.2.7.2 Lenition at clitic boundaries

Frication at the word=clitic boundary is ubiquitous; far more common than frication at the stem-suffix boundary. So, for instance, the enclitics /=kak/, /=kaːɻ/, and /=kaːk/ are almost always realized as [ɣak], [ɣaːɻ] and [ɣaːk] respectively, regardless of the preceding segment. Note that the latter two enclitics always receive primary stress, illustrating that this lenition is not only a feature of unstressed syllables. The only enclitics that do not lenite are the two emphatic discourse markers /=t̪/ and /=p/. Two factors easily explain their resilience: (1) their appearance in contexts of pragmatic emphasis (which favours fortition over lenition); (2) their position as the final element of the phonological word – and hence as syllable coda – where lenition is a feature of onsets in Kuuk Thaayorre.

2.2.7.3 Lenition at compound boundaries

The onset of the second component of a compound is usually fricated (e.g. /meːɻ-puŋk/ [meːɻ.βuŋk] 'eyebrow', /ɻiːŋ-kaːl/ [ɻɪːŋ.ɣaːl] 'leaf'). This may be an extremely recent development within the language since Hall (1968: 62) notes that "transitional vowels tend to separate contiguous consonants at syllable boundaries in compounds, when different points of articulation are involved". The examples he gives (/kaːl-puɻŋ/ 'forget' and /kul-puŋk/ 'crowd') are throughout my data pronounced [kʰaːlβuɻŋ] and [kʰulβuŋk] respectively.

2.3 Minimal pairs

This section focuses on contrasting suspicious pairs of phonemes; to provide (near-)minimal pairs demonstrating the contrast between each phoneme in each syllabic position would be unduly lengthy. It can be assumed that phonemic contrasts are maintained in all environments unless otherwise specified.

---

[44] Note that both these these words exhibit initial-syllable stress.

A contrast between each of the full inventory of obstruents is suggested by the following set of verb stems:

(9) /mi?i/   'pick up'
     /piṯiṯ/   'dream:RDP'
     /pitit/   'hold:RDP'
     /jikik/   'say:RDP'
     /ṭipir/   'exit:P.PFV'
     /picar/   'burst:P.PFV'

A minimal triplet proves the contrast between the peripheral obstruents and glide:

(10) /katp/   'grasp'
     /patp/   'hawk'
     /watp/   'dead'

The pairs in (11) and (12) demonstrate the contrast between the velar obstruent and the glottal stop:

(11) /pu?am/   'wounded'
     /pu:kam/   'new, young'

(12) /wa?ɻ/   'jellyfish'
     /wakɻ/   'follow:P.PFV'

The contrast between apical and laminal front-coronal stops is neutralized word-initially (dental pronunciation being most common), and the only word-initial palatal stops are found in marginal word classes (ideophones, interjections and loanwords; cf. §3.4, §3.5.1). Their phonemic status is, however, confirmed by contrastive use in other positions:

(13) /pa:tɻ/   'bite:P.PFV'
     /pa:ṯɻ/   'flower'
     /pa:cɻ/   'growl:NPST'

(14) /wa:ṯir/   'search:P.PFV'
     /wacir/   'correctly'

(15) /wa:t/   'incorrectly'
     /wa:ṯ/   'crow'

The palatal stop is distinguished from the palatal glide in (near-)minimal pairs such as the following:

(16) /ɟuk/ 'thing, tree'
/cuk/ 'sugar (loanword)'

(17) /puːɟ/ 'crab'
/kuːc/ 'kangaroo'

The following minimal pairs show the contrast between oral and nasal stops at each place of articulation:

(18) /man/ 'throat'
/pan/ 'bait'

(19) /in̪/ 'this'
/it̪/ 'that'

(20) /jan/ 'go:NPST'
/jat/ 'go:P.PFV'

(21) /ŋuɲan/ 'sea'
/t̪ucan/ 'scrub:DAT'

(22) /ŋul/ 'then'
/kul/ 'lap'

The contrast between bilabial, lamino-dental and velar nasals is evident in the following triplet:

(23) /mul/ 'tail'
/n̪ul/ '(s)he'
/ŋul/ 'then'

As in the oral stop series, the contrast between apical and laminal front-coronal nasals is neutralized word-initially. Example (24) shows the contrast between these two nasals in the final position:

(24) /ŋan/ 'what'
/ŋan̪/ 'me'

Apical and lamino-palatal nasals contrast preceding the palatal stop (in heterorganic and homorganic clusters respectively), as seen in the following couplets:[45]

---

[45] My thanks to Barry Alpher for confirming this contrast, and supplying audio files to support it.

(25) /minc/ 'true'
(26) /kuɲc/ 'penis'

Although no minimal pairs have yet been found to distinguish palatal and other nasals in the intervocalic position, phonemic status is strongly suggested by the following contrasts:

(27) /pinirm/ 'imagine'
    /wiɲi/ 'prawn'

(28) /kuman/ 'thigh:DAT'
    /kunanp/ 'straight'
    /ŋuɲan/ 'sea'
    /juŋaɻ/ 'swim'

The minimal pair in (29) distinguishes the two Kuuk Thaayorre rhotics:

(29) /t̪aːnpr/ 'kick:RDP:RCP'
    /t̪aːnpɻ/ 'kick:RDP:NPST'

That neither rhotic is an allophone of the apical plosive or lateral is demonstrated by the following set of minimal contrasts:

(30) /waːɻin/ 'chase'
    /waːr/ 'bad'
    /waːt/ 'incorrectly'
    /waːl/ 'silly'

Finally, it was mentioned above that the glottal stop is elided by many speakers, often producing a long vowel (as in the case of /waʔap/ à /waːp/ 'river'). Nevertheless, for some lexemes the presence or absence of a glottal stop remains synchronically contrastive, as the following shows:

(31) /koʔor/ 'spear:P.PFV'
    /koːr/ 'behind'

Advanced phonetic analysis may reveal some trace of the glottal stop even in the contexts I have described it as elided (e.g. glottalization of adjacent segments). If this is so, the retention of the glottal stop in words such as /koʔor/ 'speared' can be understood as hyperarticulation motivated by the desire to avoid ambiguity.

Turning finally to the vowels, it would again require too much space to provide a minimal pair illustrating every possible contrast. Assuming, then, that vowels are most likely to be in complementary distribution if they share the same value for either frontness or height, the following discussion will focus on proving such 'close' vowels to contrast.

Beginning with high vowels, /i/ and /u/ can be differentiated as follows:

(32) /p**i**l/ 'hip'
 /p**u**l/ 'they two'
 (cf. p**a**l 'towards')

The two mid-height vowels are contrasted in:

(33) /p**o**ɺpɻ/ 'soft'
 /p**e**ɺpɻ/ 'cover:NPST'

Non-front vowels contrast in the following:

(34) /k**u**n/ 'bottom (anatomical)'
 /k**o**n/ 'short'
 /-k**a**n/ 'up (bound root)'

Although /e/ in one ideolect sometimes corresponds to /i/ in another (§1.1.2.1), there are a few (near-)minimal pairs that demonstrate the distinction between the two to be phonemic, such as:

(35) /p**e**ɺp/ 'cover'
 /p**i**ɺp/ 'semen'
(36) /p**e**tan/ 'skin'
 /p**i**taṉ/ 'hold:SBJV'

/e/ can also be differentiated from the low central vowel as follows:

(37) /ɻ**e**:k/ 'give'
 /ɻ**a**:k/ 'place'

Finally, the fact that length is a contrastive feature for each of the vowels is evident in the following (near-)minimal pairs:

(38) /m**u**l/ 'tail'
 /m**u:**l/ 'white paint'
(39) /k**o**p/ 'below'
 /k**o:**p/ 'all'

(40) /kal/ 'carry'
/kaːl/ 'ear'

(41) /pe̯ɪp/ 'cover'
/peːp/ 'net'

(42) /jin/ 'female genitalia'
/jiːn/ 'itch'

2.4 Phonotactics

2.4.1 Epenthetic, reduced or absent vowels

Before discussion of Kuuk Thaayorre phonotactics can proceed it is important to establish the status of what were analyzed by Hall (1968) as reduced vowels,[46] but which are not transcribed as such in this grammar. This analytical difference has consequences for the analysis of possible syllable types in later sections (e.g. permissible consonant clusters and the existence of syllabic consonants). The putative phones in question will be referred to as '~vowels' throughout this discussion, in order to distinguish them from other classes of reduced vowel.

Consider, to begin with, the ~vowels in the second syllables of /ŋanc(i)[47]n/ [ŋancɨn] '1pl:excl' and /waːt̪(i)ɻ/ [waːt̪ʰəɻ] 'search:NPST'. On phonetic grounds alone, there seems little reason to transcribe such ~vowels: their quality is never contrastive,[48] and speakers do not produce a full vowel (nor lengthened schwa) when asked to pronounce a word slowly and carefully. Furthermore, when I deliberately pronounced words such as /ŋancn/ and /waːtɻ/ with a syllabic nasal and rhotic as nucleus of the final syllable, speakers approved this pronunciation as correct. Conversely, most speakers rejected pronunciations that included a full vowel. These ~vowels can in many cases be considered transitional, attributed to the aspiration on release of the preceding stop.

In favour of omitting the ~vowel from phonemic transcription, then, are the following facts:

---

[46] It should be noted, however, that Hall himself varies as to whether such vowels are included or omitted in transcription. Foote & Hall (1992) tend to include underlying vowels in transcription, Hall (1972) tends to omit them.

[47] The choice of the grapheme /i/ to represent these vowels is motivated by the transcriptions of Hall (1972) and Foote and Hall (1992), rather than by their phonetic qualities.

[48] In some cases, the reduced vowel (or absence of vowel, depending on the analysis) does contrast with an unreduced vowel (e.g. /ŋaŋk(a)n/ [ŋaŋkʰən]~[ŋaŋkʰn̩] '2sgGEN' vs. /ŋaŋkun/ [ŋaŋkʰun] '2sgDAT'). This does not prove the phonemic status of the reduced vowel, however, since the full vowel may just as well contrast with a syllabic nasal as with a reduced vowel.

1. speakers never produce a full vowel in natural or hyperarticulated speech
2. speakers accept pronunciations that omit the vowel entirely (and reject pronunciations in which a full vowel is articulated)
3. the phonetic character of the reduced vowel is entirely determined by surrounding segments (as described below)
4. some phonetic 'transitional vowel' is inevitable given surrounding segments

Illustrating points 1 and 2 is the lexeme /parɹ/, transcribed by Foote and Hall (1992) as *parr'ir*. It's not clear on what grounds Foote and Hall choose the grapheme 'i' to include as nucleus of the second syllable (nor why they transcribe a glottal stop preceding it), but every speaker I consulted was clear that this word should be pronounced [pʰarɹ̩] or occasionally [pʰarɚɹ], but never [pʰarɨɹ] or [pʰarʔɨɹ]. Supporting point 3 is the fact that ~vowels are always high following palatal stops (e.g. /ɲanc(i)n/ [ɲancɨn] '1pl:excl(NOM)'), always rounded preceding bilabial consonants (e.g. /waːṭ(i)m/ [waːṭ̥əm] 'search:P.IPFV'), and always rhotacized preceding rhotics (e.g. /parɹ/ [pʰarɚɹ] 'child'). Hall (1968: 64) himself adduces evidence of point 4, noting of the palatal stop that "before a syllable border, its affrication and aspiration help to cause the transitional vocoid which links it to the next syllable".

Such ~vowels are likely the product of one of two diachronic scenarios: (1) an originally full vowel in an unstressed (i.e. non-initial) position becomes reduced (e.g. realized as schwa); (2) an epenthetic ~vowel is inserted to reduce a consonant cluster, or a transitional ~vowel is unavoidable between a particular sequence of consonants. While the first of these scenarios offers a plausible diachronic source for ~vowels, it should be noted that these ~vowels contrast with reduced vowels synchronically produced through this very process; in fluid speech many vowels in non-initial syllables will be reduced. The difference between these reduced vowels and the ~vowels under discussion here, is that the full vowel corresponding to the former is retrievable and clearly pronounced in carefully articulated citation forms. So, for instance, although /waṉtannun/ 'where at' often sounds more like [waṉt̥ʰ(ə)n(ə)n] in rapid speech, speakers will always approximate [waṉt̥ʰannun] in careful pronunciation.[49] Both of these cases differ from the ~vowels under consideration here, which are not produced as full vowels even when the words that contain them are carefully pronounced. This can be seen in the reduced medial vowel of the second person genitive pronoun, for example. This differs from the second person dative pronoun only in the vowel of the second syllable. In the case of the dative pronoun, this vowel is indisputably the full vowel /u/; /ṉaŋkun/ [ṉaŋkʰun] '2sgDAT'. The second syllable nucleus of the genitive pronoun, however, may be analyzed as either a reduced vowel or a syllabic nasal;

---

49 Not all unstressed vowels are reduced in fast speech. Other polysyllabic words, such as /iriparop/ [ɨrɨpʰaropʰ] 'south.riverwards', are pronounced with full vowels in each syllable, despite all syllables but the first being unstressed.

/ŋaŋk(a)n/ [ŋaŋkʰən] ~ [ŋaŋkʰn̩] '2sgGEN'.[50] Although Hall (1972) usually transcribes this genitive pronoun as *nangkan*, the vowel of the second syllable is never produced as [a].[51] It should be acknowledged, however, that the distinction between ~vowels and reduced vowels proper is not always as clear cut as suggested in the discussion above. There are words that appear to fulfil all of the criteria for a ~vowel, and yet in one or two tokens in my corpus are pronounced with a full vowel.

In the absence of substantial evidence suggesting that a reduced medial ~vowel corresponds to a particular underlying full vowel, I do not view it as phonemic and consequently it is not transcribed in the example sentences herein. Many of the underlying vowels transcribed by Hall and/or Foote may indeed be sound. But since I am in most cases unable to reconstruct their rationale for ascribing reduced vowels to full vowel phonemes, I have chosen to follow their transcriptions only where they are independently substantiated.

2.4.2 Syllable types

2.4.2.1 Syllabification

There is a widely observed cross-linguistic tendency for CV (as opposed to VC) syllables to be unmarked (Jakobson 1962, Blevins 1995). This tendency is reflected in the segmentation of polysyllabic words from right to left, such that consonants found intermediate between the vowel nuclei of adjacent syllables first of all supply an onset to the syllable that follows, with remaining consonants forming the coda of the preceding syllable. Given that Kuuk Thaayorre allows a maximally one-consonant onset, to apply such an analysis to its polysyllables would result in such syllabic structures as in (43).

(43) /ŋeɪn.kan/ 'yesterday'
/kat.pir/ 'grasped'
/jom.par/ 'become'

But does this syllabification reflect the structure of the language, or the prevailing assumptions of phonological theory? Sommer (1969, 1970) proposed an alternative

---

[50] This may be considered analogous to the phonetic process in Wik Mungkan whereby "a reduced vowel combines with a following sonorant to yield a syllabic consonant" (Smith 1986: 517).
[51] There is no particular affinity between the full vowel /a/ and the reduced ~vowels under discussion here. These reduced ~vowels are variously transcribed as each of the five short vowels by Foote and Hall (1992); /kat̪(i)m/ 'bind:P.IPFV', /muŋk(u)m/ 'eat:P.IPFV', /t̪ak(a)m/ 'leave:P.IPFV', /poɪmp(o)m/ 'pour:P.IPFV', /koːc(e)m/ 'bark:P.IPFV'. Conversely, each of the five vowels can be found unreduced in unstressed syllables; /wat̪ir/ 'search.for:P.PFV', /paːn̪t̪um/ 'woman:ABL', /t̪akar/ 'leave:P.PFV', /poɪmpor/ 'pour:P.PFV', /jaker/ 'cut:P.PFV'.

pattern of syllabification for Kunjen (a close neighbour of Kuuk Thaayorre), arguing that the VC syllable should be considered basic in this language. Though this analysis was roundly criticized (Darden 1971, McCarthy and Prince 1986) and later recanted (Sommer 1981), some more recent papers (e.g. Breen and Pensalfini 1999, Tabain et al. 2004) present compelling evidence that the underlying syllable structure in Arrernte is VC(C), furnishing complex codas at the expense of onsets. In the case of Kuuk Thaayorre, the existence of onsets is undeniable. Yet there is also evidence pointing towards a preference for filling codas before supplying onsets. Consider for example the reduplicated counterparts of the three words in (44):

(44) /ŋeɻnkeɻkan/   'morning'
     /katpatpir/   'kept grasping'
     /jompompar/   'kept becoming'

If we retain an analysis under which an intervocalic sequence of consonants (e.g. /ɻnk/ in /ŋeɻnkan/) will supply an onset before coda (hereafter referred to as the 'CV analysis'),[52] we are required to explain the apparent reduplicative infixation of the syllable /keɻn/ in the word /ŋeɻn.keɻn.kan/, the syllable /pat/ in the word /kat.pat.pir/, and /pom/ in /jom.pom.par/. This could be done by stating that the reduplicative infix takes the onset of root's second syllable, followed by the rhyme of the root's first syllable. A more parsimonious alternative is offered by a left-to-right syllabification analysis (hereafter "VC analysis"), under which intervocalic consonant series fill the coda of the preceding syllable before the onset of the following one. Under this analysis, the words presented in (44) reduplicate via the infixation of the rhyme of the first syllable (cf. §2.6.2). This alternative syllabification is presented in (45).

(45) /ŋeɻnk.an/   'yesterday'
     /ŋeɻnk.eɻnk.an/   'morning'
     /katp.ir/   'grasped'
     /katp.atp.ir/   'kept grasping'
     /jomp.ar/   'become'
     /jomp.omp.ar/   'kept becoming'

The VC analysis does admit the presence of syllable onsets both word-initially (where there is no preceding coda to fill), and where the series of intervocalic consonants would violate the phonotactic restrictions on permissible consonant clusters were they to form a coda. Hence /mop.ŋun/ 'butterfly' is syllabified /mop.ŋun/ rather than

---

[52] The shorthand terms "CV-analysis" and "VC-analysis" used herein are not intended to imply that Thaayorre syllables do not contain codas or onsets respectively. Instead, these labels are meant to reflect a preference for filling onset slots versus coda slots where the two are in competition.

/mopŋ.un/, since the sequence /pŋ/ within a coda would violate the sonority hierarchy (cf. §2.4.3.3).

These data are insufficient to reach any definitive conclusions regarding the preference for CV vs. VC syllables in Kuuk Thaayorre. Further investigation – and in particular close phonetic analysis – may provide evidence that confirms one syllabification pattern as correct. It is possible, though, that Kuuk Thaayorre instead represents an intermediate step in the transition from CV-dominant (as attested in most of the world's languages) to VC-dominant (as attested in Arrernte and perhaps Kunjen), or the reverse. The following discussion will consider the implications of both CV and VC analyses wherever the two diverge.

2.4.2.2 Permissible monosyllables

The Kuuk Thaayorre lexicon contains an unusually large number of monosyllables for an Australian language. These monosyllables must be minimally bimoraic, possessing either a long vowel nucleus or a coda or both. There also appears to be a limit on the maximum syllable weight, with three-consonant codas permissible following a short vowel but not a long one. The permissible phonotactic structures of these monosyllables can be summarized as in (46).

(46)   (C)   **V** $\left\{ \begin{array}{c} : \\ C \end{array} \right\}$ (C)   (C)

Each of the monosyllables generated by (45) is exemplified in Table 4.

Table 4. Phonotactics of Kuuk Thaayorre monosyllables.[53]

V:	/iː/	'there'
CV:	/koː/	'oh (I see)!'
CV:C	/puːn/	'breeze'
CV:CC	/paːnt/	'head'
VC	/iṉ/	'this'
VCC	/ulp/	'the'
CVC	/pan/	'bait'
CVCC	/punt/	'elbow'
CVCCC	/ṉeɻŋk/	'man's child'[53]

The few Kuuk Thaayorre monosyllables lacking either onset and/or coda belong to a restricted set of word classes. The deictic adverb /iː/ 'there' is the only monosyllable in my corpus that lacks both onset and coda (V:). All remaining open monosyl-

---

[53] The term /ṉeɻŋk/ denotes a category of kin that has at its core the sons and daughters of a male ego.

lables (CV:) belong to the marginal word class of interjections (e.g. the backchannel response /koː/ 'oh, I see'). The further four onset-less monosyllables (VC and VCC) in my corpus are the 'OPTative' particle /ak/ and the three adnominal demonstratives; /iṉ/ 'this', /iṯ / 'that', and /ulp/ 'the'.[54]

2.4.2.3 Syllable types in polysyllabic words

As might be expected, the set of permissible syllable structures in Kuuk Thaayorre depends very much on whether we adopt a CV or VC analysis. For example, onset-less syllables are restricted to word-initial position under the CV analysis. Conversely, open syllables are only found word-finally under the CV analysis (and hence are never long). A further point of divergence between the two analyses is the fact that the CVCCC syllable structure (well documented for monosyllables) is only possible for polysyllabic words under a VC analysis, and even then is only ever found word-initially. Likewise, the VCCC syllable shape is only present under the VC analysis, and even then only in word-medial reduplicative infixes (cf. 2.6.2).[55] Table 5 illustrates which syllable types are attested in Kuuk Thaayorre polysyllables under both the alternative syllabification rules. Where possible, I have included examples of the syllable types in word initial, medial and final position. The relevant syllable is in boldface. Where a syllable type is only attested in polymorphemic words, breaks between morphemes are indicated by the relevant boundary marker ('–', '=' or '+').

Further to the syllable structures listed in Table 5, polysyllabic words can also contain non-initial syllables with consonantal nuclei. Only sonorants may be syllabic in Kuuk Thaayorre, thus consonantal nuclei are generally restricted to nasals and liquids (/l/, /r/ and /ɻ/). There appears to be just one exception to this generalization; the pragmatic enclitic /ṯ/, which consists simply of the dental oral stop (cf. §3.6.2). This segment may have a syllabic realization following a obstruent, as when it is suffixed to the addressee-proximate demonstrative /ulp/. The sequence of these two morphemes could be syllabified as /ul.pṯ/ under the CV analysis, or /ulp.ṯ/ under the VC analysis. The unusual phonotactic behaviour of this segment/morpheme can be attributed to its likely grammaticalization from the free distal adnominal demonstrative /iṯ/. Syllables with a consonantal nucleus are never found word-initially and hence are restricted to polysyllabic words. Table 6 presents the range of syllable structures containing a consonantal nucleus found under both CV and VC analyses.

---

[54] /ulp/, translated here as 'the', may be more accurately charaterized as an addressee-proximate demonstrative, cf. §5.3.2.1.
[55] Although the word /melnk.elnk.ar/ 'tomorrow' – which exhibits this medial syllable type under the VC analysis – is synchronically monomorphemic, its formal structure suggests a reduplicative diachronic origin.

Table 5. Range of syllable structures found in Kuuk Thaayorre polysyllables.

	Exemplar words (CV analysis)		Exemplar words (VC analysis)	
V	/o.toɲ.ci/	'hill'	/wiɲ.i/	'prawn'
	/a.ŋar/	'purposive'	/ot.oɲc.i/	'hill'
CV	/wi.ɲi/	'prawn'	/ŋat̪.n.ma/	'from me'
	/miːn.ŋa.-ni-r/	'frightened (someone)'	/puːn.ŋa/	'larrikin'
CVC	/waṉ.t̪an/	'where'	/ŋan.ip/	'father'
	/t̪ut.pin.pan/	'lizard sp.'	/miːn.ŋa-n.i-r/	'frightened (someone)'
	/ŋa.nip/	'father'	/tiːnt̪.mur/	'paralysed'
CVCC	/ŋuɻn.tuɻn.tur/	'nighttime'	/waṉt.an/	'where'
	/koɻŋ.kulm/	'string bag'	/maŋk.wark.ant/	'go circuitously'
	/weɻn.ka/	'between'		
CVCCC	*		/ɻoɻnk.r/	'light'
			/weɻnk.a/	'between'
			/melnk.elnk.ar/	'tomorrow'
VC	/iṉ.t̪ul/	'that one here'	/ot.oɲc.i/	'hill'
	/ak.pi/	'regardless'	/t̪aːp.ir.i/	'close'
			/ŋan.ip/	'father'
VCC	/iṉʔ.n̪ul/	'this one'	/iṉʔ.n̪ul/	'this one'
			/ot.oɲc.i/	'hill'
			/pin.iɻm/	'imagine'
			/koɻŋk.ulm/	'string bag'
VCCC	*		/melnk.elnk.ar/	'tomorrow'
			/ŋeɻnk.eɻnk.an/	'morning'
Vː	/iː.-l-uŋ.kar/	'from there in the north'	*	
CVː	/t̪aː.pi.ri/	'close'	*	
CVːC	/ŋoːŋ.kom/	'ignorant'	/t̪aːp.ir.i/	'close'
	/miːn.ŋa.-ni-r/	'frightened (someone)'	/miːn.ŋa-n.i-r/	'frightened (someone)'
CVːCC	/piːnt̪.-ɲan/	'going to grow'	/piːnt̪.aw.ar/	'tired'
	/ŋeːŋk.-mam/	'love'	/ŋoːŋk.om/	'ignorant'
	/puŋk.+paːnt/	'kneecap'	/puŋk.+paːnt/	'kneecap'
VːC	/iː-ŋ.kar/	'there in the north'	/iː-l.-uŋ.kar/	'coming from the north'
			/puṉt.=aːɻ/	'wingless'
VːCC	*		/iː-ŋk.ar/	'there in the north'

Table 6. Range of syllable structures containing a consonantal nucleus.

	Exemplar words (CV analysis)		Exemplar words (VC analysis)	
C̩	/weɻ.k-r̩.-ɻ/	'rubbed each other'	/weɻk.-r̩.-ɻ/ /keɻmp.l̩/	'rubbed each other'; 'corella'
CC̩	/miːn.ŋ-ɻ/ /keɻm.pl̩/	'take fright'; 'corella'	/miːn.ŋ-ɻ/	'take fright'
C̩C	*		/jo.kun.man.r̩p/	'same way'
CC̩C	/jo.kun.ma.nr̩p/	'same way'	/pr̩k/	'breaking sound [ideophone]'

Under the CV analysis, the fact that a syllable nucleus will take any immediately preceding consonant as its onset generally restricts syllables without onsets to the word-initial position. Since syllables with a consonantal nucleus are restricted to non-initial positions, this might suggest that consonantal nuclei must always be preceded by onsets under the CV analysis. This is not the case, however, since words like /weɻ.kr̩.ɻ/ 'rubbed each other' contain a series of two syllabic consonants, the second of which must comprise a syllable in and of itself since the preceding consonant is ineligible for the function of onset, being itself a syllable nucleus.

The examples of closed syllables with consonantal nuclei (i.e. CC̩C) in my data are marginal at best. They comprise particles such as /jokunman(o)rp/ 'in the same way', which may or may not contain a reduced vowel in the final syllable (cf. §2.4.1), and ideophones (which violate the phonotactic rules of Kuuk Thaayorre in a number of other ways, cf. §3.4).

2.4.3 Phonotactic constraints within the syllable

2.4.3.1 Onset

The restrictions on which of the sixteen Kuuk Thaayorre consonants may function as onset depend upon both the position of the syllable (i.e. whether or not it is word-initial) and upon whether the word has been syllabified according to the CV or VC analysis. The glottal stop, for instance, never appears word-initially and only appears as word-medial onset where the word has been syllabified according to the CV analysis. Thus the glottal onset of the second syllable in /pu.ʔam/ (with CV syllabification) is alternatively analyzed as the coda of the first syllable under the VC analysis (i.e. /puʔ.am/).

Table 7. Possible syllable onsets.

	word-initially		non-initial (CV)		non-initial (VC)	
p	/pip/	'mud'	/ak.pi/	'regardless'	*	
ṯ	/ṯeɻk/	'return'	/kemp.ṯe/	'singly'	/kemp.ṯe/	'singly'
t	*		/te.rep.-tam/	'rock-ABL'	/ter.ep.-tam/	'rock-ABL'
c	*		/wa.cir/	'properly'	*	
k	/kumun/	'thigh'	/pu.kam/	'young'	/kaɻ.-jup.=kaːɻ/	'without delay'
ʔ	*		/pu.ʔam/	'wounded'	*	
m	/mopŋuɲ/	'butterfly'	/ṯuːc.-mam/	'bush-ABL'	/ṯuːc.-mam/	'bush-ABL'
ṉ	/ṉerŋk/	'man's child'	/ko.jeṯ.ṉiṯ/	'grandfather'	/koj.eṯ.ṉiṯ/	'grandfather'
n	*		/we.neṯ/	'scared'	/ak.na/	'let me'
ɲ	(/ɲor/	'throat tickle')	/ŋu.ɲan/	'sea'	*	
ŋ	/ŋaj/	'I'	/mop.ŋun/	'butterfly'	/mop.ŋun/	'butterfly'
ɻ	/ɻiːc/	'run'	/punṯ.-ɻaːl/	'(arm)-elbow'	/punṯ.-ɻaːl/	'(arm)-elbow'
l	*		/ku.lam/	'track'	/ŋamp.lin/	'us all (excl)'
r	*		/ki.ri/	'permissive'	*	
j	/joːc/	'sop'[56]	/ko.jeṯ.ṉiṯ/	'grandfather'	/jeŋ.jor/	'knitting sticks'
w	/wuːc/	'song/dance'	/ŋa.woj/	'yes'	/maŋk.wark.ant/	'go circuitously'

2.4.3.2 Nucleus

Only sonorants (vowels, liquids, rhotics and nasals) and the dental stop /ṯ/ may function as syllable nuclei, the latter only in the form of the pragmatic enclitic /ṯ/ (used for focal emphasis). The nucleus of the initial syllable of a word must be a vowel, though this vowel can be either long or short (e.g. /waːl/ 'silly' vs. /wal/ 'dilly bag'). Long vowels are restricted to stressed syllables, which are generally word-initial (though there are exceptions, as discussed in §2.7).

Phonetic on- and off-glides are often detectable where no phonemic glide is present. For example, the ignorative /ŋene/ 'why' is often pronounced [ŋjene], and the verb /ṯiːk/ 'break' often surfaces as [ṯiːjk].

2.4.3.3 Coda

As has already been noted, Kuuk Thaayorre allows clusters of up to three consonants in the coda position.[57] There are numerous restrictions on which of the sixteen consonants may fill each of these three slots, however. To begin with, Table 8 presents the range of segments that may appear as simplex syllable codas (i.e. codas consisting

---

[56] I.e. 'be covered with fluid'.
[57] This holds under both CV and VC analyses.

of a single consonant) both word-medially and in word-final position. Under the CV analysis, all of the consonants except /ɲ/ and /ʔ/ may function as both word-medial and word-final simplex codas.[58] Under the VC analysis, these two segments may appear word-medially.

Table 8. Simplex syllable codas.

	word-medial (CV)		word-medial (VC)		word-final (simple coda)	
p	/t̪e.rep.-tam/	'rock-ABL'	/wup.an/	'temporary'	/t̪ip/	'liver'
t̪	/wa:t̪.-ŋan/	'will search'	/ŋat̪.un/	'to me'	/wa:t̪ /	'crow'
t	/put.pun/	'on top'	/put.ar/	'tree sp.'	/wa:t/	'wrongly'
c	/me:ɻ.-mic.-ɲr/	'sharp-ERG'	/kec.er/	'freshwater'	/jo:c/	'sop'
k	/ak.pi/	'regardless'	/puk.am/	'young'	/jak/	'snake'
ʔ	*		/puʔ.am/	'wounded'	*	
m	/ku.lam.-nam/	'track-ABL'	/kum.un/	'thigh'	/ɻot̪om/	'woman's child'
n̪	/wan̪.t̪an/	'where to'	/ŋan̪.ul/	'who:ERG'	/ŋan̪/	'me'
n	/mi:n.ɲɻ/	'take fright'	/kan.a/	'well'	/ŋan/	'what'
ɲ	*		/wiɲ.i/	'prawn'	*	
ŋ	/maŋ.ma.ɲal/	'happy'	/maŋmaŋ.al/	'happy'	/puŋ/	'sun'
ɻ	/t̪eɻ.ŋ-ar/	'killed'	/wa:ɻ.in/	'chase'	/ka:ɻ/	'negative'
l	/pen.kel.t̪an/	'place name'	/kul.am/	'track'	/ŋamal/	'large'
r	/kur.ca/	'cold'	/kir.i/	'permissive'	/wa:n̪tar/	'call out'
j	*		/pu:j.-il/	'crab-ERG'	/ŋe:j/	'listen'
w	/poɻmpuɻa:w.-t̪ak/	'Pormpuraaw-DAT'	/ŋaw.oj/	'yes'	/ko:w/	'nose'

A range of consonant sequences, presented in Table 9, are permissible in complex codas. The ordering of segments within the coda (and more generally the rhyme) proceeds from more sonorous to less, although some sequences of stops of (roughly) equivalent sonority (e.g. /tp/ in /watp/ 'dead') are permissible.[59] The glottal stop – which is not classified as an oral stop – is extremely restricted in its distribution. Exemplar words in Table 9 have been syllabified according to the VC analysis. Words for which a CV syllabification would reduce the cluster described are marked with a hat ('^').

---

58 Although Hall (1968: 54) finds that "only one example of the dental nasal occurs [word-finally]; /ɻu:r mopŋun̪/ 'butterfly'", I find many examples of word-final dental nasals, for instance: /ŋan̪/ 'me' (contrasting with /ŋan/ 'what'); /wan̪/ 'who' (contrasting with /wan/ 'give'), /pu:n̪/ 'sugarbag' (contrasting with /pu:n/ 'breeze').
59 Where an intervocalic sequence of consonants exhibit a marked increase in sonority, the more sonorous sound is syllabified as the onset of the following syllable (e.g. /t̪eɻk.ŋan/ 'going to leave').

Table 9. Complex syllable codas.

	C1	C2	C3	Exemplar words
1.	ɻ	(n, N̪)	(C̪)	/teɻmp/ 'saltwater', /ṉeɻŋk/ 'man's son', /koɻnt/ 'black flying fox', /koɻŋk.on/ 'string basket', /peɻp/ 'net', /poɻk/ 'big'
2.	n	p, c, k	–	/ṯanp/ 'kick', /kunk/ 'alive', /punc/ 'hunk'
3.	N̪	C̪	–	/puŋk+pa:nt/ 'kneecap', /ṯomp/ 'smoke', /ṯa:piɲc/ 'owl'
4.	l	m, n, ŋ	(k)	^/melnk.elnk.ar/ 'tomorrow', /koɻŋk.ulm/ 'string basket', peln 'they (3plNOM)'
		p, t, k	–	/ulp/ 'the', /polk/ 'big', ^/ngamal-t.am/ 'large-ABL'
5.	r	N, C	–	/ka:lk.urc/ 'cold', /wo:c.orm/ 'sacred', /park/ 'shine',
6.	C̪	ʔ	–	/iṉʔ.ṉul/ 'this one', ^/iṯʔ.ark.o/ 'wow!'
7.	t, k	p	–	/watp/ 'dead', /patp/ 'hawk', /akp/ 'despite'

The first row of Table 9 condenses a number of cluster types. The most complex of these, comprising three consonants, must have the retroflex glide in the initial position, followed by a nasal, followed by an oral stop. Where the nasal is alveolar in articulation (/n/), this may be followed by any of the oral stops. Any of the other nasals, however, can only precede a homorganic oral stop. The same is true of two-consonant clusters of nasal + oral stop (as seen in rows 2 and 3); the alveolar is the only nasal that may enter a heterorganic cluster.[60] The only oral consonant that is not found following the alveolar stop in a complex coda is the dental, which appears always to trigger place assimilation in the nasal.

The lateral approximant is attested in three-consonant complex codas where the second slot is filled by a non-palatal nasal and the third slot is optionally filled by the velar oral stop (row 4). It may also serve as initial segment of a two-consonant coda where the second segment is any non-laminal nasal or oral stop. While the lateral approximant and retroflex glide regularly appear within complex codas, the glides /w/ and /j/ are never attested preceding another segment within a coda except where a pragmatic enclitic (/=ṯ/ or /=p/) has attached to a glide-final word (e.g. in /ŋaj=ṯ/ 'I=PRAG').

The apical tap/trill may be combined with only one other segment in a coda, though this segment can be any nasal or oral stop (row 5). The glottal stop is likewise found only in two-segment clusters, and only following a dental (nasal or oral) stop (row 6). The final cluster type attested in my corpus is the sequence of an apical or velar followed by bilabial oral stop (row 7).

---

60 The pragmatic enclitics /=ṯ/ and /=p/ produce a number of possible exceptions to this rule since they may attach to words that end in nasals of other places of articulation (e.g. /ŋaṉ=p/ 'me=PRAG', /puŋ=ṯ/ 'sun=PRAG').

Finally, it is worth noting that although sequences of two nasals or two rhotics are always treated here as heterosyllabic, their pronunciation varies such that some tokens appear to suggest a complex cluster analysis. For example, the sequence /rɻ/ is found word finally both across affix boundaries, as in /waːṉtar-ɻ/ 'call.out-P.PFV', and in roots, such as /parɻ/ 'child'. The inflected verb /t̪eɻŋ-m/ 'hit-P.IPFV', meanwhile, illustrates the word-final sequence /ŋm/. Both /parɻ/ and /waːṉtar-ɻ/ are variously produced as bisyllabic, 'sesquisyllabic'[61] and (potentially) monosyllabic. There are also a number of roots that contain sequences of nasals (e.g. /miːnŋ/ 'take fright'), although their obligatory inflection allows for the analysis of the root-final nasal as second-syllable onset. Future research, and in particular acoustic phonetic analysis, may shed light on the status of these putative complex clusters of sonorants.

2.5 The word

2.5.1 Phonotactic constraints at the word level

Kuuk Thaayorre contains a particularly high number of monosyllables for an Australian language (cf. Dixon 1980: 167, 2002: 651). These words are minimally bimoraic, containing either a long vowel nucleus, a coda, or both. Kuuk Thaayorre also possesses numerous words with four or more syllables. Examples of such words – syllabified according to the CV analysis – include: /maŋk.war.kan.tɻ/ 'went circuitously'; /i.li.pa.raw/ 'from south east'; /po.te.paː.t̪ɻ/ 'shiver' (Hall 1968: 143); /wa.ram.ṉa.ma.rul/ 'he was getting worse' (Hall 1968: 145); /t̪o.t̪o.wol.na.nɻ.ul/ 'he made them keep playing' (Hall 1968: 146); /ŋeɻm.pe.na.ni.cr.t̪a/ 'nearly pushed me down' (Hall 1968: 146).

As noted in §2.4.3.1, there are a number of restrictions on word-initial segments. Namely, /r/, /t/, /n/, /ɲ/, /c/, /ɻ/ and /l/ are only attested word-initially in ideophones and English loan words. Hall (1968: 55) gives a number of examples of words beginning with these phonemes, but I do not take these exceptions to disprove the restriction for several reasons. To begin with, the procedure Hall followed in order to determine felicitous syllable structures may have led informants to attribute meaning to phonetic strings that are not part of the Kuuk Thaayorre language proper. As he puts it: "Generative lists comprising proved phonemes served to encourage informants to 'recognize' actual Thaayorr words" (Hall 1968: 127). We might infer that Hall's collaborators were asked to attribute meaning to random strings of phonemes. While

---

[61] Matisoff (1973: 86) coined the term "sesquisyllable" (literally, 'one-and-a-half syllables') to refer to words that are phonetically disyllabic, but for which the vowel of the first syllable is epenthetic rather than phonemic (and therefore omitted in most practical orthographies). I find it useful to apply this term to the syllable structure of many Thaayorre words, although in these cases it is the vowel of the second syllable that is extremely reduced and non-phonemic.

their responses may be both interesting and significant, it cannot be assumed that the 'recognized' words form part of the structured lexicon of the Kuuk Thaayorre language. Indeed, none of these forms are attested in my corpus.

Secondly, the examples with which Hall illustrates these phonemes in word-initial position appear to be almost exclusively ideophones (e.g. /liŋ/ 'flash of torch', /lak/ 'speared', /lup/ 'in', /law/ 'break', /tuːr/ 'gunshot sound'). Ideophones are well-known to flout phonotactic constraints in other Australian languages (cf. Alpher 1994, Schultze-Berndt 2001, inter alia). The exceptions to this are a couple of interjections (e.g. /ceːr/ 'sorry', used in situations of contact between proscribed relatives) and partially-assimilated loan words (e.g. /cuk/ 'sugar'). Again, we might allow that unusual phonotactic patterns may emerge in such marginal cases. Nevertheless, the fact that these phonemes appear word-initially at all suggests that the contrast between them and other stops (e.g. between the alveolar [t] and dental [t̪]) has not been neutralized as such, but rather that there is a phonotactic constraint on their appearing at the start of the lexemes of less marginal word classes.

Like the palatal obstruent, palatal nasals generally do not appear word-initially. Hall (1968: 53) gives one example of an initial palatal nasal – /ɲor/ 'throat tickle' – though the word class of this lexeme is unclear. It seems likely that /ɲor/ is some kind of ideophone or exclamation (like the words containing initial palatal stops mentioned above). In other words the absence of initial palatal nasals seems to again be due to phonotactic constraints. Further research may prove word-initial /ɲ/ to be marginal rather than disallowed, however.

Many of the small set of vowel-initial words (§2.4.2.2) have consonant-initial allomorphs, usually found following vowel-final words. The distal demonstrative /it̪/, for example, often surfaces as /ŋit̪/ in contexts such as /kuta ŋit̪/ 'that dog'. Similarly /ulp/ ~ /ŋulp/ 'the', /oŋkor/ ~ /ŋoŋkor/ 'prohibitive', /aka/ ~ /ṉaka/ 'this place' and /iːwal/ ~ /jiːwal/ 'towards'.[62] These consonant-initial allomorphs appear historically conservative, since the nature of the onset is not phonetically or morphologically predictable. Synchronically, too, we must take the consonant-initial allomorph to be basic, although these initial consonants may be deleted even following vowel-final words (i.e. /kuta it̪/ 'that dog' is also an acceptable string). The deletion of word-initial segments is also found in fast speech (§2.5.2) and encliticization (the dubitative enclitic /=okun/, for instance, is no doubt related to /jokun/ 'perhaps', see also the pronominal enclitics §3.1.2.2).

Kuuk Thaayorre possesses extremely few vowel-final verb or noun roots, but inflected words commonly end in vowels. Such inflected forms include many ergative and dative-inflected nouns, reflexive and counterfactual verbs and more. The emphatic enclitics /=pa/ and /=e/ (pronounced [ej]) also add to the number of vowel-

---

[62] Hall (1968: 64) likewise notes: "the semivowel /y/ appears intermittently before /i/ as a lenis 'prefix' in many vowel-initial directional terms: e.g. in /iːwal/ ~ /yiːwal/ 'come from there'".

final phonological words in Kuuk Thaayorre discourse (cf. §6.11.2.3). The number of vowel-final words becomes further reduced if we consider the phonetic pronunciation of syllable-final /e/ as [ej] (this frequently affects the reflexive suffix /-e/, for instance when word-final or preceding a syllabic [ɻ] marking past perfective tense/aspect, and always affects the emphatic enclitic /=e/).

I have found no evidence so far of sandhi, either internal or external.

2.5.2 Fluid speech and contractions

Although there is a strong tendency in Kuuk Thaayorre towards closed syllables, there is no elision when a vowel-final word is followed by a vowel-initial word:

(47)   ... ŋan̪   kuta-ku   angar   ŋe:j-n̪
       1sgACC   dog-ERG   WANT   hear-SBJV
       '... so the dog would hear me'
       [KTh_GJ18Jan2004 Elicitation]

In fast speech, however, vowels and consonants are often elided both word-initially and word-internally (e.g. /wan̪n̪uŋun/ 'whose' is often pronounced [waŋwun], especially by younger speakers). The Kuuk Thaayorre tendency for the onsets of word-initial syllables, rather than word-final codas, to be reduced or omitted may be unusual in a broader typological perspective (cf. Martinet 1955, Hock 1991, Keating et al. 1998, and Cho and Keating 2001). However, as noted earlier, in the Australian context initial segments seem prone to weakening (cf. Hale 1976a on Northern Paman languages; Dixon 1980 on Arrernte; and Stoakes pers. comm. on Bininj Gun-Wok). Hall (1968: 64) labels the phenomenon of word-initial onset deletion in rapid speech 'telescoping', observing that "after word-final consonants, the following C_1 is often lost [...] About 14.1% of word-initial phones, almost entirely consonants, may be omitted in normal speech" (1968: 72).

2.5.3 Phonetic effects of syllable structure

Hall (1968) includes a detailed discussion of the phonetic characteristics of consonants according to their position within the syllable. Many of his observations, however, do not accord with my own observations of Kuuk Thaayorre. It is unclear whether this is due to differences in approach, analysis, speakers consulted or changes in the language itself.

Nonetheless, Hall's (1968: 58) observation that word-initial oral stops tend to be aspirated, voiceless and 'fortis' (e.g. in /ka:l/ [kʰa:l] 'ear') holds true for my data. The onsets of subsequent syllables are also often aspirated (e.g. /pitɻ/ [pʰitʰɻ] 'hold:NPST).

Where this onset forms a homorganic stop sequence with the coda of the preceding syllable, though, it is usually unaspirated, e.g. /ṉaŋkn/ [ṉaŋkn] '2sgGEN' (cf. Hall 1968: 58). As mentioned above, the first segment(s) of a consonant cluster are usually released, except where followed by a bilabial stop (e.g. /ṯaŋkt/ [ṯaŋkʰt̚] 'pus:PRAG' but /watp/ [wat̚p] 'dead'). Word-final consonants are almost always released and optionally aspirated (word-final aspiration is usually associated with emphasis).

2.6 Reduplication

Reduplication in verbs is a productive morphological process and it may also be productive for some classes of adverb. In other word classes, however, reduplicated forms appear to be synchronically lexicalized. This section details the forms reduplication may take; its semantic effects are discussed in the relevant chapters (e.g. §7.2.4 for verbal reduplication). There are four distinct morphophonological patterns of reduplication in Kuuk Thaayorre. The first two processes (vowel lengthening §2.6.1 and rhyme reduplication §2.6.2) apply to verbs with short initial syllable vowels. The third pattern (onset-nucleus reduplication §2.6.3) only applies to verbs with an initial long vowel. The fourth (first syllable reduplication, §2.6.4) is the least productive and mostly found among adverbs. The theoretical implications of Kuuk Thaayorre's rhyme and onset-nucleus reduplication patterns have been considered by Round (2013, for Base-Reduplicant Correspondence Theory) and Gaby & Inkelas (2014, for Morphological Doubling Theory MDT). The latter also considers the implications of these patterns for syllable structure in Kuuk Thaayorre. Both of these accounts differ from Gaby's (2006) analysis of reduplication as infixation. This section does not review these theoretical debates; it simply describes the empirical evidence for all four reduplication patterns.

2.6.1 Reduplication by vowel lengthening

Verb roots that have a short initial-syllable vowel may code durative aspect by simply lengthening that vowel (cf. §7.2.4.2). This can be seen in the relationship between the verb roots and their reduplicated counterparts in (48):

(48) /jan/   'go'   /jaːn/   'keep going'
     /wun/   'lie'   /wuːn/   'go on lying'
     /muŋk/ 'eat'   /muːŋk/ 'keep eating'
     /ɹat̪/   'chop'   /ɹaːt̪/   'keep chopping'
     /pat̪/   'bite'   /paːt̪/   'keep biting'
     /jik/   'speak'   /jiːk/   'keep speaking'

For the first three of these verb roots (e.g. *jan* 'go'), vowel lengthening is the only available form of reduplication. For the others, both vowel lengthening and rhyme-reduplication are used with contrastive effect (see §7.2.4.3).

This first form of reduplication can be summarized by the rule in Figure 4, which takes the example of /paṯ/ 'bite':

C_1 V_1 $(C_2)(C_3)(C_4)$ ... → C_1 V_1: $(C_2)(C_3)(C_4)$ ...
p   a   ṯ   p   a: ṯ

Figure 4. Vowel lengthening reduplication of /paṯ/ 'bite'.

2.6.2 Rhyme reduplication

For most verbs with short initial syllable vowels, the corresponding reduplicated form exhibits what I refer to here as 'rhyme reduplication. Whether or not it is in fact the rhyme that reduplicates depends on whether one adopts a CV or VC analysis of syllabification (see §2.4.2.1). The list in (49) provides both CV and VC syllabification of polysyllabic roots to highlight this difference. This list also includes fossilized relics of the same reduplication pattern in other word classes, such as the emphatic pronoun /ṉululɪ/ 'by himself' and the adverbs /ṯintintr/ 'very slowly' and /ŋeɪnkeɪnkan/ 'morning':

(49) /kal/   'carry'   /kalal/   'keep carrying'
      /peɪp/   'cover'   /peɪpeɪp/   'keep covering'
      /katp/   'grasp'   /katpatp/   'keep grasping'
      /kunk/   'alive'   /kunkunk/   'alive [of many people]'
      /ṉul/   'he'   /ṉululɪ/   'by himself'

      /jompar/   'become'   VC: /jomp.omp.ar/   'becoming'
                                CV: /jom.pom.par/   'becoming'

      /kunut/   'remove'   VC: /kun.un.ut/   'keep removing'
                                CV: /ku.nu.nut/   'keep removing'

      /piniɪm/   'imagine'   VC: /pin.in.iɪm/   'keep imagining'
                                CV: /pi.ni.niɪm/   'keep imagining'

      /ŋeɪnkan/   'yesterday' VC: /ŋeɪnk.eɪnk.an/ 'morning'
                                CV: /ŋeɪn.keɪn.kan/ 'morning'

The rule for deriving so-called rhyme-reduplicated words is given in Figure 5, which remains agnostic as to whether C_2-C_4 are syllabified as coda and whether the reduplicant is the product of infixation or some other process (cf. Gaby & Inkelas 2014).

C_1 V_1 $(C_2)(C_3)(C_4)$ ...   → C_1 V_1 $(C_2)(C_3)(C_4)$ V_1 $(C_2)(C_3)(C_4)$ ...
p   i   ɻ m p   p   i   ɻ m p   i   ɻ m p

Figure 5. Rhyme reduplication of /piɻmp/ 'rise'

2.6.3 Onset-nucleus reduplication

Verbs that have a long initial-syllable vowel exhibit reduplication of the initial syllable onset and vowel, though the vowel of the second syllable of the reduplicated verb is always short (in keeping with Kuuk Thaayorre's restriction of long vowels to stressed syllables). As the final example of (50) demonstrates, fossilized relics of this reduplication pattern are found among other word classes, though it remains productive only for verbs:

(50) /ʈuːʈ/   'crawl'   /ʈuːʈuʈ/   'keep crawling'
      /koːpe/   'wait'   /koːkope/ 'keep waiting'
      /waːʈ/   'search'   /waːwaʈ/   'keep searching'
      /paːʈ/   'fire'   /paːpaʈ/   'hot'

It is possible to analyze the onset-nucleus reduplicant as prefixed, infixed or produced through some alternative process (e.g. morphological doubling, Inkelas & Zoll 2005). If prefixed, the vowel of the verb root must be shortened in the reduplicated verb stem, presumably through some productive phonological process which renders the vowels of all unstressed syllables short. If infixed, it must be stipulated that the onset plus the short congener of the first vowel are infixed following the first syllable. Once again, the rule presented in Figure 6 is purely descriptive, remaining neutral with respect to these analytical differences:

C_1 V_1: $(C_2)(C_3)(C_4)$ ...   → C_1 V_1: C_1 V_1 $(C_2)(C_3)(C_4)$ ...
w   aː   ʈ   w   aː   w   a   ʈ

Figure 6. Onset-nucleus reduplication of waːʈ 'search for'.

In onset-nucleus reduplication, the second manifestation of the onset (i.e. the second C_1 in Figure 6) is almost always lenited to a voiced fricative. Hence /ʈeːʈeɻk/ [ʈeːðeɻk] 'return:RDP'; /koːkope/ [kʰoːɣope] 'wait:RDP'; and /paːpaʈ/ [pʰaːβaʈ] 'hot'.

2.6.4 First syllable reduplication

The final pattern of reduplication evident in Kuuk Thaayorre involves reduplication of the first syllable in its entirety. This pattern is most common among adverbs. Most adverbs reduplicate for intensification, as seen in (51). Other syllable-reduplicated words appear to be fossilized, having no non-reduplicated counterpart (such as *ma:lmal* 'slowly').

(51) /wacir/ 'correctly'   /wacwacir/ 'just so'
     /kempṯe/ 'singly'   /kempkempṯe/ 'each one'
     /ṯil/ 'again'   /ṯilṯil/ '(yet) again'
     /putpun/ 'on top'   /putputpun/ 'right on top'
     /pal/ 'towards'   /palpal/ 'close to'
     /ko:r/ 'behind'   /ko:rkor/ 'over and over'
     /ko:p/ 'all'   /ko:pkop/ 'every single one'
     /wa:r/ 'bad'   /wa:rwa:r/ 'worse'
     */ma:l/   /ma:lmal/ 'slowly'

Figure 7 provides the descriptive rule for first syllable reduplication. As with rhyme reduplication, long vowels in the first syllable of the root correspond to short vowels of the same quality in the second syllable of the reduplicated stem.

C_1 $V_1(:)$ $(C_2)(C_3)(C_4)$ ... → C_1 $V_1:$ $(C_2)(C_3)(C_4)$ C_1 V_1 $(C_2)(C_3)(C_4)$ ...
m a: l   m a: l   m a l

Figure 7. First syllable reduplication in *ma:lmal* 'slowly'.

A small minority of lexemes allow first syllable reduplication as an alternative to rhyme reduplication (§2.6.2). This is found among words of all reduplicable word classes, as illustrated by the verb, emphatic pronoun and adverb in (52):

(52) /ŋamp/ 'we (1pl:excl)'   /ŋampŋampɹ/ ~ /ŋampampɹ/ 'ourselves (1pl:excl)'
     /ṯil/ 'again'   /ṯilṯil/ ~ /ṯilil/ '(yet) again'
     /ɹip/ 'exit'   /ɹipɹip/ ~ /ɹipip/ 'keep exiting'

2.7 Stress

The suprasegmental phonology of Kuuk Thaayorre warrants much deeper investigation than I have been able to undertake. The few observations outlined here offer a basis for future study. The interested reader is also referred to Hall (1968), which includes detailed and more richly exemplified discussion than space allows for here.

Primary stress in Kuuk Thaayorre is allocated to the first syllable of the lexical head (cf. Alpher's 1972: 71 similar claim that stress falls on the root-initial syllable in both Kuuk Thaayorre and Yir Yoront). Since Kuuk Thaayorre is a predominantly suffixing language, the initial syllable of the lexical head usually but not always corresponds to the first syllable of the phonological word. Examples of nonalignment, where the lexical head is not the word-initial morpheme, are typically found among compounds. In most cases, it is compound-final root that receives primary stress (e.g. /puŋk+páːnt/ 'kneecap [lit. knee+head]', /mèːɻ+kun+wáːr/ 'pitiful [lit. eye+guts+bad]'). The enclitics /=(k)aːk/ 'proprietive' and /=(k)aːɻ/ 'privative' likewise attract primary stress (cf. §4.2.8 and §4.2.9). These enclitics are unusual not only in receiving stress, but also in the fact that they contain long vowels, these two features being clearly related. The initial syllable of the word to which these enclitics attach will usually exhibit secondary stress, with all intervening syllables unstressed (e.g. /jìːramokunkáːk/ 'perhaps having another'[63]).

For most words, the initial, stressed syllable is followed by secondary stress on subsequent odd syllables (as noted by Dixon 1980: 128 as a common Australian stress pattern), hence /máŋkwarkàntɻ/ 'going circuitously around'. Dixon also notes that word-final syllables tend to be unstressed in Australian languages, even in words containing an odd number of syllables. Odd-syllabled Kuuk Thaayorre words vary in this respect, with the allocation of stress to final syllables seemingly dependent on: (a) the phonotactic structure of the syllable (e.g. does it contain a vowel nucleus); (b) the morphological status of the syllable (i.e. is it part of a root or suffix); and (c) the position of the word within the intonational phrase. Accordingly, /máŋk.war.kànt/ 'go circuitously around (imperative)' allocates secondary stress to the final syllable, but /ŋáṯn-m(a)n/ 'my-ERG' does not. These findings stand contrary to Hall's (1968: 61) observations that "the second morpheme tends to compete with the first and receives a stronger accent: e.g. [pòkʰón] 'nothing'" and "operative suffixes frequently receive greater stress than initial syllables of the root-morpheme: e.g. /ŋàṯn/ 'my'; cf. /ŋàṯún/ 'to me'" (1968: 151). In my data, it is exclusively the first syllable of /pókon/ that is stressed, as is the first syllable of /ŋáṯun/ '1sgDAT'.[64]

In spontaneous speech, stress patterns may be altered for discursive or stylistic effect. Hence in the 'Two Crocodiles' narrative told by DW, the word /irkuw/ 'to the west' (which usually carries stress on its initial syllable) is pronounced once with second-syllable stress:

(53) ŋul puʔam iː-r-kúw tḛɻk-ɻ
 then wounded there-towards-west return-P.PFV
 "then when he was wounded he went back to the beach"
 [KTh_**DW**-CW09Dec2002 Narrative 2Crocs]

---

63 The phonological word /jìːramokunkáːk/ can be segmented as /jiːram=okun=kaːk/ 'another= dubitative=relational.proprietive'.
64 We might speculate that Hall's collaborators stressed contrastive suffixes in an elicitation context.

The stress pattern of this word is presumably changed for contrastive effect, highlighting that the crocodile was now returning to the west, following earlier clauses' description of his movement to the east. Throughout the rest of the story (which can be found in Appendix 2), /írkuw/ 'to the west' is pronounced with the usual word-initial stress.

It has already been noted that the vowel nuclei of unstressed syllables are commonly somewhat reduced. Conversely, pragmatic emphasis is frequently marked by prosodic vowel lengthening. There is thus a certain iconic function of lengthening the initial vowel of /ŋamal/ 'large' in [ŋaːːmal] 'enormous' or /kanaŋkar/ 'long ago' > [kʰaːːnaŋkar] 'very long ago'. In the following chapters, vowels lengthened due to pragmatic emphasis (rather than being phonemically long) will be transcribed in the Pormpuraaw Orthography (§2.8) as 'Vːː' rather than 'VV'.

2.8 Orthographic conventions

2.8.1 History of Kuuk Thaayorre practical orthographies

Several practical orthographies have been employed since Kuuk Thaayorre was first written down. The first was most likely developed by Allen Hall in collaboration with speaker-linguist †Tom Foote. This orthography has been used in an impressive array of primers, readers and other literacy materials printed by the Queensland Education Department and the Jollen Press (Brisbane) for the Pormpuraaw State School, circa 1970. Although a generation of Pormpuraawans became literate in Kuuk Thaayorre by means of these publications, few remember or employ it today. Those who remain literate (or who have redeveloped their literacy) in Kuuk Thaayorre, generally employ one or more of the alternative working orthographies ('WO') used around the community. It seems likely that native speaker linguists, perhaps in collaboration with outsiders, developed these orthographies based jointly on English orthography and what they remembered of the Hall/Foote (hereafter 'HF') orthography from school. Finally, there is the so-called Pormpuraaw Orthography ('PO') developed by a committee of Thaayorre elders in consultation with the Pormpuraaw Aboriginal Council and me as part of the Cape York Peninsula Language Project. This orthography attempts to standardize the common elements of the other orthographies. It was used in the *Ngay Kuuk Thaayorre Yiik* ('I speak Kuuk Thaayorre') CD-ROM and printed materials employed by the Pormpuraaw Primary School between 2002 – 2008, and will be used to transcribe example words and sentences throughout the rest of this grammar. The phonemic inventory of Kuuk Thaayorre, as represented in PO, is as follows:

The key differences between the orthographies lie in their respective representations of the dental nasal and the palatal obstruent. (Some other differences, such as the transcription of reduced ~vowels, are reflective of analytical differences rather than differences in orthography as such.) The HF orthography represents the dental nasal as /n/ when word-initial and /h/ elsewhere, while WO and PO represent it as /nh/ in all contexts. Hence the pronoun /ṉuṉ/ 'him' is transcribed as *nuh* throughout Foote & Hall (1992), but *nhunh* in this grammar. WOs variously represent the dental nasal as /n/ and /nh/. The palatal obstruent is represented by HF as /c/, by WO as either /j/ or /ch/ or /c/, and by PO as /c/.

Although Kuuk Thaayorre remains in vibrant use in Pormpuraaw, it is seldom written. Communication is overwhelmingly oral in the community, with the written medium largely restricted to official business, all of which is conducted in English. Excluding my own work and related projects, I have only encountered written Kuuk Thaayorre in the form of: dictionaries and literacy materials prepared by Allen Hall and †Tom Foote, presently locked in a storage cupboard at the Pormpuraaw State School; two posters at the Pormpuraaw Primary Healthcare Centre, translated by Mrs Myrtle Foote; street signs and signage for Pormpur Paanthu women's centre and various other organizations; and some new catalogues and booklets produced by the Pormpuraaw Art Centre. There is significant enthusiasm in the community for increased visibility of local languages (including but not limited to Kuuk Thaayorre), and more widespread use will likely feed standardization.

2.8.2 Pormpuraaw Orthography and conventions

The following tables set out the practical renderings of the Kuuk Thaayorre consonants and vowels in PO:

Table 10. Consonants in Pormpuraaw Orthography.

	bilabial	lamino-dental	apical	lamino-palatal	velar	glottal
Obstruents	p	th	t	c	k	'
Sonorants	m	nh	n	ny	ng	
Tap/trill			rr			
Lateral			l			
Glides	(w)		r	y	w	

Table 11. Vowels in Pormpuraaw Orthography.

	front	central	back
high	i, ii		u, uu
mid	e, ee		o, oo
low		a, aa	

A few further orthographic conventions in PO require explanation before we proceed. Firstly, homorganic dental clusters are simplified as follows:

/n̪/ + /t̪/ → nth

There do not appear to be any heterorganic alveolar-dental clusters within morphemes, but where a morpheme-final alveolar nasal is followed by a morpheme-initial dental stop (most commonly the pragmatic enclitic =th), this is disambiguated from the homorganic cluster by an underscore if not an explicit marker of the morpheme boundary:

/n̪t̪/ → nth
/nt̪/ → n_th

The underscore is used in preference to a full stop in order to reserve the latter for signalling a boundary between morphemes that are together expressed by a single word in the gloss line (as within the verbal compound *thaa.riic* 'tear', literally 'mouth+run').

Homorganic velar and palatal clusters remain unsimplified:

/ŋk/ → ngk
/nk/ → nk
/ɲc/ → nyc
/nc/ → nc

Sequences of rhotics are separated by an underscore:

/rɻ/ → rr_r
/ɻr/ → r_rr

An alveolar nasal followed by a palatal glide is similarly disambiguated from the palatal nasal by an intervening underscore:

/nj/ → n_y
/ɲ/ → ny

3 Word classes

At the broadest level, Kuuk Thaayorre lexemes can be divided into four word classes – nominals, verbs, adverbs and ideophones – which are joined by a host of particles and enclitics that do not form a unified class as such. Each of the major classes is open, in the sense that it is possible to coin new nominals, verbs, adverbs and (possibly) ideophones, yet all but the ideophones possess one or more closed subclasses. Pronouns form a closed nominal subclass, for instance, and directional adverbs form a morphologically complex closed paradigm.

A lexeme is generally assigned to a word class on the basis of its potential inflection and syntactic distribution, and the many homophones in the Kuuk Thaayorre lexicon can usually be differentiated on this basis. The form *patp*, for example, is analyzed as a specific noun when it inflects for case (e.g. *patpa* 'hawk:ERG') and/or combines with a generic noun in a classifying phrase (e.g. *minh patp* 'MEAT hawk(NOM)'), but the same form is analyzed as a verb when it inflects for tense, aspect and/or mood (e.g. *patpirr* 'camp:P.PFV'). The morphosyntactic criteria used to distinguish the Kuuk Thaayorre word classes are discussed in the relevant subsections below.

3.1 Nominals

Nominals are a class of referring forms, all of which may function as the argument of a predicate and/or copula verb, and all of which[65] bear case signalling their role in the clause. Within the nominal class it is possible to identify various subclasses, particularly with respect to their position and function within the noun phrase. The syntactic structure of the noun phrase is the concern of Chapter 5, but it is worth previewing here since many of its constituents are defined in part on this basis.

While constituent order is remarkably flexible in Kuuk Thaayorre, the internal constituents of the noun phrase appear in a relatively fixed linear order, as follows:[66]

(54) NP → Pro {N$_{GN}$ N$_{SP}$ Deg Adj Deg Gen Quant Ign/Dem.Pro}-**case** Adn.Dem Pro

Figure 8 summarizes the various nominal subclasses and the hyponymic relationships that hold between them. Dashed lines represent valid alternative classifications. The divisions between subclasses are not always neat; genitive pronouns, for

---

[65] Predicate adjectives are an exception to this rule since they never bear case. Predicate adjectives can, however, function as arguments of a copula predicate (as seen in example (80) below).
[66] Abbreviations used: Pro 'Pronoun'; N$_{GN}$ 'generic noun'; N$_{SP}$ 'specific noun' ; Deg 'degree adverb'; Adj 'adjective'; Gen 'genitive pronoun'; Quant 'quantifier'; Ign 'ignorative pronoun'; Dem.Pro 'demonstrative pronoun'; Adn.Dem 'adnominal demonstrative' Pro 'pronoun'. Each of these constituents is optional.

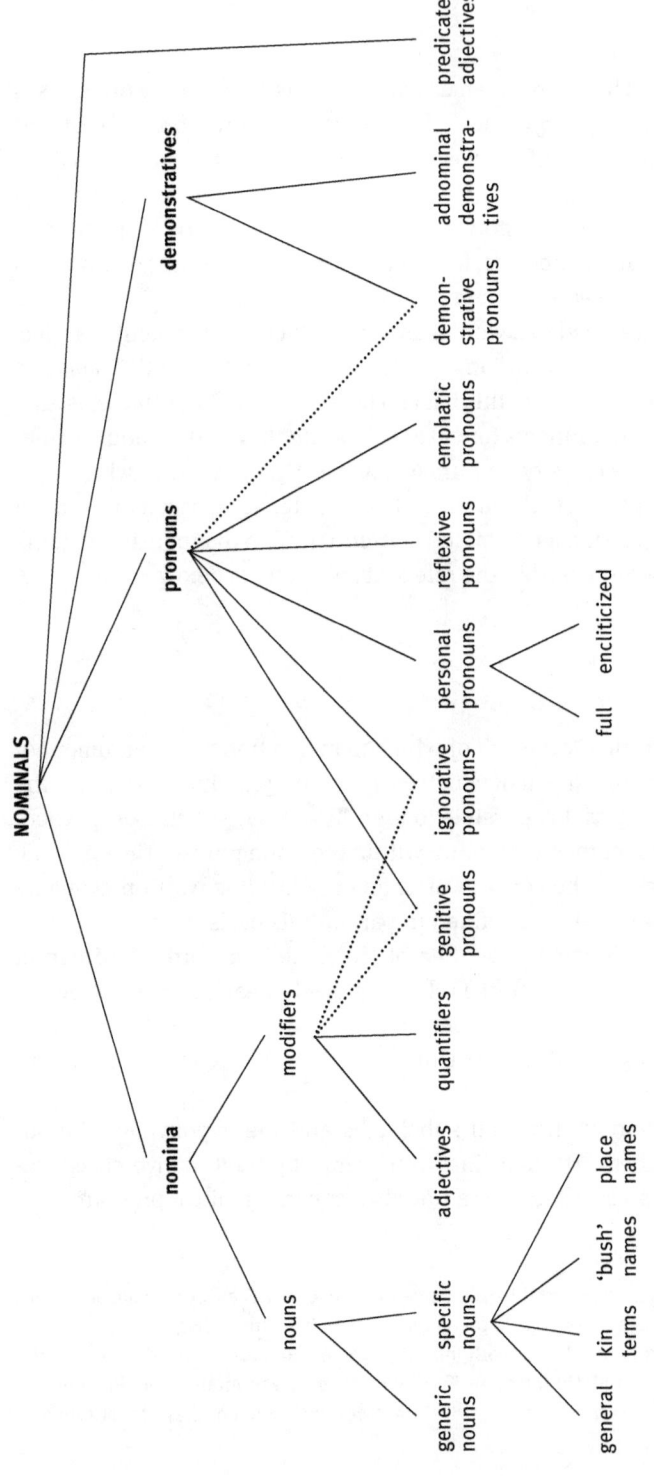

Figure 8. Nominal subclasses.

instance, could equally be considered a subclass of modifier (and hence a nomen) or a subclass of pronoun. Demonstrative pronouns similarly share characteristics of both demonstratives and pronouns, as their label suggests. The exclusive allocation of such word subclasses to an intermediate class (e.g. nomen vs. pronoun) reflects the somewhat arbitrary heuristics involved in producing a linear grammar, rather than the inherent nature of the forms in question.

3.1.1 Nomina

The term 'nomen' (pl. 'nomina') denotes a nominal subclass spanning generic nouns ('generics'), specific nouns ('specifics'), adjectives and quantifiers (cf. Wilkinson 1991). These elements are united by their shared inflectional morphology. Moreover, many lexemes may function as generic, specific and adjective in different contexts. The form *pam*, for example, can function as a generic (denoting the class of humans, as in (55)), as a specific (denoting men, as in (56)) or as an adjective (denoting maleness, as in (57)).

(55) **pam**   nhanganam
      HUMAN   mother
      '(a) mother'

(56) **pam** watp
      man   dead
      '(a) dead man'

(57) parr_r **pam**
      child   male
      '(a) boy'

Although nomina are united by their common morphology and the existence of forms such as *pam* that span the functional and syntactic range of generics, specifics and adjectives, there are clear grounds for distinguishing these three subclasses. The justification for considering forms like *pam* above as heterosemous, as well as syntactic evidence for distinct subclasses of nomen, is laid out in §6.3.

3.1.1.1 Generics
The closed nominal subclass of generics is composed of at least fifteen members. Generics occupy the initial position in the noun phrase, taking the full range of case suffixes where appropriate. In (58), for instance, the generic noun *minh* 'MEAT' is inflected for ergative case due to its being the sole exponent of the NP.

(58)   *yokun   minh-al   patha-rr   pulnan*
       perhaps MEAT-ERG   bite-P.PFV 3duACC
       'perhaps a [crocodile] got them'
       [KTh_GJ15Oct2002 Narrative PlaneSighting]

Where generic and specific nouns are paired in a 'classifying construction' (§6.2), the construction as a whole is always a hyponym of the generic. As such, generic nouns serve a categorizing function, optionally classifying entities in the world into at least fifteen generic groups. Table 12 presents a list of the generics documented to date.

Table 12. List of Kuuk Thaayorre generic nouns.

Form	Gloss	Denotation
minh	MEAT	**edible land animals:** meat, most land animals (including crocodiles and legged lizards, excluding snakes and insects), all birds.
ngat	FISH	**edible aquatic animals:** fish, crabs. **aquatic mammals:** dugong, dolphins, porpoises.
may	VEG	**edible plants:** non-meat food, a meal (which may include meat since *may* is the unmarked food generic), honey, honey bees.
ngok	LIQUID	**liquids:** water, all drinkable fluids (e.g. beer), water-based non-drinkable bodies of water (e.g. *ngok thermp* 'saltwater').
kuuk	WORD	**structured utterances:** words, languages, individual utterances, pronouncements, human speech generally, birdsong.
warrath	GRASS	**grasses**
yuk	1. TREE 2. THING	**trees:** tree species and parts and products thereof (e.g. roots, branches, sticks, dyes, etc.) **objects** (typically elongated and / or resembling sticks): microphones, cigarettes, aeroplanes, cyclones, prawns.[67]
yak	SNAKE	**snakes** (also includes snake-like vertebrates such as eels and legless lizards.)
raak	1. PLACE 2. TIME 3. OBJECT	**physical locations:** place names, geographical areas, ground, the earth, soil. **times:** diurnal phases, seasons, etc. **items of material culture:** money.
pam	1. HUMAN 2. MAN 3. MALE	**people:** humans **man:** adult male humans **male:** male humans

---

67 Prawns and shellfish – along with their discarded shells – are classified as *yuk*, by analogy with the trees and sticks they resemble. This analogy extends to labelling their edible flesh as *may*, the generic noun usually reserved for the edible parts of plants (cf. Taylor 1984: 48).

Table 12. (continued)

Form	Gloss	Denotation
paanth	1. WOMAN 2. FEMALE	**women:** adult female humans **female:** female humans
parr_r	CHILD	**juveniles:** immature humans and other species
kuta	PET	**social animals:** dogs, cats, dingoes
ngan	KIN	**relatives:** consanguineal or affinal (not classificatory) kin and surrogates.
ruurr	INSECT	**insects**

3.1.1.2 Specifics

Where a noun phrase includes both a specific and a generic, the specific noun immediately follows the generic, the two entering into a classifying construction. Taking the full range of case suffixes, specific nouns comprise the largest nominal subclass, freely incorporating newly coined, derived or borrowed terms. The formation of neologisms through nominal compounding is widespread (e.g. *meer+kay* 'spectacles', lit. 'eye+metal'), and English nouns are borrowed daily without any special morphology. Generic-specific pairings may themselves become lexicalized via compounding, producing a new specific noun which may enter a classifying construction afresh. This is seen in *ngat minh+patp* 'spotted eagle-ray', where *minh patp* means 'hawk'. Specific nouns may also be derived from verbs or phrases, e.g. by suffixing the 'nominalizer' suffix -*m* (e.g. *yuur+kath-m* 'policeman', lit. 'hand+bind-NMLZ), see §8.1.6 for further discussion of this derivational process.

Not all specific nouns combine with a generic. There is rather a cline ranging from (a) specific nouns that are unable to enter into any classifying construction (e.g. *pung* 'sun'); to (b) those that rarely co-occur with a generic (such as *[ngat] puuy* '[FISH] crab'[68]); to (c) those that are found as frequently with as without a generic (e.g. *[raak] ngurnturnturr* '[TIME] night'); to (d) those that usually occur with a generic (e.g. *minh pinc* 'MEAT crocodile'); to (e) those that are only attested with a generic (e.g. *raak rirkr* 'money [lit. OBJECT shell]'). The nature of the relationship between generic and specific nouns is considered further in §6.2 and §6.3.

---

[68] The infrequency with which the generic *ngat* 'FISH' precedes *puuy* 'crab' has lead many younger speakers to reclassify this specific noun as *minh puuy* 'MEAT crab'.

3.1.1.2.1 Referential kin terms

Of the four sets of kin terms presented in §1.3.3.1, only the referential kin terms are clearly nominal. They frequently comprise generic – specific pairings (e.g. *ngan puumi* 'KIN younger.brother' and *pam kanam* 'MALE older.brother'), and may be modified by adjectives (e.g. *ngan nhanganam mantam* 'mother's younger sister [lit. KIN mother small]') and genitive pronouns (59). They may receive case inflection, as in (60), and head argument noun phrases (59).

(59) Angelina-n   pit-m   pam   kanam   ngathn
      Angelina-ERG   keep-P.IPFV   MALE   B+   1sgGEN(ACC)
      'Angelina was in a relationship with my elder brother'
      [KTh_ACh07Nov2002 Conversation]

(60) ngay   nganip-an   yan
      1sg(NOM)   father-DAT   go:NPST
      'I'd go with my father'
      [KTh_AC10Aug2002 Conversation]

As with other specific nouns, there is a cline between those referential kin terms that never combine with generics in my data (e.g. *mokr* 'mother's elder brother') through those that rarely combine with generics ([*pam*] *nhanganip* '[MALE] father', *[ngan] pinhirr* '[KIN] father's sister') to those that obligatorily combine with generics (e.g. *pam kunyangkar* 'brother'). It is only in combination with kinship specific nouns that we find the generic noun *paanth* 'FEMALE' in opposition to *pam* 'MALE', the latter elsewhere having the gender-neutral meaning 'HUMAN'. The variability in the obligatoriness of generic terms is reflected in Table 1 in §1.3.3.1, where just the specific term is entered for some kin relations but the full classifying phrase is entered for others. The inclusion or exclusion of generic nouns in Table 1 was determined by frequency; where they are present in over 50% of tokens for that kin category in my data they are included in the table.

By contrast, vocative kin terms (such as *wanhn!* '(hey) elder brother!') may be considered a subtype of interjection, the kinship hand signs form part of the sign register, and bereavement terms, while probably nominal, are too poorly understood at present to allow classification.

3.1.1.2.2 Body part terms

Body part terms occupy a privileged position in Kuuk Thaayorre morphosyntax in several respects. Firstly, they are frequently compounded with a verbal head (§8.3), compounded with another noun (especially in the formation of referential kin terms, §1.3.3.1, also cf. Green et al. In press), or compounded with certain adverbs and particles (§9.2.6). Secondly, they enter into the part-whole apposition construction (§6.10.1).

Thirdly, they exhibit an extremely high degree of polysemy, and are used metaphorically in the description of space, landscape, human emotions and intellectual and psychological experiences (cf. Gaby 2006, 2008b). The inventory of body part terms collected to date is presented in Gaby (2006). The semantic processes involved in producing body part compounds are explored in §4.3.2.

3.1.1.2.3 Proper nouns

Traditional 'bush names' (proper names for people, and sometimes dogs) and place names for sacred sites commonly index events that occurred during the sacred epoch known to outsiders as 'the dreaming'. Owing to their spiritual significance, some of the speakers I interviewed indicated that they would prefer these names did not appear in print. In keeping with this wishes, this discussion does not include any names themselves and is accordingly rather general and brief. The interested reader can find a list of place names in Taylor (1984 and 1985).

Belying the title of this section, it would seem that there is no word (sub)class of proper nouns as such. Rather, the traditional names of both people and sacred sites are phrasal in form. These polynomial expressions usually take the form of either a complex noun phrase (e.g. generic noun, specific noun and adjective) or a subject + verb. Personal 'bush' names do not seem to be formally differentiated from place names (in particular, the names of *raak woocorrm* 'story places'). For instance, in talking about his father's bush name, Alfred Charlie at one point included the PLACE generic noun *raak* at the start of the bush name. Certainly the same principles seem to govern the composition of both kinds of name.

3.1.1.3 Adjectives

The prototypical adjective describes some quality or characteristic of an entity. Adjectives directly follow the specific noun (or generic if there is no specific noun) within the NP. Most adjectives take the usual nominal case suffixes and certain adjectives may additionally be reduplicated to indicate plurality or intensity, e.g. *kump* 'deep' > *kumpumpum* 'really deep' (Hall 1972: 92). This reduplication does not appear to be productive, however, and reduplicated forms may be separate, frozen lexical entries formed during a period when reduplication was more widespread.

3.1.1.4 Quantifiers

The five native Kuuk Thaayorre quantifiers (*thono* 'one', *kuthirr* 'two', *pinalam* 'three, several', *mong* 'many', *koop* 'all') appear to be part of an open class, despite their limited number. The class can be considered open on the grounds that loan numerals are prevalent throughout Kuuk Thaayorre speech (though obligatorily taking the suffix *-nharr*, §4.4.2). Additionally, a number of rarely used numerals (e.g. *yuur* 'five' [lit. 'hand']) are likely to be calques of English, coined due to the increasing demand for numeracy during the mission era. These possibly innovative numerals have extremely limited currency nowadays. Quantifiers are assigned a particular slot in the noun phrase and inflect for case when phrase-final. I have not yet found any evidence to suggest that numerals should be distinguished from the other quantifiers as a separate (sub)class.

The numeral quantifier *thono* 'one' is additionally employed as a reference tracking device, introducing new participants that might potentially be confused with participants already 'on scene' (cf. §6.11.2.1).

3.1.2 Pronouns

A macro-class of pronouns – subsuming personal pronouns, reflexive pronouns, emphatic pronouns, inclusory pronouns, ignorative pronouns and demonstrative pronouns – can be established on the basis of formal and indexical similarities. Demonstrative pronouns, however, share many key characteristics with adnominal demonstratives. As flagged in §3.1, my analysis allows for the dual class-membership of such forms, though it is organizationally preferable to classify them in one class or another. For this reason, demonstrative pronouns are discussed alongside adnominal demonstratives in §3.1.3.1. Bound and free personal pronouns and inclusory pronouns may only be used with reference to humans and – in some cases – higher animates (e.g. dogs).

3.1.2.1 (Free) personal pronouns

Kuuk Thaayorre personal pronouns distinguish three person values (first, second and third), three numbers (singular, dual and plural) and make a binary inclusive/exclusive distinction for dual and plural first person pronouns. Each of the eleven basic pronominal categories (formed through the various combinations of these values) further inflects for nominative/ergative, accusative, genitive, dative and ablative cases. The full paradigm of case-inflected personal pronouns is given in §5.1.1.1.

The personal pronominal paradigm is nominal in its encoding of case categories. Personal pronouns encode case through stem mutation, though, rather than hosting the case morphs suffixed to other nominal classes. The syntactic relationship between pronouns and other coreferential nominals is also much looser than that which holds between co-constituents of a NP. Pronouns are frequently repeated several times in a single clause (61), are considerably freer than other nominals with respect to word order and may either form a syntactic unit with a coreferential NP, or be apposed to it in syntactic independence (see §6.6, 6.7).[69]

---

[69] Cf. Stirling (2008) on the apposition of coreferential pronouns and noun phrases in Kala Lagaw Ya.

(61) ngay   piinthawaarr-m-r ngay   nhangknma
    1sg(NOM) tired-VBLZ-P.PFV 1sg(NOM)   2sgABL
    'I wearied of you'
    [Hall 1972: 138]

Generally speaking, personal pronouns may only be used to refer to humans and higher animates (i.e. dogs and dreamtime beings). Emphatic and demonstrative pronouns, however, are unrestricted by considerations of animacy (see §5.1.3, 5.3.1).

3.1.2.2 Enclitic pronouns

Nominative and accusative (and, marginally, dative) personal pronouns possess alternative enclitic forms that attach to a variety of word classes, usually the verb. These enclitics are in the early stages of grammaticalizing from the free personal pronouns, and share the same forms minus the initial nasal of the free pronouns. Thus the first person singular enclitic pronoun =ay in (62) is transparently derived from the first person singular free pronoun ngay. Similarly, the third person singular accusative enclitic =unh (63) derives from the corresponding free form nhunh.

(62) two   years   nhamunp   nhiin-r=ay
    two   years   in.that.place   reside-P.PFV=1sg(NOM)
    'for two years I stayed there [Darwin]'
    [KTh_AJ-GJ03Feb2004 Conversation]

(63) punth   thiika-rr=unh
    arm(ACC)   break-P.PFV=3sgACC
    '[the crocodile] broke his arm'
    [KTh_AJ-GJ03Feb2004 Conversation]

The paradigms of enclitic pronouns are given in §5.1.1.3, which also contains a discussion of their syntax.

3.1.2.3 Reflexive pronouns

Reflexive pronouns signal that the subject participant is affected by their own actions. These forms may thus be used to achieve a reflexive interpretation of a clause whether in the presence or absence of verbal reflexive coding. Reflexive pronouns decline for person and number, but do not encode case. The reflexive pronominal forms are formally very close to compounds of the corresponding genitive pronouns and nominative personal pronouns. Hence the second person singular reflexive pronoun *nhangknunt* 'yourself' is patently derived from *nhangkn* '2sgGEN' + *nhunt* '2sg(NOM)'.

The reflexive pronouns are not only used to describe self-directed ('reflexive') actions, but also events that occur without the intervention of an external agent, as in the second clause of (64).

(64) *ngul thaathi-n-r, nhululr thaathath-r*
then dry-v^-NPST 3sgRFL dry:RDP-NPST
'then you dry out [the raffia], it dries itself out [in the sun]'
[KTh_ME04Jun2005 Narrative Yencr]

The morphology and functions of reflexive pronouns are discussed in §5.1.2, while the semantics and morphosyntax of reflexive constructions more generally are discussed in §11.5.

3.1.2.4 Reciprocal subject marker, -*nharr*

The suffix -*nharr* 'RECiPROCANTs' optionally attaches to both emphatic pronouns (65) and noun-headed noun phrases (66) to mark them as the subject of a reciprocal clause.

(65) *pelpelr-nharr   rangkangk-rr-nam   pam   ith*
3plEMPH-RCPCANT question:RDP-RCP-P.IPFV men(NOM) dem:dist
'those men were questioning each other'
[Hall 1972: 107]

(66) *wakrr   parr_r ngathn-nharr*
fight:RCP kid   1sgGEN(NOM)-RCPCANT
'all my kids are fighting'
[Hall 1972: 107]

It should be noted that this form is quite rare in my corpus, so its characterization here is tentative at best. From the examples to hand, however, -*nharr* seems semantically limited to core reciprocal events, and not collective (67) or distributive events.

(67) *parr_r ngathn-mun/*-nharr   ngat   mungk-m*
kid   1sgGEN-ERG/*- RCPCANT fish(ACC) eat-P.IPFV
'my children were eating fish [together]'
[KTh_MF20Aug2002 Elicitation]

Though -*nharr* is a suffix rather than a reciprocal pronoun, it is included for discussion in this word classes chapter owing to its functional similarity to the reflexive pronouns (§3.1.2.3).

Finally, it is worth noting that the same suffix form is employed as a marker of loan numerals (§4.4.2). It is unclear at this stage whether or how these two functions are related.

3.1.2.5 Emphatic pronouns

The set of emphatic pronouns, discussed in §5.1.3, is used to focus attention on the participant(s) encoded as subject, in contrast with other potential actors. Thus in (68) the emphatic pronoun *nhulnhulr* makes clear that the stick breaks spontaneously (or from its own internal propulsion), rather than due to any external force applied by an alternative actor.

(68) yuk   thongkn   nhulnhulr rumparr-r
      THING   stick(NOM)   3sgEMPH   break$_{ITR}$-P.PFV
      'the stick broke by itself'
      [KTh_EN15Dec2002 CutBreak16]

The strong formal resemblance between the emphatic pronouns and the nominative forms of the corresponding personal pronouns suggests that the former were originally formed through reduplication of the personal pronouns, followed by the suffixation of *-r* (cf. §5.1.3). Hence *nhul(nh)ulr* 'itself' in (68) is formally related to the third person singular nominative pronoun *nhul*.

3.1.2.6 Inclusory pronouns

Inclusory pronouns refer to a nonsingular participant group, simultaneously encoding the group as a whole and picking out one or more of its members (always either speaker or addressee[s]) for individual reference. This is evident in (69), in which the inclusory pronoun *ngalngun* 'you and I [lit. you and I with you]' makes the addressee particularly prominent among the plural participant group.

(69) nhunt   ngalngun   pam.thaaw
      2sg(NOM)   1du:incl|2sgINCL   friend
      'you and I are good friends together'
      [Hall 1972: 380]

The set of inclusory pronouns (presented in Table 13) seems likely to have been formed through the encliticization of dative personal pronouns (representing the individual) to nominative personal pronouns (representing the group). Further examples and discussion of inclusory pronouns and their functions are provided in §5.1.4 and §6.8.5.

Table 13. Comparison of inclusory, nominative and dative pronouns.

Inclusory pronoun	Nominative pronoun	Dative pronoun
ngalathun 'we two including **me**'	*ngal* '1du:incl'	*ngathun* '1sg'
ngalngun 'we two including **you**'	*ngal* '1du:incl'	*nhangkun* '2sg'
ngalingathun 'we two including **me**'	*ngali* '1du:excl'	*ngathun* '1sg'
ngampathun 'we all including **me**'	*ngamp* '1pl:incl'	*ngathun* '1sg'
pelnathun 'them including **me**'	*peln* '3pl'	*ngathun* '1sg'
nhunturra 'each one of **you** all'	*nhunt* '2sg'	*nhurrnhungun* '2pl'
nhipurra 'the two of **you** all'	*nhip* '2du'	*nhurrnhungun* '2pl'

3.1.2.7 Ignorative pronouns

Ignoratives (Wierzbicka 1977, 1980) express a lack of knowledge on the part of the speaker. This may be done in order to mark a referent as indefinite (e.g. *he has something in his pocket*), or to request information from the hearer (the 'interrogative' use; e.g. *what does he have in his pocket?*). The nine Kuuk Thaayorre ignoratives form a class defined by shared semantic, distributional and functional properties. They contrast in the particular categories of knowledge they mark as lacking. Hence *ngan* 'what' corresponds to a lack of knowledge in the category THING, *wanh* 'who' to the category PERSON, and *ngene* 'why' to REASON. The more precise delineation of these semantic categories is explored in §5.2.

In addition to their core indefinite and interrogative functions, the Kuuk Thaayorre ignoratives perform the following range of functions:

a. interrogative pronoun
b. indefinite pronoun
c. relative pronoun
d. free choice pronoun
e. rhetorical particle
f. imprecision pronoun
g. apprehensive counterfactual

Ngan 'what' might therefore be alternatively be translated as 'something', 'anything', 'that', 'which', 'lest' or 'whatever'. Throughout this grammar, ignoratives are always glossed with the corresponding English interrogative term, but translated according to their specific function in the clause.

The inclusion of ignoratives within the macro-class of nominals, and more specifically pronouns, is justified functionally by the fact that they are often referring expressions (e.g. *wanh* 'somebody' in (70)), morphologically by the fact that they may inflect for case (e.g. *ngenem* 'from what cause' in (71)), and syntactically by the fact that they may fill an argument slot subcategorized for by the verb (e.g. the agent-subject *wanhul* 'who' in (72)).

(70) ulp   wanh=okun   thongko-rr
     dem:ad.prx who=DUB   arrive-P.PFV
     'somebody has arrived'
     [KTh_GJ10Jan2004 Elicitation]

(71) kiin   ulp   ngene-m?
     tooth(NOM) dem:ad.prx why-ABL
     'what happened to [your broken] tooth?'
     [KTh_EF14Dec2002 DemonstrativeScene2]

(72) paath thomp   ith   wanhul   rinti-rr
     fire   smoke(ACC) dem:dist who:ERG   burn-P.IPFV
     "who make that firesmoke?"
     [KTh_BH14Jan2004 Conversation]

The ignorative word class is syntactically heterogeneous, spanning a wider range of clausal functions and combinatorial possibilities (both morphological and syntactic) than the members of most other word classes. In some contexts, certain ignoratives (e.g. *ngan* 'what', *wanh* 'who', *ngannganr* 'how much', *wanhwanhrr* 'how many' and *wanthan* 'where') function as nominal modifiers. *Ngannganr* 'how much' thus quantifies *raak rirkr* 'money' in (73).

(73) nhunt   raak   rirkr   ngannganr pit-r
     2sg(ERG) OBJECT money(ACC)   how.much   hold-NPST
     'how much money do you have?'
     [KTh_EN15Dec2002 Elicitation]

However other ignoratives (e.g. *wanthantharr* 'how', *ngene* 'why' (74)) are more adverbial in function:

(74) nhunt   ngene yan   ii-rr-kop   Cairns-na?
     2sg(NOM) why   go:NPST there-towards-below   Cairns-DAT
     'why are you going to Cairns?'
     [KTh_EN04Aug2002 Elicitation]

As Evans (2000: 719–720), Dixon (1972: 49–58) and others have pointed out, it is cross-linguistically common for ignoratives to cross-cut other word classes (notably pronouns) established on the more conventional grounds of shared morphology and syntactic environments. The ignorative word class is nevertheless identifiable on functional and semantic grounds as a set of forms expressing lack of knowledge in a particular epistemic domain (Evans 2000: 719).

3.1.3 Demonstratives

The class of demonstratives is defined on functional grounds as the set of deictic elements that refer or restrict reference to entities in the discursive, attentional or physical environment. They may be used endophorically, exophorically and 'recognitionally' (Enfield 2003b, cf. §5.3.3). There are no common morphosyntactic criteria (beyond some formal resemblances suggesting a common etymology) that unify pronominal and adnominal demonstratives. Further, this word class is bisected by the class of pronouns under which pronominal demonstratives can be alternatively classified.

3.1.3.1 Demonstrative pronouns

Kuuk Thaayorre demonstrative pronouns function both independently as pro-nominal forms (as in 75) and as modifiers within the noun phrase (76).

(75) *inhul palkoorr inh, thamr+ratr*
this.one just.behind dem:sp.prx foot+ankle
'this one, behind here, is the ankle'
[KTh_ME02Oct2002 Elicitation]

(76) *ngat inhul ngat thermp*
fish(NOM) this.one FISH salmon
'that fish is a salmon'
[KTh_GJ28Oct2002 Elicitation]

The paradigm of demonstrative pronouns is structured around a two-way distance distinction (e.g. the proximal *inhul* 'this one' contrasts with distal *yuunhul* 'that one') and somewhat irregular inflection for case; some forms bear case through stem mutation, while others take the external case suffixes available to nomina and some other nominals. The structure of the demonstrative pronominal word is discussed in §5.3.1.1. The use of demonstrative pronouns in discourse is discussed in §5.3.3. The role of demonstrative pronouns within the noun phrase is discussed in §6.5.3.

3.1.3.2 Adnominal demonstratives

The three adnominal demonstratives – *inh ~ inh'nh* 'speaker proximate', *ulp* 'addressee proximate' and *ith* 'distal' – defy either purely spatial or purely interactional analysis. In §5.3.2.1 we will see that speakers draw on a range of spatial, interactional, cognitive ('attentional') and discourse pragmatic factors that converge upon the referent being 'proximal' to either speaker or addressee, or 'distal' to both.

Adnominal demonstratives occupy the final slot in the noun phrase (arguably as 'specifier' – see §6.6) serving to restrict the reference of the head noun (whether overt or elided). They are distinguished from other nominal modifiers (which also restrict reference) by their general insensitivity to case.

Almost all adnominal demonstratives are morphologically simplex. They may, however, combine with an optional 'attentional' prefix, *aw-* (77)–(78), and the addressee-proximate demonstrative *ulp* very occasionally bears an ergative case suffix (79), as summarized in Table 14, cf. §5.3.2.2.

(77) *paanth   aw-inh'nh   paath okon*
     woman(NOM) attn-dem:sp.prx fire   beside
     'the woman's next to the fire'
     [KTh_EC2Oct2002 Elicitation]

(78) *yal-am   kal-r   ngat   aw-ith?*
     creek-ABL carry-NPST fish(ACC) attn-dem:dist
     'are you bringing the fish from the creek?'
     [Foote and Hall: Reader 10, dialogue 1]

(79) *minh   ulp-thn   paatha-rr   nganh*
     MEAT dem:ad.prx-ERG bite-P.PFV 1sgACC
     'that dog bit me'
     [Hall 1972: 388]

Table 14. Morphological structure of adnominal demonstratives.

attentional prefix	root		ergative suffix
(aw-)	inh('nh)	'dem:sp.prx'	
	ith	'dem:dist'	
	ulp	'dem:adr.prx'	(-thn, -nthurr)

3.1.4 Predicate adjectives

Predicate adjectives are peripheral members of the nominal class. They are unlike other nominals in that they do not inflect for case. They also resemble verbs functionally, in that they predicate rather than refer and subcategorize for one or two arguments. *Pamngongkom* 'ignorant of', for example, subcategorizes for both a nominative-case subject and an accusative-case direct object, as seen in (80):

(80) *peln   nhunh   pamngongkom*
     3pl(NOM) 3sgACC ignorant.of
     'they didn't know about him [that he had arrived]'
     [KTh_GJ18Jan2004 Narrative Christmas]

Unlike verbs, though, they do not inflect for any TAM categories or undergo any of the derivational processes available to verbs. Further confirming their nominal status, predicate adjectives can function as complements in copula constructions (such as (81), headed by the copula postural verb *nhiin* 'sit').

(81) *ngay*   *walmeerem*   *angarr*   *nhiin*
      1sg(NOM)   knowledgeable.of   ANGARR   sit:NPST
      'I want to know'
      [Anon.]

The two most common predicate adjectives are nominal compounds. *Walmeerem* 'knowledgeable of' is composed of the body part terms *wal* 'brow' and *meer* 'eye', with the verbalizing/nominalizing suffix *-m* (§8.1.6). *Pamngongkom* 'ignorant of' is composed of the noun *pam* 'man (or person)' and the adjective *ngoongkom* 'ignorant'.

The syntax of predicate adjectives is discussed in §10.1.4.

3.2 Verbs

Verbs are easily identified by their distinctive morphology. All verbs inflect for at least a subset of TAM categories and a subset of derivational suffixes such as the valence increasing *-(nh)an(i)*, reciprocal *-rr* and reflexive *-e*. The morphological template for the verbal word (including enclitics in italics) is presented in Table 15, with each of the categories presented therein discussed in chapters 6 and 7. Only the root and inflectional positions (bold face in Table 15) must be filled; all other morphemes are optional.

Table 15. Morphological template of the Kuuk Thaayorre verbal word.

DERIV	**ROOT**	DERIV	DERIV	DERIV	DERIV	**INFL**	ARG	ARG	PRAG
body+	ROOT-:RDP	-VBLZ	-V^	-RFL -RCP	-GO& -RUN&	-TAM	=PRO	=PRO	=le =th =p(a) =thurr
verb roots may be compounded with a body part nominal	the bound verb root is optionally reduplicated	derives a verb from nouns, etc.	increases valency by one argument	produce a reflexive or reciprocal stem with reduced valency	one of two associated motion suffixes	either a tense / aspect or mood suffix	*first enclitic pronoun*	*second enclitic pronoun*	*discourse pragmatic markers*

Aside from body part nominals (with which verb roots may be compounded) and infixal reduplication, Kuuk Thaayorre verbal morphology is entirely suffixal. In this representation, morphemes are categorized into distinct positions, from each of which only one morpheme may appear in any single word. The relative order of the valence increaser and the reflexive/reciprocal suffixes is variable, as indicated by the diagonal line between these two derivational positions. (See §8.1.1 for a discussion of the iconic correlation between their linear order and the semantic order of application.) Finally, the enclitic pronouns and pragmatic clitics are represented in italics since these are not considered internal to the verb proper, despite forming part of the phonological verbal word.

The verb is the head of the clause, determining the tense, transitivity, mood, etc. of the clause as a whole. The verb also dictates argument structure, including the case of the arguments it subcategorizes for. Regardless of its linear position within the clause, the verb tends to attract any pronominal enclitics.[70]

The macroclass of verbs can be alternatively subcategorized according to either morphology or syntax. Morphologically, verbs fall into three conjugations. The first of these (composed mostly of transitive verbs) is by far the largest. For first conjugation verbs, the suffix *-r* signals nonpast tense. For second conjugation verbs (the majority of which are intransitive), the suffix *-r* encodes the past perfective. In addition to these two conjugations are a set of irregular verbs, for which no common inflectional pattern can be identified. The morphological distinction between verbs of the conjugations is illustrated in Table 16, and discussed in more detail in §7.1.2.

Table 16. Key differences between the three conjugations.

	1st Conjugation *mungk* 'eat'	2nd Conjugation *thongk* 'arrive'	Irregular *ya-* 'go'
Imperative	mungk	thongk	yarr
Nonpast	mungkr	thongk	yan
Past perfective	mungkarr	thongkr	yat

Syntactically, verbs may be subcategorized according to the number and type of arguments they subcategorize for, as shown in Table 17 below. Hence the intransitive verbs which take a single (nominative) subject argument are distinguished from the semi-transitive verbs which subcategorize for both a nominative subject and dative object, and both of these subcategories are distinguished from 'quasitransitive' verbs, which subcategorize for a nominative subject and accusative object. A number of additional subclasses are discussed in §10.1. The set of postural verbs may either function as

---

[70] The verb is not the only potential locus for these clitics, however, as they may be encliticized to other word classes (demonstratives, pronouns and connective *ngul*), cf. §5.1.1.3.

intransitive predicates (their diachronically prior function), predicating a particular posture of their subject argument (82), or as copula verbs, subcategorizing for a complement NP that is predicated of the subject (83).

(82) pam-al ith kuta thanpa-rr ngul kuta nhiin-r
 man-ERG dem:dist dog(ACC) kick-P.PFV then dog(NOM) sit-P.PFV
 'the man kicked the dog and the dog sat down'
 [KTh_GJ18Jan2004 Elicitation]

(83) punguk ngay mincwanc=aak nhiin-m
 last.time 1sg(NOM) sickness=ADN.PROP sit-P.IPFV
 'I was sick last week'
 [Anon.]

Table 17. Verbal subclasses by argument structure.

Valence	Verbal subclass and sub-categorization frame	Sample verbs {with sample objects}
Monovalent	Intransitive <Sbj$_{NOM}$>	riic 'run' rip 'enter' thangkar 'laugh'
Bivalent	Intransitive copula <Sbj$_{NOM}$, Subj-COMP$_{NOM}$>	nhiin 'be (< sit)' than 'be (< stand)' yomparr 'transform'
	Semitransitive <Sbj$_{NOM}$, I.Obj$_{DAT}$>	koope {wanhngun} 'wait {for someone}' ngee {wanhngun} 'listen {to someone}' nhaa {wanhngun} 'look {at someone}'
	Quasitransitive[71] <Sbj$_{NOM}$, Obj$_{ACC}$>	paarr {meerngok} 'cry {tears}' rok {mimp} 'put on {clothes}' thaangk {minh} 'ride {an animal}'
	Transitive <Sbj$_{ERG}$, Obj$_{ACC}$>	kal {yuk} 'carry {something}' matp {yuk} 'smash {something}' mungk {may} 'eat {food}'
Trivalent	Transitive copula <Sbj$_{ERG}$, Obj$_{ACC}$, Obj-COMP$_{NOM}$>	wan {yuk, ngan} 'name {something, something}'
	Semiditransitive <Sbj$_{NOM}$, Obj$_{ACC}$, I.Obj$_{DAT}$>	yik {kuuk, wanhngun} 　'say {words, to somebody}' waantharr {kuuk, wanhngun} 　'call out {words, to somebody}' wan {yuk, wanhngun} 　'give {something, to somebody}'
	Ditransitive <Sbj$_{ERG}$, Obj$_{ACC}$, Obj$_{ACC}$>	reek {wanh, yuk} 'give {somebody, something}' wan {wanh, wanh} 'tell {somebody, on somebody}'

The cline of verbal subclasses, arranged from lowest to highest valency, is presented in Table 17. Each subclass is listed with its subcategorization frame and a set of exemplar verbs.

In addition to the verbal subclasses presented here, there is the problematic case of some intransitive verbs (e.g. *patp* 'camp', seen in (84)) which optionally co-occur with seeming cognate objects (e.g. *wuuc patp* [lit. 'ceremony camp'] 'take part in a ceremonial retreat, with associated singing and dancing', seen in (85)). These would appear to pattern with the (quasitransitive) cognate object verbs were it not for the fact that the subject of, e.g., *wuuc patp* 'take part in ceremonial retreat' receives ergative case marking.

(84) *pam   ith=ul   yarra yan   patp-nhan=okun=ul*
man(NOM) dem:dist=3sg(NOM) away go:NPST camp-GO&:NPST=DUB=3sg(NOM)
"maybe that chap will hive off and pitch camp"
[Hall 1972: 85]

(85) *ngancn   wuuc   patp-m,   Conrad-n   pul,   ulp*
1pl:excl(ERG) ceremony(ACC) camp-P.IPFV Conrad-ERG 3du(ERG) dem:ad.prx
'we used to camp for the ceremony, (with) Conrad and him'
[KTh_GJ18Jan2004 Narrative Christmas]

Thus in terms of its array of arguments (and case-marking thereof), *patp* functions as either a straightforwardly intransitive verb (84) or a straightforwardly transitive verb (85). It is, therefore, best to view this as a case of verbal heterosemy despite the semantic linkage between these two uses. There are examples of verb forms that straddle other categories too. *Thaangk*, for example, may function as a semitransitive verb meaning 'climb' (subcategorizing for a nominative-case climber and a dative-case ground object or locus of climbing (86)), but also an intransitive cognate-object verb meaning 'ride' (subcategorizing for a nominative-case rider and an accusative-case vehicle (87)).

(86) *ball   ii   otonyciy-ak thaangk-ica-rr*
ball(NOM) there hill-DAT   climb-RUN&-P.PFV
'the ball went and climbed up the hill'
[KTh_GJ20Nov2002 Elicitation MoverbTriads4]

---

71 The quasitransitive class includes forms traditionally analyzed as intransitive verbs taking cognate objects (e.g. paarr {meerngok} 'cry {tears}', cf. Austin 1982) as well as clearly bivalent verbs that subcategorize for both a nominative-case subject and accusative-case (non-cognate) object, see §10.1.4 for further discussion.

(87)　*yarrman*　　*thaangk-m*　*peln*
　　　 horse(ACC)　ride-P.IPFV　3pl(NOM)
　　　 'they were riding horses'
　　　 [KTh_AJ27Jan2004 Conversation]

Although large, there is no firm evidence that the class of inflecting verbs is open. I have not recorded any neologisms formed from Kuuk Thaayorre morphemes, which is particularly significant given the wealth of nominal neologisms created during the process of bible translation in the sixties and seventies. The expression of new verbal concepts is instead achieved via the coining of complex verbs, in which an English verb or native lexeme from another word class is paired with the inflecting verb *rirk* (originally meaning 'rise', but glossed as 'DO' in this function). Many of the loan verbs take the transitive suffix *-m*. This process appears to be creating a new (open) class of coverbs, defined by their lack of inflection and co-occurrence with the 'light' verb *rirk* 'DO'.[72] (88) exemplifies a complex predicate involving a loan verb, while (89) places a Kuuk Thaayorre noun *mit* 'work' in the coverb slot:

(88)　*ngay*　　*ulp*　　　　　*net*　　　*kaar drag-m rirk*
　　　 1sg(ERG)　dem:ad.prx　net(ACC)　NEG　drag-TR　DO:NPST
　　　 'I don't drag those [fish] nets'
　　　 [KTh_AJ-**GJ**03Feb2004 Conversation]

(89)　*ngay*　　　*mit*　*rirk-m,*　　*rubbish-ak*　*ngan*
　　　 1sg(NOM)　work　DO-P.IPFV　rubbish-DAT　what
　　　 'I was working, at rubbish [collection] and stuff'
　　　 [KTh_**AJ**-GJ27Jan2004 Conversation]

Both transitive (88) and intransitive (89) complex predicates are attested, and the coverb determines argument structure. The intransitive status of *mit.rirk* 'work' is supported by the dative case-marking of the prosodically separated peripheral phrase, *rubbishak ngan* 'at rubbish [collection] and stuff' (which might otherwise be construed as a direct object). Other than the transitive suffix, the coverbs remain morphologically simplex. All TAM categories and valence-changing morphology are affixed to the light verb.

---

[72] There is a wealth of literature on coverb–light verb pairings and analogous complex predicates both cross-linguistically (e.g. Butt 1995, Alsina et al. 1996, Amberber et al. 2007) and in Australian languages in particular (e.g. Nash 1982, Wilson 1999, Schultze-Berndt 2000, McGregor 2002, Bowern 2004, 2012). Coverbs generally contribute lexical information about the event described (e.g. its manner, as seen in 87) while grammatical information (such as tense, aspect, mood and/or agreement) is realized in the inflection of the light verb (so-called because it is relatively 'light' in semantic content). These two word forms – drawn from distinct word classes – jointly predicate within a single clause (cf. Amberber et al. 2007).

The morphosyntactic subclasses of verb, including the coverbs and light verb, can be represented as in Figure 9, leaving aside the differences in argument structure (which cross cut each of these verb classes).

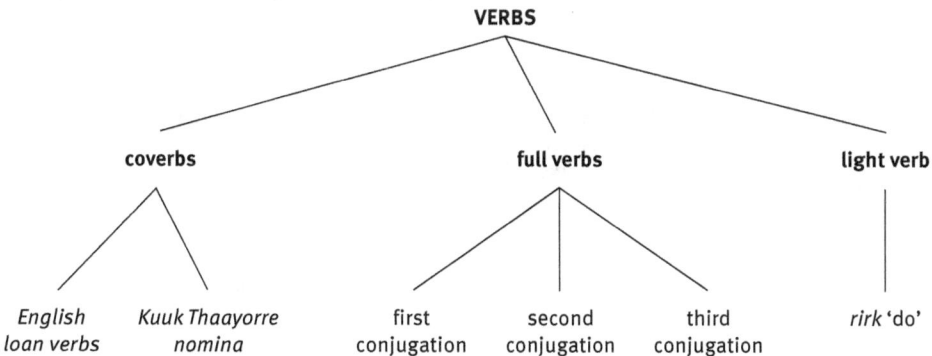

Figure 9. Morphosyntactic verbal subclasses.

3.3 Adverbs

Kuuk Thaayorre adverbs are identified primarily by their function of modifying predicates. Syntactically, adverbs tend to precede the predicate where there is one (90). Adverbs commonly appear in verbless clauses (91).

(90) nhul   maalmal yump-m   pormpr
     3sg(ERG) slowly   make-P.IPFV   house(ACC)
     'he built the house slowly [over a long period of time]'
     [KTh_GJ31Jan2004 Elicitation]

(91) yuur wacirr!
     hand correctly
     'be careful of your hands [or they might get cut on that barramundi fin]'
     [KTh_EF15Dec2002 Conversation]

While individual subclasses of adverb may display morphological uniformity, the broader adverbial class is formally, functionally and semantically heterogeneous, making impossible any general discussion of, e.g., the structure of the adverbial word. In a number of cases (e.g. deictic *pal* 'towards') the boundary between adverb and particle is fuzzy. This issue is revisited in Chapter 11; the remainder of this section will be concerned with the identification and characterization of adverbial subclasses rather than of adverbs overall. These subclasses – and the semantic relationships between them – are presented in Figure 10.

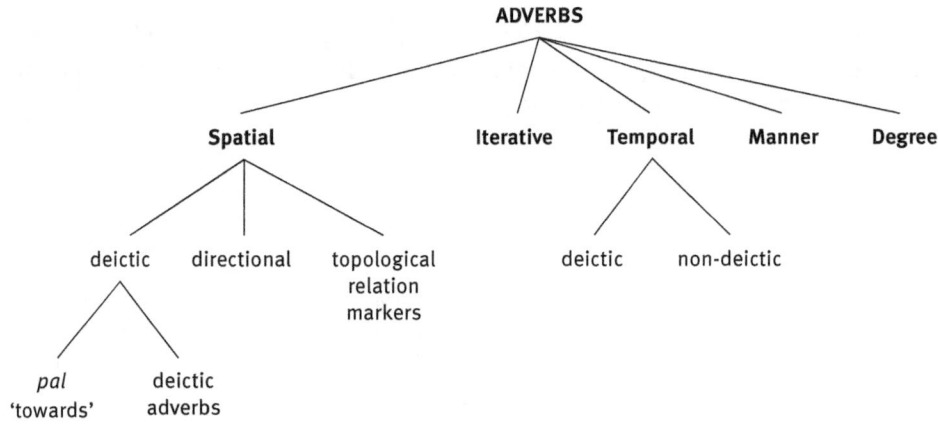

Figure 10. Adverbial subclasses.

As is evident from Figure 10, the spatial adverbial subclass is by far the most elaborated, especially given the morphological and semantic complexity of the directional paradigm it includes. There is considerable polysemy among adverbs so, for example, one sense of *kanpa* 'in front', 'before' is a topological relation marker, while a second sense belongs with the deictic temporal adverbs.

3.3.1 Spatial Adverbs

There is both formal and semantic overlap between the various subclasses of spatial adverb, and between these subclasses and the class of demonstrative pronouns (§3.1.3.1, §5.3.1). Thus the free deictic adverb *pal* 'towards' is clearly linked to the bound morpheme *-pal-*, found in: the deictic adverb *yuupal* '(coming) from far away'; the directional *palipan* 'nearby on the south bank'; and the topological relation markers *palpal* 'nearby' and *palkoorr* 'just behind'. These linkages between subclasses bespeak a long history of multidirectional grammaticalization. Nevertheless, I believe the classification presented here most accurately reflects the synchronic subdivision of spatial adverbs.

3.3.1.1 Deictic adverbs
The class of deictic adverbs is defined semantically as the set of forms that are optionally employed to locate an event with respect to the deictic centre. Though semantically and (for the most part) functionally coherent, this word class is internally heterogeneous in terms of morphological structure and relationships with other word classes. The central members of the set of deicitic adverbs (other than *pal* 'towards') can be arranged as a paradigm, as seen in Table 18:

Table 18. Paradigm of deictic adverbs.

	i'i 'here'	*ii* 'there'	*yuuw* 'far'
attentional prefix *aw-*	*aw-i'i* 'right here'	*aw-ii* 'right there'	—
with 'allative' *-rra*	*i'irra* 'to here'	*iirra* 'to there'	*yuurra* 'to far away'
compounded with *+pal* 'towards'	*i'ipal* 'from here'	*iipal* 'from there'	*yuupal* 'from far away'

Note that the attentional prefix *aw-* is shared with both the adnominal and pronominal demonstratives, while the form *pal* 'towards' (seen in the bottom row compounds) is both a free deictic adverb and a prefix in the paradigm of directional adverbs. Moreover, a ninth adverb, *yarra* 'to away', might be added to the right of Table 18's middle row. This form is likely derived from the verb root *ya-* 'go', though no equivalent forms with *aw-* or *+pal* are attested to complete the paradigm.[73] A list of further deictic spatial adverbs is given in (92), followed by some examples illustrating their use.

(92) *i'i* 'here'
i'irra 'to here'
ii 'there'
iirra 'to there'
yuuw 'far away'
yuurra 'to far away'
yarra 'away'
pal 'towards'
(i)nhaka 'here, in this place'
angunp 'there, at that place'
nheman 'from that place'

(93) ngumpurr wang ii thongk-nhat
old.lady whitefella(NOM) there arrive-GO&:P.PFV
'the white lady turned up over there'
[KTh_AC14Nov2002 Narrative LosingIrma]

---

[73] Though somewhat aberrant paradigmatically, the Thaayorre form *yarra* 'away' is reconstructable to proto-Paman **yarra* 'away' Alpher (personal communication).

(94) *paath   pal   minharr*
firewood(ACC) towards   pick.up:GO&:IMP
'bring some firewood (towards) here'
[KTh_AJ27Jan2004 Conversation / Elicitation]

(95) *ngancn   may   dinner   nhaka   mungk-r*
1pl:excl(ERG) VEG   dinner(ACC)   in.this.place eat-NPST
'(sometimes) we eat dinner here'
[KTh_AC10Aug2002 Conversation]

The semantics and functions of *pal* 'towards' are elaborated upon in §9.2.1.1, while those of the other deictic adverbs are discussed in §9.2.1.2.

3.3.1.2 Directional adverbs

In natural conversation and narrative, speakers regularly anchor the events they describe with respect to the direction along which a motion took place. The first morphological position in the directional word is obligatorily filled by one of three prefixes marking direction, the second position by one of five prefixes marking motion and/or orientation. The third position is obligatorily filled by one of eleven root morphemes. The root is followed by two optional suffix positions. The first of these further specifies the direction, for example by adding the suffix *-uw* to the stem *iiparr* 'in the south' to create *iiparruw* 'in the south-west'. The second suffix position optionally marks the river as a relevant reference point, usually the start- or endpoint of motion. Indeed, the Chapman River is itself conventionally referred to by the directional term *iiparrop*, segmented and glossed in (96).

(96) *ii-parr-op*
there-at:south-river
'the Chapman River'
[KTh_EN28Oct2002 Elicitation]

The first morpheme, *ii-*, indicates that the location is neutral with respect to distance from the deictic centre. The absence of any second-position prefix indicates a static or stable locative relationship (as opposed to movement to, towards or away from the direction in question). The bound root form *-parr* refers to the compass direction 'south', while the final suffix *-op* specifies that the location is determined with respect to the river.[74] The structure of the Kuuk Thaayorre directional word is analyzed in detail by Foote and Hall (1992: 227), and in §9.2.1.3 of this grammar.

---

[74] Thus the Chapman River is named in (95) by a directional term that would otherwise be used to locate a figure with respect to the river itself.

3.3.1.3 Topological relation markers (TRMs)

The intentionally vague label 'topological relation marker' – borrowed from Levinson and Meira (2003) – is applied to a semantically and functionally united set of Kuuk Thaayorre lexemes (97) that range from the more adverbial to the more postpositional (cf. §9.2.1.4). In the absence of firm evidence to the contrary, I tentatively categorise these lexemes as an adverbial subclass.

(97)   *koorr*   'behind, outside'
        kanpa   'in front'
        thorkorr   'far away'
        thaapirri   'nearby'
        palpal   'close'
        (put)pil   'beside'
        kop   'below'
        putpun   'on top'
        mangka   'low down by'
        wernka   'in the middle of, between'
        okon   'adjacent to'

Though the set of TRMs listed in (97) contains some pairs of antonyms (e.g. *koorr* 'behind' vs. *kanpa* 'in front'), the semantic relationships between most of the TRMs are more loose. Nevertheless, all are used in order to locate a figure with respect to a ground object. Like other adverbs, all of the TRMs may appear as the sole exponent of a location in the absence of any noun phrase referring to a ground object. Where the TRM combines with an overt NP referring to the ground object, there is significant variance in the syntactic relationships that hold between the two. In some cases (in which the TRM appears to function more like a postposition) the TRM immediately follows the ground NP. In other cases the two are free with respect to their respective positions in the clause. There is likewise significant variation – both between TRMs and between different tokens of a single TRM – as to the case-marking of the ground NP. Finally, the TRMs *kop* 'below', *mangka* 'low down by' and *(put)pil* 'beside' may optionally bear dative marking themselves, betraying their nominal origin. These three key parameters of variation (strength of syntactic bond with ground NP, case-marking of ground NP and case-marking of TRM) are explored in more detail in §9.2.1.4.

Aside from the optional case-marking of *kop* 'below', *mangka* 'low down by' and *(put)pil* 'beside', TRMs are non-inflecting forms. The body part prefix *koo-* 'nose' is optionally prefixed to TRMs in order to emphasize the directedness (i.e. frontwise orientation) of the topological relationship (see §9.2.6). In all other respects, however, TRMs are morphologically simplex forms.

Finally, it is worth noting that there is some formal and functional overlap between the TRMs and the paradigm of directional adverbs (§9.2.1.3). Indeed, the TRM *koorr* 'behind, outside' is differentiated from the bound directional root *-korr* 'behind, outside' only by the length of the vowel.

3.3.2 Temporal Adverbs

Temporal adverbs can be subdivided into:

1. deictic temporal adverbs (which locate the event with respect to the moment of speech, or an alternative deictic centre); and
2. non-deictic temporal adverbs (which locate the event with respect to the periodic cycles of days and seasons).

Each of these subclasses is considered in more depth in §9.2.2.

3.3.3 Iterative adverbs

The subclass of iterative adverbs are concerned with where the event described falls within a series of (potential) repetitions of that event. None of the iterative adverbs permit inflection, with the exception of *thil* 'again' which may be reduplicated to indicate extended iteration (i.e. *thilil* 'yet again' or 'again and again'). See §9.2.3 for further discussion.

3.3.4 Manner adverbs

Manner adverbs add information about the way in which an action was performed, often carrying implicatures as to its outcome (e.g. *waat* 'wrongly, => unsuccessfully'). Several manner adverbs are homophonous with forms in other classes. For instance *waarr* 'badly' and *min* 'well' are homophonous with the adjectives *waarr* 'bad' and *min* 'good' respectively. It is possible for some manner adverbs to reduplicate for intensification (cf. §2.6.4); no other inflection or derivation of manner adverbs is possible. The syntax and semantics of manner adverbs are considered further in §9.2.4.

3.3.5 Degree adverb

Kuuk Thaayorre possesses three degree adverbs (*minc* 'really', *mangr* 'quite, rather'[75] and *waarr* 'very'). Each of the three may be used to modify adjectives, but only *minc* may modify other adverbs. Though they are virtually synonymous, *waarr* 'very' precedes and *minc* 'really' follows the adjective they modify:

---

[75] The polysemous English adverb *quite* used to gloss *mangr* should be understood in its sense(s) 'slightly, a bit, a small amount' rather than in its intensifying sense.

(98) *inhul   ngamal minc, meer+pungk   paant   waarr ngamal!*
this.one(NOM) large   really eye+knee(NOM) head(NOM) very large
'this one [crocodile] was really big, the eyebrows on its head were really big!'
[KTh_AJ3Feb2004 Conversation]

Mangr may only combine with a restricted number of adjectives in quite constrained pragmatic contexts. In general, it must be used as a modification of a preceding statement:

(99) *ngul ulp   kunk   than-r,   mangr min   yancm ii-rr-kuw*
then dem:ad.prx alive stand-P.PFV quite good go:P.IPFV there-towards-west
'then he was alive, he was quite well when he went westward'
[KTh_**DW**-CW09Dec2002 Narrative 2Crocs]

For further discussion of degree adverbs, see §6.4 and §9.2.5.

3.4 Ideophones

Many words within the sound symbolic class of ideophones display some onomatopoeic resemblance of the event or entity they describe (e.g. *purt* 'fart') and are set apart from the intonational contour of the clause (cf. §9.3 for discussion of the prosodic and other characteristics of ideophones). Many interjections violate the phonotactic rules that apply to the rest of the lexicon (e.g. word-initial /l/ in *liiy* 'beam of light') or contain non-phonemic segments[76] (e.g. the initial segment [tʃ] in *churr* 'spear flying through air'). Ideophones also frequently draw attention to inaudible but expressive components of an event (as with *liiy* 'beam of light' above).

Ideophones do not enter into any syntactic relationship with other elements in the formation of larger phrases, but rather independently contribute information about (the sound or other evocative characteristic of) the event. Aside from reduplication (e.g. in *we'we'we'* 'bird call' Foote and Hall 1992: 235), ideophones do not participate in any morphological processes, inflectional or derivational.

At this stage it is unclear how much creative input speakers have into the form of the ideophones they use, and accordingly whether the class of ideophones is closed or open. The scarcity of ideophones in my data, particularly in comparison with the texts recorded by Foote and Hall (ms.), suggests that this class is presently in a state of decline.

---

[76] It is an interesting – and as yet unresolved – question whether a segment should be considered phonemic simply by virtue of its contrastive usage in an ideophone. Nevertheless, such segments should be considered only marginal members of the Kuuk Thaayorre phonemic inventory (i.e. members of a 'co-phonology', Inkelas 1998), given that their distribution is restricted to ideophones and interjections (cf. §3.5.1).

3.5 Particles

The remaining Kuuk Thaayorre word classes are closed, morphologically simplex (i.e. uninflecting and underived) and have fewer members than the 'major' word classes discussed above. They are for this reason collected under the heading 'particles', although this is not intended to represent a single unified word class.

3.5.1 Interjective particles

Interjections may be defined as forms belonging to no other word class that may be uttered in isolation as a complete, non-elliptical utterance. Such words may be used to greet, farewell, or attract the attention of an addressee (e.g. *wooy* 'hey! I'm over here!'); to express agreement or disagreement (e.g. *kece* 'that's wrong!'); or to express the speaker's attitude towards something in the discourse context, including the discourse itself (e.g. *ith'tharrko* 'wow!'). Like ideophones, interjections frequently contain segments found nowhere else in the Kuuk Thaayorre lexicon (e.g. the initial segment [tʃ] in *chaa* 'get away! (to dog)',[77] or the alveolar fricative /s/ in *psi'psi* 'apology before one's mother in law' (Foote and Hall 1992: 235)). Unlike ideophones, though, they do not tend to be embedded within a clause. Where interjections are uttered as part of a larger utterance, they tend to be separated from the following or preceding clause by a pause and an intonational break. This is true of both *ngeeca* and *koo* in (100).

(100) 1. *ngeeca! Win-m rirk-r!*
       hooray win-TR DO-P.PFV
       'hooray! We won [the football]!'
   2. *koo, ngamp melnkelnkarr ii-th-iparr therk*
       oh 1pl:incl(NOM) tomorrow there-to-south return:NPST
       'okay then, we'll return [to Pormpuraaw] tomorrow'
       [KTh_AC21Aug2002 Narrative WeipaFootball]

Note that the interjections *ngee* 'I see' and *koo* 'oh' – most frequently used by addressees as 'backchanneling' devices – may have etymological sources in the verb *ngeey-* 'hear' and the body part term *koow* 'nose' (which has many other grammaticalized functions, cf. Gaby 2006, §9.2.6).

The semantic classes of interjection are explored further in §9.4.

---

[77] The same interjective form (including the areally unusual segment [tʃ]) is found across Arnhem Land (Evans, personal communication).

3.5.2 Connective particles

The four Kuuk Thaayorre connectives *ngul* 'then, so, but', *ith* 'if', *akp* 'despite' and *kar* 'like' are invariant in form and have the common syntactic property of connecting clauses and/or phrases. These forms typically appear in between the two constituents they connect (101, 102, the relevant forms are highlighted in bold face).

(101) 1. *paanth   pitit-nh   wuump=ul=okun,*
         woman(ACC) keep:RDP-SBJV CDICT=3sg(ERG)=DUB
         'it would be one thing if he had a wife...'
    2. ***ngul** pul   wupan*
        but   3du(NOM) temporary
        'but they're just temporary'
        [KTh_ACh07Nov2002 Conversation]

(102) *quiet one **akp**,   ngay   kaar trust-m rirk*
      quiet one despite 1sg(ERG) NEG trust-TR DO:NPST
      'although [that crocodile] is quiet, I don't trust him'
      [KTh_GJ3Feb2004 Conversation]

Alternatively, though, the connective may appear immediately preceding the first of two or more connected clauses, cf. §12.2.1.2.

The four connectives have quite different functions in a range of complex clause types. The use of the concessive particle *akp* in concessive constructions is discussed in §12.2.3, the use of *kar* and *ith* in conditional constructions is discussed in §12.1.2.1, the role of *ith* in concessive conjunction is discussed in §12.2.3, while the use of *ngul* in simple conjunction is discussed in §12.2.1.2.

In addition to the four native Kuuk Thaayorre connectives, the English form *or* has been borrowed as a disjunctive particle (cf. §12.2.2). The Kuuk Thaayorre third person dual pronoun also appears to be developing a connective role (103), conjoining noun phrases that are functioning as a single argument (cf. §6.9.1 for discussion as to how this use of *pul* 'they two' differs from its use as a simple personal pronoun).

(103) *ngul Ebi-n   pul   Donald   pul   mi'im:rr*
       then Ivy-ERG 3du(ERG) Donald(^ERG) 3du(ERG) sing:P.PFV
       'then Ivy and Donald sang'

   Cyril   pul   mi'im-rr
   Cyril(^ERG) 3du(ERG) sing-P.PFV
   'then Ivy and Donald, the two of them sang... and Cyril sang'
   [KTh_AJ-IC-**GJ**26Nov2002 Narrative/Conversation]

3.5.3 Negative particles

Kuuk Thaayorre possesses four negative particles, grouped together here due to their shared function of negation, though they share few morphosyntactic features beyond being non-inflecting particles. The clausal negator *kaar* 'NEG' generally precedes the predicate, as does the prohibitive (negative imperative) particle *ongkorr*. The constituent negator *pokon* 'NO' is usually found immediately following the noun phrase it negates, while the contradictory interjection *kece* (~*kace*) always forms a syntactically complete clause by itself. Note that the contradictory particle is prosodically marked in receiving secondary stress.[78] *Pokon* 'NO' and *ongkorr* 'PROHIB' also double as interjections (meaning 'no/none/nothing' and 'don't!' respectively). The syntax and functions of each of these are discussed in further detail in §11.3.

3.5.4 Modal particles

While tense and aspect are encoded in verbal inflectional morphology, modal information is marked by a range of particles (as well as a couple of verbal suffixes). (104) lists the modal particles and enclitic along with their gloss and the section in which they are discussed.

(104)   kirri   'permissive'   (§11.2.1)
       wuump   'contrastive'   (§9.1.4)
       =okun   'dubitative'   (§9.1.5)
       angarr   'angarr'[79]   (§11.7.1.2)
       kar   'like'   (§9.1.3)
       ongkorr   'prohibitive'   (§11.3.4)
       minc   'against expectations (UNXP)'   (§9.1.6)

3.6 Other enclitics

Finally, there are a number of promiscuous morphemes which are relatively unrestricted with respect to the word classes to which they attach. This fact of their attaching to a wide range of words and phrases (including normally non-inflecting lexemes, such as adnominal demonstratives and particles) is taken as evidence that they are

---

[78] There is considerable inter-speaker variation in the pronunciation of this form, with *ke'ce*, *ka'ce*, and *'kace* all widespread.
[79] It is challenging to provide a succinct gloss for the particle *angarr*, but as detailed in §11.7.1.2 this form is used to express what the speaker believe would and should be the case 'in a correct world'.

enclitics rather than suffixes. All have scope over the word or phrase to which they attach, however.

3.6.1 =Nhurr 'only'

The enclitic =nhurr 'only' is used with the sense 'and nothing else', drawing attention to the limited number or scope of an entity or event. This can be seen in (105), where the speaker uses =nhurr to stress that her activities will be limited to the house.

(105) ngay   pormp-an=nhurr nhiinhin
       1sg(NOM) house-DAT-only   sit:RDP:NPST
       'I'm just going to stay at home'
       [KTh_EN06Sep2002 Conversation]

Likewise, in (106) =nhurr is used to stress that only the one man (to which the speaker turns attention in 106.2) had died.

(106) 1. ulp   three-nharr pelnan thaka-rr;   Conrad, William ngul Jack
         dem:ad.prx three-NUM   3plACC leave-P.PFV Conrad William then Jack
         'there were three of them left; Conrad, William and Jack'
      2. pam   ulp=nhurrp   James   wonp-r
         man(NOM) dem:ad.prx=only James(NOM) die-P.PFV
         'just the [one] man, James, died'
         [KTh_AJ-**IC**-GJ26Nov2002 Narrative/Conversation]

Finally, note that the adverb *yoorrnhurr* 'for the first time' is composed of the morpheme =*nhurr* 'only' suffixed to the temporal adverb *yoorr* 'now'.

3.6.2 Pragmatic/emphatic enclitics

Kuuk Thaayorre possesses seven further enclitics which may be attached to a word or phrase, primarily to accord it prominence. An initial account of these forms is presented in §6.11.2.2–§6.11.36.11.2.2. As further research is required in order to precisely delineate their respective functions, a single gloss ('PRAGmatic') is used for each of the morphemes pending a clear motivation for more specific glosses.

4 Morphology of nomina (nouns, adjectives and numerals)

Nomina comprise a nominal subclass spanning generic nouns, specific nouns, adjectives and numerals. The syntactic, functional and semantic criteria used to differentiate these nomen subclasses were discussed in §3.1.1 (see also §6.3) while their respective roles and positions in the noun phrase are outlined in 6. The present chapter is primarily concerned with the morphological structure of the nomen word, detailing the range of inflectional and derivational affixes with which nomina may combine.

The morphological structure of nomina can be summarized as in Table 19.

Table 19. Structure of the nomen word.

(deriv)*	stem	(-infl)
(nomen+)*	nomen(:RDP) verb-*m*	(-case)

The nomen word minimally consists of a root, which may optionally be reduplicated (§4.3.1). Derived nomen stems may be formed by suffixing the nominalizer -*m* to a verb stem (§8.1.6). Nomen stems can also be derived by the compounding of a nomen root and nomen stem, the latter of which may be deverbal (§4.3.2). A noun phrase-final nomen obligatorily inflects for case. The full case system is outlined in §4.1, with discussion of the various case forms and functions in §4.2. Derivational processes are outlined in §4.3, while §4.4 describes three morphemes which are neither clearly derivational nor clearly inflectional. Nomina may also host a wide range of enclitics. Pronominal enclitics are discussed in §5.1.1.3, while the various pragmatic enclitics are presented in §3.6.

4.1 Case

In Kuuk Thaayorre, case inflection is the repository of all information about grammatical relations. It also distinguishes various adjunct roles. Case therefore plays a prominent role in both morphosyntax and discourse pragmatics. Throughout this grammar, I analyze case as a property of the noun phrase, rather than just the lexeme that bears it. Accordingly, the following description of the case system should be understood to apply to all components of the noun phrase. Thus the accusative case is common to both nomina and pronominals, although formally it is unmarked for nomina (along with the nominative case) but marked for pronouns (as distinct from the nominative case, see Goddard 1982, and Blake 1994 for further justification of such an analysis).

The syncretism between nominative and accusative cases (for nomina), and nominative and ergative cases (for pronouns), is shown in Table 20's summary of Kuuk Thaayorre's tripartite core case system:

Table 20. Kuuk Thaayorre's tripartite core case system.

	Ergative	Nominative	Accusative
Nomina			
Pronouns			

In addition to the three core cases, Kuuk Thaayorre nomina inflect for the dative, genitive, ablative, comitative, proprietive and privative cases. The dative is on the boundary between core and peripheral cases, as it can be used to mark the (core) recipient argument of a ditransitive verb, as well as (peripheral) goals and other adjuncts. Table 21 presents the case-inflected forms of a representative sample of nomina, with the case-inflected forms of a personal pronoun (*nhul* 's/he') added for comparison.

Table 21. Case-inflected forms of a selection of nominals.

	paanth 'woman'	*pam* 'man'	*thok* 'cat'	*ngathn* 'my (1sggen)'	*nhul* 's/he (3sg)'
ERG	paanthu	pamal	thokn ~thokthn ~thokthurr ~thokthurr	ngathnthurr ~ngathnman ~ngathnantamn	nhul
NOM	paanth	pam	thok	ngathn	nhul
ACC	paanth	pam	thok	ngathn	nhunh
DAT	paanthun	pama ~paman ~pamak	thokthak	ngathnmak ~ngathnmun	nhangun
GEN	paanthak	pamak	thokthak	ngathnmak	nhangn
ABL	paanthum	pamam ~pamtam	thokntam	ngathnmantam	nhangnma
COM	paanthkak	pamkak	thokkak	ngathnkak	—
PROP (adn)	paanthaak	pamaak	thokaak	ngathnaak	—
PROP (rel)	paanthkaak	pamkaak	thokkaak	ngathnkaak	—
PRIV (adn)	paanthaar	pamaar	thokaar	ngathnaar	—
PRIV (rel)	paanthkaar	pamkaar	thokkaar	ngathnkaar	—

Note that both the proprietive and privative morphemes have distinct relational and adnominal forms, discussed in more detail in §4.2.8 and §4.2.9 respectively. These forms (and possibly also the comitative, §4.2.7) are encliticized – rather than suffixed – to their nominal host. They are presented together with the inflectional cases in §4.2 due to their functional similarity.

The following sections provide an overview of the formal expression of case marking in nomina (§4.1.1) and genitive pronouns functioning as adnominal modifiers (§4.1.2), followed by a more detailed consideration of both the forms and the range of semantic and syntactic functions expressed by each case category (§4.2). The case forms of free personal pronouns are detailed in §5.1.1.1.

4.1.1 Case marking of nomina

As seen in Table 21 of the previous section, many Kuuk Thaayorre nomina have a number of alternate forms for the ergative, dative and ablative cases. The nomen *pam* 'man', for example, has three dative forms; *pama*, *paman* and *pamak*. These allomorphs do not contrast with one another in any meaningful way, but rather appear to have been produced through the diachronic interaction of sound changes in general (operating across the lexicon) and the grammaticalization of case morphemes in particular. The same is true of the alternate ergative and ablative forms. The diachrony of this irregular case inflection and its implications are explored further in the relevant sections.

It is impossible to predict from the form of a nomen root the number and shape of alternate case forms it will take. It is possible, however, to predict from the ergative form of a nomen that it will have particular dative and ablative forms, even if these may alternate with (unpredictable) dative, ablative and ergative forms. Any nomen with an ergative-inflected form ending in -Vl, for instance, will have a dative form ending in -V. Table 22 thus presents the broad declensional classes into which Kuuk Thaayorre nomina can be divided. Alternate case-inflected forms of the exemplar nouns are presented in parentheses, but should not be taken to apply to the declensional class as a whole. Where my corpus includes no examples of a particular case form for the exemplar nomen, this is indicated by a dash '–' in the relevant cell. Note also that Table 22 omits proprietive, privative and comitative inflected forms since these case suffixes are morphologically invariant and therefore unaffected by declension class.

Table 23 presents a sample of irregular nomina that do not fit into any of the three major declensional classes. These nomina may combine with novel suffixes not found in the major declensional classes (as seen in the ergative form of *kuta* 'dog', *kutaku*), or they may combine with the regular suffixes seen in Table 23, but have dative and/or ablative forms that are unexpected given their ergative form (e.g. *kumun* 'thigh', which has the ergative form *kumunthurr*, but dative *kuman* rather than the expected *kumunak*).

Table 22. Major nomen declension classes.

	Ergative	Nominative	Accusative	Genitive	Dative	Ablative
Declension 1.	(n)thurr	ø	ø	(th)ak	(th)ak	(n)tam
'black'	ngotnthurr (~ngotnthn)	ngotn	ngotn	ngotnak	ngotnak	ngotntam
'many'	mongthurr	mong	mong	mongthak	mongthak	mongtam
Declension 2.	V	ø	ø	ak	Vn	Vm
'woman'	paanthu	paanth	paanth	paanthak	paanthun	paanthum
'snake'	yaka	yak	yak	yakak	yakan	yakam
'hole'	ranthi	ranth	ranth	ranthak	ranthin	ranthim
Declension 3.	Vl	ø	ø	ak	V	Vm
'man'	pamal	pam	pam	pamak	pama (~paman) (~pamak)	pamam (~pamntam)
'FISH'	ngatal	ngat	ngat	ngatak	ngata	ngatam
'WORD'	kuukul	kuuk	kuuk	—	kuuku	kuukum
'water'	ngokel	ngok	ngok	—	ngoke (~ngokak) (~ngokeln)	ngokem

Table 23. Declension of some irregular nomina.

Irregular	Ergative	Nominative	Accusative	Genitive	Dative	Ablative
'dog'	kutaku ~kutan	kuta	kuta	kutathak	kutan ~kutathak	kutakum
'thigh'	kumunthurr	kumun	kumun	kumunak	kuman	kumunmam ~kumuntam
'old lady'	ngumpurran	ngumpurr	ngumpurr	ngumpurrak	ngumpurrak	—
'raffia'	yencnthurr	yencr	yencr	yencrak	yencer	yencntam
'child'	parran	parr_r	parr_r	parr_rak	parr_rak	parrntam
'foot'	thamarr	thamr	thamr	thamrak	thamrak	thamrntam

The details of how phonologically- and lexically-determined case allomorphs are selected are discussed separately for each case. But first it is worth noting a significant formal correspondence between the ergative, dative and ablative-marked forms of second and third declension nomina. All of these forms include a lexically-specified vowel (rendered as 'V' in Table 22). That this vowel is not phonologically predictable is evident in Table 24 and Table 25, which compare the nominative and ergative forms of a range of second and third declension nomina. Note that the vowels of the ergative forms presented therein are always the same as those of the corresponding dative and ablative forms. Hence the vowel /u/ is found in the ergative, dative and ablative forms of *kaal* 'ear' (*kaalu, kaalun* and *kaalum* respectively), while the vowel /a/ is found in the ergative, dative and ablative forms of *waal* 'silly' (*waala, waalan* and *waalam* respectively).

Table 24. Nominative and ergative forms of some second declension nomina.

Nominative	Ergative	Gloss
yak	yaka	'snake'
patp	patpa	'hawk'
waal	waala	'silly'
kiin	kiina	'tooth'
peep	peepa	'net'
pork	porka	'big'
kunk	kunka	'alive'
ngeengk	ngeengka	'belly'
ruuc	ruuca	'ashes, dust'
min	mini	'good'
nhan	nhani	'sand'
meer	meere	'eye'
pot	pote	'dry'
koow	koowo	'nose'
thomp	thompo	'smoke'
paanth	paanthu	'woman'
kaal	kaalu	'ear'
raak	raaku	'place'
kam	kamu	'blood'
yuk	yuku	'tree'
minc	mincu	'true'

Table 25. Nominative and ergative forms of some third declension nomina.

Nominative	Ergative	Gloss
pam	pamal	'man'
ngat	ngatal	'FISH'
minh	minhal	'MEAT'
kun	kunal	'bum/butt, shit'
puun	puunil	'breeze'
puuy	puuyil	'crab'
pinc	pincil (~ pinci)	'saltwater croc'
ngok	ngokel	'water'
kuuk	kuukul	'word, language'

Selecting the appropriate vowel for these case-inflected forms clearly requires access to lexical, not merely phonological, properties of the word. This suggests that they may in fact be part of the root form of nomina, with the nominative/accusative nomen forms produced through subtractive morphology. This is best understood in a diachronic context. Witness the resemblance between the Kuuk Thaayorre ergative-inflected nomina presented in the second column of Table 26 and the reconstructed/cognate nominative forms presented in the third.

Table 26. Cognates of some second and third declension nomina.

Nominative	Ergative	Reconstructed and cognate forms
kaal 'ear'	kaalu	Ayapathu *kaalu* (Rigsby, personal communication).
yuk 'tree'	yuku	Pakanh *yuku* 'tree' (Rigsby p.c.).
pungk 'knee'	pungku	Pakanh *pungku* (Rigsby p.c.), Kugu Muminh *pungku* 'knee' (Gaby, field notes), Yidiɲ *bunggu* 'knee' (Dixon 1977).
kam 'blood'	kamu	Kaanytyu *kamu* 'blood' (Rigsby p.c.); Yidiɲ *gamu* 'blood' (Dixon 1991).
raak 'place'	raaku	Kugu Muminh *agu* 'place' (Gaby, field notes), Pakanh *agu* 'place' (Rigsby p.c.).
thip 'liver'	thipa	Pakanh *thipa* 'liver' (Rigsby p.c.).
pinc 'saltwater crocodile'	pinci ~ pincil	Kugu Muminh *pinci* 'salwater crocodile (Gaby, field notes).
pam 'man'	pamal	PP **pama* 'man' (Hale 1966a), Kugu Muminh *pama* 'man' (Gaby, field notes), Guugu Yimidhirr *bama* (Haviland 1979).
kuuk 'LANGUAGE'	kuukul	Kugu Muminh *kugu* 'language' (Gaby, field notes), Guugu Yimidhirr *guugu* 'language' (Haviland 1979), Yidiɲ *gugu* 'language' (Dixon 1977).
minh 'MEAT'	minhal	PP **miɲa* 'meat' (Hale 1966a), Kugu Muminh *minha* 'meat' (Gaby, field notes), Wik-Ngathan *minh* 'meat' (Sutton 1995).
ngat 'FISH'	ngatal	Kugu Muminh *nga'a* 'fish' (Gaby, field notes).
kun 'shit'	kunal	PP **kuna* 'shit' (Hale 1966a), Kugu Muminh *kuna* 'shit' (Gaby, field notes), Wik-Ngathan *kun* 'shit' (Sutton 1995).

As Table 26 shows, many of the ergative forms of Kuuk Thaayorre second declension nomina (e.g. *kaalu* 'ear:ERG') are formally identical to the corresponding nominative forms reconstructed for proto-Paman, or otherwise have cognates in the nominative forms of other Paman languages. For third declension nomina, the vowel that precedes /l/ in the ergative inflection (e.g. /a/ in *pamal* 'man:ERG') is identical to the root-final vowel of the corresponding nominative forms of other Paman languages. The comparative evidence thus points strongly towards the lexically-determined vowels being a part of the nomen root at some point in Kuuk Thaayorre's history. The historical phonological process of word-final vowel deletion[80] resulted in the loss of the root-final vowels in the nominative and accusative nomen forms. These vowels have been preserved, however, in case-inflected forms. The particular historical processes through which the present case allomorphs were formed are outlined in each subsection detailing the relevant case. While I view the nominative/accusative forms of these nomina as realised through substractive morphology, this grammar will segment and gloss nomen forms as though the nominative/accusative form is the root and other case inflections produced through concatenative morphology. This representational artifice is simply due to the difficulty of representing subtractive morphology.

Case-marking is realized only on the final eligible constituent of the noun phrase, as is fairly common across the Australian continent.[81] While some theoreticians have argued such phrasal marking indicates that the case morphs are postpositional enclitics (Anderson 2005), the formal irregularity of the Kuuk Thaayorre ergative morpheme, in particular, cannot be reconciled with such an analysis (cf. Table 24, Anderson et al. 2006).

4.1.2 Genitive pronouns inflected for relational case

While pronoun forms and functions are the subject of Chapters 5 and 6, the discussion of case marking would be incomplete without mentioning the affixation of case suffixes to genitive-form pronouns functioning as adnominal modifiers within the NP.[82] This case marking (presented in Table 27) is relatively regular.

---

[80] Independent evidence of word-final vowel deletion across the Thaayorre lexicon is provided by the verb stem allomorphy discussed in §7.1.2. This process was evidently in operation prior to Kuuk Thaayorre's separation from other members of the Southwest Pama subgroup; cf. Alpher 1972.

[81] See, for example, Diyari (Austin 1981), Yankunytjatjara (Goddard 1985) and Wik Mungkan (Sayers 1976).

[82] Gaby (2006) postulated a series of 'possessive pronouns' that were argued to be distinct from – though homorphous with – the genitive personal pronouns. This analysis was justified functionally by the putative possessive pronouns' function as adnominal modifiers, morphologically by their hosting relational case suffixes (further to their genitive/possessive form), and syntactically by their position within a noun-headed NP. This grammar departs from that analysis, finding the original justifications less persuasive than the principle of parsimony. It therefore allows that the genitive-form personal pronouns may function adnominally within a noun-headed NP, with the attendant morphological consequences.

Table 27. The case suffixes for genitive pronouns.

	suffix	*ngathn* 'my' (1sggen)
Ergative	*-thurr ~ -man ~ -antamn*	*ngathnthurr ~ngathnman ~ngathnantamn*
Nominative / Accusative	*-ø*	*ngathn*
Genitive	*-mak*	*ngathnmak*
Dative	*-mak ~ -mun ~ -man*	*ngathnmak ~ ngathnmun ~ ngathnman*
Ablative	*-mantam*	*ngathnmantam*
Proprietive (relational)	*=kaak*	*ngathnkaak*
Proprietive (adnominal)	*=aak*	*ngathnaak*
Privative (relational)	*=kaar*	*ngathnkaar*
Privative (adnominal)	*=aar*	*ngathnaar*
Comitative	*-kak*	*ngathnkak*

The forms given in Table 27 should be understood to apply to the full set of genitive pronouns. As this table shows, both ergative and dative case-marking may be achieved by a number of alternative allomorphs. The selection of allomorph is not phonologically-determined since each genitive pronoun can combine with each of the allomorphs. Neither does the variation appear to be conditioned by the animacy of the possessum and related differences in case function (i.e. marking a recipient vs. a locational goal). Thus human addressees may be possessed by a pronoun marked by either *-mak* (107) or *-mun* (108), as may an inanimate location (109 and 110 respectively).

(107) ngay   parr_r ngathn-mak yiik-r   "nhunt   kirri   yarr   rumpun!"
      1sg(NOM) child 1sgGEN-DAT say-P.PFV 2sg(NOM) PERM go:IMP beach-DAT
      'I said to my kid "you can go down to the beach"'
      [KTh_MF06Aug2002 Elicitation]

(108) ngali   pam.kunyangkar ngathn-mun nhaanhath-rr
      1du(NOM) brother   1sgGEN-DAT look.at:RDP-RCP:NPST
      'my brother and I are looking at each other'
      [KTh_MF06Aug2002 Elicitation]

(109) nhul   pormpr ngathn-mak yat
      1sg(NOM) house 1sgGEN-DAT go:P.PFV
      'he walked through my house (went in front door and out the back).'
      [KTh_GJ15Oct2002 Elicitation]

(110) nhunt   kirri yarr   iirra   raak ngathn-mun
      2sg(NOM) PERM   go:IMP to.there place 1sgGEN-DAT
      'you can go to my place (to stay there while I'm away)'
      [KTh_AJ8Feb2004 Conversation/Elicitation]

There is some very limited evidence of a fine-grained semantic difference between the forms, however. In an elicitation context, one language expert declared the form -*mak* to be ungrammatical in marking a static locative relation:

(111)   *koo,   yokun   pormpr   ngathn-man / *-mak   yokun   thaka-rr*
        oh   DUB   house   1sgGEN-DAT   DUB   leave-P.PFV
        'Oh, [you] might have left [your bag] at my house'
        [KTh_GJ15Oct2002 Elicitation]

Furthermore, on another occasion the same language expert selected the different morphs -*mun* and -*mak* when contrasting motion through a location with motion past (the outside of that location), viz (112) and (109) above. Though this may suggest that -*mak* is associated with relations of proximity and/or movement, rather than static location and/or containment, this cannot be a semantic absolute, given examples such as (110) above.

(112)   *nhul   pormpr   ngathn-man   yat*
        3sg(NOM)   house(ACC) 1sgGEN-DAT   go:P.PFV
        "he just walked past my house"
        [KTh_GJ15Oct2002 Elicitation]

The evidence to hand is insufficient to establish a locative (or perlative or other) case (sub-)category, especially given the absence of an analogous category in the case inflection of nomina (compare, for example, the use of the -*ak* dative allomorph in example 113 with -*man* in 112).

(113)   *peln   ii   pass   rirk-r   school-ak*
        3pl(NOM)   there   pass   DO-P.PFV   school-DAT
        'they (drove) past the school'
        [KTh_GJ14Oct2002 Elicitation]

It may be, though, that some of the dative functions (discussed in §4.2.5) were originally distinguished by means of these different forms, but these categories have merged for most of today's Kuuk Thaayorre speakers.

The adnominal functions of genitive pronouns and their syntactic position within the noun phrase are discussed in §6.5.

4.2 Case categories

4.2.1 Ergative

The Kuuk Thaayorre ergative case – primarily associated with the marking of transitive subjects – expresses a variety of functions by means of a variety of forms. This section will begin by considering its allomorphic variance, followed by a discussion of the syntactic, semantic and pragmatic functions of this morpheme.

Ergative case is marked by the suffixation of *-(n)thurr* to first declension nomina. The two allomorphs *-nthurr* and *-thurr* are treated here as a single suffix (in contradistinction to the ergative suffixes of other declensions) since their respective distributions are for the most part phonologically predictable. The suffix *-thurr* occurs following apical-final and nasal-final nomen stems and *-(n)thurr* occurs elsewhere (as schematized in (114)).

(114)   *-nthurr*   →   *-thurr*   / $\left\{ \begin{array}{l} [+\text{apical}] \_\_ \\ \text{N} \_\_ \end{array} \right\}$

   →   *-nthurr* /   elsewhere

Table 28 presents a sample of first declension nomina:

Table 28. Selection of first declension nomina.

Nominative	Ergative	gloss
thono	*thonthurr*	'one'
saw (/soː/)	*sawnthurr*	'saw'
ngamal	*ngamalthurr*	'large'
muul	*muulthurr*	'ochre'
government (/kapment/)	*governmentthurr*	'government'
kunyangkar	*kunyangkarthurr*	'sibling'
min	*minthurr*	'good'
mong	*mongthurr*	'many'
mantam	*mantamthurr*	'small'
pung	*pungthurr*	'sun'

There are just a handful of exceptions to the rule given in (113). These include *cane knife* /kejnajp/ which has the ergative form /kejnajpṭur/ (with the allomorph *-thurr*) although it ends in a non-apical oral stop, the nomen *thatr* 'frog' which has the ergative form *thatrnthurr* although it ends in an apical glide, and the nomen *thok* 'cat' which appears as both *thoknthurr* and *thokthurr* in my data.

The allomorph *-thurr* is homophonous with the 'FOCal' suffix (§6.11.2.2) which attaches to stems of any word class (e.g. the permissive particle in (115)) to add prominence.

(115) *koo kirri=thurr yarr*
       oh PERM=FOC go:IMP
       'get going!'
       [Foote and Hall 1992: 17]

Gaby (2010) outlines the grammaticalization pathway that likely led focal *-thurr* to be reanalyzed as an ergative case marker. Such a diachronic development is in keeping with the cross-linguistic tendency noted by Traugott and Heine (1991) for pragmatic elements to grammaticalize into grammatical units. Today, *-(n)thurr* is the most productive ergative allomorph. It is commonly used with loan words, and many younger speakers use it in place of the conservative ergative forms of less common vocabulary items. As the forces of language obsolescence favour regularization, it seems likely that *-(n)thurr* may become the standard ergative suffix with only high-frequency nomina retaining irregular inflection.

For second declension nomina, the ergative case is marked by a lexically-specified vowel. It would seem that this vowel was originally part of the nomen root, but subsequently deleted for nominative and accusative case forms. There are a number of possible explanations for the preservation of this vowel in the ergative-inflected form, each considered in detail by Gaby (2010).

Diachrony aside, it is unclear whether the nominative or ergative form of second declension nomina should be considered 'unmarked'. The fact that the final vowel of the ergative form is lexically specified makes it more economical to make the ergative form the lexical entry for second declension nomina, with the nominative/accusative form produced through subtractive morphology. Hence the Kuuk Thaayorre lexeme for 'name' would be listed as *nhampu* 'name(ERG)', with the nominative/accusative form *nhamp* 'name:NOM' formed by deletion of the root-final vowel /u/. This analysis has the added benefit of the dative and ablative suffixes being suffixed directly to the vowel-final root rather than including a lexically-determined vowel. Hence the single segment dative suffix *-n* would be attached to the root *nhampu* 'name' to produce *nhampu-n* 'name-DAT' and likewise the ablative suffix would be reduced to *-m* in *nhampu-m* 'name-ABL'. Also supporting this analysis is the retention of the ergative-marking vowel in certain fixed phrases (116) in which ergative marking is syntactically, semantically, and pragmatically anomalous.

(116) *nhamp(u)*[83] *ngay*   *Alfred Charlie*
 name(NOM) 1sg(NOM) Alfred Charlie
 'my name is Alfred Charlie'
 [KTh_AC06Aug2002 Conversation]

When it comes to representing case-inflected forms in example sentences, however, there are a number of practical arguments against taking the ergative stem as the basic form of noun roots. Subtractive morphology is difficult to represent through standard glossing conventions and may potentially mislead readers trying to parse example sentences. It is also worth noting that language experts most often, though not exclusively, give the nominative/accusative nomen form as the citation form in elicitation contexts. Accordingly, the final vowels of second and third declension ergative forms will be segmented as suffixes throughout this grammar.

The ergative form of third declension nomina consists of the nominative form followed by a lexically-specified vowel plus the segment /l/. This final segment can be reconstructed to a proto-Paman ergative suffix *-lu (Hale 1966a). We can thus account for these -Vl ergative forms by means of the historical process of vowel-final deletion described above. This development is shown in Table 29.

Table 29. Putative diachrony of third declension ergative marking.

	Nominative	Ergative
Stage 1:	pama 'man'	pama-lu
Stage 2:	pam	pama-l

If we take the ergative form as the lexical entry, the nominative/accusative forms of third declension nomina must be formed through the subtraction of the final two segments (i.e. /Vl/), and the dative forms through the subtraction of root-final /l/. Hence nominative *pam* and dative *pama* formed from the root *pamal*. This analysis is inelegant when it comes to accounting for ablative-inflected forms (e.g. *pamam*), however. These must be formed through the subtraction of root-final /l/ followed by the suffixation of -*m*. It would be more parsimonious to take the dative form *pama* 'man(DAT)' as the lexical entry. From this, the nominative/accusative can be formed through the subtraction of the final vowel (as with second declension nomina), the ergative formed through the suffixation of -*l*, and the ablative formed through suffixation of -*m*. While I take this to be the best synchronic analysis, the representational

---

83 The final vowel of *nhamp(u)* 'name' in (115) is in parentheses to indicate its optionality. When asked to pronounce this clause slowly and carefully for transcription, most language experts were clear that the final vowel should be omitted.

imperative again dictates the presentation of third declension root-final vowels as part of the case suffixes.

In addition to the three major declensional classes there are a number of nomina which have irregular ergative forms though they otherwise conform to the inflectional patterns of first declension nomina. The most common of these irregular ergative forms are: *-(a)n* (Table 30), *-thn* (Table 31) and *-arr* (which replaces the root-final segment, as shown in Table 32).

Table 30. Sample of nomina that take ergative *-(a)n*.

Nominative	Ergative	gloss
meerkole	meerkolen	'taipan'
kuta	kutan	'dog'
waarr	waarran	'bad'
parr_r	parran	'child'
yiirram	yiirraman	'other'
ngumpurr	ngumpurran	'old lady'

(117) *-(a)n* → *-n* / V __
              → *-an* / elsewhere

Table 31. Sample of nomina that take ergative *-thn*.

Nominative	Ergative	gloss
ngotn	ngotnthn	'black'
thok	thokthn	'cat'
workrr	workrrthn	'string'

Table 32. Sample of nomina that take ergative *-arr*.

Nominative	Ergative	gloss
werngr	werngarr	'boomerang'
thamr	thamarr	'foot'
yapn	yaparr	'elder sister's

There are additionally a handful of unique ergative inflections, such as *kuta-ku* 'dog-ERG' (which alternates with *kuta-n* 'dog-ERG') and *kuthirr-man* 'two-ERG'. It is worth noting here that the ablative allomorph *-m* attaches to the ergative form *kuta-ku* 'dog-ERG' > *kuta-kum* 'dog-ABL', supporting the idea that today's ergative-inflected forms were historically unmarked stems.

For irregular nomina, both ergative and nominative forms must be specified in the lexicon. I have no specific proposals as to their diachronic development, other than to note the possibly coincidental formal similarity between the ergative suffix *-thn* and pragmatic enclitic *=th*, and between ergative *-arr* and the pragmatic enclitic *-rr* (cf. §3.6.2).

The following subsections detail the syntactic, semantic and pragmatic functions of the ergative case.

4.2.1.1 Ergative – transitive subject

All transitive, semiditransitive and ditransitive verbs assign ergative case to their subject (cf. Chapter 9). Ergative case marking is thus indicative of the syntactic function of transitive subject, as seen in (118):

(118)   *pam-al   ith   yuk   raath-r*
        man-ERG DEM:DIST stick(ACC) chop:RDP-NPST
        'the man is chopping at a stick'
        [KTh_GJ15Oct2002 Elicitation Cut&Break3]

Although it is possible to offer a semantic characterization of ergative case-marking in such contexts (e.g. 'ergative – agent'), this would be somewhat misleading since the ergative case is also used to encode non-agentive transitive subjects (e.g. experiencers, as in (119)), while being omitted from the marking of significantly more agentive subjects of semi(di)transitive verbs (120):

(119)   *kuta-ku   nhul   glass   nhaanham*
        dog-ERG 3sg(ERG) glass(ACC) look.at:RDP:NPST
        'the dog is looking at the jar'
        [KTh_MF17Sep2002 Narrative FrogStory]

(120)   *ngul   nhul   ngathunyarriy yik-r   teacher: "..."*
        then   3sg(NOM) 1sgDAT   thus   say-P.PFV   teacher(NOM)
        'then the teacher said to me: "..."'
        [KTh_AJ-GJ27Jan2004 Conversation]

4.2.1.2 Ergative – Instrument

The ergative case may also mark instrumental adjunct NPs, an extremely common pattern of polysemy among Australian languages (Blake 1987, Blake 1994). This can be seen in the identical inflection of *coconut* in both (121), in which it has the grammatical function of transitive subject, and (122) in which it has the function of instrumental adjunct:

(121) pam   coconut-nthrr theernga-rr
       man(ACC)   coconut-ERG   kill-P.PFV
       'the coconut [fell and] killed the man'
       [KTh_GJ10Jan2004 Elicitation]

(122) ngay   theernga-rr=unh   coconut-nthrr
       1sg(ERG)   kill-P.PFV=3sgACC   coconut-ERG
       'I killed him with a coconut [by throwing it at him]'
       [KTh_GJ10Jan2004 Elicitation]

I view the ergative and instrumental as distinct categories (associated with distinct thematic roles) that are encoded by the polysemous ergative suffix. Foley and Van Valin (1984), McGregor (1990) and Van Valin and Wilkins (1996), however, argue for a single thematic role that spans both of these uses (labelled 'effector' in the Role and Reference Grammar framework). This argument builds upon the idea of a causal chain in which the ergative-marked effector argument (whether transitive subject or instrumental adjunct) is implicated in the causation of the event (cf. the event construal model developed by Talmy 1988). It does not seem possible, however, to provide a semantic definition of effector that will capture every ergative-marked transitive subject (e.g. (119) above), but exclude other kinds of non-ergative causers (e.g. the girl in (123) and the woman in (124)).

(123) parr_r paanth   ith   minc.munthi-rr
       child   female(NOM)   dem:dist   wash.body-P.PFV
       'the girl washed herself'
       [KTh_AJ7Feb2004 Elicitation]

(124) trouble=okun   yan   yup   paanth-um   inh'nheman
       trouble(NOM)=DUB   go:NPST   soon   woman-ABL   this.very.one:ABL
       'I might get into trouble because of this woman'
       [KTh_AC14Nov2002 Narrative LosingIrma]

Also weighing against a purely semantic account of the ergative case is the fact that instruments cannot be ergative-marked when they appear in an intransitive clause.

Hence the *yuk* 'stick' the man uses to help him walk in (125) must take dative, not ergative, case.[84]

---

[84] It could, of course, be argued that the stick in (125) is simply not construed as an instrument. The fact remains, however, that there are no intransitive clauses in which a potentially instrumental adjunct receives ergative case marking.

(125) pam   yuk-un / *u   yan
       man(NOM) stick-DAT/*ERG go:NPST
       'the man's walking with a (walking) stick'
       [KTh_GJ12Jan2004 Elicitation]

(Note that the case-marking of instruments in intransitive reflexive clauses is somewhat more complicated, §11.5).

The debate as to whether the formal identity of ergative and instrumental marking represents the syncretism of two cases, or a single case spanning two grammatical functions, or a single case with a single function will not be resolved here. Pending consensus on this topic, I shall continue to assume the existence of a single Kuuk Thaayorre case category which I label 'ergative'. (Di)transitive predicates assign this case to their subjects, but the same case may also mark instrumental adjuncts, identified here as a distinct grammatical function. The ergative case morpheme is thus associated with a range of thematic roles; namely all those associated with the subjects of transitive predicates (e.g. agent, force, effector, experiencer, etc.) as well as instrument.

4.2.1.3 Ergative – Unexpected Actor

Both purely syntactic and purely semantic accounts of ergative case-marking in Kuuk Thaayorre are challenged by examples such as (126) and (127).

(126) Parr-an   pul   kuta-ku   ngok-eln   wont-r
       child-ERG^ 3du(NOM) dog-ERG^   water-DAT fall-NPST
       'the child and the dog fall into the water'
       [KTh_MF17Sep2002 Narrative FrogStory]

(127) minh   patp   piinth.kat   waawath
       MEAT hawk(#ERG) scrap(ACC) search:RDP:NPST
       'hawks fossick for scraps'
       [KTh_AC10Aug2002 Conversation]

In (126), the subject of an intransitive clause is unexpectedly ergative-marked. For clarity, the gloss 'ERG^' will be employed where the morph occurs in such syntactically non-ergative contexts. In (127) the transitive subject is morphologically unmarked where ergative marking would be expected. Such cases where the expected ergative marking is omitted are coded '#ERG'.[85] In examples such as these, the morphological case forms exhibited are out of alignment with the grammatical function and seman-

---

[85] Following McGregor (1998), I view the omission of ergative case-marking in transitive clauses as meaningful (signalling an expected subject).

tic role of the arguments they mark. The distribution of ergative case-marking in such clauses is instead determined by pragmatic factors. Specifically, as argued in Gaby (2008), the Kuuk Thaayorre ergative case suffix may be used to mark the subject of an intransitive clause as 'unexpected', while it may be omitted if the subject of a transitive clause is 'expected'.

Pragmatic and discourse contexts similarly influence the distribution of ergative morphemes in several other Australian languages. McGregor (1998, 2006), discusses in detail the influence of discourse pragmatics on the inclusion or omission of the ergative morphemes in Gooniyandi and Warrwa respectively. He argues that the Warrwa focal ergative marker combines the functions of marking syntactic ergative case and pragmatic focus. In Rembarrnga, too, unexpected intransitive subjects may optionally be ergative-marked (Adam Saulwick, personal communication). Pensalfini (1999) argues that the Jingulu ergative markers have grammaticalized into focus markers (which now operate in parallel to ergative case markers), due to the pressures of language contact and obsolescence. Meakins and O'Shannessy (2004) similarly attribute to language contact the fact that the ergative-marking of transitive subjects may be omitted in Gurindji Kriol and Light Warlpiri. In Kuuk Thaayorre, by contrast, the pragmatic use of the ergative morpheme would appear to pre-date its syntactic function (cf. the above discussion of the diachrony of ergative morphology, Gaby 2010).

4.2.2 Nominative

The nominative case form generally signals the subject of an intransitive predicate, whether in a verbal (1278) or verbless clause (129).

(128) *puun   ii   yik   iipal*
      breeze(NOM) there   say-NPST   from.there
      'the breeze is whistling up from that way'
      [KTh_AC10Aug2002 Conversation]

(129) *ngat   inhul   pinporro*
      fish(NOM) this.one barramundi
      'this fish is a barramundi'
      [KTh_GJ28Oct2002 Elicitation]

As detailed in Chapter 9, semitransitive, quasitransitive, semiditransitive and intransitive copula verbs also subcategorize for a nominative case subject. Nomina with this case form may also have a number of adjunct roles in the clause. Thus in (130) a nominative noun phrase referring to a time of day has the role of temporal adjunct, while in (131) a nominative noun phrase referring to a time period (*kapr kuthirr* 'two moons', or 'two months') is used to indicate the duration of the event. The lack of oblique case marking on these adjunct NPs can be attributed to the fact that temporality and/or duration is inherent to their semantics, and their role in the clause therefore needs no further indication.

(130) ngul   may pucr   katpatp-m   raak ngurnturnturr
then   VEG nanda(ERG) grasp:RDP-P.IPFV TIME night
'he was feeling for nanda nuts [during] the night'
[KTh_**DW**-CW09Dec2002 Narrative 2Crocs]

(131) ngay   aka   kapr kuthirr   nhiin-m
1sg(NOM) at.this.place moon two(NOM) live-P.IPFV
'I've been here for two months'
[KTh_GJ16Dec2002 Elicitation]

Somewhat differently, in (132) the second nominative noun phrase (*bush food*, the first nominative noun phrase being the subject pronoun) refers to the instrument or catalyst for the growing event.

(132) ngancn   may bush.food   piinthi-rr
1pl:excl(NOM) VEG bush.food(NOM) grow-P.PFV
"we grow up on bush food"
[KTh_AJ-**IC**-GJ26Nov2002 Narrative/Conversation]

4.2.3 Accusative

Kuuk Thaayorre nomina exhibit a syncretism of nominative and accusative cases, in line with the ergative-absolutive marking pattern found across much of the Australian continent (cf., e.g., Dixon 1994). Thus the same unmarked nomen form is interpreted with the grammatical function of (intransitive) subject in an intransitive clause (133), but as direct object in a transitive clause (134):

(133) may puunh   wont-r   yuk-um
VEG bee(NOM) fall-NPST tree-ABL
'the bees fall from the tree'
[KTh_MF17Sep2002 Narrative FrogStory]

(134) kuta-ku may puunh   kookoc-r
dog-ERG VEG bee(ACC) bark:RDP-NPST
'the dog barks [at] the bees'
[KTh_MF17Sep2002 Narrative FrogStory]

The nominative and accusative cases are distinguished for all nominals because of their distinct forms in the pronominal paradigm (see §4.1 above). Thus the nominative-case intransitive subject of (135), *ngay*, differs from the accusative-case transitive subject of (136).

(135) ngay   kana   thaka-rr
       1sg(NOM) CMP   leave-P.PFV
       'I left Pormpuraaw'
       [KTh_BN1Oct2002 Elicitation]

(136) minh pinc-i   nganh   patha-rr
       MEAT saltwater.crocodile-ERG   1sgACC bite-P.PFV
       'A crocodile bit me'
       [KTh_EN1Oct2002 Elicitation]

The accusative form of the personal pronouns is only ever found with the grammatical function of direct object. As such, it is a useful diagnostic of clausal transitivity (cf. §10.1).

4.2.4 Genitive

The genitive case is marked by the suffix *-ak* for all nomina.[86] This form formally and functionally resembles proto-Pama-Nyungan *-ku*, which Blake (1976: 421) names the "most widespread affix to be found in Australia".[87] *-Ku* and its present-day reflexes span a number of functions, including the marking of possessors, as well as dative and allative case, leading Blake (1976: 423) to suggest its historical development from marking a 'goal of motion' to a 'purpose-beneficiary' to a possessor (among other things). This mirrors Kuuk Thaayorre *-ak*, which also encodes dative case for most nomina (and the Kuuk Thaayorre dative case spans goals, purposes, beneficiaries, locations, etc. – see §4.2.5 below). Although *-ku* and *-ak* share only a single segment, the following hypothetical scenario (taking the nomen *pam* 'man' as example) is in keeping with historical loss of word-final vowels discussed above.

---

[86] The regularity of this form is such that it could potentially be analyzed as an enclitic, given its position at the periphery of the phrase. But by analogy with the ergative, dative, and ablative inflections, I gloss this morpheme as a suffix throughout this grammar.

[87] It may be that the irregular ergative allomorph that attaches to *kuta* 'dog' (*kutaku* 'dog:ERG') descends from this original genitive morpheme.

Table 33. Putative diachrony of genitive marking of pam 'man'.

	Nominative	Genitive
Stage 1:	pama 'man'	pama-ku
Stage 2:	pam	pama-k
Stage 3:	pam	pam-ak

In stage 3 of Table 33, the formerly root-final vowel is reanalyzed as part of the genitive suffix. This is supported by the fact that the genitive inflection has been regularized such that second and third declension nomina with root-final vowels other than /a/ nevertheless take the genitive form -ak. This fourth stage of regularization is shown in Table 34, using the second declension exemplar nomen *paanth* 'woman'.

Table 34. Putative diachrony of genitive marking of paanth 'woman'.

	Nominative	Genitive
Stage 1:	paanthu 'woman'	paanthu-ku
Stage 2:	paanth	paanthu-k
Stage 3:	paanth	paanth-uk
Stage 4:	paanth	paanth-ak

The Kuuk Thaayorre genitive case expresses alienable (137) and inalienable (138) possession:

(137) *yuk   waarr.min   inh   [parr_r ngathn]-mak*
      THING thing dem:sp.prx   [child   1sgGEN]-GEN
      'my children's things' or 'these things belong to my children'
      [KTh_EN date unrecorded Elicitation]

(138) *nhangnam [nganip ngathn]-mak*
      mother   [father 1sgGEN]-GEN
      'my father's mother'
      [KTh_MF20Aug2002 Elicitation]

It is unclear in example (137) whether the genitive case functions relationally or adnominally (cf. Dench and Evans 1988). Under the relational analysis, the genitive phrase *parr_r ngathnmak* 'of my children' is predicated of *yuk waarrmin inh* 'these things', which functions as subject of the verbless clause. Alternatively, *parr_r ngathnmak* 'of my children' might function adnominally to modify *yuk waarrmin inh* 'these things', forming a complex NP; *yuk waarrmin inh parr_r ngathnmak* 'these things of my children's'. The adnominal function of the genitive case is clear in example (138), however.

In addition to marking possessors, the genitive case may also be used to encode beneficiaries. This is no doubt due to the fact that the beneficiaries of material goods are generally the future possessors of the item in question. This can be seen in the second turn of (139):[88]

(139) AA: *nhunt coffee=aak?*
      2sg(NOM) coffee=ADN.PROP
      'do you want some coffee?' (lit. 'are you coffee-having?')
   BB: *kirri ngul ngathn yump!*
      PERM then 1sgGEN do:IMP
      'yes please' (lit. 'go ahead then and make mine')
      [KTh_EN8Sep2002 Conversation]

But genitive case may also be employed to mark non-possessive beneficiaries.

(140) *parr_r inh nhunt pit ngathn*
      child(ACC) dem:sp.prx 2sg(ERG) keep:IMP 1sgGEN
      'look after this baby on my behalf [I am meant to look after it for its mother]'
      [KTh_GJ7Feb2004 Elicitation]

(141) *may inh stir-m rirk ngathn*
      VEG(ACC) dem:sp.prx stir-TR DO:IMP 1sgGEN
      'stir this food for me'
      [KTh_GJ07Feb2004 Elicitation]

Meronymic (part-whole) relationships, expressed by genitive case in many of the world's languages, are typically expressed by same-case apposition in Kuuk Thaayorre.

The syntax and semantics of this meronymic apposition is discussed in §6.9.2.

Interestingly, the Kuuk Thaayorre genitive case is only rarely encoded by a dedicated form (notably, by singular personal pronouns). There is a syncretism of genitive and dative case-marking for most nomina, and of genitive and accusative case for nonsingular pronouns.

---

[88] Note also that in the first turn of (138) the potential possessive relationship is signaled by the proprietive NP *coffee=aak* 'coffee-having'.

4.2.5 Dative

For first declension and irregular nomina (e.g. *thatr* 'frog' in 142) the dative case suffix is homophonous with the genitive. For second declension nomina the dative suffix has the form -*Vn* (or -*n* suffixed to the vowel-final ergative stem as in example 143, cf. §4.2.1). For third declension nomina (e.g. 144) dative case is signalled by a final vowel (arguably part of the root, cf. §4.2.1).

(142) nhul   parr_r   waawantharr   thatr-**ak**
      3sg(NOM)   child(NOM)   call.out:NPST   frog-DAT
      'the boy is calling out to the frog'
      [KTh_MF17Sep2002 Narrative FrogStory]

(143) pam   nhul   wanthantharr=okun yik-r   paanth-**un**
      man(NOM)   3sg(NOM)   how=DUB   say-P.PFV   woman-DAT
      'the man said something to the woman'
      [KTh_FT10Feb2004 RCP Pilot16]

(144) ngay   ngat-**a**   yan
      1sg(NOM)   fish-DAT   go:NPST
      'I'm going fishing [lit. for fish]'
      [KTh_EN04Aug2002 Conversation]

There are additionally a handful of irregular dative forms. The English loan *Cairns*, for instance, forms the irregular dative *Cairnsna* by suffixation of -*na*. The origin of this suffix is unclear. For a number of nouns the dative is formed by the mutation or insertion of a stem-final vowel (e.g. *kumun* 'thigh(NOM)' > *kuman* 'thigh:DAT'; *yencr* 'raffia(NOM)' > *yencer* 'raffia:DAT').

Functionally, the Kuuk Thaayorre dative case is very broad, spanning a range of case roles encoded by the allative, locative or other cases in other languages of the world. These roles are the subject of the following subsections.

4.2.5.1 Dative – Recipient

The dative case is named for events of giving, due to its marking the indirect object cum recipient of these events in Greek and Latin (Blake 1994: 144). The two Kuuk Thaayorre verbs of giving differ in the cases they assign to the recipient argument, however. Whereas *wan* 'give, transfer' subcategorizes for a recipient in dative case, its near-synonym *reek* 'give' subcategorizes for an accusative (direct object) recipient. This difference in the case-marking of recipients is key to the differentiation of ditransitive (e.g. *reek* 'give') from semiditransitive (e.g. *wan* 'give') verbs, as discussed in §10.1. Both of these verbs are illustrated in (145).

(145) pam   ii   reeka-rr   ngul   nhul   pam   thon-thak wani-rr
      man(ACC) there give-P.PFV   then   3sg(NOM) man   one-DAT   give-P.PFV
      '[she] gave the man there [a book], then he gave [it] to this other man'
      [KTh_FT10Feb2004 RCP Pilot5]

The dative-marked target of communicative acts (e.g. *paanthun* 'to the woman' in (142) above, and *ngathun* 'to me' in (146) below) may also be considered recipients of a sort.

(146) nhunt   ngathun   paac-r?
      2sg(NOM)   1sgDAT   growl-NPST
      'are you growling at [scolding] me?'
      [KTh_EN14Aug2002 Elicitation]

4.2.5.2 Dative – Affected party

It is cross-linguistically common for the marking of recipients and of beneficiaries to overlap, due to the fact that the recipients of material goods most usually benefit from the transfer and conversely most beneficiaries come into possession of some item. This can be seen in (147), in which the *pama* 'men:DAT' are expected to benefit from the wallaby's roasting by later receiving it:

(147) minh   ngaak-r   ngan yap-arr   pam-a   ngith
      MEAT(ACC) roast-P.PFV REL e.sister-ERG man-DAT   dem:dist
      'big sister roasted the wallaby for those men'
      [Foote and Hall: Reader 10]

Similarly, the beneficiary of (148) benefits through their later possession of the clean clothes (hence the alternative encoding of beneficiaries in genitive case, e.g. (138) above):

(148) nhunt   rirrkir ko'o-nhan   ngathun
      2sg(ERG) clean   spear-GO&:NPST   1sgDAT
      'you wash those things clean for me!'
      [Hall 1972: 132]

Beneficiaries may be dative-marked without any implication of future possession or receivership, however. In example (149), for instance, a man indirectly suggests that his 'poison' cousin (a taboo kin category) move off the path she is travelling along so that he can pass her without violating taboo. There is clearly no implicit transfer in such clauses.

(149) ngathunkulam   ak   thak-r,   ngay   ulp   yan   yuurra
      1sgDAT road(ACC) JUSS leave-NPST 1sg(NOM) dem:ad.prx go:NPST   to.far
      'would that the road be left for me, I'm going far off that way'
      [KTh_**AJ**-GJ27Jan2004 Conversation]

Likewise, *Jesus-ak* in (150) represents an inspiration, rather than a material beneficiary:

(150) ngancn   wuuc=yuk   thowol-nam   ulp   nhangun   Jesus-ak
      1sg(NOM)   dance=STUFF   perform-P.IPFV dem:ad.prx 3sgDAT   Jesus-DAT
      'we were doing those dances and things for Jesus [at Christmas]'
      [KTh_GJ18Jan2004 Narrative/Conversation Christmas]

The dative-marked participant might also be adversely affected by the event (i.e. having the role of 'maleficiary'). Hence in (151), the speaker is affected by the fish not biting in that her hopes and expectations (and dinner plans) are thwarted:

(151) thul   nganip-n   yuuw kerp-r
      woomera(NOM)   father-DAT far disappear-P.PFV
      'Dad's woomera got lost far away'
      [Hall 1972: 109]

In (152), the father is affected by the woomera's loss through being its (former) possessor.[89]

(152) ngay   ngat-a   yan,   ngat   ngathun   kaar paath-r
      1sg(NOM) fish-DAT   go:NPST   fish(NOM) 1sgDAT   NEG bite-NPST
      'I go fishing, but the fish don't bite [to my detriment]'
      "I go fishing but I don't catch any fish, nothing"
      [KTh_MF20Aug2002 Elicitation]

---

89 This possessive relationship is not explicitly coded in (151), but in (a) the speaker is explicitly marked as both possessor of the food (by the selection of a genitive-form pronoun) and maleficiary (by the dative case marker suffixed to this pronoun):

(a) *may ngathn-mak koop mungka-rr*
    VEG 1sgGEN-DAT all   eat-P.PFV
    'all my food's been eaten!'
    [KTh_GJ14Oct02 Elicitation]

This example is particularly striking as it seems to suggest that the first person pronoun is the target of three kinds of case: adnominal genitive case, reflecting the speaker's role as former possessor of the food; relational (zero-form) accusative case, reflecting the clausal role of the NP *may ngathn* 'my food' as direct object; and relational dative case marking, coding the clause-level role of the first person as a maleficiary. If this analysis is correct, the pronoun *ngathn* 'my' appears to have two quite separate roles in the clause, one within the NP headed by *may* 'food' and one outside. This is the only such example in my corpus; this topic warrants further study.

4.2.5.3 Dative – Goal

The dative case encodes all kinds of goals. Perhaps most basic of these is the endpoint of a translocation event:

(153)   *ngay*   *ii-rr-kan*   *Kowanyama-ngak yat*   *school-ak*
1sg(NOM) there-towards-above Kowanyama-DAT go:P.PFV school-DAT
'I went to Kowanyama for school'
[KTh_ME04Jun2005 Narrative Yencr]

(154)   *kar ngancngun theerk-nhan,*   *family-ak*
like 1pl:exclDAT return-GO&:NPST family-DAT
'she's going to return to us, to her family'
[KTh_AJ27Jan2004 Conversation]

The translocation may end in a simple locative relationship (as in (153), where the speaker ended up being located in Kowanyama), or in a relationship of general proximity (as in (154)), or in a relationship of containment, as in (155):

(155)   *bin-ak kaar roka-ni-rr*
bin-DAT NEG enter-V^-P.PFV
"I never put'm [cans] in the bin"
[KTh_AP8Oct2002 Conversation]

In other cases, the goal may not be the final endpoint of the motion, but it is still a goal in the sense of being the target the event is directed towards. This is true of *pama* 'for/up to the man' in the following example:

(156)   *minh ulp*   *ranci-rr*   *pam-a,*   *punth*   *patha-rr*
MEAT dem:ad.prx jump-P.PFV man-DAT arm(ACC) bite-P.PFV
'that crocodile jumped for the man and bit him on the arm'
[KTh_AJ-**GJ**03Feb2004 Conversation/Narrative DarwinTrip]

4.2.5.4 Dative – Location

The functional range of the Kuuk Thaayorre dative case spans what would usually be considered the domain of a locative case; i.e. where a figure is either temporarily situated (157) or habitually located (158):

(157)   *kumun-ak riiritp-m*
thigh-DAT separate.fibres:RDP-P.IPFV
'she was splitting [the cabbage palm raffia] on her thigh'
[KTh_ME04Jun2005 Narrative Yencr]

(158) nhul   ii-kaw   wun   H.A.C.C.-ak
      3sg(NOM)   there-at:east   live:NPST   H.A.C.C.-DAT
      'she lives over there in the east, at the H.A.C.C.'⁹⁰
      [KTh_AJ27Jan2004 Conversation]

This locative relation may be one of proximity rather than co-location per se:

(159) yuk   church-ak   thanan
      tree(NOM)   church-DAT   stand:RDP:NPST
      'the tree is next to the church'
      [KTh_EC02Oct2002 Elicitation BowPed49]

As described in §4.2.1.2, instruments generally receive ergative marking. But where a theme is saliently located on or in an instrument that impacts upon it, this instrument may instead receive dative case-marking:

(160) yuk   yenhyorr-ak   ko'om,   korngkon
      stick yenhyorr-DAT   knit:P.IPFV   string.basket(ACC)
      'then [she] knit the string basket with / on knitting sticks'
      [KTh_ME04Jun2005 Narrative Yencr]

(161) ngul   ngancn   iirra   dinghy-ak   yat
      then   1sg:excl(NOM)   to.there   dinghy-DAT   go:P.PFV
      'then we went there by / in [a] dinghy'
      [KTh_AJ9Oct2002 Conversation]

(162) ngok   kaalkurrc-ak   kuungk-r
      water   cold-DAT   wet-NPST
      '[and then you] wet [the cabbage palm raffia] with / in cold water'
      [KTh_ME04Jun2005 Narrative Yencr]

The dative morpheme in such cases does not mark the instrumental relation per se, but rather the contact between the instrument and theme (similar to the locative usage noted above).

4.2.5.5 Dative – Path (goal-focus)
As well as marking static locations and the endpoints of trajectories, the dative case may encode the path of a trajectory, as seen in the following examples:

---

90 HACC is an acronym for the 'Housing and Community Care' aged accommodation.

(163) raak-un   yan   warrath-n, yak   pil.wacirr!
      ground-DAT go:NPST   grass-DAT snake beware
      'you walk through the grass [to get pandanus], but watch out for snakes!'
      [KTh_GJ06Jun2005 Elicitation]

(164) nhul   pormpr ngathn-mak   yat,   pass rirk-r
      3sg(NOM)   house 1sg-DAT go:P.PFV pass   DO-P.PFV
      'he walked through my house (went in the front door and out the back)'
      [KTh_GJ14Oct2002 Elicitation]

This path function is shared by the ablative case, but it appears that the dative case is used where there is a focus on the endpoint of the action (e.g. the implicit goal of the pandanus in example (163)), while the ablative is used with a focus on (or shared perspective with) the point of origin (see §4.2.6.2).

4.2.5.6 Dative – Duration

In keeping with the TIME IS SPACE metaphor that pervades Kuuk Thaayorre grammar and lexicon,[91] the dative morpheme extends from marking a spatial passage (as in (163)) to marking a passage of time; i.e. the time period through which an event endures. In (165), for instance, the period *awa* 'hour' is encoded as the duration of the communication event:

(165) awa-ak   yik-m   pul   yak-am
      hour-DAT   say-P.IPFV 3du(NOM)   snake-ABL
      'they two talked for an hour about the snake'
      [Foote and Hall: Primer 9]

4.2.5.7 Dative – Purpose

The Kuuk Thaayorre dative case encodes both the endpoint of a trajectory and the motivation or expected reward for some activity (much like its English equivalent, *goal*). Thus in (166), the wallabies the men hope to catch are coded dative:

(166) pam   peln   ii   kana   yan   minh-a,   minh kothon-ak
      man(NOM) 3pl(NOM) there about.to   go:NPST MEAT-DAT MEAT wallaby-DAT
      'those men are hunting wallaby'
      [KTh_AC10Aug2002 Elicitation]

Similarly, in (167) the fiscal incentive for the selling activity is marked by dative case:

---

[91] As exemplified by the polysemous generic noun *raak* 'place, ground, earth, time'.

(167) raak.rirkr-ak sell-m rirk
money-DAT sell-TR DO:NPST
'[they] sell [it] for money'
[KTh_AJ27Jan2004 Conversation]

The desired purpose of relatively passive events may also be coded dative, as in the following example:

(168) ngay pam ngathn-mak wait rirk... ngok-e
1sg(NOM) man 1sgGEN-DAT wait DO:NPST LIQUID-DAT
'I'm waiting for my husband... for beer'
[Anon.]

In learning events, the dative-marked noun phrase encodes the body of knowledge or skill being acquired:

(169) nhul learn-m rirk-m wang ulp korngkon-ak
3sg(NOM) learn-VBLZ do-P.IPFV whitefella(NOM) dem:ad.prx string.basket-DAT
'that whitefella was learning [how to make] string baskets'
[KTh_ME04Jun2002 Narrative Yencr]

4.2.5.8 Dative – Stimulus

Closely related to its marking of goals, is the dative's use to mark the stimulus of sensory activities, i.e. the goal towards which the subject's attention is directed. Hence the dative case is used to encode the thing seen in (170), and the thing heard in (171):

(170) kaapac-ak nhaath-m ngancn
cloud-DAT look.at-P.IPFV 1pl:excl(NOM)
'we were staring at the clouds'
[KTh_GJ15Oct2002 Narrative PlaneSighting]

(171) nhunt wuump news-ak ngeey-r?
2sg(NOM) CONTR news-DAT listen.to-P.PFV
'did you listen to the news?'
[KTh_AJ-GJ03Feb2004 Conversation]

For both *nhaa-* 'look at, see' and *ngeey-* 'listen to, hear', the nominative-dative case frame alternates with an ergative-accusative case frame (see §10.1.3).

4.2.5.9 Dative – Experiencer

The experiencer of a stimulus or sensation is sometimes dative-marked:

(172)   aa,   kul.paath=pa   pam-a   ith   paapath   wun!
        yes   sweet(NOM)=PRAG   man-DAT   dem:dist   hot   lie:NPST
        'yes, [water] is sweet to someone who is hot!'
        [Foote and Hall: Primer 9]

The dative pronoun *ngathun* 'to me' in (173) can be interpreted either as a goal or as an experiencer / viewer:

(173)   may coconut   ngathun   wont-r
        VEG coconut(NOM)   1sgDAT   fall-P.PFV
        'that coconut fell on me'
        or: 'that coconut fell (and I was watching)'
        [KTh_GJ10Jan2004 Elicitation]

This usage is interesting given that the relational opposite of an experiencer – the stimulus – is also dative coded (see §4.2.5.8). I have not been able to construct any grammatical elicitation sentences that include both a dative-marked experiencer and a dative-marked stimulus. It seems that the dative-marking of stimuli can only be assigned by the predicate, whereas dative experiencers may more readily be incorporated into a clause as an adjunct.

4.2.5.10 Dative – Accompaniment

Although Kuuk Thaayorre possesses a dedicated comitative morpheme (*-kak*; see §4.2.7), the dative case is also sometimes used to comitative effect, as seen in the third line of the following example:

(174)   1. ngay   parr_r   mant   yancm
            1sg(NOM)   child   small(NOM)   go:P.IPFV
            'when I was a boy'
        2. ngay   nganam   wak-m,   kanangkarr
            1sg(ERG)   mother(ACC)   follow-P.IPFV   long.ago
            'I would follow my mother [here], long ago'
        3. ngay   nganip-an   yan
            1sg(NOM)   father-DAT   go:NPST
            'or I'd go with my father'
            [KTh_AC10Aug2002 Conversation]

Dative-marking is the only comitative strategy for personal (175) and genitive (176) pronouns, neither of which may host the comitative suffix *-kak*:

(175) nhunt   ngathun wiitl   Cairns-na
      2sg(NOM) 1sgDAT in.company Cairns-DAT
      'you'll accompany me to Cairns [won't you?]'
      [KTh_EN27Jan2004 Conversation]

(176) nhul   pam nhangn-mak
      3sg(NOM) man 3sgGEN-DAT
      'she's with her husband'
      [KTh_EN27Jan2004 Conversation]

4.2.6 Ablative

The ablative case suffix has the allomorphs *-(n)tam* ~ *-ma(m)* ~ *-Vm*.[92] Which ablative allomorph is selected cannot be predicted from the form of either the nomen stem or its ergative-inflected form. For instance, the noun *nganam* 'mother' takes the *-tam* allomorph, while the phonetically similar *pam* 'man' takes *-am*. Meanwhile, both *kumun* and *ngamal* take the ergative allomorph *-thurr*, but the ablative form of the former is *kumun-mam*, and the latter, *ngamal-tam*. Further, some nomina may be paired with multiple ablative allomorphs, even by the same speaker. Thus *yak* 'snake' may take either *-ntam* or *-am*, while *thuuc* 'scrub' (which takes the same ergative allomorph as *yak* 'snake'; *thuuca* 'scrub:ERG' and *yaka* 'snake:ERG') takes the ablative allomorph *thuuc-mam* 'scrub-ABL'. This remains a topic for further investigation.

Exceptionally, the ablative morpheme may also be suffixed to spatial and temporal adverbs (177–178, as well as 184 and 185 below), even though case inflection is generally restricted to nominals:

(177) pul   inh   kanpa-tam
      3du(NOM) dem:sp.prx before-ABL
      'they two are from before [i.e. were born before I was]'
      [KTh_GJ09Oct2002 Conversation]

(178) ball   werngka-ntam kerp-r   ngul koorr yomparru-rr
      ball(NOM) middle-ABL   disappear-P.PFV then outside transform-P.PFV
      'the ball disappeared from the middle [of the ring] and then reappeared outside'
      [KTh_GJ20Nov2002 Elicitation MoverbEnterExit8]

---

92 The vowel of this final ablative allomorph is determined by the thematic vowel of the nominal stem (cf. §4.2). Representing this allomorph as *-Vm* is in fact a simplification of the more likely case that this suffix has the form *-m*, but attaches to the allomorph of the nominal stem that includes the final thematic vowel.

The ablative case, like the dative, spans numerous thematic roles which will be outlined in the following subsections.

4.2.6.1 Ablative – Source

Ablative case-marking is used to encode sources of several kinds. The first of these is a spatial source; the point of origin for a figure that undergoes translocation:

(179) *peln   Ngumpurr.Nhiinhin-tam   theerk*
      3pl(NOM) Ngumpurr.Nhiinhin-ABL   return:NPST
      'they must be coming from Ngumpurr Nhiinhin (place name)'
      [KTh_GJ07Feb2004 Conversation / Elicitation]

(180) *parr_r   kumun-mam   wont-r   paanth-um*
      child   lap-ABL   fall-P.PFV   woman-ABL
      'the child fell from the woman's lap'
      [KTh_GJ10Jan2004 Elicitation]

In examples like (181), the ablative noun phrase represents not just a source location, but also a prior possessor:

(181) *kuta-ku   may   pam-am   pirra-rr*
      dog-ERG   VEG(ACC)   man-ABL   snatch-P.PFV
      "dog took food from man"
      [KTh_GJ19Jan2004 Elicitation]

In other cases, the ablative noun phrase represents a place of origin which is specified for identificational purposes rather than to describe motion extending outwards from it:

(182) *pam friend ngathn   pam iipal   England-tam yat*
      man friend 1sgGEN(NOM)   man from.there   England-ABL go:P.PFV
      'my friend [in Melbourne] comes from England'
      [KTh_GJ16Oct2002 MelbourneTrip Narrative]

(183) *only Kowanyama-ntam thaangk-m   peln*
      only Kowanyama-ABL   climb-P.IPFV   3pl(NOM)
      '(nobody from Pormpuraaw competed in the rodeo) only people from Kowanyama rode'
      [KTh_AJ27Jan2004 Conversation]

The source encoded in ablative case may represent a temporal origin:

(184) *kanangkarr-ntam*
       long.ago-ABL
       '[this dress is] old'
       [KTh_MF10Jan2004]

(185) *pul   inh   kanpa-tam, ngay   parr_r nhulam*
       3du(NOM)   dem:sp.prx   before-ABL 1sg(NOM)   child   youngest.offspring
       '[my two siblings] are from before [me], I am the youngest child'
       [KTh_AJ-IC-**GJ**26Nov2002 Narrative/Conversation]

Ablative case may also encode non-spatial sources of information, knowledge (186) or other states of affairs. In (187), for example, the origin of the old lady's name is traced back to the source of her tribal elders.

(186) *ngul ngancn   book-tam   ulp   thil   kaalathi-rr*
       then 1pl(NOM)   book-ABL   dem:ad.prx   recently   believe-P.PFV
       'we learned [about the plane we had seen] from a book'
       [KTh_GJ15Oct2002 PlaneSighting Narrative]

(187) *nhamp   pam ngamal-tam, pam ngotan-tam   ngumpurr   Paanthepr*
       name(NOM)   man large-ABL   man black-ABL   old.lady(NOM) Paanthepr
       'the old lady's name, Paanthepr, [was given to her by] the tribal elders'
       [KTh_AJ-**IC**-GJ26Nov2002 Narrative PormpuraawKanangkarr]

Non-spatial sources may also include the stimulus (e.g. of fear in (188)) or other external trigger or cause of an event (189 and 124).

(188) *wang-tam   ulp   nhunt   weneth   miinng-r*
       ghost-ABL   dem:ad.prx   2sg(NOM)   scared   take.fright-NPST
       'you are scared of ghosts'
       [KTh_**AJ**-GJ03Feb2004 Conversation]

(189) *kaal kam-kak   pam waal-am*
       ear   blood-COM   man silly-ABL
       'his ear was bleeding after meeting up with the mad man'
       [Foote and Hall: Primer 7]

(124') *trouble=okun yan   yup   paanth-um   inh'nheman*
        trouble=DUB   go:NPST   soon   woman-ABL   this.very.one:ABL
        'I might get into trouble from [because of] this woman'
        [KTh_AC14Nov2002 Narrative LosingIrma]

In (124), ablative case marks the woman as the ultimate cause of the trouble the speaker fears may befall him.

4.2.6.2 Ablative – Path (origin-focus)

As well as marking the point of origin from which a trajectory extends, the ablative case may be used to mark intermediate locations within a larger motion event that extends outwards from the origo:

(190)   peln   Musgrave-ma   yat
        3pl(NOM)   Musgrave-ABL   go:P.PFV
        'they went through Musgrave (en route from Pormpuraaw to Cairns)'
        [KTh_GJ14Oct2002 Elicitation DahlTMA]

(191)   paanth   window-ntam   thaathangk-r
        woman(NOM)   window-ABL   climb:RDP-NPST
        'the woman climbs [out] through the window'
        [KTh_GJ19Oct2002 Elicitation StagedEvents107]

Example (191) was uttered in the description of a video clip shot from within a room, with the woman climbing through the window to the outside. A video clip depicting the reverse event, in which the woman climbs from the outside into the room (with the video camera still located within the room), was described with dative case marking on the ground NP (see §4.2.5.5):

(192)   paanth   window-ak   thaathangk-r
        woman(NOM)   window-DAT   climb:RDP-NPST
        'the woman climbs [in] through the window'
        [KTh_GJ19Oct2002 StagedEvents146]

As well as marking intermediate points along a trajectory, the ablative case may be used to mark the scope or domain of the trajectory as a whole. This is particularly common in descriptions of particularly lengthy or extensive travels, such as the following:

(193)   1. parr_r   all over the Queensland-tam   yat:
            child(NOM)   all over the Queensland-ABL   go:P.PFV
            'we children went all over Queensland:'
        2. Aurukun, Lockhart, Weipa, Bamaga, Torres Strait, Yarrabah, Kowanyama, Normanton, Mornington Island,
            'to Aurakun, Lockhart, Weipa, Bamaga, Torres Strait, Yarrabah, Kowanyama, Normanton, Mornington Island.'
        3. parr_r   everywhere-ntam   yat   ngancn   parr_r   mant.
            child(NOM)   everywhere-ABL   go:P.PFV   1pl:excl(NOM)   child   small
            'We children went everywhere.'
            [KTh_GJ16Oct2002 Narrative]

In all such cases, the ablative-marked domain of travel (e.g. *Queenslandntam*) actually stands for a series of intermediate points along the trajectory that are subsequently enumerated.

It was noted under §4.2.5.4 above that a static relationship between a figure and ground is usually expressed by the dative marking of the ground NP. However, a handful of examples exist where the ground object is Ablative-marked:

(194) *kutpol   chair pal-kop-mam   wun*
football(NOM) chair near-at:under-ABL lie:NPST
'the ball is near the below-part of the chair [i.e. the ball is nearly under the chair]'
[KTh_GJ15Oct2002 Elicitation BowPed16]

This may reflect the speaker's recasting the static picture in terms of a larger (imagined) event, in which the chair represents a point along the ball's trajectory rather than its final resting place.

A closely related use is seen in example (195):

(195) *bush pilot-tam ulp   ngay   yat*
bush pilot-ABL dem:ad.prx 1sg(NOM) go:P.PFV
'I went by that bush pilot [light aircraft]'
[KTh_GJ16Oct2002 Narrative MelbourneTrip]

Here the ablative case is used to encode the means by which the subject participant travels – and thus the subject's immediate location at all points throughout his journey – rather than his path or a static location along it per se.

4.2.6.3 Ablative – Attribution

The ablative of attribution is related to the 'source' uses of ablative case described above. Once again, the ablative-marked entity is depicted as the ultimate origin of some other entity ('X'), but in the attributive case the identity of X is defined by the identity of its origin. In the following example, for instance, the *kirkmuk* 'black snake' is definitional of the story under discussion, through being its totemic originator:

(196) *ngay   story=nhurr   wuump wal.meerem... kirkmuk-ntam*
1sg(ERG) story(ACC)=ONLY CONTR remember   black.snake-ABL
'I only remember the story [not the song] of the black snake'
[KTh_AJ-**GJ**03Feb2004 Conversation]

In some other languages, analogous relationships are coded by the same grammatical means as are used to mark inalienable possession (cf. Chappell and McGregor 1996). Indeed, the English translation of (196) employs the possessive construction 'the story of the black snake'.

4.2.6.4 Ablative – Conversation topic

The ablative case may encode a topic of communication or cogitation:

(165') awa-ak   yik-m   pul   yak-am
       hour-DAT say-P.IPFV   3du(NOM)   snake-ABL
       'they two talked for an hour about the snake'
       [Foote and Hall: Primer 9]

This ablative function is related to the stimulus subtype of the source usage (§4.2.6.1), since the snake in (165) may be considered to stimulate or inspire the conversation much as the dog in (197) inspires the worry felt by the child:

(197) parr_r   nhul   kuta-kum   worry   rirk
      child(NOM)   3sg(NOM)   dog-ABL   work   DO:NPST
      'the child is worried about the dog'
      [KTh_MF17Sep2002 Narrative FrogStory]

4.2.6.5 Ablative – Portmanteau case

There are a number of clauses in which the ablative morpheme is attached to a noun referring to the possessor of an entity encoded as the head of a noun phrase, where the possessum (and thus the NP as a whole) has a clausal function usually signalled by overt case-marking. In (198), for example, the referent of the head noun of the initial phrase, *kuta* 'dog' has the grammatical function of transitive subject.

(198) [kuta Dan]-tam ii   kuta thok   waawarin-r
      [dog Dan]-ABL   there PET   cat(ACC)   chase:RDP-NPST
      'Dan's dog is chasing the cat there'
      [KTh_GJ14Oct2002 Elicitation]

This function of the ablative morpheme arises from the restriction of one-case-per-nomen; that any single nomen may bear at most a single case inflection. To see how this operates, consider (199) and (200), both of which express a simple possessive relationship:

(199) *kuta Dan-ak*
      dog Dan-GEN
      'Dan's dog'

(200) *kuta ngathn*
      dog 1sgGEN
      'my dog'

In both (199) and (200), an unmarked nomen representing the possessum is followed by a nomen representing the possessor; in (199) this is a genitive-case noun, in (200) a genitive pronoun. Because the genitive pronoun does not bear a case suffix as such it is eligible for case inflection where this is demanded by the role of the possessive phrase in the larger clause (cf. §6.5):

(201) [kuta ngathn]-thurr piinth   mungk-m
      [dog 1sgGEN]-ERG bone(ACC) eat-P.IPFV
      'my dog is chewing a bone'
      [KTh_EN4Aug2002 Elicitation]

However, unlike some other Australian languages (Dench and Evans 1988), Kuuk Thaayorre does not allow the concatenation of multiple case suffixes upon a single host nomen. Accordingly, where the genitive pronoun of (201) is replaced by a genitive-marked possessive nomen, it is ungrammatical to add a further, ergative, case-suffix:

(202) *[kuta Dan-ak]-thurr piinth   mungk-m
      [dog Dan-GEN]-ERG bone(ACC) eat-P.IPFV
      'Dan's dog is chewing a bone'

Instead, the sequence of genitive + ergative case marking is replaced by the ablative suffix:

(198') [kuta Dan]-tam ii   kuta thok   waawarin-r
       [dog Dan]-ABL there PET cat(ACC) chase:RDP-NPST
       'Dan's dog is chasing the cat there'
       [KTh_GJ14Oct2002 Elicitation]

(203) ith   ii-parr   [television Molly]-ntam
      DEM:DIST there-at:south [television Molly]-ABL
      nhul   kaar show.off rirk   ulp   yokunman yuk.ngat, pokon
      3sg(ERG) NEG show   DO:NPST dem:ad.prx same.way cyclone(ACC) NO
      'that television of Molly's doesn't show [news about] the cyclone either'
      [KTh_AJ-GJ03Feb2004 Conversation]

The bracketing in (198) and (203) reflects the fact that the possessum + possessor, which always appear in a fixed order, form a phrase together, the head of which is the possession (*kuta* 'dog' in (198) and *television* in (203)). The ablative morpheme in such clauses has two functions, one adnominal function within the possessive phrase and one relational function phrase-externally. The first is simply to mark the possessive relationship between the ablative-marked possessor and the unmarked possessum it follows (a function elsewhere fulfilled by the genitive case). The second function of the ablative case here is to signal the grammatical function of the possessive noun phrase as a whole; i.e. the fact that *kuta Dantam* 'dan's dog' has the function of transitive subject in (198). If the possessor were simply genitive-marked, there would be no indication that the possessive phrase functions as transitive subject. This typologically extremely rare use of a single case marker to represent two distinct roles (one within the phrase, one within the clause) is an example of what Dench and Evans (1988: 42) label a 'case portmanteau'.

An association between the ablative case and the grammatical function of transitive subject is also attested in other Australian languages. In Jaminjung, for instance, ergative case-marking of transitive subjects alternates with ablative case-marking depending on the ease with which the addressee is expected to retrieve the intended referent (Schultze-Berndt 2000). As alluded to above, however, the portmanteau use of the Kuuk Thaayorre ablative case is not restricted to the genitive + ergative combination. Rather, it can express the combination of (adnominal) genitive case with any other (relational) case. In (204), for example, the relational case assigned to *kuta Dantam* 'Dan's dog' is dative. This is made explicit in the paraphrase (b), in which the possessor is preposed to the possessum head and marked by the loan English possessive morpheme *'s*, leaving the final consituent of the NP *Dan's dog* free to bare the dative case suffix.

(204) a. *ngay   yuk   thongkn   reeka-rr,   [kuta {Dan}-tam]*
       1sg(ERG) TREE   piece(ACC) give-P.PFV [dog {Dan}-ABL]
       'I gave a stick to Dan's dog.'
    b. *ngay   yuk   thongkn   reeka-rr,   [Dan's dog]-ak*
       1sg(ERG) TREE   piece(ACC) give-P.PFV [Dan's dog]-DAT
       'I gave a stick to Dan's dog.'
       [KTh_GJ15Oct2002 Elicitation]

4.2.7 Comitative suffix -*kak*

The comitative suffix marks a NP whose referent is with (either accompanying or in spatial proximity to) another referent:

(205) *Bill   minh   way-a=th   kay-kak   yaan*
      Bill(NOM) MEAT   cuckoo.shrike-DAT-PRAG   gun-COM   go:RDP:NPST
      'Bill has gone off after a cuckoo-shrike with his gun'
      [Foote and Hall: Primer 7]

(206) *yal   pip-kak*
      creek mud-COM
      'the creek is muddy'
      [Foote and Hall: Primer 7]

It was noted in §4.2.5 that the dative case (the most common allomorph of which is -*ak*) may in some cases mark 'accompaniment', as well as 'locative' spatial proximity. This functional similarity between the dative and comitative cases is mirrored by their formal similarity, the two differing only in the initial segment (/k/) of the comitative suffix. As noted in §4.2.8, the same initial segment determines whether the proprietive and privative enclitics function relationally or adnominally. We might, therefore, expect this to be mirrored in a similar alternation between the dative and comitative suffixes, with the former functioning only adnominally and the latter only relationally. This is not borne out by my data, however, and is additionally problematized by the fact that the dative morpheme has other allomorphs formally unrelated to -*(k)ak*. Examples such as (207) and (208) illustrate the fact that the comitative typically marks the smaller object in a proximity relationship (which usually corresponds to the Figure) while the dative typically marks the larger object (usually the Ground or reference point), even when the expected Figure/Ground profile is reversed:[93]

(207) *may orange   kirk-kak*
       VEG orange(NOM) spear-COM
       'the orange [moves so that it] has the spear [inside it]'
       [KTh_GJ20Nov2002 Elicitation FigureGround19]

(208) *kirk   may orange-ak   rok-r*
       spear(NOM)   VEG orange-DAT   enter-NPST
       'the spear enters the orange'
       [KTh_GJ20Nov2002 Elicitation FigureGround19]

The formal resemblance between the comitative -*kak* and relational proprietive =*kaak* (4.2.8) – which differ only in the length of the vowel – is matched by a semantic connection. As Smith and Johnson (2000: 394) point out: "the comitative signals the inverse of the possessive, i.e. that the comitative NP accompanies or is possessed by another N or NP". Unlike Kugu Nganhcara, Kuuk Thaayorre divides this inverse-genitive territory into the comitative category (which expresses only accompaniment) and the proprietive category (which expresses only possession).[94]

---

[93] The alternation between (207) and (208) was elicited by a set of video stimuli, and is motivated by the extremely strong preference in Kuuk Thaayorre for a moving or most prominent entity to be represented as subject or unmarked topic.

[94] The semantic domains of accompaniment and possession are subtly associated elsewhere in the Kuuk Thaayorre case system, since the most widespread allomorph of the dative morpheme (which encodes accompaniment, a location, etc.) is homophonous with the genitive case suffix -*ak* (which encodes possession).

4.2.7.1 Incipient dyadic uses of comitative NPs

Dyadic forms (first labelled as such by Merlan and Heath 1982) express a relationship between two or more people. This relationship is usually one of kinship, with the dyadic term or construction making reference to 'two people, such that one calls the other K' (following Evans 2006). In Kuuk Thaayorre, this kind of dyadic interpretation is available to some comitative-marked nomina. Hence the comitative NP in (209) invokes both father and child and the relationship that obtains between them:

(209) nhanganip-kak yan
      father-COM   go:NPST
      'father and child going along'
      [KTh_GJ28Oct2002 Elicitation]

Although the kin term *nhanganip* 'father' only applies to one of the participants involved in the event, it seems that the comititative case-marking here creates a classic dyad through which the speaker refers to 'two people, such that one calls the other *nhangnip* 'father''. Similarly, the inclusory construction (§6.8.2) *pam-kak...pul* 'they two [including] the man/husband' in (210) is used not only to make reference to the two people involved in the event, but also to comment on the relationship that obtains between them (i.e. that one is man/husband to the other):

(210) pam-kak   ii   yan   pul...
      man-COM   there go:NPST 3du(NOM)
      pul   ii   yan,   kuthirr pam-kak
      3du(NOM)   there go:NPST two   man-COM
      "there go that husband and wife"
      [KTh_AC12Sep2002 Conversation]

Note that the final clause of example (209) makes explicit the fact that the total number of participants in the event is two (as opposed to the two people encoded by the dual pronoun plus the comitative-marked man). Similar extentions of comitative, proprietive and related morphology are attestested in a range of other Australian languages (cf. Breen 1976, Merlan and Heath 1982, Evans 2003b)

In all the spontaneous examples of my corpus, it is the elder relative who is named by the comitative-marked nomen. When I prompted language experts with examples formed from the term for a younger relative, asking for an English translation, I received a variety of dyadic (211) and non-dyadic (212) responses:

(211) puumn-kak pul   wakrr-nham
      B-COM   2du(NOM) fight-P.IPFV
      "two brothers fighting"
      [KTh_GJ06Dec2002 Elicitation]

(212) parr_r-kak nhip   yarr!
       child-COM 2du(NOM) go:IMP
       "you and the kids go!" (rather than 'you go with your son/daughter')
       [KTh_GJ06Dec2002 Elicitation]

4.2.8 Proprietive =aak, =kaak

The proprietive enclitics (=*aak* and =*kaak*) are used to express the fact that some entity possesses or has the NP to which =*aak* is attached (the possessum). Hence in (213), the proprietive marks *koow thorkorr* 'long nose' as possessed by *minh pink* 'bandicoot':

(213) minh pink   nhul   koow thorkorr=kaak
       MEAT bandicoot(NOM) 3sg(NOM) nose long=REL.PROP
       'the bandicoot has a long nose'
       [Hall 1972: 77]

The proprietive enclitics possess no phonologically- or lexically-conditioned allomorphs, though they are similar to the comitative morpheme -*kak* in both form and function (cf. §4.2.7). Despite functional similarities to the 'having' affixes discussed in Dixon (ed., 1976), there does not seem to be any formal similarity between =*(k)aak* and the proprietive morphemes of the fifty languages surveyed by Sutton (1976b).

Unlike other Kuuk Thaayorre case morphemes, the proprietive morpheme (and the privative below) formally distinguishes adnominal and relational functions. So where the proprietive-marked NP functions as clausal predicate (e.g. in 214), this is signalled by the use of the =*kaak* form. However, where the proprietive-marked NP functions adnominally, the =*aak* form is used (as in 215):

(214) AG: minh waath   koow pokon
           MEAT crow(NOM) nose NO
           'crows don't have a nose'
       ME: koow=kaak!
           nose=REL.PROP
           'they do have a nose!', lit. '[they are] nose-having'
           [KTh_ME02Oct2002 Conversation/Elicitation]

(215) jet   ulp   ngancn   first.time nhaath-nhat kun thomp=aak
       jet(ACC) dem:ad.prx 1pl:excl(ERG) first.time see-GO&:P.PFV bum smoke=ADN.PROP
       'it was the first time we had seen a jet with smoke coming out behind it [lit. with a smoke-having rear]'
       [KTh_GJ15Oct2002 Narrative PlaneSighting]

The contrast between adnominal and relational functions corresponds to a contrast in information structure. The adnominal form foregrounds the proprietor (i.e. *pam* 'man' in (216)), while the relational form foregrounds the relationship itself (as in (217)):

(216)   pam paanth=aak
        man woman=ADN.PROP
        'a married man'

(217)   nhul   pam=kaak
        3sg(NOM) man=REL.PROP
        'she has a husband'

Aside from the privative (§4.2.9), no other Kuuk Thaayorre case morphemes formally distinguish relational and adnominal (nor referential) functions (cf. §4.2.1–4.2.7). Such a distinction appears to be cross-linguistically uncommon, though it may have analogues in, e.g., the predicative and attributive forms of Russian adjectives (cf. Timberlake 1993, Corbett 1995).

The fact that the proprietive morpheme is an enclitic, rather than a suffix, is suggested by the fact that it may follow the dubitative enclitic =*okun* (cf. §9.1.5):

(218)   nhul   paanth yiirram=okun=kaak
        3sg(NOM) woman other(ACC)=DUB=REL.PROP
        'he might have another woman'
        [Anon.]

It may be significant that the difference between relational and adnominal forms of both the proprietive and privative morphemes hinges upon the initial segment, /k/ (always realized as [ɣ]). It may be possible to further segment these two enclitics, analyzing the initial *k-* as a 'relationalizing' prefix that transforms the proprietive and privative enclitics (=*aak* and =*aar* respectively) from markers of adnominal case to markers of relational case. Moreover, it may in fact be preferable to analyze the proprietive – and privative – morphemes as postpositions that happen to encliticize to their complement NPs. They are included within this chapter's discussion of nominal morphology, however, owing to their functional similarities to the case morphemes.

4.2.9 Privative =*aar*, =*kaar*

The PRIVative enclitics express the converse of the proprietive: lack. They attach to an NP that is lacked by another element, optionally encoded as part of a dependent-marked, privative NP:

(219) pam paanth=aar
 man woman=ADN.PRIV
 'a single man'
 [KTh_GJ15Oct2002 Elicitation]

Note that the head NP being modified by the privative-marked NP (i.e. the non-possessor) may be omitted:

(220) minh.punth=aar
 wing=ADN.PRIV
 'wingless (bird)'
 [Hall 1972: 78]

Again, there is a formal alternation between =aar and =kaar that reflects a functional alternation between the relational privative usage (220) and the adnominal (219).

(221) pam ith nhul paanth=kaar
 man(NOM) dem:dist 3sg(NOM) woman=REL.PRIV
 'he has no wife'
 [Hall 1972: 65]

The relational privative form (=kaar) bears a strong resemblance to the negative particle kaar (cf. §11.3.2), and this particle is likely the diachronic source of both privative enclitics. The clitics may be differentiated from the particle, however, on the following grounds: (a) kaar may appear clause-initially, while =kaar and =aar may not; (b) the initial segment of kaar is never reduced, while it is most frequently realized as a voiced velar fricative in the case of =kaar[95] (and not at all in the case of =aar, cf. (222) and (223) below); (c) =kaar and =aar encliticize to the final element of the NP they have scope over, while kaar tends to precede the verb (cf. §11.3.2); (d) the pragmatic enclitic =p may be encliticized to kaar (with the meaning 'not at all') but not =kaar or =aar. These forms are of course also differentiated functionally by the fact that kaar is a clausal negator, while =kaar and =aar are derivational enclitics that produce, respectively, adnominal and relational privative nomina.

(222) nhul may kaar
 [ɳul maj kaːɻ]
 3sg(ERG) VEG(ACC) NEG
 'he doesn't want any food'
 [KTh_GJ12Dec2005 Elicitation]

---

95 This frication of the segment immediately following a clitic or compound boundary is typical in Kuuk Thaayorre, cf. §2.2.7.2.

(223) nhul   may=kaar
      [n̪ul   majɣaːɻ]
      3sg(NOM) VEG=ADN.PRIV
      'he has no food' (i.e. 'he is without food')
      [KTh_GJ12Dec2005 Elicitation]

4.3 Nomen derivation

4.3.1 Reduplication

Unlike with verbs (§7.2.4), nomen reduplication does not produce a regular and predictable semantic or functional effect. With a handful of adjectives, reduplication has an intensifying or pluralizing effect:

(224) yiirram 'other'   yiirryirram 'some (pl), several'
      kump   'deep'   kumpumpum   'really deep'   (Hall 1972: 92)

There is also evidence of reduplication having been a derivational process at some earlier stage. For example, the generic-specific pairing *minh mantmant* '(small) bird' apparently derives from a reduplication of the adjective *mant* 'small'. Conversely, the adjectives *paapath* 'hot' and *kamkamu* 'red' apparently derive from the reduplication of the nouns *paath* 'fire' and *kam(-u)* 'blood(-ERG)' respectively. The semantics of these three couplets are clearly connected, though the semantic effects of reduplication appear to be neither predictable nor productive. I therefore do not consider reduplication a derivational process for nomina synchronically, but rather an etymological relic.

4.3.2 Compounding

Nomen compounding is widespread in Kuuk Thaayorre, with a comparatively large proportion of nomen stems being polymorphemic. The vast majority of these compounds involve a body part term as their first element, the second element being either a noun (225), adjective (226), verb root (227), or deverbal derived noun (228):

(225) *kun+yangkar*
      bum+calf
      'sibling'

(226) *thaa+porpr*
      mouth+soft
      'kind'

(227)　kul+path
　　　 lap+bite
　　　 'sweet'

(228)　yuur+kath-m
　　　 hand+bind-NMLZ
　　　 'policeman'

The class of words produced through compounding is not predictable from their component parts. In (226), for instance, the combination of body part term and adjective produces a compound adjective, whereas in (229) it produces a noun:

(229)　*meer+pork* (eye+big) 'star'

While bipartite compounds such as those above are the best represented in the Kuuk Thaayorre lexicon, tripartite compounds such as (230) are also not uncommon:

(230)　*meer+kun+waarr*
　　　 eye+shit+bad
　　　 'sorry, pitiful'

The degree to which Kuuk Thaayorre compounds are semantically compositional varies greatly. In most cases there is at least some semantic association between the meaning of (at least one) of the component roots and the meaning of the compound as a whole. In (226), for instance, an association between softness and kindness is not implausible. As for (225), there are (often lexicalized) associations between shins and the sibling kin relationship (Umiker-Sebeok and Sebeok 1978, Kendon 1988), possibly linked to females' ritual gashing of shins to express grief over the death of a brother (cf. the related kin sign, §1.3.3.1). A sweet taste is metonymically connected to the act of biting (227), and stars could reasonably be metaphorically described as big eyes since both stars and eyes are said to twinkle. Yet in none of these cases is the meaning of the compound fully predictable from the meanings of its component parts. All of these forms are clearly individual entries in the mental lexicon, rather than productively derived on the fly.

Not only do body part terms frequently enter into compounds describing non-corporeal entities, but many body part terms are themselves compounds of other (monomorphemic) body part terms. The semantic schemata underlying some of these combinations are cross-linguistically common (cf. Wilkins 1996, Heine 1997); such as *paant+thuur* (head+marrow) 'brain', and *pungk+paant* (knee+head) 'kneecap'. Others are more unusual; such as *thamur+thip* (foot+liver) 'sole of foot'. The Kuuk Thaayorre term *meer+paath+wirm* (eye+fire+WIRM) 'pupil', contains the same, crosslinguistically unusual pupil/flame metaphor as the Welsh pupil term, which translates literally as 'candle of the eye' (Cownie 2001, Brown and Witkowski 1981: 600).

Overwhelmingly, in Kuuk Thaayorre, the denotatum of the first element of a body part compound is related to the denotatum of the entire term by spatial contiguity and/or inclusion, while the denotatum of the second element is related via some physiological similarity, in terms of form, function or structure. So *meer+pungk* 'eyebrow' is metonymically located above the *meer* 'eye', and resembles the *pungk* 'knee' in its arched shape. *Yuur+mut* 'back of hand' is related to the *yuur* 'hand' by synecdoche, and to the *mut* 'back' by virtue of its being the inactive side, with a prominent bone structure that stabilizes its superordinate part (i.e. the hand or torso). It should be noted that the second element of these compounds is not always a body part term. It may be a 'cranberry' morpheme (as in *pil+perrk* [hip+PERRK] 'hipbone') or a noun (e.g. *man+werngr* [throat+boomerang] 'collarbone') or adjective (e.g. *yuur+ngamal* [hand+big] 'thumb') from the broader Kuuk Thaayorre vocabulary. Body part compounds may also be derived from more than two morphemes, as in: *koo+mut+pancr* (nose+back+body.hair) 'moustache'; and *ngeengk+kun+ngamal* (belly+shit+large) 'stomach, bowel'. For the former, at least, two sequential processes of derivation are indicated. The first involves *koow* 'nose' and *mut* 'back' being compounded to form *koo+mut* 'upper lip'. This output then feeds into the new compound *koo+mut* ('upper lip') + *pancr* ('body hair') > *koo+mut+pancr* 'moustache'.[96]

In compounds denoting bodily products or excreta, the first element serves to denote the source of the product. So, in *meer+ngok* (eye+water) 'tear', *meer* 'eye' represents the point of origin of the tear, rather than entering into a metonymic or synechdochic relationship with it.

The connection between excreta and their physiological origins may also be encoded via conventionalized lexical ambiguity. So, for example, *kun* means either 'bum, butt' or 'shit', while *theler* can refer to a 'womb' or 'placenta'. In the first case, it seems that the product sense ('shit') precedes the source sense ('bum') since reflexes of **kuna* 'shit' are widespread among Pama-Nyungan languages. This is just one example of conventionalized metonymic extension, a process exploited throughout Kuuk Thaayorre vocabulary (as well as those of many Australian languages). While terms for excreta are based on source/product metonymy, examples from other semantic domains are typically based on other kinds of association. *Paath*, which may mean both 'firewood' and 'fire', makes use of the actual/potential metonymy described by Dixon (1980). Similarly, the ambiguous *may puun* 'honey' or 'bee' is an example of item/index metonymy.[97]

---

[96] Word-final glides are usually deleted when part lexemes (notably *koow* 'nose' and *thaaw* 'mouth') appear as the initial component of a compound. This appears to be a purely morphophonological process.

[97] While 'bee' could be alternatively characterized as the source of its product 'honey', the fact that the term *may puun* involves the generic noun *may* 'vegetable food' (in place of the 'insect' generic noun *ruurr* expected for 'bee') suggests that the 'honey' sense is historically prior. This in turn suggests that bees came to be referred to by the 'honey' term due to their being a good index of the prized

There are finally a number of generic-specific noun pairings that seem intermediate between a compound proper and a polylexemic fixed expression. The pairing *pam thaaw* (MAN mouth) 'friend', for example, is normally pronounced with a fricated onset of the second morpheme (i.e. [pamða:w]), usually indicative of a compound juncture (cf. §2.2.7.3). This would seem to favour the compound analysis over viewing *pam thaaw* as separate lexemes forming a classifier phrase. Also supporting this analysis is the fact that a *thaaw* 'mouth' is not a type of *pam* 'MAN'. Other examples include many binomial kin terms (§1.3.3.1), as well as expressions such as *yuk ngat* (OBJECT/TREE fish) 'rainbow, rainbow serpent, cyclone'. This expression is clearly unlike a standard classifier phrase in its semantic non-compositionality, yet it does not display the phonological properties distinctive of compounds. The same is true of phrases (including phrasal verbs) such as the following:

(231)   *yuk   waarr-min*
        OBJECT   bad-good
        'thing(s), belongings'

(232)   *raak   rirkr*
        PLACE/GROUND   shell
        'money'

(233)   *pungk ko'o-rr*
        knee   spear-RCP
        'to meet, gather together'

Collocations such as these are analyzed here as fixed expressions; stored in and retrieved from the mental lexicon as a single unit with unitary (non-compositional) semantics, but articulated as phonologically distinct lexemes which may preserve some morphosyntactic independence from one another (e.g. the ability to be separated by intervening lexemes). The Kuuk Thaayorre lexicon (Foote & Hall 1992) possesses a large number of fixed expressions, a disproportionately large number of which include a body part nomen.

4.3.3 Verbalization and nominalization

The semi-productive suffix -*m* may be used to produce de-nominal verbs, but also deverbal nomina. This suffix is discussed in §8.1.6.

---

honey's location. Alternatively, it may be that bees are treated as (an inalienable) part of the honey/hive, as Evans (2003a:197) shows for Bininj Gun-Wok. The converse use in other Australian languages of animal terms to refer to plants that index the animal's location is documented by Evans (1997).

4.4 Other nomen suffixes

There are two further suffixes and an enclitic which attach only to nomina, grouped together in this section due to the fact that they are neither clearly inflectional nor clearly derivational.

4.4.1 -tharr

The only examples of *-tharr* in my corpus are associated with a craving for food or drink:

(234) ngay pungku-tharr
 1sg(NOM) knee-THARR
 'I'm hungry'

(235) ngay ngok man-tharr
 1sg(NOM) water throat-THARR
 'I'm thirsty'

Because the meaning of both *pungkutharr* 'hungry' is not obviously connected to the body part noun *pungk(u)* 'knee', I tentatively analyze *-tharr* as a derivational suffix. However, the precise meaning and functions of this form are not yet understood. This suffix may no longer be productive, with the above examples representing fixed expressions that merely preserve the relic of this erstwhile morpheme. Due to its extremely limited distribution in my data (coupled with the fact that it is seemingly unproductive), it will not be discussed further.

4.4.2 Loan numeral marker -nharr

The morpheme *-nharr* is suffixed to loan numerals, as in (236)–(237).

(236) nhul three-nharr ngat catfish kunutha-rr
 3sg(ERG) three-NUM FISH catfish(ACC) catch-P.PFV
 'she caught three catfish'
 [Anon.]

(237) ulp three-nharr pelnan thaka-rr; Conrad, William ngul Jack
 dem:ad.prx three-NUM 3plACC leave-P.PFV Conrad William then Jack
 'three of them were left [after James died]; Conrad, William and Jack'
 [KTh_AJ-**IC**-GJ26Nov2002 Narrative PormpuraawKanangkarr]

The same form is found suffixed to the subjects of reciprocal clauses (cf. §3.1.2.4).

4.4.3 =*Yuk* 'stuff'

Speakers may add the suffix =*yuk* 'STUFF' to a nomen in order to speak in general terms about a 'kind of thing' (238)–(239), or to generalize their reference to include things normally associated with the denotatum of the nomen in question (240), or to indicate reference to *type* rather than *token* (i.e. 'not a specific bull' in (241), and 'not a particular dance' in (150)):

(238)　*minh　　　ulp　　　　　ngancnhan　reeka-rr,*
　　　　MEAT(ACC)　dem:ad.prx　1sg:excl:ACC　give-P.PFV
　　　　ngat=yuk　　　　reeka-rr　　ngancnhan
　　　　fish(ACC)=STUFF　give-P.PFV　1sg:excl:ACC
　　　　'[they] gave us some meat and fish or whatever'
　　　　[KTh_GJ15Oct2002 Narrative PlaneSighting]

(239)　*kuta=yuk　　　　yuuw　yat*
　　　　dog(NOM)=STUFF　far　　go:P.PFV
　　　　"there were no people, even the dogs not there"
　　　　(lit. 'dogs and stuff had gone off')
　　　　[KTh_GJ20Jan2004 Elicitation]

(240)　*pormpr=yuk　　　　koop　thiik-nhan*
　　　　house(ACC)=STUFF　all　　break-GO&:NPST
　　　　'all the houses and things will be broken [in a cyclone]'
　　　　[KTh_AJ-**GJ**03Feb2004 Conversation]

(241)　*bull=yuk　　　　thaangk-m　　peln*
　　　　bull(ACC)=STUFF　climb-P.IPFV　3pl(NOM)
　　　　'they would ride bulls [in the rodeo]'
　　　　[KTh_AJ27Jan2004 Conversation]

(150')　*ngancn　　wuuc=yuk　　　　thowol-nam　　ulp　　　　　nhangun　Jesus-ak*
　　　　1sg(NOM)　dance=STUFF　　perform-P.PFV　dem:ad.prx　3sgDAT　　Jesus-DAT
　　　　'we were doing those dances for Jesus [at Christmas]'
　　　　[KTh_GJ18Jan2004 Conversation]

This suffix often has the pragmatic function of hedge, and is generally characteristic of a particular indirect speech style (favoured by particular individuals).

Etymologically, =*yuk* is clearly derived from the generic noun *yuk*, which denotes the class of trees and stick-like objects (e.g. cigarettes), but also a somewhat eclectic collection of (typically elongated) 'things' (including cyclones, planes, microphones, etc.). Indeed, the Kuuk Thaayorre translation of *thing* is *yuk waarr-min* 'THING bad-good'.

5 Pronouns, ignoratives and demonstratives

5.1 Pronouns

Pronouns may be divided roughly into two groups; those that inflect for case and those that do not. Personal pronouns comprise the first category, and take the form of both free pronouns and reduced enclitics. The uninflecting pronouns fall into three categories: reflexive pronouns, emphatic pronouns and inclusory pronouns. The relationships between the various categories of pronoun are represented in Figure 11.

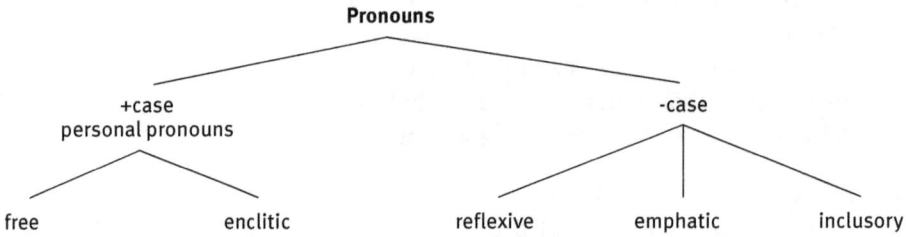

Figure 11. Relationships between categories of pronoun.

5.1.1 Personal pronouns

5.1.1.1 Morphology of free personal pronouns

The Kuuk Thaayorre paradigm of personal pronouns distinguishes three persons (first, second and third), three numbers (singular, dual and plural) and maintains an inclusive/exclusive distinction for non-singular first person pronouns. As mentioned in §4.1, pronouns exhibit a syncretism of nominative and ergative cases, with distinct accusative case forms. The unmarked (nominative and ergative) forms of all the personal pronouns are as follows:

Table 35. Nominative (= ergative) personal pronouns.

	1st Person	2nd Person	3rd Person
singular	*ngay*	*nhunt*	*nhul*
dual	*ngal* (inclusive)[98] *ngali* (exclusive)	*nhip*	*pul*
plural	*ngamp* (inclusive) *ngancn* (exclusive)	*nhurr*	*peln*

---

[98] There is no a priori reason why inclusive pronouns such as *ngal* 'you and I' should be classified first rather than second person, since they refer to both the speaker and addressee. My motivations for

The following three tables present the full, case-inflected paradigms of personal pronouns, sorted according to person.

Table 36. First person pronouns.

1st Person	singular	dual, incl	dual, excl	plural, incl	plural, excl
nominative = ergative	ngay	ngal	ngali	ngamp	ngancn
accusative	nganh	ngalin	ngalnhan	ngamplin	ngancnhan
genitive	ngathn	ngalin	ngalnhan	ngamplin	ngancnhan
dative	ngathun	ngalngun	ngalnungun	ngampulngun	ngancnungun
ablative	ngathnma	ngalnantam	ngalnantam	ngampulntam	ngancnantam

Table 37. Second person pronouns.

1st Person	singular	dual	plural
nominative = ergative	nhunt	nhip	nhurr
accusative	nhinh	nhiplin	nhurrnan
genitive	nhangkn	nhiplin	nhurrnan
dative	nhangkun	nhipulngun	nhurrnhungun
ablative	nhangknma	nhipulntam	nhurrnuntam

Table 38. Third person pronouns.

1st Person	singular	dual	plural
nominative = ergative	nhul	pul	peln
accusative	nhunh	pulnan	pelnan
genitive	nhangn	pulnan	pelnan
dative	nhangun	pulnungun	pelnungun
ablative	nhangnma	pulnuntam	pelnantam

The syntax of free personal pronouns vis-à-vis the noun phrase is discussed in §6.6.

---

presenting *ngal* 'you and I' as part of the first person paradigm are twofold. Firstly, there is the formal resemblance between the inclusive pronouns *ngal* 'you and I' and ngamp 'we (incl.)' and the other first person pronouns, each of which begins with *nga-*. The association between the phonological string *nga-* and first person pronouns is an areal feature (perhaps attributable to shared inheritance), attested by languages right around the Australian continent (cf. Dixon 1980). Secondly, there is of course a firmly entrenched tradition of classing inclusive pronouns as first person cross-linguistically, whether this be due to descriptive precedent or to independent corroborating evidence in each of the languages so described.

5.1.1.2 Functions of personal pronouns

Personal pronouns may head noun phrases, modify a head noun within the noun phrase (in genitive form), and play a determiner-like function with respect to a noun-headed noun phrase. Each of these functions is discussed in some detail in Chapter 6 (§6.6 and §6.7).

5.1.1.3 Morphosyntax of pronominal enclitics

Kuuk Thaayorre possesses an emergent class of pronominal enclitics. These reduced, phonologically dependent variants of the free pronouns are likely in the early stages of grammaticalizing into verbal cross-referencing.[99] Synchronically, though, they remain formally, syntactically and functionally very similar to the free pronouns. For this reason, they are analyzed (and glossed) as bearing case.

As Blake (1987: 103–104) observes, the pronominal clitics of Australian languages must either directly follow the first constituent of the clause (i.e. in Wackernagel's (1892) position) or attach to the verb or auxiliary. Kuuk Thaayorre clitic pronouns are frequently found in both these positions, attaching to clause-initial constituents of any word class (including particles (242, 245), demonstrative pronouns (243) and nouns (244)), or attaching to the verb, wherever it appears in the clause (245).[100] Extremely rarely, these forms attach to non-verbal hosts in non-initial positions, such as the clause-final contrastive particle in (101).

(242) ngul=ul=unh   man.pert-e   theerka-n-r   nhaknkath-an
      then=3sg(ERG)=3sgACC shoulder-ERG return-v^-NPST   camp-DAT
      'and he carried it back home on his shoulder to camp'
      [Hall 1972: 105]

(243) inh'nhul=ay   yik,   kuuk   inh'nhul
      this.very.one=1sg(NOM)   say-NPST   WORD   this.very.one
      'I'm telling this story'
      [KTh_**DW**-CW09Dec2002 Narrative 2Crocs]

---

99 The Kugu Nganhcara system of pronominal enclitics appears significantly more developed than that of Kuuk Thaayorre. Smith and Johnson (2000: 402) nevertheless surmise that they may have developed quite recently "from a situation in which unstressed but unreduced cross-referencing pronouns could occur in pre- or postverbal position". Kuuk Thaayorre appears to be following much the same diachronic development, with the difference that it appears to be the postverbal position that is becoming cemented as the preferred locus, as opposed the preverbal position now licensed in Kugu Nganhcara.

100 Noting the frequency with which pronominal enclitics select for a verbal host, Hall (1972: 378) describes them as "virtual verb suffixes".

(244) meer-e=ay   nhunh   nhaawr
     eye-ERG=1sg(ERG) 3sgACC   see:P.PFV
     'I saw her with my own eyes'
     "I seen that old lady"
     [KTh_AJ-**IC**-GJ26Nov2002 Conversation / Narrative PormpuraawKanangkarr]

(245) thil=unh   koow   rathirr=eln=unh
     again=3sgACC   nose(ACC)   chop-P.PFV=3pl(ERG)=3sgACC
     "they slashed his nose once more"
     [Hall 1972: 77]

(101') paanth   pitit-nh   wuump=ul=okun
      woman(ACC) hold:RDP-SBJV   CONTR=3sg(ERG)=DUB
      "if he had a wife, alright"
      [KTh_ACh07Nov2002 Conversation]

Enclitic pronouns, like their free counterparts, readily permit both omission and redundant repetition. The third person singular accusative enclitic =*unh* features twice in (245), for example, though either or both forms could be omitted. The nominative/ergative case forms of the pronominal enclitics are given in Table 39, while the accusative enclitic forms are given in Table 40.

Table 39. Nominative/ergative pronominal enclitics.

	1st Person	2nd Person	3rd Person
singular	=ay	=unt	=ul
dual	=al (inclusive)	=ip	=ul
	=ali (exclusive)		
plural	=amp (inclusive)	=urr	=eln
	=ancn (exclusive)		

Table 40. Accusative pronominal enclitics.

	1st Person	2nd Person	3rd Person
singular	=anh	-inh	=unh
dual	=alin (inclusive)	=iplin	=ulnun
	=alnhan (exclusive)		
plural	=amplin (inclusive)	=urrnhan	=elnan
	=ancnan (exclusive)		

Note that in each instance the enclitic pronoun is formed by the simple deletion of the initial nasal of the corresponding free pronoun. They are thus transparently the product of the fast speech phenomenon whereby the initial segments of non-sentence-initial words are reduced or lost (see §2.5.2). Indeed, there are many instances in which an unstressed post-verbal pronoun has an only faintly perceptible initial segment. Such cases are analyzed here as free pronouns, though they are an obvious source of the enclitic forms and share much in common with them.

Because they are still a nascent word class, enclitic pronouns are particularly difficult to elicit. When questioned on the subject, or asked to repeat clauses slowly and carefully, language experts are likely to replace enclitic pronouns with the corresponding free forms. However, the following observations can be made regarding order. In the vast majority of cases, only a single pronominal form is encliticized to the host lexeme. However, where two pronouns cooccur in sequence, this sequence appears determined by the competing hierarchies of person and grammatical function. Generally, a first person enclitic always precedes a second or third person subject enclitic, e.g. (246) and (247):

(246) *pal   mi'irr=ay=unh*
towards pick.up:P.PFV=1sg(ERG)=3sgACC
'I picked it up'
[Hall 1972: 95]

(247) *yup=okun   theerng-r=anh=ul*
soon=DUB hit-NPST=1sgACC=3sg(ERG)
"he might hit me before long"
[Hall 1972: 378]

Where both enclitics are non-first person, the grammatical relations hierarchy (SUBJ > OBJ > DAT) applies:

(248) *thil=unh   koow   rathirr=eln=unh*
again=3sgACC nose(ACC) chop-P.PFV=3pl(ERG)=3sgACC
"they slashed his nose once more"
[Hall 1972: 77]

5.1.2 Reflexive pronouns

5.1.2.1 Morphology of reflexive pronouns

The reflexive pronominal paradigm – which is limited to singular number – is formally related to both nominative and genitive-inflected pronouns. This is evident in the comparison of the reflexive pronouns in the third column of Table 41 with the combination of genitive and nominative pronouns in the first and second columns respectively:

Table 41. Morphology of the reflexive pronouns.

	Genitive	Nominative	Reflexive
1sg	ngathn	ngay	ngathney
2sg	nhangkn	nhunt	nhangknunt
3sg	nhangn	nhul	nhangnul

It is reasonable to assume that the diachronic origin of the Kuuk Thaayorre reflexive pronoun lies in the compounding of genitive and nominative forms. But phonological reduction at the (erstwhile) morpheme boundary, coupled with vowel shift in the first person form, suggests that the reflexive pronominal paradigm has been in existence for some time, and that these forms are synchronically monomorphemic.

Non-singular subjects of reflexive clauses are encoded by simple nominative forms in conjunction with a reflexive verb, as seen in (249)–(250).

(249) *ngali   muul-thurr   werk-ey-r*
1du.excl(NOM) white.ochre-ERG rub-RFL-P.PFV
'we painted ourselves with white ochre'
[KTh_EF15Dec2002 Elicitation]

(250) *peln   kempthe reerenng-e   peln*
3pl(NOM) singly   scratch:RDP-RFL 3pl(NOM)
'each of them is scratching himself'
[Hall 1972: 380]

5.1.2.2 Functions of reflexive pronouns

Reflexive pronouns may be the sole indicator of reflexivity in a 'pronominal reflexive construction' (described in §11.5.1 and exemplified by (251)), or they may combine with verbal reflexive marking in a 'verbal reflexive construction' (described in §11.5.2 and exemplified by (252)).

(251) *ngay   wash-m   rirk-r   ngathney*
1sg(ERG) wash-TR   DO-P.PFV   1sgRFL
'I'm washing myself'
[KTh_GJ25Oct2002 Elicitation]

(252) nhangknunt kar nhaath-e
      2sgRFL   like look.at-RFL:IMP
      'you should look at yourself!'
      [KTh_EN14Aug2002 Conversation / Elicitation]

In either case, we may assume that the reflexive pronoun is not redundant, but expresses some meaning that contributes to the interpretation of the construction as a whole. This core meaning that remains constant through all uses of the reflexive pronoun can be summarized as in (253):

(253) **Reflected action** – *the actor is affected by their own actions*

This characterization holds across all uses of the reflexive pronoun. For instance, clauses expressing 'oblique reflexivity' (i.e. where some oblique role – such as beneficiary, location, source – is ascribed to the subject participant in addition to the actor role) are never marked by the reflexive verbal suffix, but are almost always marked by the reflexive pronoun. While the subjects of such clauses do not take on an undergoer role per se, they are *affected* by their actions, either to their benefit (as in (254)) or detriment (as in (255)):

(254) ngay   may   mi'irr   ngathney
      1sg(ERG) VEG(ACC) pick.up:P.PFV 1sgRFL
      'I got myself some food'
      [Anon.]

(255) plate   ulp   nhangnul thiika-rr
      plate(ACC) dem:ad.prx 3sgRFL   break-P.PFV
      "that kid broke his own plate"
      [KTh_GJ12Jan2004 Elicitation]

5.1.3 Emphatic pronouns

5.1.3.1 Morphology of emphatic pronouns

The emphatic pronominal forms collected to date are presented in Table 42 (including three that are unattested in my data, but reported by Hall 1972). Like the reflexive pronouns, emphatic pronouns historically derive from their nominative form personal counterparts, in this case via reduplication plus suffixation of *-r* ~ *-rr* (cf. §5.2.1).[101]

---

[101] The *-rr* allomorph is generally found after alveolar nasals, the *-r* allomorph elsewhere, though some variation (e.g. *pelnpelnr* ~ *pelnpelnrr*) is evident in Hall (1972).

Here too, phonological reduction suggests that today's emphatic forms are synchronically monomorphemic.

Table 42. Emphatic pronominal forms

	Nominative pronoun	Emphatic pronoun
1sg	ngay	ngayngayr (Hall 1972: 378)
1du:incl	ngal	< unattested >
1du:excl	ngali	ngalngalir (Hall 1972: 329)
1pl:incl	ngamp	ngampngampr ~ ngampampr
1pl:excl	ngancn	< unattested >
2du	nhunt	nhuntnhuntr (Hall 1972: 379)
2du	nhip	nhipnhipr
3sg	nhul	nhulnhulr ~ nhululr
3du	pul	pulpulr
3pl	peln	pelpelr ~ pelnpelnrr

5.1.3.2 Functions of emphatic pronouns

The principal function of the Kuuk Thaayorre emphatic pronouns is to focus attention on the participant(s) encoded as subject, in contrast with other potential actors. This is exemplified by (256) and (257), the latter being particularly explicit in contrasting the participants represented by both the subject pronoun *peln* '3plNOM' and the emphatic pronoun *pelnpelnr* '3plEMPH', with the alternative group of would-be (or, rather, should-be) actants represented by *nhipnhipr* '2duEMPH':

(256) Dan   nhululr   yan   melnkelnkarr
      Dan(NOM) 3sgEMPH   go:NPST tomorrow
      'Dan will go by himself tomorrow'
      [KTh_GJ06Jun2005 Elicitation]

(257) peln=th,   pelnpelnr rirk-m,   nhipnhipr riic-m
      3pl(NOM)=PRAG   3plEMPH DO-P.IPFV   2duEMPH run-P.IPFV
      'it was them, they were all working, you two ran off'
      [Hall 1972: 308]

An emphatic pronoun may also be called for in cases where semantic features of the participant encoded as subject make it an unlikely actor (i.e. contrasting the actual actor-subject with the type of actor that might be expected by the addressee). The presence of the emphatic pronoun here rules out any alternative external actor, and can thus result in the quasi-reflexive interpretation of simple intransitive clauses such as (258).

(258) *mimp   ith   nhulnhulr thaariic-r*
cloth(NOM) dem:dist 3sgEMPH tear-P.PFV
"that piece of material is tearing up itself"
[KTh_EN3Dec2002 Elicitation Cut&Break8]

(258) was produced by a language expert in response to a video clip of a piece of cloth lying on a table, slowly (and spontaneously) tearing down the middle (Bohnemeyer et al. 2001). There are no other people or objects present in the frame, so (thanks to the wonders of video technology) the tearing of the cloth is achieved in the complete absence of external causation. This is reflected also by the language expert's subsequent translation of her Kuuk Thaayorre response; *that piece of material is tearing up itself*. The same clause minus the emphatic pronoun would be translated as something like: '[someone] tore that piece of material', implicating an external agent or force.

Reciprocal events may also be associated with emphatic pronouns for the following reason: the verb of a reciprocal clause is typically highly transitive, describing an action that proceeds from actor to highly distinct undergoer. Since reciprocal clauses pair such verbs with only a single argument, the involvement of additional actor(s) might be expected. The inclusion of an emphatic pronoun in such clauses as (259), then, stresses that it is just the one group of men who are both questioning and being questioned – the potential involvement of other participants is ruled out by *pelpelr* 'themselves'.

(259) *pelpelr=nharr   rangkangk-rr-nam   pam   ith*
3plEMPH=RCPCANT question:RDP-RCP-P.IPFV man(NOM) dem:dist
'those men were questioning each other they were'
[Hall 1972: 107]

5.1.4 Inclusory pronouns

Inclusory pronouns make simultaneous reference to a superset of participants and to a subset or individual within the superset group. Thus in (260) the inclusory pronoun *ngalathun* '1du:incl|1sg' (i.e. 'we two including me') makes the speaker particularly prominent within the first person dual inclusive subject participant group. (Note the following convention adopted for glossing inclusory pronouns: the person/number features of the superset are given to the left of the vertical line '|' and the features of the subset to the right.)

(260) *ngalathun   kuuk   yik*
1du:incl|1sg WORD(ACC) say:NPST
'you and I are speaking together in the vernacular'
[Hall 1972: 380]

No inclusory pronouns were spontaneously used in my corpus; the inclusory forms that appear in Hall (1972) are listed in Table 13 in §3.1.2.6. Further discussion of their functions and morphosyntax is provided in §6.8.5.

5.2 Ignoratives

The set of ignoratives, introduced in §3.1.2.7, primarily communicate the speaker's lack of knowledge in a particular ontological category,[102] as is made explicit in (language experts' translations of) (261) and (262). They are in this respect equivalent to the interrogative and indefinite categories of many other languages.

(261) ngay   pam.ngongkom, **wanhul**=okun. **Wanhul**=okun thaka-rr.
       1sg(NOM)   ignorant.of   who:ERG=DUB   who:ERG=DUB   leave-P.PFV
       "I don't know who, somebody must have left [that bike]"
       [KTh_AC21Aug2002 Conversation]

(262) Irene   **wanthan**=okun wun-m
       Irene(NOM)   where=DUB   lie-P.IPFV
       "I don't know where Irene stayed"
       [GJ16Oct2002 Narrative MelbourneTrip]

In addition to this lack of knowledge, ignoratives may contribute other kinds of information. Section 5.2.3 presents the inventory of functions with which the ignoratives are associated.

Table 43 presents the inventory of Kuuk Thaayorre ignoratives along with their closest English equivalent and associated ontological category. As we shall see, the Kuuk Thaayorre ignoratives span a number of functions that are served by different word classes in English (e.g. interrogatives, indefinite pronouns, free choice pronouns, etc.). I have elected to use the English interrogative forms as glosses for ignoratives throughout this grammar.

---

[102] Alternatives to the term 'ontological category' (which is used here following Jackendoff 1983: 51 and Haspelmath 1997) include 'epistemological category' (Durie 1985), 'knowledge category' (Mushin 1995) and 'epistemological domain' (Evans 2000).

Table 43. Inventory of ignoratives.

Ignorative	Translation	Ontological category
wanh	'who'	PERSON
ngan	'what'	THING
ngene	'why'	REASON
wanthan	'where to'	PLACE (w.r.t. a trajectory)
wanthanngun	'where at'	PLACE (w.r.t. a location)
wanthantharr	'how'	NATURE
ngannganr	'how much'	QUANTITY
wanhwanhrr	'how many (people)'	QUANTITY (HUMAN)
raak ngan	'when'	TIME

Section 5.2.1 is concerned with the morphological structure of ignoratives. Section 5.2.2 catalogues the semantic categories encoded by the Kuuk Thaayorre ignoratives, while §5.2.3 examines their functional ranges. The syntactic behaviour (and associated morphological modification) of ignoratives is considered in 5.2.4.

5.2.1 Morphological structure of ignoratives

The class of ignoratives can be subdivided into simple and complex expressions. The morphologically simple ignoratives are: *ngan* 'what'; *wanh* 'who'; *wanthan* 'where$_{TRJ}$'; and *ngene* 'why'. Complex ignoratives are the historical result of three processes. Firstly, two ignoratives have been derived through suffixation to the simple PLACE$_{TRJ}$ ignorative *wanthan* 'where$_{TRJ}$'; *wanthantharr* 'how'[103] and *wanthanngun* 'where$_{LOC}$'. The ignorative *wanthanngun* 'where$_{LOC}$' takes the form that would be expected if *wanthan* 'where$_{TRJ}$' were inflected for dative case. If *wanthanngun* 'where$_{LOC}$' were synchronically dative-marked, it should be associated with the endpoint of a trajectory, as is the dative-marked demonstrative pronoun in (263):

(263) *Friday, koop therk inh'nhungun Pormpuraaw-thak*
Friday all(NOM) return:NPST this.very.one:DAT Pormpuraaw-DAT
'on Friday everyone is coming back to Pormpuraaw'
[KTh_AC21Aug2002 Conversation]

Instead, it is the form *wanthan* 'where$_{TRJ}$' that encodes the endpoint of a trajectory, while the derived form *wanthanngun* 'where$_{LOC}$' refers only to static locations. For this reason, I analyze *wanthanngun* 'where$_{LOC}$' as synchronically monomorphemic. (The

---

103 This frozen *-tharr* suffix may be related to the suffix discussed in §4.4.1, thought the semantic link between these uses is not obvious.

form *wanthan* 'where$_{TRAJ}$' may itself represent lexical absorption of the dative case marker *-(a)n*. If this is true, this process of absorption must have been completed some time ago, given that the putative root form **wanth* is synchronically meaningless. Furthermore, dative case marking is never used elsewhere to mark a source or starting point, which means the lexicalized form *wanthan* 'where$_{TRJ}$' must have had time to expand its semantic range to include points of origin (as discussed in §5.2.2).

The two ignoratives corresponding to ontological categories of QUANTITY are formed through the reduplication of the corresponding simple ignorative followed by suffixation of a rhotic segment (*-r* or *-rr*); *ngannganr* 'how much' < *ngan* 'what', *wanhwanhrr* 'how many (people)' < *wanh* 'who'. The association between reduplication and plural number or distributivity is well attested cross-linguistically (e.g. Haiman 1983), but note that the same morphological process is used to derive emphatic pronouns from their corresponding personal pronouns (§3.1.2.5).

Raak ngan 'when' is a semantically transparent binomial expression, composed of the polysemous generic noun *raak* 'TIME' (also 'PLACE', 'GROUND', etc.) and the ignorative *ngan* 'what'. This collocation may be discontinuous (511), so is clearly not a compound:

(264) raak   nhul   ngan yaan=a   yarra   theerk?
       PLACE 3sg(NOM)   what go:RDP:NPST=PRAG away   return:NPST
       'what on earth time will he be going back there?'
       [Hall 1972: 139]

While contiguity is not required, the relative order of these two elements appears to be fixed. Where their order is permuted the meaning of the expression changes entirely to 'somewhere' (based on the PLACE rather than TIME meaning of *raak*), as in (265):

(265) ngul ngan raak ii-rr-kaw   ngancn   ranc-m
       then what PLACE there-towards-east   1pl:excl(NOM)   jump-P.IPFV
       'then we used to fly to somewhere in the east'
       [KTh_AJ-IC-**GJ**26Nov2002 Narrative/Conversation]

In such examples as (265), the simple ignorative *ngan* 'what' functions as an epistemic determiner modifying *raak* 'PLACE'.

Contrary to Mushin's (1995: 5) finding that the REASON category ignorative "seems to be always formed using case-marking in Australian languages", the Kuuk Thaayorre REASON ignorative *ngene* 'why' is one of only four indubitably simple ignoratives.

As discussed in §5.2.4, ignoratives with pronominal function inflect for relational case, reflecting their role in the clause.

5.2.2 Ignorative categories

Ngan 'what' is the most semantically general ignorative, and may be used to refer to any entity that falls outside the ambit of the other ignoratives. At its core, though, *ngan* 'what' refers to non-human objects and entities (266).

(266) *ant   inh   ngan?*
　　　ant(NOM) dem:sp.prx what
　　　'what [sort of] ant is this?'
　　　[KTh_EF14Dec2002 Elicitation Demonstratives3]

The category PERSON (encoded by the ignorative *wanh* 'who') includes only humans and indices[104] thereof (e.g. their names, as in (268)).

(267) *paanth   ith   wanh=okun   yan?*
　　　woman(NOM) dem:dist who=DUB   go:NPST
　　　"which is that lady there coming?"
　　　[AC21Aug2002 Conversation]

(268) *nhamp   wanh, pam nhangkn?*
　　　name(NOM) who   man 2sgGEN
　　　"what's your husband's name?"
　　　[AC21Aug2002 Conversation]

Personal names fall within the scope of *wanh* because of their function of identifying human referents, not because they are inalienable possessions. Other inalienable possessions (such as age, or body parts), and the names of non-humans are referred to using *ngan* 'what':

(269) *nhunt   age ngan?*
　　　2sg(NOM) age what
　　　'how old are you?'
　　　[KTh_EN01Oct2002 Conversation]

---

104 The term *index* is used here to refer to those things associated with people not through ownership, but through their function of 'standing for' those people, following Peirce's (1998 [1909]: 460) characterization of "Indices, which represent their objects independently of any resemblance to them, only by virtue of real connections with them". Thus a name may be used to represent a person despite its bearing no actual resemblance to that person.

(270) raak   ith   ii-kaw   ngan nhamp   wan-r?
     PLACE(ACC) dem:dist there-at:east what name(ACC) tell-NPST
     'what's the name of that place?'
     [KTh_EN02Oct2002 Conversation]

The ontological category of PLACE is subcategorized into the ignoratives *wanthanngun* 'where$_{LOC}$' (PLACE$_{LOC}$), used in reference to static locations, and *wanthan* 'where$_{TRJ}$'(PLACE$_{TRJ}$), used in reference to points on a dynamic trajectory. The PLACE$_{LOC}$ ignorative *wanthanngun* is thus used to identify a stable location defined without reference to a trajectory. This may either be due to the complete absence of trajectory (271), or because the (prior) trajectory is unimportant, as in (272) where the focus is on the eventual resting place of the figure, not the trajectory by which it arrives there:

(271) raak.pungk nhangkn   wanthanngun?
     homeland   2sg:GEN(NOM) where$_{LOC}$
     'where is your land?'
     [KTh_EN08Sep2002 Elicitation]

(272) inh   ngay   wanthanngun thak-r?
     dem:sp.prx 1sg(ERG) where$_{LOC}$ leave-NPST
     'where am I going to leave this?'
     [KTh_EN08Sep2002 Elicitation]

Wanthanngun 'where$_{LOC}$' is thus typically associated with a figure that does not move from the location in question (as in 272), but this is not always the case. The figure may come and go from a PLACE$_{LOC}$ (273) as long as it maintains a stable and ongoing relationship with this PLACE$_{LOC}$ which is not defined with respect to the trajectory.

(273) nhunt   wanthanngun   wun-m?
     2sg(NOM) where$_{LOC}$ reside-P.IPFV
     'where [in which house] were you living?'
     [KTh_GJ16Oct2002 Narrative MelbourneTrip]

The PLACE$_{TRJ}$ ignorative, *wanthan* 'where$_{TRJ}$' is used in the description of moving figures, typically with reference to the endpoint of their trajectory:

(274) nhul   wanthan=okun   yat
     3sg(NOM) where$_{TRJ}$=DUB   go:P.PFV
     "he must have gone somewhere"
     [Anon.]

It is with this reference to the endpoint of the trajectory that *wanthan* 'where$_{TRJ}$' combines with the directional particle *pal* 'towards' (§9.2.1.1), creating the collocation *wanthan pal* 'towards where' seen in (275):

(275) kapr ith wanthan pal yan
   moon(NOM) dem:dist where$_{TRJ}$ towards go:NPST
   'which way is the moon going?'
   [KTh_AC13Sep2002 Conversation]

Wanthan 'where$_{TRJ}$' also combines with *nheman* 'from there' to refer to a source (startpoint of a trajectory), as in (276):

(276) kormun inh wanthan nheman yan
   cloud(NOM) dem:sp.prx where$_{TRJ}$ from.there go:NPST
   "where this rain and this cold coming from?"
   [KTh_MF20Aug2002 Conversation]

It is possible, however, for *wanthan* 'where$_{TRJ}$' to refer to a trajectory's starting point without the explicit use of *nheman* 'from there'. In example (277), *wanthan* is used to question the place that is simultaneously the static location of the direct object *Daniel* and the origin point of the addressee/subject's trajectory. We may presume that if the referent of *wanthan* were solely a static location (instead of additionally defining the bounds of a trajectory), the locational ignorative *wanthanngun* 'where$_{LOC}$' would have been used in its place.

(277) nhunt Daniel wanthan thaka-rr?
   2sg(ERG) Daniel(ACC) where$_{TRJ}$ leave-P.PFV
   'where did you leave Daniel?'
   [KTh_AJ29Jan2004 Conversation]

In addition to referring to the poles of a trajectory, *wanthan* 'where$_{TRJ}$' may also be used to make reference to the path of the trajectory itself, as in (278):

(278) road wanthan?
   road where$_{TRJ}$
   'which road (are you taking)?'
   [Anon.]

It is worth noting how the locational semantic categories encoded by ignoratives contrast with those encoded in the case system (§4.2). While ignoratives group together goals and sources (*wanthan* PLACE$_{TRJ}$), as distinct from static locations (*wanthanngun* PLACE$_{LOC}$), it is goals and static locations that are collapsed into a single case category ('dative', §4.2.5), which is in turn differentiated from sources ('ablative', §4.2.6). In the system of directional terms (§11.4.2.3), each of these categories is differentiated from the others, with distinct terms for: (a) movement from a direction; (b) movement towards a direction; (c) static location at a direction; and (d) movement at a location (in addition to a number of further distinctions based on proximity, direction, etc.).

Just as human names may be enquired after by means of the PERSON ignorative *wanh* 'who', so too may place names be questioned by means of the place ignorative *wanthanngun* 'where$_{LOC}$', as in the following example:

(279)   *pormpr   ith   ii-kaw   wanthanngun?*
         home(NOM) dem:dist there-at:east   where$_{LOC}$
         'what's that place [called]?' or 'I can't think of the name of that place'
         [KTh_EN02Oct2002 Conversation]

The speaker is here talking about preparations for a disco to be held that evening in the women's centre, *Pormpur Paanth*, but is temporarily unable to remember its name. Its location, however, is well known to both speaker and hearer. The use of *wanthanngun* here may reflect a cultural expectation that equates knowing the name of a place with knowing its location. (A place name may alternatively be questioned by means of the THING ignorative *ngan* 'what', however, as in (270) above.)

Ngene 'why' typically refers to something desired/sought (280) or the purpose or goal of an activity (281):

(280)   *ngene?*
         why
         'what/who do you want?'
         [commonly called out from a house when a car pulls up outside]

(281)   *nhul   ngene pal   riic-r?*
         3sg(NOM)   why   towards   run-NPST
         'why/where's he running to?'
         [KTh_EN02Oct2002 Conversation]

Examples like (281) above reveal a semantic overlap between *ngene* 'why' and *wanthan* 'where$_{TRJ}$', linking the endpoint of a trajectory to its purpose. This can be attributed to the fact that the purpose of a journey can often be equated with reaching the endpoint of its trajectory (cf. the ambiguous English word *goal*). According to language experts (and substantial impressionistic evidence), *wanthan* PLACE$_{TRJ}$ and *ngene* REASON are interchangeable in contexts such as (281).

The semantic range of the English term *why* is in most Australian languages subdivided into the categories REASON (ie 'for what purpose') and CAUSE (i.e. 'due to what cause') (Dixon 1980). In Kuuk Thaayorre, however, these two categories appear collapsed, with both REASONS and CAUSES encoded by *ngene*. It is possible to disambiguate the CAUSE use of *ngene* 'why' by the optional suffixation of the ablative morpheme, however, as seen in (282).

(282) *kiin   ulp   ngene(-m)*
      tooth(NOM) dem:ad.prx   why(-ABL)
      'why is your tooth (broken)?'
      [KTh_EF14Dec2002 Eliciation Demonstratives2]

Finally, *ngene* 'why' also has the sense 'by what means' when inflected for ergative(=instrumental) case, as in (283).

(283) *yak   ith   ngene-rr   thernga-rr?*
      snake(ACC) dem:dist   why-ERG   kill-P.PFV
      'what did they kill that snake with?'
      [KTh_AJ27Jan2004 Elicitation]

This interpretation arises naturally from the interaction between ignorative and case semantics, and *ngenerr* 'by what means' is therefore not considered a complex ignorative form corresponding to its own ontological category. The ablative-marked form *ngenem* 'from what cause' is likewise considered compositional rather than a complex ignorative.

The QUANTITY ignorative, *ngannganr* 'how much', is concerned with the number or proportion of a referent group:

(284) *nhunt   ngannganr   pit-r?*
      2sg(ERG)   how.much   hold-NPST
      'how many [cigarettes] have you got?'
      [KTh_EN15Dec2002 Elicitation]

Although it is grammatical for *ngannganr* 'how much' to be used with reference to a group of humans, it is possible to explicitly refer to a human quantity by the alternative use of *wanhwanhrr* 'how many (people)' (see example (313) below).

The TIME category (expressed by the collocation *raak ngan*, literally 'TIME what') includes any period or point in time (285).

(285) *Dan   raak   ngan   pal   therk-nhan?*
      Dan(NOM)   TIME   what   towards   return-GO&:NPST
      'when / what time will Dan come back?'
      [KTh_AJ27Jan2004 Conversation]

The final ignorative lexicalized in Kuuk Thaayorre is *wanthantharr* 'how', illustrated by the following:

(286) nhunt   wanthantharr theerng-nhan?
      2sg(ERG)   how   kill-GO&:NPST
      'how are you going to kill [that fish]?'
      [GJ10Jan2004 Elicitation]

This ignorative corresponds most closely to Mushin's MANNER category, though its functional range is significantly wider than that of the English MANNER interrogative *how*, used here as its gloss. For example, in (142.1) the speaker uses *wanthantharr* in reference to the content of the man's speech, as well as the manner in which he spoke:

(287) 1. pam   nhul   wanthantharr=okun yik-r   paanth-un ith
         man(NOM)   3sg(NOM)   how=DUB   say-P.PFV woman-DAT dem:dist
         'the man said something to that woman'
      2. ngul paanth   nhul   thaangka-r
         then woman(NOM)   3sg(NOM)   smile-NPST
         'and the woman smiled'
         [KTh_FT10Feb2004 RCPpilot16]

Wanthantharr 'how' is also frequently employed to question a general state of affairs, either in the past (288), present (289) or the immediate future (290):

(288) inh'nh   wanthantharr inhul?
      dem:sp.prx   how   this.one
      'what just happened (in the movie)?'
      [KTh_GJ12Sep2002 Elicitation]

(289) Mami ngathn   ii   wanthantharr, home-ak
      mum   1sgGEN(NOM)   there   how   home-DAT
      'my mum's present state of affairs there is that she's living in a home'
      [KTh_AJ27Jan2004 Conversation]

(290) wanthantharr?
      how
      'what now?' [i.e. what shall we do]
      [KTh_AJ27Jan2004 Conversation]

As well as encoding the ontological category of MANNER, *wanthantharr* 'how' also appears to encode the category QUALITY (i.e. 'what sort of'). In clauses like (291), for instance, the speaker employs *wanthantharr* to ask what kind of house the addressee lives in, while in (292) the speaker asks the addressee what kind of tea she would like to drink:

(291) *pormpr nhangkn wanthantharr?*
house 2sgGEN(NOM) how
'what is your house like?'[105]
[KTh_GJ12Jan2004 Elicitation]

(292) *may tea nhunt wanthantharr mungk-r? milk-ak=okun or ngotn?*
VEG tea(ACC) 2sg(ERG) how eat-NPST milk-DAT=DUB or black
'how do you have your tea? With milk or black?'
[KTh_MF20Aug2002 Conversation]

Thus the categories MANNER and QUALITY can be understood as components of a single ontological category (tentatively labelled NATURE), where the MANNER subcategory refers to the nature of an event, and the QUALITY subcategory refers to the nature of an entity.

Finally, it is worth noting that although Standard Australian English possesses no exact equivalent to Kuuk Thaayorre *wanthantharr* 'how', the latter is extremely close in functional range to Pormpuraaw English *which way* (also found in most other Aboriginal English varieties).

5.2.3 Functions of ignoratives

5.2.3.1 Interrogative

The interrogative function is arguably the most basic of the ignorative functions. Here, the speaker requests information of a particular category (e.g. PLACE$_{TRJ}$ in 293) from the hearer:

(293) *nhunt wanthan pal yan?*
2sg(NOM) where$_{TRJ}$ towards go:NPST
'where are you going?'
[common greeting]

Questions in which the interlocutor is asked to pick out a member of a restricted set (translated using English *which*), are are formed by using *ngan* 'what' as modifier within a noun phrase headed by the noun denoting the (restricted) set:

---

[105] I elicited the Thaayorre sentence presented in this example by asking GJ how he would ask somebody *tell me about your house.*

(294) *kapr   ngan?*
      moon what
      'which month?'
      [KTh_ECh12Oct2002 Elicitation]

(295) *road wanthan?*
      road where$_{TRJ}$
      'which road (are you taking)?'
      [Anon.]

(296) *parr-an   ii   plate ngan   thiika-rr?*
      child-ERG   there place what(ACC)   break-P.PFV
      'which plate did the child break?'
      "what he broke plate or something? ... might be blue colour or red colour..."
      [KTh_GJ12Jan2004 Elicitation]

The ignorative *ngan* 'what', which at its core invokes ignorance in the ontological category of THING, may also be used to create a more general interrogative mood (297).

(297) *nhip   ngan truck-ak   therk-nhan?*
      2du(NOM)   what truck-DAT return-GO&:NPST
      'will you two come back by truck or what?'
      [KTh_AJ27Jan2004 Conversation]

Such examples, along with the imprecision usage of *ngan* 'what' described below, reveal it to be the most semantically general of the ignoratives.

5.2.3.2 Indefinite pronoun

The indefinite pronoun asserts the existence of some referent belonging to the relevant category. Thus in (298) the PERSON ignorative *wanhul* 'who:ERG' indicates that 'there exists some PERSON for whom it is true [that they ate it]', while in (299) the ignorative *wanthanngun* indicates 'there exists some PLACE$_{LOC}$ (in the south) for which it is true [that this thing is located there]'.

(298) *wanhul=okun   mungka-rr*
      who:ERG=DUB   eat-P.PFV
      'somebody must have eaten it'
      [KTh_GJ14Oct2002 Elicitation]

(299) *ii-parr,   somewhere raak   kuuw wanthanngun=okun*
      there-at:south   somewhere PLACE west where$_{LOC}$=DUB
      '[it's] somewhere there in the south, in the west somewhere'
      [KTh_**AJ**-GJ03Feb2004 Conversation]

In all cases where an ignorative has an indefinite function, it combines with the dubitative enclitic *=okun*. There is, therefore, never any ambiguity between the interrogative and indefinite functions. As Haspelmath (1997: 21–28) has documented, it is crosslinguistically common for indefinite pronouns to be produced through the combination of ignorative/interrogative forms with suffixes and other morphemes expressing dubitative-type semantics.

5.2.3.3 Free choice pronoun

Whereas the indefinite function involves existential quantification, the free choice pronoun use (following Vendler's 1967 terminology) approximates universal quantification (i.e. 'for any entity in this category the following is true').[106] Thus in (300) the ignorative *wanthan* indicates that 'for any PLACE$_{TRJ}$ (he leads me to), it is true [that I will follow him]').

(300) wanthan=okun yith-nh nganh, ngay ak waak-r nhunh
       where$_{TRJ}$=DUB lead-SBJV 1sgACC 1sg(ERG) OPT follow-NPST 3sgACC
       'anywhere he leads me I will follow on'
       [hymn book, origin unknown]

As with the indefinite usage, the dubitative enclitic *=okun* attaches to all ignoratives functioning as free choice pronouns.

5.2.3.4 Relative pronoun: *ngan* 'which'

Ignoratives may also function anaphorically, either to link an argument of the main clause with one in a subordinate clause (301),[107] or to connect referents across clauses (302, 303). In each of these examples, square brackets ('[...]') are used to represent boundaries between main clauses and curly brackets ('{...}') to represent the boundaries of a subordinate clause (cf. §11 for further discussion of the structure of subordinate and coordinated clauses).

(301) [yuk wele ith ii-kuw {ngan wun rump-un}]
       [THING bailer.shell(NOM) dem:dist there-at:west {what lie:INF beach-DAT}]
       'that bailer shell in the west which lies on the beach'
       [KTh_AJ-IC-GJ26Nov2002 Narrative/Conversation]

---

106 Though see Haspelmath's (1997: 48) and Vendler's (1967: 77) discussions of the truth-conditional differences between free choice indefinites and the universal quantifier.
107 I label this function of *ngan* 'what' as that of a 'relative pronoun' in the interests of cross-linguistic comparison. It should be noted, however, that (301) is the only example in which it appears in a relative clause per se. *Ngan* 'what' is more frequently found with this function in series of conjoined or independent clauses (303).

(302) [raak ith Wayenan]. [Ngan wan-r ii]
 [PLACE dem:dist Wayenan] [what tell-NPST there]
 'that place is Wayenan, that's what it's called'
 [KTh_**AJ**-IC-GJ26Nov2002 Narrative/Conversation]

(303) [Saltpan, iikaw, raak Yaath]. [Yaath ngan wanr.]
 [Saltpan, there-at-east PLACE Yaath(ACC)] [Yaath(ACC) what tell-NPST]
 '[on] the Saltpan out east, at Yaath. Yaath is what it's called'
 [KTh_AJ3Feb2004 Conversation]

The relative pronouns of Australian languages tend not to be sensitive to the semantic categories of their referent, so it is not surprising that only *ngan* 'what' is attested with relative pronoun function (as well as the rhetorical emphasis and imprecision functions described below). Attempts to elicit relative pronouns referring to humans were unsuccessful.

5.2.3.5 Rhetorical emphasis: *ngan* 'what'

N*gan* 'what' may also be used as a rhetorical device with emphatic effect. Thus in (304) it is used to tease the addressee by emphasizing the fatness of her cheeks, while in (305) it is used to complain about the noise created by construction workers nearby.

(304) inh'nh ngan thaa.put rika!
 dem:sp.prx what cheek fat
 'what fat cheeks you have!'
 [KTh_EN14Aug2002 Conversation/Elicitation]

(305) inh ngan gate peln thak-nhan-r
 dem:sp.prx what gate(ACC) 3pl(ERG) leave-v^-NPST
 "what are these people putting up the gates!"
 [KTh_ME02Oct2002 Conversation]

5.2.3.6 Imprecision: *ngan* 'what'

The THING ignorative *ngan* may also be used to mark imprecision in the speaker's choice of words. In (306), for example, the speaker wishes to mark his identification of the vessel (whether dinghy or canoe) as uncertain or inexact.

(306) ngul ngancn iirra dinghy-ak yat, ngan canoe-ak
 then 1pl:excl(NOM) to.there dinghy-DAT go:P.PFV what canoe-DAT
 'then we went off in a dinghy, or canoe or whatever'
 [KTh_AJ-IC-**GJ**26Nov2002 Narrative/Conversation]

The imprecision use of *ngan* is often found in combination with the filler use of demonstrative pronouns *inhul* 'this one' and *yuunhul* 'that one', reinforcing the fact the speaker is experiencing difficulty in retrieving the desired lexeme, as in (307):

(307) yuunhul   ith   ngan kar   pam.nhump ulp   pam.koyethnith
      that.one   dem:dist   what like old.man   dem:ad.prx great.grandfather
      ngathn
      1sgGEN
      "that thing like that old man or whatever, my Great Great grandfather"
      [KTh_AJ-**IC**-GJ26Nov2002 Narrative/Conversation]

Directly related to the generalized ignorative function of expressing a lack of knowledge, in examples like (306) and (305), the speaker temporarily lacks access to the label of the ignorative's referent, rather than lacking knowledge as to its identity.

5.2.3.7 Apprehensive counterfactual *ngene* 'why'

Ngene 'why' has a specialized usage I am labelling 'apprehensive counterfactual'. *Ngene* in these clauses expresses that something undesirable might have happened (or might happen in the future) but that it was (or should be) avoided. It is thus typically employed in the description of a lucky escape (308).

(308) ngay   nearly   punth   inh   ngene lose-m   rirk-nhan
      1sg(ERG) nearly   arm(ACC)   dem:sp.prx   why   lose-TR   DO-GO&:NPST
      "nearly lost my arm!"
      [KTh_AJ-**GJ**03Feb2004 Narrative DarwinTrip]

The apprehensive counterfactual interpretation is the product of the combination of the ignorative *ngene* 'why' with either an associated motion or counterfactual-marked verb. These apprehensive counterfactual constructions are discussed in more detail in §10.4.2.

5.2.3.8 Negative indefinite pronouns – not attested

While it is cross-linguistically common for ignoratives to function as negative indefinite pronouns (translating as, e.g., 'no one', 'nothing', or 'nowhere', cf. Haspelmath 1997 and Evans 2003b), in Kuuk Thaayorre the constituent negator *pokon* 'NO' performs this function (§11.3.3).

5.2.4 Ignorative morphosyntax

Ignoratives may function pronominally (309), adnominally (310) and quasi-adverbially (inasmuch as they modify the clause as a whole, (311)).

(309) *wanhul   church   inh   yump-m?*
       who:ERG church(ACC) dem:sp.prx   make-P.IPFV
       'who built that church?'
       [KTh_EN06Sep2002 Elicitation]

(310) *pam wanhngun kot   mit   pork   yik-m?*
       man who:DAT   God(NOM) work   big(ACC) say-P.IPFV
       'to what man did God speak of this huge task?'
       [Hall 1972: 114]

(311) *ngay   ngene=p   yithi-rr   pal?*
       1sg(ERG) why=PRAG lead-P.PFV   towards
       'why did I bring [her] here?'
       [KTh_AC14Nov2002 Narrative LosingIrma]

Where an ignorative functions adnominally, there is a strong tendency for it to directly follow the NP head. There is significant variation, however, in the case marking of both NP and ignorative. There are four logical possibilities here, all of which are attested in my data. Firstly, case may be marked on the NP head and not the following ignorative (312). Secondly, case may be marked on the ignorative but not the preceding NP head (313).[108] Thirdly, both the ignorative and NP head may be marked for case (314). Finally, it is possible for neither ignorative nor NP head to be marked for a grammatical function that would normally require signalling via case (314).

(312) *parr_r paanth-u   ngannganr wuuc   mi'im   peln?*
       child   woman-ERG   how.much   song(ACC) pick.up:P.IPFV   3pl(ERG)
       'how many of the girls were singing corroborees?'
       [Hall 1972: 114]

(313) *yuk   ngene-rr thernga-rr?*
       THING why-ERG kill-P.PFV
       'with what sort of stick did they kill him?'
       [KTh_GJ10Jan2004 Elicitation]

---

108 Remember in interpreting (313) that *ngene* 'why' corresponds to the category MEANS as well as REASON.

(314) paanth-u   wanhwanhrrul   yak   ii   theernga-rr=unh?
      woman-ERG   how.many.people:ERG   snake(ACC)   there   kill-P.PFV=3sg(ACC)
      'how many woman killed the snake?'
      [KTh_AJ27Jan2004 Elicitation]

(315) pormpr wanthan   nheman   nhul   ripi-rr?
      house   where_TRJ   from.there   3sg(NOM)   exit-P.PFV
      'which house did he come out of?'
      [KTh_EN27Jan2004 Elicitaion]

This last absence of overt case marking is always found with the three ignoratives beginning with *wanthan* (i.e. *wanthan* 'where_TRJ', *wanthanngun* 'where_LOC' and *wanthantharr* 'how'), none of which permit case inflection. Where ablative case marking of *wanthan* 'where_TRJ' may be semantically desirable, the same effect is achieved by combining this ignorative with the adverb *nheman* 'from there', as in (315).

This variation in the locus of case marking may be symptomatic of a deeper ambivalence with respect to the degree of syntactic integration of the ignorative within the noun phrase (Chapter 6).

Ignoratives functioning pronominally may also bear case, as seen in the ablative marking of *raak ngan* 'when' in (316) and the dative marking of *ngan* 'what' in (317).

(316) church   inh   raak ngan-tam   than-m?
      church(NOM)   dem:sp.prx   TIME what-ABL   stand-P.IPFV
      'how long has the church been here?'
      (lit. 'from what time has the church been standing?')
      [KTh_EN6Sep2002 Elicitation]

(317) "ngan-ak yan   ngancn?"   ngancn   ask-m   rirk-r
      what-DAT go:NPST   1sg:excl(NOM)   1sg:excl(ERG)   ask-TR   DO-P.PFV
      '"in what [kind of vehicle] will we go?", we asked'
      [KTh_GJ16Oct2002 Narrative MelbourneTrip]

Besides the variation in the presence or absence of case marking, there is also variation in the form this case marking takes. In particular, the case marking of *wanh* 'who' reinforces its status as intermediate between pronouns and (modifying) nomina. Like a nomen, the unmarked form *wanh* is used with the grammatical functions of both intransitive subject and direct object. Its ergative form, *wanhul* (seen in (308)), however, resembles the unmarked nominative/ergative third person singular pronoun, *nhul* 's/he' (perhaps pointing to a diachronic origin in the compounding of *wanh+nhul*). There are, moreover, three dative forms of *wanh* 'who' in my data. The first of these (*wanhngun*, seen in (309) above) resembles the dative inflection of personal pronouns (e.g. *ngampulngun* 'to us [plural, excl.]', *ngalngun* 'to us two [incl.]').

The second (*wanhulak*, (318)) is composed of the nomen dative suffix *-ak* attached to the ergative ignorative form, *wanhul*. Third variant (*wanhulngun*, (319)) combines both the pronominal-type and nomen-type inflections.

(318) ngul   nhul   iirra   yat,   inhul   wanhulak
      then   3sg(NOM)   to.there   go:P.PFV   this.one   who:DAT
      'then she went off, to that whatsit [other man]'
      [KTh_ACh07Nov2002 Conversation]

(319) ngat   ulp   wanhulngun   wan?
      fish(ACC)   dem:ad.prx   who:DAT   give:NPST
      'who are you giving that fish to?'
      [KTh_GJ10Jan2004 Elicitation]

The fact that two of the dative variants are built upon the (present day) ergative form *wanhul*, may suggest that *wanhul* was originally an unmarked pronominal form of the ignorative (cf. *nhul* 's/he'), and not necessarily associated with ergativity. However, its current usage points to its being – synchronically at least – ergative-marked.

While Mushin (1995: 22) asserts: "in other languages, and not just in Australian languages, there is a strong tendency for [ignoratives – AG] to occur clause-initially", the reverse is true of Kuuk Thaayorre. Although the ignoratives have no fixed position in the clause, it is extremely rare for an ignorative to appear clause-initially. Instead, they tend to precede the (usually clause-final) predicate (320), as is widespread among verb-final languages, or to occur as a clause-final complement in a verbless clause (321).

(320) paanth   ith   wanh=okun   yan?
      woman(NOM)   dem:dist   who=DUB   go:NPST
      "which is that lady there coming?"
      [KTh_AC21Aug2002 Conversation]

(321) nhunt   nhamp   wanh?
      2sg(NOM)   name(NOM)   who
      'what's your name?'
      [Anon.]

5.3 Demonstratives

At the core of the Kuuk Thaayorre demonstrative system are two pronominal demonstratives (322) and three adnominal demonstratives (323):

(322)   *inhul* 'this one'; *yuunhul* 'that one'

(323)   *ith* 'that (distal)'; *inh* 'this (speaker-proximate)'; *ulp* 'the (addressee-proximate)'

These indexical forms prototypically locate entities along a distance scale (cf. Himmelmann 1996: 210). Their wide range of functions involves indexing entities and other referents[109] according to: situational information (e.g. distance from speaker or addressee), activation status (e.g. new referents or those that are deactivated, in focus, common knowledge, etc.), or discourse function (e.g. identificational, contrastive, anaphoric, etc.). Because these functions are shared by pronominal and adnominal demonstratives, section 5.3.3's discussion of demonstrative functions considers pronominal and adnominal demonstratives together. Furthermore, although the formal and diachronic evidence suggests the split between the two subclasses is founded in the distinction between pronominal and adnominal functions, it is synchronically commonplace for the demonstrative pronouns to function adnominally and – to a lesser extent – the adnominal demonstratives to function pronominally (i.e. indexing non-elliptically).

Kuuk Thaayorre offers no evidence against Himmelmann's (1996: 206) observation that "in some languages, the pronominal forms are morphologically more complex than the adnominal ones and are clearly derived from the latter. The opposite, however, does not seem to occur". Certainly the Kuuk Thaayorre demonstrative pronouns are longer in form than the adnominal demonstratives and permit more complex and more widespread inflection. We may further speculate that the demonstrative pronoun *inh'nhul* 'this very one' was historically produced through the compounding and grammaticalization of the speaker-proximal adnominal demonstrative *inh* and the third person singular personal pronoun *nhul*. Although my corpus does not contain an obvious bridging context in which the juxtaposition of these latter two forms might have been reanalyzed as a single demonstrative pronoun – possibly due to the very existence of the proximal demonstrative pronoun – there are many instances of the distal adnominal demonstrative being immediately followed by a coreferential third person singular pronoun (324). It is easy to imagine how a new demonstrative pronoun could emerge in such contexts.

---

109 Hanks (2005) provides excellent justification for preferring the label 'demonstratum' to 'referent' for the entity indexed by a demonstrative form.

(324) *pam-al   ith   nhul   may carrot   knife-nthurr*
man-ERG dem:dist 3sg(ERG) VEG carrot(ACC) knife-ERG
thongkthongkn yakake-rr
pieces   cut:RDP-P.PFV
'the man cut the carrot into pieces with a knife'
[KTh_EN3Dec2002 Elicitation Cut&Break10]

Given the formal, semantic and functional overlap between adnominal and demonstrative pronouns, we might ask what contexts and communicative requirements differentiate them. This question is surprisingly difficult to answer, and there are indeed numerous clauses in which both adnominal and pronominal demonstratives co-index a single referent (as in (325), which additionally contains a coreferential personal pronoun).

(325) *ngul nhul   inh'nhul   ulp   kookope*
then 3sg(NOM) this.very.one dem:ad.prx wait:RDP:NPST
'this one [dog] here's waiting [for me]'
"he waitin for me"
[ECh2Oct2002 Conversation]

One obvious difference between adnominal and pronominal demonstratives is the fact that the latter are used in contrastive contexts. Thus in (326.1) the adnominal demonstrative is used initially to introduce the first referent (pandanus palm), while the pronominal demonstrative is used in (326.2) in order to contrast it with the processed pandanus fibre.

(326) 1. *inh   korngkon   wan-r   inhul*
dem:sp.prx cabbage.palm tell-NPST this.one
'this is called a *korngkon*, this one'
2. *inhul   ngancn   wan-r   yencr*
this.one 1pl:excl(NOM) tell-NPST raffia
'this one we call *yencr*'
[KTh_ME04Jun2005 Conversation / Narrative Yencr]

The discussion of demonstrative functions in §5.3.3 is preceded by a summary of the morphology, syntax and semantics of demonstrative pronouns (§5.3.1) and adnominal demonstratives (§5.3.2) respectively. Further to these forms, the particle *yarriy* 'thus' and many of the deictic spatial adverbs discussed in §3.3.1.1 and §9.2.1.2 correspond to what Dixon (2010: 221–61; 2003) labels manner demonstratives and local adverbial demonstratives respectively.

5.3.1 Demonstrative pronouns

5.3.1.1 Morphology of demonstrative pronouns

The indexical subclass of demonstrative pronouns is primarily divided into proximal and distal forms, for each of which there is an unmarked, a dative and an ablative form. The proximal forms have additional emphatic variants, as seen in Table 44.

Table 44. Core demonstrative pronouns.

	Unmarked	Dative	Ablative
proximal emphatic	*inh'nhul* 'this very one'	*inh'nhungun* 'to this very one'	*inh'nheman* 'from this very one'
proximal	*inhul* 'this one'	*inhungun* 'to this one'	*inheman* 'from this one'
distal	*yuunhul* 'that one'	*yuunhungun* 'to that one'	*yuunheman* 'from that one'

Note that the distinction between emphatic and simple proximal forms is a working hypothesis only. Alternatively, we might posit a single proximal series, with glottal stop seen in the so-called 'emphatic' forms being deleted in fast (or non-emphatic) speech. Thus the association with emphatic contexts may prove epiphenomenal; an articulatory process correlated with pragmatic contexts, rather than an emic distinction per se. This analysis is supported by the fact that only the proximal emphatic forms appear in Foote and Hall (1992) and Hall (1972). On the other hand, language experts repeating sentences slowly and carefully for the purpose of transcription do not generally insert a glottal stop into forms like *inhul* 'this one' or *inheman* 'from this one'. Moreover, Hall (1992) and Foote and Hall (1992) transcribe all instances of the adnominal demonstrative *inh* 'this' as *inh'nh* (rendered as *in'n* and *ih'h* in their respective orthographies) and lack any mention of the distal forms (e.g. *yuunhul* 'that one'). This may indicate a subsequent change in the system. The reanalysis of carefully articulated variants as coding emphasis would not be an exceptional kind of change.

The nine forms listed in Table 44 can be further decomposed into an initial morpheme coding distance, followed by a bound demonstrative pronominal root, followed by a suffix coding case. This is presented in Table 45.

Table 45. Putative prefix-root-suffix demonstrative pronominal paradigm.

prefix	root	case inflections
inh'- 'prox.emph'	*-nh-*	*-ul* (nominative, ergative, accusative)
i- 'prox'	*-nh-*	*-ungun* (dative)
yuu- 'dist'	*-nh-*	*-eman* (ablative)

The simple proximal and distal prefixes are transparently related to both the spatial adverbs *ii* 'there', *yuuw* 'far', as well as the prefixes *ii-* 'there' and *yuu-* 'far' found in the directional paradigm (§9.2.1.2) and deictic adverbs (§3.3.1.1). The case inflections *-ungun* '-DAT' and *-eman* '-ABL' likewise resemble the deictic adverbs *angun(p)* 'at/to there' and *nheman(p)* 'from there' respectively, as well as some allomorphs of the dative and ablative nominal case suffixes (§4.2.5 and §4.2.6). While there is no obvious free counterpart to the bound demonstrative pronoun root, *-nh-*, there is a suspicious resemblance between this, the emphatic proximal prefix, and the adnominal demonstrative *inh* 'this'. The attentional prefix *aw-* (which also attaches to adnominal demonstrative forms §3.1.3.2, and deictic adverbs §3.3.1.1) can precede either the proximal or proximal emphatic prefixes for additional rhetorical strength.

In addition to the nine forms presented in Table 44 and Table 45, there is a tenth demonstrative pronoun *inhaka* 'at/to this place', used to index the location of speech. This form – transparently related to the free adverbial form *(nh)aka* 'here' – can be seen in (327).

(327) inhaka   born rirk-r.
       at.this.place born DO-P.PFV
       '[all my children] were born here [in Pormpuraaw]'
       [KTh_ACh07Nov2002 Conversation]

The emphatic variant *inh'nhaka* 'at/to this very place' is also attested in my data.

While the semantic difference between the forms beginning with *i-* and those beginning with *yuu-* has thus far been characterized in terms of 'proximal' versus 'distal', the contrast between the two series is not purely spatial. Thus the referent of *inhul* 'this one' in (328) is significantly further from the locus of the speech event than is the referent of *yuunhul* 'that one (far away)' in (329).[110]

(328) raak   thaapirri **inhul**,   Station Creek
       place nearby   this.one   Station Creek
       'Station Creek, that place is nearby'
       [KTh_AC21Aug2002 Conversation]

(329) pam-al   ii   radio **yuunhul** too.high   yikika-n-r!
       man-ERG there radio that.one   too.high say:RDP-V^-NPST
       'the man over there is playing his radio too loud'
       [KTh_GJ12Jan2004 Elicitation]

What counts as 'proximal' and what 'distal' instead emerges from the interactional, physical, psychological and cultural context constructed by interlocutors in part

---

[110] See also example (621) from the same elicitation session.

through their use of the demonstratives and other indexical elements themselves (cf. Clark et al. 1983, Burenhult 2003, Enfield 2003a Hanks 2005, Cutfield 2012, inter alia). Disentangling the respective contributions of each of these factors to determining demonstrative selection is too complex a task to be achieved here. The following subsections merely outline the key semantic oppositions between demonstratives, their distributions and functions.

5.3.1.2 Syntax of demonstrative pronouns

As their name suggests, demonstrative pronouns may be used to make (non-elliptical) reference to entities (330).

(330) *inhul   ngay   thaangk-m*
      this.one   1sg(NOM)   climb-P.IPFV
      'I used to climb these ones [trees]'
      [KTh_AC04Jun20051 Conversation]

Where demonstrative pronouns are used in combination with a coreferential noun-headed noun phrase, they may either retain their pronominal function or they may function adnominally. In the first case, the pronominal demonstrative and coreferential noun phrase are apposed in the same case. While the demonstrative pronoun is usually placed immediately to the left of the noun-headed NP, and both contribute information about a single entity, the two are syntactically independent at the level of surface structure. This can be seen in (331), in which both the demonstrative pronoun *yuunhulak* 'for that one' and the following noun phrase *paath rucak ulp* 'for that ash' are inflected for dative case.

(331) *kanangkarr ngancn   kaar learnm   rirkr   yuunhul-ak*
      long.ago   1pl(NOM) NEG learn-VBLZ   DO-P.PFV   that.one-DAT
      paath ruc-ak   ulp
      fire   ash-DAT   dem:ad.prx
      'long ago we didn't learn how to do this one with ashes'
      [KTh_ME04Jun2005 Conversation]

Where the demonstrative pronoun functions adnominally, it appears within the noun-headed NP. Moreover, since it is located at the right edge of this NP, it bears the single exponent of the relational (dative) case assigned to the noun phrase as a whole. Hence in (332), the demonstrative pronoun *inhulthurr* 'this one:ERG' takes an ergative case suffix to indicate the instrumental role of the NP *pipe inhulthurr* 'this pipe', indicating that it is the final constituent of the NP. Conversely, the fact that *pipe* is not inflected for case indicates that it is not the final constituent of the NP.

(332) *pipe   inhul-thurr   log.cabin   kar   path-r   kaalkurrc*
pipe this.one-ERG log.cabin(ACC) like bite-NPST cool
'log cabin smokes coolly in this pipe'
[KTh_ME02Oct2002 Conversation]

The place of demonstrative pronouns within the noun phrase is considered further in §6.5.3 and §6.6.

5.3.2 Adnominal demonstratives

5.3.2.1 Adnominal demonstrative categories

Kuuk Thaayorre makes use of three basic adnominal demonstratives; *ith* 'that (distal)', *inh* 'this (speaker-proximate)', and *ulp* 'the (addressee-proximate)'. The semantic oppositions that distinguish these forms cannot be captured in purely spatial terms (i.e. relating demonstratives to one another along a distance scale of relative proximity to the speaker and/or addressee). As Hanks (2005: 197) has pointed out, "under many circumstances, what counts most for proper construal of the referent object is not its location but its accessibility in memory, anticipation, perception, or prior discourse". But neither can Kuuk Thaayorre demonstrative semantics be adequately captured through a purely 'interactionist' characterization.[111] The more accurate, holistic description of Kuuk Thaayorre demonstrative deixis – taking into account the multiple perspectives of interactants, their attention, shared knowledge, memory, prior discourse, physical environment, cultural context and so on – is a complex task demanding both deep qualitative and expansive quantitative study. Accordingly, the following discussion should be taken as a broad overview of some of the relevant factors, a more thoroughgoing analysis being deferred to future research.

To begin with, let us remove discourse and cultural context as far as possible by concentrating upon the situational ('exophoric') use of demonstratives to draw the addressee's attention to an entity. This situational use of demonstratives was systematically investigated through the Wilkins 1999 elicitation questionnaire, revealing a contrast between the three adnominal demonstratives in terms of accessibility to speaker and/or addressee. This is evident in the comparison of (333a–c).

---

[111] In particular, the Thaayorre deictic system defies decomposition into a set of features, such as Choi's (1999, 2001) '+/–NEW' and '+/–PROMINENT', although these features undoubtedly enter into the online construction of deictic categories.

(333) a. *yuk*   *ith*   *murk*
stick(NOM) dem:dist other's.pos[112]
'those cigarettes [on the far side of the room from you and me] are someone else's'
b. *yuk*   *inh*   *murk*
stick(NOM) dem:sp.prx other's.pos
'these cigarettes [that I hold in my hand] are someone else's'
c. *yuk*   *ulp*   *murk*
stick(NOM) dem:ad.prx other's.pos
'those cigarettes [that you are picking up over there] are someone else's'
[KTh_EN14Aug2002 Elicitation]

Ith 'that (distal)' is used to index an object that is inaccessible to both speaker and hearer. The 'speaker-proximal' demonstrative *inh* 'this' is used to index an object accessible to the speaker, while the 'addressee-proximal' demonstrative *ulp* indexes an object accessible to the addressee and not the speaker. This alternation between *inh* and *ulp* is particularly obvious in dialogue, where the same object (in the personal sphere of interlocutor A) will be referred to as *inh* by interlocutor A (signalling proximity to the speaker) but as *ulp* by interlocutor B (signalling proximity to the addressee), as seen in (334).

(334) A: *ant*   *inh*   *ngan?*
ant(NOM) dem:sp.prx what
'what kind of ant is this? [pointing to ant on her own shoulder]'
B: *mooln*   *ulp.*
small.brown.ant.sp. dem:ad.prx
'that's a *mooln*'
[KTh_EF14Dec2002 Elicitation Demonstratives3]

Where the referent is equally accessible to both speaker and addressee, the speaker-proximate form *inh* is used. The situational uses of the Kuuk Thaayorre adnominal demonstratives can be summarized as in Table 46.

Table 46. Componential analysis of adnominal demonstratives with situational use.

	ith	*inh*	*ulp*
Accessible to Speaker	−	+	−
Accessible to Addressee	−	+/−	+

---

112 The adjective *murk*, meaning 'belonging to somebody else', is glossed 'OTHER'S POSSESSION'.

These adnominal demonstratives also have a wide range of functions beyond indexing physical objects within the speech context, of course. The terms 'proximal' and 'distal' are used here for the benefit of cross-linguistic comparison, but in a broader sense than that with which they are typically used (which has strong spatial connotations). Hence what is 'proximal' is not only 'here', but also 'now', is accessible to touch and/or memory, is local in terms of culture and/or personal and familial allegiances, and so on. These contextual factors that speakers draw upon in selecting a demonstrative appear related along a cline, such that those at one end can be overridden by those towards the other. The spatial dimension ranks lowest on this cline, while the interactional dimension (in particular, the preceding discourse) ranks highly, with most other dimensions (including time) falling somewhere in between. Thus where the proximity rating of a referent is low in spatial terms but high in interactional terms we would expect the interactional feature to win out, with the proximal demonstrative being selected. This can be seen in (335.4), in which the time period referred to by *raak inh* 'this (proximal) time' is clearly temporally distal (as made explicit by the speaker in the following clause). Yet this is 'outranked' by the fact that this time period is topical and thus proximal in terms of both the speaker's and addressee's memory and attention.

(335) 1. GJ: *kaar rirk-m   ngay   mit.*
             NEG DO-P.IPFV 1sg(NOM) work
             'I wasn't able to work'
      2.   *yuunhul   ngay   money sickpay   mi'im.*
             that.one 1sg(ERG) money sickpay(ACC) pick.up:P.IPFV
             'I collected that sick pay'
      3. AG: *raak ngan?*
             TIME what
             'when was that?'
      4. GJ: *raak inh   nineteen seventy. Long time, long time minc.*
             TIME dem:sp.prx nineteen seventy long time long time really
             'this was in nineteen seventy. A long time ago, a very long time ago.'
             [KTh_AJ-**GJ**03Feb2004 Conversation]

Similarly, in (336) the speaker uses the addressee-proximate demonstrative *ulp* to index an out-of-sight location, thereby signalling her expectation that the addressee is familiar with the referent (through shared local / cultural knowledge and the context of the preceding discourse).[113]

---

[113] It is for this reason that I glossed *ulp* 'dem:fam (familiar to addressee)' in previous works.

(336) *station   ulp   ngathn*
station(NOM) dem:ad.prx 1sgGEN
'that station belongs to my family'
[KTh_EF14Dec2002 Elicitation Demonstratives25]

For similar reasons, *ulp* 'the (addressee-proximate)' is frequently used to mark narrative topics since these are expected to be within the current attention of the addressee. In (337), for example, the speaker is responding to his interlocutor's stated plan of going swimming in a lake an hour's drive away.

(337) *ngok   ulp   kaalkurrc*
water(NOM) dem:ad.prx cold
'[but] the water's cold!'
[KTh_GJ31Jan2004 Elicitation DahlTMA36]

It was noted above that in situational usage, referents that are close to both speaker and addressee are referred to using the speaker-proximal form *inh*. This does not straightforwardly extend to non-situational ('exophoric') usage, however. In each of (335.4–337), for example, the speaker refers to topics that are equally 'proximal' to both speaker's and addressee's attention, but in (335.4) he uses *inh* 'this (speaker-proximate)' and in (336)–(337) the speakers select *ulp*. Section 5.3.3 outlines more fully the range of situational and non-situational functions with which Kuuk Thaayorre demonstratives are used, relating these to the taxonomy of 'universal' demonstrative uses identified by Himmelmann (1996).

As with the corresponding demonstrative pronouns, the speaker-proximal adnominal demonstrative *inh* alternates with the form *inh'nh* in pragmatically emphatic contexts. As the speakers I consulted regard these forms as mutually substitutable, they will not be differentiated in the following discussion. Transcriptions will reflect the speakers' pronunciation of the demonstrative form, however.

5.3.2.2 Morphosyntax of adnominal demonstratives

Despite their name, adnominal demonstratives may function both in the presence (338) and absence (339) of a nomen head.

(338) *yak   ith   kaar wonp-r*
snake(NOM) dem:dist NEG die-P.PFV
'the snake didn't die'
[KTh_AJ27Jan2004 Elicitation]

(339) *kanpa inh   kerp   yup   yan!*
before dem:sp.prx finish:IMP soon go:NPST
'finish this first, go later!'
[KTh_ME04Jun2005 Conversation]

Where a head nomen is present, these demonstratives occupy a dedicated 'specifier' position at the right periphery of the NP (cf. §6.6). Case inflection precedes the adnominal demonstrative, which does not bear case itself (as seen in (340) and (341)).

(340) *[paanth-u ith] light keempe-nhan*
woman-ERG dem:dist light(ACC) extinguish-v^
'the woman turned off the light'
[KTh_AJ8Feb2004 Elicitation]

(341) *learn-m rirk-m ngay [school-ak ulp]*
learn-TR DO-P.IPFV 1sg(ERG) school-DAT dem:ad.prx
'I learned at that [bush] school'
[KTh_AJ-IC-**GJ**26Nov2002 Narrative/Conversation]

Adnominal demonstratives may also combine with pronouns. In such cases, the adnominal demonstrative functions to restrict the reference of a potentially ambiguous personal pronoun (342) or demonstrative pronoun (343).

(342) *nhul inh pam kon*
3sg(NOM) dem:sp.prx MAN short
"she's short"
[EF15Dec2002 Conversation / Elicitation]

(343) *inhul ulp, peln Donald, Cyril,*
this.one dem:ad.prx 3pl(NOM) Donald(NOM) Cyril(NOM)
peln ulp walmeerem=unh
3pl(NOM) dem:ad.prx be.knowledgeable.of=3sgACC
'these ones here, Donald and Cyril and them, they remember him'
[KTh_**AJ**-IC-GJ26Nov2002 Narrative/Conversation]

My corpora contain just a handful of examples in which the 'addressee-proximate' demonstrative is case inflected on behalf of the NP as a whole. In (344), *ulp* is marked for the ergative case of the subject argument *minh ulp* 'that dog', where it would normally be the preceding nomen (*minh* 'animal') that would inflect for case. In (345.3), *ulp* is the only exponent of the noun phrase and receives ergative case (though interestingly this is marked by a different ergative allomorph to that in (344)) to indicate its referent's role as instrument.[114]

---

[114] Indeed, this allomorphic variation, in conjunction with the extreme rarity of adnominal demonstrative case inflection, may suggest that the case marking of *ulp* 'the (addressee-proximate)' is a recent innovation.

(344) minh   ulp-thn   patha-rr   nganh
       MEAT   dem:ad.prx-ERG   bite-P.PFV 1sgACC
       'that dog bit me'
       [Hall 1972: 388]

(345) 1. yuk   wele   ith   ii-kuw   ngan wun   rump-un
         THING bailer.shell(NOM)   dem:dist there-at:west   what lie:NPST beach-DAT
         'that bailer shell in the west that is found on the beach'
      2. yokunman   use-m   rirk-m
         same.way   use-TR   DO-P.IPFV
         '[we'd] use [them] like that'
      3. ulp-nthrr   ngok   mi'im
         dem:ad.prx-ERG   water(ACC)   pick.up:P.IPFV
         '[we] would fetch water using those'
         [KTh_AJ-IC-GJ26Nov2002 Narrative/Conversation]

(Rather than revising the analysis of case marking and NP structure, it is more parsimonious to allow *ulp* in these very few, aberrant cases to appear within the N' and thus receive the case assigned to that position.)

Lastly, adnominal demonstratives are also found modifying spatial adverbs such as *iipal* 'from there' and *iirrkuw* 'there towards the west' (cf. §9.2.1.2):

(346) pam   iipal   ith   nhul   yat
       man(NOM)   from.there   dem:dist 3sg(NOM)   go:P.PFV
       'the man went from over there'
       [KTh_FT10Feb2004 Elicitation RcpPilot21]

(347) raak   min,   eh, rump,   ii-rr-kuw   inh
       PLACE   good(NOM)   eh beach(NOM) there-towards-west   dem:sp.prx
       'it's a nice place, eh, the beach towards the west there'
       [KTh_AJ27Jan2004 Conversation]

5.3.3 Functions of demonstratives

As noted above, the range of demonstrative functions can be broadly divided into situational (also labelled 'exophoric') and non-situational ('endophoric') uses.[115] Situational uses are commonly characterized as the indexation of entities within the

---

[115] Throughout this section I follow Himmelmann's (1996) terminology wherever appropriate, though this has been supplemented by additional terminology in places.

immediate speech context, though this simplification has been revealed as a convenient fiction by Hanks (2005).[116] Nevertheless, the indexation of entities in the immediate speech environment (*demonstratio ad oculos* in Bühler's 1934 terms) falls clearly within the core of situational demonstrative usage. This is illustrated by the use of the adnominal demonstrative *inh* 'this' in (348) and the pronominal demonstrative *inhul* 'this one' in (349).

(348) *Jessica, hat   inh   nhangkn?*
      Jessica hat(NOM) dem:sp.prx 2sgGEN
      'Jessica, is this hat yours?'
      [KTh_EF14Dec2002 Elicitation Demonstratives16]

(349) *ngat   inhul   ngat thermp*
      FISH(NOM) this.one FISH salmon
      'this fish is a salmon'
      [KTh_GJ28Oct2002 Elicitation]

Situational uses of demonstratives are frequently accompanied by pointing gestures towards the entity (or other referent) in question. Most situational tokens in my data have the communicative function of attention-getting, particularly where a contrast is being made between multiple potential referents. In (348), for example, the speaker is directing Jessica's attention towards a particular hat, in order to ask whether it is hers. In (349), the speaker directs the addressee towards a particular fish in order to specify its species (in contrast with other nearby fish of other species). Furthermore, my corpus is filled with demonstratives used situationally in the context of director-matcher games (e.g. elicitation tasks in which two language experts have to collaborate through verbal description to find two matching pictures), where the speaker will point to a series of pictures asking *inhul?* '[is it] this one?'. Also classed as 'situational' is the use of demonstratives to index locations (350)–(353).

(350) *may riitham   ii-kaw   inh,   Yulu*
      VEG bulguru(NOM) there-at:east dem:sp.prx Yulu
      'there's bulguru[117] just here in the east, at Yulu'
      [KTh_ME04Jun2005 Conversation / Narrative Yencr]

(351) *yuuw kaar=p   yat,   nhul   inhul*
      far   NEG=PRAG go:P.PFV 3sg(NOM) this.one
      'he hasn't gone off, he's here'
      [KTh_AJ27Jan2004 Elicitation]

---

116 Hanks (2005: 191) has instead shown deictic practice to be "an emergent construal of socially embedded deictic fields".
117 Bulguru is also known as 'water chestnut', or *Eleocharis dulcis*.

(352) camping wun-m   peln   inh'nhngun.
      camping lie-P.IPFV 3pl(NOM) this.very.one:DAT
      'people must have camped here'
      [KTh_AC10Aug2002 Conversation]

(353) pokon, inhaka   Daycare
      NO   in.this.place Daycare
      'no, [he works at nearby] Daycare [not the more distant Canteen]'
      [Anon.]

Just as the opposition between proximal and distal demonstrative forms may be used situationally to contrast referents within the (contextually defined) interactional sphere with those outside it, so too may this opposition be exploited to contrast referents existing in the present era with those in distant time periods (via the metaphorical schema WHAT IS HERE IS NOW). This use of distal demonstratives to index referents of distant time periods is often difficult to distinguish this from what Haviland (1993) terms 'local anchored space'; the situational indexation of a location that stands for an entity associated with it (e.g. referring to a deceased individual by indexing the house they once lived in, cf. Clark et. al. 1983). In (354), for example, we might assume that the selection of the distal demonstrative pronoun *yuunhul* 'those ones [far away]' was motivated by the time that has elapsed between referents' being alive and the speech event.

(354) nganip   pelnan=a   work-orr   thernga-rr koop   yuunhul
      father(ACC) 3plACC=PRAG   string-ERG kill-P.PFV all(ACC) that.one
      'those fathers [my father and his brothers] were all killed by string [sorcery]'
      [KTh_AJ-IC-GJ26Nov2002 Narrative/Conversation]

The fact that the speaker gestured eastwards (towards the traditional lands of the 'fathers') as he uttered (354), however, would seem to indicate a local anchored space use of the demonstrative.

In (355.5), the use of the distal demonstrative to refer to unfamiliar Kuuk Thaayorre dialects may also be motivated by local anchored space since the dialects are associated with lands far removed from the place of speech. Alternatively, though, the speaker may be using the distal demonstrative to emphasize the (metaphorical) distance between the dialects and his mastery thereof.

(355) 1. ngay   wuuc   kaar patpi-rr
         1sg(ERG) ceremony(ACC)   NEG camp-P.PFV
         'I didn't perform in the ceremony'

      2. wuuc   ngay   kaalpurngmat
         ceremony(ACC) 1sg(NOM)   forget:GO&:P.PFV
         'I've forgotten the songs'

3. *kaalpurngmat kaar=p,   ngay   kaar learn-m rirk-r*
   forget:P.PFV   NEG=PRAG 1sg(ERG) NEG learn-TR DO-P.PFV
   'it's not that I've forgotten, I never learned'
4. *kaar katp-m   ngay*
   NEG grasp-P.IPFV 1sg(ERG)
   'I didn't grasp [them]'
5. *theep-er   **yuunhul** too strong, theepr **yuunhul** yiirryirram*
   tongue-DAT **that.one** too strong, tongue that.one other:RDP
   'those ones are too strong on my tongue [i.e. hard to pronounce], those other dialects'
   "it a bit difficult on my tongue. Different tongues"
   [KTh_AJ-IC-**GJ**26Nov2002 Narrative/Conversation]

Bühler (1934) contrasts the more concrete indexation of entities in the speech environment (*demonstratio ad oculos*) with what he terms *deixis am phantasma*, in which the speaker takes an insiders' perspective of the event by shifting the deictic centre from the speech event to the place and time of the event itself (thereby making reference to entities outside the speech environment). This can be seen in (356), in which the speaker describes a shovel that he had at the time of the story using the proximal demonstrative, despite the fact that this shovel is nowhere near the locus of the speech event.

(356) *ngay   inh   yuk... yuk   shovel   kal-m/   man.pert-an*
      1sg(ERG)   dem:sp.prx   THING THING shovel(ACC) carry-P.IPFV   shoulder-DAT
      'I was carrying a... a shovel on my shoulder'
      [KTh_AC14Nov2002 Narrative LosingIrma]

Later in the same narrative text (357), the speaker refers to another protagonist using the distal demonstrative pronoun, in order to emphasize her physical distance from him at the time of the story (not at the time of speech).

(357) *ngul yuunhul nhaawr   "nge'!"*
      then that.one see:P.PFV hey
      'then I saw her in the distance, "hey!"'
      [KTh_AC14Nov2002 Narrative LosingIrma]

A particular form of *deixis am phantasma* is the phenomenon of "demonstrative reference to a part of the speaker's body in order to indicate where something happened to a protagonist" (Himmelmann 1996: 221). Example (358) illustrates this use of the proximal adnominal demonstrative – in conjunction with a pointing gesture – in order to specify where exactly the protagonist might have been hit by lightning. In (359), the speaker uses the same demonstrative form while clasping his own arm in order to describe the size of a crocodile's leg.

(358) paanth   inh=okun   thernga-rr
     woman(ACC) dem:sp.prx=DUB hit-P.PFV
     '[lightning] hit the woman hereabouts [points to arm]'
     [KTh_AC14Oct2002 Narrative PormprRintm]

(359) punth   inh   waarr ngamal minc
     arm(NOM) dem:sp.prx very   large really
     '[his] arm was really enormous'
     [KTh_**AJ**-GJ03Feb2004 Conversation]

Finally, Himmelmann (1996: 221) argues persuasively for classing self-reference to a linguistic unit or act (e.g. *this article, in this book*) as a subtype of situational use. Almost every Kuuk Thaayorre narrative begins with a demonstrative so used; (360.1) and (361.1) are just two of many examples illustrating this use of both the pronominal and adnominal proximal demonstratives.

(360) 1. *Inhul   yik-nhan   ngay,*
        this.one say-GO&:NPST 1sg(NOM)
        'I'm going to tell this one [story]'
     2. *nhul   minh pinc   ii-kuw,   wuurr   ko'om*
        3sg(NOM) MEAT saltie(NOM) there-at:west fishtrap(ACC) knit:P.IPFV
        'a saltwater crocodile was in the west, [he] was building a fishtrap'
        [KTh_**DW**-CW09Dec2002 Narrative 2Crocs]

(361) 1. *Inhul   kuthip   inh   wanan-nhan,*
        dem:pro:prx story(ACC) dem:sp.prx tell:RDP-GO&NPST
        'I'm going to tell this story'
     2. *ngay   kanangkarr parr_r mant...*
        1sg(NOM) long.ago   CHILD small
        'long ago [when] I was a small child...'
        [KTh_GJ16Oct2002 Narrative MelbourneTrip]

There are three major non-situational demonstrative uses. The first of these is termed 'discourse deixis' by Himmelmann (1996 – cf. Lyons' 1977 'textual deixis', Fillmore's 1982 'text reference', Dixon's 2003 'textual anaphora'). Whereas situational uses of demonstratives index entities or locations, the discourse deictic use makes reference to propositions or events. This is usually done anaphorically (as in (362), which follows the speaker's expounding at length upon the benefits of a Christian lifestyle):

(362) *try best rirk   ngancn   yuunh'nhul-ak ulp*
     try best DO:NPST 1pl:incl(NOM) that.one-DAT dem:ad.prx
     "that's why we're trying best for that thing [to go to heaven]"
     [KTh_GJ18Jan2004 Narrative Christmas]

The second non-situational demonstrative use is to track the referents (or 'protagonists') under discussion. This is usually done anaphorically; (124), for example, was uttered towards the end of a long story concerning the whereabouts of the referent, while (363) is explicit in its reference to a previously established path.

(124') *trouble=okun   yan   yup,   paanth-um   inh'nheman*
        trouble(NOM)=DUB go:NPST soon   woman-ABL   this.very.one:ABL
        'I might get into trouble from [because of] this woman'
        [KTh_AC14Nov2002 Narrative LosingIrma]

(363)   *ngay   ii-rr-korr   therk-r,   main road ith,   same road.*
        1sg(NOM) there-towards-outside return-P.PFV main road dem:dist same road
        'I went back that way along that main road, the same road [I had come down].'
        [KTh_AC14Nov2002 Narrative LosingIrma]

The use of demonstratives to introduce new participants (i.e. a cataphoric tracking use) is labelled by Himmelmann as a distinct, 'recognitional' function. Demonstratives so employed draw on assumed shared knowledge, often with an acknowledgement that the addressee may have some difficulty retrieving the intended reference (Himmelmann 1996: 231). This can be seen in (364.2), in which the speaker uses two proximal demonstratives in his first reference to the protagonist of a traditional story, with which it is reasonable to assume an addressee with a basic level of cultural fluency will be familiar.

(364) 1. *inh'nhul=ay   yik,   kuuk   inh'nhul*
         this.very.one=1sg(NOM) say-NPST WORD(ACC) this.very.one
         'I'm telling this story'
      2. *inh   minh pinc   inh'nhul*
         dem:sp.prx MEAT saltie this.very.one
         '[there was] this saltwater crocodile'
      3. *thernga-rr=unh*
         kill-P.PFV=3sgACC
         '[and they] killed him.'
         [KTh_**DW**-CW09Dec2002 Narrative 2Crocs]

While the use of *inh* 'this' and *inhul* 'this one' in example (364.2) may resemble use of the English proximal demonstrative to introduce a new entity into the discourse (termed 'new-this' by Wald 1983, and classified by Himmelmann 1996 as a kind of *Deixis am Phantasma*), these are more accurately viewed as an example of the recognitional demonstrative function, signalling the speakers expectation that the addressee should (but might not) be familiar with the referent. The Kuuk Thaayorre data do not offer any strong counterexamples to Himmelmann's (1996: 222) observation that "these *new-this*-like uses have not as yet been attested/described for languages other than English". The function of introducing new, unfamiliar referents (as does English *new-this*) is instead performed by the quantifier *thono* 'one' are discussed in §6.11.2.1.

Related to the potential retrieval problems signalled by the recognitional demonstrative use is the use of the demonstrative pronouns as fillers for an 'inaccessibile' target word or phrase (translated here using the Pormpuraaw English equivalent, *whatchamacallit*, cf. Enfield 2003b). This filler usage is discussed in §6.11.4.

6 Noun phrase syntax

6.1 Arguments for the existence of a NP

There are several clear indicators of a noun phrase structure in Kuuk Thaayorre. These include: (a) case marking; (b) internal word order; and (c) prosody. (In this respect, Kuuk Thaayorre is typical of its Cape York neighbours but unlike some other Australian languages, which lack such clear evidence of NP constituency, cf. Louagie & Verstraete 2016). To begin with, case suffixes are attached only to the final eligible constituent of the noun phrase, e.g. *ngathn* 'my' in (365):[118]

(365) *ngan puumn ngathn-thurr kuta theernga-rr*
 KIN B- 1sgGEN-ERG dog(ACC) hit-P.PFV
 'my younger brother hit a dog'
 [KTh_EN12Dec2002 Elicitation]

While the ordering of constituents in the clause is subject to pragmatic conditioning, word order within the noun phrase generally adheres to the set of phrase structure rules given in (367), each of which is explained and justified in the following subsections. Since this set of rules is somewhat complex, the simple linear order of constituents in a hypothetical maximal NP is also provided in (366).[119] Note that any case markers attach to the rightmost element within the braces { }, which is optionally followed by any adnominal demonstrative and/or pronoun.

(366) NP → Pro {N_{GN} N_{SP} Deg Adj Deg Gen Quant Ign/Dem.Pro}-**case** Adn.Dem Pro

(367) **NP** → **N'** (AdnDem)

$$\mathbf{N'} \rightarrow \left\{ \begin{array}{l} (N)\ (AdjP)^{*}\quad (N'_{GEN})\quad (Quant) \left\{ \begin{array}{l} (Dem.Pro) \\ (Ignorative) \end{array} \right\} \\ \qquad\qquad\qquad\qquad Pro \end{array} \right\}$$

$$N \rightarrow (N_{GN})\ \left\{ \begin{array}{l} (N_{SP}) \\ (N) \end{array} \right\}$$

 AdjP→ (Deg) Adj (Deg)

---

[118] This 'final eligible constituent' is the last constituent of N', any following adnominal demonstrative does not inflect for case (cf. §6.6.2).
[119] Note the abbreviations used here: Pro 'Pronoun'; N_{GN} 'generic noun'; N_{SP} 'specific noun' ; Deg 'degree adverb'; Adj 'adjective'; Gen 'genitive pronoun'; Quant 'quantifier'; Ign 'ignorative pronoun'; Dem.Pro 'demonstrative pronoun'; Adn.Dem 'adnominal demonstrative' Pro 'pronoun'

The generic noun (N_{GN}) and specific noun (N_{SP}) together enter into what I call a 'classifying construction' (see §6.2 below). This may be followed by multiple adjective phrases, composed of a head adjective and optional degree adverb(s) (§6.4). The next optional constituent may be either a genitive pronoun or N' encoding the possessor of the head noun (§6.5). This constituent is optionally followed by a quantifier and/or demonstrative (§6.5, §6.6).

Smith and Johnson (2000: 388) propose a similarly invariant NP constituent order for Kugu Nganhcara, and Wilkins (1989) and McGregor (1990) also describe the fixed ordering of NP constituents in Mparntwe Arrernte and Gooniyandi respectively.[120] As the parentheses in (367) indicate, each element of the Kuuk Thaayorre noun phrase may be omitted, including the head noun.[121] It is extremely rare (and distinctly odd-sounding) for all of the elements to co-occur in a single noun phrase, and no spontaneous examples of this have been recorded to date. Illustrating just two possible combinations of constituents, then, (365) above includes N_{GN} – N_{SP} – Pro_{GEN} and (368) below illustrates N_{GN} – N_{SP} – Adj – Adj:

(368) *minh kothon pam ngamal*
MEAT wallaby man large
'an enormous male wallaby'
[Hall 1972: 67]

Prosodically, the noun phrase is characterized by: (a) a lack of planned pauses (disfluencies notwithstanding); (b) a single intonation contour; (c) a single primary stress peak.

Discontinuous NPs, such as the direct object in (369) and the transitive subject in (370), are rare in my data, though amply attested. Note that in (370) only the final constituent of the discontinuous noun phrase <u>as a whole</u> receives relational case marking (whereas the first portion of the NP, *paanth* 'woman' is in bare form):

(369) **may** nhul **koop** mungka-rr thon-thrr
VEG(ACC) 3sg(ERG) all(ACC) eat-P.PFV one-ERG
'the one guy ate all the food!'
[AJ07/02/04 Elicitation]

(370) **paanth** ii peln **pinalam-un** theerng-m yakulp
woman there 3pl(ERG) three-ERG hit-P.IPFV snake(ACC) dem:adr.prx
'the three women there were hitting a snake'

---

120 In Kuuk Thaayorre, however, some limited permutation of NP constituents is possible for pragmatic or stylistic effect. See §6.5.2.
121 Wilkins (2000: 150) also finds that "an overt head noun is not obligatory in a noun phrase" in Arrernte.

In many of the Australian languages for which a noun phrase can be identified, these are analyzed as having an internally flat structure (see, e.g., Alpher 1973, Blake 2001b). The Kuuk Thaayorre NP, however, is frequently complex. Each NP is composed of a N' (described in §6.5 below), optionally specified by a demonstrative (see §6.6 for a syntactic analysis of the relationship between N›, demonstratives and pronouns). Below the level of N›, constituents may be organized into classifying constructions (N) and/ or adjective phrase(s) (AdjP). Each of these subcomponents is described in the following sections.

6.2 N – The classifying construction

Generic and specific nouns together enter into a 'classifying construction' which heads the noun phrase. The characterization of such a construction in terms of classification (following Wilkins 2000) is motivated firstly by the semantic function of generic nouns in categorizing entities according to their social and cultural importance. Secondly, as Smith and Johnson (2000: 420) note of Kugu Nganhcara, generic nouns are somewhat "similar, in both syntactic position and semantics, to the numeral classifiers of languages of Asia and Central America" (cf. Seifart 2010). Although generic nouns do not enter into a special relationship with quantifiers, as do most numeral classifiers, this is not a necessary criterion for classification (Craig 1986). Sands (1995) treats frequency of cooccurrence with the relevant noun as the primary criterion for being labelled a classifier, according to which the Kuuk Thaayorre construction should qualify as 'classifying'. The small number of generic nouns, along with their productive combination with newly coined or introduced specific nouns, also favours such an analysis. The following subsections outline the classifying construction's semantics, syntax, theoretical significance and role in discourse.

6.2.1 Semantics of the classifying construction

The generic noun in a classifying construction is usually in a superordinate (whether hypernymic or meronymic) relationship to the construction as a whole (and often also to the specific noun itself). So, for example, the generic noun *ngat* 'FISH' is preposed to a large number of specific nouns referring to fish species, for instance *ngat pinporro* 'barramundi', but also specific nouns referring to entities meronymically related to fish, such as *ngat thip* 'fish liver'.

This construction is fully productive, with introduced concepts readily incorporated into the classification system, usually a new specific noun paired with an existing generic noun. This is exemplified by terms such as *may punan* 'banana' (*may* 'plant food'), *minh pik* 'pig' (*minh* 'MEAT'), or the following:

(371) minh   tin.meat   mungka-rr
      MEAT   tinned.meat(ACC)   eat-P.PFV
      '[they] ate tinned meat'
      [KTh_AJ-IC-**GJ**26Nov2002 Narrative/Conversation]

In Yidinj, some specific nouns can appear with each of two generics, one of which will characterize the inherent nature of the referent, the other its function. Thus "all birds are considered edible and so may occur either with generic *minja* 'flesh food' or with the generic *djarruy* 'bird'" (Dixon 2002: 456). In Kuuk Thaayorre, too, some specific nouns may occur with multiple generic nouns. Unlike in Yidinj, however, the resulting classifying constructions make entirely different reference, rather than evoking different aspects of the same referent. So, for example, *may kermpl* 'large white berry' refers to a kind of *may* 'plant food' while *minh kermpl* 'corella' refers to a kind of *minh* 'MEAT' (the generic used with all birds). This may seem typical of a classifying system, but the fit is not perfect. In most cases where a single specific noun form can occur with multiple generic nouns, a monosemous definition of the specific noun form is impossible. For example, although the metonymic connection between *may kermpl* 'large white berry' and *minh kermpl* 'corella' may be the etymological motivation behind the shared form, this kind of sign metonymy is not sufficiently regular or predictable to allow one use of *kermpl* to be derived from the other (or a more abstract underlying sense). For this reason, I assume such specific nouns to be polysemous, with each sense selecting for a different generic noun. There are a number of homonymous specific nouns in addition to these, though they may have their origins in polysemy (or, indeed, deeper cultural and linguistic understanding may reveal links indicative of synchronic polysemy even here, see §3.1.1).

Semantically, Kuuk Thaayorre generics can be characterized as classifying the entities of the world according to humans' interaction with them, grouping together things that are manipulated or consumed in similar ways (e.g. *ngat* 'FISH', *warrath* 'grasses'), or individuals with whom particular social relations hold (e.g. *parr_r* 'CHILD', *ngan* 'KIN'). This categorization is not exhaustive, however; many specific nouns never cooccur with a generic noun (e.g. *pung* 'sun'). The semantics of each of the generic nouns are elaborated upon in §3.1.1.1.

6.2.2 Syntax of the classifying construction

There is a strict ordering restriction within the classifying construction, with generic nouns always preceding specifics. This special relationship between the two noun types is significant since, as Wilkins (2000: 162) puts it:

> In languages as renowned for their freedom of word order as the Australian languages are, any fixed ordering of elements must be considered a good candidate for a construction functioning as a unique sign with its own form, meaning and pragmatics of use.

But while the order of the generic and specific nouns is fixed in Kuuk Thaayorre, neither is obligatory in the noun phrase. The generic noun frequently occurs alone, often used anaphorically in referent-tracking, as is common in Australian languages (cf. §6.11.1). The specific noun may also occur alone; example (372) shows a specific noun used in the absence of its associated generic (*minh* 'meat'):[122]

(372)   *pinc,   nhul   kar   winwin=peey!*
        salt.croc(NOM) 3sg(NOM)   like fearsome=PRAG
        'the saltwater crocodile, that's *winwin*'
        [KTh_**AJ**-GJ03Feb2004 Elicitation/Conversation]

There is a continuum of specific nouns ranging from those that never cooccur with a generic noun (e.g. *pormpr* 'humpy, house'), to those that only very rarely occur without one (e.g. *ngat pinporro* 'barramundi'). In the middle, of course, are a large number of specific nouns that are commonly found both with and without a generic. These include *yencr* 'raffia' (which may or may not follow *yuk* 'TREE, THING') and *kaala* 'uncle (mother's younger brother)' (which is often preceded by *ngan* 'KIN'). This optionality of generic nouns can cause problems for transmission of the classifying system to younger speakers. For instance, most people I questioned who were born after 1990 were unsure of whether *puuy* 'crab' is classified as *ngat* 'FISH' or *minh* 'MEAT' or is incompatible with any generic (the majority of my elder informants prefer *ngat puuy*).

A generic-specific pairing can itself enter into a higher-level classifying construction in the specific slot. This can be seen in (373), in which the classifying construction *minh patp* 'hawk' (literally, 'MEAT hawk') follows the generic noun *ngat*:

(373)   *ngat   minh.patp*
        FISH   hawk
        'stingray sp. (devil ray)'

The structure of the classifying construction can thus be schematized as in (374). Note that the construction as a whole is labelled 'N', to convey the fact that it is the head constituent of a larger noun phrase, but also to indicate its proposed status as a lexical unit (as (373) shows).

(374)   N → (N_{GN}) $\begin{Bmatrix} (N_{SP}) \\ (N) \end{Bmatrix}$

---

[122] See (485) below for the same clause in its broader discourse context.

Within the classifying construction itself, the question of headedness is less easy to resolve. Since both generic and specific are types of nomen, both are eligible to head a noun phrase. In favour of viewing the generic as head is Kuuk Thaayorre's typological tendency towards the head-initial (hence exhibiting N–Adj, N–Rel, N–Dem, Adj–Deg, though also Deg–Adj). Semantically, too, the generic noun is always the most general of the noun phrase constituents, determining the 'type' of referent described by the phrase as a whole, with all other elements (including the specific noun) further specifying its reference. This is roughly the approach taken by Dixon (2002: 454), who argues, for Yidinj, that "the generic term ('edible animal') can be taken as head of the NP, and the specifier ('kangaroo') as a kind of modifier".

However, McGregor (1990) argues persuasively for an analysis of the Gooniyandi specific noun as head, with the generic noun fulfilling a classifying function. Following from this, Wilkins gives an analysis of the Arrernte generic noun (within a complex head of the NP) providing classification in such a way that X Y means 'the group of things called Y is one of the different kinds of things X refers to' (Wilkins 2000: 185). Supporting the analysis of the specific noun as the head of the Kuuk Thaayorre classifying construction, is the fact that the classifying construction as a whole functions as a specific noun (as seen in (373)). Nevertheless, noun phrases containing a generic nomen but no specific do not appear elliptical. On the basis of such ambivalent evidence, I choose to analyze the generic and specific nouns as co-heading the noun phrase, much as Wilkins (2000: 151) finds for Arrernte that:

> A generic noun and specific noun can enter into construction and together function as the head of the noun phrase, but either may occur on its own as the sole member of the head of the NP.

The pragmatics of selecting either generic noun, specific noun or both to head the Kuuk Thaayorre NP, are explored under §6.11.1.

6.3 N_{GN}, N_{SP}, Adj: Word classes or syntactic slots?

The monosemy bias advocated by Ruhl (1989) seeks to avoid the multiplication of senses where these can be brought together by a single definition. Following from this, it is preferable to avoid positing multiple lexical entries where a lexeme can be given a single underlying meaning. Among Australian languages, this issue is particularly pertinent in the domain of nomina, among which there is often a systematic formal and semantic relationship between lexemes in the generic, specific and adjectival word classes. Morphy (1983: 83), for instance, argues that Djapu makes no strict distinction between generic and specific nouns, but rather that these nouns are arranged along a continuum, according to the specificity of their semantics. Wilkins (2000: 155) similarly proposes that the class of generic nouns in Arrernte is semantically, rather than syntactically, defined:

any lexicalized superordinate term which has identifiable lexicalized hyponyms can indeed occur as the generic in a 'generic-specific' construction, and the set of generic nouns will therefore be coterminous with the set of lexical superordinate terms.

Likewise, among Kuuk Thaayorre nomina which we find many instances of the same form (e.g. *wang*, as illustrated below) functioning alternately as generic noun, specific noun, and/or adjective:

(375) *wang kirkunka*
WANG devil.sp
'red-legged devil'

(376) *wang*
WANG
'(a) whitefella'

(377) *parr_r paanth wang*
child female WANG
'(a) white girl'

In (375), *wang* functions as a generic noun, referring to the class of devils. In (376), *wang* is used as a specified noun, specifying that the language in question is English. *Wang* can also be used adjectivally, as in (377) where it modifies the classifying construction *parr_r paanth* 'girl'. If we are strongly biased towards monosemy, we should attempt to attribute all three uses of *wang* to a single underlying form in the mental lexicon (belonging simply to the macro-class 'nomen', cf. §3.1.1). The semantic and syntactic differences associated with these different positions in the noun phrase (currently associated with distinct word subclasses, e.g. 'generic noun' and 'adjective') being attributed not to the lexeme, but rather its role in the clause. The fact that some generic nouns may only appear in the generic slot (e.g. *ngan* 'RELATION'), and some specific nouns only in the specific slot (e.g. *kothon* 'wallaby'), would thus be attributed to the fact that their semantics are incompatible with modification or classification respectively. This is not the analysis advanced here, however. Instead, I analyze these three uses of *wang* as corresponding to three different senses, each of which belongs to a different word subclass (this relationship with word subclasses is considered further below). This heterosemic analysis has a number of advantages over a monosemic one. Firstly, it is otherwise difficult to predict exactly which nomen can appear in which slot. Why, for instance, can *kuta* 'dog, domestic animal' appear in the generic slot (e.g. in *kuta thok* 'cat'), but *puuy* 'crab' cannot? Secondly, it is difficult to provide a coherent monosemous definition of any of the multi-functional forms involved. In the examples given above – *wang*$_1$ 'DEVIL (generic noun); *wang*$_2$ 'whitefella (specific noun)'; and *wang*$_3$ 'pertaining to whitefellas (adjective)' – *wang*$_2$ is derived from *wang*₁ by a process of metaphor (WHITEFELLAS ARE DEVILS), while *wang*₃ is derived from *wang*₂ by metonymy (the English language, clothing, and other things prominently associated with whitefellas are described as *wang*₂). These differences in meaning cannot simply be attributed to the interpretation they receive according to the slot they fill.

Heterosemous definitions may be necessary to account for the functions of lexemes even within a single part of speech. For example, a comparison of (378) with (379) would seem to suggest that the generic noun *paanth* classes together all and only female entities, while *pam* classes together all and only male entities:

(378) *paanth   kunyangkar   ngathn*
      WOMAN   sibling   1sgGEN
      'my sister'

(379) *pam   kunyangkar   ngathn*
      MAN   sibling   1sgGEN
      'my brother'

However, as (380) shows, *pam* may also be paired with specific nouns referring to females:

(380) *pam   nhangnam   ngathn*
      HUMAN   mother   1sgGEN
      'my mother'

In examples such as (379), *pam* appears to more broadly refer to humankind, though it may also be used contrastively to refer to males (exhibiting a kind of auto-hyponymy). (The semantics of *pam* and the other generic nouns were discussed in more detail in §3.1.1.1.)

Whether monosemy, polysemy, or heteronymy proves the best synchronic analysis, it does seem likely that Kuuk Thaayorre forms such as *wang* and *pam* were originally monosemous, belonging to a single word class. As these words came to take on different kinds of roles in the noun phrase, they developed different senses, and vice versa. For example, where a particular noun regularly combined with other, semantically appropriate, (specific) nouns, it would come to be associated with a particular syntactic position (the 'generic slot'). This in turn might feed the establishment of distinct word classes associated with these syntactic positions. This can be understood in terms of emergence from frequency (Hopper 1987, Thompson and Hopper 2001). The analysis advanced in this grammar is that this process is not yet complete. It is nevertheless descriptively useful to assign lexemes to distinct generic, specific and adjectival subclasses of nomina for a number of reasons. Firstly, the three subclasses differ in their combinatorics and their semantic contribution to the noun phrase.

Generic nouns are semantically broad members of a small class, always a hypernym of the generic-specific pairing as a whole. Adjectives, meanwhile, tend to describe qualities or characteristics, and as such they may freely combine with all – or at least a wide range of – generics. Specifics, however, are restricted to combining with one or two generics (cf. Dixon 2002: 459).[123] Furthermore, many adjectives, but not generics or specifics, may be modified by degree adverbs (381).

(381) a. *waarr ngamal*
         very   large
         'very large'
     b. **waarr nganip*
         very   father
         'very father(ly)'

There is also evidence of the lexicalization of the (specific) noun – adjective distinction; the lexemes *yiirr ~ yiirram* 'other/different' and *mant ~ mantam* 'small' have different forms according to whether they are functioning as specific or adjective. In the first clause of (382), for example, the form *yiirr* 'other' is used as an adjective (modifying *pam* 'man'), while the longer form *yiirram* '(an) other' in the second clause corresponds with its use as a specific noun.

(382) *pam yiirr.   Yiirram riica-rr*
      man other_ADJ other_SPC go.fast-P.PFV
      '[it must have been] a different man. Someone else drove off'
      [KTh_EN27Jan2004 Conversation]

The ending *-am* could for this reason be analyzed as a suffix used to derive specific nouns from adjectives. But since it is found only in the two forms *yiirram* and *mantam*, these nouns are analyzed here as synchronically monomorphemic.

Lastly, a rather different source of evidence for heterosemy and distinct word subclasses are the numerous nomina that are apparently monosemous and restricted in the syntactic roles they may play. This is illustrated by the generic noun *ngan* 'KIN' – denoting the class of kin – which cannot function as specific noun or adjective, but only as a generic, as in (383). There is nothing inherent in its semantics that prevents such polyfunctionality. It is easy to imagine its use as a specific noun (384) or adjective (385).

---

[123] Again, though, there seems to be a cline from those (adjectives) that may combine with all the generics, to those (adjectives and specifics) that may combine with a limited number of generics, to those (adjectives and specifics) that only combine with one. It is possible to account for such a distribution by appealing to semantics, without recourse to establishing separate word classes.

(383) ngan   pinhirr
       KIN   FZ
       '(an) aunt [father's sister]'

(384) *pam   ngan
       HUMAN   relative
       'relatives'

(385) *parr_r pam   ngan
       CHILD   male relative
       'relative boys [i.e. young males within the family]'

It would seem, therefore, that *ngan* 'KIN' only functions as a generic noun precisely because it is monosemous. Where forms are associated with multiple functions (e.g. as both specific and generic noun), this is viewed as indicative of heterosemy.

6.4 AdjP – The adjective phrase

Immediately following the specific noun in the noun phrase template, are the adjective phrase(s). An adjective phrase is composed of a head adjective and (maximally two) optional degree adverbs. Of the three Kuuk Thaayorre degree adverbs, two precede the head adjective (*waarr* 'very' and *mangr* 'quite, rather'), while the other (*minc* 'really') follows (cf. §3.3.5, §9.2.5). Since the two pre-head degree adverbs are semantically incompatible, where the adjective phrase phrase contains two degree adverbs, these are always *waarr* (preceding the head) and *minc* (following it). The structure of the adjective phrase is thus:

(386) (Deg) Adj (Deg)

Example (387) illustrates an adjective phrase – the predicate of a verbless clause – in which each potential slot filled:

(387) punth   inh   [waarr ngamal minc]!
       arm(NOM) dem:sp.prx   [very   large   really]
       'this [crocodile's] arms were really very large!'
       [KTh_**AJ**-GJ03Feb2004 Conversation]

The combination of multiple adjective phrases within the NP is discussed in §6.5 below.

6.5 N' – Head noun and modifiers

6.5.1 Overview of N'

This chapter has so far considered the relative positioning of generic nouns, specific nouns, and adjective phrases. The remaining constituents of the noun phrase are genitive-inflected possessors (whether pronominal or a noun-headed N'), quantifiers and demonstrative and ignorative pronouns functioning adnominally. These two modifier slots, along with the adjective phrase(s), follow the head noun(s) to form N'. This complex structure may be substituted by a simple personal pronoun. The structure of N' can thus be summarized:

(388) $\text{N}' \rightarrow \begin{Bmatrix} \text{(N) (AdjP)* (N}'_{\text{GEN}}\text{) (Quant)} \begin{Bmatrix} \text{(Dem.Pro)} \\ \text{(Ignorative)} \end{Bmatrix} \\ \text{Pro} \end{Bmatrix}$

An (elicited) NP including four modifiers is given in (389):

(389) *kuta ngamal ngotn ngathn thono=nhurr*
 dog large black 1sgGEN one=only
 'my only big, black dog'
 [KTh_AJ27Jan2004 Elicitation, based on data from Hall 1972: 69]

A NP including a possessive N' is illustrated by (197).

(390) *nganh [[kuta [Dan]]-tam] patha-rr*
 1sgACC [[dog [Dan]$_{\text{N'}}$]$_{\text{N'}}$-ABL]$_{\text{NP}}$ bite-P.PFV
 'Dan's dog bit me'
 [KTh_GJ14Oct2002 Elicitation]

Note that the ablative case-marking at the right edge of the second N' represents a portmanteau case morpheme (as discussed in §4.2.6.5) subsuming the functions of the adnominal genitive case assigned to the right edge of the inner N' (*Dan*) and the relational ergative case assigned to the outer N' (*kuta Dan[ak]* 'Dan['s] dog'). Because the single lexeme *Dan* occupies the rightmost position of both the inner N' and outer N', the portmanteau ablative case is required to signal both case relations due to the restriction of only one case morpheme per lexeme.

The phrase structure rule given in (388) formalizes the fact that personal pronouns are of themselves equivalent to the collection of elements that can make up a noun-headed N'. They may head a noun phrase in isolation, or they may be specified by a demonstrative (as in (391)):

(391) *nhul   ulp   miracle=yuk   yump-m*
3sg(ERG) dem:ad.prx miracle(ACC)=STUFF make-P.IPFV
'he was making miracles'
[KTh_GJ18Jan2004 Narrative Christmas]

Of all the constituents of the Kuuk Thaayorre NP, the noun (i.e. the generic and/or specific head of N), and pronoun have special status as head. Any one of them may constitute a non-elliptical noun phrase in isolation, and each may be specified by a demonstrative.

6.5.2 Order of nominal modifiers

Judging by my present corpus, it is extremely marked to include more than two modifiers in a single phrase, and speakers only rarely do so. Example (389) above demonstrates the order N_{SP}–AdjP–AdjP–Pro$_{GEN}$–Quant. It is premature to make any definitive statements regarding the order of multiple adjective phrases within N', though it does seem that permutations in order are motivated by pragmatics, rather than either syntax or semantics. That is to say, there does not appear to be any requirement that, for example, adjectives denoting more fixed, stable or inherent characteristics (such as colour) precede those denoting more transient or mutable characteristics (such as age). The ordering of other modifiers likewise appears also to have much to do with information structure. Consider, for instance, the following set of permutations documented by Hall (1972: 69):

(392) a. *kirk   ngathn pork   kuthirr*
         spear   1sgGEN big   two
      b. *kirk   pork   ngathn kuthirr*
         spear   big   1sgGEN two
      c. *kirk   kuthirr pork   ngathn*
         spear   two   big   1sgGEN
      d. *kirk   ngathn kuthirr pork*
         spear   1sgGEN two   big
      e. *kirk   pork   kuthirr ngathn*
         spear   big   two   1sgGEN
      f. *kirk   kuthirr ngathn pork*
         spear   two   1sgGEN big
         'my two big spears'
         [Hall 1972: 69]

It might be expected that (393a–f) would have different interpretations, and although Hall does not provide translations per se, he does underline the second word of each gloss (giving, e.g., 'spears my big two' as the gloss of (394a)), presumably to indicate pragmatic emphasis on the head noun-adjacent constituent.

In most cases where the NP constituents appear in orders other than those set out in (388), it can be argued that they no longer comprise a single noun phrase. Compare, for example, (389) with (395), the translation of which was supplied by a language expert:

(389')   kuta   ngamal   ngotn   ngathn   thono=nhurr
         dog   large   black   1sgGEN   one=only
         'my only big, black dog'
         [KTh_AJ27Jan2004 Elicitation]

(395)   kuta   ngotn   ngamal   thono=nhurr   ngathn
         dog   black   large(NOM)   one=only   1sgGEN
         "big black dog is mine only"
         [Hall 1972: 69, translation by AJ27Jan2004]

In (395), the pronoun *ngathn* does not appear in its usual NP-internal position preceding the quantifier, but instead follows the numeral as well as the enclitic *=nhurr* (which attaches at the right edge of the NP). However, AJ's translation of (395) suggests that it is a possessive copula construction, rather than a single noun phrase. As a copula construction, (395) would be composed of two noun phrases; *kuta ngotn ngamal thono=nhurr* 'only one big black dog' and the genitive pronoun (with predicative function) *ngathn* 'is mine'. Similarly, the occasions where the quantifier *thono* 'one' follows the demonstrative specifier, which is relatively common, can be explained by *thono*'s reference tracking function (§6.11.2.1). This can be seen in (396):

(396)   parr_r   ith   thono   nhul   koow.miing   kar   nhangnip   minc
        child(NOM)   dem:dist   one   3sg(NOM)   face(NOM)   like   father   true
        'that boy [rather than his brother] looks just like his father'
        [KTh_EN02Oct2002 Elicitation]

See §6.11.2.1 for a fuller discussion of the discourse functions of *thono* 'one'.

6.5.3 Ignorative and demonstrative pronouns in N'

There are two final candidates elements that may be included within a noun-headed N'; ignorative and demonstrative pronouns. Although both these word classes commonly function – as their names suggest – as independent pronouns (constituting an N' in their own right, as in (397) and (398)), both can also function adnominally (as in (399) and (400)).

(397) **yuunhul** ngay money sick pay mi'i-m
that.one(ACC) 1sg(ERG) money sick pay(ACC) pick.up-P.IPFV
'I got that, whatsit, sick-pay'
[KTh_AJ-**GJ**03Feb2004 Conversation]

(398) minh **wanhul** mungka-rr?
MEAT(ACC) who:ERG eat-P.PFV
"who bin eating that turtle?"
[KTh_AC10Aug2002 Conversation]

(399) minh **yuunhul** mungka-rr
MEAT that.one(ACC) eat-P.PFV
'(they) ate that whatsit meat'
[KTh_**AJ**-IC-GJ26Nov2002 Conversation/Narrative PormpuraawKanangkarr]

(400) ngul minh **ngan** waak-r Papa-n?
then MEAT what(ACC) follow-NPST Papa-ERG
'I wonder what bird Dad was chasing?'
[Foote and Hall: Primer 10]

Where they function adnominally, both demonstrative pronouns and ignoratives appear at the right periphery of N', bearing the case inflection of the NP (402, 403) and preceding any adnominal demonstrative in specifier position (404).

(401) wa'ap **inhul** ii-parr-op
river this.one(NOM) there-at:south-river
'this river down in the south'
[KTh_ME28Oct2002 Conversation]

(402) pam **wanhngun** kot mit pork yik-m?
man who:DAT God(NOM) work big(ACC) say- P.IPFV
'to whom did God speak of this huge task?'
[Hall 1972: 114]

(403) yuk **ngene-rr** thernga-rr?
THING why-ERG kill-P.PFV
'with what sort of stick did they kill him?'
[KTh_GJ10Jan2004 Elicitation]

(404) man **yuunhul** inh, ngan wan-r? man+nhapn
throat that.one dem:sp.prx what tell- NPST throat+egg
'what's that part of the throat called? The windpipe'
[KTh_AJ8Feb2004 Elicitation / Conversation]

Although it might be tempting to claim that demonstrative and ignorative pronouns always occupy this slot within N' (even in examples such as (397) and (398)), this is clearly not the case. When functioning pronominally, there is no requirement of contiguity between demonstrative/ignorative pronouns and the coreferential (noun-headed) NP, and both bear case independently of one another. Thus (405) contains two dative-marked NPs (*inh'nhngun* 'to this very [place]' and *Pormpuraawthak* 'to Pormpuraaw'), with the demonstrative pronoun preceding the noun-headed NP. In (266), the ignorative pronoun follows the full NP (including specifier) *paanth ith* 'that woman'.

(405) *Friday, koop therk,*   ***inh'nhungun***   *Pormpuraaw-thak*
       Friday all   return:NPST this.very.one:DAT Pormpuraaw-DAT
       'on Friday everyone is coming back to Pormpuraaw'
       [KTh_AC21Aug2002 Conversation]

(406) *paanth*   *ith*   ***wanh=okun***   *yan?*
       woman(NOM) dem:dist who(NOM)=DUB go:NPST
       "which is that lady there coming?"
       [KTh_AC21Aug2002 Conversation]

For this reason, I analyze demonstrative and ignorative pronouns as filling an N'-internal slot when functioning adnominally, while constituting an N in and of themselves (along with personal pronouns) when functioning pronominally. This corresponds with the N'-internal position of genitive pronouns functioning adnominally vs. the use of genitive personal pronouns as N's of themselves when functioning as complements, predicates and/or clausal adjuncts (cf. §5.1.1.2).

6.6 Determination, determiners and specifiers

There has been considerable debate in the Australianist literature as to the existence of a determiner-headed DP, and the semantic and syntactic relationships between pronouns and coreferential NP/DPs (see Verstraete & Louagie 2015 for an excellent summary of this literature). The following sections consider how these questions Kuuk Thaayorre. Section 6.6.1 begins by outlining semantic evidence that both pronouns and adnominal demonstratives play a determining function with respect to the noun phrase. The following sections, §6.6.2 and §6.6.36.6.3, consider the syntax of how adnominal demonstratives and pronouns, respectively, combine with noun-headed noun phrases. Section 6.6.4 considers instances of 'over-determination', in which adnominal demonstratives are used in combination with pronouns. Section 6.6.5 concludes by considering the evidence for a determiner phrase.

6.6.1 Determination

Both adnominal demonstratives and pronouns can play a determiner-like role with respect to the noun-headed NP. Adnominal demonstratives cause a NP to have definite reference, while the presence of a pronoun makes a noun phrase specific. Hence in (407) the referent of *paanth ith* 'that woman' is definite, while in (408) the referent of *pul pam ngumpurrkak pul* 'an old man and woman' is specific, but not definite:

(407) paanth   ith   nhamp   wanh?
      woman(NOM) dem:dist   name   who
      'what is that woman's name?'
      [KTh_AC21Aug2002 Elicitation]

(408) kanangkarr pul   pam   ngumpurr-kak pul,   may-i   yat
      long.ago   3du(NOM)   man(NOM)   old.lady-COM 3du(NOM) VEG-DAT go:P.PFV
      'Once upon a time an old man and his wife went looking for food'
      [KTh_FT8Feb2004 Narrative Adoptee]

Note, however, that the presence of neither demonstrative nor pronoun is required for a NP to be a referring expression. In their absence, the NP is simply unspecified for definiteness and specificity. Such NPs may be indefinite and unspecific (as is *pam* 'HUMAN' in (409)); indefinite but specific (as is *nhayp* 'knife' in [410]); or definite and specific (as is *nganip* 'father' in (411)):

(409) pam   yuur   kuthirr=kaak
      HUMAN(NOM)   hand   two=REL.PROP
      'people have two hands'
      [KTh_GJ12Sep2002 Elicitation]

(410) ngernkan   AA   nganh   nhayp-n   yaki-rr
      yesterday [name redacted]   1sgACC   knife-ERG   cut- P.PFV
      'yesterday AA cut me with a knife'
      [Anon.]

(411) Nganip-i   yumpi-rr,   nganip   ilnen   ii
      father-ERG   made-P.PFV   father(NOM)   from.above   there
      'God made (dogs), God up there'
      [KTh_AC10Aug2002 Conversation]

While demonstratives and pronouns clearly perform a determiner-like function, the fact that they are not required for definite/specific reference might make their classification as determiners less attractive.[124] Moreover, while demonstratives and pronouns share a determiner-like function, their respective syntactic distributions are markedly different; demonstratives are tightly bound to the NP with respect to word order, while the pronouns are (arguably) syntactically free, and inflect for case independently. The respective syntactic profiles of these determining forms are outlined in the following sections.

6.6.2 Adnominal demonstrative determiners

Adnominal demonstratives appear at the right edge of the noun phrase (as per the NP rule given in (367)), but they do not host the phrase-final case inflection that signals the grammatical function of the NP as a whole.[125] Where a case-bearing noun phrase has an adnominal demonstrative as its final constituent, it is the penultimate constituent that bears the case inflection (whether this be noun, adjective, possessor or quantifier). Thus in (412), the ergative inflection appears in the middle of the noun phrase *parr_r paanthu ith* 'that girl' since *paanth* 'female' is the last element that may inflect for case:

(412)   *parr_r paanth-u   ith   may   mular   wash-m   rirk   ngok-eln*
        child female-ERG   dem:dist   VEG   yam(ACC)   wash-TR   DO:NPST   water-DAT
        'that girl washes the yam'
        [KTh_AJ7Feb2004 Elicitation]

Similarly, in (413) it is the specific noun *nhump*[126] 'elder', and not the following demonstrative, that inflects for ergative case in the noun phrase *pam nhumpu ith* 'that old man':

(413)   *yuur   pinalam   ith   sing   rirk   pam   nhump-u   ith*
        hand   three   dem:dist   sing   DO:NPST   MAN   elder-ERG   dem:dist
        'the old man sang it three times'
        [KTh_AJ27Jan2004 Elicitation]

One way to explain why it follows the case affixes, would be to analyze the demonstrative as a determiner that heads a determiner phrase with a (case-marked) NP complement (cf. Gaby 2006). In the phrase structure rules presented at the beginning of

---

124 There are precedents for analyzing similar forms as determiners, however. Alpher (1973: 281–282) similarly finds Yir Yoront noun phrases may have definite reference in the absence of demonstratives and pronouns, but continues to classify them together as determiners. Blake (2001b:417) likewise establishes for Pitta-Pitta a 'pronoun-determiner' class that heads the (determiner) phrase.
125 Two exceptions to this rule are discussed in §5.3.2.2.
126 *Nhump* 'elder' is a dialectal variant of *thuump* 'elder; grey (hair)'.

this chapter (367), however, the adnominal demonstrative is included within the NP structure as a specifier. This is largely attractive because it allows phrase-initial pronouns to be analyzed as determiners heading a DP. The syntactic function of adnominal demonstratives is considered further in §6.6.5 below.

6.6.3 Pronominal determiners

As discussed in §6.7, it is commonplace for pronouns to co-occur in the same clause with non-adjacent, coreferential, noun-headed NPs. This is analyzed as apposition. It is also commonplace, however, for pronouns to occur immediately adjacent to and within the same prosodic unit as noun-headed NPs. This is illustrated by example (414), in which *nhul* 'he' arguably forms a phrase with *parran* 'child':

(414) nhul   parr-an   kuta   mi'irr   nhul   ngamal.katpi-rr.
      3sg(ERG) child-ERG dog(ACC) pick.up:P.PFV 3sg(ERG) hug-P.PFV
      'The child picked up the dog and hugged him.'
      [KTh_MF17Sep2002 Narrative FrogStory]

Pronouns are also found immediately adjacent to coreferential noun-headed NPs, but outside their prosodic unit. Such pronouns – like those displaced from the coreferential NP – are considered syntactically apposed, though performing a determining function. Most commonly, as shown in (415), the pronoun falls clearly within the same prosodic unit as the noun-headed NP:

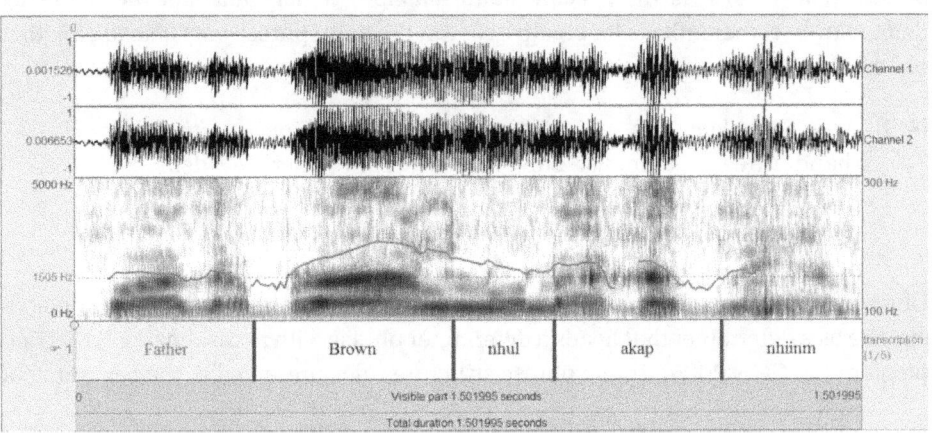

(415) *Father Brown   nhul   aka=p   nhiin-m*
      Father Brown(NOM) 3sg(NOM) here=PR sit-P.IPFV
      'Father Brown was here'
      "he was the only priest here, that Father Brown"
      [KTh_AJ-IC-GJ26Nov2002_28: 57–28: 59 Conversation]

Although the pronoun occurs at the right edge of the NP in (415), it is more commonly found at the left edge, as in the following example:[127]

(416) *ngee! nhul   ngan yapa kaar yat,   nhul   ii-korr*
       I.see 3sg(NOM) KIN Z+   NEG go:P.PFV 3sg(NOM) there-at:beyond
       'your sister didn't come to see me, she's out bush'
       [KTh_AJ08Feb2004 Elicitation]

It is possible for Kuuk Thaayorre pronouns to form a unit with proper names, such as *Father Brown* in (415) above and *Irene* in (417) and (418), representing a possible exception to Stirling and Baker's (2007) distinction between 'classic' and 'topic' determiners (cf. also Verstraete & Louagie 2015).

(417) *ngul nhul   Irene   kempthe yat*
       then 3sg(NOM) Irene(NOM) singly   go:P.PFV
       'then Irene went off on her own [to a different place]'
       [KTh_GJ16Oct2002 Narrative MelbourneTrip]

(418) *nhul   Irene   make.friend rirk-r   pelnungun family nhangn-mak*
       3sg(NOM) Irene(NOM) make.friend DO-P.PFV 3plDAT   family 3sgGEN-DAT
       'Irene made friends with her [host] family'
       [KTh_GJ16Oct2002 Narrative MelbourneTrip]

Lastly, note that – in sequences such as *pelnungun family nhangnmak* 'with her family' in (418) – pronouns with this determining function may receive non-core case marking (in this instance, dative).

6.6.4 Over-determination: pronoun + demonstrative

The combination of multiple determining elements is known as 'over-determination' (Himmelmann 2001, Plank 2003, Verstraete & Louagie 2015). Such over-determination is rife in Kuuk Thaayorre, in which multiple demonstratives and pronouns may combine not only within a particular phrase, but across multiple apposed, coreferential phrases. Examples (419)–(421) demonstrate the combination of demonstrative and pronominal determining elements:

---

[127] This supports Verstraete and Louagie's (2015) finding that in Australian languages adnominal pronouns occur most frequently at the left edge of the NP, although they are also found at the right edge as well as displaced from the NP. As they put it, "regardless of which edge they prefer, the tendency towards edge position for adnominal pronouns nicely fits in with a determining function, reflecting scope over the entire nominal expression" (Verstraete & Louagie 2015: 172).

(419) nhul   pam-al   ith   door   open   rirk
      3sg(ERG) man-ERG   dem:dist   door(ACC) open   DO:NPST
      'the man opened the door'
      [KTh_**FT**-GJ10Feb2004 Elicitation RCP9]

(420) pam   nhump   ulp   nhul   wonp-r
      man   old(NOM)   dem:ad.prx   3sg(NOM)   die-P.PFV
      'the old man died'
      [KTh_AJ-IC-**GJ**26Nov2002 Narrative/Conversation]

(421) paanth-u   ith   nhul   yuk   thongkn   thiika-rr
      woman-ERG   dem:dist   3sg(ERG)   thing   stick(ACC)   break-P.PFV
      'that woman broke a stick'
      [KTh_GJ15Oct2002 Elicitation Cut&Break19]

Note that in (419) the pronoun precedes the NP, while in (421) it follows, but in both cases the adnominal demonstrative occurs immediately to the right of the noun. This is consistent with a phrase structure in which the demonstrative is closer to the head noun than is the pronoun, a tendency among Australian languages noted by Verstraete & Louagie (2015: 174). This fact underlies the determiner phrase structure proposed in §6.6.5 below.

Before moving on, however, it should be noted that adnominal demonstratives and pronouns can combine in the absence of any noun or other NP constituent. This is illustrated by the following pair of examples, taken from an extended group narrative told by three siblings. In example (422.1), the speaker adds the demonstrative *inh* 'this' to the pronoun *nhul* 'she' in order to unambiguously refer to the woman sitting next to him.[128] Later in the same discussion (423), the speaker adds the addressee proximal form *ulp* to the first person plural pronoun *ngancn*, in order to disambiguate the three siblings involved in the storytelling (and who are thus 'proximal' to the linguist/addressee) from the previous generation of elders who also feature in the story:

(422) 1. nhul   inh   kanpa-tam   inh.
         3sg(NOM) dem:sp.prx   first-ABL   dem:sp.prx
         'she here's the first (born).'
     2. pul   inh   kanpa-tam
        3du(NOM) dem:sp.prx   first-ABL
        'The two of them were first.'
        "she's eldest, first, Albert too"
        [KTh_AJ-IC-**GJ**26Nov2002 Narrative/Conversation]

---

128 This is followed by the use of the dual pronoun, to add reference to the speaker's brother (who sits to the other side of their sister).

(423) ngancn   ulp   parr_r   ngan   yancm
      1pl(NOM) dem:ad.prx   child   what   go:P.IPFV
      'we were kids [then]'
      [KTh_AJ-IC-**GJ**26Nov2002 Narrative/Conversation]

In both cases, the demonstrative seems to play a determining function vis-à-vis the pronoun, rather than the reverse. This question is revisited in the next section.

6.6.5 Determiner phrase

One way to account for the facts outlined above is to propose a determiner phrase (DP) headed by a NP-adjacent pronoun. This explains why adnominal demonstratives, as specifiers of NP, must always appear closer to the noun-head than pronouns. The relevant phrase structure rules are as follows (note that for transparency, I use the abbreviation 'Pro' rather than 'D' for the personal pronoun head of DP):

(424) **DP** → (Pro) , (NP)
      NP → N' (AdnDem)

As formalized in this DP rule, the pronoun head can either precede or follow NP, but where it follows it will always appear to the right of any adnominal demonstrative. Furthermore, the noun-headed NP is optional in DP, so personal pronouns may constitute an NP in and of themselves. In DPs consisting of a pronoun and adnominal demonstrative alone (as in examples (422) and (423)), the adnominal demonstrative represents the only constituent of NP (since all NP constituents are optional, per the phrase structure rules in (367) above). In clauses where the NP and pronoun are separated by other clausal constituents, the pronoun would form a DP in isolation which is apposed to the NP (the two forming a discontinuous DP at some higher level, with the NP as complement).

The mapping of this phrase structure rule onto actual examples is shown by (425), in which the pronoun forms a phrase with the immediately preceding NP, and (426), in which the pronoun forms a DP in isolation:

(425) pam   -al   ith   nhul   may   carrots   yakake:rr
      [[[man]_N' -ERG   dem:dist]_NP   3sg(ERG)]_DP   [[VEG carrots]_N ACC]_NP   cut:RDP:P.PFV
      'the man cut up the carrots'
      [KTh_EN03Dec2002 Elicitation Cut&Break10]

(426) parr_r   inh   yan   peln   school-thak
      [child]_N' (NOM) dem:sp.prx]_NP   go:NPST   [3pl(NOM)]_DP   school-DAT
      'these children (nowadays) go to school'
      [KTh_AJ-IC-**GJ**26Nov2002 Narrative/Conversation]

An advantage of the DP rule proposed in (424), is that Pro can be removed from the suite of NP rules proposed in (367) (in which Pro can substitute for the noun-headed constituents of N'). This simplification of the NP rules comes at a cost, however. Two advantages of retaining Pro at N' are as follows: (1) it allows for the generalization that referential case is always and only marked at the right edge of N', thereby capturing the inflectional behaviour of both nomina and pronouns; and (2) it allows for the generalization that a genitive-inflected N' (whether noun-headed or pronominal) may be recursively inserted as a possessive modifier within N'.

If we retain the pronoun's place within N', the structures consisting solely of pronoun and adnominal demonstrative (seen in (422) and (423)) would alternatively be analyzed as a single NP headed by a pronoun in N' followed by the adnominal demonstrative in specifier position. It is possible to abandon the DP altogether, analyzing all pairings of coreferential pronouns and noun-headed NPs as instances of the apposition of two syntactically independent phrases. Under this analysis, the clause given in example (425), then, would instead be parsed as in (427):

(427) pam   -al   ith   nhul   may carrots   yakakerr
      [KTh_[man]$_{N'}$ -ERG dem:dist]$_{NP}$ [[3sg]$_{N'}$ ERG]$_{NP}$ [[[VEG carrots]$_{N}$]$_{N}$ACC]$_{NP}$ cut:RDP:P.PFV
      'that man cut up the carrots'
      [KTh_EN03Dec2002 Elicitation Cut&Break10]

The question of whether pronouns head a DP in Kuuk Thaayorre is of theoretical rather than descriptive interest, and as such will not be considered at any more length. It is sufficient to simply observe that the function performed by these pronouns is one of determination, and that there is a significant degree of prosodic integration with adjacent noun-headed NPs. Indeed, much as clitics exhibit mixed behaviour at the level of the word (being phonologically dependent but syntactically independent), these Kuuk Thaayorre pronouns exhibit mixed behaviour at the level of the phrase (being semantically and prosodically integrated but syntactically more free). Much as clitics often represent a midway point along the grammaticalization pathway from free word to affix, so too the Kuuk Thaayorre pronoun may be midway between heading an independent, apposed phrase and being integrated into a higher-level phrase.

The remainder of this grammar will assume the phrase structure rules in (367), analyzing coreferential NPs and pronouns as syntactically apposed to one another whether adjacent or discontinuous.

6.7 Wholly coreferential NPs

6.7.1 Apposition via referential case

It is commonplace in Kuuk Thaayorre for multiple coreferential NPs to stand in a relation of apposition to one another within a single clause, thereby together comprising an argument. In (428), for example, the two noun phrases *parr_r inh* 'these kids' and *peln* 'they' do not form a continuous syntactic phrase, yet both contribute information about the same group of participants. Similarly, in (429) *peln* 'they' is coreferential with the clause-initially phrase *pam mong minc ith* 'those very many men'.

(428) *may   nhul   koop   mungka-rrthon-thrr*
      VEG(ACC) 3sg(ERG) all(ACC) eat-P.PFV   one-ERG
      'the one guy ate all the food!'
      [AJ07/02/04 Elicitation]

(429) *pam mong minc   ith   ii   yan   peln*
      man many really(NOM) dem:dist there go:NPST 3pl(NOM)
      'a lot of men are walking along there'
      [KTh_AJ07Feb2004 Elicitation]

It is also common for (coreferential) free pronouns to be repeated several times in a single clause, as in (430):

(430) *nhul   parr_rpaanth   nhul   yancm*
      3sg(NOM) child woman(NOM) 3sg(NOM) go:P.IPFV
      'she was a young girl [then]'
      [KTh_AJ-GJ-**IC**26Nov2002 Narrative/Conversation]

6.7.2 Peripheral phrases

In addition to the apposition of multiple pronouns or pronoun and noun phrase, it is often common for speakers to repeat part or all of a nomen-headed noun phrase at the beginning or end of the clause and prosodically separated from it. These semantically redundant noun phrases are similar to those labelled "afterthoughts" in Gooniyandi (McGregor 1990), and "codas" and "postscripts" in Kugu Nganhcara (Smith and Johnson 2000). None of these labels are appropriate to Kuuk Thaayorre, however, since in this language the extraposed phrase may precede as well as follow the main clause. Illustrating both these orders, a peripheral phrase (*kuta* 'dog') precedes the first clause of (431), while the peripheral phrase (*kuta mant* 'small dog') follows the second main clause:

(431) 1. **kuta, kuta**   ith   riiric-r!
         dog dog(NOM) dem:dist run:RDP-NPST
         'that dog's running past'
      2. **kuta**   riiran theetherk,   **kuta mant**
         dog(NOM) alone return:RDP:NPST dog small
         'that dog's going back alone, (just a) small puppy'
         [KTh_AC21Aug2002 Conversation]

For this reason, I label them 'peripheral phrases', while acknowledging their formal and functional similarity to the aforementioned categories described in other Australian languages.

Peripheral phrases are distinguished by their prosodic independence from the main clause; they fall outside the latter's intonational contour and are usually separated from it by a short pause. Peripheral phrases generally do not carry the relevant case marking for their (associated) role inside the clause. This is illustrated by (432), in which the location referred to by the peripheral phrase *raak inh* 'this place' would receive dative case marking if it were part of the main clause.

(432) *raak   inh,   Paangunth, angunp   kerp-r*
      PLACE dem:sp.prx Paangunth in.that.place finish-P.PFV
      'this place, Paangunth, (she) disappeared there'
      [KTh_AC14Nov2002 Narrative LosingIrma]

It is possible, however, for the case marking of peripheral phrases to reflect their role in the clause, as in the following:

(433) *pam   peln   ii   kana   yan   minh-a,   minh kothon-ak*
      man(NOM) 3pl(NOM) there about.to go:NPST MEAT-DAT MEAT wallaby-DAT
      'those men are hunting wallaby'
      [KTh_AC10Aug2002 Elicitation]

The repetition of coreferential noun phrases is so ubiquitous in the speech of certain individuals that it can become difficult to draw a line between peripheral phrases and main clauses. Example (434) contains maximally seven clauses (bounded by pauses), only the last of which contains a verb (*therk* 'return'). It would be possible, then, to view this final clause (434.5) as the main clause, and each of the preceding phrases in (434.1)–(434.4) as peripheral phrases, each of which contributes to specifying the reference of the subject pronoun *peln* 'they':

(434) 1. *thil   peln   ii-l-ungkarr,   par_r   inhul   peln*
again 3pl(NOM) there-from-north child(NOM) this.one 3pl(NOM)
'those children [coming] again from the north'
2. *Dan   mangka...*
Dan(NOM) mob
'Dan and them'
3. *Dan,   peln   parr_r   inhul*
Dan(NOM) 3pl(NOM) child(NOM) this.one
'Dan and those children, they...'
4. *parr_r mant   inhul   peln*
child small(NOM) this.one 3pl(NOM)
'those small children'
5. *peln   Friday yup   therk   ii-l-ungkarr*
3pl(NOM) Friday soon return:NPST there-from-north
'they'll come back from the North [Weipa] on Friday'
[KTh_AC21Aug2002 Narrative WeipaFootball]

6.8 The inclusory construction

Inclusory constructions are employed to make explicit reference to a particular individual or individuals within a larger participant group. This is illustrated by (435), in which the referent of *wangath* 'doctor' is included within the participant group referred to by *ngali* 'we two':

(435) *ngali   wangath-an hour-ak   ngat   pit-m*
1du:excl(ERG) doctor-ERG hour-DAT fish(ACC) hold-P.IPFV
'The doctor and I were fishing for an hour'
[Foote and Hall: Reader 10]

Kuuk Thaayorre is unusual in having several alternative inclusory constructions (cf. Singer 2001). Each of these is composed of a pronoun referring to the superset of participants, which is apposed to one or more NPs referring to the subset(s) to which attention is drawn. The key morphosyntactic difference between the different inclusory constructions is the case-marking of the subset noun phrase, as detailed in the following sections.

Analogous constructions have been documented in a wide range of languages, for example by Lichtenberk (2000), Schwartz (1988), and Singer (2001). In her typology of inclusory constructions in Australian languages, Singer (2001: 22–25) offers the following defining features of inclusory constructions: (1) the relationship between superset and subset is one of proper inclusion; (2) entailments of the predicate always hold for the superset and subset; (3) the superset is encoded by a pronoun; (4) the inclusory construction is equivalent to a single argument of a single predicate. These features straightforwardly apply to each of the Kuuk Thaayorre inclusory constructions, though not the inclusory pronouns (§6.8.5) in which both superset and subset are encoded by a single pronoun. In all the Kuuk Thaayorre inclusory constructions, the number and person features of the argument as a whole match those of the superset pronoun, suggesting that it is the pronoun that is the head of the construction and the subset NP the complement.

6.8.1 The simple inclusory construction

In the simple inclusory construction, superset and subset are represented by distinct NPs that are apposed in the same case. This is illustrated by (436), which contains three coreferential noun phrases representing the superset (*ngali* 'we two', twice instantiated, and *kuthirr* 'the two (of us)') and one NP representing the subset *I.C.* (a personal name). All four noun phrases are in nominative case, assigned by the intransitive verb *yan* 'go' to its subject argument:

(436)   ngali   I. C.   ngali   yat   kuthirr
        1du:excl(NOM) I. C.(NOM)   1du:excl(NOM) go:P.PFV   two(NOM)
        'I. C. and I went, the two of us'
        [KTh_GJ16Oct2002 Narrative MelbourneTrip]

The simple Thaayorre inclusory construction is so labelled because of its relative lack of morphological marking (compared with the comitative, dative and ergative inclusory constructions). The term is not intended to signify cognitive primacy or diachronic priority.

Inclusory constructions are most frequently associated with the grammatical function of subject. They may have other grammatical functions, however, as the following examples show.

(437)   ngalinan   pam thuump-ak   inhul
        1du:excl:GEN   man elder-GEN   this.one
        'this one is my husband's and mine'
        [KTh_FT8Feb2004 Narrative Adoptee]

(438)   ngay   pulnun   Barry-ak   nhaawr
        1sg(NOM) 3duDAT   Barry-DAT see:P.PFV
        'I saw him and Barry'
        [KTh_EN27Jan2004 Conversation]

In (437), the inclusory construction encodes possessors, while in (438) the inclusory construction has the grammatical function of indirect object.[129]

While the subset NP most commonly appears immediately following the superset pronoun, the two need not be contiguous nor in this order. In (439), for instance, the subset *ngan waanharr* 'elder brother' and superset *ngali* 'we two' are separated by the verb:

(439) wey, ngali yancm ngan waanharr iipal
 hey 1du:excl(NOM) go:P.IPFV KIN e.brother(NOM) from.there
 'hey, my brother and I have come here'
 [Foote: Narrative KutaWoochorrm]

It is difficult, then, to analyze superset and subset as forming a single noun phrase. Within the theoretical framework of LFG, it could be argued that the superset and subset NPs form a single unit filling an argument position in the f-structure representation, but that they do not form a single constituent at the level of c-structure. Like the part-whole construction (described in §6.10.1 below), it seems that the linkage of the two phrases to a single argument slot (and thus grammatical function) is achieved through their agreeing in case. This fits the characterization of 'referential case' proposed by Dench and Evans (1988: 13):

> The referential case function involves the marking of some NP or adverb in agreement with some other (usually core) NP in the same clause... the identically marked words are separate constituents.

The superset noun phrase in a simple inclusory construction is commonly a first or second person dual pronoun. In such cases, one referent is specified by the subset NP, and the other is fully recoverable as either the speaker or addressee respectively. The simple inclusory construction is thus used frequently in discourse to introduce new participants, or to clarify the membership of a nonsingular participant group. In example (440), an inclusory construction formed from a second person dual pronoun is used specifically in order to request the identity of the second, non-addressee participant:

(440) nhip wanh wun ii-kaw
 2du(NOM) who(NOM) reside:NPST there-at:east
 'who do you live with?'
 [KTh_MC21Jan2004 Conversation]

---

[129] Note that although the subset NP in (438) is marked by dative case, this is not considered an example of the dative inclusory construction (described in §6.8.3 below). In (438), the dative case is assigned by the verb to its argument (and the subset agrees with the superset pronoun in referential dative case), rather than the case marker being used to comment on the relationship that obtains between the participants.

6.8.2 The comitative inclusory construction

The noun phrase referring to the subset may be marked by the comitative suffix -*kak*, as seen in example (441).

(441) 1. *pam-kak   ii   yan   pul*
man-COM   there go:NPST 3du(NOM)
'that husband and wife are going along'
2. *pul   ii   yan,   kuthirr,   pam-kak*
3du(NOM) there go:NPST two(NOM)   man-COM
'they two are going along there, two of them, husband and wife'
[KTh_AC12Sep2002]

In (441.1), the participants are identified by means of both the nominative pronoun *pul* 'they two' (referring to the superset) and the comitative noun phrase *pamkak* 'with man' (the 'man' being a subset of the subject participant group). Crucially, one of the participants (the man) is referred to by both the subject pronoun *pul* 'they two' and the adjunct NP *pamkak* 'with the man'. This contrasts with a literal translation of (441.1); *they two are going along with the man*, which in English entails three rather than two participants, since the reference of the adjunct PP *with the man* must not overlap with the reference of the subject NP *they two*. An analogous construction is also available in Kuuk Thaayorre, with the comitative adjunct referring to a participant wholly distinct from that referred to by the subject NP. Disjoint reference is also possible in Kuuk Thaayorre, as seen in (442), in which the reference of the subject pronoun *ngay* 'I' is wholly distinct from that of the comitative adjunct *pam puukath-kak* 'with an initiated man':

(442) *pam puukath-kak   wak-m   ngay*
man initiated-COM follow-P.IPFV 1sg(ERG)
'I was hunting with an initiated man'
[Foote and Hall: Primer 10]

Why, then, would a speaker choose to utter the comitative inclusory construction over the simple inclusory construction, or a clause in which subject and adjunct have disjunct reference? The Kuuk Thaayorre comitative inclusory construction is advantageous in the following respects. Firstly, the fact that the subject pronoun *pul* 'they two' in (441) incorporates both participants in its reference captures the fact that both the man and woman participate in the event in the same way (i.e. they are both walking), and thus a single relationship holds between them and the predicate. The nominative case assigned to the subject pronoun – which is the head of the inclusory construction – is hence relational case, marking a dependency relationship between the noun phrase and predicate. Meanwhile, the dependent comitative NP allows the speaker to simultaneously comment on the relationship that holds between the respective subject participants (adnominal case). In (441) above, for example, the comitative adjunct is used to imply that the subject participants are married. The noun *pam* means both 'man' and 'husband', and the clauses in (441) were uttered both to point out to the addressee a couple walking past, and (more importantly) to communicate the relationship that held between them. This is an implicature, though, and not an entailment.[130] Where the superset pronoun is plural (as opposed to dual), the implicature of marriage is no longer present:[131]

(443) *pam-kak ngancn yat*
 man-COM 1pl(NOM) go:P.PFV
 'we went with the man'
 [KTh_GJ06Dec2002 Elicitation]

The comitative inclusory construction may also be used to implicate non-familial relationships. In (444), for instance, both the participants represented by the dual pronoun *nhip* 'you two' are exhorted to engage in the same activity. The extraposition of one of these in the comitative adjunct *parr_r-kak* 'with the child', suggests that an unequal relationship holds between the two. Specifically, we may infer from (444) that the child is less centrally involved in the event, which is to be initiated by the addressee (the unspecified member of the superset pronoun *nhip* 'you two'). The choice of construction thus places responsibility on the addressee for the actualization of the event, and the involvement of the subset 'child'.

(444) *parr_r-kak nhip yarr!*
 child-COM 2du(NOM) go:IMP
 'you go with that child'
 [KTh_GJ06Dec2002 Elicitation]

This construction is not exotic: both Schwartz (1988) and Singer (2001) find many languages in their samples employ an adnominal case (often comitative, dative or instrumental cases, or some other marker of nominal conjunction) to relate subset NPs to the superset. Russian, for example, possesses a construction in which a subset NP (in instrumental case, signifying accompaniment) complements a free pronoun representing the superset:

---

130 Evans (2006) also discusses the development of a similar dyad sense through the hardening of implicature to entailment.
131 Note also that comitative inclusory constructions containing plural superset pronouns are often indistinguishable from simple comitative constructions in which the referent of the comitative phrase is not included within the reference of the plural pronoun.

(445) my   s   vami   gde.to   vstrecha-l-i-s'
      1plNOM with 2pl¹³²:INSTR somewhere meet-PST-PL-RFL
      'you and I have met somewhere'
      [film title]

See §4.2.7.1 for a discussion of the incipient dyadic function of the comitative inclusory construction.

6.8.3 The dative inclusory construction

The dative inclusory construction is structurally very similar to the comitative inclusory construction; the two differ only in the eponymous case assigned to the subset NP. The dative inclusory construction is exemplified by (446), in which the head NP *ngali* 'we two' is followed by its dative-marked complement *pam kunyangkar ngathn-mun* 'at my brother':

(446) ngali   pam kunyangkar ngathn-mun nhaanhath-rr
      1du:excl(NOM) MAN sibling   1sgGEN-DAT look.at-RCP:NPST
      'my brother and I are looking at each other'
      [KTh_MF06Aug2002 Elicitation]

The dative inclusory construction is often found in reciprocal clauses derived from base verbs that subcategorize for a (dative-marked) indirect object. In (446), for example, both participants are associated with two semantic roles (agent and goal) and also two cases (nominative and dative). The ascription of two semantic roles to a single argument is licensed by the reciprocal construction (marked by the verbal suffix *-rr*). The two participants are thus encoded as a single subject argument, encoded by a pronominal head and dative complement. Rather than analyzing the dative-marked subset NP as complement to the superset pronoun (the former being related to the latter via adnominal case), we might wish to view the nominative pronoun and dative NP as separate arguments corresponding to those in the subcategorization frame of the underived verb root *nhaa-* 'look <NOM, DAT>'. The fact that the referent of the dative-marked subset NP is included within the reference of the subject pronoun, however, makes such an analysis problematic, as does the fact that reciprocal derivation by the suffix *-rr* would normally result in the deletion of one argument under coreference with the subject. This leads us to another interesting point. Reciprocal derivation (by the verbal suffix *-rr*) is generally only available to verbs that subcatego-

---

132 The Russian second person plural pronoun is used as a respectful second person singular form.

rize for an (accusative) direct object (i.e. transitive and ditransitive verbs). The comitative inclusory construction, however, is only available to verbs that subcategorize for a (dative) 'indirect object' (i.e. extended intransitive and extended transitive verbs). The verb root *nhaa-* is polysemous, functioning as a transitive verb with the sense 'look at, see' (with the associated <ERG, ACC> subcategorization frame), but also as an extended intransitive verb with the sense 'look' (with the associated <NOM, DAT> subcategorization frame). In (446) it would seem that the reciprocalization of the verb is licensed by the transitive sense of *nhaa-*, but the dative inclusory construction is licensed by its extended intransitive sense. The theoretical implications of this for our analysis of valency, reciprocalization and case warrant further consideration.

As well as appearing in reciprocal-marked clauses, the dative inclusory construction can be found in the description of semantically symmetric (i.e. reciprocated) events that may not be formally coded as such by the verbal suffix *-rr*. In (447), for example, the verb *yik* 'say' is an extended intransitive verb (subcategorizing for a nominative subject, dative indirect object and optional cognate object, filled here by *kuuk* 'WORD'), and is thus ineligible for reciprocal derivation by *-rr*. Nevertheless, the symmetry of the conversing event is encoded by the fact that both participants are encoded as a single argument. That two semantic roles are associated with this argument is meanwhile expressed by the dative marking of the subset NP. This makes it is clear that the two brothers are directing their speech to one another, rather than broadcasting simultaneously.

(447) pul   pam kunyangkar nhangn-mun   kuuk   yiik
      3du(NOM) MAN sibling   3sgGEN-DAT   WORD(ACC) say:RDP:NPST
      'he and his brother are talking to one another'
      [KTh_MF06Aug2002 Elicitation]

The dative inclusory construction can thus be considered a valid strategy for encoding reciprocity (a 'double role marking' strategy per Evans' (2008) structural typology of reciprocals) since its use entails symmetry of relations between participants. (This entailment depends, however, upon the construction being interpreted with its inclusory sense. If the hearer does not interpret the subject pronoun and dative NP as overlapping in their reference, (447) could alternatively be interpreted as 'they two$_i$ were talking to his brother$_j$'.)

6.8.4 The ergative inclusory construction

The ergative inclusory construction is the final construction in which the subset NP is marked as a dependent of the superset pronoun by adnominal case. As discussed in §4.2.1.3 (and more extensively in Gaby 2008a, 2010) the ergative morpheme has some pragmatic, as well as syntactic, functions. One of these is to mark a subject referent that is likely to be 'unexpected'[133] by the addressee. Accordingly, where the addressee is anticipated to have difficulty retrieving or predicting the reference of some subset of a plural referent group, the speaker will often employ an inclusory construction in which the relevant subset NP is ergative-marked. Note that the ergative inclusory construction is attested only where the complete NP has the grammatical function of intransitive subject. If the grammatical function were transitive subject, there would be no way of distinguishing an ergative inclusory construction from a simple (appositional) inclusory construction.

Exemplifying the ergative inclusory construction is (448), in which the subset NP *Edwardnthurr* 'Edward' is ergative-marked.

(448) *AA nhul driver. Ngali mit rirk BB-nthurr*
AA 3sg(NOM) driver(NOM) 2du:excl(NOM) work DO:NPST BB-ERG
'AA is the driver. We two work, [me and] BB'
[KTh_AJ27Jan2004 Conversation – names redacted]

The intransitive subject subset of (448) (*BB*) is ergative-marked due to discourse pragmatic considerations, rather than intra-clausal morphosyntax or semantics. Because the first clause of (448) has set up AA as topic, when the second clause goes on to state 'we two work' the addressee might be misled into thinking that the speaker is referring to himself and AA, rather than himself and BB. For this reason, the speaker affixes the ergative marker to *BB* to stress the fact that (perhaps contrary to the addressee's expectations) he is the subject of the second clause.

As well as introducing an entirely new subject referent, the ergative inclusory construction may be used to signal a change in membership of a plural subject group. Example (449) is excerpted from a story about the narrator's childhood, recounting the time he and his siblings first saw a plane. The enduring topic of the whole narrative is *ngancn* 'we', which is used most of the time in reference to the speaker and his siblings (as it is in (449.1). In the second line of the example, however, the referential scope of *ngancn* 'we' expands to include the speaker's parents. To mark this unexpected shift in reference, the two new participants in (449.2) are encoded by ergative-marked subset NPs; *nganipi* 'father' and *mami ngathnman* 'my mum':

---

133 A subject is defined as 'unexpected' where it refers to a newly introduced (or re-introduced) participant in a section of discourse that has had a stable protagonist/topic chain that has been displaced by this new participant, as characterized by McGregor's (1998: 516) 'Expected Actor Principle':

The episode protagonist is – once it has been established – the expected (and unmarked) Actor of each foregrounded narrative clause of the episode; any other Actor is unexpected.

(449) 1. *ngancn   kanangkarr parr_r mant*
       3pl:excl(NOM) long.ago   child   small(NOM)
       'when we used to be small kids'
  2. *ngul ngancn   nganip-i   ngancn,   mami ngathn-man ngancn...*
       then 1pl:excl(NOM) father-ERG^ 1pl:excl(NOM) mum 1sgGEN-ERG^ 1pl:excl(NOM)
       'we, including Dad and Mum...'
  3. *ngancn   ii-rr-kaw   yat*
       1pl:excl(NOM) there-towards-west go:P.PFV
       'we went out bush'
       [GJ15Oct2002 Narrative PlaneSighting]

What is particularly interesting about these examples, is that they show that case marking remains sensitive to information status even within arguments, so that where two subparts of a single argument differ in givenness, this can be represented by different case marking.

6.8.5 Inclusory pronouns

The inclusory pronoun construction is discussed here because of its functional similarity to the other kinds of inclusory construction. Syntactically, however, it is entirely dissimilar. Inclusory pronouns express, in a single lexeme, both a superset group with the grammatical function of subject and a subset of that group which has an additional oblique grammatical function (hereafter referred to as the 'subject superset' and 'oblique subset' respectively). An example of this is (259), in which the inclusory pronoun *ngalathun* makes reference to both a dual subject superset (equivalent to the personal pronoun *ngal* 'we two (inclusive)') and a singular oblique subset (equivalent to *ngathun* 'to me'):

(450) *ngalathun   kuuk   yik*
      1du:incl|1sg WORD(ACC) say:NPST
      'you and I are speaking together in the vernacular'
      [Hall 1972: 380]

Inclusory pronouns are attested so far only in the work of Hall (1972), and further investigation is required to fully explain their semantics and morphosyntax. Pending this, however, the following observations can be made. Firstly, the inclusory pronouns appear to be the product of dative case pronouns encliticizing to, and later fusing with, nominative personal pronouns (see Table 13 in §3.1.2.6). Synchronically, the pronouns appear to be monomorphemic, rather than productively derived, since phonological reduction and modification have in some cases obscured the source morphemes. Nevertheless, it is useful for the discussion below to discuss the inclusory pronouns in terms of two component parts: an initial element drawn from the nominative paradigm (the features of which are glossed to the left of '|'); and a second element drawn from the dative paradigm (the features of which are glossed to the right of '|'). It is acknowledged, however, that this most likely does not reflect the synchronic morphological status of these forms.[134]

The fact that the apparent case-marking of the component elements is not assigned by the predicate is evident in the following example, in which the plural group went <u>with</u> the speaker (a relationship elsewhere coded comitative) rather than <u>to</u> the speaker (elsewhere coded dative):

(451) pelnathun   kanpa   yaat
       3pl|1sgINCL before go:RDP:P.PFV
       'they and I all went previously'
       [Hall 1972: 381]

There is a semantic distinction between those inclusory pronouns in which the initial (nominative) element refers to the superset, and those in which it refers to the subset (cf. §3.1.2.6). Where the subset follows the superset, the inclusory pronoun appears to focus attention on the subset referent. This is evident in (452) and (453).

(452) ngamp   ngerngkan ngampathun   thangkar-nam   raak   min-m
       1pl:incl(NOM) yesterday 1pl:incl|1sgINCL laugh-P.IPFV   thing   good-ABL
       'all of us had a roaring good time yesterday from those jokes with me'
       [Hall 1972: 380]

(453) nhunt   ngalngun   pam.thaaw
       2sg(NOM)   1du:incl|2sgINCL   friend(NOM)
       'you and I are good friends together'
       [Hall 1972: 380]

Note also that examples (452) and (453) present what could be analyzed as an inclusory pronoun construction embedded within a simple inclusory construction. The simple inclusory construction requires that a pronoun referring to the superset be apposed to one or more NPs referring to subset(s), but since the inclusory pronoun in itself refers to both superset and subset separately, it can be apposed to pronouns referring to either the superset (e.g. *ngamp* in (452)) or the subset (e.g. *nhunt* in (453)).

---

[134] It may be that these inclusory pronouns originated as reciprocal pronouns (cf. the formally analogous reflexive pronouns §5.1.2), but then generalized to other contexts (e.g. sociative, as in (451) below).

The semantics of the inclusory pronouns in which the subset precedes the superset, are less easily specified. Like other inclusory pronouns, they may focus attention on the subset (454).

(454) *nhipurra   yarr*
    2du|2plINCL go:IMP
    'just two of you all go'
    [Hall 1972: 381]

Examples like (454) differ from other uses of inclusory pronouns, however, in that the verb predicates over only the subset and not the superset encoded by the inclusory pronoun. Conversely, in cases like (455) the individualization of the plural subject group by means of the inclusory pronoun actually appears intended to stress that the message applies to each individual member of the superset and not just a subset.

(455) *nhunturra pam; paanth nhunturra; ongkorr reepon   murk=th*
    2sg|2pl   man   woman 2sg|2pl   PROHIB steal:IMP others'.poss=PRAG
    'every one of you men – and women – don't steal what's another's'
    [Hall 1972: 380]

It should be noted here that there is some formal irregularity in the composition of these two inclusory pronouns; *nhunturra* '2sg|2pl' and *nhipurra* '2du|2pl'. In both cases, the first formative represents the subset, rather than the superset as with the other inclusory pronouns. Moreover, the second formative (*-urra*) resembles the unmarked nominative form *nhurr* '2pl(NOM)' rather than the corresponding dative free personal pronoun *nhurrnhungun*.[135] It is worth noting, however, that the suffix *-a* marks the dative case for some declensions of free noun (e.g. *pama* 'to the man').

Finally, note that the lexeme *pelnathun* 'they and I' is labelled an 'inclusory pronoun' due to its formal resemblance of the other inclusory pronouns, despite the fact that the label is in this case somewhat of a misnomer. Used in clauses such as (451), the dative referent *-athun* 'to me' is not actually a subset of the plural nominative form *peln* 'they', but rather specifies an additional participant who acts in conjunction with the participants referred to by the superset:

(451') *pelnathun   kanpa   yaat*
    3pl|1sgINCL before go:RDP:P.PFV
    'they and I all went previously'
    [Hall 1972: 381]

---

[135] The similarity here is even stronger given that the nominative second person plural pronoun takes the form *nhurra ~ nyurra* in around a hundred other Australian languages (Dixon 1980: 153).

6.9 Nominal coordination

Studies of nominal coordination differ greatly in scope. Haspelmath (2007: 1) defines coordination extremely broadly, as:

> Syntactic constructions in which two or more units of the same type are combined into a larger unit and still have the same semantic relations with other surrounding elements.

Haspelmath (2007) considers inclusory constructions such as those described in §6.8 as a coordinate subtype. Others (e.g. Stassen 2000) explicitly exclude inclusory constructions from their considerations of nominal coordination. The following sections describe a range of constructions in which multiple entities, each encoded by separate noun phrases, have the same role in the clause. Some of the constructions discussed may not be classified as nominal coordination proper, but their functional similarity warrants their presentation here for comparison. There are, however, many strong similarities between some coordinate constructions described below and the corresponding inclusory constructions. These will be indicated where appropriate.

6.9.1 Conjunction by coordinator

It appears that the nominative third person dual pronoun *pul* 'they two' is acquiring the function of a coordinator. Consider, for instance, example (456):

(456) *parr-an   pul   kuta-ku   nhaanham   nhunh   thatr*
child-ERG   3du(ERG)   dog-ERG   look.at:NPST 3sgACC   frog(ACC)
'the child and the dog are looking at the frog'
[KTh_MF17Sep2002 Narrative FrogStory]

Pul may here be functioning as a coordinator, conjoining the two NPs *parran* 'the child' and *kutaku* 'dog'. Alternatively, it may be that *pul* 'they two' is a simple subject pronoun, apposed to two subset NPs that identify the two individuals it refers to. On the evidence of examples such as (456) alone, there would be no need to posit this coordinator function of *pul*. However, there are a very small number of examples in which *pul* is used to conjoin a plural (not dual) number of participants. In such cases as these, it is difficult to retain an analysis of *pul* as a (dual number) subject pronoun:

(457) 1. *ngul Ebi-n   pul   Donald   mi'imrr...*[136]
         then Ivy-^ERG   3du(NOM)   Donald(NOM)   sang
         'so Ivy and Donald sang'
     2. *Cyril   pul   mi'imrr*
         Cyril(NOM)   3du(NOM)   sang
         'and Cyril sang'
         [KTh_AJ-IC-**GJ**26Nov2002 Narrative/Conversation]

The second clause of (457) is separated from the first by a short pause. It would seem that the speaker originally formulated the initial clause to stand alone, then remembered a third participant, Cyril. It would be incorrect to assume that the use of the dual pronoun here is a speech error, though, as *pul* appears after the speaker has remembered and mentioned the third participant. If it were functioning as a subject pronoun, then, we would expect it to take the form *peln* '3pl(NOM)' in (457.2), reflecting that it refers to three participants overall, or *nhul* '3sg(NOM)', if it were to refer just to Cyril. The fact that the speaker instead continues to employ *pul* '3du(NOM)' to add a third actor, suggests that *pul* is functioning as a coordinator. The grammaticalization of coordinators from (usually dual, third person) pronouns is attested in a number of Australian languages, including Tiwi (Osborne 1974), Ngandi (Heath 1978), Arrernte (Wilkins 1989), Kayardild (Evans 1995a), and neighbouring Kugu Nganhcara (Smith and Johnson 2000). Unlike the coordinators of many of these languages, however, Kuuk Thaayorre *pul* does not occupy a fixed position with respect to the coordinands, and nor do the coordinands occupy a fixed position relative to each other. In (457.1) and (457.2), the coordinator immediately follows the first coordinand (and in (457.1) it immediately precedes the second). In (458), however, *pul* precedes the second coordinand (*nganamu* 'mother'), but both are separated from the first coordinand (*nganipi* 'father') by the verb and its object. In (459), *pul* follows the two coordinands (*paanth thono* 'a woman' and '*pam* 'man'), which are adjacent:

(458) *nganip-i   ngancan   thaka-rr   pul   nganam-u*
      father-ERG   1pl:excl:ACC   leave-P.PFV   3du(ERG)   mother-ERG
      'Dad and mum left us'
      [KTh_GJ15Oct2002 Narrative PlaneSighting]

---

136 The verb *mi'i* 'pick up, sing' is irregular. The expected form in this example would be either *mi'im* 'sing:P.IPFV' or *mi'irr* 'sing-P.PFV'. The form *mi'imrr* would usually correspond to the nonpast form of a reciprocal derived verb. Reciprocal marking would be semantically compatible with the collaborative nature of the performance described, but it is unclear why the verb should be in unmarked nonpast tense. The same irregular verb form is found in other contexts too, with various tense/aspect features.

(459) paanth   thono   pam   pul   mimp   katp-r
     woman   one(NOM) man(NOM) 3du(NOM) cloth(ACC) grasp-NPST
     'a woman and man are holding up a piece of cloth'
     [KTh_EN15Dec2002 Elicitation Cut&Break12]

With respect to word order, then, *pul* appears to behave more like a Kuuk Thaayorre free pronoun than a conventional coordinator. There are further indications that this putative coordinator function of *pul* is not yet fully developed. To begin with, *pul* is only ever used with third person referents, and in most cases it conjoins only two NPs. This is unlike Kayardild, for example, where the second person dual pronoun *birra* – when functioning as conjunction – can combine with a first person pronoun as in *ngada birr* (1sg CONJ) 'me too' (Evans 1995a:20).

The final piece of evidence that Kuuk Thaayorre *pul* has not yet fully grammaticalized as a coordinator, is the fact that it is only used to conjoin NPs with the grammatical function of subject, as befits its erstwhile nominative/ergative case form. Where non-subject arguments are conjoined, alternative coordination strategies are employed, such as the borrowed English conjunction *and*.

(460) *Daniel-ak   and Alice-ak   pulnungun kaar=p   nhaaw-r*
     Daniel-DAT and Alice-DAT   3duDAT   NEG=PRAG   see:P.PFV
     'haven't you seen Daniel and Alice?'
     [KTh_GJ10Jan2004 Conversation]

Time will tell whether *pul* will eventually develop into a fully-fledged coordinator. For the purposes of this grammar, I will continue to treat it as a personal pronoun apposed to the coordinands.

6.9.2 Asyndetic conjunction (referential case linkage)

As mentioned in the preceding section, it is not possible to use *pul* '3du(NOM)' as coordinator where the coordinands have a grammatical function other than subject, or where a coordinand is first or second person. In such cases, there are a range of options available to the speaker. The first of these is asyndetic conjunction, or the simple apposition of coordinands in the same case. This is illustrated by (461), in which three noun phrases (*nguk* 'hook', *yuk* 'thing' and *wal* 'bag') are coordinated as a single object argument:

(461) *nguk,   yuk,   wal   kal-r   pul*
     hook(ACC) thing(ACC) bag(ACC) carry-P.PFV 3du(ERG)
     'the two of them carried hooks and things in their bags'
     [Foote and Hall: Reader 10]

Although the three coordinands in (461) are adjacent, this is not a necessary condition for coordination. In (462), for instance, one coordinand (*kirk* 'spear') precedes the verb, while the other (*thul=yuk* 'woomera-kind-of-things') follows:

(462) ngul   ngay   kirk   kempthe kal-m   thul=yuk
      then   1sg(ERG)   spear(ACC) singly   carry-P.IPFV woomera(ACC)=STUFF
      'I used to carry spears and woomeras separately'
      [KTh_**AJ**-IC-GJ26Nov2002 Narrative PormpuraawKanangkarr]

Similarly, in (463) one coordinand (*nganipn* 'to Dad') appears clause-initially while the other (*nganamun* 'to Mum') is clause-final:

(463) nganip-n   ngancn   yik-nhat   nganam-un
      father-DAT   1pl:excl(NOM)   say-GO&:P.PFV   mother-DAT
      'we said to Dad and Mum'
      [KTh_GJ15Oct2002 Narrative PlaneSighting]

Coordinated noun phrases may be apposed to one another regardless of their role in the clause (e.g. object in (462) or indirect object in (463)). The fact that the noun phrases stand in apposition is marked by referential case (i.e. they must take the same case); word order plays no role in marking coordination.

6.9.3 Conjunction by adnominal case linkage

Section 6.8 presented a number of inclusory constructions in which an individual included within the reference of a non-singular pronoun is also referred to by a separate (subset) noun phrase marked by adnominal case as a dependent of the (superset) pronoun. Inherent in the definition of inclusory constructions, is the fact that at least one member of the superset is referred to only by the superset pronoun. In Kuuk Thaayorre, however, there are many examples of clauses structurally similar to inclusory constructions, but in which each member of the superset is explicitly referred to by a separate NP. In all such clauses recorded to date, the superset includes only two participants. These constructions are discussed in the following sections.

6.9.3.1 Comitative conjunction

Section 6.8.2 presented the comitative inclusory construction, in which the subset NP is marked as a comitative dependent of the (ergative or nominative) superset subject. Where both superset participants are enumerated, one agrees with the relational case of the superset pronoun via referential case linkage (cf. §6.7), while the other receives adnominal comitative case-marking:

(464) kanangkarr pul   pam   ngumpurr-kak pul   may-i   yat
      long.ago   3du(NOM)   man(NOM) old.lady-COM 3du(NOM)   VEG-DAT go:P.PFV
      'long ago an old man and his wife went out to gather food'
      [KTh_FT8Feb2004 Narrative Adoptee]

Like the comitative inclusory construction, the comitative conjunction construction appears to be used in order to imply that a particular relationship holds between participants. In (464), for instance, the two participants are married. We may assume that the comitative conjunction construction is used here instead of the corresponding inclusory construction because the addressee could not be expected to retrieve the reference of either participant from the superset pronoun alone. Taken from the first line of a text, (464) serves to introduce two new topics, and as such explicit reference to the individuals involved is preferred.

6.9.3.2 Dative conjunction

It is also common for one subset NP to receive dative marking (as per the dative inclusory construction, §6.8.3) and the other to receive the case-marking appropriate to the grammatical function of the argument as a whole. This can be seen in (465), in which the first subset NP *Jimmynthurr* 'Jimmy' agrees with the superset pronoun *pul* 'they two' (twice instantiated) in ergative case, while the second subset NP *Johnnyn* 'at Johnny' is dative-marked:

(465) Jimmy-nthurr Johnny-n   pul   ngerngkan thanp-rr-r   pul
      Jimmy-ERG   Johnny-DAT   3du(ERG)   yesterday kick-RCP-P.PFV 3du(ERG)
      'Jimmy and Johnny kicked each other yesterday'
      [Hall 1972: 244]

Such clauses thus contain subject elements in different cases. The fact that dative case-marking is adnominal in function, rather than being assigned by the predicate (i.e. relational), is evidenced by the construction's compatibility with clauses headed by a verb that does not subcategorize for an indirect object (e.g. (465) above). Along with the dative inclusory construction, dative conjunction is employed in the description of semantically symmetric events (whether formally coded reciprocal (465) or not (466)), and is the only strategy for marking the symmetry of a relationship not encoded by a transitive verb. Thus the relationship of adjacency described by (466) (i.e. that the two participants sit <u>beside</u> one another) – usually marked by dative case in non-symmetric clauses – is made 'reciprocal' through dative conjunction.

(466) pam   ith   pul   paanth-ak   nhiinat   pul
      man   dem:dist 3du(NOM)   woman-DAT   sit:GO&:P.PFV   3du(NOM)
      'the man and the woman went and sat down next to each other'
      [KTh_ICh25Jan2005 Elicitation RCP]

The dative suffix on the subset *paanthak* 'to/at the woman' thus captures the relationship of adjacency, while the fact that both participants are included within the reference of the superset subject pronoun *pul* 'they two' marks the event as symmetrical. This reciprocal strategy has analogues in the binomial quantifiers used to encode reciprocity in languages such as French and Russian, in which case roles are mapped onto different components (e.g. in French *l'un à l'autre* 'the one to the other') regardless of the fact that each participant plays both roles.

6.9.4 Concessive conjunction

I have found no examples of the concessive conjunction of noun phrases or adjectival phrases. This is instead achieved by means of the concessive conjunction of clauses, as can be seen in the following example:

(467) *pam   nhangnam ngathn   nhul   pam   kon*
      HUMAN   mother   1sgGEN(NOM) 3sg(NOM) HUMAN   short
      ngul nhul   piintharrn
      but   2sg(NOM) strong
      'my mother's short but strong'
      [KTh_GJ12Jan2004 Elicitation]

Rather than merely contrasting the characteristics 'short' and 'strong' (as in the English translation), the Kuuk Thaayorre construction contrasts two full propositions: *pam nhangnam ngathn nhul pam kon* 'my mother is short'; and *nhul piintharrn* 'she's strong'. The role of the coordinator *ngul* 'then, but' in clausal conjunction is described in §12.2.1.2.

6.9.5 Disjunction

Nominal disjunction is achieved by means of the modal enclitic, *=okun* 'DUBitative'. The disjunctive function of *=okun* can be seen in (468):

(468) *nhunt   wanthanngun nhiinan,   Cairns=okun, Melbourne=okun*
      2sg(NOM) where$_{LOC}$ sit:GO&:NPST Cairns=DUB   Melbourne=DUB
      'where are you going to live, Cairns or Melbourne?'
      [KTh_MF20Aug2002 Conversation]

=Okun (discussed in §9.1.5) introduces a possible world or state-of-affairs which the speaker does not have sufficient evidence to assert. As such, its closest English translation is 'maybe'. Thus, if we interpret the ignorative *wanthanngun* 'where' as an

indefinite pronoun (one of its core functions, cf. §5.2.3.2), example (468) could alternatively be translated 'you are going to live somewhere, maybe Cairns, maybe Melbourne'. This reflects the indirect style of questioning that is polite in many speech contexts (cf. §1.3.3.2).

Because =*okun* is encliticized to both of the disjunct noun phrases in (468), it may be tempting to analyze this construction as bisyndetic coordination (with both coordinands being marked by the coordinator =*okun*). =*Okun* need not be encliticized to both coordinands, however, as (8) shows:

(8') 1. *T.A.   ngancn   katpi-rr*
          T.A.(ACC) 1pl:excl(ERG) grasp-P.PFV
          'we caught T.A. [airline]'
      2. *T.A.=okun   Ansett   katpi-rr=okun*
          T.A.(ACC)=dub   Ansett(ACC) grasp-P.PFV=DUB
          'either T.A. or Ansett [airline]'
          [KTh_GJ16Oct2002 Narrative MelbourneTrip]

Although =*okun* appears twice in (8), it is encliticized to only the first of the coordinands and to the verb. This suggests that it is clausal in scope, rather than directly marking coordinands. However, it should be noted that in every recorded example in my corpus, =*okun* is attached to the first coordinand as well as at least one other clausal constituent. In many examples, though, it is also encliticized to other clausal constituents, as in (8) and the following:

(469) *ngul=okun   kunk=okun   pul   watp=okun   pul*
       then=DUB   alive=DUB   3du(NOM)   dead=DUB   3du(NOM)
       '(I don't know whether) they two are alive or dead'
       [KTh_GJ16Oct2002 Narrative MelbourneTrip]

Finally, the English loan *or* is frequently used to achieve nominal disjunction (as well as clausal disjunction – cf. 11.2.3), though usually alongside the dubitative enclitic, as in the following:

(470) *may   tea   nhunt   wanthantharr mungk-r?*
       VEG   tea(ACC) 2du(ERG)   how   eat-NPST
       milk=aak=okun   or ngotn?
       milk=ADN.PROP=DUB or black
       'how do you take your tea? White or black?'
       [KTh_MF20Aug2002 Conversation]

6.10 Possession

6.10.1 Part-whole apposition (referential case linkage)

Section 6.8 discussed the apposition of partially coreferential NPs that refer to part and whole of a participant group (i.e. subset and superset). The part-whole apposition described here involves a different kind of partial coreference: reference to part and whole of a single entity. In this construction, a NP and/or pronoun referring to the whole entity is apposed to a NP in the same case referring to a part of that entity. This is exemplified by (471), a clause headed by an intransitive verb, *rokr* 'entered', that subcategorizes for a single argument in nominative case:

(471) *kuta   nhul   paant   glass-ak   rok-r*
      dog(NOM)   3sg(NOM)   head(NOM)   glass-DAT   enter-P.PFV
      'the dog put his head into the jar'
      [KTh_MF17Sep2002 Narrative FrogStory]

The three nominative noun phrases – *kuta* 'dog', *nhul* 'he', and *paant* 'head' – together comprise the subject argument, each contributing different kinds of information. *Kuta* 'dog' identifies the participant involved in the event, while *paant* 'head' specifies the part of the dog that enters the jar. *Nhul* 'he' makes the reference specific, aiding reference tracking throughout the narrative. All indexes of a person (e.g. their name, voice, shadow and footprints) are treated as 'part' of them for the purposes of this construction (as seen in examples (476) and (475) below).

The meronymic apposition of noun phrases referring to part and whole is a crosslinguistically common strategy for representing inalienable possession, particularly across the Australian continent. Analogous constructions in other Australian languages have been labelled 'External Possession' (eg. McGregor 1998 for Nyulnyulan languages), the 'favorite construction' (e.g. Hale 1981 for Warlpiri), and 'inalienable possession' (e.g. Austin 1981 for Diyari, Goddard 1982 for Yidiɲ, and Evans 1996 for Mayali). Each of these constructions functions to link both possessor and possessum to a single argument of a predicate. Researchers differ, however, as to the relative status of whole and part. Evans (1996: 87) asserts that the Mayali "part and whole are syntactically in apposition, with 'head' like properties shared between the part and the whole". Hale (1981) also argues for an appositional analysis of Warlpiri part and whole nominals, with both being linked to the same argument position of the verb. Unlike Evans, though, Hale (1981: 338) views the whole NP as head, proposing that the part NP may function as a secondary predicate with scope over the whole NP. Harvey (1996: 134) provisionally adopts a similar analysis of the Warray construction, under which the whole is head and the part modifier.

What, then, is the syntactic relationship between whole and part NPs in Kuuk Thaayorre? To begin with, the two noun phrases do not occupy a fixed position relative to each other. While they are often contiguous (as in example (471) above), they need not be. In (472), for example, the pronoun representing the possessor (*nhinh* 'you') appears clause-initially, while the possessum *name nhangkn* 'your name' does not appear until after the predicate.

(472) nhinh   ngay   wuump walmeerem name nhangkn   ngay
      2sgACC   1sg(NOM) CONTR remember   name 2sgGEN(ACC) 1sg(NOM)
      'I remember your name'
      [KTh_AC21Aug2002 Conversation]

The reverse ordering of part and whole is seen in example (244), in which the part NP (*koow* 'nose') occurs clause-initially, and the whole NP (=*unh* 'him') follows at the end of the clause:

(473) koow   rathi-rr=eln=unh
      nose(ACC) chopped=3pl(ERG)=3sgACC
      'they chopped his nose off'
      [Hall 1972: 77]

It seems clear, then, that part and whole are referred to by separate NPs. How, then, are these phrases related? We might assume that the two NPs form a unit at some level of representation. Such an analysis raises the question of what is the head of the larger unit; both part and whole NPs exhibit some characteristics associated with heads. In favour of the whole as head, where a pronominal enclitic is attached to the verb this always agrees with the whole and not the part:

(474) yuur   stitch-m   rirk-r=anh
      hand(ACC) stitch-TR DO-P.PFV=1sgACC
      'they put stitches in my hand'
      [KTh_AJ-**GJ**03Feb2004 Narrative DarwinTrip]

If the part were the syntactic head, we would expect the pronominal enclitic to agree with it in (third) person, but instead we find the enclitic =*anh* '1sgACC' attached to the verb. Similarly, wherever the meronymic construction contains a free pronoun, it must have the person and number of the whole, rather than the part.

On the other hand, what is predicated of the part need not be entailed of the whole, suggesting that the part NP has head status (cf. McGregor 1985, Evans 1996, Harvey 1996). In (471), repeated below, it is not true that the whole dog goes into the glass, only its head:

(471')   kuta   nhul   paant   glass-ak   rok-r
         dog(NOM)   3sg(NOM)   head(NOM)   glass-DAT   enter-P.PFV
         'the dog puts his head into the jar'
         [KTh_MF17Sep2002 Narrative FrogStory]

But it is true to say that the dog enters the glass inasmuch as its head does, which is no doubt a motivation for these kinds of constructions. Example (475), however, illustrates a clear case of impact upon part and not whole.

(475)   kamp-an[137]   yarr   pam-an
         track-DAT   go:IMP   man-DAT
         'we must walk in his tracks'
         [Foote and Hall: Reader 9]

Example (476) presents another clause in which the predicate apparently has scope over the part but not the whole. This clause was uttered by one of my friends and collaborators, who knew the referent of the whole expression, *pam nhangkn* 'your husband', very well, but had temporarily forgotten his *nhamp* 'name'.

(476)   ngay   pam nhangkn   nhamp   ngay   pamngongkom
         1sg(NOM)   man 2sgGEN(ACC)   name(ACC)   1sg(NOM)   ignorant.of
         'I've forgotten your husband's name'
         [KTh_AC21Aug2002 Conversation]

However, to claim that the predicate does not have scope over the whole argument in clauses such as (476), may be to misapply English rules of entailment to Kuuk Thaayorre. In English, the statement *I don't remember your husband* entails that the speaker does not remember the person as a whole, not just one aspect of them. The same is not necessarily true of Kuuk Thaayorre, though. Example (477) was uttered by a friend shortly after I had arrived in Pormpuraaw:

(477)   ngay   nhinh   pamngoongkom
         1sg(NOM)   2sgACC   be.ignorant
         'I didn't know you (were here)'
         [Anon.]

---

137 Note that two allomorphs of the dative suffix (*-an* and *-ak*) are associated with the noun *kamp* 'track', as seen in (475) and (478) respectively. Their usage is determined by the age and dialect of the speaker, rather than any semantic or functional contrast.

As she herself explained, she meant that she did not know I was coming Pormpuraaw, not that she didn't know who I was. In Kuuk Thaayorre, then, 'I don't know you' can mean 'I don't know something to do with you'. Even where a part is not specified, then, something predicated of an argument that refers to a whole, may in fact apply only to one part or aspect of that whole. If this is true, then it seems even more plausible that the whole is head, and the part is complement at some level of representation. Alternatively, it is possible to analyze the meronymic construction as double-headed, with part and whole both functioning as heads with a single grammatical function, but not operating as a single syntactic unit. Such an analysis fits Dench and Evans's (1988) characterization of referential case (cf. §6.7).

Finally, it should be noted that the NPs referring to part and whole may in some cases form a higher-level noun phrase, as in (478).

(478)   nhunt   [minh kothon   thamr kamp]-ak   thanan   ulp
        2sg(NOM)   [MEAT wallaby foot   track]-DAT stand:RDP:NPST   dem:ad.prx
        'you're standing on wallaby tracks'
        [KTh_AJ27Jan2004 Elicitation]

Here, the whole *minh kothon* 'wallaby' and the part *thamr kamp* 'tracks' form a single phrase (marked by square brackets), as evidenced by their contiguity and – most importantly – the presence of only a single suffix marking dative case. The syntax of apposed, partially coreferential NPs is discussed further in Gaby 2005.

6.10.2 Possessum-head (adnominal case linkage)

Section 6.5 above discussed the role of genitive pronouns in the noun phrase, pointing out that they occupy a particular nominal modifier slot and may bear the relational case suffix assigned to the phrase as a whole. (479) is an example of a clause containing a genitive pronoun.

(479)   kuta nhangkn   wanthan?
        dog   2sgGEN(NOM)   where
        'where's your dog?'
        [Anon.]

The genitive pronoun, *nhangkn* 'your', is a dependent modifier within the NP headed by the possessum *kuta* 'dog'. Possessum NPs may alternatively be modified by noun-headed NPs in the genitive case (as in 480), the two forming a complex possessive NP.

(480) *yulu Yuwi-ak*
apple Hughie-GEN
'Hughie's apple'
[Foote and Hall: Primer 8]

Where the possessive NP has a role in the clause that requires overt case-marking, the form this takes is determined by the word class of the possessor. Where the possessor is represented by a genitive pronoun, grammatical function is signalled by the relevant case morpheme attaching to the genitive pronoun, as in the following:

(481) *ngay   [pam ngathn-mak] wait rirk...   ngok-e*
1sg(NOM) [man 1sgGEN-DAT] wait do:NPST beer-DAT
'I'm waiting for my husband... for beer'
[Anon.]

Where the possessor is represented by a genitive-marked noun, however, the grammatical function of the possessum may be marked in one of two ways. Firstly, and only where the possessum has an oblique case role, both possessor and possessum may be encoded as separate adjunct arguments. In example (482), for example, both *pamak* 'to the man' and *pormpan* 'to the house' are marked by dative case, their status as independent adjuncts confirmed by their separation by *ii* 'there':

(482) *ngal   iirra   yat   pam-ak   ii   pormp-an.*
1du:incl(NOM) to.there go:P.PFV man-DAT there house-DAT
Pormpr nhangn-mun.
house   3sgGEN-DAT
'we went to that man's house'
"you 'n' me go over there where that man house"
[KTh_AJ27Jan2004 Elicitation]

The possessive relationship that obtains between the man and his house is only implied by the first line of (482).[138] This stands in contrast to its paraphrasing in the second clause, in which the possessor is encoded by a pronoun. Recall that genitive pronouns, unlike genitive-inflected nomina, can be inflected for relational case. Here, the possessor and possessum are represented in a single phrase *pormpr nhangnmun* 'to his house', to which the dative case is suffixed only once (phrase-finally, to the

---

138 Under the analysis presented herein, this construction is syntactically different from the (same case) part-whole apposition construction discussed in §6.10.1 though the two are identical at the surface level.

genitive pronoun). This single phrase simultaneously encodes the possessive relationship and oblique case role.

The second means by which a possessor noun can reflect the grammatical function of its possessum is through the use of ablative case marking, as described in detail in §4.2.6.5.

6.11 Noun phrases and discourse structure

6.11.1 Anaphora and cataphora

6.11.1.1 Demonstrative pronouns

The various situational and non-situational uses of demonstrative pronouns were detailed in §5.3.3. These included the use of demonstrative pronouns as substitution anaphora and cataphora, as well as in anaphoric reference tracking and with cataphoric 'recognitional' function.

6.11.1.2 Generic nouns and the classifying construction

Both Wilkins (2000) and Dixon (2002) report anaphoric functions of generic nouns, which may be employed to refer back to a generic-specific pairing. This can be seen in (483), where the full classifying construction is used in the first reference to the saltwater crocodile *minh pinc* (in line 1), with the generic *minh* used as anaphor in line 3:

(483) 1. kar **minh pinc** pam.thaawarra=eey. mmm.
like MEAT salt.croc(NOM) dangerous-=PRAG mmm
'Saltwater crocodiles, for instance, are very dangerous'
2. ngay news-ak ngay nhaath-m,
1sg(NOM) news-DAT 1sg(NOM) see-P.IPFV
'I saw on the news...'
3. Cairns iikop, pam farmer, nhul **minh** tourist-ak meeren-r.
Cairns at.down man farmer 3sg(ERG) MEAT(ACC) tourist-DAT show-P.PFV
'down in Cairns a farmer had been showing the tourists crocodiles'
4. tourist-ak meeren-m.
tourist-DAT show-P.IPFV
'was showing the tourists...'
5. nhul minh yarriy katp-m
3sg(ERG) MEAT(ACC) thus grasp-P.IPFV
'he was holding [chicken] meat like this [for the crocodiles]'
6. ngul **minh pinc** ulp ranci-rr punth aka patha-rr.
then MEAT salt.croc(NOM) dem:ad.prx jump-P.PFV arm(ACC) here bite-P.PFV
'when that crocodile jumped up and bit his arm here'
[KTh_AJ-GJ03Feb2004 Conversation]

Interestingly, in line (483.5) the same generic noun as was used to refer to the crocodiles, *minh* 'MEAT', is used to refer to the chicken meat being fed to the crocodiles. This renders the generic noun ambiguous. For this reason, the immediately subsequent reference to the crocodiles reverts to the full classifying phrase *minh pinc* 'saltwater crocodile' (483.6) rather than the generic noun alone.

Generic nouns may also be used cataphorically, introducing a new referent that subsequently receives further specification by a full classifying construction. This often occurs within a single clause, as illustrated by example (166), repeated below. Here, the main clause makes a general statement about the men's hunting for meat, while the particular animal they are hunting is specified by a full classifying construction in a peripheral phrase. In (484), too, the fronted NP *minh=yuk* 'meat sort of thing' introduces the referent in the most general way possible; the kind of meat is specified post-verbally:

(166')   *pam   peln   ii   kana   yan   minh-a,   minh   kothon-ak*
         man(NOM)   3pl(NOM)   there   about.to   go:NPST   MEAT-DAT MEAT   wallaby-DAT
         'those men are hunting wallaby'
         [KTh_AC10Aug2002 Conversation/Elicitation]

(484)   *minh=yuk   kaamp-m   ngancn   minh   kothon*
        meat=THING   roast-P.IPFV   1pl:excl(ERG)   MEAT   wallaby(ACC)
        'we used to roast meat things, (like) wallaby'
        [KTh_AJ030204 Conversation/Narrative]

Kuuk Thaayorre is somewhat unusual in also allowing specific nouns to appear without any generic. Although there is a strong preference for some specific nouns (including *pinc* 'saltwater crocodile') to be preceded by their generic, this is not a syntactic requirement, pace Dixon (2002: 455):

> In Ea1, Kuuk Thaayorre, a specific noun never occurs alone, without the appropriate generic. At first mention in a text we find minh ('edible animal': GENERIC NOUN) kothon ('wallaby': SPECIFIER) but at later mentions the wallaby is referred to just by minh (Hall 1972: 70–1) .

The specific noun *pinc* 'saltwater crocodile', appears as the sole constituent of the noun phrase in the third line of example (485), despite the fact that its associated generic noun (*minh* 'meat') appears nowhere in the discourse context:

(485)   1. *kar   inh   waarr.min-tam   yak-ntam*
           like   dem:sp.prx   thing-ABL   snake-ABL
           'like from things, from snakes'
        2. *nhunt   weneth=peey   miinng-r*
           2sg(NOM)   scared=PRAG   take.fright-NPST
           'you take fright from them'

3. *pinc,   nhul   kar   winwin=peey!*
   salt.croc(NOM) 3sg(NOM) like fearsome=PRAG
   'the saltwater crocodile, it's *winwin*'
4. *nhunt   weneth   miinng-r*
   2sg(NOM)   fright   happen-NPST
   'you're scared [of it]'
   [KTh_**AJ**-GJ03Feb2004 Conversation]

6.11.2 Focus markers

Kuuk Thaayorre possesses a number of free and enclitic forms the functions of which all fall within the broad discourse pragmatic domain of focus. Further research is required to distinguish these forms in terms of their more precise functions and distribution. In the meantime, the following sections lay out the basic characteristics of each one.

6.11.2.1 *thono* 'one'

The quantifier *thono* 'one' has grammaticalized into a focus marker (glossed as 'ONE' in small caps to distinguish it from the quantifier use).[139] This particle functions akin to an indefinite-specific marker, introducing participants as 'new' and 'unexpected'. The participant may be unexpected either because it arrives on the scene 'out of the blue' (i.e. without foreshadowing) or because it contrasts with an existing participant with which it might potentially be confused (usually because of identical referring expressions). The first of these scenarios is illustrated by (486). After hearing only of the speaker's own travels in (486.1-.4), our attention is diverted to an unforeshadowed new actor by the use of *thono* in (486.5) who takes over from the speaker as topic.

(486) 1. *ngay   ii-rr-kuw   Darwin-ak   yat=ay,   1970.*
        1sg(NOM) there-towards-west Darwin-DAT go:P.PFV=1sg(NOM) 1970
        'I went west to Darwin in 1970'
     2. *ngul   1969 Cyclone Tracy-n   thiika-rr.*
        then   1969 Cyclone Tracy-ERG   break-P.PFV
        'in 1969 Cyclone Tracy had destroyed it'
     3. *Darwin   ulp   thiika-rr.*
        Darwin(ACC) dem:ad.prx   break-P.PFV
        'it destroyed Darwin'
     4. *ngay   ii-rr-kuw   yat   1970.*
        1sg(NOM) there-towards-west   go:P.PFV 1970
        'I went there to the west in 1970'

---

139 It is cross-linguistically common for reference-tracking forms with similar functions to grammaticalize from the numeral 'one' (e.g. German *ein* 'one', Russian *odin* 'one' and even English *an* < *one*).

5. ngul pam **thono**, mark   meerenm   rip.
   then man ONE   mark(ACC) show-P.IPFV scar(ACC)
   '[there was] a man, [who] showed [me] a mark, a scar'
6. glass-n   ke'err=unh.
   glass-ERG spear:P.PFV =3sgACC
   'glass had cut him'
7. Taxi driver, pam ngotn.
   taxi driver man black
   '[he was] a taxi driver, a black man'
8. Taxi driver   glass-n   ke'err.
   taxi driver(ACC) glass-ERG spear:P.PFV
   'the taxi driver had got cut by glass'
   [KTh_AJ-**GJ**03Feb2004 Narrative DarwinTrip]

There is nothing in the preceding discourse or the addressee's background knowledge that would lead them to anticipate the introduction of this new participant. Neither does the addressee know anything of the identity of the *pam* 'man' until they are told in line 7 that he is a taxi driver. The presence of *thono* immediately following this first mention of *pam* 'man' in line 3 thus marks him as an entirely new participant for whom the addressee should not search for an antecedent. This use of *thono* on the first mention of a new protagonist – especially one that might potentially be confused with previously mentioned protagonists – is very common.

(487) 1. nhul   pam-al   ith   door   open rirk
         3sg(ERG) man-ERG   dem:dist   door(ACC) open DO:NPST
         'the man opened the door'
     2. pam   nhul   **thono** ith   pal   yat,
         man(NOM) 3sg(NOM)   ONE   dem:dist   towards   go:P.PFV
         'this other man came in'
     3. ngul   kuthirr   pul   thanat   koo.miing
         then   two(NOM)   3du(NOM)   stand:GO&P.PFV   face
         'then the two of them stood face to face'
         [KTh_**FT**-GJ 10Feb2004 Elicitation RCP9]

Example (488.2) illustrates the use of *thono* as a marker of contrastive focus. Again, *thono* follows the first reference to a new participant, *yuk dye ith* 'that dye'. Here, though, the discussion of dyes is not off topic. The potential for confusion instead arises from the availability of a (false) antecedent, the *kormpr dye* (488.1). *Thono* is therefore used to stress that the noun phrase it follows refers to an entirely new participant, once again warning the addressee not to look for an antecedent in the previous discourse.

(488) 1. kormpr   wuump yiirram ii-kuw   mi'imrr,[140]   rump-un
        root.sp.   CONTR other   there-at:west   pick.up:NPST   beach-DAT
        'we get *kormpr* dye on the western side, we get it at the beach'
     2. yuk   dye   ith   **thono=th**
        THING   dye   dem:dist   ONE=PRAG
        'whereas there's that other dye'
     3. yuk   ith   ii-kaw,   yuk   wurrk   wan-r
        THING(NOM)   dem:dist   there-at:east   THING   wurrk(ACC)   tell-NPST
        'that dye in the east, [we] call it *wurrk*'
        [KTh_ME04Jun2005 Conversation / Narrative Yencr]

Syntactically, this use of *thono* 'ONE' differs from the quantifier use *thono* 'one' in that it appears immediately following the noun phrase it modifies, rather than appearing within the noun phrase in the quantifier slot. This is clear in (488.2), where *thono* would precede the adnominal demonstrative *ith* 'that' if it were functioning as quantifier.

6.11.2.2 =*thurr* 'focus'

The primary function of =*thurr* 'FOCUS' is to mark a pragmatically prominent clausal word or constituent.[141] Frequently found in contrastive contexts, the encliticization of =*thurr* attracts attention to one element of a phrase at the expense of the phrase as a whole. So in (489), it is not the fact that the participants in question have a father that is newsworthy, but rather the singularity of this father (i.e. the fact that they share one father, despite having two different mothers). Accordingly, the emphatic =*thurr* is attached to the lexeme *thono* 'one':

(489) nhangnam   yiirr-ntam.   Nganip   thon=thurr
      mother   different-ABL   father   one=FOC
      'they're from different mothers [but] one father'
      [Anon.]

Similarly, the newsworthy information in (490) is the fact that the man's face is nice, not that he has a (nice) face:

(490) *pam*   *ith*   *koow.miing*   *min=thurr*
      man(NOM)   dem:dist   face   good=FOC
      'that man has a nice face'
      [KTh_EN02Oct2002 Conversation]

---

140 See footnote 134 above on this irregular verb form.
141 The form =*thurr* (when not functioning as an ergative marker) is glossed by Foote and Hall (1992: 16–18) as 'go on!', 'isn't it?', 'indeed!', 'enough', 'you think?', 'with' and 'good enough' and by Hall (1972: 140) as 'hortative'.

Though the same phonological form, =*thurr*, also functions as a marker of ergative case (§4.2.1), the focal morpheme can be differentiated from the case morpheme on formal as well as functional grounds. Firstly, the focal enclitic is formally invariant, while the ergative suffix has many allomorphs (including the phonetically similar -*nthurr*). The combinatorics of the two morphemes also differ widely; the ergative suffix appears only in the inflection of nomen stems, while the focal enclitic may take a much wider range of hosts. For instance, the latter but not the former may attach to nomina already inflected for case (e.g. dative-marked *thiiya* 'for a pee' in (491)). Unlike many Australian languages (cf. Dench and Evans 1988, Dench 1995b), Kuuk Thaayorre does not allow multiple case-marking and it is therefore impossible to attach a case morph to an already case-marked noun (cf. the use of ablative marking as a portmanteau case discussed in §4.2.6.5).

(491) *ngay   thiiy-a=thurr   yan*
 1sg(NOM) urine-DAT=FOC go:NPST
 'I'm going for a pee'
 [Anon.]

As well as attaching to already-inflected nomen stems, =*thurr* may also be encliticized to non-nominal clausal elements which are ineligible for case inflection. In (114), for example, =*thurr* is attached to the permissive particle, which permits no inflection, while in (493) it is attached to a verb:

(492) *koo kirri=thurr yarr*
 oh PERM=FOC go:IMP
 'get going!'
 [Foote and Hall 1992: 17]

(493) *ngay   yaan=thurr!*
 1sg(NOM) go:RDP:NPST=FOC
 'I'll go right now!'
 [Hall 1972: 140]

It should be noted that the directionality of grammaticalization in this case has not been established, so while it may be the focal usage of =*thurr* is a case of advanced grammaticalization of the ergative morpheme, it may equally be that the original function of =*thurr* was to mark focus, from which ergative case use has subsequently grammaticalized (cf. Gaby 2010, §4.2.1). The latter course is more in line with the tendency of pragmatic or lexical elements to grammaticalize into grammatical units (Traugott and Heine 1991).

6.11.2.3 Other focal enclitics

Further to *thono* and *=thurr*, three enclitic forms may be used to add prominence to a word, constituent or clause. Their precise functions – particularly in contrast with one another and *=thurr* – warrant further investigation. In the meantime, they are all glossed '=PRAG' to reflect their quintessentially pragmatic function. The three forms in question are listed in (494):

(494) =rr
=le(y)[142]
=e(y)

The first of these forms, *-rr*, may share an etymological source with the focus marker *=thurr* described in the previous section. Fittingly, then, it is commonly found in cases of contrast, as illustrated by examples (495) and (496).

(495) ngancn   nhiplin   ngeeyr   kar yak-a   patha-rr,
 1pl:excl(ERG) 2duACC hear:P.PFV like snake-ERG bite-P.PFV
 kar minh-al=**rr**   patha-rr
 like MEAT-ERG=PRAG bite-P.PFV
 'we thought you might have been bitten by a snake, or bitten by a crocodile'
 [KTh_GJ15Oct2002 Narrative PlaneSighting]

(496) ulp   parr_r pam=**rr**   pokon
 dem:ad.prx CHILD male=PRAG NO
 'this isn't a boy!'
 [KTh_ACh07Nov2002 Conversation]

Example (496) is taken from ACh's description of a conversation between her and and her husband following the birth of their daughter (whom he mistook for a son). *Pam* 'male' thus contrasts with the actual sex of the baby.

The second enclitic, *=ley*, seen in examples (497) to (500), bears a strong resemblance to the third, *=ey*, seen in examples (501) to (503). There is no obvious functional difference between the two, and they occur in the same phonetic environments (e.g. following [r] in examples (500) and (501)). One difference is that only *=ey* follows the topic enclitics described in the following section. It is for this fact alone that I represent the two forms as distinct enclitics, rather than as allomorphs; *=(l)ey*.

---

142 Both *=ley* and *=ey* are usually pronounced with a final palatal glide, this is common among syllables ending in /e/, so the glide is most likely epenthetic.

(497) kuuk   letters   learn   rirk=**ley**!
      WORD   letters(ACC) learn   DO:IMP=PRAG
      'learn the letters!'
      [KTh_MF10Jan2004 Elicitation]

(498) ngamp   yoorr inh   thurma=**ley**
      1pl:incl(NOM)   now   dem:sp.prx   together=PRAG
      'now we're here together'
      [KTh_FT10Feb2004 Elicitation RcpPilot13]

(499) Ngul ngay   thil   mit=kaar=**ley**   nhiin-m   ulp
      then 1sg(NOM) again   work=REL.PRIV=PRAG   sit-P.IPFV   dem:ad.prx
      'then I was without a job again'
      [KTh_GJ27Jan2004 Conversation]

(500) ngul yoorr raak   yiirr=**ley**   yomparr-r
      then now   PLACE   other=PRAG   transform-P.PFV
      'now it [Pormpuraaw] has become a different town'
      [KTh_AJ-IC-**GJ**26Nov2002 Narrative/Conversation]

(501) pik kuthirr=**ey**
      pig two=PRAG
      'there are two pigs'
      [KTh_GJ12Jan2004 ManAndTree3]

(502) tourist   ulp   weneth miinngr=**ey**!
      tourist(NOM)   dem:ad.prx   scared take.fright=PRAG
      'the tourists were all scared!'
      [KTh_AJ-**GJ**03Feb2004 Conversation]

(503) 1. kar   inh   waarrmin-tam yak-ntam
         like   dem:sp.prx   thing-ABL   snake-ABL
         nhunt   weneth=**p**=**ey**   miinng-r
         2sg(NOM)   scared=PRAG=PRAG   take.fright-NPST
         'you're scared of things like snakes'
      2. Pinc,   nhul   kar   winwin=**p**=**ey**!
         saltie(NOM)   3sg(NOM)   like   fearsome=PRAG=PRAG
         'or crocodiles are scary'
         [KTh_**AJ**-GJ03Feb2004 Conversation / Elicitation]

Both =*le* and =*e* appear to select for predicates, whether the verb itself (as in, e.g., (497) and (502)); a noun marked by the relational privative enclitic (499); a nominal predicate in a verbless copula clause (e.g. (501), (501) and (503.2)); a secondary predicate (503.1) or predicative complement (500) in a verb-headed clause. These focal enclitics always appear at the right edge of the word. Thus they follow all inflectional categories, such as case and tense/aspect/mood (509). These forms are also evident in a number of frozen lexemes or expressions (e.g. *-rr* and *-p* in *yokunmanrrp* 'in the just same way').

6.11.3 Other discourse pragmatic enclitics

The three pragmatic enclitics gathered together in this section are even more opaque in function than the focal enclitics of the previous section. These forms – listed in (504) – are likewise glossed '=PRAG' in order to reflect the prematurity of their analysis at this stage.

(504) =*p*
=*th*
=*a*

The first two forms may have their origins in the speaker- and addressee-proximal demonstrative forms (*ulp* and *ith*) respectively.[143] Proximal demonstratives seem a particularly likely source for markers of topicality, though both the distributions and functions of these forms seem considerably wider than those of a typical topic marker. All three of these pragmatic enclitics attach to hosts from a wide range of word classes, for instance: particles (505); demonstratives (507); personal names (506); pronouns (508, 511); case-inflected nomina (495); verbs (508, 510); and adverbs (512). This distribution is notably wider than that of the focal particles described above.

(505) *missed-m rirk-r pelnan, ngay yarriy=**p** nhiin-m.*
miss-TR DO-P.PFV 3plACC 1sg(NOM) thus=PRAG sit-P.IPFV
'I missed them [my family], that's how I was feeling'.
[KTh_GJ16Oct2002 Narrative MelbourneTrip]

(506) *pam nhump ith William=**th** wonp-r*
man elder(NOM) dem:dist William=PRAG die-P.PFV
'that old man, William, died'
[KTh_AJ-IC-GJ26Nov2002 Narrative/Conversation]

---

[143] It is possible that the combination of *-p* and *-a* (forming *-pa*, as seen in (509)) is in fact a reduction of *pam* 'man'. Although there is little evidence of this from the Thaayorre data alone, Verstraete (2005) points out possible parallels in the development of reflexes of Paman *pama* 'man' into, e.g., emphatic pronouns in other Cape York languages (e.g. Olkolo, Sommer 1972: 93–94).

(507) *Ngawoy, kar Friday ulp   yokunmanrrp big day ulp=**th***
       yes   like Friday   dem:ad.prx same.way   big day dem:ad.prx=PRAG
       'yes, Friday is also a big day there [at the Canteen]'
       [KTh_AJ27Jan2004 Conversation]

(508) *ngay=**th**   thele   nhiin=**p***
       1sg(NOM)=PRAG   in.turn sit:NPST=PRAG
       'it's my turn to sit next'
       [Hall 1972: 140]

(509) *paath   waarr rint-nh=**p**=**a***
       fire(ACC) really burn-SBJV=PRAG=PRAG
       'so that we can make a fire'
       [KTh_AJ27Jan2004 Elicitation]

Note that both the pragmatic enclitics *-a* and *-ey* may appear either in isolation as in (510), (511) below and (501), (502) above, or in conjunction with the enclitics *-p* (509) and *-th* (512).

(510) *raak nhul   ngan yaan=**a**   yarra therk?*
       TIME 3sg(NOM) what go:RDP:NPST=PRAG   away return:NPST
       "what on earth time will he be going back there?"
       [Hall 1972: 139]

(511) *nganip   pelnan=**a**   work-orr   thernga-rr   koop   yuunhul*
       father(ACC) 3plACC=PRAG string-ERG kill-P.PFV   all   that.one
       'those fathers [my father and his brothers] were all killed by string [sorcery]'
       [KTh_AJ-**IC**-GJ26Nov2002 Narrative/Conversation]

(512) *ngay   kar palpal=**th**=**a**   learn-m   rirk-m*
       1sg(ERG) like nearby=PRAG=PRAG   learn-TR DO-P.IPFV
       "I kept on learning English"
       [KTh_AJ-IC-**GJ**26Nov2002 Narrative/Conversation]

6.11.4 'Filler' (*whatchamacallit*) terms

Demonstrative pronouns commonly serve as fillers when a speaker cannot or will not utter the target word or phrase. The closest equivalents in English are *whatchamacallit*, *wossname*, *whatsit* and the like (cf. Enfield 2003b), though they are unsurprisingly nonidentical in distribution to their Kuuk Thaayorre counterparts.

The target word that is substituted by a filler term may be inaccessible for one of two reasons. Firstly, it may be inaccessible to the speaker due to a problem of memory or lexical retrieval (e.g. 'tip of the tongue' phenomena). The filler term is used here to fill the gap in the flow of speech. In (513), for example, the speaker had temporarily forgotten the Kuuk Thaayorre term for *windpipe* (which I had asked him to translate). He therefore employs the filler form *yuunhul* 'that one' while touching his own windpipe.

(513) man   **yuunhul** inh,   ngan wan-r?   man+nhapn
       throat(ACC) that.one   dem:sp.prx   what tell-NPST throat+egg
       'what's this throat-whatchamacallit called? The windpipe'
       [KTh_AJ08Feb2004 Elicitation / Conversation]

Secondly, the target term may be inaccessible to the <u>addressee</u>. For example, they may lack conceptual or identificational information that is necessary for them to interpret the target term, if used. This can be seen in (514), in which the demonstrative *yuunhul* 'that one' precedes the kin term *pam meermele* 'poison cousin' in order to signal to the addressee that she is not expected to be familiar with this term or its significance, which the speaker then goes on to explain.

(514) kar **yuunhul**, pam meermele   nhul,   kar   nganc-le   ulp
       like that.one   MAN FZS   3sg(NOM) like   sacred=PRAG dem:ad.prx
       'like that whatchamacallit, *pam meermele* [cousin], that's a kind of poison relationship'
       [KTh_AJ27Jan2004 Elicitation / Conversation]

In many cases, such as example (515.2), the target term may be at once inaccessible to both speaker (who can't think of the right word) and addressee (who is unfamiliar with or not anticipating the word and/or referent):

(515) 1. ngok   inh   yoorr tap water-tam   mungk-r   inh
          water(ACC)   dem:sp.prx now   tap water-ABL   drink-NPST   dem:sp.prx
          'nowadays we drink this tap water here'
       2. ngancn   yuunhul   mungk-m   ngok,   ngok   menc   mungk-m
          1pl:excl(ERG) that.one   drink-P.IPFV water... water well(ACC) drink-P.IPFV
          'we used to drink that [other]... well water'
          [KTh_AJ-IC-**GJ**26Nov2002 Narrative/Conversation]

This distinction between inaccessibility to speaker versus addressee does not affect the choice of filler term, as demonstrated by the use of the distal demonstrative pronoun in (513) and (514) above. Nor is the choice of filler term affected by the terms' semantics in their basic situational use. In the case of *yuunhul* 'that one', this is amply demonstrated by example (513); it is impossible to construe the windpipe of a speaker's own body as spatially 'distal'. Instead, the choice between proximal and distal forms reflects how the speaker chooses to respond to the inaccessibility.

The proximal demonstrative *inhul* 'this one' is used to avoid disruption to the flow of speech (where the target lexeme is unnecessary or undesirable to the speaker's communicative goals). The distal demonstrative *yuunhul* 'that one', meanwhile, is used to signal that the inaccessibility of the target lexeme (whether to speaker or addressee) is disruptive to the flow of speech, and must be repaired before proceeding. Illustrating the first of these scenarios are many examples like (513) above, in which the speaker is not immediately able to supply the word I am attempting to elicit and record. Since the purpose of the work session is to record such lexical items, this lexical retrieval failure is clearly disruptive to the speaker's communicative goals. This is further illustrated by AJ's turn in example (516):

(516) AG: *nhunt   ngene katpi-rr?*
        2sg(NOM) how grasp-P.PFV
        'how did you catch [the prawns]?'
   AJ: ***yuunhul**=yuk... peep   ngancn   drag-m rirk-m*
        that.one= STUFF net(ACC) 1pl:excl(ERG) drag-TR DO-P.IPFV
        'with a whatsit... we were dragging a net'
        [KTh_AJ27Jan2004 Conversation]

It is not always the case that the speaker has a particular target lexeme in mind (which they fail to immediately verbalize), in some cases the speaker experiences trouble thinking of an example of a semantic field, or in defining a term. This can be seen in the following example, in which I begin by asking the language expert to explain a term he had just used in the prior discourse:

(517) AG: *winwin   kar ngan?*
        WINWIN(NOM) like what
        'what's winwin'
   AJ: *kar **yuunhul** ngan=yuk*
        like that.one what=STUFF
        'like those whatsits'
        ***yuunhul** kar wang ngan   nhaath-nhan, wang   yomprr*
        that.one like ghost what(ACC) see-GO&:NPST ghost(NOM) appear:NPST
        'like when you see a whatsit, when spirits appear'
        [KTh_**AJ**-GJ03Feb2004 Conversation / Elicitation]

It should be noted that the speaker not only uses the demonstrative pronoun as filler here, but combines this with repeated use of the ignorative pronoun *ngan* 'what' (see also the use of *wanhulak* 'to whom' in (354) below). As befits this pragmatic context, the various ignorative pronouns – which express a lack of knowledge in a particular category – are frequently found in combination with or in place of the 'filler' demonstrative pronouns.

Moving now to the proximal demonstrative pronoun, *inhul* 'this one', this form is used to signal that there is no need to disrupt the conversation in order to retrieve or explain the target lexeme. In some cases (owing to bereavement and/or kinship taboo) it would be inappropriate for the speaker to utter the lexeme in question. In example (518), for instance, the speaker obliquely refers to a sister of Donald and Cyril by using the plural (rather than dual) pronoun *peln* 'they' in an inclusory construction, coupled with the proximal demonstrative filler *inhul* 'this one'. The example might thus be translated 'This *whatsitsname* [who you know but I must not name, associated with Donald and Cyril] remembers him [and will be able to tell you about him when you later meet with her]':

(518) **inhul**   ulp,   peln
      this.one   dem:ad.prx   3pl(NOM)
      Donald, Cyril, peln   ulp   walmeerem=unh
      Donald Cyril 3pl(NOM) dem:ad.prx remember=3sgACC
      'those ones, Donald and Cyril and whatsitsname, they all remember him'
      [KTh_AJ26Nov2002 Conversation]

The speaker may use *inhul* 'this one' as a filler to avoid disrupting the conversation even where the addressee is not familiar with the target referent and does not have the means to establish the intended reference from discourse context. In (318) below, for example, the speaker describes an extra-marital affair without naming the man involved, due either to discretion or to the fact that I (her interlocutor) would not have been familiar with the man in question even if he were identified, or both:

(318') ngul   nhul   iirra   yat,   inhul   wanhulak
       then   3sg(NOM)   to.there   go:P.PFV   this.one   who:DAT
       'then she went off, to that whatsit [other man]'
       [KTh_ACh07Nov2002 Conversation]

As noted above, this filler usage of demonstrative pronouns is semantically and pragmatically related to ignorative pronouns (§5.2), but also the nominal enclitic *=yuk* 'STUFF' (§4.4.3) and the associative use of the Topological Relation Marker *mangka* 'low, mob' (§9.2.1.4). There are also notable commonalities with the discourse uses of both demonstrative pronouns and adnominal demonstratives (§5.3.3).

7 Verbal inflection

7.1 The verbal word

Kuuk Thaayorre verb stems may be either simplex (consisting solely of a verb root) or complex. Complex, polymorphemic verb stems may be formed either by compounding a (reduced) body part noun with a verb root, or by suffixing one or more derivational suffixes to the verb root. All forms of verbal derivation are considered in 8.

7.1.1 Overview of inflectional categories

As noted in §3.2, the verbal word may contain a maximum of one inflectional suffix (expressing some combination of tense, aspect and/or mood).[144] These inflectional suffixes follow any derivational morphology, as predicted by Greenberg (1963: 93). The inflectional suffixes are divided into those expressing modal categories alone, and those expressing tense/aspect. There is a binary tense split between 'past' and 'nonpast'. The 'past' tense in turn bifurcates into two aspects – perfective and imperfective – as schematized in Figure 12:

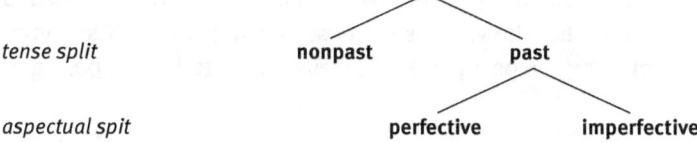

tense split nonpast past

aspectual spit perfective imperfective

Figure 12. Tense/aspect categories encoded by the Kuuk Thaayorre verb.

There are thus three indicative tense/aspect categories encoded by Kuuk Thaayorre suffixes, further to the aspectual effects of optional root reduplication (see §7.2.4): past perfective, past imperfective and nonpast. The nonpast category is neutral with respect to mood (i.e. it may express a realis event in progress at the time of utterance, or equally an irrealis desire or expectation for the future), but both past tense affixes are necessarily realis. Further to these are five modal suffixes which occur in the same position as tense/aspect inflection, but are neutral with respect to tense and aspect. The modal categories encoded are: Imperative ('IMP'), subjunctive ('SBJV'), purposive ('PURP') counterfactual ('CTF'), and imminence ('IMM').[145] Further to these inflectional

---

[144] This suffix may, however, combine with root reduplication expressing verbal aspect.
[145] The verbal categories proposed here differ considerably from those put forward by Hall (1972). Compare, for example, my three-way distinction between past perfective, past imperfective and non-

categories, this chapter also includes consideration of the arguably derivational process of reduplication due to its function of marking aspectual categories (§7.2.4).

7.1.2 Verbal conjugations

The conjugation class of a verb stem determines which allomorphs of the tense/aspect morphemes it combines with. The suffix form *-r*, for example, signifies nonpast tense when suffixed to a conjugation 1 verb, but signifies past perfective tense/aspect when suffixed to a verb of conjugation 2. The majority of Kuuk Thaayorre verbs belong to conjugation 1, but the number of conjugation 2 verbs is significant. Although the second conjugation is smaller in membership than the first, there is no evidence that this is a closed class; new verbs derived by the 'verbalizing' suffix *-m* are generally assigned to the second conjugation. In addition to these two major conjugation classes, there are a handful of irregular verbs, the inflection of which must be learned on a verb-by-verb basis.

The conjugation membership of complex (polymorphemic) verb stems is determined solely by the final morpheme, whether this be the root (as above) or a derivational suffix. Accordingly, all verb stems derived by suffixation of valence-increasing *-(nha)n(i)* belong to conjugation 1, regardless of the conjugation of the root from which they are derived. Derivational morphemes, like roots, are therefore assigned to a particular conjugation class. That the valence increaser belongs to the first conjugation can be seen by comparing the past perfective forms of the following base and valence-increased verbs:

(519) *rok-r* 'enter-P.PFV' (Conj2)   >   *roka-ni-rr* 'enter-v^-P.PFV' (Conj1)
(520) *piinthi-rr* 'grow-P.PFV' (Conj1)   >   *piinthi-ni-rr* 'grow-v^-P.PFV' (Conj1)

The second conjugation verb, *rok* 'enter' converts to first conjugation through suffixation of the conjugation 1 valence increaser *-(nha)n(i)*. The reverse conversion is evident in examples (521) and (522), in which the second conjugation reflexive suffix derives a second conjugation stem from first conjugation roots:[146]

(521) *katpi-rr* 'grasp-P.PFV' (Conj1)   >   *katp-ey-r* 'grasp-RFL-P.PFV' (Conj2)
(522) *thernga-rr* 'hit-P.PFV' (Conj1)   >   *therng-ey-r* 'hit-RFL-P.PFV' (Conj2)

---

past tense/aspect (which have different forms for the different conjugations) with Hall's (1972: 86) distinctions between past, present and future tenses and nonspecific, realis and irrealis (plus punctiliar and continuous) aspects. These are not simple differences in terminology, but rather reflect a much deeper cleavage in analysis. Since the discussion of each divergence would lead to an overly convoluted exposition, only the most pertinent departures will be flagged.

146 Since none of the second conjugation roots are fully bivalent, they cannot be reflexivized.

Moreover, all verb stems derived through the second associated motion derivation belong to the first conjugation, regardless of the valency of the stems to which they attach.[147] Hence, the associated motion 2 verb stem in (523) – derived from the transitive root *mungk* 'eat' – conjugates no differently from that in (524) – derived from the intransitive root *rok* 'enter':

(523) anyway mungk-ica-rr, pungkutharr
anyway eat-RUN&-P.PFV hungry
'I went and ate [the fish] anyway, because I was hungry'
[KTh_AJ27Jan2004 conversation]

(524) ball werngka rok-ica-rr
ball(NOM) middle enter-RUN&-P.PFV
'the ball went into the middle (of the enclosure)'
[KTh_GJ20Nov2002 MoverbEnterExit18]

Table 47, Table 48, and Table 49 present the imperative, nonpast and past perfective inflections of some common Kuuk Thaayorre verbs belonging to the first, second, and irregular conjugations respectively.

The assignation of verb roots to conjugation classes is lexically-determined. There is, however, a strong correlation between conjugation class and valency, according with Dixon's (1980, 2002: 233) observation that the conjugation classes of many Australian languages are predominantly (though usually not exclusively) composed of verbs with a particular transitivity value. Conjugation 2 verbs are almost exclusively monovalent (exceptions include *wene* 'want, become' and *yik* 'say', which are semi-transitive and semiditransitive respectively, and the postural verbs, which may take complements in their copula and ascriptive functions – see §10.2). Similarly, while conjugation 1 is made up predominantly of polyvalent verbs, there are some notable exceptions (e.g. *riic* 'run', *piinth* 'grow', etc.). Further supporting a non-binding association between conjugation and valency, the valence-reducing reflexive and reciprocal suffixes both derive second conjugation stems, while the valence increasing morpheme derives a first conjugation stem. This link is strengthened by the fact that intransitive verbs created by the verbalizing suffix -*m* belong to conjugation 2, while transitive verbs created by -*m* 'VerBaLiZer' belong to conjugation 1. Hence the suffix -*r* signifies present tense in (525.2) (indicating that the verbalizer has derived a transitive, first conjugation stem *pinirm* 'imagine'), but past perfective in (526) (indicating that the derived second conjugation stem *piinthawaarrm* 'tire' is intransitive).

---

147 The first associated motion morpheme derives irregular verb stems following the inflectional pattern of *yan* 'go'.

Table 47. Imperative, nonpast and past perfective forms of first conjugation verbs.

Conjugation 1: -r 'npst' / -rr 'p.pfv'			
IMP		NPST	P.PFV
kal 'carry (tr)'		*kalr*	*kalirr*
katp 'grasp (tr)'		*katpr*	*katpirr*
koont 'deprive (ditr)'		*koontr*	*koonterr*
matp 'smash (tr)'		*matpr*	*matparr*
mi'i 'pick up (tr)'		*mi'ir*	*mi'irr*
miinng 'take fright (semitr)'		*miinngr*	*miinngarr*
mungk 'eat (tr)'		*mungkr*	*mungkarr*
munth 'sink (intr)'		*munthr*	*munthirr*
path 'bite (tr)'		*pathr*	*patharr*
patp 'camp (intr)'		*patpr*	*patpirr*
pic 'burst (intr)'		*picr*	*picarr*
piinth 'grow (intr)'		*piinthr*	*piinthirr*
pit 'keep (tr)'		*pitr*	*pitarr*
pinirm 'dream (tr)'		*pinirmr*	*pinirmirr*
pirk 'peel (tr)'		*pirkr*	*pirkarr*
rath 'chop (tr)'		*rathr*	*rathirr*
reek 'give (ditr)'		*reekr*	*reekarr*
riic 'run (intr)'		*riicr*	*riicarr*
rint 'cook, burn (tr)'		*rintr*	*rintirr*
thaa.raak 'place/stand (tr)'		*thaa+raakr*	*thaa+raakirr*
thaangk 'climb (intr)'		*thaangkr*	*thaangkarr*
thaath 'scorch'(tr)		*thaathr*	*thaathirr*
thak 'leave' (tr)		*thakr*	*thakarr*
therng 'hit' (tr)		*therngr*	*therngarr*
thunp 'throw' (tr)		*thunpr*	*thunpirr*
thuuth 'pull' (tr)		*thuuthr*	*thuutharr*
waath 'seek' (tr)		*waathr*	*waathirr*
wak 'follow' (tr)		*wakr*	*wakirr*
wan 'call' (ditr)		*wanr*	*wanirr*
wunp 'lay' (tr)		*wunpr*	*wunparr*
yith 'lead' (tr)		*yithr*	*yithirr*
yoongk 'hang'(tr)		*yoongkr*	*yoongkerr*
yump 'do' (tr)		*yumpr*	*yumpirr*
-(nha)n(i) 'V^'	[any verb stem ending in the valence increasing suffix]	*-(a)nr*	*-(a)nirr*
-ic(a) 'RUN&'	[any verb stem ending in the second series of Associate Motion suffixes]	*-icr*	*-icarr*

Table 48. Imperative, nonpast and past perfective forms of second conjugation verbs.

Conjugation 2: -ø 'npst' / -r 'p.pfv'

IMP	NPST	P.PFV
kerp 'finish (intr)'	*kerp*	*kerpr*
koope 'wait (intr)'	*koope*	*koopeyr*
kooc 'bark (tr)'	*kooc*	*koocr*
nhiin 'sit (intr)'	*nhiin*	*nhiinr*
paarr 'cry, be born (intr)'	*paarr*	*paarr_r*
rirk 'rise, DO (INTR)'	*rirk*	*rirkr*
rumparr 'break (intr)'	*rumparr*	*rumparr_r*
than 'stand (intr)'	*than*	*thanr*
therk 'return (intr)'	*therk*	*therkr*
thongk 'arrive (intr)'	*thongk*	*thongkr*
thowol 'play (intr)'	*thowol*	*thowolr*
waantharr 'call out for (intr)'	*waantharr*	*waantharr_r*
wene 'become' (semitr)	*wene*	*weneyr*
wonp 'die (intr)'	*wonp*	*wonpr*
wont 'fall (intr)'	*wont*	*wontr*
wun 'lie (intr)'	*wun*	*no P.PFV*
yik 'say' (semitr)	*yik*	*yikr*
yoongke 'hang (intr)'	*yoongke*	*yoongker*
yuuc 'ache (intr)'	*yuuc*	*yuucr*
-e 'RFL' [any verb stem formed through reflexive derivation]	*-e*	*-ey-r*
-rr 'RCP' [any verb stem formed through reciprocal derivation]	*-rr*	*-rr-r*

Table 49. Imperative, nonpast and past perfective forms of common irregular verbs.

Irregular

IMP	NPST	P.PFV
ke'e 'spear (tr)'	*ke'er*	*ke'err ~ ko'orr*
ngeey 'hear (tr)'	*ngeem*	*ngeeyr*
*unattested in IMP (except as derived Go&) 'see (tr)'	*nham*	*nhaawr*
yarr 'go (intr)'	*yan*	*yat*
-nharr 'GO&' [any verb stem formed through first associated motion derivation]	*-nhan*	*-nhat*

(525) 1. *ngay ulp net kaar drag-m rirk, iikuw*
1sg(ERG) dem:ad.prx net(ACC) NEG drag-TR DO:NPST there:at:west
rump-un
beach-DAT
'I don't drag net down on the beach'
2. *kar ngay minh ulp pininir-m-r*
like 1sg(ERG) MEAT(ACC) dem:ad.prx dream-VBLZ-NPST
'because I imagine/think about those crocodiles'
[KTh_GJ3Feb2004 conversation]

(526) *ngay piinthawaarr-m-r ngay nhangknma*
1sg(NOM) tired-VBLZ-P.PFV 1sg(NOM) 2sgABL
'I wearied of you'
[Hall 1972: 138]

While there are also some extremely weak correlations between conjugation, aktionsart and token frequency, these can be attributed either to coincidence or to a correlation with valency.

Kuuk Thaayorre verb stems have fixed and stable conjugation membership. There are, however, a small number of exceptions evident in the works of Foote and Hall. In the following three examples, bivalent verbs derived by the valence increasing morpheme (suffixed to an originally second conjugation root) appear to be inflecting as a second conjugation stem, with the suffix *-r* apparently encoding past perfective:

(527) *ngul=(nh)ul=(nh)unh man-pert-e theerka-n-r nhaknkath-an*
then=3sg(ERG)=3sg(ACC) shoulder-ERG return-V^-P.PFV home-DAT
'and he carried it back home on his shoulder to camp'
[Hall 1972: 105]

(528) *ngay nhunh pam pork wene-nhan-r*
1sg(ERG) 3sgACC man big become-V^-P.PFV
'I caused him to become great'
[Hall 1972: 131]

(529) *nganip-i thul nhangn yuuw kerpa-n-r*
father-ERG woomera 3sgGEN(ACC) far finish-V^-P.PFV
'Dad lost his woomera far away from here'
[Hall 1972: 108]

Although it might be tempting to search for reasons why these particular verb stems might be more likely to retain the conjugation class (2) of the root, it should be noted that in my data there are plenty of examples of these same verb roots combining with the valence increaser to produce first conjugation stems, as in (530):

(530) pam thon-thrr find-m   rirk-r,   therka-ni-rr   parr_r   ulp
      man one-ERG   find-VBLZ DO-P.PFV return-V^-P.PFV child(ACC) dem:ad.prx
      'one man found the child and brought him back'
      [KTh_FT8Feb2004 Narrative Adoptee]

I therefore set aside counterexamples such as (527)–(529), assuming that they are the product of ideolectal or pragmatic factors (e.g. the -r suffix may in fact represent nonpast tense, used in these apparently past contexts for now unreconstructable discursive effect).

Table 50 presents the full range of TAM-inflected forms of an exemplar of each of the two major conjugations.

Table 50. Conjugation of two typical Kuuk Thaayorre verbs.

	path 'bite (Conj1)'	*rirk* 'rise, do (Conj2)'
Nonpast; -r ~ -ø	pathr	rirk
Past perfective; -rr ~ -r	patharr	rirkr
Past imperfective; -(nha)m	pathm	rirkm
Reduplicated; [cf. §2.6]	pathath ~ paath	rirkirk
Imperative; -ø	path	rirk
Subjunctive; -nh	pathnh	rirknh
Counterfactual; -nhata	pathnhata	rirknhata
Purposive; -nhatha	pathnhatha	rirknhatha
Imminence; -rrth(a)	pathrrth(a)	rirkrrtha

Table 51 presents the conjugations of the most common irregular verbs.

Table 51. Conjugation of the five most common Kuuk Thaayorre irregular verbs.

Root	*ya-* 'go'	*ngee-* 'hear'	*nhaa-* 'see'	*mi'i* 'pick up'	*ke'e* 'spear'
Nonpast	yan	ngeem	nham	mi'ir	ke'er
Past perfective	yat	ngeeyr	nhaawr	mi'irr	ke'err ~ ko'orr
Past imperfective	yancm	ngeeym	nhaathm	mi'im	ko'om
Reduplicated	yaan	ngeengem	nhaanham	—	—
Imperative	yarr	ngeey	nham	mi'irr	ko'o
Subjunctive	yancnh	ngeeynh	nhaathnh	?	?
Counterfactual	yatath	ngeeynhata	nhaathnhata	?	?
Purposive	?	ngeeynhatha	nhaathnhatha	?	?
Imminence	yarrtha	?ngeeyrrtha	nhaathrrtha	?	?

Throughout this grammar, verb roots are transcribed with either of two alternative forms; a thematic vowel-final form seen in the contexts of past perfective inflection (for first conjugation verbs) and valence increasing derivation, the other ('reduced') form found elsewhere. Table 52 presents these two root forms in combination with some common inflectional and derivational suffixes.

Table 52. Alternative root allomorphs of some first conjugation verbs.

Reduced root	V-final root
mungk 'eat:IMP'; *mungk-r* 'eat-NPST'	*mungka-rr* 'eat-P.PFV'; *mungka-n(i)-* 'eat-v^'
path 'bite:IMP'; *path-r* 'bite-NPST'	*mungka-rr* 'eat-P.PFV'; *mungka-n(i)-* 'eat-v^'
rok 'enter:IMP'; *rok-r* 'enter-P.PFV'	*roka-n(i)-* 'enter-v^'
rip 'exit:IMP'; *rip-r* 'exit-P.PFV'	*ripi-n(i)-* 'exit-v^'
therng 'hit:IMP'; *therng-r* 'hit-NPST'	*thernga-rr* 'hit-P.PFV'; *thernga-n(i)* 'hit-v^'
waath 'search.for:IMP'; *waath-r* 'search.for-NPST'	*waathi-rr* 'search.for-P.PFV'; *waathi-n(i)-* 'search.for-v^'
yump 'do:IMP'; *yump-r* 'do-NPST'	*yumpi-rr* 'do-P.PFV'; *yumpi-n(i)* 'do-v^'
yak 'cut:IMP'; *yak-r* 'cut-NPST'	*yake-rr* 'cut-P.PFV'; *yake-n(i)-* 'cut-v^'

This apparent root allomorphy can be analyzed in one of three ways. The analysis followed here is one of subtractive morphology. Specifically, I analyze the vowel-final allomorph as the lexical entry. The consonant-final allomorph is produced through the deletion of the final vowel, as specified by the relevant suffix. The imperative verbal form, for example, is formed through this final vowel-deletion alone. Such an analysis mirrors that applied to nomina with respect to the subtractive morphology of case inflection (cf. §4.1.1 and §4.2.1). As with nomina, the representational difficulties associated with a subtractive analysis lead me to segment and gloss verb roots in a manner that does not fully reflect this analysis. Specifically, the root-final vowel is simply omitted from the citation form and any other instance in which it has been deleted.

An alternative analysis would attribute the putative root-final vowels to the suffix that follows them. Hence the past perfective morpheme would have allomorphs: *-arr* (following verb roots such as *path* 'bite'); *-err* (following verb roots such *yak* 'cut'); *-irr* (following verb roots such as *waath* 'search for'); and so on. Such an analysis would require that each verb root be assigned to a conjugation subclasses that determines the suffix allomorphs with which it may combine. So, for instance, *path* 'bite' would be a member of conjugation subclass-a, *yak* 'cut' would be a member of conjugation subclass-e, *waath* 'search for' would be a member of conjugation subclass-i, and so on. These subclasses are required because the suffix allomorph that is selected cannot be predicted by the phonotactics of the verb root. Such an analysis is serviceable, if inelegant.

The third and final analysis would enter two alternative root forms into the lexicon, specifying that the consonant-final allomorph be selected for, e.g., imperative inflections, and the vowel-final allomorph be selected as input for, e.g., valence increasing derivation. Again, this analysis is serviceable, though less parsimonious than the first analysis which posits only a single lexical entry for each verb.

In the following discussion of verbal inflection and derivation, reference will be made to 'vowel-extended' verb root forms (such as *waathi-* 'search for' and *mungka-* 'eat') and 'bare' verb root forms (such as *waath* 'search for', *mungk* 'eat' and *mi'i* 'pick up').

7.2 Tense and aspect

Kuuk Thaayorre verbal morphology marks two distinctions in tense and three in aspect. Rather than being encoded by dedicated morphemes severally, these five tense/aspect categories overlap, and hence are considered together in this section. As mentioned in §7.1, the two past tense morphemes contrast in (im)perfectivity, while the nonpast morpheme simply encodes tense (often with modal implicature). Reduplicative verb root mutation (discussed under §7.2.4) encodes aspect alone. The following sections detail the semantics of these tense/aspect categories.

7.2.1 Nonpast

The nonpast tense is encoded by the bare root or stem for conjugation 1 verbs, and by adding the suffix *-r* to the bare root or stem for conjugation 2 verbs. The nonpast-inflected forms of the most common irregular verbs and exemplars of the two major conjugation classes (*path* 'bite' for conjugation 1 and *rirk* 'rise' for conjugation 2) are presented in Table 47, Table 48 and Table 49.

The tense system of Kuuk Thaayorre does not distinguish events that are in progress at the time of speech from those that are expected to occur at some point following the speech event. As Comrie (1985: 49) notes, such a binary tense split between nonpast and past is common. However, the term 'nonpast' to describe the broader Kuuk Thaayorre category may be somewhat of a misnomer. In order to explain why, let us first consider the range of event types that receive nonpast marking.

Firstly, the nonpast morpheme may be used in the description of events that have not yet occurred at the time of speech, but are expected to occur sometime afterwards:

(531) *ngay   nhangun yup   yik*
      1sg(NOM) 3sgDAT later say:NPST
      'I will tell her later'
      [KTh_MF20Aug2002 Conversation]

An event may also be encoded by the nonpast morpheme if its duration overlaps with the speech event. In example (532), for example, the speech event and the event described are necessarily coextensive:

(532) ngay   nhangkun yiik
       1sg(NOM) 2sgDAT   say:RDP:NPST
       'I'm talking to you'
       [Anon.]

Less perfect overlap between the speech event and the event described is also permissible. In (533) the speech event intersects the described event (since the speaker must necessarily have broken off his discussion with the white girl in order to utter this clause to the addressee):

(533) ngay   paanth wang-a   yiik
       1sg(NOM) woman   whitefella-DAT say:RDPNPST
       'I'm talking to the white girl'
       [KTh_AC22Jul2002 Conversation]

Although the term 'nonpast' suggests incompatibility with events that extend backwards in time, this is not the case in Kuuk Thaayorre. Example (534) illustrates the use of the nonpast tense to describe an event that spans past, present and future:

(534) ngul ngay   ulp   kuuk wang   yiik
       then 1sg(NOM) dem:ad.prx WORD whitefella(ACC) say:RDP:NPST
       'since that time I can speak English'
       [KTh_AJ-IC-**GJ**26Nov2002 Conversation/Narrative]

Like examples (532) and (533), (534) describes an event that overlaps in duration with the speech event. It is not crosslinguistically unusual for a morpheme that encodes present-tense events to also encode events that extend backwards (as well as forwards) in time. As Comrie (1985: 38) observes, the basic present-tense category "invariably locates a situation at the present moment, and says nothing beyond that. In particular, it does not say that the same situation does not continue beyond the present moment, nor that it did not hold in the past". While the Kuuk Thaayorre nonpast morpheme may itself say nothing about whether or not the situation held in the past, the label 'nonpast' does imply that it did not. If the uses of this tense category cannot be unified by the fact that they all encode events or situations that did not hold in the past, is it possible to provide a monosemous definition of the nonpast morpheme? Or should the nonpast category instead be subdivided into the (polysemous) senses 'Present' and 'Future'? I propose that a monosemous characterization of this category can be sketched as follows. If we imagine a timeline, upon which the beginning of the speech event (or alternative deictic anchor) is labelled 'BSp', any event encoded by the two past tense/aspects must occur during the period prior to 'BSp', while any event encoded by the nonpast morpheme must occur for a period of time that includes the period following 'BSp'. This can be represented diagrammatically as follows:

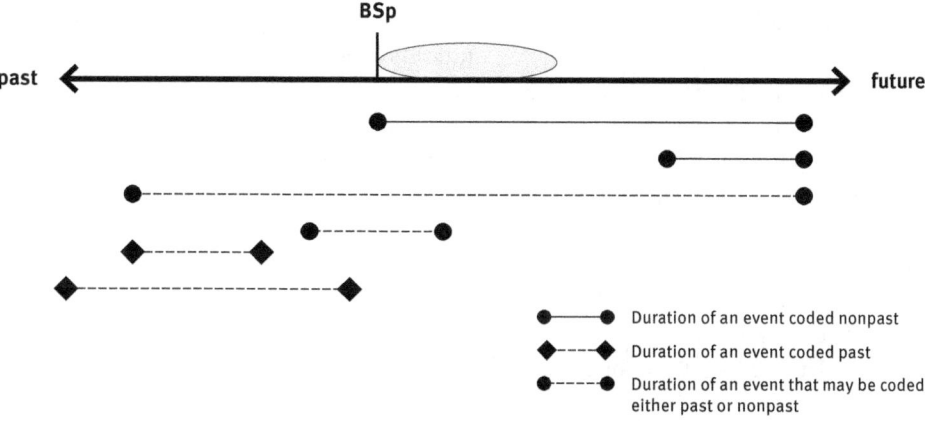

Figure 13. The division between Kuuk Thaayorre 'past' and 'nonpast' categories.

If we take the grey oblong to represent the duration of the speech event, the crucial point in determining nonpast coding is the vertical line marking the beginning of the speech event ('BSp'). If the event described has ended to the left of (and therefore prior to) this vertical line, it may not be encoded nonpast. If, however, the event has not ended by this point (including where it has not yet begun), it is eligible for nonpast marking. In other words, any event marked 'nonpast' has not yet ended by the start of the speech event. All the circle-ended lines below the diagram fall into this category. The term 'nonpast', then, should be understood as applying to events that do occur in the non-past period (i.e. the period that is not prior to the deictic anchor), rather than to events that do not occur in the past. Conversely, events that do occur in the period preceding the beginning of the speech event 'BSp' (represented by dashed lines below the timeline in Figure 13) may be encoded by one of the past tense morphemes. An event that spans both the period prior to BSp and the period following it should theoretically be compatible with either nonpast or past tense marking. Implausible though this may sound – that a single event could alternatively be marked past or nonpast – this is in fact what we find. Such events are represented in Figure 13 by dashed lines with terminal circles. The choice between tenses is motivated by which period the speaker wishes to emphasize. So in (534) above, the speaker chooses to stress his current fluency in English (which results from an event in the past). In (535), however, the speaker focuses on the fact that her bag was lying 'here' in the past (the whole time she was looking for it), instead of on the fact that it remains 'here' during the speech act:

(535) ngay   kana   wuwirr   bag   ngathn
      1sg(ERG) finish find:P.PFV   bag   1sgGEN(ACC)
      inh'nhaka   wun-m   yuk-un   mangka-n
      at.this.place lie-P.IPFV   tree-DAT low-DAT
      'I've found my bag, [it] was lying under the tree here'
      [KTh_MF20Aug2002 Elicitation]

Similarly, generalizations about typical behaviour may be phrased in either the nonpast (536) or the past imperfective (537):

(536) mit   pork rirk   ngancn
      work   big   DO:NPST 1pl:excl(NOM)
      'we work hard'
      [KTh_AJ27Jan2004 Conversation]

(537) kuta thok-n   kookoc-m?   Pokon, kaar kookoc-m
      PET cat-^ERG   bark:RDP-P.IPFV   NO   NEG   bark:RDP-P.IPFV
      'do cats *bark*? No, they don't bark'
      [KTh_GJ31Jan2004 Elicitation DahlTMA76]

Compare the latter example, in which an inductive generalization is phrased in the past tense (presumably because it was made on the basis of past observations), with the English colloquial phrasing of generalizations in the future (*a dog'll bark but a cat won't*), predicting expected behaviour rather than describing past observations. Predictably, it is only the past imperfective, not the perfective, which can describe events that extend beyond the beginning of speech. This follows from the fact that perfective event must have been completed (see §7.2.2). It should finally be noted that the nonpast categories of neighbouring Yir Yoront and Kugu Nganhcara also include in their scope events that begin in the past and endure into the future.[148]

Although I do not view the present and future tenses as distinct subsenses of the nonpast morpheme, Kuuk Thaayorre speakers are of course able to distinguish events occurring at the time of speech from those that will occur subsequently. Where disambiguation is required, this is done by clausal particles (e.g. *yoorr* 'now', *yup* 'soon

---

[148] Although Smith & Johnson (2000: 408) label the equivalent Kugu Nganhcara tense *present*, they do acknowledge that it "might be more appropriately named nonpast; it indicates not only present events and states but also those of the future (in conjunction with the particle (yu)pa... and those with no specific timeframe (e.g. Wallabies eat grass)".

after', or *ngul* 'later'), rather than coded in verbal morphology. This can be seen in the following interchange, where I misunderstood the language expert's initial request and she subsequently clarified using *yup* 'soon after':

(538) ME: *pal   kal=pa!*
          towards carry:IMP=PRAG
          'bring [the cabbage palm leaves] here!'
      AG: [gets up to leave]
      ME: *kace, kana   yan   nhunt=a*
          CDICT about.to go:NPST 2sg(NOM)=PRAG
          'no, [you're] about to go'
      AG: *kana   yan   yoorr, or...?*
          about.to go:NPST now   or
          'go now, or...?'
      ME: *yup! ngal   thurma   yarr=ey!*
          soon 1du:incl(NOM) together go:IMP=PRAG
          'soon [i.e. not yet]! We'll go together!'
          ngal   yarr   thurma,
          1du:incl(NOM) go:IMP together
          'we'll go together'
          kanpa inh   kerp,   yup   yan
          first   dem:sp.prx finish:IMP soon go:NPST
          'finish this first, go soon'
          [KTh_ME04Jun2005 Conversation (interruption to Narrative)]

Since the nonpast tense may be used to describe both events overlapping in time with the speech event and events that will occur in the time following the speech event, it might be expected that this tense should also encode events beginning at the time of speech and enduring into the future. However, because such events are strongly associated with inceptive aspect, they are almost always marked as such (e.g. by an associated motion suffix – see §8.1.4). Rare exceptions to this usually involve the verb *ya-* 'go', which for reasons of etymology may not combine with the associated motion suffixes, in combination with the particle *kana* 'about to' (§9.1.1):

(539) *ngamp   kana   yan   ngat-a*
      1pl:incl(NOM) about.to go:NPST fish-DAT
      'let's go fishing' / 'we're about to go fishing'
      [KTh_MF10Jan2004 Elicitation / Conversation]

(540) *ngay   kana   yan*
      1sg(NOM) about.to go:NPST
      'I'm going now'
      [most common farewell/leave-taking expression in Kuuk Thaayorre]

(541) paath   ulp   kana   keempe-nhan   yup!
      fire(NOM) dem:ad.prx about.to extinguish-GO&:NPST soon
      'that fire's going to go out soon'
      [KTh_AJ8Feb2004 Elicitation]

While both the subjunctive and associated motion suffixes may be used to encode hope, desire or intention more explicitly, the nonpast tense often has a modal implicature. In the following example, for instance, the speaker expresses his desire to go to Melbourne simply by means of a nonpast verb (and an English loan adverb):

(542) ngay   yan,   ngay   yan.   Ngay   willing ngay   yan
      1sg(NOM) go:NPST 1sg(NOM) go:NPST 1sg(NOM) willing 1sg(NOM) go:NPST
      'I want to go [to Melbourne]. I'm willing [to do this], I want to go'
      [KTh_GJ16Oct2002 Narrative MelbourneTrip]

The nonpast tense combines with various other forms to form larger constructions (e.g. to express desiderative mood, §11.7.211). These are discussed in Chapter 10.

7.2.2 Past perfective

The past perfective is marked by the suffixation of -rr to the vowel-extended root/stem of first conjugation verbs, and the suffixation of -r to the bare root/stem of second conjugation verbs (see examples in Table 47, Table 48 and Table 49). The past perfective tense/aspect not only locates the event described at a time prior to the speech event (or alternative deictic anchor), but also indicates that it has been completed. So, for instance, in (543) the past perfective suffix -rr indicates both that the chopping event has already occurred, but also that the stick was successfully chopped; the chopping event was not interrupted or abandoned prior to completion:

(543) nhul   thongkn kuthirr   rathi-rr
      3sg(ERG) piece   two(ACC) chop-P.PFV
      'he chopped (the stick) into two halves'
      [KTh_EF15Dec2002 Elicitation Cut&Break2]

This Kuuk Thaayorre tense/aspect can also encode some events that will not take place until after the time of utterance (unlike the past perfective categories of some other languages, e.g. Kugu Nganhcara; Smith and Johnson 2000: 410). This can occur where the speaker establishes some future deictic centre, with respect to which the event described is anchored. From the perspective of this deictic centre anchor, then, the described event (will have) already occurred in its entirety. Example (544) is accordingly framed with respect to some postulated time of death, at which time the addressee will receive the gift of eternal life, provided that they have (perfectively, in the past) believed in Jesus:

(544) ith   kar   nhunt   kar   trust-m   rirk-r   nhunh,
       if   like 2sg(NOM)   like trust-VBLZ   DO-P.PFV   3sg(ACC)
       believe-m   rirk-r   nhunh
       believe-VBLZ   DO-P.PFV   3sg(ACC)
       'if you have trusted and believed him [you will have eternal life]'
       [KTh_GJ18Jan2004 Narrative Christmas]

This last usage is quite rare, however. In the vast majority of cases, the past perfective is anchored by the speech act (otherwise it might better be analyzed as encoding perfective aspect alone).

The past perfective tense/aspect marks an event as telic, transforming (usually) an activity verb into an achievement or accomplishment. In (545), for instance, the speaker is describing a bush trip on which he lost his companion. Although *wak* 'follow' normally encodes an activity, he marks it past perfective to emphasize the point at which her route diverged from his. That is to say, instead of describing the activity of following the track (i.e. in the past imperfective: *nhul kulam yiirr wakm* 'she followed/was walking along a different track'), the speaker focuses our attention on the moment of separation, where she turned from one track to another:

(545) nhul   kulam yiirr   waki-rr
       3sg(ERG)   path   other(ACC)   follow-P.PFV
       'she followed a different path'
       [KTh_AC14Nov2002 Narrative LosingIrma]

When combined with a past perfective verb, the particle *kana* has the meaning 'finished', adding emphasis to the completion of the event (cf. §9.1.1). This can be seen in examples such as the following:

(546) ngay   kana   thaka-rr
       1sg(NOM)   finish leave-P.PFV
       'I left Pormpuraaw'
       [KTh_BN1Oct2002 conversation]

(547) yuk   kana   kerp-r
       cigarette   finish finish-P.PFV
       'the smokes are all gone'
       [KTh_BN1Oct2002 conversation]

7.2.3 Past imperfective

The past imperfective morpheme attaches to the bare root form of verbs, taking one of the following three allomorphs: *-nham ~ -nam ~ -m*. The last (hereafter 'reduced') allomorph attaches to most high frequency stems, including those ending in:

- /p/ (e.g. *yump-m* 'make-P.IPFV')
- /th/ (e.g. *waath-m* 'search-P.IPFV')
- /t/ (e.g. *pit-m* 'keep-P.IPFV')
- /rr/ (e.g. *paarr-m* 'cry-P.IPFV')
- /l/ (e.g. *kal-m* 'carry- P.IPFV')
- /c/ (e.g. *riic-m* 'run-P.IPFV')
- /k/ (e.g. *wak-m* 'follow-P.IPFV')
- /n/ (e.g. *wan-m* 'tell-P.IPFV')
- /ng/ (e.g. *theerng-m* 'hit-P.IPFV')

While there does not seem to be any phonological basis for the selection of the reduced past imperfective allomorph, the allomorphy between the 'full' forms *-nham* and *-nam*, can be predicted from the final segment of the verb stem. The 'full' allomorph *-nam* occurs following stems that end in alveolar and retroflex phonemes, with *-nham* found elsewhere. The conditioning of the full allomorphs can thus be summarized:

-nham → *-nam* / C __
[+alveolar]

→ *-nham* / elsewhere

Table 53 gives the past imperfective inflections of the seven exemplar verbs:

Table 53. Seven Kuuk Thaayorre verbs inflected for the past imperfective.

Root	Past imperfective	Meaning
ke'e	ko'om	'was spearing'
mi'i	mi'im	'was picking up'
ngee-	ngeeym	'was hearing'
nhaa-	nhaathm	'was seeing'
ya-	yancm	'was going'
path	pathm	'was biting'
rirk	rirkm	'was rising'

Whereas the past perfective emphasizes the completion or closure of an event, the past imperfective shifts the perspective to the internal duration of the event. Typically for an imperfective, it is used to encode "actions conceived as extending over a period of time, continuously or at intervals" (Matthews 1997), where those actions occurred over a time period inclusive of a time prior to the speech event (or alternative deictic anchor). The following examples illustrate the use of the past imperfective to encode continuously enduring activities (548 and 549), states (550), and actions iterated over a period of time (551):

(548) yuk   shovel   kal-m   man.pert-an
      THING   shovel(ACC) carry-P.IPFV   shoulder-DAT
      'I was carrying a shovel on my shoulder'
      [KTh_AC14Nov2002 Narrative LosingIrma]

(549) yuu-rr-iparr   wun-m   ngancn...   Thaayorre
      far-towards-south   lie-P.IPFV   1pl:excl(NOM)   Thaayorre
      'we Thaayorre used to live a long way to the South'
      [KTh_AC22Jul2002 Narrative Kanangkarr]

(550) ngay   kanpa yat,   ngok   inh   paapath   wun-m
      1sg(NOM) before go:P.PFV water(NOM)   dem:sp.prx   hot   lie-P.IPFV
      '[when] I went down before the water was warm'
      [KTh_GJ31Jan2004 Elicitation DahlTMA33]

(551) 1. werngr   ulp   thunp-m
         boomerang(ACC)   dem:ad.prx   throw-P.IPFV
         '[they] kept throwing the boomerang'
      2. ulp   koo-pal=p   therk-m
         dem:ad.prx   nose-towards=PRAG   return-P.IPFV
         'but it kept coming back'
         [KTh_AC13Sep2002 Narrative Werngr]

Being atelic, most states and activities strongly favour past imperfective marking (e.g. 548–550). A telic event (achievement or accomplishment) marked past imperfective must have endured over time in one of three ways. Firstly, the whole telic event may have been iterated a number of times, as in (551) above and also (552):

(552) "koowe, koowe"   waantharr-m=ay
      cooee   cooee   call.out-P.IPFV=1sg(NOM)
      'I kept calling out "cooee, cooee"'
      [KTh_AC14Nov2002 Narrative LosingIrma]

The choice of representing each of (551) and (552) in the past imperfective rather than past perfective tense/aspect signifies that the actions of throwing a boomerang (and it returning), and calling out 'cooee', respectively, were each repeated a number of times, not that each action endured in itself.

Similar to this iterative usage is the employment of the past imperfective tense/aspect in the description of an activity, achievement or accomplishment in order to mark habitual aspect. Like the iterative, I take habitual aspect to encode an event that was repeated a number of times. What differentiates the habitual, then, is the fact that the event was repeated over a long (often unspecified) period of time, rather than as subevents of a larger macroevent. So in (553), the speaker is not remarking on any one particular event or set of events of eating, but is rather stating that the Thaayorre people used to frequently and habitually eat the particular food over a nonspecified period of time:

(553) *may   ngancn   mungk-m*
      VEG(ACC) 1pl:excl(ERG)   eat-P.IPFV
      'we used to eat that food'
      [KTh_AJ-IC-**GJ**26Nov2002 Conversation/Narrative PormpuraawKanangkarr]

This habitual usage of the past imperfective often appears to contain an implicature that the event occurred only prior to the time of speech (as does the English imperfect; *we used to eat that food* similarly implicates but does not entail *we no longer eat that food*). The implicature in Kuuk Thaayorre seems significantly weaker, however. As discussed in §7.2.1 above, the past tense component of its meaning simply asserts that the event did occur prior to the speech event, not that it did not also occur during or following the speech event. Not only is it possible to defeat the implicature 'we no longer eat that food' in (553), but the past imperfective tense may also be used to make generalizations that unambiguously hold throughout time, as in the following two examples:

(537') *kuta   thok-n   kookoc-m?   Pokon, kaar kookoc-m*
       PET   cat-ERG   bark:RDP-P.IPFV   NO   NEG   bark:RDP-P.IPFV
       'do cats *bark*? No, they don't bark'
       [KTh_GJ31Jan2004 Elicitation DahlTMA76]

(554) *kuta   ith   nhul   pungkutharr than-m,*
      dog(NOM)   dem:dist   3sg(NOM)   hungry   stand-P.IPFV
      nhul   kookoc-m
      3sg(NOM)   bark:RDP-P.IPFV
      'when [my] dog's hungry he barks'
      [KTh_GJ31Jan2004 Elicitation DahlTMA74]

It is important to note here that, although it is perfectly grammatical to employ the past imperfective in generalization clauses such as those above, it remains more common to use the nonpast tense, as in the following:

(555) *ngay   ngernkernkernkan   rirk*
       1sg(NOM)   morning:RDP   rise:NPST
       'I get up early each morning'
       [KTh_GJ31Jan2004 Elicitation DahlTMA71]

(556) *ngay   may   rat   mungk-r   min*
       1sg(ERG)   VEG   sugarbag(ACC)   eat-NPST   good
       'I really like sugarbag'
       [KTh_AC10Aug2002 Conversation]

The key difference between the past imperfect and the nonpast lies in whether emphasis is placed on the period prior to the speech event (in the case of the former) or the period during and following the speech event (in the case of the latter). There is no prima facie reason why one tense or the other should be favoured for the coding of events that span past, present and future. What, then, determines their respective usages? It is not possible to make any definitive statements based on the extremely small number of exemples in my data. However, there does seem to be some correlation between animacy and verbal tense/aspect. Verbs that have a human subject (as in (555) and (556))[149] are only attested with nonpast tense marking in these 'generalization' clauses. Where the subject is nonhuman, both nonpast and past imperfective verbal marking seems acceptable. Why should this be so? It was suggested above that the past imperfective coding of generalizations suggests that the speaker has based their induction on the basis of past observations (i.e. in (554), when my dog has been hungry in the past it has barked, with the implicature that it is also likely to do so in the future). It may be that speakers are more confident to predict the behaviour of human agents without explicit reference to their past behaviour, while a speaker wishing to generalize about the behaviour of animals (and inanimate forces) is more inclined to rely upon past observations.

It was noted in §7.2.2 that the past perfective is used to encode telic events, even with verb lexemes that more commonly describe atelic activities or states. Conversely, the final function of the past imperfective is to focus on the (atelic) internal duration

---

149 While the subject of both [555] and [556] is first person, this need not be the case. An example of a third person subject with a nonpast verb in a generalization clause is as follows:

(a) *nhul   radio   ngee<nge>m*
    3sg(ERG)   radio(ACC)   listen<RDP>:NPST
    'he listens to the radio [every day after breakfast]'

of (what would normally be) an accomplishment, rather than on its completion. So in (557), the speaker chooses to focus on the process of building a house (and its overlap with his waiting), while in (558) the accomplishment of building a fishtrap was interrupted before it could reach completion, thus transforming it into an activity:

(557) nhul   pormpr   yump-m
      3sg(ERG) house(ACC)   make-P.IPFV
      ngul ngay   kulam-an   kookope-nham
      then 1sg(NOM)   road-DAT   wait:RDP-P.IPFV
      'while he was building the house I was waiting for him on the road'
      [KTh_GJ31Jan2004 Elicitation DahlTMA28]

(558) 1. nhul   minh pinj   ii-kuw,   wuurr   ko'o-m
         3sg(NOM)   MEAT saltw.croc(NOM)   there-at:west   fishtrap(ACC) spear-P.IPFV
         'the saltwater crocodile was in the west, making a fishtrap'[150]
      2. minh kanharr   riica-rr   ii-rr-kuw
         MEAT freshw.croc(NOM) run-P.PFV   there-towards-west
         '[when] the freshwater crocodile came west'
      3. mun-ica-rr   ii-rr-kaw
         send-RUN&-P.PFV   there-towards-east
         'and ordered him to go inland'
         [KTh_**DW**-CW09Dec2002 Narrative 2Crocs]

Aside from its role in making generalizations, the various uses of the past imperfective are quite standard. Of Kuuk Thaayorre's nearest neighbours, both Yir Yoront and Kugu Nganhcara appear to have roughly analogous verbal categories, though neither is labelled past imperfective. The Kugu Nganhcara category is labelled by Smith and Johnson (2000: 410) as the 'historic', of which they note:

the historic is an invariant verb form, formed with the suffix -nhum for all persons and numbers. The function of the historic is not well understood. It is used frequently in story telling and can usually be interpreted duratively

It seems highly likely that Kugu Nganhcara *-nhum* is cognate with Kuuk Thaayorre *-(nha)m*, and indeed all the examples given by Smith and Johnson (2000: 410) following the above statement seem compatible with the present characterization of the past imperfective, for example:

(559) nganhca   thaaran   thangki-nhum
      1plexcNOM   3plDAT   arrive-HIST
      'we used to go and visit them'

---

150 The verb *ke'e ~ ko'o* 'spear' is used to describe any form of manufacture by means of spear-like instruments (e.g. knitting), including the construction of fishtraps.

(560) ngaya   ngaka   uyu   mungga-nhum
       1sgNOM   water [alcohol] much   drink-HIST
       'I had a big drink / I was drinking a lot'

Before moving on to consider the other aspect and mood categories encoded by Kuuk Thaayorre, it is worth briefly considering the homophony of past imperfect tense/aspect and ablative case (§4.2.6). Both display the same partially phonologically-conditioned allomorphy, as illustrated by the following examples of nouns in ablative case:

(561) ngul   Laura-**nham**   pal   therk
       then   Laura-ABL   towards   return:NPST
       'then [they] will come back here from Laura'
       [KTh_EN15Dec2002 Elicitation]

(562) raak   kanangkarr-**nam**
       time   long.ago-ABL
       '[the church has been there] for a long time'
       [KTh_EN06Sep2002 Elicitation]

(563) parr_r   kumun-mam   wont-r   paanthu-**m**
       child(NOM)   lap-ABL   fall-NPST   woman-ABL
       'the child falls from the woman's lap'
       [KTh_GJ10Jan2004 Elicitation]

Like the past imperfective morpheme, the ablative allomorph *-nham* usually follows a vowel-extended stem (561), *-nam* follows alveolar or retroflex segments (562), and *-Vm* occurs in most other cases (563). The ablative morpheme, however, possesses the additional morphemes *-mam* (seen on *kumunmam* 'from the lap') and *-(n)tam*, the distribution of which is not fully understood at this stage. Nevertheless, the clear parallelism between past imperfective and ablative morphology begs the question, what do the two share in semantics? Being aspectually imperfective, events encoded by the past imperfective necessarily endure over a period of time; beginning at some point in the past and extending forwards from there. It is easy to imagine how these (target) temporal semantics might be conceptualized in terms of a more concrete physical trajectory (i.e. the past tense beginning point in time is depicted as a physical location from which the event extends). Indeed, English speakers similarly use the preposition *from* with both spatial and temporal senses, along with various other spatio-temporal metaphors as evident in the preceding sentences. Other Australian languages also exhibit this connection between a spatial origin and past tense (cf. Dench and Evans 1988).

7.2.4 Reduplication

The morphophonology of reduplication was discussed in detail in §2.6. To briefly recapitulate this discussion, there are three main patterns of reduplication that apply to verbs, the form depending primarily upon the length of the first-syllable vowel. Verb roots with a long vowel in the initial syllable exhibit reduplication of the initial onset + vowel (with the vowel of the second syllable realized as short). Hence *waath* 'search (for)' > *waawath* 'search:RDP'. Verb roots with a short initial vowel, most commonly reduplicate by repeating the rhyme of the initial syllable immediately following the first syllable coda, hence *thangkr* 'laugh' > *thangkangkr* 'laugh:RDP'. A few verbs with short initial vowels may either additionally or alternatively express reduplication by simply lengthening the initial vowel; *mungk* 'eat' > *muungk* 'eat:RDP'. Where a single verb root may exploit two different models of reduplication (i.e. both infixation of initial-syllable rhyme and lengthening of the initial vowel), it seems that each is ascribed just one of the two functions of reduplication ('iterative' and 'durative' aspect, as described below). The semantic contrast between alternative forms of reduplication will be explored in §7.2.4.3.

The iconic relationship between the form of verbal reduplication, and the semantics of repeated or enduring events has been well documented (see, for example, Moravcsik 1978, Anderson 1982 and Wilkins 1989: 248–249). The two functions of verbal reduplication in Kuuk Thaayorre are rather standard; to express iterative and durative aspects. Both of these can be understood as marking an event's extension through time: with durative aspect, a single instantiation of the event has an extended internal temporal structure, whereas iterative aspect encodes multiple instantiations of the same event which together form a single macroevent. Similar categories are encoded by reduplication in neighbouring languages, too. In Kugu Nganhcara, "verbs can reduplicate in all tenses and aspects to indicate continuous (or repeated) action" (Smith and Johnson 2000: 411), while in Yir Yoront, reduplication indicates continuative and distributive aspects among other senses (Alpher 1991: 46).

7.2.4.1 Iterative reduplication

The iterative function of reduplication is frequently seen in the encoding of events that involve a number of participants or a number of (identical) actions repeated by a single participant. The former case is illustrated by (564), in which a large number of bees exit their hive, with each exiting only once. The latter is illustrated by (565), in which a single agent repeated chops a single carrot into a number of pieces:

(564) *may puunh   ulp   ranth-im   ripip-r*
      VEG bee(NOM) dem:ad.prx hole-ABL exit:RDP-NPST
      'those bees are flying out of the hole'
      [KTh_MF17Sep2002 FrogStory]

(565) *pam-al   ith   nhul   may   carrot   knife-nthurr*
man-ERG   dem:dist   3sg(ERG)   VEG   carrot(ACC)   knife-ERG
thongkthongkn   yakake-rr
half:RDP   cut:RDP-P.PFV
'that man cut the carrot into many pieces'
[KTh_EN03Dec2002 Cut&Break10]

In both these examples, the crucial factor conditioning reduplication is distribution over events, rather than distribution over participants or activities. That is to say, the verb *rip* 'exit' is reduplicated in (564) because the event of a bee exiting the tree is repeated a number of times, while in (565), the man cutting the carrot is repeated as a whole a number of times. This contrasts with the non-reduplicated verbs used to describe, for instance, elicitation video clips (Bohnemeyer et al. 2001) in which a man repeatedly chops at a branch of a tree, eventually separating it from the tree trunk (566). This indicates that, because accomplishment cut/break verbs such as *yak* 'cut' and *rath* 'chop' entail the separation of the undergoer into pieces, the event as a whole (including the division of the undergoer) must be iterated to warrant verbal reduplication, rather than simply the cutting or chopping action.

(566) *pam-al   ith   keynayp-thrr   yuk   thongkn   rathi-rr*
man-ERG   dem:dist   cane.knife-ERG   TREE   piece(ACC)   chop-P.PFV
'the man cut the branch off with a cane knife'
[KTh_EN03Dec2002 Cut&Break3]

Iterative aspect may be expressed by either rhyme reduplication, as seen in (564) and (565), or by reduplication of the onset+vowel, as seen in the following:

(567) *yuk   pungk-un   thiithik-r*
stick   knee-DAT   break:RDP-NPST
'he repeatedly breaks the stick on his knee'
[KTh_GJ15Oct2002 CutBreak5]

My data contains no instance of reduplication by vowel lengthening encoding iterative aspect, even where the lengthened initial vowel is the only reduplication strategy available to the particular verb. Vowel lengthening, then, appears to be solely associated with durative aspect (§7.2.4.2). This may be due to the aktionsart of the particular verbs that permit only this form of reduplication, namely: *wun* 'lie'; *yan* 'go'; and *mungk* 'eat'. *Wun* 'lie' inherently describes a state, in both its basic and copula usages. *Yan* 'go' and *mungk* 'eat' both describe activities, though *yan* may also be stative when functioning as copula. The latter two verbs may also encode accomplishment events, but even such telic going and eating events cannot be marked as iterative via reduplication. Consider the following example:

(568) ngay   may pucr   kaar=p   thaka-rr,   ngay   koop mungka-rr
      1sg(ERG) VEG nunda(ACC) NEG=PRAG   leave-P.PFV 1sg(ERG)   all   eat-P.PFV
      'I didn't leave any nunda nuts [for anyone else], I ate every one'
      [KTh_GJ7Feb2004 Elicitation]

It might be expected that *mungk* 'eat' would be reduplicated in (568) because the subject ate a large number of nunda nuts in sequence. Of course it could be that the speaker in neither of these cases wanted to focus attention upon aspect, however it seems improbable that it is pure coincidence that these two verbs (along with *wun* 'lie') are nowhere marked for iteration throughout my corpus.

7.2.4.2 Durative reduplication

As indicated above, reduplication can also mark an event as enduring over time. This is particularly common with stative verbs; *nhiin* 'sit, reside', *than* 'stand, be situated' and *wun* 'lie, live' are almost always reduplicated with durative effect:

(569) kana=le   nhul   aka   nhiinhin   thonmarr
      finish=PRAG   3sg(NOM)   here   reside:RDP:NPST always
      'that's it, she's going to live here from now on'
      [KTh_AJ27Jan2004 Conversation]

(570) nhul   kuuk=aar=nhurr=p   thanan-m
      3sg(NOM)   word=ADN.PRIV=only=PRAG   stand:RDP-P.IPFV
      'she kept quiet'
      [KTh_AC14Nov2002 Narrative LosingIrma]

Although it is more frequently found in the description of nonpast events, durative aspect can also be marked on past tense verbs (570).

Durative aspect – like iterative – may be expressed by either rhyme reduplication (570 above), onset+vowel reduplication (571), or vowel lengthening (573 below):

(571) pam minh.puth waawath-r
      MAN boss(ACC) search:RDP-NPST
      '[that dog] is looking for his owner'
      [KTh_AC21Aug2002 Conversation]

7.2.4.3 Contrast between alternative reduplicative forms

It has already been established that both rhyme reduplication and onset+vowel reduplication may express both iterative and durative aspects. It has also been noted that reduplication via vowel lengthening marks durative aspect alone. Where a verb permits both rhyme reduplication and vowel lengthening as alternative reduplication strategies, it appears that the former is functionally restricted to marking only iterative aspect, leaving durative aspect to be encoded by vowel lengthening alone.[151] For example, the verb *rath* 'chop' may be 'reduplicated' as either *raath* or *rathath*, where the former vowel-lengthening is associated with an enduring event, whereas reduplication proper (i.e. *rathath*) is associated with iteration. This is evident in the contrast between the following sentences:

(572) *pam-al   ith   may carrot   knife ngamal-thrr koop rathathi-rr*
man-ERG dem:dist VEG carrot(ACC) knife large-ERG all chop:RDP-P.PFV
'that man kept cutting up the carrot [i.e. into many pieces] with a big knife'
[KTh_EN03Dec2002 Cut&Break6]

(573) *pam-al   ith   yuk   raath-r*
man-ERG dem:dist stick(ACC) chop:RDP-NPST
'that man kept chopping at the stick [until it eventually broke off the tree]'
[KTh_GJ15Oct2002 Cut&Break3]

In (572), the full chopping event (i.e. bringing a blade into abrupt, forceful contact with the carrot, causing separation) is repeated a number of times, resulting in the carrot ending up in many pieces. These multiple (iterated) accomplishments are encoded as predicted by rhyme reduplication. In (573), by contrast, the repeated chopping actions cumulate to produce a single event of severance of stick from tree. The event described here, then, represents only a single accomplishment, the extended internal duration of which is coded by vowel lengthening.

Similarly, the verb *path* 'bite' may be alternatively reduplicated as *pathath* 'bite repeatedly' (in (574) and (575)) and *paath-* '(ongoing) biting' (in (576)):

(574) *kuta   ith   yiin=p   pathath-e*
dog(NOM) dem:dist itch=PRAG bite:RDP-RFL:NPST
'that dog keeps biting itself'
[KTh_AC21Aug2002 Conversation]

(575) *yiki, ngat-al pathath-m   iipal*
yikes fish-ERG bite:RDP-P.IPFV from.there
'hey! The fish are beginning to bite now'
[Foote and Hall: Primer 10]

---

151 Note that it is logically impossible for a verb to permit both vowel-lengthening and onset+vowel reduplication since the latter occurs only with verbs of which the initial syllable vowel is already long.

(576) *kuta-ku   nhul   thok   ulp   paath-r*
dog-ERG 3sg(ERG) cat(ACC) dem:ad.prx bite:RDP-NPST
'the dog's biting the cat'
[KTh_LF18Sep2002 Conversation]

As noted above, the rhyme reduplication of *path* 'bite' may indicate iteration of the full event involving the same participants (as in (574), where a single dog bites itself repeatedly), or of multiple participants performing the same action (as in (575), where a number of different fish bite the bait). Example (576), meanwhile, describes a single event of biting that endures throughout the speech act. One might infer that durative marking here emphasizes the current relevance of the event, with the implicature that the addressee should intervene to save the cat.

Inferences as to the respective distributions of the two reduplication types are based here on only a rather small number of examples. Further research may show the interaction between the two to be more subtle. Note that in one or two examples, reduplication seems to have other effects, such as marking inceptive aspect in the following example:

(577) *paath   kal-r   yaat pil-un,   pathatha-n-ir*
firewood(ACC) carry-P.PFV yard side-DAT bite:RDP-V^-NPST
'they carried firewood up to the yard and began to blow up a fire'
('they carried firewood to the yard, causing [the fire] to bite [the wood]')
[Foote and Hall: Reader 9]

This example could be fitted into the analysis presented here, however, if we assume that the speaker was describing the subject participants' repeatedly blowing on the fire. If this is so, we must also assume that the reduplication has scope over the predicate as a whole (thus applying after the valence-increasing morpheme to create the predicate 'repeatedly make bite') rather than having scope only over the verb root (with the valence-increasing morpheme only afterwards deriving the predicate 'make repeatedly bite'). Because reduplication is a non-linear process (changing the form of the verb root, rather than appearing as one of a sequence of suffixes), it can be considered exempt from the general iconic tendency – in Kuuk Thaayorre and elsewhere (cf. Haiman 1980, 1983) – for 'innermost' affixes to apply before those towards the periphery. Indeed, in all other cases where reduplication cooccurs with derivational suffixes, reduplication always appears to encode the aspect of the event as a whole. This is evident in the following clause, which describes rangers and policeman repeatedly causing the fast motion of supplies, rather than causing supplies to repeatedly move quickly:

(578) kar   ranger   kar   policeman   may=yuk
      like   ranger(#ERG)   like policeman(#ERG)   VEG(ACC)=STUFF
      everywhere   riirica-n-r
      everywhere   run:RDP-V^-NPST
      'the rangers and policemen were moving food and stuff everywhere [during the cyclone]'
      [KTh_**AJ**-GJ03Feb2004 Conversation]

Wilkins (1989: 242–249) also describes a number of alternative forms of verbal reduplication in Mparntwe Arrernte (up to two of which may be employed by a single verb). These four reduplication strategies differ from those described here in their form, combination with other verbal suffixes, and semantic functions. Nevertheless, in both cases the repective functional loads of alternative reduplicated forms may be considered iconic. Wilkins (1989: 249) observes of Arrernte:

> reduplication of final elements in the verb stem corresponds to the verb stem event being achieved over and over again (i.e. the event repeatedly comes to an end [...]), while reduplication of initial elements of the verb stem corresponds to the event continuing to begin without ever being achieved.

In Kuuk Thaayorre, lengthening of the root vowel in verbs like *mungk* > *muungk* 'eat' and *rath* > *raath* 'chop' signifies a lengthening of the event, a single instantiation of which stretches through time. Conversely, repetition of the initial syllable's rhyme corresponds to repetition of the event as a whole.

7.2.4.4 Alternatives to reduplication

Iterative and durative aspects may alternatively be marked by repetition of either the full verb or some other clausal element, as in (579)–(580):

(579) *ii-rr-kan,   nhaawr,   nhaawr,   nhaawr...*
      there-towards-up see:P.PFV   see:P.PFV   see:P.PFV
      '[the boomerang] went up and they watched and watched and watched [it]'
      [KTh_AC22Jul2002 Narrative Werngr]

(580) *train   ulp   yancm   yancm   yancm...*
      train(NOM)   dem:ad.prx   go:P.IPFV   go:P.IPFV   go:P.IPFV
      'the train kept going and going and going'
      [KTh_GJ16Oct2002 Narrative MelbourneTrip]

Reduplicated verbs may themselves undergo repetition for additional emphasis of duration:

(581) *peln   kookope,   kookope...*
      3pl(NOM) wait:RDP:NPST wait:RDP:NPST
      'they waited and waited'
      [KTh_GJ16Oct2002 Narrative MelbourneTrip]

These repeated verbs display a characteristic intonational rise on each token. The same intonation contour and semantic effect is evident in examples where just the verb is repeated (579)–(580) as well as in instances of clausal repetition. For instance, in (582b) enclitic and full pronouns intervene between tokens of the verb *yumpirr* 'made':

(582) 1. *stitch-m   rirk-r=anh*
         stitch-VBLZ DO-P.PFV=1sgACC
         'they stitched me up'
      2. *ngul   nganh   yumpi-rr   peln,   yumpi-rr=anh   yumpi-rr,   kana*
         then   1sgACC make-P.PFV 3pl(ERG) make-P.PFV=3sgACC make-P.PFV finish
         'they stitched me and stitched me, finished [the wound was sealed]'
         [KTh_AJ-**GJ**03Feb2004 Conversation / Narrative]

Although (582b) could be viewed as describing multiple subevents of stitching, I believe it is more likely that the repetition of the verb (and argument) rather emphasizes the extended duration of the macro-event, as evident in the translation.

In Yir Yoront, Alpher (1973) notes, "a continuing action can be described by repeating the verb in the nonpast tense. If the action consists of repeated discrete parts, each repetition of the verb is taken to indicate a repetition of the action". In Kuuk Thaayorre, however, repeated verbs tend to represent enduring activities or states. Iteration of a punctual (achievement or semelfactive) event is more often achieved by repeating a clausal element – usually representing the result state – as in the following:

(583) *ngancn   yuk   kumun   rath-m*
      1pl:excl(ERG) TREE root(ACC) chop-P.IPFV
      thongkn thongkn thongkn rath-m
      half   half   half   chop-P.IPFV
      'we used to chop the roots into many pieces [to poison fish]'
      [KTh_AC26Nov2002 Narrative Kanangkarr]

7.3 Mood

7.3.1 Imperative

Kuuk Thaayorre possesses only a single imperative verb inflection. However, this (and the nonpast inflection) interacts with clausal particles to distinguish second person imperatives, prohibitives, third person jussives and first person hortatives. This section describes the morphology of the imperative verb form. The morphosyntax and semantics of the constructions used to express imperative, hortative and jussive moods are detailed in §11.2, and the prohibitive in §11.3.4.

The imperative form of almost all verbs is identical to that of the root. The only exceptions encountered so far are the following irregular verbs:

Root	Imperative	Meaning
ke'e	ko'o	'spear!'
mi'i	mi'irr	'pick (it) up!'
nhaa-	nhaam	'look!'
ya-	yarr	'go!'

Verb stems formed through suffixation of derivational morphemes (aside from the first associated motion morpheme) do not receive any special imperative marking, but rather imperative mood is signalled by the absence of other tense/aspect/mood inflection. Hence in (584) and (585) the final morpheme of the imperative verb is a derivational suffix:

(584) *nganh yak watp-a ongkorr miinnga-n!*
1sgACC snake dead-ERG PROHIB take.fright-v^:IMP
'don't scare me with that dead snake'
[KTh_GJ10Jan2004 Elicitation]

(585) *ongkorr yika-n-rr*
PROHIB say-v^-RCP:IMP
'don't tease each other'
[Anon.]

Following from the imperative form of *ya-* > *yarr* 'go!', the imperative ending of a verb that has undergone first associated motion derivation (§8.1.4.1) is *-nharr* 'GO&:IMP'. This form is illustrated in many of the following examples, since a particular affinity is shared between the inceptive aspect marked by the associated motion morpheme and imperative mood (which marks an event the speaker urges should be initiated in the immediate future).

7.3.2 Subjunctive

Definitions of the subjunctive mood are commonly vague, but generally combine some semantic notion of non-factivity with the syntactic feature of occurring in embedded clauses (cf. Matthews 1997: 360; Palmer 2001). The Kuuk Thaayorre subjunctive category is used to encode desire (586), purpose (587), intention (588), potential (or 'hypothetical', as in 589) and ability (590), as seen in the following examples:

(586) ngay   paath-meer   waarr   rint-nh
      1sg(ERG) fire-eye(ACC) WAARR   burn-SBJV
      'I really want to make a campfire'
      [KTh_AJ27Jan2004 Elicitation]

(587) ngay   money   save-m   rirk
      1sg(ERG) money(ACC)   save-TR DO:NPST
      'I'm saving money'
      ngay   raak   Cairns-na   angarr   yanc-nh
      1sg(NOM) PLACE   Cairns-DAT ANGARR   go:SBJV
      'so that I can go to Cairns to see old Dr Hall'
      [KTh_GJ18Jan2004 Elicitation]

(588) ngay   minc min waantharr-r   nganh   kuta-ku   angarr   ngeey-nh
      1sg(ERG) very good call.out-P.PFV   1sgACC   dog-ERG   ANGARR   hear-SBJV
      'I called out good and loud so the dog would hear me'
      [KTh_GJ18Jan2004 Elicitation]

(589) kar nhunt   yancnh   inh   truck-ak,   nhaathnhancnh   nhunt
      like 2sg(NOM) go:SBJV   dem:sp.prx   truck-DAT   see:GO&:SBJV   2sg(ERG)
      "if you go you will see it for yourself"
      [KTh_AJ27Jan2004 Conversation]

(590) ngay   rok-nh   ii-rr-kan   wanthan?
      1sg(NOM) enter-SBJV   there-towards-inside   where.to
      "I enter-can in where?"
      [Hall 1972: 146]

All of these uses may be characterized as expressing "something other than a statement of what is certain", which Palmer (2001: 360) claims to be the central role of many subjunctive markers. The subjunctive form commonly appears in the second clause of a complex structure, as in the following:

(591) [ngal   paath   minharr]
      1du:incl(ERG) firewood(ACC) pick.up:GO&:IMP
      [paath   waarr rint-nh=pa]
      fire(ACC) very burn-SBJV=PRAG
      'let's go and get firewood [so as to] build a fire'
      [KTh_AJ27Jan2004 Elicitation/Conversation]

Alternatively the subjunctive clause (this time representing an imagined hypothetical world) can precede the clause representing the contrasting actual state of affairs (cf. §12.1.2.3):

(101') paanth   pitit-nh   wuump=ul=okun
       woman(ACC) hold:RDP-SBJV   CONTR=3sg(ERG)=DUB
       "if he had a wife, alright"
       ngul pul   wupan
       but 3du(NOM) temporary
       "they just temporary"
       [KTh_ACh07Nov2002 Conversation]

It is also possible for the subjunctive clauses to comprise a complete utterance, as in (586) above and (592) below. This may be the result of 'insubordination' (Evans 1995a:438, 2007); the use of a subordinate clause as a main clause.

(592) ngamp   kunk angarr nhiin-nh   muthathan
      1pl:incl(NOM) alive ANGARR reside-SBJV forever
      'we [strive] to live forever'
      [KTh_GJ18Jan2004 Narrative Christmas]

Note that Hall glosses both -nh and -nha at times *desiderative* and at other times *potential*. I believe it is preferable to subsume these two moods as distinct functions of a single subjunctive category, especially given the diachronic links between this morpheme and the associated motion (§8.1.4) and other modal (§7.3.6) suffixes.[152]

---

[152] An alternative candidate label for this category is *irrealis*, however, this term is used to label quite a different category in Yir Yoront. Like the Kuuk Thaayorre subjunctive, the Yir Yoront irrealis indicates that the event was desired, intended or expected, but unlike the Kuuk Thaayorre subjunctive category, the Yir Yoront irrealis entails that the event was not or will not be carried out. This clearly does not apply to examples such as (588), in which the intended effect was achieved, or (589) which was issued as a directive to go to the place described (and thus conveys that the 'seeing' event *should* occur in the future, rather than marking that it won't). The Kuuk Thaayorre subjunctive category is semantically and syntactically more akin to the Yir Yoront 'Desiderative' (Alpher 1991).

7.3.3 Counterfactual

The counterfactual suffix, *-nhata*, encodes an event that was (at some point) desired, intended or expected, but which did not or will not occur.[153] This is illustrated by (593), the description of an elicitation video clip in which a man cutting an orange also cuts his finger with the knife. By means of counterfactual marking, the speaker conveys her inference as to the man's intended outcome (i.e. cutting the orange), simultaneously noting that this did not occur:

(593) 1. *yiki   pam   ith   nhul   minc may orange*
         yikes man(#ERG) dem:dist 3sg(ERG) really VEG orange(ACC)
         knife-nthurr yak-nhata=th
         knife-ERG   cut-CTF=PRAG
         'that man meant to cut the orange with a knife'
    2. *ngul nhul   yiirrar   yuur   nhangn   yake-rr   minc   waarr*
         but   3sg(ERG) instead hand   3sgGEN(ACC) cut-P.PFV really   bad
         'but instead he cut his finger really badly'
         [KTh_EN15Dec2002 Elicitation Cut&Break18]

The counterfactual can also encode an event that might be expected to occur in the future, but that will not:

(594) *parr-an   ith   peln   yup   thangkangkr-nhata*
       child-ERG^ dem:dist 3pl(NOM) soon   laugh:RDP-CTF
       'those children are suppressing laughter
       [i.e. they won't laugh although they want to]'
       [KTh_GJ18Jan2004 Elicitation]

Hall's (1972: 209) description lists the allomorphs of this morpheme *-(nh)atath ~ -natath*, while I find the final segment /th/ to be frequently absent. For this reason, I analyze the string *-nhatath* in (593) above to be composed of the counterfactual suffix *-nhata* followed by the pragmatic focus enclitic *=th*. I also diverge from Hall's analysis in terminology. Although Hall labels this category 'subjunctive mood', I prefer to reserve that term for the morpheme *-nh(a)*. The more narrow label *counterfactual* neatly encapsulates the range of contexts the longer form *-nhata* is found in, both from my own data and the clauses given by Hall (1972: 209–212) as examples of subjunctive mood, such as the following (glossed to reflect the present analysis):

---

[153] It is in this respect very similar to the Yir Yoront irrealis category (Alpher 1973: 252–253)

(595) nhunt   panh   pormp-nhata=th
       2sg(ERG) vomit(ACC)   pour-CTF=PRAG
       'you would have vomited'
       [Hall 1972: 209]

(596) ngay   minc   kal-nhatath, thaka-rr   (nga)y
       1sg(ERG)   really carry-CTF   leave-P.PFV 1sg(ERG)
       'I would have taken it but I left it'
       [Hall 1972: 210]

(597) peln   ngul   ngene=p   thothowol-natha=th   thaapirri ranth pork-an
       3pl(NOM)   later why=PRAG   play:RDP-CTF=PRAG   close   hole   big-DAT
       'how lucky it was those kids didn't play near the big hole!'
       [Hall 1972: 211]

Note that the Kugu Nganhcara 'Nonfactual' enclitic =*monh* (Smith and Johnson 2000: 441) also appears to have essentially the same function as the Kuuk Thaayorre counterfactual suffix and Yir Yoront irrealis suffix. The Kuuk Thaayorre particle *kar* may also be used with a counterfactual-like effect, discussed further in §9.1.3.

7.3.4 Purposive

The use of simple subjunctive inflection often has a purposive interpretation, as seen in (587) above. Alternatively, purposive mood can be explicitly encoded by the morpheme *nhatha*, as in the following:

(598) ngay   kuta   ngathn   piinth   reeka-rr   mungk-nhatha
       1sg(ERG)   dog   1sgGEN(ACC)   bone(ACC)   give-P.PFV eat-PURP
       'I gave my dog a bone to eat'
       [KTh_EN04Aug2002 Elicitation]

Most commonly, the main verb of this construction (*reekarr* 'gave' in (598)) describes some action performed in order to bring about the event described by the purposive clause. Accordingly in (598) the speaker describes giving her dog a bone so that her dog could eat that bone. It is not always the case that the subject of the purposive verb is the one who desires the event to take place. Thus in (598) it is the speaker who desires the dog to eat the bone, not necessarily the dog.

As well as describing the goal or intended result of an action, a purposive verb can represent the desired, intended or inherent function of an object. This is evident in the following:

(599) *kaal   kuuk   ngeey-nhatha*
      ear(NOM) word(ACC) listen-PURP
      'ears are for listening'
      [KTh_GJ19Nov2002 Elicitation]

Further examples of purposive inflection can be found in §12.1.2.2.

7.3.5 Imminence

The imminence morpheme marks an event that has not yet occurred, but is expected to do so in the immediate future unless someone or something prevents it. This is exemplified by the following:

(600) *kuta thok-thun nhul   kuta   ngulyirr kanthi-rrtha*
      PET cat-ERG   3sg(ERG)   dog(ACC) soon   scratch-IMM
      'the cat is about to scratch the dog'
      [KTh_LF18Sep2002 Conversation]

(601) *nhul=okun   nganh   path-nhancrrth*
      3sg(ERG)=DUB   1sgACC   bite-GO&:IMM
      "maybe he wanna bite me" [i.e. 'I expect him to bite me if I don't prevent it']
      [KTh_AJ-GJ03Feb2004 Conversation]

It is not immediately obvious whether 'imminence' is a modal or tense category. Like a tense, it locates the event in the immediate future of the speech event. On the other hand, through the imminence morpheme the speaker expresses some degree of certainty that the event will occur unless measures are taken to avoid it. This makes it seem more modal. The fact that the imminence suffix *-rrtha* shares its final syllable (*-tha*) with the purposive, leads me to analyze this morpheme as part of a broader modal system (cf. §7.3.6).

The label 'imminence' appears to have been coined by Hall (1972: 156) for the category described here. I have continued to use it, as it captures both temporal immediacy and modal near inevitability. Further, it has no connotations of the event's being undesirable, which is important since imminent-marked events can also be desirable, as in the following:

(602) *nhurr   may   muungk-rrtha*
      2pl(ERG) VEG(ACC)   eat-IMM
      'you are about to dine'
      [Hall 1972: 123]

The imminence category thus differs from the apprehensive and evitative categories of some other Australian languages (e.g. Kayardild [Evans 1995a], Warlpiri [Nash 1980] and Ngandi [Baker 1999]).

7.3.6 Semantic overview of the modal affixes

The counterfactual, purposive and imminence suffixes (*-nhata*, *-nhatha* and *-rrtha* respectively) are not only phonologically similar, but also share similar functions. All three describe nonfactive events (i.e. events that have not actually occurred), but each has different emphases and entailments. The counterfactual entails that this nonfactive event has not and will not occur, the purposive focuses on the fact that [someone] intends the event to occur (remaining neutral as to whether or not it will), while the imminence suffix expresses that the event will occur unless prevented.

The counterfactual and purposive inflections differ only in their penultimate segment (/t/ versus /th/), and it is possible that the two functions were once shared by a single morpheme. Examples such as (593) show the overlap between the two semantic categories:

(593') *yiki   pam ith   nhul   minc may orange   knife-nthurr yak-nhata-th*
yikes man dem:dist 3sg(ERG) really VEG orange(ACC) knife-ERG   cut-CTF-PR
ngul nhul   yiirrar   yuur nhangn   yake-rr   minc waarr
then 3sg(ERG) instead hand 3sgGEN(ACC) cut-P.PFV really bad
'that man meant to cut the orange with a knife, but instead he cut his finger really badly'
[KTh_EN15Dec2002 Elicitation Cut&Break18]

The counterfactual-marked verb, *yaknhatath* 'intended to cut but didn't' represents both the (purposive) accomplishment the actor intended to bring about by his action (i.e. cutting the orange), as well as a (counterfactual) event that did not occur, contrary to expectations.

The functional common ground between the purposive (*-nhatha*) and imminence (*-rrtha*) morphemes – which share the ending /tha/ – can be seen in the following example:

(603) *kuta thok-thun nhul   kuta   ngulyirr kanthi-rrtha*
PET cat-ERG   3sg(ERG) dog(ACC) soon   scratch-IMM
'the cat is about to scratch the dog'
[KTh_LF18Sep2002 Conversation]

The imminence-marked verb *kanthirrtha* 'about to scratch', encodes an event that is both intended by its subject (purposive), but also highly likely to occur unless measures are taken to avoid it.

Although these three suffixes are presented above as monomorphemic, it seems likely that – at some stage of the language's history – they were composed of at least two morphemes. The first syllable of both the counterfactual and purposive suffixes, is homophonous with the subjunctive morpheme (*-nh[a]*), which is particularly significant given the semantic commonality between the three. All (can) denote irrealis states of affairs. Like counterfactual clauses, subjunctive clauses can refer to hypothetical events that did not and will not occur, as in (101) above. Similarly, subjunctive verbs are often used to describe a purpose or desired outcome (586), with the purposive suffix transforming this implicature into an entailment. We might therefore choose to reanalyze the counterfactual morpheme as having the form *-ta* (only suffixed to a subjunctive stem), and the purposive as *-tha* (also attached to a subjunctive stem). Such an analysis reveals the morphological similarity between the purposive and imminence morphemes, the latter currently analyzed as *-rrtha*. If we assume that the latter segments of *-rrtha* 'imminence' actually represent the same morpheme as is suffixed to the subjunctive verb to create the purposive, it might be better to recast the function of this *-tha*. For example, labelling *-tha* 'intention', would allow this morpheme to combine with a subjunctive-inflected verb to denote 'purposive' (i.e. a nonfactive event that is intended), but also to combine with what we'll call an 'immediate' morpheme, *-rr*, to denote 'imminence' (i.e. an intended event that is temporally immediate). Such a system can be schematized as follows:

Table 54. Putative polymorphemic analysis of Kuuk Thaayorre modal affixes.

	-tha 'intention'	*-ta* 'counterfactual'
-nha 'subjunctive'	*-nha-tha* 'purposive'	*-nha-ta* 'counterfactual'
-rr 'immediate'	*-rr-tha* 'imminence'	

There may well have existed a system much like this at some stage of the language's history, but synchronically a monomorphemic analysis of the counterfactual, purposive and imminence suffixes seems more parsimonious. One reason for this is the fact that neither *-ta* nor *-tha* may be affixed to the verb directly, without either the subjunctive suffix or *-rr* intervening. A second factor weighing against segmenting these forms, is the fact that the morpheme *-rr* is homophonous with both the reciprocal and past perfective suffixes, yet neither of these could compositionally produce the semantics of the 'imminence' category when combined with *-tha* 'Intention'. A segmental approach would therefore introduce a new morpheme *-rr*, which only ever appears preceding the 'intention' suffix. It therefore seems clearer to postulate three monomorphemic suffixes (*-nhata* 'counterfactual', *-nhatha* 'purposive', and *-rrtha* 'imminence'), while noting their likely diachronic origins.

7.4 Infinitive

For any verb, the infinitive form is identical to the imperative. This is true for regular and irregular verb roots (604), as well as derived verb stems (605).

(604) a. *kal!*   b. *kal*
           carry:IMP   carry:INF
           'carry [it]!'   'carrying'

(605) a. *roka-n!*   b. *roka-n*
           enter-V^:IMP   enter-V^:INF
           'put [it] in!'   'putting [it] in'

This generalization holds even where the imperative inflection is non-zero in form. Thus the marked imperative allomorph of the associated motion morpheme *-nharr* doubles as an infinitive form, suffixed to the verb *nhaath* 'see' in the subordinate clause of (606).

(606) *ngul nhul   meer+kay   rok-r   minc nhaath-nharr*
       then 3sg(NOM) eye+metal(ACC) enter-P.PFV really see-GO&:INF
       'he put on glasses on so he could see properly'
       [KTh_GJ18Jan2004 Elicitation]

Infinitive verbs head subordinate clauses (such as 607), the functions and morphosyntax of which are discussed in §12.1.1.1.

(607) "*Ngay   iirra   ritar   yat,   kumun therk,   thuuthu-n-m.*
       1sg(NOM) to.there gammon go:P.PFV thigh   return:INF pull-V^-P.IPFV
       "'I just went for a bit over there to stretch my legs'"
       [KTh_AC14Nov2002 Narrative LosingIrma]

8 Verbal derivation

This chapter surveys the range of morphemes used to derive new verbal stems. These include morphemes that reconfigure argument structure and/or affect valency (including the valence increaser, reflexive, and reciprocal suffixes; §8.1.1–8.1.3), associated motion morphemes which add motion-related semantics to those encoded by the verb root (§8.1.4), suffixes that derive non-finite verbs for use in subordinate clauses (§8.1.5), and a peculiar suffix that may derive nouns from verbs as well as verbs from nouns (8.1.6). Also considered within the auspices of verbal derivation is the light verb *rirk* 'DO', which combines with forms of various word classes (and languages) to produce complex predicates (§8.2). Lastly, §8.3 considers the frequent compounding of body part terms to verb roots and the attendant semantic consequences.

8.1 Derivational suffixes

A number of derivational suffixes may be attached to Kuuk Thaayorre verb roots. All of these derive a new lexeme, but only one (the nominalizer/verbalizer *-m*) results in a change in lexical category. This chapter considers 'verbal derivation' in the broadest possible sense, including in its scope:

- all derivational morphemes that affix to a verbal root or stem
- (including those with a nominal output)
- all derivational morphemes and processes that derive a new verb stem
- elements that may be compounded with verb roots to produce a new verbal stem

Table 15 in §3.2 provided an overview of the range of inflectional and derivational morphemes that may appear within the Kuuk Thaayorre verbal word. The relevant derivational positions are summarized as Table 55:

Table 55. Derivational positions in the Kuuk Thaayorre verb.

COMPOUND	**ROOT**	DERIV	DERIV	DERIV	DERIV
BodyPart+	**ROOT**	-VBLZ	-V^	-RFL -RCP	-GO& -RUN&
verb roots may be compounded with a nominal element		derives a verb from nouns, etc.	valence increasing suffix; increases valency by one	produce a reflexive or reciprocal stem with reduced valency	Two associated motion suffixes

There are no obligatory derivational morphemes, so all morphemes listed in Table 55 except the root are optional. Where two morphemes are listed within a single position in Table 55, there are no attestations of the two co-occurring in a single verb stem. So, for instance, I have been unable to record any instances of a verb root that undergoes both reflexive and reciprocal derivation, or of both the associated motion morphemes combining in a single verb stem. The valence increasing suffix, meanwhile, can combine with either one of the reflexive/reciprocal morphemes, but the ordering of the morphemes is variable (see §8.1.1). Otherwise, the exponents of the various morpheme positions may freely combine provided they occur in the order set out in Table 55. While no examples have been recorded illustrating the combination of four derivational suffixes in a single word, the following examples each contain three:

(608) *ngancn   nhunh   kaar=p   yoongk-e-nhan-nhan   yuk-un*
  1pl(ERG) 3sgACC   NEG=PRAG   hang-RFL-V^-GO&:NPST   tree-DAT
  'we won't make him hang himself in the tree'
  [Hall 1972: 391]

(609) *pulnhan   yup   nhaath-nhan-rr-nhan=unt*
  3du(ACC) soon   see-V^-RCP-GO&:NPST=you(ERG)
  'you'll soon be making them two see each other'
  [Hall 1972: 392]

8.1.1 Valence increaser

Only one of the Kuuk Thaayorre derivational suffixes increases the valency of the verb stem. This can be seen in the comparison of (610) and (611), the first of which includes the inflected simple root *rok* 'enter', which subcategorizes for a single intransitive subject argument, the second of which includes the derived stem *rokan* 'cause to enter', which subcategorizes for both transitive subject and object:

(610) *bullet   tunnel-ak   rok-r*
  bullet(NOM) tunnel-DAT enter-P.PFV
  'the bullet went into the tunnel'
  [KTh_GJ20Nov2002 MoverbEnterExit17]

(611) *nhul   kuta   pormp-an   roka-ni-rr*
  3sg(ERG) dog(ACC) house-DAT enter-V^-P.PFV
  'he put the dog in the house'
  [KTh_GJ14Oct2002 Elicitation]

In the majority of instances of its use, V^ has a causative interpretation, adding an agent argument (encoded as transitive subject) that causes a theme (the erstwhile intransitive subject, now encoded as direct object) to undergo the activity or state-change described by the verb root. This is evident in the contrast between *rok* 'enter' and *rokan* 'cause to enter' above, but also in the contrast between *thaa.riic* 'tear (predicated of some saliently 2-dimensional material) and *thaa.riican* 'cause (some saliently 2-dimensional material) to tear (predicated of an agent or force)', as in the following:

(612) nhul   mimp   thaa.riica-ni-rr
       3sg(ERG)   cloth(ACC) tear-v^-P.PFV
       'she tore the cloth'
       [KTh_EF15Dec2002 Cut&Break1]

There are many instances, however, in which the valence increaser (hereafter, v^) has a different effect on argument structure. For instance, when v^ is added to the verb *yungar* 'swim', it is the locative adjunct that is promoted to direct object, while the intransitive actor-subject simply becomes transitive actor-subject:

(613) ngay   ngerngkan yungar-nata=th wa'ap-n
       1sg(NOM)   yesterday swim-CTF=PR   river-DAT
       'I would have swum in the river yesterday (but...)'
       [Hall 1972: 122]

(614) wa'ap   inh   ngancn   yungar-nan-m
       river(ACC)   dem:sp.prx   1pl(ERG)   swim-v^-P.IPFV
       'we used to swim that river (i.e. cross it by swimming)'
       [KTh_ME04Jun2005 Narrative Yencr]

In this case, valence increase not only alters the argument structure of *yungar* 'swim', but also results in a semantic/Aktionsart shift from describing the activity of swimming (613), to describing the accomplishment of swimming across a river in order to reach the other side (614).

When v^ is added to the verb *thowol* 'play' (seen in its underived form in (615)), meanwhile, it can introduce a direct object encoding either the theme (616) or a comitative argument (617):

(615) thowol-nam ngancn   parr_r mant
       play-P.IPFV 1pl:excl(NOM) child small(NOM)
       'we little kids were playing'
       [KTh_GJ15Oct2002 Narrative PlaneSighting]

(616) Anisha, ulp   ngan thowol-nan-r?
       Anisha dem:ad.prx what play-v^-NPST
       'Anisha, what's that you're playing with?'
       [KTh_EF14Dec2002 DemonstrativeScene18]

(617) nhul   parr_r   ii   thowol-nan-r
       3sg(ERG) child(ACC) there   play-v^-NPST
       'he'll be playing with those kids (when we get there)'
       [KTh_GJ31Jan2004 Elicitation DahlTMA]

When asked, the language expert allowed that (617) could also describe a man (as an external agent) causing children to play. However, its more natural interpretation (and the one intended by the speaker), is that the man and children are playing together (albeit with greater responsibility for instigating the game attributed to the man). The activity performed by the agent (encoded as transitive subject) is thus the same as that performed by the intransitive subject of the underived verb. Note that the difference in the semantic effect of valence increase between (617) and (612) cannot be attributed to verbal semantics alone. If this were the case, each verb root should allow only a single interpretation when combined with v^. The contrast between (616) and (617), however, demonstrates the compatibility of individual verb roots with multiple patterns of argument structure reconfiguration as a result of valence increasing derivation. In (616), v^ adds an inanimate instrument, while in (617) it adds comitative participants.

In a bivalent clause derived by v^, it is not always clear which of the arguments has been introduced and which corresponds to the single argument of the original monovalent clause. Consider (618), for instance:

(618) kar ranger   kar policeman   may=yuk
       like ranger(#ERG) like policeman(#ERG) VEG(ACC)=STUFF
       everywhere riirica-n-r
       everywhere run:RDP-v^-NPST
       'the rangers and policemen were moving [distributing] food and stuff everywhere [during the cyclone]'
       [KTh_**AJ**-GJ03Feb2004 Conversation]

It is possible to view v^ as introducing either a comitative argument (i.e. 'the rangers and policemen run around *with food and things*'), or an agent/causer (i.e. 'the rangers and policemen cause the food and things to move quickly [around the village]'). Under the first interpretation, the subject of the intransitive clause would correspond to the subject of the derived transitive clause, with the comitative argument *may=yuk* '(with) food and things' introduced. This follows the same pattern as seen in (619), in which it must be the comitative argument that is introduced by v^:

(619) ngal   iirra   therka-n
       1du:incl(ERG) to.there return-v^:IMP
       'let's bring [him] back [to camp]' (i.e. 'let's return to camp with him')
       [KTh_FT8Feb2004 Narrative Adoptee]

That it is the transitive subject *ngal* 'we two' that corresponds to the intransitive subject of the underived clause, is clear from the narrative context in which (619) was uttered. This clause forms part of a story about an elderly husband and wife who had gone out bush looking for food when they came upon an abandoned baby, at which point the wife says to her husband *ngal irra therkan* 'let's bring him back'. In this context, the subject of the valence-increased verb stem *therkan* 'return with' (i.e. *ngal* 'we two') must correspond to the subject of the original intransitive verb; the baby would not be able to 'return' since it had not come from the camp in the first place. It is therefore clear that the baby is introduced as a comitative argument.

Under the second interpretation of (618), it is the agent/causer subject argument (*kar ranger kar policeman* 'like rangers or policemen') that has been introduced, with the subject of the intransitive clause corresponding to the theme-object (*may=yuk* 'food and things'). This would follow the pattern seen in (620), where it is the direct object of the derived transitive clause ('the book') that corresponds to the subject of the intransitive clause ('the book returned'):

(620) book   ulp   pal   therka-ni-rr
      book(ACC)   dem:ad.prx   towards   return-v^-P.PFV
      '[he] returned the book [to her]'
      [KTh_FT10Feb2004 Elicitation RcpPilot5]

It is clear in this case that the valence-increasing derivation has added an agent/causer since the subject argument (the elided '[he]') does not himself return. Rather, he remains in the same place, while causing the theme argument ('the book') to return.

Rather than spanning a range of distinct functions, I view v^ as semantically nonspecific, simply increasing the number of arguments in the verb's subcategorization frame by one. The grammatical function of this new argument is determined by the verb root, rather than v^ itself. Some verb roots (labelled here 'type 1') undergo subject-to-object derivation (e.g. *thaariic* 'tear'), others ('type 2') undergo subject-to-subject derivation (e.g. *yungar* 'swim'). There remain further verbs ('type 3') which permit both patterns of derivation (e.g. *thowol* 'play', *therk* 'return and *riic* 'run'). For these verbs, the argument introduced by v^ may have one of a number of potential thematic roles. I assume that the mapping of argument/roles to grammatical function is determined for such verbs by the thematic role hierarchy (cf. Givón 1984, 2001; Bresnan and Kanerva 1989; Grimshaw 1990; Simpson 1991). Where the verb root in question permits more than one so-derived argument structure (as with *thowol* 'play'), the correct interpretation must be gleaned through attention to a combination of contextual information, semantic features of the introduced argument (e.g. animacy) and the addressee's inferential abilities. In example (616), for instance, it is natural to assume that the inanimate referent of *ngan* 'what' represents a theme/instrument with which Anisha is playing, while in (617) the subject is interpreted as engaging in the playing event along with the animate direct object *parr_r* 'children', rather than playing them like instruments.

In some cases, v^ derivation is associated with so significant a shift in verbal semantics, the derived verb must be regarded as lexicalized. Suffixation of v^ to the verb *yik* 'say', for example, can result in a number of seemingly lexicalized interpretations, in addition to the more compositionally derived sense of 'cause to make noise' seen in (621). In (622), for example, *yika-n* 'say-v^' means 'teach', which is far narrower in sense than 'cause to say'.

(621) pam-al   ii   yuunhul   radio   too.high yikika-n-r
      man-ERG there that.one radio(ACC) too.high say:RDP-v^-NPST
      'the man over there is playing his radio too loud'
      [KTh_GJ12Jan2004 Elicitation]

(622) nhunt   nganh   yikan-r
      2sg(ERG) 1sgACC say-v^-NPST
      'you're teaching me'
      [KTh_LF26Aug2003 Elicitation]

Yikan can also mean 'tease', with the result that (623) could alternatively have been translated as 'you are teasing me'. One specific form of teasing – tickling – may also be referred to by means of *yika-n* 'say-v^', as seen in the following:

(623) ngeengk   yika-ni-rr   ngul plate   runca-rr
      belly(ACC) say-v^-P.PFV then plate(NOM) collide-P.PFV
      '[he] tickled [her] belly and the plate hit [the ground]'
      [KTh_GJ19Oct2002 Elicitation StagedEvents78]

The meanings 'make speak', 'teach' and 'tease' seem too saliently different for the derived verb *yika-n* 'say-v^' to simply be vague. That is to say, it seems unlikely that a speaker uttering (622) would intend to express a category of event that includes teasing and tickling as well as teaching. Instead, it seems more plausible to posit ambiguity between a number of distinct senses.

Verb stems created by suffixation of v^ belong to the first conjugation class. Although all of the examples above involve a verb root undergoing valence increase, there is some evidence that this morpheme may attach directly to members of other word classes.[154] For example, the verb *meeren* 'show (something to someone)', seen in example (624) below, is apparently derived from the body part noun *meer(e)* 'eye' + *-(nh)an(i)* 'v^':

---

[154] The Kugu Nganhcara causative morpheme combines productively with nouns, adjectives and quantifiers – as well as verb roots – to produce transitive verbs (Smith & Johnson 2000: 427). The Kuuk Thaayorre valence increasing morpheme seems considerably more restricted in its combinatorics.

(624) pam   farmer, nhul   minh   tourist-ak   meere-n-m
      man   farmer 3sg(ERG) meat   tourist-DAT eye-V^-P.IPFV
      'a farmer was showing some tourists crocodiles'
      [KTh_AJ-**GJ**03Feb2004 Conversation]

Such cases are rare, however, and the form *meeren* 'show' appears to be lexicalized as a verb root rather than productively derived via valence increase.

In most cases, the valence increasing morpheme is the first derivational suffix to follow the verb root. As flagged above, however, there is some variation in the respective order of valence increaser and the reflexive/reciprocal morphemes. This can be seen in the comparison of (625) with (626), the first of which exhibits V^-RFL ordering, the second exhibits the reverse RFL-V^ order. Note that V^ has causative semantics in both these examples.

(625) ngay   ngathney   mungka-n-ey-r   merrethen
      1sg(ERG)   1sgRFL   consume-V^-RFL-P.PFV   medicine(ACC)
      'I made myself swallow the medicine'
      [Hall 1972: 392]

(626) ngancn   nhunh   kaar=p   yoongk-e-nhan-nan   yuk-un
      1pl(ERG)   3sgACC   NEG=PRAG   hang-RFL-V^-GO&:NPST   tree-DAT
      'we won't make him hang himself in the tree'
      [Hall 1972: 391]

The tendency for 'innermost' verbal affixes to apply semantically before those towards the periphery has long been recognized (e.g. Haiman 1980, 1983; Baker 1985).[155] This iconicity is reflected by the examples above, in both of which the 'inner' affix applies first. Accordingly, the order RFL-V^ expresses 'cause X to do V to X', where X is the subject participant and V is the event described by the verb. Conversely, the order V^-RFL expresses 'X causes X to do V' – in other words the reflexive affix has scope over the causation rather than the event (cf. Hyman 2003 on similar motivations for suffix ordering in Bantu languages).

---

155 Though see Evans (1995a) on an exception to this in the Australian language Kayardild.

8.1.2 Reflexive

The reflexive suffix -*e* 'RFL' primarily marks an action as self-directed (as in 627):

(627) ngay   nhaanhath-e
       1sg(NOM=ERG)   look.at:RDP-RFL:NPST
       'I'm looking at myself'

The reflexive suffix is, however, highly polysemous. The full range of event types associated with this morpheme is discussed in §11.5, as is the morphosyntax of the broader reflexive construction.

Reflexive derivation creates a second conjugation verb stem, with a zero-marked nonpast tense (as in (627) above). The past imperfective is marked by the full allomorph -*nham* (§7.2.3) and the past perfective by -*r* (§7.2.2):

(628) ngay   ngat-a   ngay[156]   yak-e-nham
       1sg(NOM)   fish-DAT   1sg(NOM)   cut-RFL-P.IPFV
       'I cut myself [while] fishing'
       [KTh_EN28Oct2002 Elicitation]

(629) nhul   yarriy katp-ey-r,   'iitharrkoo, kam   inh!'
       3sg(NOM)   thus   grasp-RFL-P.PFV   wow   blood   dem:sp.prx
       'he touched himself [on the arm] like this [and realized] "hey, I'm bleeding!"'
       [KTh_AJ-**GJ**03Feb2004 Narrative DarwinTrip]

As reflected in the transcription, an epenthetic palatal glide always intervenes between the reflexive suffix and past perfective morpheme (with the verb in (629) pronounced something like [katpejɪ]).

8.1.3 Reciprocal

The reciprocal suffix primarily marks events as symmetric.[157] The term 'symmetric' may be applied to any event-type involving (minimally) two participants and in which participant A both acts upon participant B and is acted upon by B,[158] as seen in the following:

---

[156] As discussed in §6.7, it is commonplace for there to be multiple exponents of a single argument within the Thaayorre clause. The repetition of *ngay* 'I' here, then, is unrelated to reflexivity.
[157] I borrow this term from König and Kokutani (2006).
[158] Where more than two participants are involved, I will class as symmetric any event in which the majority of participants both act upon, and are acted upon by, other participants. Exactly how

(630) paanth   pinalam   ith   ngamal.katp-rr peln
      woman   three(NOM)   dem:dist   hug-RCP:NPST   3pl(NOM)
      'the three women hug each other'
      [KTh_FT10Feb2004 RCP20]

This definition is intentionally semantic in orientation since the match between symmetric semantics and reciprocal coding is inexact. Hence §11.6 details a range of distinct functions associated with the reciprocal morpheme, as well as the potential for symmetric events to be encoded by non-reciprocal constructions.

Derivation of a reciprocal verb by suffixing -rr creates a stem of conjugation 2. Hence the nonpast tense is unmarked (as in (630) above) and the past perfective marked by the suffix -r:

(631) pul   yoorr   yith-rr-r   ii-rr-kuw   rump-un
      3du(NOM)   today   lead-RCP-P.PFV   there-towards-west   beach-DAT
      'those two led each other to the beach today'
      [Hall 1972: 108]

8.1.4 Associated motion

The category of 'associated motion' was first labelled as such by Koch (1984: 23) in his discussion of Kaytetye and other Australian languages.[159] Quite common among Pama-Nyungan languages, the functional range of associated motion morphemes varies from language to language. Most, if not all, of these morphemes can be used to mark the event described by the verb root as accompanied by some kind of motion (typically a change in location). This is illustrated by the following Kuuk Thaayorre example, which describes an event of fishing that will occur following motion to the river:

(632) ngay   ii-kuw-op-in   line   pit-nhan
      1sg(NOM)   there-at:west-river-DAT   line(ACC)   keep-GO&:NPST
      'I'm going [in order] to fish at the westwards river'
      [KTh_AC10Aug2002 Elicitation]

Kuuk Thaayorre possesses two associated motion morphemes which are etymologically related to the free motion verbs ya- 'go' and riic 'run'. The first associated motion

---

the reciprocal semantic prototype should be characterized is an empirical question that is, I believe, yet to be satisfactorily established. The definition given above is, however, a satisfactory heuristic for present purposes. This issue is revisited in §11.6.2.

159 Similar categories found on other continents have been labelled 'Andative' and 'Venitive' (cf. Lehmann 1983).

morpheme (*-nha-* 'GO&') combines the marking of associated motion and TAM inflection into a series of portmanteau suffixes. This can be attributed to the morpheme's origin as an irregular verb, the TAM inflection of which is not easily distinguished from the verb root. The second associated motion morpheme (*-(nh)ic(a)* 'RUN&') derives a straightforwardly first conjugation verb. The contrast between the two is evident in the comparison between (633) and (634), the past perfective morpheme being segmentable in the latter but not the former:

(633) *ngumpurr wang   ii   thongk-nhat*
       old.lady   whitefella(NOM) there   arrive-GO&:P.PFV
       'the old white lady's just arrived there'
       [KTh_AC14Nov2002 Narrative LosingIrma]

(634) *ngul yuparr   kaar=p   kuta pam.thaawarra kana   thongk-ica-rr*
       then later:prag NEG=PRAG dog cheeky(NOM)   finish arrive-RUN&-P.PFV
       'and no later [than he said that] the cheeky dog arrived'
       [Foote: Kuta Woochorrm]

Both of the associated motion morphemes can express aspectual information as well as associated motion proper (i.e. that the event described by the verb root also involves some change of place). The following sections detail these semantic categories, as well as the morphology and inferred etymology of the two morphemes.

8.1.4.1 *-nha-* 'go&'

As flagged in the previous section, the first associated motion morpheme (hereafter 'GO&') combines with TAM inflection to produce a series of portmanteau suffixes. These are presented in Table 56:

Table 56. Comparison of TAM inflections of *ya-* 'go' and the GO& morpheme.

	-nha- 'go&'	*ya-* 'go'
Nonpast	*-nhan*	*yan*
Past perfective	*-nhat*	*yat*
Imperative	*-nharr*	*yarr*
Subjunctive	*-nhancnh*	*yancnh*

That this morpheme has grammaticalized from the free verb *ya-* 'go' is clear only from a comparison of the tense inflection of the two. *Ya-* is a highly irregular verb; no other verb has a present tense marked by *-n*, a past perfective marked *-t* or an imperative marked *-rr*. The initial segment of the GO& motion morpheme, /nh/, is likely to have once marked subjunctive mood. This fits with an inferred construction at an earlier stage of the language's development, in which a subjunctive verb (encoding an intended event) combined with a motion verb. Illustrating this proposed development, (635) presents a hypothetical stage I clause in which a subjunctive verb is immediately followed by a motion verb. It is suggested that such a construction formed the basis for the (spontaneously uttered) associated motion verb seen in (636):

(635) *ngay   yukurra   kirk   wuump kath-nh   yan
        1sg(ERG) next.time spear(ACC) CONTR bind-SBJV go:NPST
        'next time I'll go and make a spear'

(636) ngay   yukurra   kirk   wuump kath-nhan
        1sg(ERG) next.time spear(ACC) CONTR bind-GO&:NPST
        'next time I'm going to make a spear'
        [KTh_AJ27Jan2004 Conversation]

No such serialization of subjunctive verb + motion verb is attested in my data, but such a construction could well have been superseded (and thus made obsolete) by the monolexemic associated motion verb. An alternative source of the initial -nh(a), however, might be the Pama-Nyungan nominalizer -nh(th)a- (Evans 1988), a reflex of which combines with the Warlpiri verb ya- 'go' to produce a similar associated motion category (Simpson 2002).

Associated motion derivation has no effect on valency, with the derived stem retaining the original valency of the root or stem to which the associated motion morpheme is suffixed. This is evidenced by the transitive verb *kath-nhan* 'tie-GO&:NPST' in (636), which is derived from the transitive root *kath* 'tie', and by the intransitive verb *thaangk-nhan* 'climb-GO&:NPST' (derived from the intransitive root *thaangk* 'climb') in the following example:

(637) ball   otonyciy mantam-ak   thaangk-nhan
        ball(NOM) hill   small-DAT   climb-GO&:NPST
        'the ball goes and climbs the small hill'
        [KTh_EN03Dec2002 Moland3]

The GO& morpheme has three major functions which can be summarized as follows (with V representing the action described by the verb root to which the GO& morpheme attaches):[160]

---

[160] My characterization of these functions borrows heavily from Alpher's (1973, 1991: 51) description of the Yir Yoront associated motion category.

1. **Motion** (*following motion do V*)
2. **Aspectual-inceptive** (*from a state of inaction do V*)
3. **Modal-dynamic** (*willingly do V*, or *be able to do V*)

The first, 'motion' usage is most closely connected to the origins of *-nha-* as a free motion verb. As seen in the following example, the GO& morpheme functions in this way to mark an event that occurs following a change in location:

(638) ngul raak yiirr waath-nhat
then place other(ACC) search-GO&:P.PFV
'then they went to find another place'
"they walk all the way, till they bin find another place"
[KTh_AC22Jul2002 Conversation / Narrative]

Although we might expect this morpheme also to encode an event that occurs <u>during</u> (rather than *following*) motion, this is nowhere attested in my corpus. Attempts to elicit an associated motion clause describing an activity that occurs simultaneously with motion, resulted instead in biclausal constructions such as the following:

(639) pam ith riic-m, nhul paanth nhaawr
man(NOM) dem:dist run-P.IPFV 3sg(ERG) woman(ACC) look.at:P.PFV
'the man looks at the woman as he's running along'
[KTh_GJ18Jan2004 Elicitation]

The second function of the GO& morpheme is labelled here 'aspectual-inceptive'. The morpheme here focuses attention upon the initiation of the event described by the verb root. Hence (640) was used in the description of one of a series of pictures depicting an apple falling from a tree. In the particular picture described in (640), the apple was in mid-air just below the branch it had been hanging from:

(640) may yulu wont-nhan ya-rr-kop
VEG apple(NOM) fall-GO&:NPST going-towards-below
'the apple is starting to fall downwards'
[Anon.]

GO& morphology is also found with this aspectual-inceptive function at the beginning of almost every story, as in the following two examples:

(641) ngay nhangkun kuthip wanan-nhan
1sg(NOM) 2sgDAT story(ACC) call:RDP-GO&:NPST
'I'll tell you a story...'
[KTh_GJ25Oct2002 Narrative]

(642) *inhul   yik-nhan   ngay,   nhul   minh pinc   ii-kuw*
this.one say-GO&:NPST 1sg(NOM) 3sg(NOM) meat saltie(NOM) there-at:west
'I'm about to tell this [story, in which] the saltwater crocodile is in the west...'
[KTh_**DW**-CW09Dec2002 Narrative 2Crocs]

The aspectual-inceptive usage is also seen in examples like (643), in which the GO& morpheme focuses our attention on the inception of the event in order to stress the protagonist's surprise at what he saw:

(643) *next morning ngay   rirk-r*
next morning 1sg(NOM) rise-P.PFV
ngay   nhaath-nhat   punth   mark   inh
1sg(ERG) see-GO&:P.PFV arm(ACC) mark(ACC) dem:sp.prx
'the next morning I got up and [suddenly] I saw this mark on my arm'
[KTh_AJ-**GJ**03Feb2004 Conversation]

The final function ascribed to the GO& morpheme is termed here 'modal-dynamic', and relates to the ability or willingness of the subject participant to perform the action described by the verb root. This function is only found within the desiderative construction, described in detail in §11.7.3.

8.1.4.2 *-(nh)ic* 'run&'

The second associated motion morpheme, *-(nh)ic*, derives historically from the free motion verb *riic* 'run'.[161] Like the GO& morpheme, the first segment of the suffix may well reflect erstwhile subjunctive inflection. However, this initial segment is frequently omitted (see, e.g., (644) below). Suffixation of this morpheme derives a verb stem of the first conjugation class, with fully regular tense/aspect/mood inflection. The fact that the two associated motion suffixes assign the resultant verb stems to different conjugation classes, is the product of their diachronic origins, in particular the conjugation class of the source verb, rather than signalling any semantico-syntactic distinction (e.g. in valence, which is unaffected by associated motion derivation as noted above).

The second associated motion morpheme (hereafter, 'RUN&') is attested with two of the three functions associated with the GO& morpheme:

1. **Motion** (*following motion do V*)
2. **Aspectual-inceptive** (*from a state of inaction do V*)

---

161 This is observed by Hall (1972: 126), who notes "it seems likely that the urgency morpheme /-(nh)ic/ derives from /(r)iic/ 'run', a verbroot, according to one informant. This is feasible, for with elision of the C1 and then later substitution of the common verb suffix particle /-n-/ after a vowel in verbclasses IV-III, it is explained rationally."

The motion function is evident in (644) and (645), both of which describe an activity that took or should take place following a change in location by the subject participant:

(644) *minh kanharr riica-rr ii-rr-kuw*
MEAT freshwater.croc(NOM) run-P.PFV there-towards-west
mun-ica-rr ii-rr-kaw
summon-RUN&-P.PFV there-towards-east
'the freshwater crocodile went westwards and summoned [the saltwater crocodile] to the east'
[KTh_**DW**-CW09Dec2002 Narrative 2Crocs]

(645) *nhunt yaarra thowol-nic!*
2sg(NOM) to:there play-RUN&:IMP
'you run away and play!'
[Hall 1972: 126]

The use of an associated motion morpheme with aspectual-inceptive function in order to express surprise or the suddenness of an event was noted above for GO&. This can also be seen in examples like the following:

(634') *ngul yuparr kaar=p kuta pam.thaawarra kana thongk-ica-rr*
then later NEG=PRAG dog cheeky(NOM) finish arrive-RUN&-P.PFV
'and no later [than he said that] the cheeky dog arrived'
[Foote: Kuta Woochorrm]

The semantic contrast between the first and second associated motion morphemes is not immediately obvious. It seems that RUN& is more frequently used with the motion sense than GO&, while the GO& morpheme is more frequently used with the aspectual-inceptive sense than the second. We might also expect there to be some emphasis on speed of motion given that this is the primary dimension of contrast between the two free verbs from which these morphemes grammaticalized. However, there is no clear evidence that such a speed-based contrast exists. The only suggestion that this might be the case, is the tendency for the RUN& morpheme to coincide with the free verb *riic* 'run' – and the GO& morpheme with the free verb *ya-* 'go' – in tightly linked clauses (e.g. (644) above). The categorical boundary between the respective functional ranges of these two morphemes warrants further investigation.

8.1.5 Subordinate

The subordinate suffix, *-marr* (~*-namarr*), is attested only in earlier recordings of the Kuuk Thaayorre language (e.g. Hall 1972) and does not feature in my data. For this reason, my discussion of subordinate verbs will be brief and somewhat speculative.

The functions of the subordinate clauses marked by *-marr* are discussed in more detail in §12.1.1.2.

Hall (1972: 193) labels *-marr* 'visible contemporaneous' due to its commonly heading the complement clause of a perception verb, as in (646):

(646) *ngay   pam   ith   nhaawr   ngat   kal-marr*
1sg(ERG)   man(ACC)   dem:dist   see:P.PFV fish(ACC)   carry-SBD
'I saw those men carrying fish'
[Hall 1972: 125]

It is thus reasonable to assume that *-marr* marks the carrying event as occurring at the same time as (i.e. 'contemporaneous' with) the viewing event, and within the sights of the subject of the matrix clause (*ngay* 'I'). However, I have chosen to eschew this label in favour of the more general 'subordinate' since these conditions of simultaneity and visibility often seem irrelevant to the event being encoded. In (647) it is not necessary for Jesus to be seen for it to be true that he was handcuffed when sent to Caiaphas.

(647) *Annas-an   nhunh   Jesus   punth   kath-marr   muth.wunpa-rr*
Annas-ERG   3sg(ACC)   Jesus(ACC)   arm(ACC)   bind-SBD   send-P.PFV
nhangun   Caiaphas-ak
3sgDAT   Caiaphas-DAT
'Annas sent Jesus handcuffed to Caiaphas'
[Foote and Hall 1992]

In (648), too, the subordinator *-marr* appears to simply mark the verb as head of a subordinate clause.

(648) *nhul   yaan   yungar-namarr*
3sg(NOM)   go:RDP:NPST   swim-SBD
'he will go swimming'
[Hall 1972: 147]

8.1.6 Verbalization and nominalization

There are three ways to create a verb stem from a nominal root in Kuuk Thaayorre: (1) suffixation of the verbalizer *-m*; (2) suffixation of the valence increaser *-(nha)n(i)*; (3) zero derivation. Since the first and the third of these strategies are also employed to derive nominal stems from verbal roots, it is most parsimonious to discuss these two processes – of verbalization on the one hand and nominalization on the other – in the same section.

The first way to create a verb stem from a nominal root is suffixation of *-m*, glossed here 'VerBalizeR'. For example, the verb stem *ngeengkm* 'love' is derived from the noun root *ngeengk* 'belly'. This morpheme can attach not only to a simplex, monomorphemic root but also to compounds, as in *kaal-purng-m* (lit. 'ear-blocked-VBLZ') 'forget'.[162] Significantly, this is the only Kuuk Thaayorre derivational morpheme that appears to create verb stems belonging to both of the major conjugation classes (see discussion in §7.1.2). The assignation of *-m*-derived stems to conjugation classes seems to correlate with valency; with those (like *pinirm* 'dream') assigned to the first conjugation class being bivalent, and those (like *piinthawaarrm* 'tire') assigned to the second being monovalent. The first conjugation morphology of the monovalent *waarrm* 'become bad' (649) represents an exception to this generalization, however:

(649) 1. *['i gotta cleanm rirkm straight out, otherwise 'i might get, you know]*
['you've got to clean them straight away, otherwise they might, you know']
2. yup   waarr-m-r
soon   bad-VBLZ-NPST
'[they] will spoil'
[KTh_ME04Jun2005 Narrative/Conversation Yencr]

Many verb stems derived through this process involve nominal roots referring to parts of the body. The semantic relationships between nominal roots and derived verb stems vary in their transparency. While the event of tiring (described by *piinthawaarrm* 'tire') is obviously connected to the characteristic of being *piinthawaarr* 'tired', the connection between the belly and love (lexicalized in *ngeengkm* 'love, lit. belly-VBLZ') or a blocked ear and forgetting (lexicalized in *kaal-purng-m* 'forget, lit. ear-blocked-VBLZ') is based in conventionalized metaphor. It is unclear whether the process of verbalization remains productive. Certainly, there are numerous cases of apparent lexicalization. Take, for example, the predicate adjectives *walmeerem* 'know' and *pamngongkom* 'be ignorant of'. The former can be decomposed into two body part nouns (*wal* 'forehead' and *meer* 'eye') plus the verbalizer *-m*. However, the product of their combination is not an inflectable verb stem, nor is the derived meaning 'know' compositional. In the case of *pamngongkom* 'be ignorant of', there is no corresponding noun *ngongk(o)*, though Kugu Nganhcara *ngonggolo* 'ignorant' is likely cognate.[163] This suffix is also likely implicated in the creation of the adverb *porprm* 'excessively' from the adjective *porpr* 'soft'.

The verbalizer morpheme itself has cognate forms in neighbouring Yir Yoront and Kugu Nganhcara. In Yir Yoront, "the derivative suffix *-m ... forms a verb of the L[dental] conjugation" (Alpher 1973: 241), while the Kugu Nganhcara patrilects

---

162 The Kuuk Thaayorre predicate *kaal-purng-m* (ear-blocked-VBLZ) 'forget' is strikingly similar in semantics and etymology to the 'forget' verbs of dozens of Australian languages, not least Yir Yoront *pin=porng+vm* (ear=stopped.up+m) 'forget' (Alpher 1991: 724).
163 The first element, *pam*, is a noun meaning 'man', but may used here in its apprehensive sense, expressing a state or event that would best be avoided.

possess an 'intransitive' morpheme *-ma*, that both appears on (already) intransitive verbs and creates intransitive verbs from adjectives (Smith & Johnson 2000).

The coincidental homophony of the Kuuk Thaayorre verbalizer *-m* and the common Kriol transitive verb suffix *-(i)m* poses a certain analytical problem. It is difficult to decide to which of these should be attributed the suffix that attaches to the English loan verbs that combine with the light verb *rirk* 'DO' in collocations such as *trainm rirk* 'train':

(650) *school-mam pelnan ulp train-m rirk*
school-ABL 3plACC dem:ad.prx train-? DO:NPST
'he's training the kids from the school'
[KTh_ME02Oct2002 Conversation]

Indeed, the fortuitous confluence of these two forms may have facilitated the incorporation of numerous English loan verbs into the Kuuk Thaayorre lexicon. However, the fact that the morpheme *-m* is not suffixed to intransitive English loan verbs (651) suggests that the suffix *-m* in (525) is a different morpheme to that in, e.g., (526) above.

(651) *minh ulp peln breed.up rirk-r*
meat(NOM) dem:ad.prx 3pl(NOM) breed.up DO-P.PFV
'those [crocodiles] bred up (i.e. multiplied)'
[KTh_AJ-GJ03Feb2004 Conversation]

For this reason, I posit a distinct morpheme *-m* 'transitive verbalizer' which attaches only to transitive English loan verbs (which then combine with the light verb *rirk* 'DO' to form an inflecting verbal complex, see §8.2 below).

As flagged above, the form *-m* may also derive a nominal stem from a verbal root. Because the derivational processes of verbalization and nominalization are clearly distinct, I view the two morphemes as homophonous, glossing the nominalizer *-m* 'NMLZ'. The most frequently encountered example of nominalization is the noun *yuur+kath-m* (hand+bind-NMLZ) 'policeman'. Apart from this one noun, nominalization via the nominalizer is rare, tending to involve a whole phrase rather than a simple verb root. So while the nominalizer is suffixed only to the verb *thak* 'leave' in (652) below, the noun it forms must be considered phrasal (i.e. *raak rirkr thak-m* [THING money leave- NMLZ] 'treasury [i.e. the place money is left]').

(652) *nhul wun pormprranth raak rirkir thak-m-an*
3sg(NOM) live:NPST house hole THING money leave-NMLZ-DAT
raak yuur mong-on
time hand many-DAT
'he stays in the treasury room for ages and ages'
[Hall 1972: 74]

Note that the dative case suffix (which only attaches to nominal stems) is attached to the derived stem *thakm*. This shows that *thakm* is the final element of the larger noun phrase *pormpr ranth raak rirkr thakman* '(in the) treasury room' (see §6 for discussion of the internal structure of noun phrases). This is a complex noun phrase with the following hierarchical structure:

Table 57. Syntactic structure of *pormpr ranth raak rirkir thak-m-an* 'treasury room'.

NP 'treasury room'				
N' 'room'		N' 'treasury'		
N 'room'		N 'money'		AdjP 'left'
pormpr N_{GN} 'house'	ranth N_{SP} 'hole'	raak N_{GN} 'thing'	rirkr N_{SP} 'shell'	thakm Adj 'left.thing'

New verbs may also be created by the suffixation of the valence increasing morpheme (v^) to a nominal root, as noted in §8.1.1. For example, the ditransitive verb *meeren* 'show' is both formally and semantically related to the body part noun *meer* 'eye'. Similarly *pakun-* 'bury' < *pak* 'grave'. It is possible that this process is no longer productive. Every neologism of this kind that I proposed to language experts (e.g. *kuthirran 'halve' < *kuthirr* 'half') was rejected.

8.2 Complex predicates

The inflecting 'light verb' *rirk* 'DO' combines with (a small number of) Kuuk Thaayorre nouns and wide range of English loan words and phrases to form complex verb structures, as illustrated by example (653):[164]

---

[164] The word class termed *light verb* (Grimshaw & Mester 1988, Butt & Geuder 2001) varies enormously across languages (compare, for example, English [Brugman 1988], Japanese [Grimshaw and Mester 1988], Chinese [Butt & Gueder 2001], Bardi [Bowern 2004]), but in all cases refers to a class of verbs that are in some sense 'lexically weak' or semantically deficient. This term is attractive in the description of Thaayorre *rirk* both because it specifies the semantic broadness of this lexeme, and because it does not specify anything further. Labels more commonly employed in the Australian context (e.g. *generic verb* [Jaminjung, Schultze-Berndt 2000], *inflecting verb* [Wagiman, Wilson 1999 and Mawng, Singer 2006], *finite verb* [Ngan'gityemerri, Reid 2000], *verb* [Ngalakgan, Baker 1999] and *auxiliary* [Warlpiri, Simpson 1991]) tend to describe more complex and well-developed systems, usually involving a number of verb forms that may be used contrastively as part of a paradigmatic set.

(653) ongkorr worry rirk
 PROHIB worry DO:IMP
 'don't worry!'
 [KTh_GJ28Oct2002 Elicitation]

As a free verb, *rirk* 'rise' is an intransitive predicate that describes upward motion, as can be seen in the following examples:

(654) kuta kana rirk-r. Kanpa wut wun-m
 dog(NOM) CMP rise-P.PFV before asleep lie-P.IPFV
 'The dog's got up. It was sleeping before'
 [KTh_AC21Aug2002 Conversation]

(655) minh ii yuk ranth-im rirk-r
 bird(NOM) there TREE hole-ABL rise-P.PFV
 'the bird flew out of its hole in the tree'
 [KTh_GJ28Oct2002 Elicitation]

It may also combine with bare Kuuk Thaayorre nouns to produce a complex verb, e.g. *mit rirk* 'work' and *pancr rirk* 'be shame (embarrassed)' in the following examples:[165]

(656) ngal muth-wiitl mit rirk-m
 1du:incl(NOM) neck-jointly work DO-P.IPFV
 'we were working together'
 [KTh_EN27Jan2004 Elicitation]

(657) ngay pancr rirk-m=ay
 1sg(NOM) body.hair DO-P.IPFV=1sg(NOM)
 'I was shame'
 [KTh_GJ16Oct2002 Narrative MelbourneTrip]

---

[165] The Aboriginal English adjective 'shame' is not to be confused with English *be ashamed*, see Harkins (1990) for an account of its semantics. We might tentatively speculate that this construction has its origins in an expression like *pancr rirk* 'be shame'. This would involve a bridging context in which the term *pancr* 'body hair' functions originally as a body part apposed (in nominative case) to the whole undergoer subject *ngay* 'I', as per (a) below. This would then be reanalyzed as a complex verb as per (b):

(a) ngay pancr rirk-m=ay
 1sg(NOM) body.hair(NOM) rise-P.IPFV=1sg(NOM)
 'my body hair rose (stood on end)'
(b) ngay pancr rirk-m=ay
 1sg(NOM) body.hair DO-P.IPFV=1sg(NOM)
 'I was shame'
 [GJ16/10/02 Narrative MelbourneTrip]

Since the Kuuk Thaayorre verbalizing suffix -*m* (§8.1.6) is only marginally productive, English loans are unable to function as full verbs in and of themselves. The relevant verbal inflections must therefore be hosted by the light verb, *rirk*. This accords with Dixon's (2002: 210) observation that:

> loans from English are almost always (or always?) taken into Australian languages as free forms. This means that English verbs are borrowed in the form of nouns or adjectives, which must then be verbalized in order to function as verbs.

English-origin nouns and adjectives – as well as verbs – frequently combine with *rirk* 'DO' in order to produce complex Kuuk Thaayorre verb forms. There is no obvious difference in form or meaning according to which word class the loan word is sourced from; all function as verbs in combination with *rirk* 'DO'. The following examples illustrate *rirk* 'DO' in combination with forms that, respectively, belong to the following word classes in the source language, English: adjective (658); noun (660); verb (661, 662); phrasal verb (663); verb + direct object (418):

(658) *drunk   rirk-r   ngul   ngay   AA   thanpa-rr*
       drunk   DO-P.PFV   then   1sg(ERG)   [name redacted](ACC)   hit-P.PFV
       'I got drunk and punched AA'
       [Anon.]

(659) *peln   glad   rirk-r*
       3pl(NOM)   glad   DO-P.PFV
       'they were glad' [or: they expressed being glad, e.g. by cheering]
       [KTh_GJ16Oct2002 Narrative MelbourneTrip]

(660) *Celebration   rirk-r   nhangun,   birthday.of.Christ   nhangun*
       celebration   DO-P.PFV   3sgDAT   birthday.of.Christ   3sgDAT
       'we celebrated for him, for the birthday of Christ'
       [KTh_GJ18Jan2004 Narrative ChristmasStory]

(661) *ngay   minc.ngul   knock.off   rirk,   three.o'clock*
       1sg(NOM)   afternoon   knock.off   DO:NPST   three.o'clock
       'I knock off in the afternoon, at three o'clock'
       [KTh_AJ27Jan2004 Conversation]

(662) *peep   ngancn   drag-m   rirk-m*
       net(ACC)   1pl:excl(ERG)   drag-TR   DO-P.IPFV
       'we were dragging nets'
       [KTh_AJ27Jan2004 Conversation]

(663) yup   find.out rirk   ii-parr
     soon   find.out DO-NPST there-at:south
     '(we'll) find out soon down in the south'
     [KTh_GJ16Oct2002 Narrative MelbourneTrip]

(418') nhul   Irene   make.friend rirk-r   pelnungun family nhangn-mak
      3sg(NOM)   Irene(NOM)   make.friend DO-P.PFV   3plDAT   family 3sgGEN-DAT
      'Irene made friends with her [host] family'
      [KTh_GJ16Oct2002 Narrative MelbourneTrip]

The valence of the complex predicate as a whole is determined entirely by the loan verb, which is marked by *-m* if transitive (662) and unmarked if intransitive (661). This transitive marker is generally restricted to verbal loans (as opposed to loan adjectives and loans of other word classes). Example (664) may appear to be an exception to this rule, but *off* is widely used as a transitive verb in Pormpuraaw English, which is presumably the source of the loan.

(664) ulp   light koopkop   off-m   rirk-nhan   ulp
     dem:adr.fam   light all:RDP(ACC) off-TR   DO-GO&:NPST   dem:adr.fam
     'all the lights will be turned off [in the cyclone]'
     "everything light will be off"
     [KTh_**AJ**-GJ03Feb2004 Conversation]

The loan word and *rirk* may in fact form a single lexical unit (through either compounding or the suffixation of *-rirk*), which would indicate *rirk*'s grammaticalization into a new (loan-)verbalizing suffix. This stands in contradistinction to the combination of *rirk* and native Kuuk Thaayorre nominals, which are commonly separated by modal operators (such as *kaar* 'NEG' in (665)) and may be inverted in pragmatically marked or emphatic contexts (as are *mit* 'work' and *rirk* in (334)):

(665) nhunt   yoorr   mit   kaar rirk?
     2sg(NOM)   today   work   NEG   DO:NPST
     'do you want to do some work today?'
     [KTh_EN8Sep2002 Elicitation]

(666) kaar rirk-m   ngay   mit
     NEG   DO-P.IPFV   1sg(NOM)   work
     'I wasn't able to work'
     [KTh_AJ-**GJ**03Feb2004 Conversation]

When English loans are paired with *rirk*, by contrast, their order is never inverted in my data. Nor are there examples of the two being separated by other words. Notably, *kaar* 'NEGative' – which almost always appears in immediately pre-verbal position – always precedes the English loan verb (as in 525 above). Further, in many recorded utterances, the English loan + *rirk* appear to form a single phonological unit (often with the initial segment of *rirk* elided). In other utterances, however, the two are articulated distinctly. Hence these complex verbs are transcribed as bipartite expressions throughout this grammar, though it is noted that *rirk* may be in the process of grammaticalizing into a derivational loan verbalizer. (In the meantime, it is unclear which part of the bipartite structure represents the head. On the one hand, it is the loan preverb that determines theta-role assignment and the transitivity of the clause. On the other hand, it is the inflecting light verb that encodes clausal aspect.)

8.3 Body part noun + verb compounds

Kuuk Thaayorre possesses a large number of verbal compounds composed of (at least one) body part noun followed by an inflecting verb root (as seen in (667) below). The compounding of the two morphemes (as opposed to simple juxtaposition) is suggested by the frequent phonological reduction of the body part term (hereafter BPT), and its restriction to the immediately pre-verbal position (discussed further below). The meaning of the compound also usually (but not always) differs from that of the verb root. The process of deriving such compounds does not appear to affect valency, which is determined by that of the verb root. Conjugation membership is also determined by this verb root (or any following derivational affixes), as would be expected of the final morpheme of the verb stem.

(667) *bottle table-ak thaa+raaki-rr*
  bottle(ACC) table-DAT mouth+PLACE-P.PFV
  'she put the bottle on the table'
  [KTh_GJ20Nov2002 Elicitation CausedPositions20]

Only a limited number of body parts have been attested in verbal compounds so far (viz: *koo(w)* 'nose', *thaa(w)* 'mouth', *man* 'throat', *muth* 'back of neck', *yuur* 'hand', *meer* 'eye', *mut* 'back', and *pungk* 'knee'), but there is no reason prima facie to assume that these form a closed subset of body part terms.

The derived semantics of body part + verb compounds fall into four main categories:

1. the body part represents the instrument or theme involved in the event;
2. a feature of the event (particularly a result state) in some way resembles the body part;
3. the semantic contribution of the body part noun is unclear, with the semantics of the compound very similar to that of the verb root; or

4. the derived semantics of the compound are non-compositional, reflecting the semantics of neither body part nor verb root directly.

Each of these four categories will be discussed in turn.

8.3.1 Body part = instrument or theme

Complex stems in which the body part noun represents an instrument often involve only a slight refinement of the verb's meaning. The verb *mungk-* 'eat, drink', for example, is disambiguated by compounding with *thaa* 'mouth'; meaning only 'eat'. Compounding *wan* 'tell, name' with the body part *yuur* 'hand' specifies that a referent is indexed or communicated by being 'pointed out' rather than through language. The verb *thaa.punyc* 'kiss' is formed by compounding the verb *punyc* 'suck' with the active body part *thaa(w)* 'mouth'. Note that the semantics of this compound verb are not strictly compositional; *thaa.punyc* 'kiss' may describe kissing someone on the cheek or elsewhere, so *thaa(w)* 'mouth' must refer to the instrument rather than the undergoer of the event. This does not account for the semantic shift from 'suck' to 'kiss', however, since sucking always involves the mouth (as does drinking, above). That *thaa+punyc* 'mouth+suck' refers specifically to kissing, then, is purely conventional. This is true of almost all Kuuk Thaayorre body part + verb compounds.

Further examples of compounds in which the BPT represents an instrument or theme are given in Table 58. The first column gives the Kuuk Thaayorre predicate (and, where the translation relies upon them, core arguments), the second column gives a morpheme-by-morpheme gloss, and the third an English translation / approximate. Where a form does not occur in isolation, it appears in the gloss in capitals.

Table 58. Some complex verbs in which the BPT represents an instrument or theme.

#	Complex verb	Gloss	English translation
1	*koo+mi'i*	nose+pick.up	recognize (someone's face)
2	*koo+munth*	nose+sink	wash face
3	*koo+than*	nose+stand	sneeze
4	*kuuk man+kerp*	word throat+finish	be dumb
5	*meer+maak*	eye+tread[165]	blind (somebody)
6	*meer+munth*	eye+sink	blink
7	*meer+nhaath*	eye+see	stare

---

[166] The verb *maak*, glossed here as 'tread', may also mean 'trample', and is commonly used to describe the process of feeling for things (e.g. freshwater mussels) with one's feet. In light of the compound *mut-maak* (back-tread) 'lie somebody down', it may mean something more like 'press against the ground'.

Table 58. (continued)

#	Complex verb	Gloss	English translation
8	mut+maak	back+tread	lie somebody down
9	mut+rirk	back+rise	get out of bed, hunt
10	pungk+therk	knee+return	"right round sit down"
11	thaa+mungk	mouth+consume	eat
12	thaa+munth	mouth+sink	drown
13	thaa+pac	mouth+complain	argue
14	thaa+pirr	mouth+strip	reply
15	thaa+punyc	mouth+suck	kiss
16	thaa+ratprr	mouth+RATP	fan fire
17	thaa+theepr	mouth+defecate	spit
18	thaa+whistle+thunp	mouth+whistle+throw	whistle
19	yuur+(koo+)wan	hand+(nose+)tell	point out

Although the body part seems to represent the instrument in lines 3, 10, 14 and 16, the semantic contribution of the verb is unclear. The verb *pirr* 'strip, peel' (in *thaa+pirr* 'reply'), for instance, typically describes removing the skin from fruit or the bark from a tree, and seems to have little to do with the communicative act of replying. In cases such as 1, 2, 5 and 8, the body seems involved in the event more as a theme or undergoer than an instrument. In 1, for instance, recognizing a person has more to do with the face of the person recognized than the face of the person doing the recognizing (apart from their eyes, the active person part).

8.3.2 Feature of body part = feature of event / result state

There are two key semantic patterns in this category. One is for the morpheme *thaa* 'mouth' to metaphorically indicate a hole or gap that appears as the result of the activity described by the complex predicate as a whole (i.e. opening, in the case of *thaa+raw*, or tearing in the case of *thaa+riic*). The second semantic subclass involves person parts associated with the orientation or direction of the action, namely *koo* 'nose' and *man* 'throat'. This is a somewhat hazy definition based on the assumption that the nose – due to its protrusion from the front of the face – is associated with activities directed outward along the body's sagittal axis (e.g. attacking and pointing in lines 1 and 5). Note that this last example, *yuur+koo+wan* (hand+nose+tell) 'point out' combines two levels of compounding. Firstly, *koo(w)* 'nose' is compounded with *wan* (a verb used to describe a range of event types, including the recounting of tales and naming a person or thing, cf. §10.1.8) to provide the directionality of the event (extending outwards from the body). This is subsequently compounded with the BPT *yuur* 'hand', which provides the instrumental body part involved in the event (the person or thing is pointed out by the hand). The throat – due to its location at the front of the body, and association with the chest (Gaby 2006) – is presumably associated with the activity of 'staring downwards' (in line 2), which extends outwards and downwards from the eye origin.

Table 59. Complex verbs in which a feature of the BPT represents a feature of the event.

	Complex verb	Gloss	English translation
1.	koo+thak	nose+leave	attack
2.	man+wewerngkr	throat+middle:RDP	stare (downwards)
3.	thaa+raw	mouth+dig	open (e.g. a door, a pen)
4.	thaa+riic	mouth+go.fast	tear, crack (e.g. of material)
5.	yuur+koo+wan	hand+nose+tell;name	point out

8.3.3 Contribution of body part unclear

There is not always a clear change in semantics as a result of BPT + verb root compounding. The BPT *thaa* 'mouth', for example, appears to contribute little to the predicate *thaa+ranc* 'jump' (lit. 'mouth+jump') in the following example:

(668)   *minh   kothon   kana=th=p   ke'e-rr   thaa+ranci-rr=p*
         meat wallaby(NOM) finish=PRAG=PRAG spear-P.PFV mouth+jump-P.PFV=PRAG
         'this wallaby here really got speared and jumped'
         [Hall 1972: 140]

In this example and the following, only the analysis of a very large corpus will illuminate precisely how these verbal compounds differ in sense and distribution from the underived verb root since the speakers consulted have not been aware of a substantive difference in meaning.

(669)   *parr_r   ii   koo+thaka-rr*
         child(ACC) there nose+leave-P.PFV
         'that kid got left behind'
         [KTh_GJ28Oct2002 Elicitation]

(670)   *referee-n   thaa+thunp-r*
         referee-ERG mouth+throw-NPST
         'the referee is shoving [the man] along'
         [KTh_GJ19Oct2002 Elicitation StagedEvents80]

8.3.4 Meaning non-compositional

In the vast majority of BPT + verb root compounds, there is no straightforward relationship between the meaning of the compound as a whole and those of its components. So the event of helping somebody seems to have little to do with noses or growing, yet the verbal compound *koo+piinth* 'help' is formed by compounding *koo(w)* 'nose' with the verb root *piinth* 'grow' (homophonous with the BPT *piinth* 'bone'). Further examples of non-compositional complex predicates are presented in Table 60.

Table 60. Some semantically non-compositional complex verbs.

	Complex verb	Gloss	English translation
1.	muth+wunp	back.of.neck+put	'send (someone, somewhere)'
2.	man+ke'e	throat+spear	'owe'
3.	meer+thiik	eye+break	'pretend; copy'
4.	koo+rok	nose+enter	'hide'
5.	thaa+raak	mouth+place	'stand (something) up'

8.3.5 Related functions of body part terms

A closely related phenomenon to the compounding of body part terms and verb roots is the formation of phrasal verbs in which a phonologically independent (often case-marked) body part term is preposed to an inflected verb. *Kiina raak* (tooth:ERG place) 'swear' (671) is one such phrasal verb. Like verbal compounds, the semantics of these phrasal verbs tend to differ significantly from those of the verb roots they contain. Also like those in verbal compounds, the semantic contribution of the body part term involved may be either transparent (e.g. representing an instrument, as in (672)) or opaque (as in (673)):

(671) nhunt   nganh   kiin-a   raak-r
      2sg(ERG) 1sgACC tooth-ERG place-NPST
      'you're swearing at me'
      [KTh_EN14Aug2002 Elicitation]

(672) pul   meer-e   nhaanhath-rr
      3du(ERG) eye-ERG see:RDP-RCP
      'they're staring at each other'
      [KTh_MF06Aug2002 Elicitation]

(673) *piinth+thaaw theetherk-e*
bone+mouth return:RDP-RFL:NPST
'[he's] stretching'
[KTh_GJ19Oct2002 Elicitation StagedEvents123]

BPTs also combine with non-verbal lexical roots in somewhat similar ways to the cases described above. For example, there are an enormous number of nominal compounds involving person parts as their first element (e.g. *meer+ngok* [eye+water] 'tears', in which the BPT *meer* 'eye' represents the source of the compound referent). BPTs are also commonly prefixed – possibly with their orientation/direction function – to spatial adverbs, as in the following example:

(674) *ngul nheman=p meer-ii-kan ngancn thowol-nam*
then from.there=PRAG eye-there-at:up 1pl:excl(NOM) play-P.IPFV
"from then, we were playing as high up as the sky"
[KTh_GJ15Oct2002 Narrative PlaneSighting]

9 Particles and adverbs

9.1 Particles

This chapter considers the particles and adverbs that play a key role in Kuuk Thaayorre grammar. It focuses on those of high frequency and/or particular significance with regard to the formation of complex constructions, excluding those discussed in detail in other chapters (e.g. *ngul* 'then', considered at length in §12.2.1.2; *kirri* 'permissive', discussed in §11.2.1; *ak* 'optative', discussed in §11.2.2; the particle usage of *waarr* (elsewhere meaning 'bad(ly)'), discussed in §11.7.1.3; and the particle *angarr*, which is used to describe how the world ought to be, discussed in §11.7.1.2). The full range of adverbs and particles are summarized in §3.3 and §3.5.

9.1.1 *Kana* 'well'

The ubiquitous Kuuk Thaayorre particle *kana* has five distinct meanings. Which of these obtains in a particular clause depends on the clausal predicate and – where this predicate is a verb – tense/aspect marking. The following characterization of the semantics of Kuuk Thaayorre *kana* draws heavily on Alpher's (1991: 152) description of the cognate Yir Yoront *kana*, but makes some significant departures. Table 61 summarizes the five functions of *kana*, listed according to its role in the clause (including aspectual features of the verbal head where *kana* is not itself the main predicate). Note that the alternative translations of *kana* given in Table 61 should be taken to reflect an inexact match between the semantics of *kana* and those of the English translations. They are not intended to signify that there are two distinct senses of the Kuuk Thaayorre particle.

Table 61. The five functions of *kana*.

	Role in the clause	Meaning	Antonym
1.	Nonverbal predicate	'well', '(in a) good (state)'	*waarr* 'bad'
2.	Interjection or nonverbal predicate	'finished', 'enough'	*ngaathirr* 'ongoing'
3.	Particle in a clause with a past perfective verb	'finished', '(successfully) done'	*ngaathirr* 'ongoing' *kaar* 'NEGative' *waat* 'wrongly'
4.	Particle in a clause with a nonpast verb	'about to'	*yukurra* 'next time'
5.	Discourse particle	'OK'	—

The first function of *kana* is as a nonverbal predicate meaning 'well' or '(in a) good (state)'. It is used with this sense in the Kuuk Thaayorre greeting *nhunt kana?* (2sgNOM well) 'are you well?'. In addition to this highly routinized usage, *kana* can also be used to mean 'good' in contexts like the following:

(675) bag inh kana, min
bag(NOM) dem:sp.prx well good
'this bag's pretty good'
[KTh_EF14Dec2002 Elicitation Demonstratives8]

This sense fits within the antonymic scale between *min* 'good' and *waarr* 'bad'. *Min* 'good' is slightly stronger in its positive semantics, and is more commonly used in emphatic contexts, as can be seen in the following:

(676) 1. AG: nhul minc-wanc=kaak?
     3sg(NOM) body-ache=REL.PROP
     'is she sick?'
  2. AJ: pokon, mami ngathn min!
     NO mum 1sg(NOM) good
     'no, my mum's well!'
     [KTh_AJ27Jan2004 Conversation]

The somewhat downgraded level of satisfaction indicated by *kana* can be seen in the second line of the following utterance:

(677) 1. *Ngul ngay pirrkunc kuthirr katpi-rr, mantam.*
   then 1sg(NOM) SPECIES two(ACC) grasp-P.PFV small(ACC)
   'then I caught two *pirrkunc* fish, small ones'
  2. *ngay kana, good.enough inh*
   1sg(NOM) well good.enough dem:sp.prx
   'I was satisfied, this is good enough'
  3. *ngay paath thiika-rr angunp,*
   1sg(NOM) firewood(ACC) break-P.PFV in.that.place
   'I made a fire there'
  4. *anyway mungk-ica-rr, pungkurtharr. Awoy.*
   anyway eat-RUN&-P.PFV hungry yes
   'and went and ate them anyway, as I was hungry. That's right'
   [KTh_AJ27Jan2004 Conversation]

The second function of *kana* is as an interjection or nonverbal predicate meaning 'finished' or 'enough'. Again, it seems that these two meanings, though distinct in English, may fall within a single, vague Kuuk Thaayorre sense that conveys an idea of completion of an event or a substance. Hence I was often asked by language experts – whose patience had been worn by an endless sequence of elicitation videos – *kana, or ngaathirr?* '(are we) finished or still going?'. *Kana* 'finished' can also be predicated of an argument, such as *kuthip* 'story' in the first clause of (678).

(678)   *kana*   *kuthip*   *inh.*   *Kana kerp-r.*
       finished story(NOM) dem:sp.prx CMP finish-P.PFV
       'that's the end of the story'
       [KTh_GJ16Oct2002 MelbourneStory]

Many narratives end with the simple statement *kana* 'finished', analogous to the English phrase 'the end'.

This sense of 'finished' is closely linked to *kana*'s function when combined with a past perfective-inflected verb. Glossed 'COMpletive', this third function of *kana* indicates that the event described has (been) finished or completed, as seen in the second clause of (678) above. This is frequently accompanied by an implicature of 'successfully completed', no doubt fostered by *kana*'s first sense, 'well'. Example (679.1) demonstrates the use of *kana* to mark a fully completed event, while (679.2) illustrates the use of its antonym *ngaathirr* 'ongoing'.

(679)   1. *Pormpr nhangkn*   *kana yumpi-rr?*
          house 2sgGEN(ACC) CMP make-P.PFV
          'have (they) finished building your house yet?'
     2. *Pokon. Ngaathirr.*
          NO   ongoing
          'no – they're still going.'
          [KTh_EN8Sep2002 Elicitation]

The perfective aspect of the verb is strongly emphasized by this function of *kana*, making *kaar* 'NEGative', which negates the event's completion, another of its antonyms. So strong is *kana*'s association with telic events, its presence in a clause headed by a past imperfective verb is ungrammatical. Hence the language expert rejected the following clause, which I had proposed with a putative meaning 'what have you been doing (since I last saw you)?':

(680)   **nhunt*   *ngan kana yump-m?*
       2sg(NOM) what CMP do-P.IPFV
       [KTh_ME02Oct2002 Elicitation]

It is, however, grammatical for *kana* to combine with a non-perfective verb in nonpast tense. In this case, *kana* has the meaning of 'about to', or 'on the point of'. Hence the typical Kuuk Thaayorre farewell; *ngay kana yan* (1sg[NOM] about.to go:NPST) 'I'm going'. *Kana* in this function frequently combines with a verb stem derived by the first associated motion morpheme (as in (681)), which is hardly surprising given the latter's use to mark inceptive aspect.

(681) *paath   ulp   kana   keemp-e-nhan   yup!*
fire(NOM) dem:ad.prx about.to extinguish-RFL-GO&:NPST soon
'that fire's going to go out soon'
[KTh_AJ8Feb2004 Elicitation]

Rarely, *kana* is used with this sense in the absence of a verb (i.e. as an interjection). The following interchange – which was prompted by my collaborator's asking me whether we were going to work together – exemplifies this usage (which is clearly not ambiguous with the 'finished' or 'well' interjection functions):

(682) AG: *raak ngan?*
TIME what
'when?'
GJ: *kana*
about.to
'now'
[KTh_GJ12Jan2004 Conversation]

This function of referring to an (imminent) future event by means of a particle otherwise associated with completed, finished events might at first seem odd. As Comrie (1985: 20) notes, however, in many languages around the world "the past tense can be used for imminent future events. Thus in Russian, the usual expression for use when one is about to leave is *ja pošël*, literally 'I left' even though this is clearly not literally true".

There is just one example in my corpus in which *kana* combines with a nonpast verb, but does not appear to carry this meaning of immediacy. Indeed, my analysis of the meaning of *kana* in such contexts led to the following misunderstanding of language expert ME's utterance in line 3:

(683) 1. ME: *pal   kal=p=a!*
towards carry=PRAG=PRAG
'bring [the Cabbage Palm leaves] here!'
2.   [AG gets up to leave]
3. ME: *kace, **kana**   yan   nhunt=a*
WRONG **about.to** go:NPST 2sg(NOM)=PRAG
'no, [you're] about to go'
4. AG: *kana   yan   yoorr, or...?*
about.to go:NPST now   or
'go now, or...?'

5. ME: *yup! ngal thurma yarr=ey! ngal*
   soon 1du:incl(NOM) together go:IMP=PRAG 1du:incl(NOM)
   yarr thurma
   go:IMP together
   'soon [i.e. not yet]! We'll go together! We'll go together,'
6. ME: *kanpa inh kerp, yup yan*
   first dem:sp.prx finish:IMP soon go:NPST
   '[we'll] finish this first, [then] go soon'
   [KTh_ME04Jun2005 Narrative Yencr-interruption]

I remain unsure as to the exact function of *kana* in this instance. Although the 'about to' sense would seem to have antonyms in both *yup* 'soon' and *yukurra* 'next time', the use of *kana* in the second clause of (683) is clearly compatible with *yup* 'soon'.[167]

Finally, *kana* also functions as a discourse particle, glossed here as 'OK'. Like its English gloss, *kana* has a range of discourse functions, most prominently marking a particular kind of discourse boundary, termed here 'thematic break'. This thematic break does not necessarily represent a change of topic (in the non-technical sense), but indicates that the state of affairs described by a clause or series thereof has been fully established, and that the subsequent clause(s) will go on to establish a different state of affairs. Such a break usually involves some change in the time or place of the events at issue. This is best illustrated by example:

(684) 1. *Mami ngathn ulp ii wun wanthan=th.*
   Mum 1sgGEN(NOM) dem:ad.prx there live:NPST where=PRAG
   'my mum lives there somewhere.'
2. *Julatten. Ulp home-ak.*
   Julatten dem:ad.prx home-DAT
   'in Julatten. In a home there.'
3. *Ngul **kana**=le mami ngathn pal therk-nhan. Monday.*
   then OK=PRAG mum 1sgGEN(NOM) towards return-GO&:NPST Monday
   'So my mum's going to come back, on Monday.'
4. ***Kana**=le nhul aka nhiinhin thonmarr.*
   OK=PRAG 3sg(NOM) here reside:RDP:NPST forever
   '[But this time] she's going to stay [in Pormpuraaw] forever'.
   [KTh_AJ27Jan2004 Conversation]

---

167 There would seem to be an interesting parallel between this usage of *kana* and one use of English *directly*, as noted by a character in Peter Carey's *Illywhacker* (1985 [1999]: 68):

> I was always offended by what I understood to be the Irish sense of the word 'directly' which did not mean, as it appeared to, something that would be done in a direct manner, immediately, without delay, but rather the opposite – it would be done indirectly, after taking time, having a smoke, wandering about, having a piss down the back and then approaching the object under discussion along a meandering sort of a path. It meant maybe. Or later.

The first two lines of (684) establish where the speaker's mother currently resides. Having done this, the speaker goes on to state that his mother will be coming back to Pormpuraaw on Monday, using *kana=le* 'OK' to mark the shift from describing her living in Julatten to her coming to Pormpuraaw. In the fourth line, this particle is employed to mark a further shift in focus from her travelling to Pormpuraaw to the fact that she will thereafter be living in Pormpuraaw. The same can be seen in (685), an excerpt from a story about the first time the speaker and his siblings had seen a plane:

(685) 1. "*pam-an ngan=okun yancm ulp*"
man-DAT what=DUB go:P.IPFV dem:ad.prx
'[we said:] "oh man, what could that thing be, going along?" '
2. "*yoorrnhurr nhaath-nhat ngamp ulp*"
first.time see-GO&:P.PFV 1pl:incl(NOM) dem:ad.prx
'"it's the first time we've seen that" '
3. *ngancn ulp **kana**.*
1pl:excl(NOM) dem:ad.prx **ok**
"then we alright."
4. ***Kana**, may ulp ngancn mungka-rr*
ok VEG dem:ad.prx 1pl:excl(NOM) eat-P.PFV
'Okay, we ate some food.'
5. *therk-m ulp ngancn nhakankath-an*
return-P.IPFV dem:ad.prx 1pl:excl(NOM) home-DAT
'and we went home'
6. ***kana**=le nhamump.*
ok=PRAG there
"from there okay."
7. (*Ngul ngancn ulp nhemanp still schoolak ngancn jet inhul book ulp nhaathm ngancn parran*)
('then when we were still at school, we kids saw that jet in a book.')
[KTh_GJ15Oct2002 Narrative PlaneSighting]

In the third line, *kana* 'OK' marks that the speaker believes that he has successfully established the first episode of this extract, the sighting of the plane, and intends to move on to describe the next part of the story. The significance of the break between the plane sighting and the children going back to camp to eat is emphasized by using *kana* 'OK' both as the head of the clause *ngancn ulp kana* (translated by the speaker as "then we alright") and to start the following line. *Kana* 'OK' then reappears in the sixth line, to mark a further thematic break between the return to normal life (as described in lines 3 and 4) and the later seeing a plane in a schoolbook (in line 6). In all of these cases, I take *kana*'s primary function as marking this thematic break, rather than expressing that things are 'alright' (as the language expert's literal translation of line 3 might suggest). This is supported by the fact that *kana* 'OK' is frequently used in the description of states and events that the speaker clearly does not support. For example, example (686) quotes the speech of a group of people looking for a man who went missing during a bush trip. One of the search party points out the tracks of the missing man near a river, then uses *kana* 'OK' to mark a moment of realization, as he infers that the man was taken by a crocodile:

(686) "*koo, inhungun... Awoy, kana, minh-al katpa-rr, minh-al patha-rr.*"
oh   dem:pro:DAT yes OK meat-ERG grasp-P.PFV meat-ERG bite-P.PFV
'oh, [look] there... yes, okay, a crocodile (must have) got him, a crocodile bit him'
[KTh_AC13Sep2002 Conversation]

Clearly the quoted speaker does not think that it is 'okay' that the man was taken by a crocodile. Like the 'finished' sense of *kana* detailed above, *kana* 'OK' seems to carry some sense of completion or conclusion, but in this case it relates more to the full establishment of a proposition or a discourse episode than to the perfectivity of the event described.[168]

It is striking how similar are the functions of Kuuk Thaayorre *kana*, Yir Yoront *kana* and Kugu Nganhcara *kana* (as well as cognate terms in other more distant languages, e.g. *kan* in Wik Mungkan [Sayers 1976] and Wik Ngathan [Sutton 1995], *gana* in Yidiny [Dixon 1977], Djabugay [Alpher 2004b] and Guugu Yimidhirr [Haviland 1979], and *kana* in Pakanh [Alpher 2004b],). This, together with cognate forms in a wide range of other Pama-Nyungan languages (albeit with quite different meanings), leads Alpher (2004b:424) to reconstruct **kana* 'finished, ready'.

9.1.2 *Yarriy* 'thus'

The particle *yarriy* 'thus' is typically used in order to integrate a quote, enactment or other representation of an event into spoken discourse. Through the use of *yarriy*, the speaker asserts that the indexed item illustrates the point they are trying to make. In most cases *yarriy* is translatable by the English *thus*, *like this* or *like that*. Example (687) illustrates the use of *yarriy* to introduce quoted speech:

---

[168] The kinds of discourse boundaries marked by *kana* 'ok' are not typologically unusual (cf. Stirling 2001). To take just a few examples, significant shifts in time, setting or points of view are commonly marked by 'differential subject' marking (Stirling 1993) or the switch from zero topic anaphora to full NPs in Chamorro (Scancarelli 1985) and Hebrew (Ariel 1990). It is likely that these discourse boundaries also have implications for Thaayorre anaphoric expression, but a quantitative study showing this is yet to be carried out. The particle *alright* in Pormpuraaw English (and many other varieties of Aboriginal English) also functions in a very similar way. This discourse usage of Kuuk Thaayorre *kana* also has a close parallel in the use of Bininj Gun-Wok *bonj* (Evans 1992).

(687) *peln   yarriy yik-r:*   "*ongkorr pancr   rirk*"
       3pl(NOM) thus say-P.PFV "PROHIB shame DO:IMP"
       'they said: "don't be shy"'
       [KTh_GJ16Oct2002 Narrative MelbourneTrip]

The form *yarriy* is historically derived from the imperative form of the verb *yan* 'go' (*yarr*), plus the particle *ii* 'there'. The form *yarri'i* (cf. *i'i* 'here') is also attested and is assumed to contrast with *yarriy* either semantically or discursively. The exact nature of this contrast is as yet unknown, however, since *yarri'i* is poorly represented in my data and therefore will not be discussed further. The variants *yarriy* and *arriy*, however, appear to be in free variation with both often used by a single speaker. For consistency, I transcribe both as the conservative allomorph *yarriy* since the contrast appears to be purely phonetic.

The different kinds of quotation or illustration that *yarriy* may introduce are outlined below. Following that is a discussion of the morphosyntax of the constuction(s).

9.1.2.1 Illustration: quoted speech

Yarriy may combine with a range of verbs describing speech, in order to introduce a quotation, such as in (688)–(689):

(688) *nhunt   yarriy yik*   *ngathun* "*pam ngathn   nhamp Dan*"
       2sg(NOM) thus   speak:IMP   1sgDAT   man   1sgGEN(NOM) name Dan"
       'you [should] say to me "my man's name is Dan"'
       [KTh_AC21Aug2002 Conversation]

(689) *ngay   explain-m   rirk-m...   yarriy:*
       1sg(ERG) explain-TR do-P.IPFV   thus
       "*wacirr   thowol   kutpol   inhul*"
       correctly play:IMP   football(ACC) this.one
       'I was explaining to them, like this: "play football properly!"'
       [KTh_AC21Aug2002 Conversation]

The verb of the main clause is frequently left out, in a construction similar to the colloquial English quotative construction *s/he was like, "X"*, as illustrated by (690):

(690) *nhul   yarriy kaar=p*   "*woy! Ngay   awi'i*"
       3sg(NOM) thus   NEG=PRAG   hey   1sg(NOM)   here
       'she never said "hey, I'm here!"'
       [KTh_AC14Nov2002 Narrative LosingIrma]

Example (690) also demonstrates that *yarriy* may be negated.

9.1.2.2 Illustration: quoted thought

The use of *yarriy* in reporting a thought or belief is very close to the introduction of quotative speech:

(691) ngancn   yarriy ngeey-m: "kee! [...]"
       1pl:excl(NOM) thus   think-P.IPFV hey
       'then we were thinking: "hey! [maybe Dad and Mum have had an accident]"'
       [KTh_GJ15Oct2002 Narrative PlaneSighting]

9.1.2.3 Illustration: verbal description

Yarriy may be used to anaphorically refer to a verbal description. As it can be taken for granted that most verbal descriptions are illustrations of some kind, this function can be taken as emphasizing that the particular description is really key to the matter at hand. This is exemplified by (505), the second clause of which stresses that the emotion was an ongoing state, rather than a momentary experience:

(505') missed-m rirk-r   pelnan. Ngay   yarriy=p   nhiin-m.
        miss-TR   do-P.PFV   3plACC 1sg(NOM)   thus=PRAG   sit-P.IPFV
        'I missed them [my family]. That's how I was feeling'.
        [KTh_GJ16Oct2002 Narrative MelbourneTrip]

In (692), the purpose of *yarriy* is to exhort the audience to follow the verbal instructions given previously:

(692) wacirr thowol   kutpol   inhul.   Yarriy nhurr!
       right   play:IMP   football(ACC) this.one   thus   2pl(ERG)
       'play football properly! You [should do it] like that'
       [KTh_AC21Aug2002 Conversation]

9.1.2.4 Illustration: pantomimic gesture

There is widespread use of pantomimic gesture in Kuuk Thaayorre narratives. Where a speaker wants to draw particular attention to their enactment, or explicitly point out that it represents the action of a protagonist, they may introduce (or sometimes follow) it with *yarriy*.

(693) ngul ulp   ngay   raak   koorre nhaawr,   yarriy!
       then dem:ad.prx 1sg(NOM)   PLACE behind look.at:P.PFV   thus
       'then I looked back, like this!' [speaker turns to look over his shoulder]
       [KTh_AC14Nov2002 Narrative LosingIrma]

(694) yarriy punth wan-r rirk
     thus arm(NOM) tell-P.PFV DO:NPST
     [speaker raises hand] 'like this she pointed'
     [KTh_GJ16Oct2002 Narrative MelbourneTrip]

9.1.2.5 Illustration: live action/event

Finally, a master demonstrating their craft to a novice (e.g. an elder showing schoolchildren how to make a spear), will repeatedly utter *yarriy!* – often in isolation – to draw attention to a particular action. Similarly, if a speaker notices an event in their surrounds which illustrates their point (e.g. if they are talking about how birds eat a particular fruit, then they see a bird eating this fruit), they might point and utter *yarriy!*.

9.1.2.6 Morphosyntax of *yarriy* 'thus'

Although word order is not rigidly fixed, *yarriy* tends to appear in one of three positions: (a) immediately preceding a predicate referring to the event illustrated (i.e. before *wont* 'fall' if it is the falling that is being mimed, or before *yik* 'speak' if it is speech that is being quoted, e.g. (688)); (b) immediately preceding or following (sometimes with overlap) the illustration itself (whether the illustration is a non-verbal gesture/enactment or a verbal quotation, e.g. (693)); or (c) in place of the constituent anaphorically referred to, e.g. (505). The first (and, oftentimes, the third) of these positions corresponds with that of adverbs, which might be predicted given *yarriy*'s somewhat adverbial role in the clause. This order may be permuted, though, where *yarriy* is in particular focus, as in the following example:

(695) yarriy ngay yik-r ...
     thus 1sg(NOM) speak-P.PFV
     'And I said: ...'
     [KTh_GJ16Oct2002 Narrative MelbourneTrip]

9.1.3 Analogical *kar* 'like'

The particle *kar* is a connective used to liken one phrase or clause to another. Most often, as in (696), *kar* 'like'connects two noun phrases; this is taken to be its primary function.

(696) nhul koo.miing kar pam nhangnip nhangn
     3sg(NOM) face(NOM) like man father 3sgGEN
     'he looks like his father' (lit. 'he is like his father in the face')
     [KTh_ACh05Oct2002 Conversation]

Although they differ in vowel length, *kar* 'like' may be historically related to the negative particle *kaar*. The semantics of the two are plausibly related since, as Smith and Johnson (2000: 437) put it: "if X is merely LIKE Y, then X is NOT Y". Historical reconstruction would be required to prove this, but it is conceivable that the vowel was either lengthened due to the obligatory stress attributed to the negative particle, or shortened in this unstressed position. In Kugu Nganhcara a single form (*ka'i*) is used for both this semblative function and negation, likewise the Wik Mungkan negator *ke'*, which can also mean 'similar to' (Ray forthcoming). The Kayardild particle *maraka* encodes a similar association between 'like' and 'counterfactual' (Evans 1995a: 378–382).

As a highly grammaticalized element, *kar* has many functions. I take the most basic of these to be likening one (head) NP to another (modifying) NP which is immediately preceded by *kar*. The fact that two separate NPs are involved is indicated by the fact that both must take the case-marking relevant to the head NP's role in the clause, as seen in (697).

(697) wa'ar   pam.thaawaarr-an   nhul   kar   paath-thurr
      jellyfish dangerous-ERG   3sg(ERG)   like fire-ERG
      thaathi-rr   nganh   yangkar
      sting-P.PFV   1sgACC   leg(ACC)
      'the venomous jellyfish stung me on the leg like fire'
      [Hall 1972: 104]

However, the two constituents also seem to form a higher-level NP, as evidenced by the fact that the proprietive enclitic =*kaak* in example (698) attaches to the second NP, although it is the first (or both NPs together) which it modifies semantically (i.e. the addressee has a face, not a baby):

(698) nhunt   koo.miing   kar   parr_r   meenmrr=kaak
      2sg(NOM)   face   like   child   baby=REL.PROP
      'you have a face like a baby'
      [Anon.]

As well as co-occurring with a verbal predicate and under the scope of the relational proprietive (e.g. (697) and (698)), *kar* also appears with a predicate-like function in verbless clauses:

(699) kuta   kar   pam
      dog(NOM)   like   man
      'dogs are like people'
      [KTh_AC10Aug2002 Conversation]

It may also be used to introduce an illustrative example (similar to English *like* or *for instance*), with the meaning 'the following is an example of what I am talking about'. In (700), then, the speaker indexes a nearby dog as a token of the class of dogs he is talking about.

(700) *kuta... kar kuta ngith wun... nganip-i yumpi-rr*
dog like dog(NOM) dem:dist lie:NPST father-ERG make-P.PFV
'dogs, like that dog over there, god up there made [them]'
[KTh_AC10Aug2002 Conversation]

In other clauses, the illustrative example might be a fictional 'for instance' description of the type of event that might occur (as seen in (701), uttered by the speaker as an example of he and his brother's being close), or to make a generalized statement about an entity (702).

(701) *kar mimp wuuthaw*
like clothes(ACC) share:NPST
'for instance [we might] share clothes'
[KTh_EN09Oct2002 Conversation]

(702) *pipe inhul-thurr log cabin kar path-r kaal.kurrc*
pipe this.one-ERG log cabin(ACC) like bite-NPST cool
'with this pipe, log cabin [tobacco] smokes coolly'
[KTh_ME02Oct2002 Conversation]

The rest of this section will be spent detailing the more extended functions of this particle. Firstly, *kar* has a hedge-like usage (703)–(704) which is closely related to its basic likening function.

(703) *peln kar pormp-an pit-r inside*
3pl(ERG) like house-DAT keep-NPST inside
'they [crocodiles] live in something like a house underwater'
[KTh_AC13Sep2002 Conversation]

(704) *pam thono... kar ii-th-iparr turn, thono ii-rr-ikarr*[169]
man one(NOM) like there-to-south turn one(NOM) there-towards-north
'one man is... sort of turned south, and one to the north'
[Anon. Elicitation Man&Tree]

---

[169] I attribute the use here of the unconventional allomorph of *ungkarr* 'north' (?*ikarr*) used here to the age of the speaker (~thirteen). There seems to be some regularization of the directional paradigm among younger speakers that will not be explored further here.

The second extended function of *kar* is to introduce an explanation:

(705) *ngamp   nhangun   kaalath,   kar kulam thono   angarr   yancnh*
       1pl:incl(NOM) 3sgDAT   believe:IMP   like path one(ACC) ANGARR   go:SBJ
       'we must believe in him, because [he is the] one path [we] can go by'
       [KTh_GJ18Jan2004 Narrative Christmas]

The English particle *as* exhibits a similar polysemic link between likening and explanation (e.g. *her hands are cold as ice* versus *he couldn't leave as he was stuck to the chair*).

The third extended use I call 'fictive'. With this use, *kar* typically marks the report of erroneous (previously held) beliefs:

(706) *ngay   kar ngeey-m   nhunt   kar sixteen=nhurr=p*
       1sg(ERG)   like think-P.IPFV   2sg(NOM)   like sixteen=ONLY=PRAG
       'I thought you were just sixteen'
       [Anon., confirmed LN02Oct2002]

It seems that, with this function at least, *kar* takes the whole clause in its scope, as evidenced by its varied placement in examples (707)–(708).

(707) *nhiplin kar yak-a   patha-rr.   Kar minh-al=rr   patha-rr*
       2sgACC   like snake-ERG   bite-P.PFV like MEAT-ERG=PRAG   bite-P.PFV
       "[we thought] you two might have been bitten by a snake or by a crocodile."
       [KTh_GJ15Oct2002 Narrative PlaneSighting]

(708) *ngay   ngeey-r   kar parr_r   nhurr   thaa+munthi-rr*
       1sg(ERG) hear-P.PFV   like child(NOM)   2pl(NOM)   mouth+sink-P.PFV
       'I thought you kids had drowned!'
       [KTh_GJ15Oct2002 Narrative PlaneSighting]

This 'fictive' function could be viewed as a subtype of irrealis. *Kar* 'like' also appears in (irrealis) clauses with (directive) deontic mood such as (709).

(709) *nhangknnhunt   kar nhaath-e*
       2sgRFL   like look.at-RFL:NPST
       'you should look at yourself!' [retort to teasing]
       [KTh_EN14Aug2002 Conversation]

The final extended function of *kar*, the marking of conditionality, is also associated with irrealis aspect. This can be seen in the following:

(710) ngay   kar   pormp-an   therk-nhan
      1sg(NOM) like   house-DAT return-GO&:NPST
      ngay   kuta   ngathn   piinth   reek-nhan
      1sg(ERG) dog   1sg(ACC)   bone(ACC)   give-GO&:NPST
      "If I go home I'll give my dog a bone"
      [KTh_EN04Aug2002 Elicitation]

The counterfactual implicature associated with the 'fictive' usage is weakened to neutral status here. The use of *kar* 'like' in subordinate conditional clauses is explored in (§12.1.2.1).

9.1.4 Contrastive *wuump*

By including the particle *wuump* in a clause, the speaker contrasts two states of affairs. In its basic function, *wuump* is used to contrast two entities or scenarios (either real or imagined). This contrastive construction may be either biclausal or monoclausal.

In the biclausal construction, the focused clause (expressing that which is central to the speaker's message) occurs <u>without</u> *wuump* (711.2), while the background against which it is set contains *wuump* (711.1). The focused clause may either precede (711) or follow (711.2) the background clause:

(711) 1. nhinh   ngay   wuump   wal.meerem   name   nhangkn
         2sgACC   1sg(NOM)   CONTR   remember   name   2sgGEN(ACC)
         ngay,   Alice   nhunt...
         1sg(NOM) Alice   2sg(NOM)
         'I know your name, you're Alice...'
      2. ngay   pam nhangkn   nhamp   ngay   pam.ngongkom
         1sg(NOM)   man 2sgGEN(ACC)   name(ACC)   1sg(NOM)   lack.knowledge.of
         '[but] I can't remember the name of your man'
         [KTh_AC21Aug2002 Conversation]

(712) yoorr kaar=p   nhiina-n-r   pokon, kanangkarr wuump
      now   NEG=PRAG sit-V^-P.PFV   NO   long.ago   CONTR
      'today we don't plant [those vegetables]. Unlike the old days'
      [KTh_AC22Jul2002 Narrative]

In the monoclausal construction, the situation described is contrasted with an alternative situation that has either been established previously in the discourse, or is pragmatically understood:

(713) *yoorr wuump peln   yan   high.school-ak*
 now CONTR 3pl(NOM) go:NPST high.school-DAT
 'nowadays they go to high school [unlike in my day]'
 [KTh_AJ-IC-**GJ**26Nov2002 Narrative/Conversation]

Wuump may also be combined with the dubitative enclitic =*okun* (§9.1.5) to contrast one situation or event with another possible, potential, or imagined alternative situation or event:

(101') *paanth   pitit-nh   wuump=ul=okun*
 woman(ACC) hold:RDP-SBJV CONTR=3sg(ERG)=DUB
 "if he had a wife, alright"
 ngul pul   wupan
 then 3du(NOM) temporary
 "they just temporary"
 [KTh_ACh05Oct2002]

The interrogative function of *wuump* can be understood as asking the addressee to confirm whether the state of affairs described is true or desirable (in contrast to an implied alternative state of affairs). Consider the following:

(714) *ngay   may   wuump rint-nh   ngampalin*
 1sg(ERG) VEG(ACC) CONTR cook-SBJV 1pl:incl:DAT
 'shall I cook something for us?'
 [KTh_MF20Aug2002 Elicitation]

(715) *ngay   wal ngathn   waawath-r,*
 1sg(ERG) bag 1sgGEN(ACC) search:RDP-NPST
 nhunt   wuump nhaawr?
 2sg(ERG) CONTR look.at:P.PFV
 'I'm looking for my bag. Have you seen it?'
 [KTh_MF20Aug2002 Elicitation]

In (714) the interlocutor is asked to choose between a situation in which the speaker prepares some food, and an implied alternative scenario of the food's not being cooked. In (715), the speaker asks whether the addressee has seen her bag (or not). *Wuump*'s interrogative function is thus related to the basic use inasmuch as it presents the addressee with two contrastive scenarios between which they are asked to choose.

Wuump may appear in any position in the clause. Variations in word order do not appear to affect its scope.

9.1.5 Dubitative =okun

The DUBitative enclitic =*okun* is related to other epistemic forms (notably ignorative pronouns (§5.2) and *wuump* 'contrastive' (§9.1.4)) by its association with a lack of knowledge on the speaker's part, as made explicit in (716).

(716) ngawiiyokun ngan=okun!
       I.don't.know what=DUB
       "I don't know what it could be"
       [KTh_GJ15Oct2002 Narrative PlaneSighting]

=*Okun* is frequently used to disambiguate the indefinite interpretation of ignoratives from their many other functions (e.g. interrogative). Hence the indefinite interpretation of *wanhul* 'who' in (717) and of *wanthanngun* 'where at' in (718.2):

(717) wanhul=okun mungka-rr
       who=DUB   eat-P.PFV
       'somebody must've eaten it'
       [KTh_MF20Aug2002 Elicitation]

(718) 1. ngay   wal   waawath-r,
           1sg(NOM)   bag(ACC)   search:RDP-NPST
           'I'm looking for my bag'
       2. ngay   wanthanngun=okun   thaka-rr
           1sg(NOM)   where$_{LOC}$=DUB   leave-P.PFV
           'I left it somewhere'
           [KTh_MF20Aug2002 Elicitation]

In the absence of an ignorative, =*okun* generally functions to introduce a possible world or state-of-affairs which the speaker does not have sufficient evidence to assert. It can thus be understood as modally non-committal. This use is seen in the simple expression of possibility (e.g. in (719)–(720)), avoiding any commitment as to the likelihood of an event's transpiring, seen in the following examples:

(719) yup=okun   ngay   yan   Waar.Paant-ak
       soon=DUB   1sg(NOM) go:NPST Waar.Paant-DAT
       'maybe later I'll go out to Waar-Paant'
       [KTh_ECh02Oct2002 Conversation]

(720) trouble=okun yan   yup
       trouble=DUB   go:NPST soon
       'I might get into trouble' [lit. trouble might come]
       [KTh_AC14Nov2002 Narrative LosingIrma]

The possible world described might alternatively represent an abstraction of the kinds of events that happen in the real world, in opposition to specific instantiations that have happened (this is a function also performed by *kar* 'like', §9.1.3). This can be seen in (721), in which the speaker reflects on the kinds of behaviour that typify fraternal relationships.

(721) *pul   pam.kunyangkar=okun   wuth-nhan*
       2du(NOM) brother(NOM)=DUB   share-GO&NPST
       'brothers might share [things]'
       [KTh_GJ06Dec2002 Elicitation]

=*Okun* may also be employed in the description of a fact or event that the speaker imagines to be the case – or to at least be possible – but does not have sufficient evidence to judge (722).

(722) *city   ngamal=okun, kar   Cairns ulp*
       city   big=DUB   like Cairns dem:ad.prx
       yoorr   yokunmanorrp   ngamal yomparru-rr
       now   same.way   big   transform-P.PFV
         "it [Melbourne] might be a big place like Cairns now"
       [KTh_GJ16Oct2002 Narrative MelbourneTrip]

This latter use is related to =*okun*'s function as a hedge. This hedge function is seen in example (723), in which the speaker describes a scene from a mythical story in which a woman is attacked by bolts of lightning. The verbal description transcribed here was accompanied by gestures to the speaker's arms and legs at the points at which he imagines (but has no evidence to prove) the girl might have been injured.

(723) *paanth   inh=okun   thernga-rr, pirka-rr,*
       woman(ACC) dem:sp.prx=DUB   hit-P.PFV   swipe-P.PFV
       thatparr,   thutha-rr   prrk!
       lightening pull-P.PFV IDPH
       'this woman might have had this arm hit, struck by lightning, struck off, whack!'
       "he break this arm, and this one... lightning no friend"
       [KTh_AC14Oct2002 Narrative PormprRintm]

In example (724), a language expert is describing a video clip in which a man is tending a pot on a fire. He suggests that he might be making tea, but is unsure of the actual contents of the pot and therefore attaches the dubitative clitic to mark the tea as being presumed rather than known.

(724) *may tea=okun riint-r*
VEG tea(ACC)=DUB cook-NPST
'he's making tea, perhaps'
[KTh_GJ19Oct2002 Elicitation StagedEvents140]

=Okun is also commonly employed to express disjunction, with which function it always appears at least twice in the clause, though not necessarily on the coordinands (8). Disjunction is nowadays largely achieved using the English loanword *or*, often in conjunction with *=okun* (292):

(8) 1. *T.A. ngancn katpi-rr*
T.A.(ACC) 1pl:excl(ERG) grasp-P.PFV
'we caught T.A. [airline]'
2. *T.A.=okun Ansett katpi-rr=okun*
T.A.(ACC)=dub Ansett(ACC) grasp-P.PFV=DUB
'either T.A. or Ansett [airline]'
[KTh_GJ16Oct2002 Narrative MelbourneTrip]

(292') *may tea nhunt wanthantharr mungk-r? milk-ak=okun or ngotn?*
VEG tea(ACC) 2sg(ERG) how eat-NPST milk-DAT=DUB or black
'how do you have your tea? with milk or black?'
[KTh_MF20Aug2002 Conversation]

=Okun also combines with the NEGative particle *kaar* to form an 'impossiblity construction'. This is described in §11.3.2.

=Okun's status as an enclitic (rather than a suffix or free particle) is evidenced by four key facts:

1. it may never occur clause-initially;
2. it may intervene between a nomen and another enclitic (e.g. proprietive *=kaak*, (725), cf. §4.2.8);
3. it never intervenes between a nomen and an affixed case marker (726);
4. it attaches to forms of almost any word class (as seen in the examples above)

(725) *nhul paanth yiirram=okun=kaak*
3sg(NOM) woman different(ACC)=DUB=REL.PROP
'maybe he has another woman'
[Anon.]

(726) *yak-a=okun patha-rr*
snake-ERG=DUB bite-P.PFV
'a snake might have bitten [them]'
[KTh_GJ15Oct2002 Narrative PlaneSighting]

9.1.6 *Minc* 'against expectations'

The form *minc* has already been introduced as an adjective meaning 'true' and an adverb meaning 'really' (cf. §3.3.5). This form also functions as a particle to contrast expectations or intentions with events as they actually transpire.[170] I label this arguably 'mirative' (DeLancey 1997) sense of *minc* 'against expectations' ('UNXP'). Hence in (727), *minc* appears in a clause describing the intended event of orange-cutting that was in fact thwarted by the actor-subject's cutting his finger instead. Similarly, in (728) *minc* appears in a clause describing a boy looking in a hole expecting to find a frog in it, which contrasts with the actual outcome of his finding a rat emerging from it:

(727) yiki!   pam   ith
      yikes   man(ERG^)   dem:dist
      nhul   minc   may   orange   knife-nthurr   yak-nhata=th
      3sg(ERG)   UNXP   VEG   orange(ACC)   knife-ERG   cut-CTF=PR
      'yikes! That man meant to cut the orange with the knife [but cut his finger]'
      [KTh_EN15Dec2002 Elicitation Cut&Break18]

(728) nhul   minc   thatr   waath-m   ngul   minh   kaal   ripi-rr
      3sg(ERG)   UNXP   frog(ACC)   search-P.IPFV then   MEAT   rat(NOM)   exit-P.PFV
      'he was looking for the frog but a rat came out [of the hole]'
      [KTh_MF17Sep2002 Narrative FrogStory]

This function of *minc* relates to its function as a degree verb, in which is emphasizes the (often unexpected) degree to which something is true (cf. §9.2.5). In examples such as (727)–(728) above, *minc* 'against expectations' somewhat resembles a counterfactual particle, in that it marks an irrealis event that contrasts with an actualized state of affairs. It may seem curious that a form that also means 'true' should be used with seemingly irrealis force. However, *minc* does not mark the counterfactual state of affairs per se, but rather the <u>contrast</u> between the actual state of affairs and those expected (not unlike English *actually*). Hence in clauses like (729.2), *minc* 'against expectations' appears within a clause describing the <u>actual</u> state of affairs (the same is also seen in example (214) above):

(729) 1. nhunt   money-ak   yik-m,   ngay   kana   yoorr   reek-nhata=th
         2sg(NOM)   money-DAT   say-P.IPFV   1sg(ERG)   CMP   today   give-CTF=PR
         'you asked for money, I would have given you [some]'

---

170 This is somewhat similar to the Kayardild form *nginja*, used to describe things going against the expected outcome (e.g. a lack of rain despite the presence of black clouds; see Evans 1995a: 382–384).

2. | ngay | money | ngay | pokon | minc |
    |------|-------|------|-------|------|
    | 1sg(NOM) | money(ACC) | 1sg(NOM) | NO | UNXP |

    'but I have no money'
    [KTh_DJ04Feb2004 Elicitation]

In examples like (729), *minc* appears in a clause that is adjacent to an explicitly counterfactual-marked clause. This is by no means a requirement, however. In examples like (730) (and (214) above), there is no explicit mention of an irrealis, expected, counterfactual state of affairs – the contrast between expectations and actual events is only signalled by the presence of *minc* 'against expectations'.

(730) | parr_r | minc | ith | nhaath-nharr | pul |
      |--------|------|-----|--------------|-----|
      | child(ACC) | UNXP | dem:dist | see-GO&:IMP | 3du(ERG) |

'[to their surprise] they saw this child [alone in the bush]'
[KTh_FT08Feb2004 Narrative Adoptee]

Example (730) raises the somewhat perplexing fact that *minc* 'against expectations' appears to intrude within a noun phrase (in this case, *parr_r ith* 'this child'), although the particle is clausal in scope. This could perhaps be explained by arguing that *parr_r* 'a child' and *ith* 'that' form independent noun phrases, though this is very much a post hoc explanation.

9.2 Adverbs

9.2.1 Spatial adverbs

9.2.1.1 *Pal* 'towards'

The most frequently used spatial adverb is *pal* 'towards', which marks the event described as oriented towards a deictic centre. The default deictic centre is the locus of the speech event, which encompasses the locations of both speaker and addressee(s). This can be seen in the following:

(731) | piinth-r | ngul | nhul | pal=ul | yan |
      |----------|------|------|--------|-----|
      | grow-NPST | then | 3sg(NOM) | towards=3sg(NOM) | go:NPST |

"when he [cyclone] grows up then he come"
[KTh_**AJ**-GJ03Feb2004 Conversation]

The speaker employs *pal* 'towards' in example (731) in order to describe the movement of the cyclone nearing Pormpuraaw, where the speech event took place. However, the locus of the deictic centre frequently shifts. A fairly minimal shift (seen in (284) and (733)) involves a narrowing from the speech event as a whole (encompassing both speaker and addressee) to whichever of the interlocutors is not involved as either theme (or 'figure', in Talmy's 1978 sense) or source of the motion event described. Thus in clauses with a second person figure-subject (732) *pal* typically describes orientation towards the speaker. Conversely, in clauses with a first person subject (733) *pal* typically describes orientation towards the addressee:

(732) nhunt   raak   ngan   pal   therk-nhan?
      2sg(NOM)   TIME   what   towards   return-GO&:NPST
      'when will you come back?'
      [KTh_AJ27Jan2004 Conversation]

(733) ngay   pal   kalal
      1sg(ERG)   towards   carry:RDP:NPST
      'I'll bring [it] to you'
      [KTh_BN1Oct2002 Conversation]

These patterns of interpretation are the result of pragmatic implicature, rather than forming part of the lexical semantics of *pal*. These implicatures stem from the dual facts that *pal* 'towards' marks events as 'oriented towards the deictic centre', and that the default deictic centre is the speech event. Thus when one member of this speech event (i.e. either speaker or addressee) is themself the figure whose motion is being tracked, the deictic centre shifts to the other interlocutor. So because (732) describes the return of the addressee, she cannot herself form the reference point, leaving the speaker alone implicated as reference point. Example (732) thus describes the movement of the addressee towards the speaker at a future point in time. This implicature is sufficiently strong that *pal* 'towards' is often the sole clue to the identity of an elided recipient argument. Hence (734) is a common way to make a request.

(734) ngok   pal   reek
      beer(ACC)   towards   give:IMP
      'give me a beer'
      [Anon.]

This implicature is defeasible, however.[171] Example (735), for instance, was uttered to instruct the addressee to pick up the ball (towards herself) rather than to move the ball (up) towards the speaker:

---

[171] Indeed, it is probably the fact that the first person recipient is implied rather than overtly encoded that makes this such a common format for requests. This fits with the tendency – both among the Thaayorre and worldwide – to avoid explicit mention of the addressee in polite/indirectness requests.

(735) ball   ulp   pal   mi'irr
      ball(ACC) dem:ad.prx   towards   pick.up:IMP
      'pick up that ball!'
      [KTh_EF14Dec2002 Elicitation / Conversation]

The deictic centre can further shift to a locus independent of both speaker and addressee. This is illustrated by example (736), uttered by EN to a group of people in a house after her cousin ran out of the house and past us down the road.

(736) nhul   ngene   pal   riic-r?
      3sg(NOM)   why   towards   run-NFUT
      'why/where's he running to?'
      [KTh_EN02Oct2002 Conversation]

The subject here is demonstrably moving away from the locus of the speech event, rather than towards it. It seems here that it is the ignorative *ngene* 'why/where' that anchors the deictic particle *pal*.

The deictic centre may alternatively be established by the preceding discourse. Example (737) is taken from a traditional narrative in which a large group of men tried to throw away a boomerang but it kept returning to them. By the time the speaker comes to utter (737), then, it is clear that the story's protagonists (the group of men) form the deictic centre towards which *pal* orients the boomerang's movement:

(737) 1. *thunp-m   peln...*
         throw-P.IPFV   3pl(ERG)
         'they kept throwing [it]'
      2. *pokon! Werngr   pal=p   therk-m*
         NO   boomerang(NOM) towards=PRAG   return-P.IPFV
         'but it didn't work! The boomerang kept returning [to them]'
         [KTh_AC13Sep2002 Narrative Werngr]

Similarly, where a clause contains a locative expression explicitly specifying the goal of the event (e.g. the dative-case NP in (738)), this is the reference point anchoring *pal*:

(738) *paath-un   yaki-rr   pal*
      fire-DAT   cut-P.PFV   towards
      '[she] slices [it] into the flames'
      [Foote and Hall: Primer 9]

Although analogous deictic forms in other languages are often glossed 'hither' – implying motion towards the speaker – their actual usage may not diverge significantly from that of Kuuk Thaayorre *pal*. The cognate Kugu Nganhcara form *pala* certainly appears to have a similar functional range (Smith and Johnson 2000: 452), as do the deictic forms of some more areally and genetically distant languages. The English deictic verb *come*, for instance, may be used to describe motion towards a reference point other than the deictic centre where this reference point has especial discourse salience, as in (739) (cf. Fillmore 1975).

(739) *After four hours of wandering lost in the woods, he* ***came*** *to a clearing*

Pal 'towards' appears in a number of compounds and conventionalized collocations. The first of these, *wanthan pal* 'which direction?' (lit. 'where$_{TRJ}$ towards') is found in the standard Kuuk Thaayorre greeting.

(740) nhunt   wanthan pal   yan?
       2sg(NOM) where$_{TRJ}$ towards go:NPST
       'which way are you going?'
       [KTh_common greeting]

As noted above, ignoratives with interrogative function (such as *wanthan* 'where$_{TRJ}$') are generally interpreted as deictic centre (thus anchoring *pal* 'towards), though they only rarely coincide with the location of the speaker and/or addressee.

The second collocation, *thakr pal* 'facing' (lit. 'front.of.torso towards') describes the static orientation of a figure with an inherent front side (e.g. the people in example (741)):

(741) peln   thakr pal   nhiinhin
       3pl(NOM) front towards   sit:RDP:NPST
       'they are sitting facing [us, the viewers]'
       [KTh_FT10Feb2004 Elicitation RcpPilot8]

The collocation *thakr pal* 'facing' typically describes an orientation towards the speech event, much as does *pal* 'towards' alone. But again, this deictic centre may shift, being alternatively anchored by interrogative ignoratives such as *wanthan* 'where$_{DIR}$' in the following example:

(742) pam inthul,   yuk   punth mal-an   kaatp-r,
       man this.one:EMPH   stick(ACC) arm   right-DAT grasp:RDP-NPST
       nhul   thakr wanthan pal   thanan?
       3sg(NOM)   front where$_{TRJ}$ towards stand:RDP:NPST
       'this man, holding a stick in [his] right hand, which way is he facing'
       [KTh_DJ04Feb2004 Elicitation Man&Tree]

In addition to these two collocations, *pal* 'towards' may be compounded with the deictic adverbs *i'i* 'here', *ii* 'there' and *yuuw* 'far' to form *i'ipal* '[coming] from here', *iipal* '[coming] from there' and *yuupal* '[coming] from far [away]' respectively, as discussed in §9.2.1.2 below, and it is the etymological source of one of the directional prefixes (§9.2.1.3).

9.2.1.2 Other spatial deictic adverbs

Spatial deictic adverbs – a subclass that includes *pal* 'towards' above (cf. §3.3.1.1) – are optional clausal elements that locate the event (or entity in verbless clauses) with respect to physical distance from the deictic centre. The three core forms *i'i* 'here', *ii* 'there', and *yuuw* 'far' form a neat paradigmatic set, as follows:[172]

Table 62. Paradigm of core spatial deictic adverbs.

	i'i 'here'	*ii* 'there'	*yuuw* 'far'
attentional prefix *aw-*	*aw-i'i* 'right here'	*aw-ii* 'right there'	—
allative suffix *-rra*	*i'irra* 'to here'	*iirra* 'to there'	*yuurra* 'to far away'
compounded with *pal* 'towards'	*i'ipal* 'from here'	*iipal* 'from there'	*yuupal* 'from far away'

The distribution of the bare root forms *i'i*, *ii* and *yuuw* – with or without the attentional prefix – is equivalent to that of a dative-case noun phrase. They may thus function as an optional adjunct in an otherwise complete clause (743), or as the locative complement in a locative construction (744), cf. §10.2.5:

(743) *kuta Dan-tam ii   kuta thok   wawarin-r*
dog Dan-ABL there PET cat(ACC) chase:RDP-NPST
'Dan's dog is chasing the cat'
[KTh_LF12Nov2002 Elicitation]

(744) *ngay   aw-i'i*
1sg(NOM) ATTN-here
'I'm right here!'
[KTh_EN04Aug2002]

---

[172] This was first observed by Hall (1972: 442), who adds an additional 'Locative, moving' category, marked by the suffix *-wurra*. Since this form does not appear in my data,, it is not discussed here.

Allative-marked deictic spatial adverbs may fulfil a subset of the syntactic roles performed by dative-marked NPs; namely, representing the path or endpoint of the event described (745). Spatial deictic adverbs compounded with *pal* 'towards', meanwhile, fulfil a subset of the syntactic roles performed by ablative-marked NPs; namely, representing the spatial origin of an event involving motion (746). Note that it is common for spatial deictic adverbs to be apposed to such case-marked NPs, as in (746):

(745) ngay   iirra   yat,   Saturday
      1sg(NOM) to.there go:P.PFV Saturday
      'I went there [to the beach] on Saturday'
      [KTh_AJ27Jan2004 Conversation]

(746) ngay   iipal   Melbourne-mam yat   punguk
      1sg(NOM) from.there Melbourne-ABL go:P.PFV last.time
      'I came up from Melbourne a couple of weeks back'
      [KTh_MF17Sep2002 Elicitation]

There are also rare instances in which a spatial deictic adverb functions as an adnominal modifier, appearing within the noun phrase immediately preceding the (specifier) demonstrative slot:

(747) pam yuupal   ulp=th
      man from.far dem:ad.prx=PRAG
      'those men from far away'
      [Hall 1972: 73]

There are three further deictic adverbs that do not fit neatly within the paradigm: *nhaka* 'in this place', *angunp* 'in that place' and *nheman* 'from that place'. See discussion in §5.3.1.1 of the morphological and functional relationships between these three adverbs and the demonstrative pronouns. The adverbs *ii* 'there' and *yuuw* 'far' are etymologically related to the prefixes *ii-* 'there/proximal' and *yuu-* 'far/distal', which attach to demonstrative pronouns (§5.3.1.1) and directional adverbs (§9.2.1.3). Conversely, the proximal demonstrative pronoun, *inhul* 'this one', in some cases functions as a local adverbial demonstrative (cf. Dixon 2010: 221–61; 2003), sometimes with the attentional prefix *aw-* (749). The speaker of (748) noted that *awi'i* 'right here' could be substituted for *inhul* 'this one' in this example without any noteable change in meaning.

(748) raak rirkr   inhul
      thing shell(NOM) this.one
      'the money [you are looking for] is here'
      [KTh_LN04Aug2002 Elilcitation]

(749) ngay   pinharr Alice aw-inhul
     1sg(NOM) FZ   Alice attn.-this.one
     'I'm Aunt Alice here [description of hand-shaking greeting formula]'
     [KTh_FT10Feb2004 Elicitation RcpPilot13]

9.2.1.3 Directionals

Directionals comprise a set of morphologically complex clausal adjuncts used to locate an entity or event (hereafter referred to as 'figure') with respect to a reference point (hereafter referred to as 'ground') calculated according to one or more of: (a) the set of cardinal directions; (b) the up–down axis defined by gravity; (c) certain geographical landmarks (notably the river); (d) intrinsic features of the ground object. Their morphological inflection may add information about whether the figure is static or in motion, approaching or moving away from the deictic centre, as well as its distance from the deictic centre in the direction described.

Directionals minimally consist of a bound directional root (e.g. *-parr* 'north', *-ungkarr* 'south', etc.) plus an initial prefix coding distance from the deictic centre (i.e. *ii-* 'there (unmarked)', *pal-* 'near' or *yuu-* 'far away'). There are three further, optional morpheme positions, the functions of which are detailed below. The structure of the directional word is summarized in Table 63.

Table 63. Morphological structure of the directional word.

Position 1	Position 2	Position 3	Position 4	Position 5
distance/motion	(orientation)[172]	directional root	(secondary direction)	(river reference)
ii- 'there'	*th-* / *k-* 'to'	*-ungkarr* 'N'	*-uw* 'W'	*-op* 'river'
yuu- 'far'	*-rr* 'towards'	*-iparr* 'S'	*-aw* 'E'	
pal- 'near'	*-l* 'from'	*-kaw* 'E'		
ya- 'going', 'away'	*-ø* 'at'	*-kuw* 'W'		
		-ipan 'Sbank'		
		-kan₁ 'Nbank'		
		-kop 'below'		
		-kan₂ 'above'		
		-korr 'behind/beyond/outside'		
		-kan₃ 'inside'		

Examples (750)–(752) illustrate the contrast between the prefixes in the first, 'distance/motion' position: *ii-* 'there' (750), *yuu-* 'far' (549), *pal-* 'near' (751) and *ya-* 'going' (752):

---

[173] The morphemes of the orientation slot are optional except following *ya-*, which may not immediately precede the directional root.

(750) nhul   ith   ngan   ii-korr   yump-r
      3sg(NOM) dem:dist what   there-at:outside   do-NPST
      'what's that he's making outside?'
      [KTh_EN15Dec2002]

(549') yuu-rr-iparr   wun-m   ngancn...   Thaayorre
       far-towards-south live-P.IPFV 1pl:excl(NOM) Thaayorre
       'we Thaayorre used to live a long way to the south'
       [KTh_AC22Jul2002 Narrative]

(751) pam nhump   nhul   pal-ipan   wonp-r   raak.mele
      man elder(NOM) 3sg(NOM) near-Sbank die-P.PFV homeland
      'the oldfella died just there on the south side of the river, in his homeland'
      [KTh_AJ-**IC**-GJ26Nov2002 Conversation/Narrative]

(752) ya-rr-kuw   yat=ay
      going-towards-west   go:P.PFV=1sg(NOM)
      'I went westwards'
      [KTh_**DW**-CW09Dec2002 Narrative 2Crocs]

The most frequently used prefix, *ii-* 'there', is unmarked for distance, though it carries an implicature of being neither saliently near nor far away due to its paradigmatic opposition to *pal-* and *yuu-*. The four prefixes vary somewhat in their morphological distribution. *ii-* and *yuu-* can form a complete directional term with just a directional root (750) but can also combine with the full range of prefixes in the 'orientation of motion' position (757). *Pal-* can also form a complete directional term with just a directional root (751), but it cannot occur with any of the 'orientation of motion' prefixes. *Ya-* is rarely used in my data, and only appears preceding an 'orientation of motion' prefix (752).

The second directional position is optional. The morphemes of this position are distinguished as follows: (a) *rr-* marks movement towards a place or in a direction, with a focus on the path (753); (b) *th-* marks motion to a place, with a focus on the goal (754); and (c) *l-* marks motion from a place, with a focus on the source (755). The absence of any overt morpheme in this position signifies simple location (756). Because this meaning does not appear to be defeasible (i.e. motion to, towards or from a location is always overtly coded by one of the second position morphemes), Table 63 lists a zero morpheme encoding 'at'. (This zero is not viewed as morphologically substantive, however, and is not transcribed in example sentences.)

(753) *Monday holiday, ngernkan, ngay   ii-rr-iparr-op   yancm*
Monday holiday yesterday 1sg(NOM) there-towards-south-river go:P.IPFV
'on the holiday Monday yesterday, I went down south, riverwards'
[KTh_AJ27Jan2004 Conversation]

(754) *koo ngamp   melnkelnkarr ii-th-iparr   therk*
oh 1pl:incl(NOM) tomorrow   there-to-south return:NPST
'okay, tomorrow we're going to return south [to Pormpuraaw]'
[KTh_AC21Aug2002 Conversation]

(755) *ii-l-ungkarr   yancm,   ngancn   ii-l-iparr   yancm*
there-from-north go:P.IPFV 1pl:excl(NOM) there-from-south go:P.IPFV
'they [Munkan people] came from the north, we came from the south'
[KTh_AC21Aug2002 Conversation]

(756) *ngat   ii-kan   glass-ak   yan*
fish(NOM) there-at:inside glass-DAT go:NPST
'the fish is swimming around inside the glass bowl'
[KTh_EC2Oct2002 BowPed32]

Although *rr-* and *th-* are typically found in the description of motion events, both morphemes are also attested with a 'fictive motion' function. Hence in (757), *iithiparr* 'to the south' is used to describe the traditional lands to which the speaker's family belongs. Although this clause does not describe a motion event per se, the use of the *th-* 'to' directional prefix makes the distance between the speech event and the location described more vivid (much as does the equivalent usage of 'to the south' in the English translation):

(757) *ngancn   ii-th-iparr   wun-m*
1pl(NOM) there-to-south live-P.IPFV
'we [Thaayorre] used to live to the south'
[KTh_AC21Aug2002 Conversation]

Similarly, in (758.2) the 'towards' prefix *rr-* combines with the 'going' prefix *ya-* to denote a broader area (as would be traversed by a moving entity) rather than a specific location. This is done in part to hedge the statement made (i.e. expressing that the hospital was somewhere near where the current plumbers' shed is, not necessarily the same exact location):

(758) 1. *Dennis O'Connor ngan plumbers' shed   ith   thanan...*
         Dennis O'Connor what plumbers' shed(NOM) dem:dist stand:RDP:NPST
         '[where] that Dennis O'Connor or whatever plumbers' shed is...'

2. *ya-rr-iparr-op   than-m.*
   away-towards-south-river stand-P.IPFV
   'around there near the river in the south.'
3. *Nhamunp   kanpa   hospital   than-m*
   at.that.place before hospital(NOM) stand-P.IPFV
   'The hospital used to be there before'
   [KTh_GJ27Jan2004 Conversation]

The third position in the directional word is filled by the set of obligatory directional roots. The first four of these encode the cardinal directions (*-ungkarr* 'north' (755), *-iparr* 'south' (754), *-kuw* 'west' (759) and *-kaw* 'east' (760)). Although, for simplicity, I translate these four forms with their closest English equivalents *north*, *south*, *west* and *east*, it should be noted that the axis labelled 'north' – 'south' is in Kuuk Thaayorre rotated thirty-five degrees clockwise, parallel to the local coastline.

(759) *ii-rr-kuw-op   thuuthuth-m*
       there-towards-west-river crawl:RDP-P.IPFV
       '[the saltwater crocodile] went crawling west towards the river'
       [KTh_**DW**-CW09Dec2002 Narrative 2Crocs]

(760) *ball   otonyciy mantam-ak   thaangk-nhan*
       ball(NOM) hill   small-DAT   climb-GO&:NPST
       ngul renp-nhan   ii-rr-kaw
       then descend-GO&:NPST   there-towards-east
       'the ball goes and climbs the little hill and then goes down it to the east'
       [KTh_EN03Dec2002 Elicitation Moland3]

The next two directional roots, *-kan* 'north bank' (761) and *-ipan* 'south bank' (762.3), refer to the banks of the Chapman river, just south of Pormpuraaw.

(761) *raak   woocorrm   nhumpa-ni-rr   **ii-kan**   Ngumpurr.Nhiinhin*
       place   sacred(ACC) disturbed-V^-P.PFV   there-at:N.bank   place.name
       '[you] stirred up that story place[174] on the north riverbank, Ngumpurr Nhiinhin'
       [KTh_MF20Aug2002 Conversation]

(762) 1. *dinghy pokon, ngancn   canoe   use-m   rirk-m*
         dinghy NO   1pl:excl(ERG)   canoe(ACC)   use-VBLZ   DO-P.IPFV
         '[we had] no dingies, we used to use canoes'

---

174 Sacred sites of ritual significance are usually referred to as 'story places' in Pormpuraaw English.

2. kar yarra New Guinea use-m   rirk-m
   like away New Guinea use-VBLZ DO-P.IPFV
   'like [they] would use off in New Guinea'
3. canoe yokunman-ak ngancn   cross-m   rirk-m   **ii-th-ipan**
   canoe likewise-DAT 1pl:excl(NOM) cross-VBLZ DO-P.IPFV there-to-s.bank
   'we would cross to the south bank in the same kind of canoe'
   [KTh_AJ-IC-**GJ**26Nov2002 Narrative/Conversation]

A further five directional roots encode relational categories defined by the intrinsic characteristics of reference objects (e.g. a house) or local geography. *-Kop* 'down', for example, refers to an area underneath (763) or below (764) the deictic centre or ground object.

(763) peln   raak   ranth-in   pit-r   ii-rr-kop
       3pl(ERG) place   hole-DAT   keep-NPST   there-towards-down
       'they [crocodiles] keep [dead bodies] in underwater caves'
       [KTh_AC13Sep2002 Narrative]

(764) yik-r   ngancnngun: "city Melbourne inh   ii-kop   ii!"
       say-P.PFV 1pl:excl:DAT   city Melbourne dem:sp.prx   there-at:down   there
       '[the pilot] said to us "that's the city of Melbourne down there!"'
       [KTh_GJ16Oct2002 Narrative MelbourneTrip]

These two meanings – 'underneath' and 'below' – can be considered contextual interpretations of a single sense; 'down'. It is similarly possible to offer a monosemous analysis of *-korr* 'beyond', although this directional root spans the etic categories 'behind', 'outside', 'out bush', as seen in (765), (766) and (767) respectively.

(765) nhul   ii-rr-korr   pal   chair-thak   move   rirk-r
       3sg(NOM)   there-towards-beyond   towards   chair-DAT   move   DO-P.PFV
       'she moved backwards [i.e. behind herself] in her chair towards the camera'
       [KTh_EN3Dec2002 Elicitation Cut&Break7]

(766) *Ngul thuc-an   ii-rr-kan   rok-nhan*
       then bush-DAT   there-towards-inside   enter-GO&:NPST
       ngul rip-nhan   ii-rr-korr
       then exit-GO&:NPST   there-towards-outside
       '[the ball] goes into the bushes and then [rolls] outside them again'
       [KTh_EN03Dec2002 Elicitation Moland1]

(767) ngul   ngancn   ii-korr=nhurr   kaamp-m   bush-ak
      then   1pl:excl(NOM)   there-at:outside=ONLY   roast-P.IPFV bush-DAT
      'in those days we'd cook our food [in ground ovens] just out bush there'
      [KTh_AJ-IC-**GJ**26Nov2002 Narrative/Conversation]

-*korr* might be characterized as coding locations as outside the familiar, visible, or 'experienced' environment, in a form of "boundary deixis" (Hoffman 2013).

The final root form, -*kan*, has three distinct senses that defy amalgamation: 'up' (768), 'inside' (769), as well as the 'north bank' sense discussed above (761).

(768) ngancn   pal-kan   thowol-nam
      1pl:excl(NOM)   near-at:up   play-P.IPFV
      'we were playing a little way up [in a tree]'
      [KTh_GJ16Oct2002 PlaneNarrative]

(769) nge'!   ngumpurr   ii-kan   wun
      hey   old.lady(NOM)   there-at:inside   lie:NPST
      '[surprised:] hey! The old woman's lying indoors'
      [KTh_ME02Oct2002 Conversation]

Each of these senses is antonymically related to another of the directional roots: -*kan* 'up' to -*kop* 'down'; -*kan* 'inside' to -*korr* 'beyond'; and -*kan* 'north bank' to -*ipan* 'south bank'.

Towns in the region are conventionally associated with directional terms via metaphors that seem to have their bases in the river flow. Hence Kowanyama (to the southeast of Pormpuraaw) is referred to as -*kan* 'up, in' (770), presumably because it is inland and upriver. By contrast, Cairns is -*kop* 'down' (771), presumably because it is on the (eastern) side of the Great Dividing Range, and hence locally downriver. This contrasts with the pervasive English schema, NORTH IS UP.

(770) ngay   ii-rr-kan   yan,   Kowanyama
      1sg(NOM)   there-towards-up   go:NPST   Kowanyama
      'I'm going up to Kowanyama'
      [KTh_AC22Jul2002 Conversation / Elicitation]

(771) awoy,   ngok   ii-kop   wuump
      yes   water(NOM)   there-at:down   CONTR
      'yes, by contrast [there is] hard liquor down [in Cairns]'
      [KTh_AJ27Jan2004 Conversation]

The penultimate position in the Kuuk Thaayorre directional word is optionally filled by a secondary cardinal direction morpheme. Specifically, the directional roots *ungkarr* 'north' and *-parr* 'south' can combine with the suffixes *-uw* and *-aw* (cf. the roots *-kaw* 'east' and *-kuw* 'west') to produce *-ungkarr-aw* 'northeast', *-ungkarr-uw* 'northwest', *parr-aw* 'southeast' (772), and *-parr-uw* 'southwest'. These (and the suffix of the fifth and final position) are only found following one of the four cardinal direction roots.

(772)   *pam*   *kanangkarr yungar-nam wa'ap*   *ulp*   *ii-parr-aw*
        man(NOM) long.ago   swim-P.IPFV river(ACC) dem:ad.prx there-at:south-east
        'long ago, people used to swim across that river in the southeast'
        [KTh_ME04Jun2005 Narrative Yencr]

The final directional position is optionally filled by the suffix *-op*, which indicates a general association with a river (neither bank in particular, and not necessarily the Chapman River):

(773)   *ith*   *ii-parr-op*   *wa'ap-n*   *mong*   *ulp*   *wun*
        dem:dist there-at:south-river river-DAT many dem:ad.prx lie:NPST
        'at that place on the river down south, there are lots of fish'
        [KTh_AJ3Feb2004 Conversation]

(774)   *korngkon*   *ii-kaw*   *ith*,
        cabbage.palm(NOM) there-at:east dem:dist
        mong   *thanan*   *ii-ngkarr-op,*   Rita.
        many(NOM) stand:RDP:NPST there-at:north-river Rita
        'there are cabbage palms in the east, and lots in the north by the river, at Rita.'
        [KTh_ME04Jun2005 Narrative Yencr]

The Kuuk Thaayorre directionals are high frequency items, often occurring as an adjunct in an otherwise complete clause, as in the following:

(775)   *ngamp*   *ii-rr-kuw*   *ngat-a*   *yan*
        1pl:incl(NOM) there-towards-west fish-DAT go:NPST
        'let's go fishing westwards'
        [KTh_AJ27Jan2004 Elicitation/Conversation]

The only case in which a directional is syntactically required is when functioning as locative complement, and even here it could be substituted by a case-marked noun phrase of other spatial adverb. This locative complement use is illustrated by both (757.1) (in which the main predicate, *wun* 'live', subcategorizes for a locative complement) and (757.2), a verbless locative construction:

(757') 1. ngancn   ii-th-iparr   wun-m
        1pl:excl(NOM) there-to-south live-P.IPFV
        'we [Kuuk Thaayorre] used to live in the south'
    2. peln   ii-rr-ungkarr
        3pl(NOM)   there-towards-north
        'they were towards the north'
        [KTh_AC22Jul2002 Narrative]

Finally, directionals may function as nominal modifiers. In this function, they appear immediately following the full NP, as in the following:

(776) pormpr   ith   ii-kaw   wanthanngun?
      house(NOM) dem:dist there-at:east where$_{LOC}$
      'what's the name of that eastern building?'
      [KTh_EN14Dec2002 Conversation]

(777) bucket   ith   ii-korr   ngathn
      bucket(NOM) dem:dist there-at:beyond 1sgGEN
      'that bucket outside is mine'
      [KTh_EN14Dec2002 Elicitation Demonstrative21]

Examples such as (778) are difficult to classify. On the one hand, the directional here may perform a kind of synecdochic modification of *pormpr* 'house' (i.e. directing the addressee to shut the westward [part of the] house). Alternatively, it may be a simple clausal adjunct (i.e. directing the addressee to perform the house-shutting over there in the west).

(778) pormpr   ii-kuw   thaa+ngeth-ic!
      house(ACC) there-at:west mouth+close-run&:IMP
      'go and close the west [door] of the house!'
      [KTh_ME02Oct2002 Conversation]

9.2.1.4 Topological relation markers (TRMs)

The Kuuk Thaayorre 'topological relation markers' (introduced in §3.3.1.3), are related along a cline from the more clearly adverbial (e.g. *kanpa* 'in front' and *koorr* 'behind' in (779)) to the more clearly postpositional (e.g. *mangkan* 'low' (780)):[175]

---

[175] Smith and Johnson (2000: 417) label analogous Kugu Nganhcara forms 'adverbial operators'.

(779) kuta   kanpa   yan,   kuta thok   pal   koorr   yan
       dog(NOM)   in.front go:NPST PET cat(NOM) towards behind   go:NPST
       'dog walking in front, the cat walking behind'
       [KTh_EN13Aug2002 Elicitation Up&Down]

(780) rope   yuk-un   mangka-n   katha-rr
       rope(ACC)   tree-DAT   low-DAT   bind-P.PFV
       'the rope is tied around the base of the tree'
       [KTh_GJ15Oct2002 Elicitation BowPed55]

The set of topological relation markers has as its core: *(put)pil* 'beside', *wernka* 'between', *kanpa* 'in front', *putpun* 'on top', *koorr* 'behind, outside', *palpal* 'near', *thaapirri* 'close' and *mangka* 'low'. (The peripheral members of this word class will be discussed below.) Each member of this somewhat heterogeneous collection may appear both as the sole exponent of a location (781), or in combination with a ground NP (782), apparently forming a complex locative expression (though see discussion below):

(781) ngul ulp   dye   thak-r   putpun
       then dem:ad.prx dye(ACC)   leave-NPST   on.top
       'then you leave that dye on top [of the cabbage palm shoots]'
       [KTh_ME04Jun2005 Narrative Yencr]

(782) kormun   ii   putpun   otonyciy-ak
       storm(NOM)   there   on.top   hill-DAT
       'the cloud is over the mountain'
       [KTh_GJ15Oct2002 Elicitation BowPed36]

TRMs vary in whether their relationship to the ground NP is reflected morphologically. *(Put)pil* 'beside' and *mangka* 'low' take dative case marking when combined with a dative NP (e.g. in (783) and (780) above), while *wernka* 'between', *kanpa* 'in front', *koorr* 'behind, outside', *palpal* 'near', *thaapirri* 'close' and *putpun* 'on top' do not.[176] This is illustrated by the comparison of (783) with (784):

(783) yuk   pormpr   pil-un   thanan
       tree(NOM)   house   beside-DAT   stand:RDP:NPST
       'the tree is beside the house'
       [KTh_GJ15Oct2002 Elicitation BowPed49]

---

176 It should be noted, however, that *putpun* 'on top' appears to carry a fused locative suffix *-un*.

(784) *yuk   pormpr thaapirri thanan*
      tree(NOM) house   close   stand:RDP:NPST
      'the tree is close to the house'
      [KTh_GJ15Oct2002 Elicitation BowPed49]

Despite their differences, in both these examples the TRMs function much like postpositions. This postpositional analysis is problematized by two factors, however. The first of these is the fact that word order is not fixed, with the TRM sometimes following the ground object but at other times preceding it (785):

(785) *yuk   inh   putpun otonyciy thanan*
      tree(NOM) dem:sp.prx on.top hill   stand:RDP:NPST
      'the tree is on top of the mountain'
      [KTh_GJ15Oct2002 BowPed]

In clauses like (785), it cannot be the syntactic position of the TRM that disambiguates which of *yuk inh* 'this tree' and *otonyciy* 'hill' is the ground object and which is figure. This is done instead by the combination of world knowledge (trees are located on hills, not the reverse) and the extremely strong information-structure preference for figure NPs to precede ground NPs. Furthermore, in examples (786) and (787) the TRM is separated from the ground NP by the verb, with the order ground–verb–TRM in (786), and the order TRM–verb–ground in (787):

(786) *kuta thok   nhul   chair-thak nhiinhin   putpun*
      PET   cat(NOM) 3sg(NOM) chair-DAT   sit:RDP:NPST on.top
      'the cat is sitting on top of a chair'
      [KTh_LF12Nov2002 Narrative Up&Down]

(787) *parrr   nhul   putpun thanan   therrep-ak, waawantharr*
      child(NOM) 3sg(NOM) on.top stand:RDP:NPST rock-DAT   call.out:RDP:NPST
      'the boy is standing on top of a rock, calling out'
      [KTh_MF17Sep2002 Narrative FrogStory]

Significantly, though, where the TRM and ground NP are not adjacent, the ground NP always inflects for case. The ground NP may also be case-marked when adjacent to the TRM, but this is not obligatory. While we might expect this case-marking to be assigned by the TRM/postposition, this does not seem to be the case. Each of the TRMs may be paired with ground NPs in a range of cases. *Putpun* 'on top', for example, is paired with an unmarked ground NP in (785), a ground NP in dative case in (786) and (787), and a ground NP in ablative case in (788):

(788)   light   putpun   table-tam
        light(NOM)   on.top   table-ABL
        'the light hangs over the table'
        [KTh_GJ15Oct2002 BowPed13]

There is a correlation between the case of the ground NP and the relationship that obtains between it and the figure NP. Where figure and ground are in contact (or saliently connected/close to one another) this tends to be reflected by a dative-marked ground NP (e.g. in (786) and in (789)). This stands in opposition to the use of ablative case to signify that the figure and ground are at a distance from one another, though still related topologically as encoded by the TRM (e.g. in (788) and (790)):

(789)   may yulu   bowl-ak   werngka   wun
        VEG apple(NOM)   bowl-DAT   middle   lie:NPST
        'the apple is in the middle of the bowl'
        [KTh_GJ6Dec2002 Elicitation CntSeries]

(790)   pormpr   wernka   thanan   fence-tam.   Fence   pal-korr
        house(NOM)   middle   stand:RDP:NPST fence-ABL   fence(NOM)   near-at:outside
        'the house is surrounded by the fence. The fence is round the outside'
        [KTh_GJ15Oct2002 Elicitation BowPed60]

There are a small number of exceptions to this generalization (e.g. (782)), which can be explained by the fact that dative case is assigned to ground NPs by default, but may optionally be replaced by ablative case in order to add further relational information. Thus the case marking of the ground NP can be understood as semantically motivated, independently contributing to the characterization of the topological relationship that holds between figure and ground.

Although directionals (§9.2.1.3) form a distinct class (based on their shared morphological template), these terms also share many of the functions of TRMs. Consider, for example, the parallelism between the use of *putpun* in the first clauses of (786), and the use of *palkop* in the second:

(786') 1.   kuta   thok   nhul   chair-thak nhiinhin   putpun
            PET   cat(NOM)   3sg(NOM)   chair-DAT   sit:RDP:NPST   on.top
            'the cat is sitting on top of a chair'
       2.   minh   kaal   nhul   pal-kop   nhiinhin   chair-thak
            MEAT   rat(NOM)   3sg(NOM)   near-at:below   sit:RDP:NPST   chair-DAT
            'the rat sits underneath the chair'
            [KTh_LF12Nov2002 Narrative Up&Down]

The same can be seen in the comparison between TRM *putpun* 'on top' and direction *yuukan* 'far above' in (791):

(791) 1. minh   kaal   nhul   pormp-an   putpun   thaathangk-r,
         MEAT   rat(NOM)   3sg(NOM)   house-DAT   on.top   climb:RDP-NPST
         'the rat is climbing up the roof'
      2. kuta   thok   nhul   yuu-kan   nhiinhin   nhangun
         PET   cat(NOM)   3sg(NOM)   far-at:above sit:RDP:NPST   3sgDAT
         'the cat is sitting above him'
         [KTh_LF12Nov2002 Narrative Up&Down]

Moreover, both TRMs and directionals can be marked by case suffixes, showing them to have a nominal-like function. Hence *wernka* 'middle' in (792) refers more accurately to 'the middle area', and *palkop* 'just under' (lit. 'near below') refers to the region underneath the chair in (793):

(792) ball   werngka-ntam   kerp-r   ngul   koorr   yomparr-r
      ball(NOM)   middle-ABL   disappear-P.PFV   then   outside   appear-NPST
      'the ball disappears from the middle (of the walled area), then appears outside'
      [KTh_GJ20Nov2002 Elicitation MoverbEnterExit8]

(793) kutpol   chair   pal-kop-mam   wun
      football(NOM) chair   near-at:under-ABL   lie:NPST
      'there's a football just under the chair'
      [KTh_GJ15Oct2002 Elicitation BowPed16]

As noted in §3.3.1.3, there is further a clear etymological relationship between the TRM *koorr* 'behind, outside' and the directional root -*korr* 'behind, beyond, outside'.

Finally, it is worth noting that *mangka* 'low' also has an associative use, particularly when paired with a proper name:

(794) thil   peln   ii-l-ungkarr   parr_r   inhul   peln,   Dan mangka...
      again   3pl(NOM)   there-from-north   child(NOM)   this.one   3pl(NOM)   Dan low
      'these children will [come back] again from the north, Dan mob'
      [i.e. Dan and the people associated with him]'
      [KTh_AC21Aug2002 Conversation]

So what motivates the association between the spatial relation 'low' and the associative plural category? It could be that the physical postures of being seated or supine are generally adopted only around friends and family. Strangers are more likely to encounter one another upright. Whether or not this etymological speculation is well-founded, a similar association is found in certain English varieties, where to be *down with* someone or something expresses familiarity, intimacy, affection and/or loyalty, as seen in the lyric: "I'm still **down** with my homies from the hometown" (Shakur 1991, emphasis added).

9.2.2 Temporal adverbs

Temporal adverbs locate an event in time with respect to the speech event or alternative reference point. While Hall (1971: 96) divides temporal adverbs into 'aspectual' and 'calendar' forms, I divide these expressions into those concerned with relative time (temporal adverbs) and those concerned with the number and structure of repetitions of an event (iterative adverbs).

9.2.2.1 Deictic temporal adverbs

Deictic temporals (listed in (795)) relate the event described to the origo (usually the time of speech) in terms of either: (a) simple temporal proximity (e.g. *thil* 'recently'); or (b) contextually determined temporal intervals (e.g. *punguk* 'last time', which may refer to the previous week, the previous year, and so on, depending on context). A number of forms can function with either interpretations (e.g. *yup* can refer either to simple proximal future time, or to the period immediately following a period that includes the speech act).

(795) *yoorr*   'today, now, nowadays'
       thonmarr   'always'
       muthathan   'forever'
       thil   'recently'
       kanpa   'before, previously'
       kanangkarr   'long ago'
       melnkelnkarr   'tomorrow'
       ngernkan   'yesterday'
       yup   'soon, in the impending period'
       punguk   'last time' (often used to translate *last week*)
       yukurra   'later on, next time' (often used to translate *next week*)

Although the length of time intervening between the reference time and the deictic centre varies for each of the adverbs above (e.g. one day in the case of *ngernkan* 'yesterday', but years in the case of *kanangkarr* 'long ago'), for each of these adverbs, retrieval of the reference time is dependent upon knowing the time of the speech event or alternative deictic centre. What was *yup* 'soon' a fortnight ago may be *punguk* 'last time' now. The terms *yukurra* 'next time' and *punguk* 'last time' are frequently used to translate *next week* and *last week* respectively, though these terms can also be used with reference to periods of other lengths.

9.2.2.2 Non-deictic temporal adverbs

Non-deictic temporals are concerned with periodicity, locating events with respect to their position in the diurnal (796) or seasonal (797) cycle.[177] They can be fully understood out of context since they make reference to a point in a cyclic period calculated independently of the speech (or any other) event.

(796) *(raak) miing*   'daytime'
       (raak) ngurnturnturr   'nighttime'
       raak meerngernk   'pre-dawn morning' (lit. 'TIME eye-morn')
       raak patpirr   'sunrise' (lit. 'TIME camp-P.PFV')
       ngernkernkernkan   'dawn/really early morning' (lit. 'yesterday:RDP:RDP-DAT')
       ngernkernkan   'dawn-9.30ish' (lit. 'yesterday:RDP-DAT')
       raak pung putpun   '9.30am – 1pm' (lit. 'TIME sun on.top')
       mincngul   'afternoon' (lit. 'true-then')
       meerngernka reeknhan   'sunrise/sunset' (lit. 'eye-yesterday give-GO&:NPST')
       raak wutan   'midnight' (lit. 'TIME sleep-DAT')

(797) *raak karrtam*   'wet time [broadly defined]'
       raak warreekaman   'wet season [~December-February]'
       raak wurripan   'dry-wet [~March-May]'
       raak kaalkurrc   'cold time [~June-August]' (lit. 'time ear-cold')
       raak paapath   'hot time [~September-November]' (lit. 'TIME fire:RDP')

Unlike the deictic temporals, almost all of these terms are polymorphemic (incorporating, e.g., the body part terms *kaal* 'ear', *meer* 'eye', as well as frequent use of reduplication) and many are polylexemic. Even *ngurnturnturr* 'nighttime' structurally resembles a reduplication (though there is no present-day corresponding form **ngurnturr*). Further, many of the non-deictic temporals co-occur with the generic noun *raak* 'TIME' in what looks like a classifying construction (§6.2). But while they may resemble nominals (and in particular, specific nouns) in this respect, the semantics, functions and clausal syntax of these expressions justifies their inclusion within the adverbial macroclass (cf. §9.2.2). For example, were *raak ngurnturnturr* functioning as a temporal adjunct NP – rather than adverbial expression – in (798), it would obligatorily carry case-marking.

---

[177] These lists have been greatly informed by discussions with John Taylor regarding the extensional ranges of the Thaayorre seasonal (non-deictic temporal) terms (cf. Taylor 1984).

(798) ngul may pucr   katpatp-m   raak ngurnturnturr
      then VEG nunda(ACC) grasp:RDP-P.IPFV time night
      "he was feeling for nunda nuts during the night"
      [KTh_**DW**-CW09Dec2002 Narrative 2Crocs]

9.2.3 Iterative adverbs

Members of the small set of iterative adverbs relate the event in question to other (potential) instantiations of that event. Specifically, these adverbs refer to repetition (e.g. *thil* 'again') or originality (e.g. *yoorrnhurr* 'for the first time'):

(799) *yoorr=nhurr*   'for the first time' (lit. 'now=only')
       (yuur) kuthrrka 'twice'   (lit. '[hand] two-KA')
       yuur pinalam   'a few times'   (lit. 'hand three')
       yuur mongrron   'many times'   (lit. 'hand many-RRON')
       thil ~ thilil   'again'   (cf. *thil* 'recently')

Each of these iterative adverbs is either homophonous with or derived from a form in another word class, as indicated in the literal translations above. *Yuur pinalam* 'a few times' is transparently composed of the nominals *yuur* 'hand' and *pinalam* 'three'. *Kuthrrka* 'twice' is undoubtedly related to the numeral *kuthirr* 'two', although the derivational process it has undergone is opaque (*-ka* appears to be a cranberry morph). Similarly, *mong* 'many' > *yuur mongrron*. *Yoorrnhurr* is formed by fusing the enclitic *=nhurr* 'only' to the temporal adverbial *yoorr* 'now'. *Thil* 'again' (often reduplicated as *thilil*) is polysemous with the temporal adverb *thil* 'recently'. Although there is a semantic connection between the two (in that something repeated is made immediate, rather than simply in the past), these are clearly separate senses. This can be seen in the contrast between (800), in which *thil* has only the iterative sense 'again', and (801), in which *thil* has only the temporal sense 'recently'.

(800) thil   waantharr-r   "koowe, Irma, Irma!"
      again call.out-P.PFV   cooee   Irma   Irma
      'again [I] called out "cooee, Irma, Irma!"'
      (not 'I recently called out "cooee, Irma, Irma!"')
      [KTh_AC14Nov2002 Narrative LosingIrma]

(801) may   inh   wang-am   thil   thongk-nhat
      VEG(NOM) dem:sp.prx whitefella-ABL recently arrive-GO&:P.PFV
      "whitefella food come lately"
      'the white people's food arrived recently [to this area]'
      (not 'the white people's food arrived [to this area] again')
      [KTh_AJ-IC-**GJ**26Nov2002 Narrative/Conversation]

There is no constructional disambiguation of the two senses, which must be distinguished by pragmatic context.

9.2.4 Manner adverbs

Only a small number of manner adverbs appear in my data, pertaining mainly to speed and effectiveness:

(802) *waat*   'wrongly'
      wacirr   'correctly, effectively'
      ritar   'without purpose, gammon do something'
      porprm   'excessively'
      petpan   'fast'
      therp   'hastily'
      maalmal   'slowly'
      thintintrr   'very slowly'
      kampan   'peacefully'
      kempthe   'singly'
      yoorrp   'that way'
      yarriy   'like this, thus'
      waarr   'badly'
      min   'well'
      minc   'really, strongly, with increased impact, force or deliberation'

Manner adverbs do not take any inflectional affixes, and only two may be reduplicated for emphasis (cf. §2.6.4). The semantic contrast between unreduplicated (803) and reduplicated (804) forms of *kempthe* 'singly' is illustrated by the following examples:

(803) ngul ngay   kirk   kempthe kal-m   thul=yuk
      then 1sg(NOM) spear(ACC) singly   carry-P.IPFV   woomera(ACC)=STUFF
      'I was carrying spears and a woomera separately'
      [KTh_AC14Nov2002 Narrative LosingIrma]

(804) kempkempthe yan   peln
      singly:RDP   go:NPST   3pl(NOM)
      'all of the men are walking'
      [KTh_AJ7Feb2004 Elicitation]

While the semantic connection between individuation (803) and universal quantification (804) may not be immediately obvious, it can be explained by the fact that both require attention to each member of a larger group. Example (804) was uttered as part of an elicitation series focused on quantification, immediately after a number of clauses describing 'most of the men' or 'some of the men' performing an activity. Set in opposition to vagueness with respect to the number of participants involved, the statement in (804) predicates 'walking' of each member of the subject group individually. The same can be seen in the relationship between English *single* and *every single (one)*.

The manner adverbs *yoorrp* 'that way' and *yarriy* 'in this way' in some respects resemble interjections, as they frequently occur in complete isolation, drawing attention to a non-verbal aspect of the speech context, or some preceding or following clause (cf. §9.1.2).[178] Their adverbial status, however, is clear in examples such as the following:

(805) yoorrp   yancm,   pirmp-nhat,   ngul   ngay   yarriy   turn   rirk-r
      like.that go:P.IPFV   rise-GO&:P.PFV   then   1sg(NOM) like.this turn   DO-P.PFV
      '[the croc] was going along like that and popped up, so I turned like this'
      [KTh_**AJ**-GJ03Feb2004 Conversation]

Both *min* 'well' and *waarr* 'badly' often retain the evaluative semantics of their homophonous adjectival counterparts (*min* 'good' and *waarr* 'bad') when functioning adverbially. This can be seen in (25), which describes an activity performed well, and (26) in which the activity is performed ineffectually:

(806) nhunt   kana   min   yump-r
      3sg(ERG)   about.to   well   do-NPST
      'you are getting better [at talking language]'
      [KTh_LF18Sep2002 Conversation/Elicitation]

(807) yuk.thongkn   minc[179]   waarr   thiika-rr
      stick(ACC)   really   badly   break-P.PFV
      '[she] broke the stick ineffectually'
      [KTh_EN15Dec2002 Elicitcation: Cut&Break25]

Note that while *waarr* (in this function) and *waat* 'wrongly' both describe ineffective actions, *waarr* is used when the activity has been carried out but the effect on the patient is incomplete, whereas *waat* is used when the patient is unaffected or the activity is otherwise judged entirely miscarried:

---

178 Some other manner adverbs also appear in interjection-like contexts, such as the exclamation *waat!* 'missed [it]!'
179 *minc* 'really' is used here as a degree adverb (intensifying the manner adverb *waarr* 'badly'), rather than with its manner adverbial sense.

(808) waat   patha-rr!
      wrongly bite-P.PFV
      '[the snake] nearly bit you!'
      [KTh_AC14Oct2002 Conversation/Narrative]

(809) waat   yik-r   ngan yapa
      wrongly say-P.PFV   kin e.sister
      'big sister was wrong'
      [Foote and Hall; Reader 9]

The adverb *porprm* 'excessively' appears to be derived from the adjective *porpr* 'soft' through the suffixation of *-m*. This is particularly curious given that the derivational suffix *-m* may alternatively function as a nominalizer (attaching to verbs in order to produce nouns) and a verbalizer (attaching to nouns in order to produce verbs) – see §8.1.6.

9.2.5 Degree adverbs

The three Kuuk Thaayorre degree adverbs are presented in Table 64, along with the parts of speech they modify. The rightmost column of Table 64 lists whether or not the degree adverb can also function as a manner adverb, modifying verbs. This is included for comparison only and should not be understood as a degree adverbial function.

Table 64. Functional ranges of Kuuk Thaayorre degree adverbs.

modifies:	adjective	adverb	(verb)
minc 'really'	√	√	√
waarr 'very'	√	x	√
mangr 'rather'	√	x	x

Minc 'really' has the widest functional range, modifying adjectives (810), adverbs (811), and – as a manner adverb meaning 'with intensity' – verbs (812). Although *minc* always appears following the adjective it modifies, when modifying an adverb or verb *minc* appears in the pre-head position.

(810) *trooper   ngamal minc*
      trooper(NOM) big   really
      'the trooper was really big'
      [KTh_ACh07Nov2002 Conversation]

(811) yuk   thongkn   minc   waarr   thiika-rr
      tree   piece(ACC)   really badly   break-P.PFV
      '[he] broke the stick really badly (so the pieces were still attached)'
      [KTh_EN15Dec2002 Elicitation Cut&Break25]

(812) nhul   meerkay   rok-r   minc   nhaawr
      3sg(NOM)   glasses(ACC)   enter-P.PFV   really see:P.PFV
      'he put on his glasses and saw properly'
      [KTh_GJ18Jan2004 Elicitation]

When functioning as a manner adverb, *waarr* means 'badly' (811). As a degree adverb it means 'very', and may only modify adjectives (813). In this function, the degree adverbs *waarr* and *minc* can combine (see §6.4 for discussion of the role of degree adverbs within the adjective phrase):

(813) punth   inh   waarr ngamal minc!
      arm(NOM)   dem:sp.prx   very   large   really
      'this [crocodile's] arms were really very large!'
      [KTh_**AJ**-GJ03Feb2004 Conversation]

Mangr 'rather' has the most restricted functional range, modifying adjectives alone (814).

(814) ngul ulp   kunk than-r,   mangr   min   yancm   ii-rr-kuw
      then dem:ad.prx   alive stand-P.PFV   rather good   go:P.IPFV   there-towards-west
      'then he [saltwater crocodile] was alive, he was quite okay when he went west'
      [KTh_**DW**-CW09Dec2002 Narrative 2Crocs]

Of the three degree adverbs, only *minc* 'really' appears to modify other adverbs. For example, it may follow temporal or iterative adverbs (e.g. *kanangkarr* 'long ago' > *kanangkarr minc* 'a very long time ago', and *yoorrnhurr* 'for the first time' > *yoorrnhurr minc* 'the very first time'), or precede manner adverbs (815).

(815) ngay   minc   min   waantharr-r   nganh   kuta-ku   angarr   ngeey-nh
      1sg(NOM)   really well call.out-P.PFV 1sgACC dog-ERG   ANGARR   hear-SBJV
      'I shouted good and loud so the dog would hear me'
      [KTh_GJ18Jan2004 Elicitation]

The fact that *minc* 'really' appears in the post-head position when modifying temporal and iterative adverbs is further evidence of their nominal origin.

9.2.6 Body part prefixes to adverbs

Body part terms – in particular *koo* 'nose'[180] – are frequently compounded with deictic adverbs (816), directionals (817) and topological relation markers (818):

(816)   ngul **koo**-pal   otonyciy mantam-ak pal-kop   ranth-in rok-nhan
      then nose-towards hill   small-DAT   near-at:down hole-DAT enter-GO&:NPST
      'then coming over the hill, (the ball) comes down and enters the hole
      [KTh_EN03Dec2002 Moland3]

(817)   ngul nheman=p   **meer**-ii-kan   ngancn   thowol-nam
      then from.there=PRAG eye-there-at:up 1pl:excl(NOM) play-P.IPFV
      "then we were playing right up high [in the tree]"
      [KTh_GJ15Oct2002 Narrative PlaneSighting]

(818)   kuta thok   nhul   **koo**-kanpa   nhiinhin   nhangun kuta-thak
      pet cat(NOM) 3sg(NOM) nose-before sit:RDP:NPST 3sgDAT   dog-DAT
      'the cat is sitting in front of the dog'
      [KTh_LF12Nov2002 Narrative Up&Down]

There are also examples of body parts being compounded with other adverbial subclasses (as well as nouns and verbs – cf. §4.3.2 and §8.3)4.3.2. In the following example, for instance, *pil* 'hip' is prefixed to the manner adverbial *wacirr* 'correctly' in order to create the idiomatic 'be careful':

(819)   raak-un   yan   warrath-n, yak   pil-wacirr!
      ground-DAT go:NPST grass-DAT snake hip-properly
      'walk through the grass, but watch out for snakes!'
      [KTh_GJ06Jun2005 Elicitation]

---

[180] For clarity, I shall continue to gloss body part terms such as *koo(w)* as, e.g., 'nose' here, although I do not mean to suggest that speakers have this literal meaning of the morpheme in mind when they use it in such contexts.

9.3 Ideophones

Ideophones are sound-symbolic elements that "depict sensory imagery" (Dingemanse 2015: 654) to make one's utterance more vivid and engaging. Kuuk Thaayorre ideophones typically appear adjacent to the verb, either immediately preceding it (820) or immediately following (821):

(820) *nhul   minh kothon   tup   ke'err!*
 3sg(ERG) meat wallaby(ACC) IDPH spear-P.PFV
 'he speared the wallaby, thwack!'
 [Hall 1972: 142]

(821) *paanth   inh=okun   thernga-rr, pirka-rr,*
 woman(ACC) dem:sp.prx=DUB hit-P.PFV   strip-P.PFV
 thatpa-rr   thutha-rr   prrk!
 lightning(NOM) strike-P.PFV IDPH
 '[lightning] hit the woman around here [points to arm], stripped [her], the lightning struck – prrk!'
 [KTh_AC14Oct2002 Narrative PormprRintm]

Functionally, ideophones range from the mimetic – usually onomatopoeic – reference to the sound created by an event (e.g. *purrp* to describe something falling into water), to the more opaque reference to movements, result states, attitudes, and so on that entail no audible sound (e.g. *ke'* 'surprised'). Although they tend to be embedded within the clause, ideophones do not enter into any syntactic relationship with other clausal constituents to form larger units, nor are they ever subcategorized for by a predicate.

Ideophones are best identified through their unusual phonetic, phonotactic and prosodic features. Many contain non-phonemic segments (e.g. [tʃ] as the initial segment of *churr* 'spear flying through air'), or combinations of segments that violate the phonotactic constraints that apply to the rest of the lexicon (e.g. allowing [l] word-initially in *liiy* 'flash of light'). Prosodically, ideophones are 'performatively foregrounded' (Nuckolls 1996) through being uttered at a higher pitch, at higher intensity than the rest of the clause that contains them, and through being separated from adjacent lexemes by a short pause.[181] Impressionistically, there appears to be a correlation between the timing of ideophones and mimetic/expressive gestures, though this remains to be quantitatively studied (cf. Kita 2001). Despite their syntactic and functional similarity to secondary predicates (which similarly appear adjacent to the

---

[181] Schultze-Berndt (2001: 367) notes similar the similar usage of 'expressive prosody' to mark ideophone-like elements in Jaminjung.

main predicate and commonly contribute information about result states), these phonetic and prosodic features distinguish ideophones as a special class, as does the fact that ideophones are never co-opted from other word classes (unlike the frequent use of adjectives as secondary predicates).

Ideophones are most likely an open word class that may be added to by creative speakers (cf. §3.4). There are no clear examples of newly coined ideophones in my corpus, however, and their usage appears to be declining among younger speakers.

9.4 Interjections

Wilkins (1992b: 124) proposes a formal definition of the interjection as a lexical item "which (commonly and) conventionally constitutes an utterance on its own, (typically) does not enter into construction with other word classes, is (usually) monomorphemic, and (generally) does not host inflectional or derivational morphemes." Section §3.5.10 above introduced a number of Kuuk Thaayorre particles that fit this formal prototype. This section will instead focus upon the functional subclasses of interjection, including both polymorphemic forms and forms that enter into constructions with other word classes (such atypical forms are presented in parentheses in the lists below). These forms are nevertheless unified by their dual functions of drawing the addressee's attention to something in the speech context (including the immediately preceding discourse) while also simultaneously expressing the speaker's attitudes and/or communicative intentions (Ameka 1992: 107, Enfield 2007: 310). The list provided here is incomplete, but demonstrates the functional range of Kuuk Thaayorre interjections.

The expressive interjections index the speaker's affect or attitude towards something in the speech context. This context includes the immediately preceding discourse, as when *ngeeca* 'hooray' is uttered as a response to good news delivered by the interlocutor:

(822) *ngeeca*   'hooray'
      yiki   'yikes'
      (*meer.kun.waarr* 'poor thing')

The last of these expressions, *meer.kun.waarr* 'poor thing', is used to express compassion towards a pitiful target. This interjection is formally atypical in its being a compound of three nomina (*meer* 'eye', *kun* 'bum', *waarr* 'bad'); it is for this reason presented in parentheses. The interjection *yiki* 'yikes!' is – impressionistically – among the most frequent Kuuk Thaayorre expressions. It is typically uttered as a response to something disgusting, frightening or entirely unexpected. The speaker need not display a negative affect towards the unexpected event or entity, but it should be sufficiently unexpected to have provoked a startle response in them. This form may also be used to alert addressees to something noteworthy or dangerous in their surrounds (e.g. *yiki, yak!* 'yikes, a snake!'). In this respect it resembles the set of conative interjections, which are uttered to provoke a response from the addressee (823). For example, the interjection *chaa!* 'get away!' – pronounced with a phonologically exceptional voiceless palato-alveolar affricate (cf. §3.5.1) – is used to shoo away dogs. Other conative interjections are used for attention-getting, greeting and leave taking:

(823) *chaa* 'get away [to dog]'
(ongkorr 'don't')
ee' 'hey'
wooy 'hey, I'm over here'
koowe 'cooee' (used over larger distances than *wooy*)
yawo 'goodbye'
wuurrwurr 'goodbye' (claimed to be a more conservative farewell)

The prohibitive particle *ongkorr* is placed in parentheses owing to its frequently entering into constructions with other forms, cf. §3.5.1. The negative interjection *pokon* 'no' is likewise marked by parentheses in (826) below, since it functions as both an interjection and a constituent negator (in which latter function it syntactically combines with an NP). The use of these two forms as interjections could be viewed as elliptical. For similar reasons, the monolexemic utterances *thak* 'leave it!' or *kuukaar* 'be quiet!' (in which the adnominal privative enclitic *=aar* is attached to the generic noun *kuuk* 'WORD') are not prototypical interjections on the grounds that: (a) they are members of other word classes (*thak* 'leave' being a verb, *kuukaar* being a nomen); (b) *kuukaar* 'be quiet!' is morphologically complex (comprised of nominal root *kuuk* 'word' and privative *=aar*); and (c) they can combine with other morphemes or lexemes in a clause, as seen in (824)–(825):

(824) *aawoy, nhunt kuuk=aar nhiinhin*
yes 2sg(NOM) WORD=ADN.PRIV sit:RDP:NPST
'yes, you're sitting silent'
[KTh_ME02Oct2002 Conversation]

(825) *pormp-an thaka-rr*
house-DAT leave-P.PFV
'I left [my cigarettes] at home'
[KTh_BN1Oct2002 Elicitation]

The set of discourse-oriented forms in (826) include markers of agreement and disagreement, backchannel devices and response markers. Prosody plays an important role here in marking, e.g., the degree of surprise or unexpectedness communicated by *koo* 'oh, I see'. This remains an important area for further research.

(826)   *ngawoy ~ aawoy*   'yes'
      kece   'that's wrong'
      (*pokon*   'no')
      ith'tharrko   'wow, how amazing'
      'e'   'woah! [often as backchannel]'
      mmm   'mm [often as backchannel]'
      ngee   'I see [usually as backchannel]'
      koo   'oh, I see [usually as backchannel]'

Lastly, there are a number of forms used as response cries during traditional song and dance performance, or used by the singer to conclude a song cycle. For example, the optionally reduplicated interjection *cheerr(cherr)* is uttered by the singer at the end of certain *wuuc* 'traditional song', such as the Rainbow song performed by †Alice Chillagoe. The same form may also be uttered as an apology for finding oneself in the presence of someone in a proscribed kin category. Foote and Hall (1992: 235) likewise list *psi'psi'* as an "apology made in presence of mother in law".

10 Syntax of the simple clause

The Kuuk Thaayorre clause consists minimally of a predicating constituent and the core arguments it subcategorizes for, any of which may be elided. The predicating constituent can be a verb, adjective, noun, demonstrative pronoun or locational adverb/particle. Core arguments take the form of noun phrases (see Chapter 6), and are marked for the case assigned by the predicate. The frequent ellipsis of all clausal constituents renders both adjuncts and subcategorized-for arguments 'optional'. Accordingly, the distinction between transitive, intransitive and other clause types is made in Kuuk Thaayorre on the basis of potential, rather than actual, syntactic configurations. Namely, a clause is considered intransitive if it cannot include an accusative-case argument, transitive if it can include one and only one accusative-case argument and ditransitive if it can include two.[182] Criteria for identifying intermediate levels of transitivity (e.g. semitransitive clauses) are discussed in the relevant subsections.

This chapter is primarily organized according to both the word class and valency of the predicate, with a few principled exceptions. Verb-headed clauses are grouped together in §10.1, but this section also includes discussion of clauses headed by quasitransitive predicate adjectives (§10.1.4.1). Postural, locative, copula and existential clauses are considered separately in §10.2. These clause types share a number of key formal and functional features, including the optionality of a locative/copula/existential verb.

10.1 Verb-headed clauses

Table 65 (modified from Table 17 above) gives an overview of the subclasses of verb that may head the Kuuk Thaayorre simple clause, along with their subcategorization frame and two examples. The verbal clauses are named for the subclass of verb that heads them (thus an intransitive clause is headed by an intransitive verb, and so on).

As Table 65 shows, verb-headed clauses span a range of levels of transitivity. The poles of this cline are easily identified, with intransitive verbal clauses headed by monovalent verbs that subcategorize for only a single, nominative-case argument (exemplified by (827)). At the other end of the cline, ditransitive clauses are headed by trivalent verbs that subcategorize for three arguments; an ergative-case subject and two accusative-case objects (exemplified by (828)).

---

[182] Since the accusative case is unmarked for nomina (along with the nominative case), the optional inclusion of accusative pronouns in the clause is a frequently-used diagnostic for transitivity. This heuristic is made problematic, however, by the fact that pronouns may only rarely encode inanimate entities.

Table 65. Verbal subclasses and subcategorization frames.

Valence	Verbal subclass and subcategorization frame	Sample verbs	{with sample objects}
Monovalent	Intransitive <Sbj$_{NOM}$>	*riic* 'run' *rip* 'enter' *thangkar* 'laugh'	
Bivalent	Intransitive copula <Sbj$_{NOM}$, Subj-COMP$_{NOM}$>	*nhiin* 'be (< sit)' *than* 'be (< stand)' *yomparr* 'transform'	
	Semitransitive <Sbj$_{NOM}$, I.Obj$_{DAT}$>	*koope {wanhngun}* 'wait for {someone}' *ngee {wanhngun}* 'listen to {someone}' *nhaa {wanhngun}* 'look at {someone}'	
	Quasitransitive <Sbj$_{NOM}$, Obj$_{ACC}$>	*paarr {meerngok}* 'cry {tears}' *rok {mimp}* 'put on {clothes}' *thaangk {minh}* 'ride {an animal}'	
	Transitive <Sbj$_{ERG}$, Obj$_{ACC}$>	*kal {yuk}* 'carry {something}' *matp {yuk}* 'smash {something}' *mungk {may}* 'eat {food}'	
Trivalent	Transitive copula <Sbj$_{ERG}$, Obj$_{ACC}$, Obj-COMP$_{NOM}$>	*wan {yuk, ngan}* 'name {something, something}'	
	Semiditransitive <Sbj$_{NOM}$, Obj$_{ACC}$, I.Obj$_{DAT}$>	*yik {kuuk, wanhngun}* 'say {words, to somebody}' *waantharr {kuuk, wanhngun}* 'call out {words, to somebody}' *wan {yuk, wanhngun}* 'give {something, to somebody}'	
	Ditransitive <Sbj$_{ERG}$, Obj$_{ACC}$, Obj$_{ACC}$>	*reek {wanh, yuk}* 'give {somebody, something}' *wan {wanh, wanh}* 'tell {somebody, on somebody}'	

(827) *pam thuump thangkar porprm*
man elder(NOM) laugh:NPST excessively
'the old man laughs too much!'
[KTh_EN08Sep2002 Conversation]

(828) *ngay kuta ngathn piinth reeka-rr mungk-nhatha*
1sg(ERG) dog 1sgGEN(ACC) bone(ACC) give-P.PFV eat-PURP
'I gave my dog a bone to eat'
[KTh_KTh_EN04Aug2002 Elicitation]

It is frequently difficult to assign verbs and clauses to the subcategories that fall between these two poles, however. For example, it can be difficult to identify whether a dative-marked noun phrase has been subcategorized for by a semitransitive verb, or whether it simply represents a dative adjunct to an intransitive verb. Such issues are considered in detail in the relevant subsections below.

Although ergative Australian languages rarely permit alternation between intransitive and transitive case frames (Dixon 1980: 378), a couple of Kuuk Thaayorre verb forms span these two subclasses (albeit with different senses; cf. Guerssel et al. 1985, Evans 1995a:339–347 and Dench 1995a on similar alternations in the accusative languages Lardil, Kayardild and Martuthunira respectively). Further verbs exhibit alternations between other verbal subclasses; Table 66 lists some common examples.

Table 66. Verbal subclass alternations.

verb	intransitive	quasitransitive	semitransitive	transitive	semiditransitive
thaangk	'climb'			'ride'	
thowol	'play'			'dance'	
nhaa			'look at'	'see'	
ngeey			'listen to'	'hear'	
mi'i				'pick up'	'tell (story)'
rok	'enter'	'put on (clothing)'			
patp	'camp'			'participate in ceremonial camp'	

For the purposes of the following discussion, it is necessary to provide a brief working definition of the core grammatical relations in Kuuk Thaayorre, identifying the key criteria by which they may be identified. Every Kuuk Thaayorre verb subcategorizes for a subject argument, and these may span a range of semantic roles including agent, theme, experiencer and patient. Subjects are identified according to five morphosyntactic criteria:

1. Animate subjects may be encoded by nominative/ergative personal pronouns;
2. Subjects receive the semantic role of the erstwhile direct object in reflexive and reciprocal clauses;
3. The subject of a type 1 intransitive verb root corresponds to the direct object when that verb undergoes valence increasing derivation by -*n(i)* 'v^' (the 'valence increasing' morpheme, cf. §8.1.1);
4. Conversely, the new participant introduced through the valence increasing derivation of a type 1 intransitive verb is encoded as subject (cf. Blake 1987: 68, Austin 1996).
5. The subject of a type 2 intransitive verb root corresponds to the subject of the transitive verb derived through the suffixation of -*n(i)* 'v^'.

The reflexive clause (829) illustrates the first and second criteria, inasmuch as the subject argument (encoded by the nominative/ergative pronoun *nhul* 'he') is attributed the role of undergoer as well as actor.

(829) *nhul   yarriy   katp-ey-r*
      3sg(NOM/ERG) thus   grasp-RFL-P.PFV
      'he grabbed himself [on the arm] like this'
      [KTh_AJ-**GJ**03Feb2004 Conversation]

Illustrating the third and fourth criteria, when type 1 intransitive verbs undergo valence-increasing derivation through the suffixation of *-n(i)* 'v^' a new participant is introduced as subject, while the erstwhile intransitive subject is demoted to object. Thus the subject of the type 1 intransitive verb *rok(a)* 'enter' encodes the figure that 'enters' a particular ground. The subject of the derived verb *rokan(i)* 'insert', however, encodes the agent that causes the figure to enter the ground. The figure is meanwhile encoded as direct object of the derived verb.

Finally, the fifth criterion for identifying a subject argument is the fact that the (nominative-case) subject of a type 2 intransitive verb root corresponds to the (ergative-case) subject of the transitive verb derived through the suffixation of *-n(i)* 'v^'. Hence the subject of the type 2 intransitive verb *therk(a)* 'return' encodes the figure that 'returns', as does the subject of the derived transitive verb *therkan(i)* 'return with'.

Direct objects can be characterized according to four morphosyntactic criteria:

1. Objects are assigned accusative-case;
2. Animate objects may be encoded by accusative-form pronouns;
3. Objects feed reflexive and reciprocal derivation;
4. The subject of a type 1 intransitive verb root corresponds to the direct object when that verb undergoes valence increasing derivation by *-(nh)an(i)* 'v^'.

The first and second criteria are illustrated by *nhinh* 'you' in (830).

(830) *ngay   nhinh   yukurra   nhaath-nhan*
      1sg(ERG) 2sgACC   next.time   see-GO&:NPST
      'I'll see you next time'
      [KTh_MF06Aug2002 Elicitation]

The third criterion is illustrated by (829), while the fourth is illustrated by verbs like *rok(a)* 'enter' mentioned above.

Indirect objects take dative case and may be pronominal in form. They are unable to feed reflexive/reciprocal derivation and do not feature in valence increasing derivations. It is extremely difficult to differentiate bona fide indirect objects from for dative adjuncts that are not subcategorized for. This issue is revisited in §10.1.3.

Subject- and object-complements take the form of a noun phrase in unmarked nominative/accusative case,[183] and may not be encoded by pronouns, nor feed reflexive/reciprocal derivation, nor be introduced through valence increase.

10.1.1 Intransitive clauses

Kuuk Thaayorre intransitive verbs typically describe movements, motion and activities that are contained within or expressed through the subject participant's body (e.g. laughing, growing, crawling and falling). Intransitive clauses are commonly elaborated by adverbs (831), particles and/or adjunct NPs (832).

(831) *werngr   pal=p   therk-m*
    boomerang(NOM) towards=PRAG return-P.IPFV
    'the boomerang kept coming back'
    [KTh_AC05Aug2002 Narrative WerngrStory]

(832) *yak   ranth-im   ripi-rr*
    snake(NOM) hole-ABL exit-P.PFV
    'the snake came out of its hole'
    [KTh_GJ28Oct2002 Elicitation]

Intransitive clauses may also be headed by reflexive verbs derived from transitive roots, as in (833).

(833) *kuta   ngith   pathath-e*
    dog(NOM) dem:dist bite:RDP-RFL:NPST
    'that dog is biting itself'
    [KTh_AC21Aug2002 Conversation]

Reciprocal clauses derived from base transitive verbs also contain only a single core argument, but this is usually ergative-marked. These clauses therefore cannot be considered fully intransitive. Reflexive and reciprocal clauses are discussed further in §11.5 and §11.6 respectively.

---

183 I assume that subject complements agree with the (intransitive) subject in nominative case and object-complements agree with the direct object in accusative case. But since both of these cases are unmarked for non-pronominal NPs (and complements may not be encoded as pronouns), it is impossible to distinguish the two.

10.1.2 Intransitive copula clauses

In the typical copula clause, a postural verb alternates with a verbless structure. Accordingly, these clause types are discussed in §10.2.4. There are a couple of additional verbs that may feature in intransitive copula clauses, discussed in §10.2.4.1

10.1.3 Semitransitive clauses

Austin (1993, 1996) identifies for many Australian languages a class of verbs intermediate in transitivity between the fully intransitive and the fully transitive.[184] Verbs of this subclass subcategorize for both a subject marked for the case normally assigned to the subjects of intransitive clauses (i.e. nominative in Kuuk Thaayorre), as well as a complement in dative (=locative) case. Though Kuuk Thaayorre undoubtedly possesses verbs that fit this characterization (as seen in (145)), it is difficult if not impossible to prove that the dative NP is the subcategorized-for complement of a semitransitive clause and not just an optional adjunct of an intransitive clause.

(834) nhunt   ngathun paac-r?
       2sg(NOM)   1sgDAT   growl-NPST
       'are you telling me off?'
       "are you growling me?"
       [KTh_EN14Aug2002]

In many languages there exist reliable criteria for distinguishing these two scenarios, such as: the optionality of the dative NP; its placement with respect to other clausal constituents; and its ability to feed syntactic derivations such as the passive or reciprocal. None of these criteria prove useful in Kuuk Thaayorre, however. To begin with, the criterion of optionality is not helpful since any argument (core or otherwise) may be freely elided.[185] Thus it is equally acceptable to omit or include the dative pronouns in both (835), an arguably semitransitive clause, and (836), an uncontroversially intransitive clause. Further, the undoubtedly subcategorized-for subjects of both clauses may also be elided.

(835) nhul   ngathun kookope
       3sg(NOM)   1sgDAT   wait:RDP:NPST
       'he's waiting for me'
       [KTh_EC02Oct2002 Elicitation]

---

[184] Austin (1993) labels this subclass 'extended intransitive verbs'.
[185] Native speakers consulted did not offer any intuitions as to the difference between elided 'obligatory' elements, and optional elements that were simply unrealized.

(836) ngamp   ulp   ii-rr-kan   yan   nhangun
      1pl:incl(NOM) dem:ad.prx   there-towards-up   go:NPST   3sgDAT
      'we'll go up there to him'
      [KTh_GJ18Jan2004 Narrative Christmas]

Permuting constituent order has no syntactic effect, consequently there are no restrictions on the placement of dative adjuncts as opposed to the putative dative complements of semitransitive clauses. There may be some differences between the two in terms of the relative frequencies with which they appear in the preverbal position, however. In the semi-controlled pragmatic context of elicitation, decontextualized example sentences most frequently exhibit the constituent order SOV. We might therefore expect subcategorized-for indirect objects to precede the verb (like direct objects) more frequently than do adjunct NPs. The examination of a small subset of my corpus supports this (as illustrated by (835)–(836)). But this tendency should not be overstated, given both the small size of the sample and the relatively large number of counterexamples this sample contained. In (837), for instance, the putative dative complement follows the verb, while in (838) a dative adjunct immediately precedes it.

(837) nhunt   yarriy yik   ngathun: "..."
      2sg(NOM)   thus   say:IMP   1sgDAT
      'you should say it to me like this: "..."'
      [KTh_AC21Aug2002 Conversation]

(838) ngumpurr   ulp   meer+thak-en   ngathun   wonp-r
      old.lady(NOM) dem:ad.prx   eye+front-DAT   1sgDAT   die-P.PFV
      "she died in front of my eyes"
      [KTh_AJ-IC-GJ26Nov2002 Conversation / Narrative PormpuraawKanangkarr]

The third possible test for complement versus adjunct status – the ability to feed valency change – is also problematic. Reciprocal constructions might be expected to offer the best testing ground in this regard.[186] But since reciprocal derivation may only be fed by (accusative-case) direct objects in Kuuk Thaayorre, it does not differentiate between the putative subcategorized-for dative complements of semitransitive verbs and dative adjuncts. Thus neither *paac* 'tell off', *koope* 'wait for' can form reciprocal stems through the suffixation of the reciprocal morpheme *-rr* (*paacrr 'tell each other off', *kooperr 'wait for each other').

---

[186] Reflexive constructions shed no more light on this subject than do reciprocal constructions, but are significantly more complex for didactic purposes owing to their range of extended, middle-like functions, as discussed in §11.5. There is no passive construction in Kuuk Thaayorre.

In the absence of any better arguments, I have elected to treat as semitransitive any verbs whose meaning seems to require a dative-marked argument (whether this is overtly present in the clause or elided). Such a heuristic is undeniably subjective, however. Pending a sounder basis for their identification, judgements as to whether or not the dative-marked arguments are semantically required are based partly on the semantic function of the dative-marking. Illustrating the former, if a dative argument were not part of the subcategorization frame of *koope* 'wait (for)' we would expect any dative-marked adjuncts in clauses it heads to carry one of the thematic roles usually encoded by dative case (e.g. recipient, beneficiary, etc., cf. §4.2.5).[187] The fact that the dative case-marking of *ngathun* 'for me' in (835) does not straightforwardly encode the semantic role of beneficiary, location or similar, is taken to indicate that the precise role *ngathun* 'for me' plays is specified in the verbal semantics of *koope* 'wait (for)' (and specifically, is part of its subcategorization frame). Cross-linguistic comparison is also invoked in the judgement of whether or not the dative-marked NP is required by the verb. For instance, many of the putative semitransitive verbs considered here and in §9.1.7 (e.g. *paac* 'tell off', *yik* 'say', *waantharr* 'call out to', *nhaa* 'look at' and *ngeey* 'listen to') may be broadly characterized as verbs of communication and perception, the two semantic subclasses noted by Austin to frequently head semitransitive clauses in Australian languages.

It is worth noting that it is common among Australian languages for these perception verbs to exhibit an alternation between semitransitive and transitive argument structures (cf. Blake 1987: 28–29, Morphy 1983, Evans 1995a: 344–345, Evans and Wilkins 2000). This is true of both Kuuk Thaayorre *nhaa* 'see; look at' and *ngeey* 'hear; listen to', which are associated with two alternative subcategorization frames. The transitive frame <NP_{ERG}, NP_{ACC}> is illustrated in (839), while the semitransitive frame <NP_{NOM}, NP_{DAT}> is seen in (840).

(839) *minh   kothon-thrr   pam   nhaanham*
       MEAT   wallaby-ERG   man(ACC)   see:RDP:NPST
       'the wallaby's watching the man'
       [KTh_GJ11Jan2004 Elicitation]

(840) *paanth   box-ak   nhaath-nharr*
       woman(NOM)   box-DAT   look.at-GO&:INF
       'the woman is looking at the box'
       [KTh_GJ11Jan2004 Elicitation]

---

187 As Andrews (1982: 4) puts it, adjuncts have "an invariant way of contributing to the meaning of the sentence, and appear whenever they are semantically appropriate".

10.1.4 Quasitransitive clauses

Like transitive verbs, quasitransitive verbs subcategorize for a direct object in accusative case.[188] Like intransitive verbs, however, the subject of a quasitransitive verb is always in unmarked nominative case. This is exemplified by (841).

(841) pam   may   thaa+theerp-r
      man(NOM)   VEG(ACC)   MOUTH+spit-p.PFV
      'the man spat out the food'
      [KTh_GJ15Oct2002 Elicitation]

Many verbs of the quasitransitive subclass fit Austin's (1982) characterization of 'cognate object' verbs. Such verbs place tight restrictions on the semantic field from which the accusative 'cognate object' NP may be drawn. *Cry*, for example, is an English cognate object verb which usually patterns as an intransitive verb but may also take the object *tears* (or a metaphorical expression thereof). Kuuk Thaayorre quasitransitive verbs can be ranked along a continuum according to how restricted is the semantic field from which the direct object may be drawn. At the most restricted end of this continuum are verbs that may be unequivocally classified as cognate object verbs. However, the verb and noun are never formally cognate in Kuuk Thaayorre, as Austin (1982) allows may be the case. The 'cognate object' of the verb *paarr* 'cry', for instance, appears restricted to the compound nomen *meerngok* 'tears' (lit. 'eye-water'). I have nevertheless classified such verbs here as 'quasitransitive' in preference to 'cognate object' because of the large number of verbs with the <Sbj$_{NOM}$, Obj$_{ACC}$> subcategorization frame for which there is no tight semantic restriction on the nomen(s) that may function as direct object. The intransitive verb *rok* 'enter', for example, may combine with a direct object drawn from the semantic field of apparel (i.e. clothing, glasses, hats, etc.) with the meaning 'put on' as in (842).

(842) nhunt   rok   thamr   puut
      2sg(NOM)   enter:IMP   FOOT   boot(ACC)
      'put on these shoes!'
      [KTh_AC21Aug2002 Conversation]

Similarly, the intransitive verb *thaangk* 'climb' has the meaning 'ride' when paired with a direct object representing any straddled vehicle (e.g. horse, bull, bicycle, motorcycle, etc.). To claim that such a verb fits Austin's (1982) semantic characterization of a cognate object verb is to make problematic the boundary between such verbs and straightforwardly transitive verbs (like English *ride*) that place semantic

---

188 Blake (1987) discusses analogous clauses as a type of 'minority construction'.

restrictions on their direct object. Conversely, invoking semantics rather than simply argument structure would require the inclusion of verbs like *thowol* 'play' and *patp* 'camp'. These normally straightforwardly intransitive verbs (843) may optionally appear with an accusative NP *wuuc* 'ceremony'. Yet despite the fact that this accusative NP is semantically restricted to a single lexeme (and thus bears the hallmarks of a cognate object clause), the presence of this accusative NP always coincides with the ergative case-marking of the subject NP, as in (844).

(843) *parr_r   ith   peln   wanthan pal   thowowol*
child(NOM) dem:dist 3pl(NOM) where$_{TRJ}$ towards play:RDP:NPST
"where them kid, chasing round"
'where are those kids playing?'
[KTh_AJ27Jan2004 Elicitation]

(844) *ngali   Johnny-n   wuuc   thowol-nam*
1du:excl(ERG) Johnny-ERG ceremony(ACC) dance-P.IPFV
'Johnny and I performed the traditional dance'
[KTh_GJ18Jan2004 Conversation]

For these reasons, I define Kuuk Thaayorre quasitransitive verbs and clauses purely according to their nominative-accusative argument structure, regardless of whether or not they draw an object from a restricted semantic field. On the basis of their argument structure, then, I class heterosemous verbs like *thowol* 'play; dance' as straightforwardly intransitive (subcategorizing for a single, nominative-case argument) in clauses like (843), and straightforwardly transitive (subcategorizing for an ergative-case subject and accusative-case direct object) in clauses like (844).

10.1.4.1 Bivalent predicate adjectives

Kuuk Thaayorre possesses two predicate adjectives that refer to psychological states; *walmeerem* 'knowing, knowledgeable (with respect to)' and its antonym *pamngong-kom* 'ignorant (with respect to)'.[189]

(711') 1. *nhinh   ngay   wuump wal.meerem   name nhangkn   ngay,*
2sgACC 1sg(NOM) CONTR knowledgeable.of name 2sgGEN(ACC) 1sg(NOM)
Alice nhunt...
Alice 2sg(NOM)
'I know your name, you're Alice...'

---

[189] Cf. Evans (1995a: 231–232) on the similar Kayardild transitive predicate nominals *mungurru* 'knowing, knowledgeable' and *burdumbanyi* 'ignorant, not knowing'.

2. ngay   pam nhangkn   nhamp   ngay   pam.ngongkom
   1sg(NOM) man 2sgGEN(ACC) name(ACC) 1sg(NOM) ignorant.of
   '[but] I can't remember the name of your man'
   [KTh_AC21Aug2002 Conversation]

Both *pamngoongkom* (711.1) and *walmeerem* (711.2) are bivalent, subcategorizing for two core arguments. Since they assign nominative case to the subject argument (and accusative to the object), they are analyzed as heading quasitransitive clauses.

Although predicate adjectives cannot inflect for case like other nominals, neither can they inflect for the tense/aspect/mood categories marked on verbs. Instead, where the speaker wishes to explicitly mark the clause for TAM the predicate adjective must function as complement to a copula posture verb, as in (845) and (846).

(845) engine   parr_r   pamngongkom   yancm.
      engine(ACC) child(NOM) ignorant.of   go:P.IPFV
      '(we) children didn't know about (jet) engines'
      [KTh_GJ15Oct2002 Narrative PlaneSighting]

(846) ngay   walmeerem   angarr   nhiin-nh
      1sg(NOM) knowledgeable.of ANGARR live-SBJV
      'I want to know'
      [Anon.]

Finally, it is important to note some significant differences between the semantics of these predicate adjectives and those of the English psych verb (*know*) used to translate them. As alluded to in §6.10.1, *know* is far more expansive in its scope than either of the Kuuk Thaayorre predicate adjectives. Hence to translate (847) as 'I know your father' would be misleading since the English wording suggests the speaker has a particular level of personal familiarity with the object referent. The Kuuk Thaayorre clause, however, only entails that the speaker is 'knowledgeable with respect to' one particular aspect of the object referent (in this particular discursive context, his identity).

(847) ngay   pam nhangnip nhangkn   walmeerem
      1sg(NOM) MAN father   2sgGEN(ACC) knowledgeable.of
      'I know (who) your father (is)'
      [KTh_GJ12Jan2004 Elicitation]

It would be equally misleading to translate the first clause of (848.1) as 'I don't know you' (although this is one possible interpretation of the clause) since the speaker goes on in (848.2) to make explicit the particular personal trait with respect to which he had previously been ignorant.

(848) 1. *ngay   nhinh   pam.ngongkom!*
       1sg(NOM) 2sgACC ignorant.of
       'I didn't know [that] about you!'
    2. *nhunt   ngok   kaarkarurr   mungk-r!*
       2sg(NOM) water(ACC) surprising   drink-NPST
       '(I didn't know) you drank beer!'
       [KTh_AJ27Jan2004 Conversation]

10.1.5 Transitive clauses

The predicates that head transitive clauses subcategorize for an ergative-case subject NP and a single accusative-case direct object, as illustrated by (849):

(849) *kuta-ku   pam   kookoc-r*
      dog-ERG   man(ACC)   bark:RDP-NPST
      'the dog is barking at the man'
      [KTh_GJ11Jan2004 Elicitation]

Transitive clauses may be derived by adding the valence-increasing morpheme (cf. §8.1.1) to an intransitive verb, as in (850):

(850) *book   ulp   pal   therka-ni-rr*
      book(ACC) dem:ad.prx   towards   return-V^-P.PFV
      '(he) took the book back'
      [KTh_FT10Feb2004 Elicitation RcpPilot5]

10.1.6 Transitive copula clauses

Transitive copula clauses are headed by verbs that subcategorize for both an accusative-case direct object and an accusative object-complement, in addition to an ergative-case subject. Only one transitive copula verb has been identified to date, *wan* 'name {something, a name}', as seen in (851)–(852).

(851) *yak   ngancn   kirkmuk   wan-r*
      snake(ACC) 1pl:excl(ERG) black.snake(ACC) name-NPST
      'we call that snake *kirkmuk*'
      [KTh_AJ-**GJ**03Feb2004 Conversation]

(852) *pam nhump   Louie   wan-r*
      man elder(ACC) Louie(ACC) name-NPST
      'the old man's name is Louie [lit. '(we) call the old man Louie']'
      [KTh_AJ-**IC**-GJ26Nov2002 Conversation / Narrative PormpuraawKanangkarr]

10.1.7 Semiditransitive clauses

The class of semitransitive verbs, which subcategorize for a nominative-case subject and dative-case complement, was introduced in §10.1.3. This section is concerned with clauses headed by verbs that subcategorize for both a dative-case and an accusative-case complement in addition to their nominative-case subject. Many verbs of this subclass fit traditional characterizations of ditransitive verbs, e.g. *wan* 'give' in (853).[190]

(853) *nhul   pam   thon-thak   wani-rr   book   ulp*
       3sg(NOM) man   one-DAT   give-P.PFV   book(ACC) dem:ad.prx
       'he gave the book to another man'
       [KTh_FT10Feb2004 Elicitation RcpPilot5]

Others, like quasitransitive verbs, subcategorize for a direct object from an extremely restricted semantic fields. The verb *mi'im {kuthip}* 'tell {a story}' in example (854), for instance, appears to allow only the nomen *kuthip* 'story' as its direct object.[191]

(854) *nhul   ngathun kuthip   mi'im,   glass-n   yaki-rr   yuk.ngat-am*
       3sg(NOM) 1sgDAT   story(ACC) pick.up:P.IPFV glass-ERG cut-P.PFV cyclone-ABL
       'he told me a story, [about] when glass cut him in a cyclone'
       [KTh_AJ-**GJ**03Feb2004 Conversation]

Many verbs of this class are drawn from the semantic field of communication, a domain Austin (1982) associates with cognate object verbs (cf. §10.1.4). The verb *yik* 'say', for instance, subcategorizes for a (typically human) dative complement referring to the addressee of the communication event (855) as well as an accusative object drawn from the semantic fields of language and utterance types (856).

(855) *ngawoy ngay   nhangun   yup   yik   Alison-ak*
       yes   1sg(NOM)   3sgDAT   soon   say:NPST   Alison-DAT
       'I'll speak to Alison'
       [KTh_MF20Aug2002 Conversation]

(856) *paanth   wang   inh   kuuk   Thaayorre   yiik*
       woman   whitefella(NOM)   dem:sp.prx WORD   Thaayorre(ACC)   speak:RDP:NPST
       'this white girl speaks language'
       [Anon.]

---

[190] Although the Recipient subcategorized for by *wan* 'give' is always marked by dative case, the near-synonym *reek* 'give' subcategorizes for two accusative-case arguments, cf. §10.1.8.
[191] The same, heterosemous form also functions as transitive verb meaning either 'pick up (something)' or 'sing (a ceremonial song)', with which functions it does not subcategorize for an indirect object.

The same difficulties in testing whether or not the dative NP is subcategorized for obtain in semitransitive cognate object clauses as in semitransitive clauses. Here, too, the dative complement is freely omissible, can appear in any position with respect to other clausal constituents, and cannot feed reciprocalization.

10.1.8 Ditransitive clauses

Fully ditransitive clauses containing three overt core argument NPs (one in ergative case, two in accusative), are very rare in Kuuk Thaayorre discourse. All such examples in my corpus (e.g. (857)) were uttered in an elicitation context (albeit often as a spontaneous response to, e.g., visual stimuli).

(857) *nganip-i nganh koonte-rr minh kothon*
father-ERG 1sgACC deprive-P.PFV MEAT wallaby(ACC)
'Dad deprived me of wallaby [i.e. killed one and refused to share it]'
[KTh_GJ7Feb2004 Elicitation]

Kuuk Thaayorre possesses two apparently synonymous verbs that encode events of giving; *reek* 'give' and *wan* 'give'. However, only the former may head a ditransitive clause (as in (858)).

(858) *pal nganh nhunh ritar reek*
towards 1sgACC 3sgACC gammon give:IMP
'give me him [the baby] for a bit'
[KTh_GJ10Jan2004 Elicitation]

Wan 'give' is a semiditransitive verb, subcategorizing for a dative complement (encoding the recipient) and an accusative object (encoding the theme), as in (859).

(859) *ngathun thono wan*
1sgDAT one(ACC) give:IMP
'give me one [cigarette]'
[KTh_GJ10Jan2004 Elicitation]

The verb form *wan* is heterosemous. As well as its function as a semitransitive verb with the meaning 'give' seen in (859), and as a transitive copula verb with the meaning 'name' (discussed in §10.1.6), it may also function as a bona fide trivalent verb with the meaning 'tell on' (860).

(860) *nganh   nhunh   wan*
    1sgACC 3sgACC tell.on:IMP
    'tell him about me'
    [KTh_GJ10Jan2004 Elicitation]

10.2 Locative, copula and existential constructions

10.2.1 Background

Locative, copula and existential clauses are discussed together in this section because the three clause types share many properties, one of which is the optionality of the verb. This optionality makes useless the verbal/verbless distinction maintained elsewhere in this chapter. Where a locative/copula/existential construction does contain a verb, this is selected from the class of five 'postural' verbs (§10.2.2).[192] Selection of the particular postural verb employed is determined by constructional and pragmatic considerations in conjunction with semantic features of the subject argument.

It is cross-linguistically common for postural verbs such as *sit*, *stand*, and *lie* to have grammaticalized functions (e.g. as copula verbs or aspect markers). The regularity with which these postural verbs operate as a linker in locative constructions, in particular, led Ameka and Levinson (2007) to coin the label 'postural-type language'. Postural-type languages are found in families as diverse as Germanic, Siouan, Guaykuruan, Papuan (families and isolates) and both the Pama-Nyungan and non-Pama-Nyungan languages of Australia. The grammaticalized functions of posture verbs have attracted a number of studies, both typological (e.g. Newman 2002 and Ameka & Levinson 2007) and focused on particular languages (e.g. Hellwig 2003 and the papers collected by Newman, ed., 2002). The particularities of the Kuuk Thaayorre postural verbs (in their grammaticalized functions) in some respects fit the trends noted in the aforementioned publications, but in other respects Kuuk Thaayorre is quite unusual.

Before detailing the locative/copula/existential constructions in which Kuuk Thaayorre postural verbs appear, the class of postural verbs is introduced in §10.2.1, with their respective semantics explored in §9.2.2.

---

[192] Viz: *than* 'stand; *nhiin* 'sit'; *wun* 'lie'; *yan* 'go'; and *yooyongke* 'hang'. I refer to this verb class by the general title 'postural' despite the fact that neither *yan* 'go' nor *yooyongke* 'hang' really encodes postural semantics. This is for two reason: (a) the other verbs in the class primarily describe posture; and (b) the class in general displays similarities of function with the 'postural verbs' of many other languages, to whose grammaticalized functions much attention has been paid in recent typological literature (see, for example, Newman 2002).

10.2.2 The set of postural verbs

Kuuk Thaayorre possesses only three postural verbs in the strict sense of describing the configuration of the human body; *than* 'stand', *nhiin* 'sit' and *wun* 'lie'. These three verbs are hereafter referred to as the 'core' postural verbs. Unlike the posture verbs of some other Australian languages (cf., e.g., Reid 2002 on Ngan'gityemerri), the Kuuk Thaayorre set may be used to describe a change of posture in addition to their stative sense:

(861)   *nhiin*
        lie:NPST/IMP
        'sit down!' or 'he/she is sitting'

The fourth verb included in the broader class of postural verbs is *yoongke* 'hang'. Typically used to describe inanimate objects suspended from a surface or object, *yoongke* similarly allows both active and stative interpretations of the unmarked stem. But unlike the core postural verbs, the unmarked form *yoongke* may also function as a transitive, active verb with the theme argument or figure (corresponding to the subject of the intransitive clause) realized as direct object (863):[193]

(862)   *may yulu   yuk-un   yooyongke*
        VEG apple(NOM) stick-DAT hang:RDP:NPST
        'the apple is (hanging) on the branch'
        [KTh_GJ15Oct2002 Elicitation BowPed45]

(863)   *paanth-u   yuk   ith   yuk-un   yoongke-rr*
        woman-ERG thing(ACC) dem:dist stick-DAT hang-P.PFV
        'the woman hung that [rope] over the branch'
        [KTh_GJ19Oct2002 Elicitation CausedPositions38]

The fifth and final verb in the postural class is *yan* 'go'. As a full verb, *yan* patterns with verbs of motion, such as *riic* 'run', *thaangk* 'climb', or *thuuth* 'crawl'. But in its extended functions copula and locative predicate, *yan* 'go' is paradigmatically opposed to the other postural verbs.

---

[193] This alternation is somewhat surprising, given *yoongke*'s apparent absorption of the reflexive suffix *-e*, which usually has a detransitivizing effect.

10.2.2.1 Secondary senses of *nhiin* 'sit' and *wun* 'lie'

In addition to their basic postural sense, both *nhiin* 'sit' and *wun* 'lie' can be used to mean, roughly, 'live'. 'Sit' and 'lie' verbs are attested with this extended use across the Australian continent, as Dixon (1980: 116) notes:

> In most Australian languages 'to sit' ... [is] used with the general sense 'to stay, to settle down', where no particular posture is indicated; but in Wik Munkan wun- 'to lie' appears to be the unmarked term, that also has the sense 'to stay'.

In Kuuk Thaayorre, both *nhiin* 'sit' and *wun* 'lie' are extended in this way, though they differ in their extended meaning. Wun_2 (glossed 'reside') is restricted to the description of a person's relationship to their home, or immediate domestic sphere. $Nhiin_2$ (glossed 'live'), however, is associated with the broader environmental context of one's daily life. The difference between the two can be seen in the following examples:

(864) nhunt   wanthanngun   wun?
      2sg(NOM)   where$_{LOC}$ reside:NPST
      'where [i.e. in which house] do you live?'
      [KTh_EN06Sep2002 Elicitation / Conversation]

(865) nganam ngathn   angunp   nhiinhin
      mother 1sgGEN(NOM)   there   live:RDP:NPST
      'my mother lives there [in Melbourne]'
      [KTh_ME02Oct2002 Elicitation]

There is some persistence of the meaning of wun_1 'lie' that leads wun_2 'reside' to be associated with the place where one sleeps. Likewise, $nhiin_2$ 'live' is associated with the place where one spends one's 'upright' hours due to the semantic persistence of $nhiin_1$ 'sit'. This explains why both verbs may be used to describe a person's relationship to their house (i.e. *nhiin* could be felicitously substituted for *wun* in (272)), but why only *nhiin* can be used to describe a person's relationship to their home city (i.e. *wun* could not be used for (865)).

Dixon (1980: 120) suggests that, for Walmatjari at least, the copula function of the cognate *wuna* 'lie' derives from the secondary sense 'stay, settle, exist'. In Kuuk Thaayorre, it seems that both the original verbs wun_1 'lie'/ $nhiin_1$ 'sit' and the extended wun_2 'reside'/ $nhiin_2$ 'live' have independently extended to function as copula/locative predicates. This accounts for the broader distribution of the forms *nhiin* and *wun* in copula/locative constructions in comparison with *than* 'stand', as evident in the discussion below. (These verbs will hereafter be differentiated by subscript numerals only as necessary).

10.2.3 The postural construction

I assume that the original (and in some respects, basic) function of the postural verbs was to head a postural construction. This construction predicates a particular physical configuration of a figure, and consists minimally of a postural verb and an (optionally elided) subject, as in (861) above. It is thus a subtype of intransitive verbal clause (§10.1.1). A more elaborated postural construction (including locative adjuncts, topological relation markers, and/or directional adverbs) is illustrated by (866)–(867).

(866) *kuta thok   nhul   chair-thak nhiinhin   putpun*
      PET cat(NOM) 3sg(NOM)   chair-DAT   sit:RDP:NPST   on.top
      'the cat is sitting on top of the chair'
      [KTh_LF12Nov2002 Narrative Up&Down]

(867) *kuta thok   pal-korr   thanan*
      PET cat(NOM) near-at:outside   stand:RDP:NPST
      'the cat's standing outside'
      [KTh_LF12Nov2002 Narrative Up&Down]

Though the choice of postural verb is primarily motivated by the current posture or configuration of the figure itself, selection is also restricted by the figure's animacy. Specifically, *nhiin* 'sit' may not be used to describe an inanimate figure, whatever its configuration:

(868) a. **cup*   table-ak   werngka   nhiinhin*
          cup(NOM)   table-DAT   middle   sit:RDP:NPST
          'the cup is sitting in the middle of the table'
      b. *cup   table-ak   werngka   wun*
          cup(NOM)   table-DAT   middle   lie:NPST
          'the cup is lying in the middle of the table'
      c. *cup   table-ak   werngka   thanan*
          cup(NOM)   table-DAT   middle   stand:RDP:NPST
          'the cup is standing in the middle of the table'
          [KTh_GJ6Dec2002 Elicitation Sup09]

10.2.4 The copula construction

The Kuuk Thaayorre copula construction is composed of an optional copula verb, a nominative subject and an (unmarked) complement that is predicated of the subject argument. The copula construction has two key functions. The first is to predicate a characteristic (encoded as complement) of an entity (encoded as subject). The characteristic encoded as complement may be either a simple adjective (869) or a full, noun-headed NP (870)–(871).

(869) *kiin   ulp   waarr!*
      tooth(NOM) dem:ad.prx bad
      '[your] tooth is rotten!'
      [KTh_EF14Dec2002 Elicitation Demonstratives2]

(870) *yuk   wakam   merngor   min*
      TREE tree.sp.(NOM) shade   good
      'the club tree gives good shade'
      [KTh_JCo09Jan2004 Conversation / Elicitation]

(871) *wang   nhamp   Mr Burton nhamp*
      whitefella(NOM) name(NOM) Mr Burton name
      'the white man's name was Mr Burton'
      [KTh_GJ16Oct2002 Narrative MelbourneTrip]

The order of constituents in such clauses is typically subject–predicate, however the reverse order is also attested (the full context of 872 is provided in example 711 above):

(872) *Alice nhunt...*
      Alice 2sg(NOM)
      'you're Alice...'

(873) *kana   kuthip   inh*
      finished story(NOM) dem:sp.prx
      'that's the end of the story'
      [KTh_GJ16Oct2002 MelbourneStory]

None of the copula examples presented thus far has included a copula verb. I label such verbless copula clauses 'unmarked' because they contain less morphophonological material than verb-headed copula clauses. Although these clauses are typically used to describe normal, predictable and easily comprehended contexts (and thus may also be characterized as pragmatically 'unmarked' in the Gricean sense), the distinction made here between 'marked' and 'unmarked' copula clauses is a purely formal one that makes no pragmatic claims. Hence the situations and events described by means of marked copula clauses (i.e. those containing an overt postural verb) need not be pragmatically aberrant. The overt verb might be required simply to express tense, for example, as seen in the contrast between (874) and (875).

(874) *ngay   parr_r mant*
      1sg(NOM) child small
      'I [am] a small kid'

(875) *ngay   parr_r mant yancm*
      1sg(NOM) child small go:P.IPFV
      '[when] I was a small kid'
      [KTh_AC10Aug2002 Narrative ChapmanEra]

To minimize terminological confusion, clauses describing predictable, un-noteworthy states of affairs are henceforth referred to as 'default', and the verb contained therein will be referred to as 'default verbs'. This is an important distinction since default clauses may nevertheless be (morphophonologically) marked (e.g. for tense, as in (875)). The rest of this section will be devoted to the criteria that determine which (if any) of the posture verbs is selected as copula for a particular clause.

The selection of posture verb for a marked copula clause depends first of all on the animacy of the subject referent. For all animate entities, the default copula verb is *yan* 'go'. It is for this reason that the default construction used in (875) above includes the verb *yan* 'go'. The fact that *yan* 'go' is used to describe default situations that are in line with the addressee's expectations of the world (as opposed to, e.g. *wun* 'lie') is clear in the comparison of (876) and (877). While the speaker explicitly mentions his being an infant in (876) (through the noun *menmrr* 'baby'), in (877) this is implied by the use of the non-default posture verb *wun* 'lie' since babies are the only kind of 'small child' whose canonical posture is lying.

(876) *ngay   parr_r menmrr yancm*
      1sg(NOM) child baby   go:P.IPFV
      'I was a baby'
      [Anon.]

(877) *ngay   parr_r mant wun-um*
      1sg(NOM) child small lie-P.IPFV
      'I was a baby'
      [Anon.]

Similarly, the following phrases imply illness of varying levels of severity through the choice of posture verb:

(878) a. *punguk   ngay   mincwanc=aak   yancm*
         last.time 1sg(NOM) sickness=ADN.PROP go:P.IPFV
         'I was sick last week'

b. *punguk   ngay   mincwanc=aak   wun-m*
   last.time 1sg(NOM) sickness=ADN.PROP lie-P.IPFV
   'I was lying sick in bed last week'
   [Anon.]

In (82a), the selection of the default posture verb *yan* 'go' tells us nothing about the degree of illness (except that it was not particularly noteworthy, and so unlikely to be severe). Example (82b) suggests more serious illness (implying that the speaker was bedridden).

The addressee may similarly exploit the connotations of the non-default verbs in examples (879) and (880) to infer the state of the subject referent:

(879) *nhul   ngok murm yan*
      3sg(NOM) beer drunk go:NPST
      'he's drunk'
      [KTh_AP9Oct2002 Conversation]

(880) *nhul   ngok murm wun*
      3sg(NOM) beer drunk lie:NPST
      'he's paralytically drunk'
      [KTh_AP9Oct2002 Conversation]

Wun 'lie' and *nhiin* 'sit' can also be used as non-default verbs without any connotations of posture. This seems to stem from their secondary senses (i.e. 'reside' and 'live' respectively), and they are therefore glossed as such. In this usage, *nhiin* 'live' implies an ongoing, enduring state (881)–(882), while the state denoted by *wun* 'reside' seems to denote states that are more transient (884)–(885).

(881) *nhul   muthathan kunk nhiinhin*
      3sg(NOM) forever   alive live:RDP:NPST
      'he [Jesus] lives forever'
      [KTh_GJ18Jan2004 Narrative Christmas]

(882) *missed-m rirk-r   pelnan, ngay   yarriy=p nhiin-m*
      miss-TR   DO-P.PFV 3plACC 2sg(NOM) thus   live-P.IPFV
      'I missed them, that's how I was [feeling]'
      [KTh_GJ16Oct2002 Narrative MelbourneTrip]

(883) *minh kaal   nhul   mantam minc   nhiinhin*
      MEAT rat(NOM) 3sg(NOM) small   really live:RDP:NPST
      'the rat is really small'
      [KTh_LF12Nov2002 Narrative Up&Down]

(884) *"aa, kul.paath=pa pam-a   ith   paapath wun!"*
ah   sweet=PRAG man-DAT dem:dist hot   reside:NPST
"mm, [the water tastes] sweet to someone who is hot!"
[Foote and Hall: Primer 9]

(885) 1. *pam   watp-a   yat   pal   pul*
man   dead-DAT go:P.PFV towards   3du(NOM)
'the pair came for the corpse'
2. *Pat   pam-kak   pal-pil   wun=ul*
Pat(NOM) man-COM   beside   reside:NPST=3sg(NOM)
'Pat is alongside with another man'
[Foote and Hall: Primer 9]

This distinction could be cast in terms of the distinction between individual-level and stage-level predication, with *nhiin* 'live' corresponding to the former (i.e. describing a stable, permanent characteristic or state that holds throughout the existence of that individual) and *wun* 'reside' to the latter (i.e. describing a transient characteristic or state that holds only for the duration of a particular period of time, or 'stage'). However, this appears to be an implicature of these verbs, rather than an inherent part of their lexical semantics. In (882), for instance, the speaker uses *nhiin* 'live' to emphasize the duration and intensity of his feeling, though this represented a 'stage' rather than a permanent state. Moreover, examples (886)–(887) appear to contradict both these associations since (886) refers to a state that lasts only very temporarily, while the dog referred to in (887) had clearly been mangy for some considerable time:

(886) *ngongkom   nhiin*
ignorant   live:IMP
'close your eyes! [temporarily, in order to play hide and seek]'
[KTh_EN08Sep2002 Elicitation]

(887) *kuta   ngith   meer.kun.waarr   wun*
dog(NOM) dem:dist pitiful   reside:NPST
'that dog is pitiful'
"I sorry for that dog"
[KTh_AC21Aug2002 Conversation]

It is possible, however, that the speaker of (886) deliberately used *nhiin* 'live' to stress that the addressee should keep their eyes shut for a (sufficiently) prolonged period, not just momentarily. Likewise, the speaker of (887) might have (somewhat hopefully) wished to depict the dog's sorry state as only temporary.

Where the subject referent of a copula clause is inanimate, the selection of copula verb is determined by its 'canonical' posture. So, for instance, a tree canonically 'stands', and so any clause predicating some characteristic (or the identity) of a tree will include the verb *than* 'stand' (where the clause is marked). Buildings are similarly described as 'standing' (888), whereas water canonically 'lies' (889) and nanda nuts canonically 'hang' (890).

(888) *pormpr   kanpa ngamal thana-m*
house(NOM) before big   stand-P.IPFV
'the house used to be big [before it was destroyed]'
[KTh_GJ31Jan2004 Elicitation DahlTMA3]

(889) *Ngernkan kaal-kurrc. Ngernkan ngok   kaal-kurrc wun-m*
yesterday cold   Yesterday water(NOM) cold   lie-P.IPFV
'yesterday it [the water] was cold. Yesterday the water was cold'
[KTh_GJ31Jan2004 Elicitation DahlTMA32]

(890) *may pucr   kul-path yooyongke*
VEG nanda(NOM) sweet   hang:RDP:NPST
'nanda nuts are sweet'
[Anon.]

In some cases, the default verb employed in copula constructions with an inanimate subject does not belong to the set of postural verbs. In (891), for example, the most appropriate verb for the subject *wal* 'bag' is *kal* 'carry'.

(891) *wal   ith   kanpa min kal-m*
bag(NOM=ACC) dem:dist before good carry-P.IPFV
'this bag used to [be] good'
[Anon.]

This is not simply because bags are most often in a carrying posture (in fact, they are probably 'lying' on a surface the majority of the time), but rather because the quality of the bag is judged with respect to carrying it. Interestingly, the same verb is used to ascribe qualities to (human) eyes (892). We might infer from this that the eyes are understood by Kuuk Thaayorre speakers to be 'carried' by the skull.

(892) 1. *meer ngathn   yoorr waarr,*
eye 1sgGEN(NOM) today bad,
'I have bad eyesight nowadays'
2. *ngul meer ngathn   kanpa min kal-m*
but eye 1sgGEN(NOM=ACC) before good carry-P.IPFV
'but my eyes used to be good'
[Anon.]

It is unclear in these examples whether the putative copula subject is in the nominative case (as would be expected), or in the accusative case normally assigned to the theme argument of *kal* 'carry'. If the latter, (891) and (892b) should not be considered copula clauses proper. However the former case would suggest that *kal* is here functioning with an intransitive case frame and should be included within the set of postural verbs.

Example (892) notwithstanding, inalienably possessed parts are generally categorially equivalent to their wholes, in terms of the copula verb selected. So where the subject NP refers to an inanimate part (e.g. a name) of a larger animate entity (e.g. a dog), the selection of default copula verb is determined by the larger entity as a whole. Thus in (893) the copula verb *yan* 'go' is selected as the default copula verb for animates.

(893)   *nhamp*   *ulp*   *Buddy*   *yancm*
        name(NOM)   dem:ad.prx   Buddy   go:P.IPFV
        '[my childhood dog's] name was Buddy'
        [Anon.]

The same holds for the relationship between product and source. Accordingly, in (894), the choice of default copula verb is determined by characteristics of the source-complement (*wat* 'tea tree', which prototypically 'stands') rather than of the product-subject (*yuk thinycirr* 'drinking vessel', which prototypically 'lies').

(894)   *yuk*   *thinycirr*   *wat*   *inh*   *thanan*
        THING   vessel(NOM)   tea.tree   dem:sp.prx   stand:RDP:NPST
        'these drinking vessels are [made from] tea tree'
        [KTh_**AJ**-IC-GJ26Nov2002 Conversation/Narrative]

Finally, it should be noted that constituent order in copula clauses is mutable, though the order subject–complement–(postural verb) is by far the most common.

10.2.4.1 Additional copula clauses

Kuuk Thaayorre also possesses two further copula verbs which are not subject to the paradigmatic and morphosyntactic generalizations that apply to postural copulas. These two verbs (*wene* 'become' and *yomparr* 'transform') have inchoative and/or transformational semantics. Like postural copulas, though, they subcategorize for a complement in addition to their nominative-case subject. In (895) this complement is a simple adjective, while in (896) it is a full noun phrase. The copula complement may alternatively take the form of an adverb (897):

(895) ak piinth-r, ngamal wene
OPT grow-NPST large become:NPST
"let it [cyclone] grow, let it become large"
[KTh_**AJ**-GJ03Feb2004 Conversation]

(896) town ngamal yomparru-rr peln
town large transform-P.PFV 3pl(NOM)
'they have become a large town'
[KTh_AJ27Jan2004 Conversation]

(897) ball werngka-ntam kerp-r ngul koorr yomparru-rr
ball(NOM) middle-ABL finish-P.PFV then outside transform-P.PFV
'the ball disappeared from the middle then appeared [lit. became] outside'
[KTh_GJ20Nov2002 Elicitation MoverbEnterExit8]

10.2.5 The locative construction

The locative construction is used to locate or position a figure (encoded as subject) with respect to a particular ground (encoded as dative-case complement, as seen in (898)):

(898) nhul Post.Office-ak yat
3sg(NOM) Post.Office-DAT go:P.PFV
'he is at [lit. went to] the Post Office'
[KTh_GJ10Dec2002 Elicitation]

The principles according to which the postural verb is selected for a locative clause differ from those that determine the selection of copula verbs. One commonality between the two, however, is the fact that higher animate subjects almost always take the posture verb *yan* 'go' in locative constructions, as in (898). The only exception to this, is where a person is being located at their home, in which case *nhiin* 'live' or *wun* 'reside' may be used:

(899) nhul pormp-an wun / nhiinhin
3sg(NOM) house-DAT lie:NPST / sit:RDP:NPST
'he's at home'
[KTh_GJ10Dec2002 Elicitation]

To use any verb other than *yan* 'go' to locate a person outside their home, forces the clause to be interpreted as a postural construction, as can be seen in (900):

(900) *nhul   Post.Office-ak   thanan*
       3sg(NOM)   Post.Office-DAT   stand:RDP:NPST
       'he's standing near / on top of the Post Office' (not 'he's at the Post Office')
       [KTh_GJ10Dec2002 Elicitation]

Although both postural and locative clauses may contain a nominative NP, a dative NP and a postural verb (compare, for example, (898) with (900)), the two can be differentiated both syntactically and semantically. Syntactically, the postural verb is obligatory in the postural clause but not the locative, while the dative NP is an optional adjunct in the postural clause but an obligatory complement in the locative clause. Semantically, the postural construction entails the posture predicated of the subject NP, while no posture is entailed where a locative construction contains a default postural verb. The different structures of the two constructions can be summarized as in (901).

(901) Postural construction: (SUBJECT$_{NOM}$), (ADJUNCT$_{DAT}$), VERB$_{POSTURAL}$
       Locative construction: (SUBJECT$_{NOM}$), COMPLEMENT$_{DAT}$, (VERB$_{POSTURAL}$)

The selection of default postural verb is a little more complicated when the subject is animate, and must take into account certain features of the subject referent. The first relevant distinction is whether or not the object is 'moveable'. If not, the verb selected must reflect the fixed posture of the object. So, for instance, any object suspended from a surface must be described as *yooyongke* 'hanging'. There is no default/non-default distinction available for such objects; if a verb is overtly realized, it will be *yooyongke* 'hang' (as in (902)).

(902) *may   yulu   yuk-un   yooyongke*
       VEG   apple(NOM)   tree-DAT   hang:RDP:NPST
       'there are apples on the tree'
       [KTh_GJ15Oct2002 Elicitation BowPed27]

Similarly, trees or buildings that are fixed in a 'standing' position must be located by means of the verb *than* 'stand' (as in (903) and (904)).

(903) *yuk   pormpr pil-un   thanan*
       tree(NOM)   house hip-DAT   stand:RDP:NPST
       'the tree is [lit 'stands'] beside the house'
       [KTh_GJ15Oct2002 Elicitation BowPed49]

(904) *hospital   ii-kuw-an   inh   than-m*
       hospital(NOM)   there-at:west-DAT   dem:sp.prx   stand-P.IPFV
       'the hospital used to be there in the west'
       [KTh_GJ27Jan2004 Conversation]

For all moveable inanimate objects, the pragmatically unmarked verb is *wun* 'lie', and any such object positioned on a surface may be described using *wun* regardless of its actual posture. So, for example, a bottle standing on a tabletop would be described using *thanan* 'stand' in a postural construction (in order to draw attention specifically to its posture, as in (905)), but in a locative construction (used to locate the bottle with respect to the ground 'table', as in (906)), the verb *wun* is used:

(905) *bottle   table-ak   thanan*
      bottle(NOM) table-DAT   stand:RDP:NPST
      'the bottle is standing on the table'
      [KTh_GJ19Oct2002 CausedPositions25]

(906) *bottle   table-ak   wun*
      bottle(NOM) table-DAT   lie:NPST
      'the bottle is on the table'
      [KTh_GJ19Oct2002 CausedPositions14]

Note that (906) could be uttered equally felicitously in the description of either an upright bottle or a bottle lying on its side. Conversely, to merely locate a nanda nut in a tree the default verb *yoongke* 'hang' should be used, as seen in (902). To use the verb *wun* 'lie' (as in (907)) would entail that the nut has been placed on top of a branch, rather than hanging from the tree in its prototypical posture.

(907) *may pucr   yuk-un   wun*
      VEG nanda(NOM)   tree-DAT   lie:NPST
      'a nanda nut is [balanced] on the tree'
      [KTh_GJ15Oct2002 Elicitation]

Interestingly, lower animates (i.e. non-human animals, usually excluding 'social animals' such as dogs and, for some speakers, cats) appear to be more flexible with respect to the verbs that may be used to locate them. In particular, the locative posture verbs *nhiin* 'sit' and *than* 'stand' are frequently used in cases where verbal semantics conflict with the actual posture of the subject referent:

(908) *kuta thoknhul   koo-kanpa   nhiinhin   nhangun kuta-thak*
      PET cat 3sg(NOM) nose-in.front sit:RDP:NPST   3sgDAT   dog-DAT
      'the cat is <u>standing</u> in front of the dog'
      [KTh_LF12Nov2002 Narrative Up&Down]

It is unclear at this stage what motivates verb selection in such cases.

One further characteristic of the locative construction is that a locational adverb or particle may be substituted for the dative-marked noun phrase. This can be seen in example (909), in which the location of the subject/figure is indicated by the adverb *awi'i* 'here':

(909) *ngay aw-i'i*
1sg(NOM) ATTN-here
'I'm here!'

10.2.6 Existential construction

The existential construction is used to declare the existence of or to draw attention to some entity. Although in many respects structurally similar to the postural, copula and locative constructions, it differs from these in having no complement. In fact, the existential construction consists minimally of the subject/topic (whose existence is asserted), with an optional (postural verb) predicate, as in (910).

(910) *yak!*
snake
'[there's a] snake!'

As (911) demonstrates, the existential construction (911a) can be ambiguous with the copula (911b).

(911) a. *puun min*
breeze good
'[there is a] nice breeze'
b. *puun min*
breeze(NOM) good
'the breeze is nice'
[KTh_MF20Aug2002 Elicitation / Conversation]

Where an existential clause contains a verb, this appears to be selected according to the same principles as apply to copula clauses. Since existential clauses overwhelmingly take inanimate subjects, the verb in an existential clause tends to reflect the canonical posture of its sole argument, as in (315):

(912) *church inh raak ngan-tam than-m?*
church dem:dist TIME what-ABL stand-P.IPFV
'how long has the church been [in existence]?'
[KTh_EN06Sep2002 Elicitation]

Significantly, Kuuk Thaayorre existential clauses may only be negated by the constituent negator *pokon* 'NO' (913), and not by the clausal negator *kaar* 'NEG'.

(913) *kanangkarr pormpr pokon*
long.ago house NO
'before, there were no houses'
[KTh_AC06Aug2002 Conversation / Narrative Kanangkarr]

This fact differentiates Kuuk Thaayorre existential clauses from their (ascriptive) copula counterparts, in which negation may alternatively be achieved by means of the clausal negator *kaar* 'NEG' (914) or the constituent negator (915).

(914) *nhunt God kaar=p*
2sg(NOM) God NEG=PRAG
'you're not God!'
[KTh_GJ18Jan2004 Narrative Christmas]

(915) *ulp parr_r pam=rr pokon*
dem:ad.prx child male=PRAG NO
'this isn't a boy [it's a girl]'
[KTh_ACh07Nov2002 Conversation / Narrative]

11 Non-basic, non-complex clauses

This chapter considers eight classes of non-basic (but also non-complex) clause. First, it presents the interrogative constructions used to solicit information, while §11.2 identifies the constructions used to issue commands (whether imperative, hortative or jussive). Section 11.3 surveys a range of distinct strategies for forming negative clauses. Section 11.4, meanwhile, presents the two apprehensive constructions. Reflexive and reciprocal clauses are discussed in §11.5 and §11.6 respectively, while a range of up to twelve distinct desiderative constructions (used to express a wish, hope or desire) are detailed in §11.7. Lastly, §11.8 concludes with a discussion of secondary predicates, which span this chapter's focus on monoclausal constructions and Chapter 12's focus on complex clauses.

11.1 Interrogative constructions

There are three types of interrogative construction, all characterized by a distinctive intonation contour: (a) clauses containing an ignorative (e.g. *wanthanngun* 'where at' in (916), cf. §5.2); (b) clauses containing ConTRastive *wuump* (example (917), cf. §9.1.4); (c) clauses that are morphosyntactically identical to the corresponding declarative clause (918):

(916) raak pungk pelnan   wanthanngun?
place knee   3plGEN(NOM) whereLOC
'where is their land?'
[KTh_EN08Sep2002 Elicitation]

(917) Alfred Charlie   nhunt   wuump nhaawr
Alfred Charlie(ACC) 2sg(ERG) CONTR   see:P.PFV
'have you seen Alfred Charlie?'
[KTh_JCo12Sep2002 Conversation]

(918) kirkmuk   nhunt   heard.about rirk-r?
black.snake(ACC) 2sg(ERG) heard.about DO-P.PFV
'have you heard about *kirkmuk*?'
[KTh_GJ27Jan2004 Conversation]

In each of these constructions, one or more constituents is marked by focal intonation; a small dip in pitch, followed by a sharp rise with a high peak, followed by a gradual lowering of pitch. This distinctive prosodic contour is found in a number of clause types, but is strongly associated with interrogation. In the first interrogative construction, it is always the ignorative that attracts focal intonation, while focal intonation is centred on *wuump* in the second construction. The domain of focal intonation in the third interrogative construction is determined by the scope of interrogation. In (918), for instance, the domain of focal intonation coincides with the predicate *heard about rirkr* 'have heard about'.

Interrogation is just one of the many ignorative functions discussed in §5.2.3. The role of *wuump* 'contrastive' in interrogative clauses is discussed in §9.1.4.

11.2 Imperative, prohibitive, hortative and jussive constructions

The following sections (and the analysis presented within them) proceed from the premise that there is such a thing as a morphologically imperative verb form which is distinct from the imperative function. The former typically combines with a second person subject, but under some circumstances may combine with a first or third person subject. The latter, however, entails an (at least partially) second person subject (first person exhortations being classed as hortative and third person ones jussive).

11.2.1 Imperative (and prohibitive) constructions

The morphology of imperative inflection was discussed in §7.3.1. Clauses including an imperative verb may function to issue commands (919), prohibit an action (920), make requests (921), or to offer or give permission (922). Of these, only prohibitive clauses attract focal intonation, which centres upon the prohibitive particle *ongkorr* (discussed in §11.3.4).

(919) *koowe, pal   kar.yup.kaar   yarr!*
       cooee towards without.delay go:IMP
       'cooee, Come here right away!'
       [KTh_AC14Nov2002 Narrative LosingIrma]

(920) *plate   ongkorr matp!*
       plate(ACC) PROHIB smash:IMP
       'don't smash that plate!'
       [KTh_AC27Aug2002 Elicitation]

(921) *nhangun may   yump   ngathnma*
       3sgDAT   VEG(ACC) make:IMP 1sgABL
       'make him some food on my behalf'
       [KTh_EN14Aug2002 conversation]

(922) nhunt   mungk   inh,   ngay   kana   mungka-rr ngeengk-ngaac
      2sg(ERG) eat:IMP dem:sp.prx   1sg(ERG) finish eat-P.PFV belly-full
      'you eat this food, I've already eaten, I'm full'
      [KTh_AJ08Feb2004 Elicitation]

All these imperative subfunctions bar prohibition may be achieved by combining imperative verbal inflection with PERMissive *kirri*:

(923) kirri   ko'o
      PERM   spear:IMP
      'spear it!'
      [KTh_MF10Jan2004 Elicitation]

(924) a. nhunt   coffee=aak?
         2sg(NOM)   coffee=ADN.PROP
         'do you want some coffee?'
      b. kirri   ngul ngathn   yump!
         PERM   then   1sgGEN(ACC)   make:IMP
         'yes please!' (lit. 'go ahead and make mine')
         [KTh_EN8Sep2002 Elicitation]

(925) nhunt   kirri yarr   iirra   raak   ngathn-mun
      2sg(NOM)   PERM   go:IMP to.there   PLACE   1sgGEN-DAT
      'you can stay at my place [while I'm away]'
      [KTh_AJ08Feb2004 Elicitation]

Although *kirri* can occur in isolation as a response to a request (meaning something like 'go ahead!'), any full clause containing this particle must contain an imperative verb. I take this, together with the fact that *kirri* does not affect the modal force of the clause, but rather only increases politeness, as evidence that a clause containing *kirri* should not be viewed as a separate construction, but rather a subtype of the imperative construction.

Prohibition is effected by combining an imperative verb with the PROHIBitive particle *ongkorr* (926), or the use of *ongkorr* alone in a verbless clause (927):

(926) therng   ongkorr kuta!
      hit:IMP   PROHIB   dog(ACC)
      'don't hit dogs!'
      [KTh_AC21Aug2002 Conversation]

(927) yorrp   ongkorr!
      this.way PROHIB
      'don't do that!'
      [KTh_AC14Nov2002 Narrative LosingIrma]

Imperative clauses cannot be negated by means of the negative particle *kaar*. I consider clauses containing *ongkorr*, then, as simply a negated imperative clause, rather than a distinct construction.

11.2.2 Jussive and hortative

Jussive mood is expressed by a construction comprising a verb inflected for nonpast tense – not imperative mood – combined with the OPTative particle *ak*.[194] This is illustrated by examples (928) – (932):

(928) raak   ongkorr nhumpan,   ak   wun!
      PLACE(ACC)   PROHIB disturb-V^:IMP OPT lie:NPST
      'don't stir up the place, let it lie!'
      [KTh_MF20Aug2002 Conversation]

(929) ngul ngay   let-m   rirk-r...   ak   yan!
      then 1sg(ERG) let-VBLZ   DO-P.PFV   OPT go:NPST
      'I let [the fishing line go] ... may it go!'
      [KTh_AJ27Jan2004 Conversation]

(930) inh   kaar therk-nhan,
      dem:sp.prx   NEG   return-GO&:NPST
      paanth   thonmarr ak   nhiinan
      woman(NOM)   always   OPT sit:GO&:NPST
      'this [woman] won't go back. May the woman stay here forever!'
      [KTh_AJ27Jan2004 Conversation]

(931) ak   wun!
      JUSS lie:NPST
      'let them lie!' (i.e. don't move my clothes from the washing machine)
      [KTh_EN8Feb2004 Conversation]

---

194 This particle may well be cognate with the Kugu Nganhcara form *(ma)-ku*, of which Smith and Johnson (2000: 437–438) note that "third person imperatives (i.e. jussives) require the particle *(ma)-ku*, which may also optionally appear with first person imperatives (hortatives)".

(932) ak piinth-r, ngamal wene
OPT grow-NPST big become:NPST
"let it [cyclone] grow, let it become big"
[KTh_**AJ**-GJ03Feb2004 Conversation]

This same construction is also used in apparently hortative contexts (i.e. with first person subjects). Example (933), for instance, has a first person singular subject, while (934) has a first person dual exclusive subject:

(933) ngay ak kal-r iipal
1sg(ERG) OPT carry-NPST from.there
'I'll carry it home'
[Foote KutaWoochorrm]

(934) ngawoy, ngali ritar ak nhiin, ngumpurr
yes 1du:excl(NOM) gammon OPT sit:NPST old.lady
yes, let us sit a bit, old lady
[Foote KutaWoochorrm]

Although jussives and hortatives are etically distinct, in both cases the speaker expresses the hope or the expectation that nothing will intervene to prevent the situation or event described from transpiring. Interestingly, though, clauses with first person inclusive subjects behave as (second person) imperatives rather than (first person exclusive) hortatives. That is to say, the inclusion or exclusion of the addressee is in this respect more significant than the inclusion or exclusion of the speaker. Hence (935)–(937) contain an imperative-marked verb:

(935) kuuwiy ngal yarr!
hey 1du:incl(NOM) go:IMP
'come on, let's go!'
[KTh_FT08Feb2004 Narrative Adoptee]

(936) ngamp mangmangal yarr!
1pl:incl(NOM) happy go:IMP
'let's be happy!'
[KTh_GJ03Oct2002 Narrative ComposedSong]

(937) ngal yarr thurma,
1du:incl(NOM) go:IMP together
'we'll go together'
[KTh_ME04Jun2005 Narrative (interruption)]

The Kuuk Thaayorre modal system, then, groups inclusive subjects with second person (imperative) subjects, while exclusive subjects (e.g. *ngali* '[s]he and I') group with first person (jussive) subjects. This makes sense when we consider that an imperative clause with an inclusive subject, like a second person imperative, makes demands of the addressee (with all the attendant interactional considerations, such as face). Hortative/jussive clauses with first person (exclusive) and third person subjects, however, demand nothing of the addressee. It is logical, then, that a primary cleavage here should fall as it does in Kuuk Thaayorre.

Examples such as (938) and (939) might at first appear to express second person imperatives by means of the jussive construction:

(938) *yuk   aw-ith   kath; ak   yaak-r*
       tree(NOM) ATTN-dem:dist   rotten OPT cut:RDP-NPST
       "that tree is dead; saw it down!"
       [Foote and Hall: Primer 8]

(939) *ee'! ngathun kulam   ak   thak-r,*
       hey   1sgDAT path(ACC) OPT   leave-NPST
       ngay   ulp   yan   yuurra
       1sg(NOM) dem:ad.prx go:NPST far.to.there
       (to poison cousin:) 'leave the road for me, I'm going that way'
       [KTh_AJ27Jan2004 Conversation]

However, I would argue that both examples are grammatically jussive though used in the indirect expression of an order/request/command speech act. Although I am unaware of the context of utterance for (938), it seems natural for the speaker to express a general wish for the tree to be sawn down, without specifying that it should be the addressee who does so. This might be either from a desire to protect the negative face of the addressee (by avoiding a direct command, cf. Brown and Levinson 1987), or from a genuine lack of concern as to who, of a large group of potential agents, should execute the sawing. (938) might therefore be paraphrased 'that tree is dead, let it be sawn down!'. In the case of (939), it is clearly plausible that in such socially sensitive contexts as speaking to a poison cousin, direct imperatives should be avoided, being instead replaced by the more indirect expression of a desire for a particular event to occur. (939) might therefore be better translated as 'let it be that [you] leave the road, I'm going over there'. Palmer (2001: 82) notes that "there are often two kinds of command in languages with mood systems, but differing in terms of politeness". This supports the notion that the combination of the optative particle with an (implied) second person subject is associated with heightened politeness.

Finally, the jussive construction may be used in narrative to express the intention or purpose of a protagonist. So, for example, in (940) the protagonists are described as searching for firewood, and the following jussive clause might be interpreted as the will of the protagonists, rather than the speaker as such (i.e. 'they were looking for firewood that they might light a fire'):

(940) *paath   waath-m   pul   ak   pathatha-n-r*
      fire(ACC) search-P.IPFV   3du(ERG) OPT   bite:RDP-V^-NPST
      'they looked for firewood to light [a fire with]'
      [Foote and Hall: Reader 9]

Note that in such examples, the verb of the jussive clause must be inflected for nonpast tense, despite the event described's being located in the past.

11.3 Negation

Negation may be achieved in Kuuk Thaayorre in a number of ways. To begin with, there are two negative interjections (*kece* 'CONTRADICTORY' and *pokon* 'NO', discussed in §11.3.1) which are antonymically related to the affirmative interjection *ngawoy* 'yes'. The form *pokon* 'NO' also functions as a constituent negator (effecting, e.g., existential negation), as does the privative enclitic *=(k)aar*. The morphosyntactic, semantic and pragmatic differences between these two are considered in §11.3.3. Clausal negation is achieved by means of the NEGative particle *kaar*, discussed in §11.3.2.

11.3.1 Negative interjections

Both *kece* 'CONTRADICtory' and *pokon* 'NO' function as negative interjections. *Pokon* is the unmarked of the two, frequently occurring as an answer to questions (941) or to contradict a statement perceived to be incorrect (942):

(941) A: *nhunt   rump-un   yan?*
         2sg(NOM)   beach-DAT   go:NPST
         'are you going to the beach?'
      B: *pokon*
         NO
         'no.'
         [Anon.]

(942) A: *ngay   kar   ngeeym   nhunt   kar   sixteen=nhurr=p*
         1sg(NOM)   like think:P.IPFV   2sg(NOM)   like   sixteen=ONLY=PRAG
         'I thought you were just sixteen'

B: *pokon! Ngay   twenty-four*
   NO   1sg(NOM) twenty-four
   'no! I'm twenty-four'
   [Anon., confirmed LN02Oct2002]

Pokon 'NO' is also used to add emphasis to an already negated clause (this function is related to its constituent negation function, see §11.3.3):

(943) *yoorr ngancn   may   kaar=p   nhiina-n-r,   pokon!*
       now   1pl:excl(NOM) VEG(ACC)   NEG=PRAG   sit-Vᴬ-NPST   NO
       'today we don't plant any of that food, not at all / none of it!'
       [KTh_AC22Jul2002 Narrative ChapmanEra]

Kece is pragmatically stronger than *pokon*, carrying a contradictory connotation often translated in Pormpuraaw English as "you don't know!". Consequently, *kece* is usually an inappropriate response to a question, and is more typically uttered as an objection to a statement made previously by either the addressee or the speaker themself:

(944) A: *ball   ith   ngathn*
          ball(NOM)   dem:dist   1sgGEN
          'that ball is mine'
       B: *kece!   Ball   ulp   ngathn!*
          CDICT   ball(NOM)   dem:ad.prx   1sgGEN
          'no, the ball's *mine*'
          [KTh_EF14Dec2002 Elicitation Demonstratives13]

The proposition contradicted by *kece* may be implied rather than explicitly articulated by a prior statement. Hence in (945.3) AJ refutes the implicature in line (945.2) that the place under discussion is far away:

(945) 1. AJ: *[...] raak min, ee, rump, ii-kuw   inh*
              place good eh beach there-at:west   dem:sp.prx
              '[...] it's a good place, isn't it, just down on the beach in the west'
       2. AG: *ngay   kaar yat   ngay   truck pokon.*
              1sg(NOM)   NEG go:P.PFV   1sg(NOM)   truck NO
              'I haven't been, I don't have a truck'
       3. AJ: *kece!   inh   thaapirri*
              CDICT   dem:sp.prx   close
              'you're mistaken! It's nearby'
              [AJ27Jan2004 Conversation]

These two interjections are the only negators that can form a clause in isolation. But while *kece* never forms a phrase or constituent with other clausal elements, *pokon* also functions as a negator of constituents, as discussed in §11.3.3.

11.3.2 Clausal negation

A verbal clause can only be negated by the particle *kaar* 'NEGative'. Typically, *kaar* is found in immediately pre-verbal position, but it may also occur in clauses where the verb is elided (e.g. 946). *Kaar* cannot constitute a clause in isolation, but due to the optional omission of consituents, a negative clause can minimally consist of *kaar* + argument (e.g. 946) or *kaar* + verb (e.g. 947):

(946) *ngay   kaar*
       1sg(NOM) NEG
       'I don't [want to go to the outstation]'
       (also a felicitous refusal of offered cigarettes, etc.)
       [KTh_EC02Oct2002 Conversation]

(947) *yarra kaar yat*
       away NEG go:P.PFV
       '[he] didn't run off'
       [Foote and Hall: Primer 9]

In examples where the verb is omitted, such as (946), *kaar* functions with a negative desiderative force (as noted by Hall 1972: 90).[195] The role of *kaar* in a desiderative construction is discussed in §11.7.5.2.

Where a negative clause is headed by a verb, there is an overwhelming tendency for *kaar* 'NEGative' to appear in the immediately preverbal position (an initial text count of verb-headed clauses revealed ninety-eight cases in which *kaar* preceded the verb, and only three in which the predicate occurred first). Where *kaar* immediately

---

[195] Hall (1972: 90) characterizes the modal use of *kaar* as follows: "when used alone as head, the negative often substitutes for the desiderative "wish", in a negative sense, /Nunt ka:r?/ 'you refuse?' "Don't you want to?"". In cases where *kaar* is added to a verbless copula clause, there is no modal implicature. This may or may not be evidence that such copula clauses are basically verbal in nature (since they may be verb headed in certain contexts, cf. §10.2.4), with the verb simply elided in the present tense:

(a) *ngay   mincminc   kaar=p*
    1sg(NOM)   correct   NEG=PRAG
    'I'm not sure'
    [KTh_JCo13Nov02 Conversation]

precedes the verb, it has narrow scope over the verb alone. Hence example (948) describes many people not succeeding, rather than not many people succeeding:

(948) mong-thurr kaar win-m   rirk-r
      many-ERG   NEG   succeed-VBLZ DO-P.PFV
      'a lot of people couldn't do it [i.e. each person tried and failed]'
      [KTh_AC13Sep2002 Narrative Werngr]

In the clauses in which *kaar* follows the verbal head, *kaar* appears to have wider scope. Consider the second line of example (949), in which the speaker makes explicit his intention to negate the clause as a whole (i.e. 'NOT[I have forgotten]', rather than 'I have NOT[forgotten]'):

(949) 1. wuuc   ngay   kaal-purng-m-at
         song(ACC) 1sg(NOM)   ear-closed-VBLZ-GO&:P.PFV
         'I've forgotten the traditional songs'
      2. kaal-purng-m-at   kaar-p
         ear-close-VBLZ-GO&:P.PFV NEG=PRAG
         '[actually] it's not that I've forgotten'
      3. ngay   kaar learn-m   rirk-r
         1sg(NOM)   NEG   learn-VBLZ DO-P.PFV
         'I never learned [them]'
         [KTh_AJ-IC-**GJ**26Nov2002 Narrative/Conversation]

This broad-scope negation in (949.2) contrasts with the narrow-scope negation of (949.3), in which *kaar* precedes the verb.

11.3.2.1 Impossibility construction

In order to express an inability or impossibility (as opposed to unwillingness), the clausal negator *kaar* enters into a construction with the DUBitative enclitic =*okun*. This can be seen in example (950), which was uttered in an elicitation context when the speaker was asked to imagine that she had been planning (and wanted) to walk down to the beach to go fishing, but had hurt her foot and was not able to walk there.

(950) ngay   yancnh=paa   rump-un,   ngay   kaar=okun yan
      1sg(NOM)   go:SBJV=EMPH   beach-DAT 1sg(NOM)   NEG=DUB   go:NPST
      'I would walk to the beach but I can't go (i.e. it is not the case that I might go)'
      [KTh_MF06Aug2002 Elicitation]

Dubitative =*okun* is a modal enclitic used to express a lack of knowledge on the speaker's part (discussed in §9.1.5), as seen in the following:

(951) ngay   rump-un   yan=okun
      1sg(NOM) beach-DAT go:NPST=DUB
      'maybe I'll go to the beach [I don't know whether or not this will happen]'
      [KTh_MF24Sep2002 Elicitation]

If =*okun* expresses 'possibly X', the collocation *kaar=okun* expresses 'NOT {possibly X}', with the negative particle having scope over the dubitative enclitic, rather than the reverse. Interestingly, when the speaker of (950) was asked to translate the example sentence, she rendered it in Pormpuraaw English as follows:

(952) *I might walk down the beach but I mightn't go. I want to walk down the beach but I mightn't go down now.*

The original translation is rather misleading since the scope of *mightn't* in Pormpuraaw English is broader than that of the Standard Australian English equivalent. For the latter, *I mightn't go* also allows *I might go* (i.e. 'possibly {NOT X}'), whereas in Pormpuraaw English this is equivalent to *it is not the case that I might go* (i.e. 'NOT {possibly X}'). This broad scope can also be seen in example (953):

(953) kece, Mum, ngul=okun kaar wang-a   kaar=okun let-m   rirk
      CDICT Mum   then=DUB   NEG whitefella-ERG NEG=DUB let-VBLZ DO:NPST
      'No, Mum, the whitefellas won't let me'
      [KTh_ACh05Oct2002 Conversation]

I believe that this broad scope is a feature of *kaar=okun* as a restricted collocation used in the formation of an 'impossibility construction', rather than compositionally derived from the scope of either *kaar* or =*okun* in their respective independent usages.

11.3.3 Constituent negation

The particle *pokon* may has already been introduced as an interjection used to contradict prior statements or answer a polar question in the negative (see §11.3.1). The same particle can also be used either in combination with a noun phrase or in place of it in order to negate that constituent. or as the sole exponent of a constituent. Where it combines with a NP, it usually follows it directly (as in (954)), but it is also possible for other elements to intervene (as in (955)):

(954) lights pokon, money pokon
      lights NO   money NO
      '[we had] no lights, no money'
      [KTh_**AJ**-IC-GJ26Nov2002 Conversation / Narrative PormpuraawKanangkarr]

(955) yuk   ngay   pokon
      stick   1sg(NOM)   NO
      'I don't have any cigarettes'
      [KTh_AC14Oct2002 Conversation]

While this constituent negation is often used to express a negative possessive relation between the constituent and a potential possessor (as with both (954) and (955)), this is not the only use of the construction. For example, in (956) the speaker describes the first meeting of her husband and their newborn daughter. *Pokon* here is used to refute the husband's misapprehension that the baby was male, not to deny a possessive relationship:

(956) ulp   parr_r pam=rr   pokon
      dem:ad.prx   child   male=PRAG   NO
      ' "this is not a boy (i.e. it is a girl)" '
      " "there is no boy one!" "
      [KTh_ACh07Nov2002 Conversation]

Where *pokon* is the sole exponent of an argument, it expresses indefinite semantics associated with existential negation; 'nothing', 'no one', 'none'. This can be seen in the following clauses, in which *pokon* functions as complement in a verbless copula construction:

(957) ngay   pokon, ngay   kaar born rirk-r   same.time raak ulp
      1sg(NOM)   NO   1sg(NOM)   NEG   born DO-P.PFV   same.time TIME dem:ad.prx
      'I was nothing [i.e. not in existence]. I wasn't born at that time'
      [KTh_ACh07Nov2002 Conversation]

(958) kuta=yuk   yuuw yat, kuta   ii   pokon
      dog(NOM)=STUFF   far go:P.PFV dog(NOM) there NO
      "there were no people, even the dogs not there"
      [KTh_GJ12Jan2004 Elicitation/Conversation]

Where *pokon* is uttered as a response to an open-ended question (as opposed to the polar interrogatives discussed in §11.3.1), it is with this indefinite sense:

(959) A: nhunt   ngan yump-r   minc.ngul?
         2sg(NOM)   what do-NPST   afternoon
         'what will you do this afternoon?'
      B: pokon, ngay   pormp-an=nhurr   nhiin-nan
         NO   1sg(NOM)   house-DAT=ONLY   sit-GO&:NPST
         'nothing, I'm just going to sit at home'
         [KTh_EN06Sep2002 Elicitation / Conversation]

Though they are in the same semantic neighbourhood, *pokon* contrasts with the PRIVative enclitics =*kaar* and =*aar* in several respects. Compare, for instance, (960a) and (960b):

(960) a. *pam.kunyangkar pormpr pokon*
       brother(NOM)   house   NO
       'my brother [has] no house [right now]'
   b. *pam.kunyangkar pormpr=aar*
       brother(NOM)   house=PRIV
       'my brother is homeless'
       [KTh_MF20Aug2002 Elicitation]

Pokon tends to be associated with the lack of more temporary, alienable ownership (as with cigarettes, money), and =*aar* with a lacking stable and permanent association (as with body parts, spouses, cars). This appears to be only an implicature, however, as both forms are potentially compatible with the full range of possessive relations.

Pokon, =*kaar* and =*aar* also differ in their focal effects. *Pokon* contributes a focus on the possessum it modifies, as would be expected of a constituent negator. Accordingly, example (961) below focuses attention on the dog that the man lacks. The relational privative =*kaar*, on the other hand, focuses attention on the relationship itself (as befits a form most likely derived from a clausal negator). Thus the privative construction in (962) focuses attention on the possessive relationship of dog-having that is absent. The adnominal privative form =*aar* gives focal prominence to the possessor, with (963) focusing attention on the man who lacks a dog:

(961) *pam   kuta pokon*
      man(NOM) dog NO
      'the man has **no dog**'

(962) *pam   kuta=kaar*
      man(NOM) dog=REL.PRIV
      'the man **doesn't have** a dog'

(963) *pam   kuta=aar*
      man(NOM) dog=ADN.PRIV
      'the **dogless** man'
      [KTh_GJ12Dec2005 Elicitation]

This contrast in focus explains the pragmatic association of the respective markers with more vs less alienable possessive relationships. So, for instance, if the privative relation is employed to tell the hearer something about the (non)possessor, then the hearer is likely to assume that the state or situation described is something significant for the possessor, and therefore likely to be ongoing or permanent (e.g. lacking an ear is more likely to be described as an identifying characteristic of a person than lacking cigarettes).

11.3.4 Prohibition

The prohibitive construction minimally comprises an imperative-inflected verb in conjunction with the PROHIBitive particle *ongkorr*. Constituent order within the prohibitive construction is pragmatically determined, with the particle preceding the verb in (964) but following it in (965):[196]

(964) *theerng ongkorr, kuta!*
hit:IMP PROHIB dog(ACC)
'don't hit that dog!'
"no more hitim with a stick, them dog"
[KTh_AC21Aug2002 Conversation]

(965) *nhunt ongkorr yarr raak nganc-an*
2sg(ACC) PROHIB go:IMP PLACE sacred-DAT
'don't go to that poison place'
[KTh_GJ14Oct2002 Elicitation / Conversation]

See §11.2.1 for further examples of prohibition.

11.3.5 Negative constructions as a politeness strategy

In English, an interrogative construction (usually containing a modal verb) is frequently used to make requests (e.g. *would you shut that window for me?*) and offers (e.g. *would you like some tea?*). In Kuuk Thaayorre, these communicative functions are frequently achieved by means of negative constructions, as seen in the following:

(966) *nhunt yoorr mit kaar rirk?*
2sg(NOM) today work NEG DO:NPST
'would you work [with me] today?' (lit. 'you won't work today')
[KTh_EN8Sep2002 Elicitation / Conversation]

---

[196] There does not seem to be any preference for the prohibitive particle to occupy second position in the clause. Thus the exclamation *ongkorr mungk!* (PROHIB eat:IMP) 'don't eat that!' is perfectly well-formed.

(967) nhunt   kaar   mungk-nhan
      2sg(ERG)   NEG   eat-GO&:NPST
      'would you like something to eat?' (lit. 'you're not going to eat')
      [Foote and Hall: Reader]

(968) yuk   pokon
      thing   NO
      'could you give me a cigarette?' (lit. '[you have] no cigarettes')
      [Anon.]

Thus the ironic declaration in (966) ('you won't work for me') in fact implicates the speaker's desire for the opposite state of affairs ('you will work for me'). Similarly in (967) the declaration that the addressee will not eat in fact represents an indirect offer of food. Example (968) is even less direct, whereby the speaker requests a cigarette by declaring its nonexistence. These examples should be understood in the context of a sociolinguistic setting in which direct commands and questions are dispreferred for certain topics and social/kin relationships in order to protect negative face (in the sense of Brown and Levinson 1987, cf. Gaby forthcoming).

11.4 Apprehensive constructions

11.4.1 *Pam* and 'potential detriment'

Apprehensive clauses describe a (possible or actualized) event that might have (had) a negative impact.[197] This can be seen in (969) and the second clause of (970):

(969) ongkorr!   pam   path-nhan!
      PROHIB   DETR   bite-GO&:NPST
      'don't [pull that cat's tail]! [It] might bite!'
      [KTh_GJ31Jan2004 Elicitation]

(970) gas.bottle   kar   kunut-r,   in.case   pam   fly-m   rirk-nhan
      gas.bottle(ACC) like   remove-NPST   in.case   DETR   fly-VBLZ DO-GO&:NPST
      '[we'll] take out all the gas bottles, in case they fly [in the cyclone]'
      [KTh_AJ03Feb2004 Conversation]

The possible event in (970) is the gas bottles flying around, while the negative impact (that they might cause damage or injury) is only implied by the presence of *pam*.

---

[197] This usage of *pam* is noted by Hall (1972: 142) and labelled 'indefinite threat'.

Although the form *pam* is elsewhere a noun meaning 'man', it appears to have undergone semantic bleaching in this constructional context, conveying the event's potentially having some detrimental effect on a particular person or (in this case) people in general. The individual potentially harmed can be spelled out, however, as in (971.2):

(971) 1. *thaapirri kaar=p nhunt katp-nhan=unh*
close NEG=PRAG 2sg(ERG) grasp-GO&:NPST=3sgACC
'don't you go holding it [crocodile] close'
2. *ngul nhinh pam paath-r. Awoy.*
then 2sgACC DETR bite-NPST yes
'or it might bite you. True'.
[KTh_AJ-**GJ**03Feb2004 Conversation]

Such examples make it clear that *pam* does not fill an argument position (e.g. representing a non-specific referent). Given its bare form, *pam* could only occupy one of two argument slots: intransitive subject or transitive object. The fact that (971b) is a transitive clause rules out the former, while the specification of a second person direct object (*nhinh* 'you') rules out the latter. Further, while (971b) spells out the potential detrimental occurrence (i.e. that the crocodile might bite the addressee), *pam* 'DETR' also appears in clauses describing the cause of the detrimental occurrence (only indirectly alluding to the potential harm). Thus in clauses such as (972), *pam* 'DETR' is the only overt signal that the event described might have some negative impact on the speaker:

(972) *pam nhunt ngene yat?*
DETR 2sg(NOM) why go:P.PFV
'why on earth did you go off (to my potential detriment)?'
[KTh_AC14Nov2002 Narrative LosingIrma]

This example is taken from a story told by Alfred Charlie, in which he describes taking a white woman on a bush trip (the full transcript of which is given in **Appendix 2**). The woman went missing only to later reappear, saying that she had just wanted to stretch her legs. In (972), Charlie quotes himself admonishing her for leaving him and potentially getting him in trouble (for losing her). Slightly later in the story (973), he employs another potential detriment construction, though this time it focuses on the detrimental effect itself rather than its cause:

(973) *ooh, yorrp ongkorr! Ngay pam court-ak yup yan*
oh like.that PROHIB 1sg(NOM) DETR court-DAT soon go:NPST
'oh, don't do such things! I might have had to go to court'
[KTh_AC14Nov2002 Narrative LosingIrma]

Owing to its morphological isolation and syntactic independence, *pam* 'DETR' is analyzed as a clausal particle. Aside from the presence of this particle, the potential detriment construction takes the form of a regular declarative clause.

It is finally worth noting that this construction probably underlies the common fixed expression *pam thaawarra* 'dangerous', now used adjectivally. Although *thaawarra* is synchronically unanalysable, it may well derive from a compound *thaaw* 'mouth' and *waarr* 'bad' – especially since many things so-labelled are dangerous because they bite (e.g. dogs, crocodiles).

11.4.2 Counterfactual apprehensive construction

The second type of apprehensive construction in Kuuk Thaayorre is formed through the combination of the ignorative *ngene* 'why' with a verb marked either by counterfactual inflection or by the first associated motion morpheme (in nonpast tense). These 'counterfactual apprehensive' clauses both express that something undesirable might have happened (or might happen in the future), and that it was (or should be) avoided. This construction is thus typically employed in the description of a lucky escape.

(974) *ngay   nearly punth   inh   ngene lose-m   rirk-nhan*
      1sg(ERG) nearly arm(ACC) dem:sp.prx why   lose-TR DO-GO&:NPST
      "nearly lost my arm!"
      [KTh_AJ-**GJ**03Feb2004 Conversation]

(975) *ngul ngene peln   thaaw-muunth-nhan*
      then why   3pl(NOM) mouth-sink-GO&:NPST
      'lucky if they don't get drowned!'
      [Hall 1972: 112]

(976) *ngul ngene=p   yungar-natath?*
      later why=PRAG swim-CTF
      'lucky he didn't swim (near the crocodiles)!'
      [Hall 1972: 112]

The modal information that the unfortunate event was or might still be avoided is contributed by the verbal (associated motion or counterfactual) inflection, while the ignorative *ngene* contributes to the apprehensive sense of a potentially dangerous situation.

11.5 Reflexive constructions

Reflexive events prototypically involve an actor-subject directing their actions towards themself, rather than towards an external object. There are two reflexive constructions in Kuuk Thaayorre. The first, 'pronominal reflexive construction' (977) is defined by the presence of a reflexive pronoun (cf. §5.1.2) and the absence of any verbal morphology coding the reflexive or reciprocal. The second, 'verbal reflexive construction' (978) is defined by the presence of the reflexive verbal suffix -*e*:

(977) *ngay   wash-m   rirk-r   ngathney*
 1sg(ERG) wash-TR DO-P.PFV 1sgRFL
 'I'm washing myself'
 [KTh_GJ25Oct2002 Elicitation]

(978) *kuta   ngith   pathath-e*
 dog(NOM) dem:dist bite:RDP-RFL:NPST
 'that dog is biting himself'
 [KTh_AC21Aug2002 Conversation]

Section 11.5.1 describes the pronominal reflexive construction. This remainder of this section will be concerned with the verbal reflexive construction, with §11.5.2 outlining its basic morphosyntax, and the following subsections focusing upon its semantic subsenses.

11.5.1 The pronominal reflexive construction

The paradigm of reflexive pronouns was given in §5.1.2.1. In all cases of their use, reflexive pronouns express what I call 'reflected action', the fact that the actor-subject is affected by their own actions. They may be affected as undergoer (as in (977) above) or as beneficiary, as in (979):

(979) *ngay   may   mi'irr   ngathney*
 1sg(ERG) VEG(ACC) pick.up:P.PFV 1sgRFL
 'I got myself some food'
 [Anon.]

In clauses such as (977) above the reflexive pronoun fills one of the argument slots subcategorized for by the verb. As examples like (979) demonstrate, though, the reflexive pronoun need not take the place of a core argument. Instead, the reflexive pronoun may apparently fill any of the (core or oblique) functions other than subject. Reflexive pronouns thus do not appear to affect clausal transitivity, filling an argument slot where they substituting for the direct object (977), but simply marking the affectedness of the subject where an argument slot is unavailable (979).

It is common for a reflexive pronoun to supplement verbal marking in a verbal reflexive clause (e.g. (984) below) or a reciprocal clause (e.g. (1008) below).

11.5.2 Morphosyntax of the verbal reflexive construction

As shown in §8.1.2, reflexive derivation creates a second conjugation verb stem. Although this conjugation class is primarily associated with intransitive verbs, the verbal reflexive construction is somewhat ambivalent with respect to transitivity. Oftentimes, as in example (978) above, the subject of the verbal reflexive clause is in unmarked nominative case, signalling that the clause is intransitive. Other verbal reflexive clauses, however, contain an ergative-marked subject. This is particularly common where the subject is acting upon a part of themselves, where this part is encoded as an accusative direct object. Such clauses (e.g. 980) appear to be straightforwardly transitive:

(980) pam-al ith koow katpatp-e
man-ERG dem:dist nose(ACC) grasp:RDP-RFL:NPST
'that man is holding [his] nose'
[KTh_FT10Feb2004 RcpPilot8]

It is cross-linguistically common (particularly on the Australian continent) for reflexive and reciprocal clauses to display mixed and/or variable indicators of transitivity (cf. Evans et al., 2007). In Kuuk Thaayorre, there is a strong correlation between explicit reference to the undergoer (in a separate NP to that representing the actor) and the ergative-accusative case-frame indicative of transitive clauses. Complicating the analysis of transitivity somewhat, are verbal reflexive clauses containing two unmarked arguments. Such clauses (illustrated by (981), presented with two alternative glosses) arise from the differing patterns of case syncretism in the pronominal paradigm (in which the distinction between nominative and ergative is collapsed, cf. §5.1.1.1) as opposed to nominals (for which both nominative and accusative cases are unmarked, cf. §4.2).

(981) ngay punth inh yak-ey-r
1sg(ERG) arm(ACC) dem:sp.prx cut-RFL-P.PFV
1sg(NOM) arm(NOM) dem:sp.prx cut-RFL-P.PFV
'I cut myself on the arm'
[KTh_AJ-**GJ**03Feb2004 Conversation]

There are two possible analyses of such clauses. Firstly, they might be analyzed as instances of the transitive reflexive construction, containing an unmarked ergative subject argument (in this case, *ngay* 'I') and an unmarked accusative direct object (in this case *punth inh* 'this arm'), as reflected by the upper of the two gloss lines above. Secondly, the two noun phrases could be analyzed as forming a single argument through same-case (nominative) apposition, as reflected by the lower gloss line. The apposition of noun phrases representing part and whole of a single entity is common in Kuuk Thaayorre (as discussed extensively in §6.10.1), but there is a crucial difference between the representation of part and whole in reflexive clauses such as (981), and an argument composed of part and whole NPs apposed in the same case. In an appositional construction, the same relationship obtains between the predicate and both part and whole. That is to say, the predicate has scope over the whole referent inasmuch as the involved part is taken to stand for the whole (hence the part cannot be affected or agentive without the whole also being affected or agentive by implication). Accordingly, in (471) the dog enters the jar inasmuch as its head does:

(471') *kuta   nhul   paant   glass-ak   rok-r*
  dog(NOM) 3sg(NOM) head(NOM) glass-DAT enter-NPST
  'the dog puts his head into the jar'
  [KTh_MF17Sep2002 Narrative FrogStory]

In reflexive clauses such as (981) above, however, the whole referent plays a very different role to the part argument. Indeed, the whole (as actor) acts upon the part (as undergoer). I therefore analyze clauses such as (981) as transitive, with the whole subject in unmarked ergative case and the part object in unmarked accusative case.

There is thus a neat correspondence between ergative subject marking in reflexive clauses with two overt arguments (representing whole and part of a single entity – as in (980) above) and nominative subject non-marking in reflexive clauses with a single overt argument (as in (978)):

(978') *kuta   ngith   pathath-e*
  dog(NOM) dem:dist bite:RDP-RFL:NPST
  'that dog is biting himself'
  [KTh_AC21Aug2002 Conversation]

Reflexive constructions in which whole and part are explicitly referred to by separate NPs are transitive; here the subject referent is conceived of as saliently distinct from the object referent they act upon, while their overlapping reference is signalled by the presence of the reflexive suffix. A reflexive construction containing only a single subject argument, however, is syntactically intransitive. Only one entity is involved in the event, but the fact that they are involved in this event in two ways (and therefore assigned two distinct theta roles) is signalled by the reflexive suffix. To reflect this, we establish two verbal reflexive sub-constructions: (1) an intransitive 'core reflexive' construction containing a reflexive-marked verb and a single (nominative) subject argument; and (2) a transitive 'partitive object' construction comprising a reflexive-marked verb, an (ergative) subject argument and an (accusative) direct object. Transitivity is thus a property of these (sub)constructions, rather than an inherent feature of the reflexive derivational process:

Core reflexive construction: V-*e* <SUBJ$_{NOM}$, (Rfl.Pro)>
Partitive object construction: V-*e* <SUBJ-whole$_{ERG}$, OBJ-part$_{ACC}$, (Rfl.Pro)>

There is one exception to this neat division of reflexive clauses into transitive and intransitive constructions. Where the reflexive clause includes an instrumental adjunct, the subject generally takes ergative case marking, even in the absence of a direct object:

(982) *pam-al   yuk-u   reenng-e-nham*
      man-ERG stick-ERG scratch-RFL-P.IPFV
      'the man was scratching himself with a stick'
      [KTh_GJ12Dec2005 Elicitation]

This might perhaps be linked to Kuuk Thaayorre's general restriction – common among Australian languages[198] – of instrument NPs to transitive clauses (cf. §4.2.1.2). That is to say any Kuuk Thaayorre reflexive clause containing an instrument NP must behave as transitive (with regard to the case-marking of the subject), even in the absence of an overt direct object. Where the instrument NP represents a body part of the reflexive subject, the subject NP may either receive the expected ergative case-marking (as in (983)) or be unmarked (as in (984)):

(983) *pam-al   yuur-u   reenng-e-nham*
      man-ERG hand-ERG scratch-RFL-P.IPFV
      'the man was scratching himself with his hand'
      [KTh_GJ12Dec2005 Elicitation]

(984) *pam   yuur-u   reenng-e-nham   nhangnul*
      man(NOM=ACC) hand-ERG scratch-RFL-P.IPFV 3sgRFL
      'the man was scratching himself with his hand'
      [KTh_GJ12Dec2005 Elicitation]

The fact that ergative marking is obligatory in (982) but optional in (984) might be attributed to the semantic difference between an inanimate instrument (982) and a

---

198 E.g. Yalarnnga (Blake 1987: 57) and Alyawarr (Yallop 1977: 72). The fact that instrument NPs <u>are</u> allowable in (derived) intransitive reflexive/reciprocal clauses in languages such as Alyawarr, is taken by Evans et al. (2007) to be an indicator of 'mixed transitivity'.

body part instrument (984). In the case of the former, the actor-subject is more highly agentive – despite the lack of external direct object – because they must manipulate the instrument-object. By contrast, there is less agentivity involved in clauses like (984) since the body part (hand) is merely the active part of the subject referent, rather than an external object that the subject acts upon.[199] The many wrinkles in the mapping from argument structure to clausal transitivity in reflexive and reciprocal clauses warrant further research (cf. Evans et al., 2007).

The following sections outline the various event types that may be encoded by the verbal reflexive constructions.

11.5.3 Core reflexive

The first, 'core reflexive' sense can be characterized as follows:

Self-directed action; (each) single participant is both actor and undergoer of a single (sub)event.

This sense includes events in which a single participant acts upon themself as a whole (985), or in which each member of a non-singular participant group acts upon themself individually (986):

(985) *ngay   perp-e-nha   mimp-a*
      1sg(NOM) cover-RFL-SBJV cloth-ERG
      'I want to cover myself with a blanket'
      [Hall 1972: 106]

(986) *nhurr   kempthe katp-ey-r*
      2pl(NOM) singly   grasp-RFL-NPST
      'you're each touching yourselves'
      [Hall 1972: 380]

Although the verbal reflexive construction is defined by the presence of *-e* 'RFL', the reflexive-derived verb frequently co-occurs with a reflexive pronoun (described in §5.1.2), used to reinforce the core reflexive interpretation (in contradistinction to other

---

[199] It may alternatively be that *yuuru* 'hand' in (984) is in fact in ergative case (not instrumental), itself representing the transitive subject. Correspondingly, *pam* 'man' would be in unmarked accusative case, representing the direct object. This might also explain the strongly preferred (possibly obligatory) presence of the reflexive pronoun, in order to stress that the hand scratching the man is part of the man himself. Such an explanation could be tested by the substitution of a pronoun for *pam* (since pronouns distinguish nominative and accusative cases). This remains to be investigated.

senses with which the reflexive suffix may be used – see discussion below). Reflexive pronouns in such clauses appear to have an emphatic function, stressing that the event is or should be self-directed rather than directed towards others, as seen in the following example:

(987) nhangknunt   kar   nhaath-e
       2sgRFL   like   look.at-RFL:IMP
       'you should look at yourself!'
       [KTh_EN14Aug2002 Elicitation/Conversation]

11.5.4 Partitive object

Reflexive events in which the actor-subject acts upon a part of themself (as opposed to their whole self) are labelled 'partitive object' (following Geniušienė 1987). Both (980)–(981) above and (988) below are examples of the partitive object (sub)construction:

(988) ngay   muth   rint-e
       1sg(ERG)   back.of.neck(ACC)   cook-RFL:NPST
       'I'm warming my neck (to get rid of bad dream)'
       [KTh_AC10Aug2002 Conversation / Elicitation]

11.5.5 Collective reflexive

The 'collective reflexive' (following Gast and Haas 2008) can be characterized as follows:

> *The activity is carried out internally to the subject group, at least one member of which is both actor and undergoer.*

Here, two or more participants are engaged in an activity, but their respective roles are underspecified. While this use of the reflexive suffix entails that both actor and undergoer roles are ascribed to the group of participants encoded as subject (as is true of many of the senses associated with -*e* 'RFL'), it also entails that at least one of these participants is both actor and undergoer of a single subevent. This is illustrated by example (989):

(989) ngali   muul-thurr   werk-ey-r
       1du:excl(NOM=ERG) white.ochre-ERG   rub-RFL-P.PFV
       'we two painted ourselves and/or each other with white ochre'
       [KTh_EF15Dec2002 Elicitation – prompted by Hall 1972]

A strictly core reflexive interpretation of (989) would entail that each participant paints themself with white ochre (as diagrammatically represented in Figure 14). However, the same clause could be interpreted as collective reflexive (a), describing an event in which a single person paints both themself and a second person (Figure 15b) or – equally felicitously – an event where a single person is painted by both themself and a second person (Figure 15c). It is interesting to note that these latter, collective reflexive senses are better rendered by the English reciprocal construction (as in the translation of (989)) than by the reflexive.

Figure 14. Core reflexive.

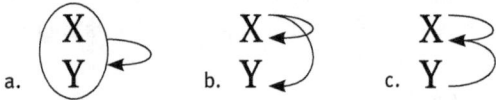

Figure 15. Collective reflexive.

The principal difference between the collective reflexive and a core reflexive clause with plural subject, can be summarized as whether reflexivity is applied to the subject group as a whole (collective reflexive; Figure 15a), or to each individual within the subject group (core reflexive, Figure 14). The collective reflexive sense, as schematized in Figure 15a, is in fact vague as to the exact relations that may hold between individuals within the subject group. Taking a group of two participants for example, it is possible that each member of the group both acts and is acted upon (as in the core reflexive, Figure 14), or that just one member acts upon both themself and the other member (Figure 15b), or that both members act upon just one member of the group (Figure 15c). The number of possible subrelations of course expands geometrically with any increase in the number of group members. Reflexivity thus applied to an entire group, without specifying the exact relationships that hold between members of that group, may well prove a bridging context for the extension of reflexive constructions to encode the reciprocal category, or the reverse.

Kuuk Thaayorre is not novel in extending its verbal reflexive construction to encode this collective reflexive category. Indeed, Gast and Haas (2008) document numerous examples of collective reflexivity in Germanic and Romance languages, wherein a reflexive relation holds for an entire group, rather than for an individual. This also helps to explain some of the apparent anomalies discussed in §11.5.8.

11.5.6 Medio-passive

The 'medio-passive' (following Geniušienė 1987) use of *-e* 'RFL' backgrounds the actor participant in order to focus attention on the undergoer:

The actor is backgrounded or unknown, with focus placed on the undergoer.

This usage is illustrated by (990), in which neither the actor nor the (whole) undergoer is specified, but it is implausible that the hair acted upon itself:

(990) *yangan   kaal-ak   kath-ey-r*
       hair(NOM=ACC)   ear-DAT   bind-RFL-P.PFV
       '[his] hair is tied over [his] ears'
       [KTh_GJ15Oct2002 Elicitation BowPed46]

Uttered in the description of an elicitation drawing, it is particularly clear that the person who had tied the man's hair is neither known nor relevant to the description.

11.5.7 Deagentive

The 'deagentive' use of the reflexive suffix is closely related to the medio-passive inasmuch as the undergoer is especially prominent in both. The deagentive sense, however, does not imply the existence of an agentive actor that is simply too unimportant (or unknown) to be represented as subject. Instead, the effect on the undergoer has been caused spontaneously or accidentally without the involvement of any external actor or force, as in (991):

(991) *minh   ith   kirk-an   runc-ey-r*
       animal(NOM) dem:dist   spear-DAT collide-RFL-P.PFV
       "wallaby collided into a spear [leaning on a rock]"
       [KTh_GJ10Jan2004 Elicitation]

Hence, the deagentive sense can be characterized as follows:

The undergoer is affected by a spontaneous or accidental event.

11.5.8 Further extended uses of the verbal reflexive construction

Some of the events described by means of the verbal reflexive construction fit none of the above categories exactly. Example (992), for instance, combines features of both the collective reflexive and medio-passive senses of *-e*:

(992) *pul*   *runc-ey-r*
       2du(NOM=ERG) collide-RFL-P.PFV
       'they two collided with one other'
       [KTh_GJ19Oct2002 Elicitation StagedEvents5]

Like a collective reflexive event, (992) describes a scene in which one member of the subject group is responsible for an action that affects both members (it was uttered in the description of a video clip in which a person looking the other way walks into another, stationary person). Like a medio-passive clause, there is no attribution of blame: the focus in (992) is not on the cause of the event, but rather on its effect on the two participants encoded as subject. What the collective reflexive and medio-passive senses have in common, is the lack of specificity with which the actor is identified – whether it is omitted (in the case of the medio-passive) or subsumed in a single actor-undergoer participant group (in the case of the collective reflexive). There is therefore no distinguishing of the individual roles played by participants, and the event is implied to be accidental.

In (993), too, the reflexive morpheme marks the event as being carried out internally to the subject group, implying that the precise assignation of roles to participants within that group is of little importance:

(993) *pul*   *kuthip*   *mi'im-r*   *mut.thongkn*   *reerek-e*
       3du(ERG)   story(ACC)   tell-P.PFV   back(NOM=ACC)   give:RDP-RFL:INF
       'they two are telling each other stories standing back to back'
       ("they give one another their back")
       [KTh_GJ19Oct2002 StagedEvents43]

We might expect that examples such as (992) and (993), in which a nonsingular number of participants both act and are acted upon by one another, would be encoded by the reciprocal construction (as indeed they are rendered in English). Yet like the reflexive functions described above, both these reflexive-marked symmetric events share a focus on an event that occurs between two individuals (and which is dependent on their mutual involvement), without distinguishing the respective contributions of the individuals to the event. Indeed, the employment of -*e* to mark apparently symmetric[200] events appears to be favoured where three conditions are met: (a) the occurrence of the event depends on each of the participants playing a particular role; (b) there is a blurring of the individual roles played by participants; and (c) there is close contact between the participants. For example, the event described

---

200 Following König and Kokutani (2006), I use the term *symmetric* to refer to any semantically-reciprocal event, broadly defined. Precisely what I take to be the semantics of the core reciprocal category is expounded upon under §11.6.2 below.

by (994) is dependent on the mutual cooperation of participants (both delousers and delousees), the description is vague as to who is removing lice from whom, and there is close physical contact:

(994) peln   korpn   nhaanhath-e
       3du(NOM=ERG) louse(ACC) look.at:RDP-RFL:NPST
       'they are checking (each other) for lice'
       [KTh_ICh25Jan2005 Elicitation RCP]

Example (995) is slightly different. Here, the blurring of roles is less significant than for (994), but there is a high level of mutual involvement and close contact:

(995) pul   nhaanhath-e
       3du(NOM=ERG) look.at:RDP-RFL:NPST
       'they are looking (into) each other('s eyes)'
       [KTh_ICh25Jan2005 Elicitation RCP]

(996) pul   meer-e   nhaath-rr-r
       3du(NOM=ERG) eye-ERG   look.at-RCP-P.PFV
       'they looked at each other (in sequence)'
       [KTh_ICh25Jan2005 Elicitation RCP]

If we compare (995) to a reciprocal clause like (996), the crucial difference is the fact that in (995) the two participants look into each other's eyes. This is significant for two reasons. Firstly, making eye contact is dependent upon the mutual cooperation of participants, who must both look in the right place at the right time (condition [a]). Secondly, although there is no physical contact, sustaining eye contact over a period of time is an intimate act (especially in Kuuk Thaayorre culture, which favours the avoidance of eye-contact in many contexts). The condition of 'close contact' is thus also satisfied.

These conditions (mutual involvement; blurring of roles; close contact) favour a perspective from which the (plural) participants are viewed as a single homogeneous set, rather than their being individualized. This, then, relates back to the 'collective reflexive' sense, in which the actions of the participant group as a whole are directed back upon that participant group. It was suggested above that the collective reflexive could be schematized as follows:

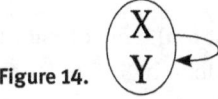
Figure 14.

In light of examples such as (992) and (993)–(995), we might extend this characterization of 'group reflexivity' to include cases in which participants act only upon each other (traditionally conceived 'reciprocal' events), as follows:

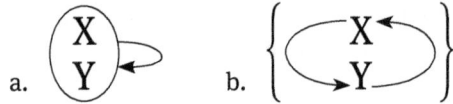

Figure 15.

11.5.9 Lexical reflexives

There are a number of (compound) verbs that entail reflexivity even in the absence of overt reflexive marking. The verb root *munth* 'sink', for instance, combines with one of two preposed body parts to form the phrasal verbs *koo+munth* (nose+sink) 'wash one's (own) face' and *minc+munth* (body+sink) 'wash oneself', as seen in the following example:

(997) parr_r paanth   ith   minc+munthi-rr
      child   female(NOM) dem:dist body+sink-P.PFV
      'the girl washed herself'
      [KTh_AJ07Feb2004 Elicitation]

That reflexivity is specified in the semantics of these phrasal verbs – rather than being merely a contextual implicature – is clear from the fact that neither can be used to describe an other-directed event. Washing a child or a car is described entirely differently (using *wothoth* 'clean', or the English loan *wash-m*).

In the vast majority of cases, however, a self-directed event will be explicitly coded as such. This includes prototypically self-directed events such as 'scratching' and 'stretching', which are often described by unmarked 'naturally reflexive' verbs in other languages (Geniušienė 1987):

(998) piinth+thaaw theetherk-e
      bone+mouth   return:RDP-RFL:NPST
      '[he's] stretching'
      [KTh_GJ19Oct2002 Elicitation StagedEvents123]

This preference for explicitly coding reflexivity stands in contrast to the encoding of symmetric (semantically reciprocal) events, which is frequently done by implicature or the use of an unmarked, 'lexical reciprocal' verb (cf. §11.6.7–11.6.8).

11.6 The reciprocal construction

11.6.1 Morphosyntax of the reciprocal construction

The reciprocal construction is defined by the presence of the reciprocal verbal suffix, introduced in §8.1.3. The core function of this suffix and construction is to mark an event in which each member of a nonsingular subject participant group directs their actions towards other member(s) of the same subject group, as in (999):

(999) *pul ngamal.katp-rr-ica-rr*
1du(NOM) hug-RCP-GO&-P.PFV
'they two went and hugged each other'
[KTh_ICh25Jan2005 Elicitation RCP23]

The suffix *-rr* is polysemous, though I will consistently gloss it as 'RCP' here. This morpheme enters into different subconstructions according to the sense with which it is used. These subconstructions will be introduced in the relevant subsections below.

Reciprocal-marked verbs are frequently reduplicated, as seen in (1000) below. There is a particular affinity between iterative aspect – marked by verbal reduplication – and reciprocal events, since the latter typically involve a plurality of subevents and relations. The overlapping distribution of the reciprocal morpheme and verbal reduplication is therefore unsurprising, although each may also occur in the absence of the other.

(1000) *ngal nhaanhath-rr*
1du:incl(NOM=ERG) look.at:RDP-RCP:NPST
'we two are looking at each other'
[KTh_ME09Feb2004 Elicitation]

The optional 'reciprocant' enclitic (glossed as 'RCPCANT') is sometimes attached to the subject of a reciprocal clause (such as (1001)). This morpheme, discussed in more detail in §3.1.2.4, is considered supplementary to and not definitional of the reciprocal construction.

(1001) *wakrr parr_r ngathn=nharr*
fight:RCP child 1sgGEN(NOM)=RCPCANT
'my kids are all fighting'
[Anon.]

11.6.2 Core reciprocal

I take the core function of the reciprocal construction to be the encoding of events in which each member of a participant group both acts upon and is acted upon by another member of that participant group. For a participant group containing just two individuals, this can be characterized as follows:

The actor of one instantiation of the event is also the undergoer of another instantiation of the same event type (i.e. A1=U2) while the undergoer of the first instantiation is the actor of the second (U1=A2)

This event-type is exemplified by (108), repeated here:

(108') ngali   pam.kunyangkar ngathn-mun   nhaanhath-rr
       1du(NOM)   brother   1sgGEN-DAT   look.at:RDP-RCP:NPST
       'my brother and I are looking at each other'
       [KTh_MF06Aug2002 Elicitation]

The standard reciprocal construction has the following form:

(1002) **Reciprocal construction₁**: V-rr <SUBJ$_{NOM}$>

But where the input to reciprocal derivation is trivalent, or an indirect argument is bound instead of the direct object, the reciprocal construction can be represented thus:

(1003) **Reciprocal construction₂**: V-rr <SUBJ$_{ERG}$, OBJ$_{ACC}$>

11.6.3 Co-participation

The 'co-participation'sense involves a number of actors participating in the same event alongside one another. Further, for an event to be classified co-partipatory, each participant must orient their actions with respect to the other participant(s); there must be <u>mutual engagement</u> in the activity, not a series of independent actions:

Participants act with respect to one another

This can be seen in (1004), an event-type characterized as 'naturally reciprocal' by Kemmer (1993: 18):

(1004) ngamp   pungk.ko'o-rr-nan
        1pl:incl(NOM=ERG) gather-RCP-GO&:NPST
        'we'll all meet up'
        [KTh_EF15Dec2002 Elicitation]

Other examples, like (1005), fit Creissels and Nouguier-Voisin's (2008: 292) characterization of 'unspecified co-participation', which involves "two or more participants that may assume distinct roles, but the construction by itself leaves open the precise role assumed by some of them, and role recognition crucially relies on lexical and/or pragmatic factors":

(1005) pul   yoorr yith-rr-r   ii-rr-kuw   rump-un
        3du(NOM=ERG)   today lead-RCP-P.PFV there-towards-west   beach-DAT
        'those two went together to the beach today'
        [Hall 1972: 108]

It is highly unlikely that this pair of actors would either take turns in leading the other, or would both lead and be led simultaneously. Instead, by choosing to represent the event by means of a reciprocal construction, the speaker asserts that an event of mutually-orientated leading occurred between the two participants, but that the precise assignment of roles is unimportant.

There is some similarity between co-participation and the collective reflexive sense discussed in §11.5.5. Both of these event types involve a plurality of participants engaged in an event with at least two roles, without assigning particular roles to individuals. This affinity between reflexive and reciprocal semantics will be revisited in §11.6.6.

11.6.4 Asymmetric-converse

The asymmetric-converse sense, like co-participation, entails the mutual orientation of two or more participants. A key difference between the two is the grammatical function with which the participants are encoded. In intransitive co-participation clauses (e.g. (1004) above), all core participants are encoded as subject, while in the transitive asymmetric-converse clauses only a subset of participants are represented as subject, while others are encoded either as direct object (as in (1006)) or in some oblique case.

(1006) pam-al   ulp   nhunh   paanth   ulp
        man-ERG   dem:ad.prx 3sgACC woman(ACC) dem:ad.prx
        koorr   waak-rr   nhul
        behind   follow:RDP-RCP:NPST 3sg(ERG)
        'that man is following along behind that woman'
        [KTh_FT10Feb2004 Elicitation RcpPilot26]

The above example sentence was uttered in response to a video clip (Evans et al. 2004) in which a woman was walking down a corridor, repeatedly looking over her shoulder for a man who was clandestinely following her. The crucial point here, is that both the woman being followed and the following man are playing an active role in the event; each continually monitoring the actions of the other. A more straightforward case of unilateral following would most likely be encoded by a straightforward transitive clause involving the underived verb *wak* 'follow' or *waarin* 'chase'.

The semantics and construction associated with the asymmetric reciprocal sense can be characterized as follows:

The subject's involvement in the activity entails the converse involvement of another participant(s)

(1007) **Reciprocal construction3**: V-rr <SUBJ$_{ERG}$, OBJ$_{ACC}$>

The grammatical encoding of involved participants as separate arguments (as opposed to all key participants being encoded as subject in co-participation clauses) reflects an important semantic difference between the asymmetric-converse and co-participation senses. Namely, participants in asymmetric-converse events are differently involved in that event, adopting mutually dependent but converse roles in a single activity.

11.6.5 Distributive

The final function with which *-rr* 'RCP' is attested in my data, is the marking of distributive aspect, as seen in (1008):

(1008)   *ngamp*   *yiirryirram nhangnul kunanpun-rr-nan*   *nhangun*
        1pl:incl(NOM=ERG) each   3sgRFL   report-RCP-GO&:NPST 3sgDAT
        'we each will give an account of ourselves to Him'
        [Hall 1972: 392]

The event encoded by (1008) involves distribution over both participants and sub-events. It is this that is marked by suffixing *-rr* to the verb, while the fact that the participants are reporting on themselves rather than each other (as the reciprocal morphology would suggest), is made clear by the inclusion of the reflexive pronoun. It is particularly interesting that the singular form of the reflexive pronoun is used in (1008), in conjunction with the adverb *yiirryirram* 'each' (or 'severally') to refer to a plural number of actors. A more accurate translation of this clause, then, would be something like 'Each of us will report on himself to Him', the individuation of each member of the subject group by the singular reflexive pronoun and *yiirryirram* 'each' reinforcing the distributive aspect marked by *-rr*.

11.6.6 Extended uses of the reciprocal suffix

As noted earlier in this section, the subjects of reciprocal clauses tend to be highly agentive. This focus on the agentive subject, coupled with the fact that reciprocal events usually impact upon the subject itself, often leads to the reciprocal subject being contrasted with other more probable agents, and thus carrying some connotation of the subject representing an 'unexpected agent'. For example, (1009) describes the highly unusual event of a woman deliberately taking her feet in her hands and breaking them. The more usual scenario of a woman breaking her foot accidentally (e.g. by treading on uneven ground or dropping something heavy on it) would be described either by a verbal reflexive construction (with deagentive sense) or by the intransitive verb *rumparr* 'break'.

(1009) *paanth-u   thamr   nhangnul   thiik-rr-r*
        woman-ERG foot(ACC) 3sgRFL   break-RCP-P.PFV
        'the woman broke her own feet'
        [KTh_GJ11Jan2004 Elicitation]

The highly marked nature of the scene described, then, is matched by the employ of a marked construction; the reciprocal suffix (signalling high agentivity, and an unexpected agent) plus reflexive pronoun (entailing that the subject is affected by her own action). (1010) similarly describes a scene in which the addressee is likely to expect an agent other than the one referred to by the subject pronoun:

(1010) *ngay   ngathney   mungka-n-rr-r   merrethen*
        1sg(ERG) 1sgRFL   consume-v^-RCP-P.PFV medicine(ACC)
        'I made myself swallow the medicine'
        [Hall 1972: 392]

To describe a pragmatically neutral scene of medicine-taking, the base transitive verb *mungk* 'eat/drink' would most likely be used. The expression of force — by means of the valence increasing suffix *-(nh)an(i)* — would most usually entail another participant causing the speaker/subject to ingest the medicine. The fact that it is the speaker who is (agentively) acting upon himself is thus pragmatically marked, and this is once again signalled by the use of the reciprocal suffix (marking the highly agentive subject that contrasts with the expected agent) coupled with the reflexive pronoun (entailing that it is the speaker who is affected by his own action). The use of *-rr* to mark an event with a surprising subject referent is also seen in examples (1008), (1011) and (1012), each of which exhibits the use of reflexive pronouns to disambiguate a *rr*-marked self-directed event.

(1011) *pam thono   tup   ko'o-rr-r   nhangnul watp*
       man one(NOM) IDPH spear-RCP-PST 3sgRFL   dead
       'one man speared himself dead, whack!'
       [Hall 1972: 137]

(1012) *nhunt   riiran nhangknunt kaar=p*
       2sg(NOM=ERG) alone 2sgRFL   NEG=PRAG
       kunk thana-n-rr-nancnh
       alive stand-v^-RCP-GO&:SBJV
       'you can't rescue yourself all alone'
       [Hall 1972: 392]

As in (1009) and (1010), the reciprocal suffix appears to mark the subject referent of (1012) as an unlikely agent. This makes sense since the very purpose of (1012) is to declare the impossibility of coreferent rescuer and rescuee.

11.6.7 Lexical reciprocals

My corpus contains only one monomorphemic verb form that strictly entails symmetry. This verb is *wuuthaw* 'share', used typically to describe the communal distribution of food, but also events like the following:

(1013) *kar mimp   wuuthaw*
       like cloth(ACC) share:NPST
       '[we] share clothes, for instance'
       [KTh_AP9Oct2002 Conversation]

There are two futher *lexicalized* reciprocal verbs, which appear to be frozen forms originally composed of verb root + reciprocal suffix, but which are no longer semantically compositional. These are *wakrr* 'fight' (< *wak* 'follow' + *rr* 'RCP') and *pungk-ko'orr-* 'meet up' (< *pungk* 'knee' + *ko'o* 'spear' + *rr* 'RCP').

11.6.8 Reciprocal by implicature

Semantically reciprocal ('symmetric') events need not be marked reciprocal at all. In (1014), for instance, a symmetric event is encoded by a simple intransitive clause ('he and his brother are talking') which nevertheless has a strong implicature of symmetry due to the absence of a specified external recipient:

(1014) *pul   pam.kunyangkar   nhangn-mun   kuuk   yiik*
       3du(NOM)   brother 3sgGEN-DAT   word(ACC)   say:RDP:NPST
       'he and his brother are talking (to each other)'
       [KTh_MF06Aug2002 Elicitation]

The same is true of (1015):

(1015) *parr_r ith   peln   thaa+whistle   thunp-r*
       kid   dem:dist   3pl(ERG)   mouth+whistle(ACC) throw-NPST
       'those kids are whistling at each other'
       [KTh_EN08Sep2002 Conversation / Elicitation]

In English, the sentence *those kids are whistling* would rarely (if ever) carry a reciprocal implicature since the default interpretation is that the kids are whistling a tune to themselves. In Kuuk Thaayorre, the symmetry of the event is implicated because of the common practice of whistling to attract and sustain someone's attention (especially during courtship).

How closely the event described corresponds to the usual state of affairs seems directly related to the presence or absence of overt reciprocal marking. An event of two people hugging one another (or a group of people hugging a new arrival, etc.) is not typically marked by the reciprocal suffix:

(1016) *peln   ngamal.kaatp-r*
       3pl(NOM)   hug-NPST
       'they all hug'
       [KTh_AJ24Jan2005 Elicitation RCP2]

On the other hand, an event in which three people hug simultaneously does receive overt reciprocal marking since this is not a usual or predictable state of affairs:

(1017) *paanth pinalam   ith   ngamal.katp-rr   peln*
       woman three(NOM)   dem:dist   hug-RCP:NPST   3pl(NOM)
       'the three women hug each other'
       [KTh_FT10Feb2004 Elicitation RCP20]

11.7 Desiderative construction

Kuuk Thaayorre speakers may express desiderative mood using one of twelve[201] constructions. Only one of these constructions can be considered a dedicated desiderative construction. Table 67 summarizes these twelve constructions, grouping them by the inflection of the main verb (seen in the first column). The second column lists any particle or adverb that is definitional of the construction, while the third column specifies the subsection in which the particular construction is introduced.

Table 67. Summary of constructions used to express desiderative mood.

Verb form	Particle	Ref.
Subjunctive (SBJV)	–	§11.7.1.1
	angarr	§11.7.1.2
	waarr	§11.7.1.3
	wanthan	§11.7.1.4
Nonpast (NPST)	–	§11.7.2.1
	ak	§11.7.2.3
	angarr	§11.7.2.2
Associated motion (GO&)	–	§11.7.3.1
	waarr	§11.7.3.2
Verbless clause	–	§11.7.5.1
	kaar	§11.7.5.2

Gaby (forthcoming) considers both the diachrony of this proliferation of desiderative constructions, as well as the question of whether desiderative mood is entailed or merely implicated by these constructions.

11.7.1 Subjunctive desiderative constructions

11.7.1.1 Simple subjunctive

Examples (1018–1020) illustrate the use of subjunctive inflection to express desired events.

(1018) ngay   yancnh=paa   rump-un,   ngay   kaar=okun yan
       1sg(NOM)   go:SBJV=PRAG   beach-DAT   1sg(NOM)   NEG=DUB   go:NPST
       'I want to walk to the beach but I can't go (i.e. it is not the case that I might go)'
       [KTh_MF06Aug2002 Elicitation]

---

[201] Technically, current speakers of Kuuk Thaayorre choose between only ten of these constructions, since the construction described in §11.7.1.4 has fallen out of use.

(1019) ngay   minh   wak-nh   koorr
       1sg(NOM) MEAT(ACC)   follow-SBJV outside
       'I want to hunt wallaby out there'
       [Hall 1972: 121]

(1020) ngay   may maak   muungknh
       1sg(ERG) VEG blackberry(ACC)   eat:SBJV
       'I want to eat some blackberries'
       [Hall 1972: 101]

The use of subjunctive verbs to head main clauses (as in the examples above), is presumed to be the result of 'insubordination'.[202] The encoding of desired events as (subordinate) purposive clauses seems a plausible bridging context for this development.

11.7.1.2 Subjunctive + *angarr*

Subjunctive verbs may also combine with the particle *angarr* to express desiderative mood, as seen in (1021):

(1021) ngay   soft drink   angarr   mungk-nh
       1sg(ERG) soft drink(ACC) ANGARR   drink-SBJV
       'I want a soft drink'
       [KTh_GJ18Jan2004 Elicitation]

Subjunctive inflection was described in §7.3.2 above. The particle *angarr* is elsewhere found in statements of general purpose and of correct behavior or states (1022–1023):

(1022) angarr   yoorrp ongkorr nhiin!
       ANGARR   thus   PROHIB   sit:IMP
       'don't just sit there!'
       [KTh_EN8Sep2002 Conversation]

(1023) photo kuthirr angarr   aka, ey? Awoy.
       photo two   ANGARR   here eh yes
       'there should be two photos here, eh? Okay'.
       [Anon.]

We can posit the following general meaning of *angarr*, constant across its uses in subjunctive and other clause types: "in a world where things are as they should be, X would obtain". This accounts for the desiderative interpretation of (1021) (i.e. in a world

---

[202] I.e. the use of a subordinate clause as a main clause, cf. Evans (1995a: 438)

where things are as they should be, I would be drinking a soft drink), the judgement expressed in (1022) (i.e. in a world where things are as they should be, you would not be sitting), the description in (1023) (i.e. in a world where things are as they should be, there would be two photos here). Such an account of *angarr*'s semantics also explains the other modal interpretations of the subjunctive + *angarr* construction. The purposive subordinate clause in (1024) can thus be re-translated "in a world where things are as they should be, the dog would have heard me (given that I called out loudly)".

(1024) ngay   minc min   waantharr-r   nganh   kuta-ku   angarr   ngeey-nh
       1sg(ERG) very good call.out-P.PFV   1sgACC   dog-ERG   ANGARR   hear-SBJV
       'I called out loudly so the dog would hear me'
       [KTh_GJ18Jan2004 Elicitation]

Angarr is also employed in the acceptance of offers where the kin relations between interlocutors allow for relative informality and directness. Example (1025), for instance, was uttered by my classificatory sister in response to my offer of cheese or tomato in her sandwich:

(1025) kuthirr angarr
       two   ANGARR
       'both please.'
       [KTh_EN8Sep2002 Conversation]

In conclusion, then, the subjunctive + *angarr* construction carries a modal entailment which describes a range of states of affairs including but not limited to those desired.

11.7.1.3 Subjunctive + *waarr*

The third construction with a modal entailment amenable to desiderative interpretation, involves the pairing of a subjunctive verb with the adverbial form *waarr*. Originally an adjective meaning 'bad', *waarr*'s closest independent function is as an intensifier adverb (translated as 'very'). The *waarr* found in this modal construction, however, is considerably further grammaticalized. It makes no compositional contribution to the modal construction other than possibly the intensification of the desire. All examples of this construction in my corpus, including (1026), are ambiguous between desiderative and purposive readings.

(1026) ngal   paath   minharr
       1du:incl(ERG)   firewood(ACC) pick.up:GO&:IMP
       paath   waarr   rint-nh=pa
       fire(ACC)   WAARR   burn-SBJV=PRAG
       'let's go and get firewood [so we can] build a fire'
       [KTh_AJ27Jan2004 Elicitation/Conversation]

The etymological link between *waarr* 'bad' and the desiderative construction is no doubt mediated by the intensifier function of this form (*waarr* 'very'). As both Alpher (1972) and Sommer (1978) have observed, there is a recurrent extension of the word meaning 'bad' to refer to 'great abundance' among the languages of Cape York Peninsula. Indeed, the Kugu Nganhcara particle *waya* (which, like its cognate *waarr*, also functions as an adjective meaning 'bad') enters into a very similar construction: "the irrealis is used in conjunction with the particle *waya* to mark desideratives" (Smith and Johnson 2000: 409).

11.7.1.4 Subjunctive + *wanthan*

The pairing of a subjunctive verb with the interrogative/indefinite form *wanthan* 'where' to express desiderative mood (as in examples 15–16), is attested only in the work of Hall (1972).

(1027) *ngay   thaank-nh   ii-rr-kan   wanthan*
       1sg(NOM) climb-SBJV there-towards-north   where
       'I want to do some climbing'
       [Hall 1972: 116]

(1028) *ngay   wanthan   thangkar-nha*
       1sg(NOM) where   laugh-SBJV
       'I want to roar with mirth'
       [Hall 1972: 116]

It may be that this construction unambiguously entailed desiderative mood. The presence of *wanthan* 'where', however, suggests this was not the original meaning of the bridging context from construction, at least. Examples like (1027), for instance, might once have served as a compositional to constructional meanings (i.e. compositionally meaning 'where can I climb?', but carrying an implicature that the speaker wanted to climb).

11.7.2 Nonpast desiderative constructions

11.7.2.1 Simple nonpast

Nonpast clauses commonly carry an implicature that the described event is desired or desirable, as in the following examples:

(1029) *ngay   ngat-a   yan*
       1sg(NOM) fish-DAT   go:NPST
       'I want to go fishing!' (but also: 'I am going fishing')
       [KTh_MF06Aug2002 Elicitation]

(1030) ngay   yan,   ngay   yan.   Ngay   willing   ngay   yan
       1sg(NOM) go:NPST 1sg(NOM) go:NPST 1sg(NOM) willing 1sg(NOM) go:NPST
       'I want to go [to Melbourne]. I'm willing [to do this], I want to go'
       [KTh_GJ16Oct2002 Narrative MelbourneTrip]

(1031) nhunt   muth piinth   kaar   muungk-r?
       2sg(ERG)   neck bone(ACC)   NEG   eat-NPST
       'don't you like eating neck-bone?' (but also: 'aren't you eating neck-bone?')
       [Hall 1972: 115]

There is nothing in such clauses to favor the desiderative interpretation over a declarative one, though this is usually clear from context.

11.7.2.2 Nonpast + *angarr*

The particle *angarr* is elsewhere found in statements of correct behavior or states (roughly meaning "in a world where things are as they should be, X would obtain"). Used in combination with a nonpast verb form, *angarr* can be used to mark a desired outcome or state, as in (81), repeated here:

(81') ngay   walmeerem   angarr   nhiin
      1sg(NOM) knowledgeable.of   ANGARR   sit:NPST
      'I want to know'
      [Anon.]

11.7.2.3 Nonpast + *ak*

A nonpast-inflected verb may be paired with the particle *ak* to describe a desired event that is intended to result from some other event, as seen in (1032) and (1033).

(1032) paath   waath-m   pul   ak   pathatha-n-r
       fire(ACC)   search-P.IPFV   3du(ERG)   AK   bite:RDP-V^-NPST
       'they looked for firewood to light [lit. make bite]'
       [Foote and Hall Ms.: Reader 10 KuthipD]

(1033) ngay   money   save-m   rirk
       1sg(ERG)   money(ACC)   save-TR   DO:NPST
       'I'm saving money'
       ngay   raak   Cairns-na   angarr   yancnh
       1sg(NOM)   PLACE   Cairns-DAT   ANGARR   go:SBJV
       'so that I can go to Cairns'
       [KTh_GJ18Jan2004 Elicitation]

As with the subjunctive + *angarr* construction, there is an obvious affinity between purposive and desiderative interpretations. *Angarr* and *ak* may also be combined, as in the following request for permission:

(1034) *ngay   yuk   angarr   ak=p   paath-r?*
       1sg(ERG) cigarette(ACC) ANGARR AK=PRAG bite-NPST
       'is it alright if I smoke?'
       [KTh_EN14Aug2002 Conversation]

The particle OPTative *ak* (discussed in §11.2.2) is otherwise associated with hortative and jussive moods.

11.7.3 Associated motion desiderative constructions

11.7.3.1 Simple associated motion (nonpast)
First associated motion morphology (referred to throughout this section as 'associated motion morphology' for brevity) is primarily employed to describe events that will occur following a change in location or to focus attention upon the initiation of the event described by the verb root (see §8.1.4.1).

Since one most often initiates or travels to events that one wants to occur, the desiderative interpretation of nonpast clauses like (1035)–(1036) is easily understood.

(1035) *ngay   wut   wunan*
       1sg(NOM) asleep lie:GO&:NPST
       'I want to sleep'
       [KTh_FT7Sep2002 Conversation]

(1036) *nhunt   may   mungk-nhan?*
       2sg(ERG) VEG(ACC) eat-GO&:NPST
       'would you like something to eat?'
       (but also: 'are you going to eat something?', 'will you eat something?')
       [KTh_EN8Sep2002 Conversation]

Associated motion morphology may only have a desiderative interpretation when inflected for nonpast tense. It may also combine with the particle *waarr* to reinforce the desiderative interpretation, as outlined in the next section.

11.7.3.2 Associated motion (nonpast) + *waarr*
The combination of the particle *waarr* and an associated motion verb form inflected for nonpast tense, allows both desiderative (1037) and potential (1038) interpretations.

(1037) ngay   raak   waarr   nhaath-nhan, Melbourne raak   kar   ngan
      1sg(NOM) place   WAARR   see-GO&:NPST Melbourne place like what
      '[as a child] I wanted to see that place, what sort of place Melbourne is'
      [KTh_GJ16Oct2002 Narrative MelbourneTrip]

(1038) nhurr   win-m   rirk-nhan   waarr!
      2pl(ERG) win-v^   DO-GO&:NPST   WAARR
      '"you can win!" (shouted at football players)'
      [KTh_AC21Aug2002 Narrative]

From the examples in my corpus, the particle *waarr* precedes the verb in desiderative clauses (such as 1037 and the examples in §11.7.1.3), but may follow it elsewhere (1038). As was noted above, *waarr* has its etymological source in the adjective *waarr* 'bad' and the adverb *waarr* 'very'. Though the adverbial *waarr* may seem semantically close to this usage, there are two reasons to view the putative particle found in desiderative clauses as synchronically distinct. Firstly, the adverb *waarr* functions to modify adjectives, not verbs. Secondly, any notional intensification in desiderative clauses is associated with the desiderative mood itself, rather than the verb. Thus in example (1037), the speaker didn't aspire to an intensified experience of seeing, but rather the desire he experienced (to see Melbourne) was intensely experienced.

Note that nonpast tense inflection is a crucial component of this construction (as also seen in §11.7.3.1). Nonpast inflection is found even in semantically anomalous contexts like (1037), which describes a past desire held by the speaker as a child (before he travelled to Melbourne).

11.7.4 Purposive desiderative construction

Both 'insubordinate' (Evans 2007) purposive verbs (1039) and those in subordinate clauses can be used to describe desired events:

(1039) parr-an   ith   peln   yup   thangkangkarr-natha
      child-ERG dem:dist   3pl(NOM)   soon   laugh:RDP-PURP
      'those kids want to laugh [but can't, because they're in class]'
      [KTh_GJ18Jan2004 Elicitation]

11.7.5 Verbless desiderative constructions

11.7.5.1 Simple verbless clauses

Clauses with non-verbal predicates may likewise carry a desiderative implicature. In (1040), for instance, it is clear from context that the addressee does not have a coffee, thus implicating the question of whether or not they might like one.

(1040) *nhunt   coffee=kaak?*
　　　 2sg(NOM) coffee=REL.PROP[203]
　　　 'do you want some coffee?' (but also: 'do you have any coffee?')
　　　 [KTh_EN8Sep2002 Conversation]

11.7.5.2 Verbless + *kaar*

The only clauses in my corpus that unambiguously entail that an event is (not) desired, contain the verbal negator, *kaar*, in the absence of the main verb. An extremely high-frequency example of this construction is (1041), the simple pairing of the first person singular subject pronoun and the verbal negator.

(1041) *ngay   kaar*
　　　 1sg(NOM) NEG
　　　 'I don't want to [go to the outstation]'
　　　 [KTh_EC02Oct2002 Conversation]

Example (1042) highlights the singularity of this construction. The particle *wut* (glossed as 'asleep') is otherwise found always and only in the presence of the verb *wun* 'lie'. It is impossible to describe someone as *wut nhiinhin* 'sitting asleep', for example, or to use *wut* as an adnominal adjective or as an ascriptive predicate. Yet just in this context, it is possible to use *wut* in the absence of *wun*.

(1042) *yuk-yuk-un   wun-m   pung-um   pul*
　　　 tree-tree-DAT lie-P.IPFV   sun-ABL   3du(NOM)
　　　 'they two lay amongst the trees away from the sun'
　　　 ngul pul   pung-un   kaar wut
　　　 then 3du(NOM)   sun-DAT   NEG   asleep
　　　 'since they didn't [want to] sleep in the sun'
　　　 [Foote and Hall Ms.; Reader 10; kuthip D]

Potential and other modal categories may not be encoded by this construction.

---

203 The Relational Proprietive enclitic (glossed 'REL.PROP') derives predicates of possession from nouns. Thus, *nhul paanth=kaak* (3sgNOM woman=REL.PROP) 'he has a wife, (lit. he is wife-having)'. This morpheme is discussed in §4.2.8.

11.8 Secondary predication

11.8.1 Depictive construction

In the Kuuk Thaayorre depictive construction, the main predicate of the clause (almost always a verb) is supplemented by a secondary predicate, which predicates on one of the verbal arguments. Hence in (1043), both *rancirr* 'landed' and *pungkurtharr* 'hungry' are predicated of the single subject argument *ngancn* 'we':

(1043) *pungkurtharr   ngancn   ranci-rr*
       hungry   1pl:excl(NOM)   jump-P.PFV
       'we were hungry when we landed (by plane)'
       [KTh_GJ16Oct2002 Narrative MelbourneTrip]

This secondary predicating element is most often a simple adjective (e.g. *pungkurtharr* 'hungry' in (1043) and *weneth* 'scared' in (1044)), but may be also be a more elaborated noun phrase (e.g. *punth kon* 'short-armed' in (1044)).

(1044) *punth kon   nhul   koorr   kanpa   riic-m   weneth*
       arm   short   3sg(NOM)   behind in.front   run-P.IPFV   scared
       'he ran back and forth, scared, with his severed arm [after a crocodile attack]'
       [KTh_AJ-GJ03Feb2004 Conversation]

As Schultze-Berndt and Himmelmann (2004) have shown, depictives are often similar to adverbial expressions. Depictives, however, assign a property to a participant of the main predicate, requiring that "the two predicates share a central participant and all circumstantial information" (Schultze-Berndt and Himmelman 2004: 69), whereas adverbials modify the predication overall. Hence the depictive *pungkurtharr* 'hungry' in (1043) tells us about the ongoing state of the participants (*ngancn* 'we') rather than about the event of landing. Similarly, in (1045) lightness is predicated of the child, not of the manner in which he is picked up:

(1045) *parr_r   inh   ngay   roorngkrr   mi'irr*
       child(ACC)   dem:sp.prx   1sg(ERG)   light   pick.up:NPST
       "this kid feels light when I pick him up"
       [KTh_EN27Jan2004 Elicitation]

The secondary predicate may have scope over the complement of the main predicate (as in 1045), the subject of an intransitive clause (1043), or the subject of a transitive clause (1046):

(1046) *Ngay   ngoongkom pit-m,   pokon*
       1sg(ERG) ignorant   hold-P.IPFV NO
       'I was holding [a fishing line], ignorant [of the crocodile nearby]'
       [KTh_**AJ**-GJ03Feb2004 Conversation]

Depictive secondary predication is thus not restricted to the 'internal arguments' as has been claimed elsewhere.

It is common among Australian languages (e.g. Yankunytjatjara, Goddard 1985; Martuthunira, Dench 1995a) for depictive constructions to be used to mark events as occurring at a particular stage of the subject's life, as in the following:

(1047) *ngay   parr_r   yik-m,   "ngay   yan"*
       1sg(NOM) child(NOM)   say-P.IPFV 1sg(NOM) go:NPST
       'I said, as a child, "I want to go!"'
       [KTh_GJ16Oct2002 Narrative MelbourneTrip]

There is just one example in my data in which an apparent depictive secondary predicate is morphologically marked (in this instance, for dative case):

(1048) *ngul ulp   may   kunk-un mungk-m*
       then dem:ad.prx VEG(ACC) raw-DAT eat-P.PFV
       'then he was eating the fruit raw'
       [KTh_**DW**-CW09Dec2002 Narrative 2Crocs]

Nichols (1978) notes that the instrumental case may be used to mark depictive secondary predicates in Russian. The marking of *kunkun* 'alive:DAT' in (1048) may represent an analogous use of the dative case in Kuuk Thaayorre. However it is also possible that it is the result of misspeech or misunderstanding.

11.8.2 Resultative construction

In the resultative construction, the secondary predicate is much more tightly bound to the verb semantically than it is in a depictive construction.[204] Thus in (1049) the secondary predicate *watp* 'dead' not only contributes information about the object

---

[204] Winkler (1997) views resultatives as a subtype of complex predicate since both the main predicate and secondary predicate contribute information about a single macro-event. So in (1049), the verb *ke'e* 'spear' and the adjective *watp* 'dead' combine to form a complex accomplishment predicate 'kill (something) by spearing'. This seems a plausible analysis, but the resultative construction is nevertheless discussed here owing to its structural similarity to the depictive construction.

argument *kuta* 'dog' (i.e. that it is dead), but also about the event itself (i.e. that the dog came to be dead through the act of spearing):

(1049) watp   ke'e-rr   nhunh   kuta   ngulp
       dead   spear-P.PFV   3sgACC dogACC dem:ad.prx
       'that dog's been speared dead'
       [Foote ms. Kuta Woochorrm]

It has been claimed that secondary predicates may only be predicated on the internal argument, whether it be intransitive subject or transitive object (see, e.g., Simpson's (1983) 'direct object restriction'). This has been shown to be false (e.g. in Gooniyandi (McGregor 1990) and Yankunytjatjara (Goddard 1985), cf. Dench and Evans 1988). However, I have not yet recorded any Kuuk Thaayorre clauses in which a resultative secondary predicate has scope over the transitive subject. Example (1050), for instance, unambiguously describes the speaker-undergoer becoming bloody as a result of being punched:[205]

(1050) nhul   nganh   yuur-u   theernga-rr kam
       3sg(ERG) 1sgACC hand-ERG   hit-P.PFV   blood
       "he hit me with the hand and blood"
       i.e. 'he hit me with his hand and I bled'
       * 'he hit me with his hand and it [his hand] bled'
       [KTh_GJ10Jan2004 Elicitation]

If we instead wished to describe the assailant's hand becoming bloody as a result of the punch, we would need to employ a biclausal construction such as the following:

(1051) nhul   theernga-rr=anh   ngul nhul   yuur kam   [yooc]   than-m
       3sg(NOM) hit-P.PFV=3sgACC   then 3sg(NOM) hand blood sopping stand-P.IPFV
       'he hit me with his hand and then his hand was [dripping] with blood'
       [KTh_GJ10Jan2004 Elicitation]

Finally, it should be noted that my data contains numerous examples that in many ways resemble a resultative construction, but that are not. In (1052), for example, the fact that a pause intervenes between the main clause and the adjective *watp* 'dead',

---

205 It should be acknowledged that I never prompted language experts with a clause in which the resultative secondary predicate agrees with the transitive subject in ergative case (which is required of secondary predicates in, e.g., Gooniyandi). It seems likely, however, that language experts would have offered such a clause alongside the many paraphrases of (1051) preferred, were it grammatical.

suggests that *watp* is in fact a clause in and of itself (i.e. '[and he was] dead!') rather than a secondary predicate within the main clause:

(1052) ngul   nhul   pam.kunyangkar   nhangnman-thurr   kat   ke'err...   watp
      then   3sg(ERG)   brother   3sgGEN-ERG   IDPH   spear-P.PFV   dead
      'then his brother speared him with a whack... dead'
      [Foote: Kuta Woochorrm]

12 Complex clauses

This chapter details the ways in which complex clauses may be formed through coordination and subordination. Subordination and coordination are generally used to express complex relationships between distinct events. Though in principle subordination and coordination are entirely distinct syntactic clauses, in some cases it can be difficult to distinguish which of the two structures applies.

12.1 Subordination

Subordinate clauses take a number of different forms in Kuuk Thaayorre. There is no direct correspondence between the structure of the subordinate clause and its function. However, each of the functions performed by the two non-finite subordinate clause types, for example, may also be performed by an unmarked finite subordinate clause. Table 68 presents the five subordinate clause types, listing the range of functions expressed by each. The conditional and purposive subordinate clause types (in italics) are subtypes of adverbial clause.

Table 68. Subordinate clause types.

Subordinate clauses				
non-finite		**finite**		
infinitive	-*marr*-marked	unmarked	purposive-marked	subjunctive-marked
1. relative	1. relative	1. complement	1. complement	1. adverbial
2. adverbial	2. adverbial	2. relative	2. adverbial	*a) conditional*
	a) purposive	3. adverbial	*a) purposive*	*b) purposive*
		a) conditional		
		b) purposive		

The location of the subordinate clause with respect to the main clause is determined by its function. A relative clause will always appear immediately following the relativized NP, regardless of whether it is finite or non-finite. Relative clauses are therefore frequently embedded within the main clause. Conditional subordinate clauses are always the initial constituent of the sentence, appearing at the left periphery of the main clause. All other subordinate clauses always appear at the right periphery of the main clause. In the example sentences throughout this section, square brackets '[]' will be used to mark sentence boundaries, and curly brackets '{}' to mark the boundaries of subordinate clauses.

12.1.1 Non-finite subordinate clauses

12.1.1.1 Infinitive subordinate clauses

Infinitive subordinate clauses are headed by an infinitive-inflected verb. The infinitive verb forms are identical to the corresponding imperative forms. Hence in (1053), the infinitive verb *kalal* is homophonous with the reduplicated imperative form *kalal* 'carry (repeatedly)!', and differs from the root form *kal* 'carry' only in its reduplication. This reduplication is independently (semantically) motivated and not implicated in the process of subordination.

(1053) *[parr_r   nhul   rirk-r   {kuta   keren   kalal}]*
       [child(NOM) 3sg(NOM) arise-P.PFV {dog(ACC) up.high carry:RDP:INF}]
       'The child got up, carrying the dog up high'
       [KTh_MF17Sep2002 Narrative FrogStory]

For second conjugation verbs, the infinitive form is homophonous with not only the imperative verb form, but also the nonpast tense. It is therefore much more difficult – if not impossible – to distinguish infinitive subordinate clauses from finite subordinate clauses (cf. §12.1.2.1). This is illustrated by (1054), which fills all the criteria for both subordinate clause types.

(1054) *[parr_r   nhul   putpun   thanan   therrep-ak*
       [child(NOM) 3sg(NOM) on.top   stand:RDP:NPST   rock-DAT
       {waawantharr }]
       {call.out:RDP:NPST/INF}]
       'The boy is standing on a rock, calling out'
       [KTh_MF17Sep2002 Narrative FrogStory]

Infinitive subordinate clauses frequently serve an adverbial function (1054) or purposive function (1055–1056), in both of which cases the subordinate clause must appear at the right periphery of the main clause. For other clauses, such as (1057), a relative clause interpretation seems most apt.

(1055) *[ya-rr-uw   yat=ay,   {ngul   thanc   nhaath-nharr}]*
       [away-towards-west go:P.PFV=1sg(NOM) {then tree.sp(ACC) see-GO&:INF}]
       'I [saltwater crocodile] went Westwards to see the Thanc tree'
       [KTh_**DW**-CW09Dec2002 Narrative 2Crocs]

(1056) *[ngul   nhul   meer+kay   rok-r   {minc   nhaath-nharr}]*
       [then 3sg(NOM) eye+metal(ACC) enter-P.PFV {really see-GO&:INF}]
       'he put on glasses on so he could see properly'
       [KTh_GJ18Jan2004 Elicitation]

(1057) [ngawiyokun   yuk   inh   {ngan wan }   wun]
       [I.don't.know THING(NOM) dem:sp.prx {what call:INF} lie:NPST]
       'I don't know what this thing, which is called what?, is'
       [KTh_AC10Aug2002 Conversation]

The complex clause in (1057) is rather challenging to parse. It was uttered by language expert Alfred Charlie in response to questioning about the Kuuk Thaayorre labels for various objects, and directly follows his stating *ngawiyokun ngan=okun* 'I don't know what it could be'. AC then mutters (1057) to himself in an attempt to jog his memory. In this pragmatic context, then, the relative clause analysis suggested by the English translation seems most appropriate. This semantic analysis is supported by the syntactic embedding of the subordinate clause directly following the relativized NP *yuk inh* 'this thing', a syntactic position reserved solely for relative clauses in Kuuk Thaayorre.

12.1.1.2 Subordinate verbs marked by *-marr*

Kuuk Thaayorre once possessed a dedicated verbal suffix (*-marr ~ -namarr*) that marked the head of a subordinate clause. This morpheme is not attested in my corpus, which suggests that it is only very rarely used and possibly being lost. On the basis of the data in Hall (1972), however, we can identify a number of functions associated with *marr*-marked subordinate clauses.

Most of the examples presented in Hall (1972)[206] are translated by English clausal complements of perception verbs (doubtless the motivation behind Hall's glossing *-marr* as 'visible contemporaneous'). This is illustrated by (1058), in which the subordinate clause describes the event seen by the subject of the matrix clause.

(1058) [ngay   pam   ith   nhaawr   {ngat   kal-marr}]
       [1sg(ERG) man(ACC) dem:dist see:P.PFV {fish(ACC) carry-SBD}]
       'I saw those men [while they were] carrying fish'
       [Hall 1972: 125]

Closer inspection of (1058), however, reveals the complement clause analysis to be inappropriate. The direct object argument of the main clause verb *nhaawr* 'saw' is not filled by a clause, but rather by the noun phrase *pam ith* 'those men'. It cannot be argued that this noun phrase forms part of a discontinuous subordinate clause (headed by *kalmarr* 'carrying') since if this were the case it should receive ergative case marking as the subject of a transitive verb. Likewise, in (1059) – where the subordinate verb is embedded within the main clause – the agents of the carrying event (i.e. the elided subject of the subordinate clause) are encoded as the direct object of the main clause in accusative case.

---

206 Hall (1972: 193) labels *-marr ~ -namarr* a 'visible contemporaneous' verbal suffix.

(1059) *[ngali   pelnan   {kal-marr}   nhaath-m]*
       [1du(ERG) 3plACC   {carry-SBD} watch-P.IPFV]
       'we two watched them carrying it'
       [Hall 1972: 402]

Although the subordinate clauses of (1058) and (1059) are semantically amenable to both a relative clause and adverbial clause analysis, their respective placements within the main clause suggest the two are fundamentally different.[207] Across all of Kuuk Thaayorre's subordinate clause types, the generalization holds that a relative clause will immediately follow the relativized NP, while an adverbial clause will appear at the right periphery of the main clause. If this generalization extends to *-marr*-marked subordinate clauses – and there is no reason why it should not – example (1058), in which the subordinate clause appears at the right periphery of the main clause, can most plausibly be analyzed as an adverbial clause (Hale's 1976b 'T-relative'), controlled by the object of the main clause. The adverbial function of *-marr*-marked subordinate clauses is further illustrated by (1060). Here the adverbial clause is again controlled by the direct object of the main clause (encoded by an accusative noun phrase [*pam meerkunwaarr* 'the depressed man'] and pronominal enclitic [*=unh* 'him']) which is overtly coded as subject of the subordinate clause (by the nominative pronominal enclitic =*ul* 'he'), thus demonstrating that the pivot argument need not be gapped.

(1060) *[pul   pam meerkunwaarr nhaawr=unh   {yoongk-e-namarr=ul}]*
       [3du(ERG) man   pitiful(ACC)   see:P.PFV=3sgACC {hang-RFL-SBD-3sg(NOM)}]
       'they two saw the depressed man hanging himself'
       [Hall 1972: 146]

Example (1059), however, is best analyzed as a relative clause (i.e. as a type of 'NP-relative' in Hale's 1976b terminology), given its syntactic placement immediately following the relativized pronoun *pelnan* 'them'. Example (1061) likewise illustrates the relative clause structure.

(1061) *[ngay   {thamr   thiinth-marr} riiric-r]*
       [1sg(NOM) {foot(NOM)   cramp-SBD}   run:RDP-NPST]
       'I, who am cramping in the foot, am running'
       [Hall 1972: 402]

Interestingly, the part-whole apposition of *ngay* 'I' and *thamr* 'foot' in example (1061) is distributed over two clauses. The noun phrase referring to the whole has

---

[207] Cf. Hale (1976), papers in Austin (ed. 1988) and Nordlinger (2006) on the problem of distinguishing these subordinate clause functions in Australian languages.

the grammatical function of main clause subject (the main clause being *ngay riiricr* 'I'm running'), while the subordinate clause contains the part NP, apposed to the null anaphor of the relativized pronoun in nominative case. (See §6.10.1 for discussion of the syntax and semantics of part-whole apposition).

A third distinct function of the subordinate-marked verb is to encode purpose. Unlike the adverbial clauses considered above, these purposive complex clauses do not assume temporal identity between main and subordinate clause, but rather the subordinate clause is an intended (and subsequent) outcome of the main clause. In the case of (648), the swimming event is the intended result of the motion event.

(1062) *[nhul   yaan   {yungar-namarr}]*
       3sg(NOM) go:RDP:NPST   swim-SBD
       'he will go swimming'
       [Hall 1972: 147]

Like adverbial subordinate clauses, however, the purposive subordinate clause must appear at the right periphery of the main clause.

12.1.2 Finite subordinate clauses

12.1.2.1 Unmarked finite subordinate clauses

Unmarked finite subordinate clauses, as their name suggests, bear no morphological coding of their subordinate status. The verbs that head them bear the same TAM inflections as verbs of main clauses, with the regular TAM interpretation, and there are no restrictions on the overt realization and case marking of the arguments they subcategorize for. The syntactic restrictions on the placement of subordinate clauses with respect to the main clause do apply, however, with relative clauses immediately following the relativized NP, conditional clauses appearing at the left periphery of the main clause and subordinate clauses with all other functions appearing at the right periphery of the main clause, as noted above.

In the tradition of Hale's (1976b) seminal analysis of the 'adjoined relative clause' type in Warlpiri, the grammars of most Australian languages include reference to a generalized (subordinate) clause type that spans both adverbial and (NP-)relative functions, much like the Kuuk Thaayorre unmarked finite subordinate clause. It is not uncommon for these clause types to lack explicit coding of their subordinate status, which may often be established only through detailed morphosyntactic analysis (e.g. McGregor 1988, Nordlinger 2006). In contrast to the other subordinate clause types discussed here, the criteria for identifying unmarked finite subordinate clauses in Kuuk Thaayorre vary according to the function of the clause. For some functions, there are clear and convincing indicators that the, e.g., unmarked complement clause should be considered subordinate. For other functions it is less clear. The syntactic analysis of the unmarked finite subordinate clause type is therefore divided according to its various functions below.

a) Complement clause function

The contents of cogitation and communication are frequently encoded by complement clauses, as seen in example (1063).

(1063) *[ngay   kar ngeey-m[208]   {kar nhunt   sixteen=nhurr=p}]*
       [1sg(ERG) like thought-P.IPFV {like 2sg(NOM) sixteen=only=PRAG}]
       'I thought you were only sixteen!'
       [Anon., confirmed EN02Oct2002]

Note that the inclusion of the particle *kar* 'like' in both main and subordinate clause signals that the thought was mistaken rather than marking or otherwise contributing to the syntactic fact of subordination. This is only one of many disparate functions of *kar* 'like', each of which is discussed in §9.1.3. *Kar* 'like' is similarly embedded within the complement clause in (1064) in order to mark a (reported) erroneous supposition.

(1064) *[ngul nganip   yik-r   pul   nganam-u*
       [then father(NOM) say-P.PFV 3du(NOM)   mother-ERG^
       {kar parr_r   nhurr   thaa+munthi-rr}]
       {like child(NOM)   2pl(NOM)   mouth+sink-P.PFV}]
       'then Dad and Mum said "[we thought] you kids had drowned"'
       [KTh_GJ15Oct2002 Narrative PlaneSighting]

It is typical for the thought processes of a third person to be reported as quoted speech, as in (1064). This might be attributed to an unwillingness to presume to know the thoughts of another person, beyond their own recounting of them. This extends to nonhuman sentient beings (e.g. the dog in (1065)), who have clearly not communicated their thoughts to the narrator through speech. This may reflect the fact that this usage has become so grammaticalized that *yik* is now a polysemous verb meaning both 'say' and 'think'.

(1065) *[nhul   yik-r   {thatr=okun   ranth-in   ngaathirr   wun}]*
       [3sg(NOM) say-P.PFV   {frog=DUB   hole-DAT   still   lie:NPST}]
       'he [the dog] thought the frog was still in the hole'
       [KTh_MF17Sep2002 Narrative FrogStory]

---

208 Nb. this verb is polysemous, also meaning 'hear, listen to'.

Note that the deictic centres of the main and subordinate clause are almost always distinct. Hence in (1064) a second person pronoun is used to refer to the narrator and his siblings, not the audience of the matrix speech event. While in (1065) the subordinate clause has nonpast tense, calculated from the perspective of the past perfective thinking event encoded by the main clause.

Despite their representation as quotations, the complement clauses of (1064) and (1065) should still be considered subordinate. These complement clauses remain integrated into the prosodic contour of the main clause, and function as one of the subcategorized-for arguments of *yik* 'say'. An alternative, non-subordinate construction is available for quoting reported speech, in which *yarriy* 'thus' (described in §9.1.2) is used to frame the quote. In this construction *yarriy* 'thus' fills the complement slot of *yik* 'say' (which subcategorizes for an object encoding words, language or speech), with the reported speech following as a coordinated main clause:

(1066) *[ngul   nhul   ngathun yarriy yik-r   teacher:]*
       [then   3sg(NOM)   1sgDAT thus   say-P.PFV teacher(NOM)]
       ["kece! wut=okun   wun"]
       [CDICT sleep=DUB lie:NPST]
       'then the teacher said this to me: "no! [She] might be asleep"'
       [KTh_AJ27Jan2004 Conversation]

In clauses such as (1066), there is a clear prosodic break between the clause that introduces the quotation and the quotation itself. The speaker of (1066) further takes great pains to imitate the protagonist quoted, with the prosodic contour of the quoted clause *kece wut=okun wun* 'no, she might be asleep' matching that of a complete and independent utterance. This differs greatly from the subordinate clause *thatr=okun ranthin ngaathirr wun* 'the frog might still be in the hole' in (1065), which is fully integrated into the prosodic contour of the main clause. The existence of this alternative structure is further validation of the subordinate status of some unmarked finite clauses.

b) Relative clause function
Unmarked finite clauses may also function as relative clauses. Unlike the unmarked complement clauses discussed above, unmarked relative clauses are typically embedded within the main clause, directly following the NP they modify. This can be seen in (1067), in which the relative clause *thangkarnam* '[who] was laughing' appears immediately following the NP head it modifies (*pam ith* 'that man'), and separating this NP from the verb of the main clause (*yat* 'went'), of which it is subject.

(1067) *[pam   ith   {thangkar-nam} yuuw yat]*
[man(NOM) dem:dist {laugh-P.IPFV} far   go:P.PFV]
'the man who was laughing went off'
[KTh_GJ18Jan2004 Elicitation]

To avoid the analysis of *thangkarnam* 'was laughing' as subordinate, one could argue that (1067) instead comprises a sequence of two coordinated main clauses; *pam ith thangkarnam* 'that man was laughing' and *yuuw yat* '[he] went off'. It is in keeping with standard Kuuk Thaayorre discourse structure for the topic (the man) to be omitted in the second clause. In favour of parsing (1067) as a single (complex) clause, however, is the fact that it forms a single intonation phrase, with no discernable break at the putative clausal juncture between *thangkarnam* and *yuuw*.

Additional evidence that unmarked relative clauses like *thangkarnam* 'was laughing' are subordinated is furnished by the behaviour of copula constructions. As discussed in §10.2, copula clauses may be formed through the simple juxtaposition of two noun phrases, or they may contain one of a number of (usually postural) verbs functioning as overt copula. Example (1068) show a verbless copula clause functioning as an embedded relative clause. In (1069), the adverb *kanangkarr* 'long ago' is added to differentiate the time period referred to by the relative clause and that of the main clause.

(1068) *[pam   ith   {minh.thop}   thanan]*
[man(NOM) dem:dist {good.hunter} stand:NPST]
'that man who is a good hunter is standing there'[209]
[KTh_GJ11Jan2004 Elicitation]

(1069) *[pam   ith   {kanangkarr minh.thop}   thanan]*
[man(NOM) dem:dist {long.ago   good.hunter} stand:RDP:NPST]
'that man [currently] standing there [used to be a] good hunter'
[KTh_GJ11Jan2004 Elicitation]

The fact that *kanangkarr* 'long ago' may be inserted with scope over just the embedded relative clause without conflicting with the nonpast inflection of the head verb of the main clause *thanan* 'is standing', is further evidence that the relative copula clause is both distinct from and subordinate to the main clause (as opposed to both (1068) and (1069) forming simplex main clauses headed by the copula verb *thanan* 'standing').

---

209 Note that the embedded subordinate clause provides the new information, while it is the main clause that helps the addressee identify the intended referent. This is unlike the better documented functions of relative clauses cross-linguistically, and also goes against McKay's (1988) observation that the Rembarrnga (relative and other) subordinate clauses are used in order to provide background information.

It is also possible to embed a verb-headed relative clause within a copula main clause. In example (1070), for example, the relative clause *wut wun* 'is sleeping' is embedded within the verbless copula clause *pam pam nhangnip ngathn* 'the man is my father':

(1070) *[pam   {wut   wun}   pam   nhangnip   ngathn]*
[man(NOM) {asleep lie:NPST} HUMAN father 1sgGEN]
'the man who is sleeping is my father'
[KTh_GJ12Jan2004 Elicitation]

Where the relativized NP is followed only by the subordinate clause it is impossible to syntactically distinguish the relative subordinate clause function from the adverbial. In (1071), for example, we can infer the subordinate clause's relative function (a) only from the fact that it is used to restrict the reference of the noun phrase it follows. The same utterance could alternatively be parsed as an adverbial clause (1071b) or complement clause (1071c).

(1071) a. *[ngay   pam.ngongkom paanth   ith   {iipal   ii   yan}]*
[1sg(NOM) ignorant.of woman(ACC) dem:dist {this.way there go:NPST}]
'I don't know that woman who is coming this way'
b. *[ngay   pam.ngongkom paanth   ith   {iipal   ii   yan}]*
[1sg(NOM) ignorant.of woman(ACC) dem:dist {this.way there go:NPST}]
'I don't know that woman, [while] she is coming this way'
c. *[ngay   pam.ngongkom {paanth   ith   iipal   ii*
[1sg(NOM) ignorant.of {woman(NOM) dem:dist this.way there
yan}]
go:NPST}]
'I didn't know that the woman is coming this way'
[KTh_AC21Aug2002 Conversation / Elicitation]

c) Adverbial function

The third function typically associated with generalized subordinate clause types in Australian languages (after Hale 1976b) is the adverbial clause. This function is illustrated by example (1072), which includes a subordinate adverbial relative clause *kutaku waawarinr* '[while] dogs chased [him]'.

(1072) *[ngay   pam   ii   nhaawr   {kuta-ku   waawarin-r}]*
[1sg(ERG) man(ACC) there see:P.PFV {dog-ERG chase-P.PFV}]
'I watched that man [while he] was chased by the dogs'
[KTh_GJ18Jan2004 Elicitation]

Unlike the complement clauses described above, adverbial subordinate clauses do not fill a subcategorized-for argument slot. Instead, this argument slot is filled within the main clause by the NP *pam* 'man', while the subordinate clause that immediately follows the main clause merely provides contextual information about the event the man was involved in when he was seen. It is difficult to conclusively establish the dependency relation between the main clause *ngay pam ii nhaawr* 'I saw the man' and the putative subordinate adverbial clause *kutaku waawarinr* 'dogs chased (him)'. As has been established, the elision of the undergoer-object of the second clause ('the man') does not entail that the clause is subordinate. Core arguments are freely elided in Kuuk Thaayorre discourse, especially where overtly mentioned in a preceding clause. Nevertheless, I analyze the second clause as subordinate on the grounds that: (a) there is no pause between the two clauses, which fall within a single intonational phrase; and (b) the verb of the complement clause must share the TAM values of the verb of the main clause. Hence *nhaawr* 'saw' and *waawarinr* 'chased' in (1072) are both past perfective, while *thanan* 'standing' and *waawantharr* 'calling out' in (1073) are both nonpast,[210] as are *wontr* 'falls' and *nhiin* 'sitting' in (1074).

(1073) *[Parr_r   nhul   putpun thanan   therrep-ak, {waawantharr }]*
       [child(NOM) 3sg(NOM) on.top stand:RDP:NPST rock-DAT   {call.out:NPST}]
       'The boy is standing on a rock, calling out'
       [KTh_MF17Sep2002 Narrative FrogStory]

(1074) *[Parr_r   nhul   wont-r   {thakr nhiin}]*
       [child(NOM) 3sg(NOM) fall-NPST {front sit:NPST}]
       'the boy falls face down.'
       [KTh_MF17Sep2002 Narrative FrogStory]

The same can be seen in example (1075), which contains two conjoined main clauses (separated by square brackets), the second of which includes a subordinate complement clause (surrounded by curly brackets). The head verbs of all three clauses are inflected for past perfective tense/aspect, but whist there is a clearly discernable prosodic break preceding the second main clause (i.e. between *nhiinm* 'were sitting' and *ngul* 'then'), there is none preceding the subordinate clause (i.e. between *ngeeym* 'was hearing' and *thangkarnam* 'was laughing').

---

[210] Though as noted in §12.1.1.1, *waawantharr* 'calling out' might also be analyzed as an infinitive verb.

(1075) *[ngancn   mong   nhiin-m]*
[1pl:excl(NOM) many(NOM)   sit-P.IPFV]
[ngul ngay   ngeey-m   {thangkar-nam}]
[then 1sg(ERG) hear-P.IPFV {laugh-P.IPFV}]
'we were all sitting together when I heard someone laughing'
[KTh_GJ18Jan2004 Elicitation]

A further piece of evidence that these adverbial clauses are subordinate to, rather than merely coordinated with, the preceding main clause, is the fact that the adverbial clause must always appear at the right periphery of the main clause, even where this ordering is anti-iconic with respect to the sequence of the events described (as in (1076)). The ordering of independent clauses in natural discourse would normally be expected to mirror the temporal order of the events they describe (cf. Jakobson 1966, Haiman 1985).

(1076) *[plate   rinca-rr   {pul   runc-ey-r}]*
[plate(ACC) smash-P.PFV {3du(NOM) collide-RFL-P.PFV}]
'the plate was smashed after/because they bumped'
[KTh_GJ19Oct2002 Elicitation StagedEvents5]

The conditional and purposive functions – detailed in the sections below – can be considered subtypes of the adverbial subordinate clause.

d) Conditional function

Complex clauses expressing a conditional relationship between two events share several key features. Firstly, the protasis (condition clause) always precedes the apodosis (describing the possible outcome). Although these are the only subordinate clauses to appear at the left periphery of the main clause, this syntactic position is typologically common for conditional clauses (Diessel 2005). Secondly, the Kuuk Thaayorre protasis is almost always marked by *kar* 'like' (the many functions of which are explored in §9.1.3), optionally in conjunction with *ith* 'if' (as seen in (1077) and (1078)). The one example in my corpus in which the conditional clause does not contain *kar* 'like' is given in (1079).

(1077) *[{ith kar kuta ngathn   ulp   pormp-an}*
[{if   like dog 1sgGEN(NOM) dem:ad.prx house-DAT}]
ngay   piinth   reek-nhan]
1sg(ERG) bone(ACC) give-GO&:NPST]
'if my dog's at home [when I get there], I'll give him a bone'
[KTh_EN04Aug2002 Elicitation]

(1078) *[{ith   kar   nhunt   kar   trust-m   rirk-r   nhunh, believe-m   rirk-r*
       [{if   like 2sg(NOM)   like trust-TR DO-P.PFV 3sgACC believe-TR DO-P.PFV
       nhunh,}   nhunt   ulp   kunk   nhiinhan   muthathan]
       3sgACC} 2sg(NOM) dem:ad.prx alive   reside:GO&:NPST   forever]
       'if you have trusted him, and believed in him, you'll have eternal life'
       "if you really believe in him you'll have eternal life"
       [KTh_GJ18Jan2004 Narrative Christmas]

(1079) *[{nhunt   may   ulp   mungk-nhan}   nhunt   wonp-nhan]*
       [{2sg(ERG) VEG(ACC) dem:ad.prx eat-GO&:NPST} 2sg(NOM) die-GO&:NPST]
       'if you eat these berries you'll die'
       [KTh_GJ31Jan2004 Elicitation]

Neither of these features suggests that the conditional clause (protasis) is subordinate to the clause describing the outcome (apodosis). The ordering of condition/protasis before outcome/apodosis is in all recorded cases iconic, and the same ordering would therefore be expected of coordinated clauses as well. Speakers further exhibit considerable freedom in assigning TAM values to the two clauses. In (1078), for instance, the protasis is past tense, while the aposodis is future. In favour of analyzing the condition-protasis clauses as subordinate, however, is the prosodic and semantic integration of the two clauses. While it is possible for clauses containing the polyfunctional form *kar* to stand alone as complete utterances (1080), this never occurs where *kar* 'like' has conditional function (cf. §9.1.3).

(1080) *thele   yoorr   kar   ngan?*
       in.turn   today   like   what
       "what's going to happen today?"
       [KTh_GJ7Feb2004 Elicitation]

Similarly, the prosodic contour of the *kar*-marked condition clauses also marks them as incomplete without a following outcome clause.

e) Purposive function

Despite the existence of dedicated purposive verbal morphology (and the associated 'purposive finite subordinate clause' structure – see §12.1.2.2 below), the unmarked finite subordinate clause may also be used with purposive function. As with the conditional function described above, there is little evidence of subordination for this construction type, other than the single intonation contour applied to the complex clause as a whole (e.g. in (1081)) and the parallels with other unmarked finite subordinate clause types.

(1081) [*minh*   *ulp*   *ranci-rr*   *pam-a*   *{punth*   *patha-rr}]*
        [MEAT(NOM) dem:ad.prx jump-P.PFV man-DAT {arm(ACC) bite-P.PFV}]
        "then that crocodile jumped for the man to bite [him on] the arm"
        [KTh_GJ27Jan2004 Conversation]

It is worth noting here that, although *pama* 'to the man' and *punth* 'arm' in (1081) have overlapping reference, they are not in part-whole apposition, but rather have entirely separate grammatical functions in two different clauses, as evidenced by their different case-marking. The possessive relationship that exists between them must thus be understood pragmatically. Likewise, there is no overt marking in (1081) of the fact that the subordinate clause represents the purpose or aim of the event described by the main clause. In other cases, such as (1032), the purposive function of the unmarked finite subordinate clause is made explicit by the inclusion of the optative particle *ak*.

(1032') [*paath*   *waath-m*   *pul*   *{ak*   *pathatha-n-r}]*
        [fire(ACC) search-P.IPFV 3du(ERG) {OPT bite:RDP-V^-NPST}]
        'they looked for firewood to light [lit. make bite]'
        [Foote and Hall: Reader 9]

Purposive subordinate clauses always appear at the right periphery of the main clause.

12.1.2.2 Purposive-marked subordinate clauses

Purposive-marked (finite) subordinate clauses share both the purposive and complement clause functions of unmarked finite subordinate clauses. They are labelled 'purposive' due to the explicit purposive marking of the subordinate verb, in keeping with the form-based labels applied to all the Kuuk Thaayorre subordinate clause types. The purposive function is illustrated by (1082), which also illustrates the obligatory placement of the purposive subordinate clause at the right periphery of the main clause.

(1082) [*nhul*   *ii*   *yat*   *{kuuk*   *yik-nhatha Allen Hall-ak}]*
        [3sg(NOM) there go:P.PFV {WORD(ACC) say-PURP Allen Hall-DAT}]
        'he went there to speak to Allen Hall'
        [KTh_GJ18Jan2004 Elicitation]

Although there the purposive-marked subordinate clause in (1082) shares its subject with the main clause, this is not a necessary condition. In (1083), for example, the (elided) subject of the subordinate clause is coreferential with one of the two objects of the ditransitive main clause (*kuta ngathn* 'my dog').

(1083) [*ngay*   *kuta ngathn*   *piinth*   *reeka-rr*   *{mungk-nhatha}]*
        [1sg(ERG) dog 1sgGEN(ACC) bone(ACC) give-P.PFV {eat-PURP}]
        'I gave my dog a bone to eat'
        [KTh_EN04Aug2002 Elicitation]

Example (1084) could be similarly characterized purposive (with the sense 'the man helped me for the purpose that I should be able to walk'), but it might alternatively signal an adverbial function of the purposive subordinate clause (with the sense 'the man helped me while I was walking').

(1084) *[pam-al   ii   yuur+reekarr=anh   {ngay   yencnhatha}]*
      [man-ERG there hand+give-P.PFV=1sgACC {1sg(NOM)   go:PURP}]
      'the man helped me to walk'
      [KTh_GJ18Jan2004 Elicitation]

In example (1085), a purposive subordinate clause functions as clausal complement, supplying the direct object of the speech event encoded by the main clause.

(1085) *[Sakala   yiik-r*
      [Sakala(NOM)   say:RDP-P.PFV
      {nhul   kuuk   yiik-nhatha   nhangun}]
      {3sg(NOM)   WORD(ACC)   say:RDP-PURP 3sgDAT}]
      'Sakala_i said he_j should talk to him_k'
      [KTh_GJ18Jan2004 Elicitation]

See §7.3.4 for further discussion of the purposive verbal category.

12.1.2.3 Subjunctive-marked subordinate clauses

Subordinate clauses headed by a subjunctive verb may also have purposive function. Purposive semantics are primarily contributed by the particle *angarr*, which must immediately precede a subjunctive-marked verb as in (1024) and (587), repeated below.

(1024') *[ngay   minc min   waantharr-r   {nganh   kuta-ku   angarr   ngeey-nh}]*
      [1sg(ERG) very good   call.out-P.PFV {1sgACC   dog-ERG ANGARR   hear-SBJV}]
      'I called out loudly so the dog would hear me'
      [KTh_GJ18Jan2004 Elicitation]

(587') *[ngay   money   save-m   rirk*
      [1sg(ERG) money(ACC) save-TR   DO:NPST
      'I'm saving money'
      {ngay   raak   Cairns-na   angarr   yancnh}]
      {1sg(NOM) PLACE   Cairns-DAT ANGARR   go:SBJV}]
      'so that I can go to Cairns'
      [KTh_GJ18Jan2004 Elicitation]

Example (1086) illustrates the conditional use of the subjunctive subordinate clause. Like the unmarked finite subordinate clauses with conditional function, the condition-protasis is marked by *kar* 'like' and must appear at the left periphery of the main clause.

(1086) *[{kar   nhunt   yancnh   inh   truck-ak}   nhaath-nhancnh nhunt]*
       [{like   2sg(NOM)   go:SBJV dem:sp.prx   truck-DAT} see-GO&:SBJV   2sg(ERG)]
       'if you were to go by truck, you would see it'
       "if you go you will see it for yourself"
       [KTh_AJ27Jan2004 Conversation]

12.2 Coordination

Since most Kuuk Thaayorre clauses are headed by a verb, clausal coordination entails verbal coordination. A distinction between the two may be useful in those languages where serial verbs (which share arguments) can be differentiated from the coordination of full clauses composed of predicates and their arguments. This is not a relevant distinction in Kuuk Thaayorre, however, as will become evident in the following sections.

The following discussion is organized firstly according to the three principal types of coordination: conjunction, disjunction and concessive conjunction. Within each of these sections, subsections are organized according to the morphosyntactic features of the various alternative constructions. Brief mention will be made of analogous structures used in nominal coordination where appropriate, but for a more complete discussion of nominal coordination see §6.9.

12.2.1 Conjunction

12.2.1.1 Asyndetic conjunction

Asyndetic conjunction – the juxtaposition of clauses without any explicit marker of conjunction – is the most common form of clausal coordination in Kuuk Thaayorre. In all cases, the ordering of clauses is iconic, with the first clause describing an event that precedes the second temporally, as in:

(1087) *[pam   ith=ul   yarra   yan]*
       [man(NOM) dem:dist=3sg(NOM)   away   go:NPST]
       [patp-nhan=okun=ul]
       [camp-GO&:NPST=DUB=3sg(NOM)]
       'maybe that chap will hive off and pitch camp'
       [Hall 1972: 85]

It is often difficult to distinguish complex clauses formed through asyndetic clausal conjunction from those containing an unmarked finite subordinate clause, especially where we lack access to prosodic cues. In examples like (1087), for instance, there is a fairly loose relationship between the events described and the two clauses could equally stand alone. In example (1088), however, the conjoined clauses share their two arguments, which frame the two adjacent verbs.

(1088) *pam   thon-thurr   find-m   rirk-r   therka-ni-rr   parr_r   ulp*
man   one-ERG   find-TR   DO-P.PFV   return-V^-P.PFV   child(ACC)   dem:ad.prx
'one man found the child and brought him back'
[KTh_FT8Feb2004 Narrative Adoptee]

In a sequence of coordinated clauses, we would normally expect to find arguments overtly represented in the initial clause, with zero anaphora in the second clause. In (1088), though, the subject of both clauses is realized in the initial position of the main clause, while the direct object of both main and subordinate clauses (*parr_r ulp* 'that child') appears only at the right periphery of the subordinate clause. This points to a closer nexus between the clauses than we might expect of a coordinate construction.[211]

Asyndetic conjunction may also be employed to express comparison. In the absence of comparative or superlative adjectives or adverbs (with the minor exception of *mangr* 'rather'), comparison can only be made in Kuuk Thaayorre by contrasting two independent statements. This is illustrated by both the elicited example (1089), and the spontaneous utterance (1090), in which the speaker wished to stress the enormous size of a crocodile he had seen by comparing it to a table near where we were sitting:

(1089) *John   pam   thorkorr,   Bill   pam   kon*
John(NOM)   MAN   long   Bill(NOM)   MAN   short
'John is taller than Bill'
[KTh_GJ14Oct2002 Elicitation]

(1090) *inhul   mantam,   nhul   nga:::mal*
this.one   small   3sg(NOM)   big
'it [the crocodile] was bigger than this [table]'
(lit. 'this one is small, he was big')
[KTh_**AJ**-GJ03Feb2004 Conversation]

---

[211] Further research may reveal a distinct verbal conjunction structure – as distinct from clausal conjunction – of which (1088) would be an example.

12.2.1.2 Ngul-marked conjunction

Conjunction of clauses may be marked by the connective *ngul* 'then'. As its gloss suggests, *ngul* 'then' typically expresses a temporal relationship between events, appearing at the beginning of a clause that sequentially follows some other event:

(1091) *ulp   wacacirr   collect-m   rirk   ngul kath-r*
       dem:ad.prx properly:RDP   collect-TR   DO:NPST   then bind-NPST
       "everything gotta be collected and tie'm up"
       [KTh_**AJ**-GJ03Feb2004 Conversation]

However, it is not entailed that the event described by the *ngul*-marked clause is subsequent to the event described by the preceding (unmarked) clause. In (1092), for example, *ngul* appears in the clause describing the events of 1969, which clearly preceded the events of 1970 (described in the previous clause).

(1092) 1. *ngay   ii-rr-kuw   Darwin-ak   yat=ay,   1970.*
          1sg(NOM) there-towards-west   Darwin-DAT   go:P.PFV=1sg(NOM) 1970
          'I went west to Darwin in 1970'
       2. *ngul 1969 Cyclone Tracy-n   thiika-rr.*
          then 1969 Cyclone Tracy-ERG   break-P.PFV
          'in 1969 Cyclone Tracy had destroyed it'
          [KTh_AJ-**GJ**03Feb2002 Conversation]

Both parataxis and *ngul*-marked conjunction may be used to much the same ends. This is evident in the following passage; the first pair of clauses are juxtaposed with no connective (most likely because they are paraphrases), the second pair are connected by *ngul* 'then', while (1093.3), which essentially rephrases (1093.2), contains no connective:

(1093) 1. *ak   piinth-r,   ngamal   wene*
          OPT   grow-NPST   big   become:NPST
          "let it [cyclone] grow, let it become big"
       2. *piinth-r,   **ngul**   nhul   pal=ul   yan*
          grow-NPST   then   3sg(NOM)   towards=3sg(NOM)   go:NPST
          "when he grows up then he come"
          'it will grow, then it will come'
       3. *piintharrn ngan   yomparr-nhan   pal=ul   yan*
          strong   what   become-GO&:NPST   towards=3sg(NOM)   go:NPST
          "when he gets strong he'll come then"
          [KTh_**AJ**-GJ03Feb2004 Conversation]

Example (1094) illustrates the typical usage of *ngul* across a more extended sequence of clauses. *Ngul* first appears at the start of a turn in line (1094.4), but the same speaker uses it again within the same turn in line (1094.6), then again at the start of his next turn, (1094.11):

(1094) 1. AJ: *Dan raak ngan pal therk-nhan?*
 Dan TIME what towards return-GO&:NPST
 'when will Dan come back?'
 2. AG: *ngay pamngongkom,*
 1sg(NOM) ignorant.of
 'I don't know'
 3. AG: *nhul mit rirk Melbourne-ak, meerkunwaarr!*
 3sg(NOM) work DO:NPST Melbourne-DAT pitiful
 'he's working in Melbourne, poor thing!'
 4. AJ: ***ngul** ngathun, teacher thono [...],*
 so 1sgDAT teacher one(NOM)
 'so anyway, this teacher [said] to me... [pause for repair]'
 5. AJ: *ngay yik-nhat yarriy "Alice wanthan?"*
 1sg(NOM) say-GO&:P.PFV thus "Alice where$_{TRJ}$"
 'I said "where's Alice?"'
 6. AJ: ***ngul** nhul ngathun yarriy yik-r*
 then 3sg(NOM) 1sgDAT thus say-P.PFV
 'and he said to me:'
 7. AJ: *"Alice yuuw yat!"*
 Alice(NOM) far.away go:P.PFV
 '"Alice has gone away"'
 8. AJ: *"wanthan pal yat?"*
 where$_{TRJ}$ towards go:P.PFV
 '"where has she gone to?" [I asked]'
 9. AJ: *"ii-rr-iparr, Melbourne-ak yat"*
 there-towards-south Melbourne-DAT go:P.PFV
 '"[she's] gone to Melbourne"'
 10. AG: *pokon!*
 NO
 'no!'
 11. AJ: ***ngul** ngay yarriy yik-r "kece!"*
 then 1sg(NOM) thus say-P.PFV CDICT
 'then I said "you're wrong!"'
 [KTh_AJ27Jan2004 Conversation]

Each time that it appears in this dialogue, *ngul* 'then' indicates a different degree of connection between clauses. Illustrating the loosest degree of connection, AJ employs *ngul* at the beginning of his second turn (1094d) to introduce a clause that is not obviously connected to the preceding discourse. *Ngul* here functions to express that the following statement nevertheless has current relevance. In (1094k), AJ once again employs *ngul* at the very beginning of a reported turn, but this time it introduces a clause that fits more tightly into the chronological sequence of the incident he is relating. Illustrating the tightest degree of connection between clauses, *ngul* appears immediately between clauses ([1094e] and [1094f]), which are tightly linked both thematically and chronologically, being a description of an answer and response between the two participants.

The cognate form *ngula* 'then, afterwards' is similarly used to conjoin clauses describing sequentially-related events in Kugu Nganhcara (Smith and Johnson 2000: 434) and Warlpiri (Nash 1980), cf. Gaby & Manning 2013.

12.2.2 Disjunction

Disjunction may be achieved by simple parataxis, as seen in the following:

(1095) nhiplin   kar   yak-a   patha-rr,   kar   minh-al=rr   patha-rr
       2duACC   like snake-ERG   bite-P.PFV like   meat-ERG=PRAG   bite-P.PFV
       "[we] thought you might have been eaten by a crocodile, or bitten by a snake."
       [KTh_GJ15Oct2002 Narrative PlaneSighting]

Although nominal disjunction is frequently achieved by encliticizing the dubitative enclitic =*okun* to both coordinands, this does not seem to be a strategy for clausal[212] disjunction. Instead, most instances of clausal disjunction in present day speech include the English loan *or*:

(1096) raak   inhul   thurma   wun-an   or wanthantharr?
       place   this.one   together   reside-GO&:NPST   or how
       'will we stay here together or what?'
       [KTh_GJ16Oct2002 Narrative MelbourneTrip]

Interestingly, the distribution of *or* in clausal disjunction seems to mirror the distribution of =*okun* 'dubitative' in nominal disjunction somewhat. In example (b), for instance, *or* appears on both coordinands, whereas in English it would only appear on the second (at the juncture between the two). Note that the presence of the dubitative enclitic, =*okun*, in the first clause does not mark it as a coordinand, but is rather functioning with its modal sense, indicating that the speaker is unsure of whether or not the event will occur.

---

[212] Throughout this section, 'clausal' should be taken to mean 'clausal and/or verbal'.

(1097) ngay   ii-rr-kuw=okun   yan;
       1sg(NOM)   there-towards-west=DUB   go:NPST
       'I might go west'
       or ngay   rump-un   yan,   or ngay   waap-n   yan
       or 1sg(NOM)   beach-DAT go:NPST or 1sg(NOM) river-DAT go:NPST
       'I might go to the beach, or I might go to the river'
       [KTh_GJ16Oct2002 Narrative MelbourneTrip]

Like Kuuk Thaayorre, Kugu Nganhcara traditionally expressed disjunction asyndetically, but "an innovative alternative construction for disjunction uses the borrowed English conjunction *oo* 'or'" (Smith and Johnson 2000: 434).

12.2.3 Concessive conjunction

Concessive/adversative constructions are rarely reported for Australian languages As with the other subtypes of clausal coordination, concessive conjunction may be achieved by parataxis:

(1098) *ith nhunt   wurrur   pirk-r   yuur   punth   thamr*
       if   2sg(ERG) WURRUR   poke-P.PFV   hand(ACC) arm(ACC) foot(ACC)
       yangkar=okun, yiin=p   kaar=p
       calf(ACC)=DUB itch=PRAG NEG=PRAG
       'if you have a rash on hands or feet, but it is not itchy'
       [KTh_Health Centre Poster – source unknown]

(Note the form *ith* is used here to establish an irrealis proposition, not to mark concessive conjunction – cf. §3.5.2).

While Kuuk Thaayorre lacks a dedicated concessive connective, concessive conjunction is strongly implied by the inclusion of either *akp* 'despite' or contrastive *wuump* in one of the two clauses.

(1099) *quiet one akp,   ngay   kaar trust-m   rirk*
       quiet one despite 1sg(ERG)   NEG   trust-TR DO:NPST
       'although [that crocodile] may be quiet, I don't trust him'
       [KTh_GJ3Feb2004 Conversation]

(711') 1. *nhinh   ngay   wuump wal.meerem name nhangkn   ngay,*
          2sgACC   1sg(NOM)   CONTR remember   name 2sgGEN(ACC)   1sg(NOM)
          Alice nhunt...
          Alice 2sg(NOM)
          'I know your name, you're Alice...'

2. *ngay   pam nhangkn   nhamp   ngay   pam.ngongkom*
   1sg(NOM) man 2sgGEN(ACC) name(ACC) 1sg(NOM) ignorant.of
   '[but] I can't remember the name of your man'
   [KTh_AC21Aug2002 Conversation]

The semantics and functions of these two particles are discussed in §9.1, and will not be elaborated upon here.

It was suggested in §12.2.1.2 that the primary function of *ngul* 'then' is to indicate temporal sequence. *Ngul* can also be used to express concessive disjunction. The third clause of (100), for example, illustrates a concessive usage of *ngul* in a clause describing a temporally prior state of affairs (cf. also example 100 above for the use of *ngul* to contrast hypothetical and real, rather than temporally connected, contexts).

(1100) 1. *hospital   ii-kuw-an   inh   than-m*
          hospital(NOM) there-at:west-DAT dem:sp.prx stand-P.IPFV
          'the hospital used to be there in the west'
       2. *ith   hall   ith   thanan,*
          dem:dist hall(NOM) dem:dist stand:RDP:NPST
          'the hall stands there now'
       3. *ngul yumpi-rr   kanpa ii-kuw-an   ith   than-m.*
          but   make-P.PFV first   there-at:west-DAT dem:dist stand-P.IPFV
          'but [the hospital] was built there first, standing there in the west'.
          [KTh_AJ27Jan2004 Conversation]

References

Alpher, Barry. 1972. On the genetic subgrouping of the languages of southwestern Cape York Peninsula, Australia. In *Oceanic Linguistics* 11(2). 67–87.
Alpher, Barry. 1973. Son of ergative: The Yir Yoront language of northeast Australia. Unpublished PhD thesis: Cornell.
Alpher, Barry. 1991. *Yir-Yoront Lexicon*. Berlin/New York: Mouton de Gruyter.
Alpher, Barry. 1994. Yir-Yoront ideophones. In J. Ohala (ed.), *Sound Symbolism*, 161–177. Cambridge: Cambridge University Press.
Alpher, Barry. 2004a. Pama-Nyungan: Phonological reconstruction and status as a phylogenetic group. In C. Bowern and H. Koch (eds.), *Australian languages: Classification and the Comparative Method*, 93–126. Amsterdam: John Benjamins.
Alpher, Barry. 2004b. Proto-Pama-Nyungan etyma. In C. Bowern and H. Koch (eds.), *Australian Languages: Classification and the Comparative Method*, 387–570. Amsterdam: John Benjamins.
Alsina, Alex, Joan Bresnan and Peter Sells. (eds.). 1996. *Complex Predicates*. Stanford: CSLI Publications.
Amberber, Mengistu, Brett Baker and Mark Harvey. 2007. Complex predication and the coverb construction. In J. Lynch, J. Siegel and D. Eades (eds.), *Language Description, History and Development: Linguistic Indulgence in Memory of Terry Crowley*, 209–219. Amsterdam: John Benjamins.
Ameka, Felix. 1992. Interjections: The universal yet neglected part of speech. *Journal of Pragmatics* 18(2–3). 101–118.
Ameka, Felix. and Stephen. Levinson. 2007. Introduction: The typology and semantics of locative predicates – posturals, positionals, and other beasts. *Linguistics* 45(5). 847–871.
Anderson, Lloyd. 1982. Universals of aspect and parts of speech: Parallels between signed and spoken languages. In Paul Hopper (ed.), *Tense-Aspect: Between Semantics and Pragmatics*, 91–114. Amsterdam: John Benjamins.
Anderson, Stephen. 2005. *Aspects of the Theory of Clitics*. Oxford: Oxford University Press.
Anderson, Stephen, Lea Brown, Alice Gaby and Jacqueline Lecarme. 2006. Life on the edge: There's morphology there after all. *Lingue e linguaggio* 1. 1–16.
Andrews, Avery. 1982. Long distance agreement in modern Icelandic. In Pauline Jacobson and Geoffrey Pullum (eds.), *The Nature of Syntactic Representation*, 1–34. Dordrecht: Reidel.
Ariel, Mira. 1990. *Accessing Noun Phrase Antecedents*. Cambridge: Cambridge University Press.
Arthur, Jay. 1997. *Aboriginal English: A Cultural Study*. Oxford: Oxford University Press.
Austin, Peter. 1981. *A Grammar of Diyari, South Australia*. Cambridge: Cambridge University Press.
Austin, Peter. 1982. Transitivity and cognate objects in Australian languages. In Paul Hopper and Sandra Thompson (eds.), *Studies in Transitivity*, 37–48. New York: Academic Press.
Austin, Peter. (ed.). 1988. *Complex Sentence Constructions in Australian Languages*. Typological studies in language 15. Amsterdam: John Benjamins.
Austin, Peter. 1993. *A Grammar of the Mantharta Languages, Western Australia*. La Trobe University, manuscript.
Austin, Peter. 1997. Causatives and applicatives in Australian Aboriginal languages. In Kazuto Matsumura and Tooru Hayashi (eds.), *The Dative and Related Phenomena*, 165–225. Tokyo: Hituzi Syobo.
Austin, Peter and Joan Bresnan. 1996. Non-configurationality in Australian Aboriginal languages, *Natural Language and Linguistic Theory* 14. 215–268.
Australian Bureau of Statistics (ABS). 2010. *National Regional Profile: Pormpuraaw (S) (Statistical Local Area). Classifications code: 350106070*. Retrieved from: http://www.abs.gov.au/AUSSTATS/abs@.nsf/Previousproducts/350106070Population/People12004-2008?opendocument&tabname=Summary&prodno=350106070&issue=2004–2008

Australian Government Bureau of Meteorology (BOM). 2016. *Climate Statistics for Australian Locations: Summary Statistics KOWANYAMA AIRPORT*. Retrived from: http://www.bom.gov.au/climate/averages/tables/cw_029038.shtml.

Australian Institute of Aboriginal and Torres Strait Islander Studies (AIATSIS). 2014. *AUSTLANG: Australian Indigenous Languages Database*. Retrieved from: http://austlang.aiatsis.gov.au/main.php?code=Y69.

Australian Institute of Aboriginal and Torres Strait Islander Studies (AIATSIS). 2005. *National Indigenous Languages Survey Report 2005*. Canberra: Department of Communications, Information Technology and the Arts. Retrieved from: http://arts.gov.au/sites/default/files/pdfs/nils-report-2005.pdf

Baker, Brett. 1999. Word structure in Ngalakgan. Unpublished PhD thesis. Sydney University of Sydney.

Baker, Mark. 1985. The mirror principle and morphosyntactic explanation. *Linguistic Inquiry* 16. 373–416.

Barras, Claude, Edouard Geoffrois, Zhibiao Wu and Mark Liberman. 1998. Transcriber: A free tool for segmenting, labeling and transcribing speech. *Proceedings of LREC 1998, the First International Conference on Language Resources and Evaluation*, 1373–1376. Granada, Spain.

Black, Paul. 1995. *The Dance of Language: Some Practical Linguistic Approaches*. Darwin: Centre for Studies of Language in Education, Northern Territory University.

Blake, Barry. 1976. Rapporteur's introduction and summary (Topic C: the bivalent suffix *-ku*). In Robert Dixon (ed.), *Grammatical Categories in Australian Languages*, 421–423. Canberra: Australian Institute of Aboriginal Studies Press.

Blake, Barry. 1979a. Pitta-Pitta. In Robert Dixon and Barry Blake (eds.), *Handbook of Australian Languages, Vol. 1*, 183–242. Canberra: A.N.U. Press.

Blake, Barry. 1979b. *A Kalkatungu Grammar*. Canberra: Pacific Linguistics.

Blake, Barry. 1983. Structure and word order in Kalkatungu: The anatomy of a flat language. *Australian Journal of Linguistics* 3. 143–175.

Blake, Barry. 1987. *Australian Aboriginal Grammar*. London: Croom Helm.

Blake, Barry. 1994. *Case*. Cambridge: Cambridge University Press.

Blake, Barry. 2001a. *Case* (2nd edition). Cambridge: Cambridge University Press.

Blake, Barry. 2001b. The noun phrase in Australian languages. In Jane Simpson, David Nash, Mary Laughren, Peter Austin and Barry Alpher (eds.), *Forty years on: Ken Hale and Australian languages*, 415–426. Canberra: Pacific Linguistics.

Blevins, Juliette. 1995. The syllable in phonological theory. In John Goldsmith (ed.), *The Handbook of Phonological Theory*, 206–244. Cambridge: Blackwell.

Bohnemeyer, Jürgen. 2001. Motionland. In Stephen Levinson and Nick Enfield (eds.), *Field Manual 2001*, 93–95. Nijmegen: Max Planck Institute for Psycholinguistics, Language & Cognition Group.

Bohnemeyer, Jürgen, Melissa Bowerman and Penelope Brown. 2001. Cut and break clips, version 3. In Stephen Levinson and Nick Enfield (eds.), *Field Manual 2001*, 90–96. Nijmegen: Max Planck Institute for Psycholinguistics, Language & Cognition Group.

Bowern, Claire. 2004. Bardi verb morphology in historical perspective. Unpublished PhD dissertation. Harvard University.

Bowern, Claire. 2012. *A Grammar of Bardi*. Berlin/Boston: De Gruyter Mouton.

Bowern, Claire and Quentin Atkinson. 2012. Computational Phylogenetics and the Internal Structure of Pama-Nyungan. *Language* 88. 817–845.

Brandl, Maria and Michael Walsh. 1982. Speakers of many tongues: Toward understanding multilingualism among Aboriginal Australians. *International Journal of the Sociology of Language* 36. 71–81.

Breen, Gavan. 1992. Some problems in Kukatj phonology. *Australian Journal of Linguistics* 12(1). 1–43.

Breen, Gavan and Rob Pensalfini. 1999. Arrernte: A language with no syllable onsets. *Linguistic Inquiry* 30(1). 1–25.

Bresnan, Joan and Jonni Kanerva. 1989. Locative inversion in Chichewa: A case study of factorization in grammar. *Linguistic Inquiry* 20. 1–50.
Brown, Cecil and Stanley Witkowksi. 1981. Figurative language in a universalist perspective. *American Ethnologist* 8(3): *Symbolism and Cognition*. 596–615.
Brown, Penelope and Stephen Levinson. 1987. Politeness: Some universals in language usage. Cambridge: Cambridge University Press.
Brugman, Claudia. 1988. The syntax and semantics of HAVE and its complements. Unpublished PhD thesis, UCLA, Berkeley.
Bühler, Karl. 1982 [1934]. The deictic field of language and deictic words. Reprinted in Robert Jarvella and Wolfgang Klein (eds.). *Speech, Place, and Action: Studies in Deixis and Related Topics*, 9–30. New York: John Wiley & Sons Ltd.
Burenhult, Niclas. 2003. Attention, accessibility, and the addressee: The case of the Jahai demonstrative *ton*. *Pragmatics* 13(3/4). 363–379.
Burenhult, Niclas. 2006. Body part terms in Jahai. *Language Sciences* 28(2/3). 162–180.
Butcher, Andrew. 2006. Australian Aboriginal languages: Consonant-salient phonologies and the 'place-of-articulation imperative'. In Jonathan Harrington and Marija Tabain (eds): *Speech Production: Models, Phonetic Processes and Techniques*, 187–210. New York: Psychology Press.
Butt, Miriam. 1995. *The Structure of Complex Predicates*. Stanford: CSLI.
Butt, Miriam and Wilhelm Geuder. 2001. On the (semi)lexical status of light verbs. In Norbert Corver and Henk van Riemsdijk (eds.), *Semi-Lexical Categories: The Function of Content Words and the Content of Function Words*, 323–369. Berlin/New York: Mouton de Gruyter.
Capell, Arthur. 1963. *Linguistic Survey of Australia*. Canberra: Australian Institute of Aboriginal Studies.
Capell, Arthur. 1976. Rapporteur's introduction and summary (Topic E: Simple and compound verbs – conjugation by auxiliaries in Australian verbal systems). In Robert Dixon (ed.), *Grammatical Categories in Australian Languages*, 615–624. Canberra: Australian Institute of Aboriginal Studies Press.
Capell, Arthur. 1979. Languages and creoles in Australia. *Sociologia Internationalis* 17. 141–161.
Chappell, Hilary and William McGregor. 1996. Introduction: Prolegomena to a theory of inalienability. In Hilary Chappell and William McGregor (eds.), *The Grammar of Inalienability*, 3–31. Berlin/New York: Mouton de Gruyter.
Carew, Margaret. 2016. Gun-ngaypa rrawa 'my country': Intercultural alliances in language research. Unpublished PhD thesis. Melbourne: Monash University.
Carey, Peter. 1999 [1985]. *Illywhacker*. Brisbane: University of Queensland Press.
Charlie, Alfred, Celia Holroyd, Gilbert Jack, Doris Ned, Jerry Ned, Cyril William, Donald William, Alice Gaby and Daniel Hirst. 2003. *Wuuch/Wanum: Songs of Pormpuraaw*. Audio CD. Pormpuraaw: Pormpuraaw Community Council.
Cho, Taehong and Patricia Keating. 2001. Articulatory and acoustic studies on domain-initial strengthening in Korean. *Journal of Phonetics* 29. 155–190.
Choi, Hye-Won. 1999. *Optimizing Structure in Context: Scrambling and Information Structure*. Stanford: CSLI Publications.
Choi, Hye-Won. 2001. Phrase structure, information structure and resolution of mismatch. In Peter Sells (ed.), *Formal and Empirical Issues in Optimality Theoretic Syntax*, 17–62. Stanford: CSLI Publications.
Chomsky, Noam. 1965. *Aspects of the Theory of Syntax*. Cambridge, MA: MIT Press.
Clark, Herbert, Robert Schreuder and Samuel Buttrick. 1983. Common ground and the understanding of demonstrative reference. *Journal of Verbal Learning and Verbal Behavior* 22. 245–258.
Comrie, Bernard. 1985. *Tense*. Cambridge: Cambridge University Press.
Comrie, Bernard, Martin Haspelmath and Balthasar Bickel. 2003. Leipzig glossing rules. Online: https://www.eva.mpg.de/lingua/resources/glossing-rules.php. Accessed 3rd July 2015.

Corbett, Greville. 1995. Agreement. In Joachim Jacobs, Arnim von Stechow, Wolfgang Sternefeld and Theo Vennemann (eds.), *Syntax: An International Handbook of Contemporary Research*, 1235–1244. Berlin/New York: Mouton de Gruyter.
Cownie, Andrew. 2001. A dictionary of Welsh and English idiomatic phrases. Cardiff: University of Wales Press.
Craig, Colette. 1986. Jacaltec noun classifiers. A study in language and culture. In Colette Craig (ed.), *Noun Classes and Categorization*, 263–295. Amsterdam: John Benjamins.
Creissels, Denis and Sylvie Nouguier-Voisin. 2008. Valency-changing operations in Wolof and the notion of co-participation. In Ekkehard König and Volker Gast (eds.), *Reciprocals and Reflexives: Cross-Linguistic and Theoretical Explorations*, 289–305. Berlin/New York: Mouton de Gruyter.
Cristofaro, Sonia. 2006. The organization of reference grammars: A typologist user's point of view. In Felix Ameka, Alan Dench and Nicholas Evans (eds.), *Catching Language: The Standing Challenge of Grammar Writing*, 137–170. Berlin/New York: Mouton de Gruyter.
Cutfield, Sarah. 2012. Demonstratives in Dalabon: A language of southwestern Arnhem Land. PhD thesis. Melbourne: Monash University.
Dahl, Östen. 1985. *Tense and Aspect Systems*. Oxford: Blackwell.
Dalrymple, Mary, Makoto Kanazawa, Yookyung Kim, Sam Mchombo and Stanley Peters. 1998. Reciprocal Expressions and the Concept of Reciprocity. *Linguistics & Philosophy* 21(2). 159–210.
Darden, Bill. 1971. A note on Sommer's claim that there exist languages without CV syllables. *International Journal of Aboriginal Linguistics* 37. 126–128.
DeLancey, Scott. 1997. Mirativity: The grammatical marking of unexpected information. *Linguistic Typology* 1(1). 33–52. doi:10.1515/lity.1997.1.1.33.
Dench, Alan. 1995a. *Martuthunira: A Language of the Pilbara Region of Western Australia*. Canberra: Pacific Linguistics, Series C: 125.
Dench, Alan. 1995b. Suffixaufnahme and apparent ellipsis in Martuthunira. In Frans Plank (ed.), *Double Case*, 380–395. Oxford: Oxford University Press.
Dench, Alan and Nicholas Evans. 1988. Multiple case-marking in Australian languages. *Australian Journal of Linguistics* 8. 1–47.
Diessel, Holger. 1999. *Demonstratives: Form, Function, and Grammaticalization*. Amsterdam: John Benjamins.
Diessel, Holger. 2001. The ordering distribution of main and adverbial clauses: A typological study. *Language* 77. 343–365.
Diessel, Holger. 2005. Competing motivations for the ordering of main and adverbial clauses. *Linguistics* 43(3). 449–470.
Dingemanse, Mark. 2012. Advances in the cross-linguistic study of ideophones. *Language and Linguistics Compass* 6. 654–672. doi:10.1002/lnc3.361
Dixon, Robert. 1972. *The Dyirbal language of North Queensland*. Cambridge: Cambridge University Press.
Dixon, Robert. 1977. *A grammar of Yidiɲ*. Cambridge: Cambridge University Press.
Dixon, Robert. 1980. *The languages of Australia*. Cambridge: Cambridge University Press.
Dixon, Robert. 1991. *Words of Our Country: Stories, Place Names and Vocabulary*. St. Lucia: University of Queensland Press.
Dixon, Robert. 1997. *The Rise and Fall of Languages*. Cambridge: Cambridge University Press.
Dixon, Robert. 2002. *Australian Languages: Their Nature and Development*. New York: Cambridge University Press.
Dixon, Robert. 2003. Demonstratives. A cross-linguistic typology. *Studies in Language* 27. 61–112.
Dryer, Matthew. 2006. Descriptive theories, explanatory theories, and basic linguistic theory. In Felix Ameka, Alan Dench and Nicholas Evans (eds.), *Catching language: The Standing Challenge of Grammar Writing*, 235–268. Berlin/New York: Mouton de Gruyter.
DuBois, John. 1987. The discourse basis of ergativity. *Language* 63(4). 805–855.

Durie, Mark. 1985. *A Grammar of Acehnese: On The Basis of a Dialect of North Aceh*. Dordrecht: Foris.
Enfield, Nick. 2002. Semantic analysis of body parts in emotion terminology: Avoiding the exoticisms of 'obstinate monosemy' and 'online extension'. *Pragmatics and Cognition* 10(1/2). 81–102.
Enfield, Nick. 2003a. Demonstratives in space and interaction: Data from Lao speakers and implications for semantic analysis. *Language* 79(1). 82–117.
Enfield, Nick. 2003b. The definition of WHAT-d'you-call-it: Semantics and pragmatics of 'recognitional deixis'. *Journal of Pragmatics* 35. 101–117.
Evans, Nicholas. 1988. Arguments for Pama-Nyungan as a subgroup, with particular reference to initial laminalization. In Nicholas Evans and Steve Johnson (eds.), *Aboriginal Linguistics* 1. 91–110.
Evans, Nicholas. 1990. Without this child: Some regularities of semantic change in the Australian linguistic area. In Peter Austin, Robert Dixon, Tom Dutton and Isobel White (eds.), *Language and History: Essays in Honour of Luise Hercus*, 137–155. Canberra: Pacific Linguistics (Series C-116).
Evans, Nicholas. 1992. 'Wanjh! bonj! nja!': Sequential organization and social deixis in Mayali interjections. *Journal of Pragmatics* 18(2/3). 71–89.
Evans, Nicholas. 1995a. *A Grammar of Kayardild*. Berlin/New York: Mouton de Gruyter.
Evans, Nicholas. 1995b. Multiple case in Kayardild: Anti-iconicity and the diachronic filter. In Frans Plank (ed.), *Double Case. Agreement by Suffixaufnahme*, 396–428. Oxford: Oxford University Press.
Evans, Nicholas. 1995c. Current issues in Australian phonology. In John Goldsmith (ed.), *Handbook of Phonological Theory*, 723–761. Oxford: Blackwell.
Evans, Nicholas. 1996. The syntax and semantics of body part incorporation in Mayali. In Hilary Chappell and William McGregor (eds.), *The Grammar of Inalienability: A Typological Perspective on Body Part Terms and the Part-Whole Relation*, 65–109. Berlin/New York: Mouton de Gruyter.
Evans, Nicholas. 2000. Word classes in the world's languages. In Geert Booij, Christian Lehmann and Joachim Mugdan (eds.), *Morphology: A Handbook on Inflection and Word Formation*, 708–732. Berlin/New York: Mouton de Gruyter.
Evans, Nicholas. 2003a. *Bininj Gun-Wok: A Pan-Dialectal Grammar of Mayali, Kunwinjku and Kune*. Canberra: Pacific Linguistics.
Evans, Nicholas. 2003b. *An Interesting Couple: The Semantic Development of Dyad Morphemes*. Köln: Institut für Sprachwissenschaft (Arbeitspapier 47, Neue Folge).
Evans, Nicholas. 2006. Dyad constructions. In Keith Brown (ed.), *Encyclopaedia of Language and Linguistics* (2nd Edition). Oxford: Elsevier.
Evans, Nicholas. 2007. Insubordination and its functions. In Irina Nikolaeva and Frans Plank (eds.), *Finiteness – Theoretical and Empirical Foundations*, 366–431. Oxford: Oxford University Press.
Evans, Nicholas. 2008. Reciprocal constructions: Towards a structural typology. In Ekkehard König and Volker Gast (eds.), *Reciprocals and Reflexives: Cross-linguistic and Theoretical Explorations*. Berlin/New York: Mouton de Gruyter.
Evans, Nicholas and Alan Dench. 2006. Grammaticography: The art and craft of writing grammars. In Felix Ameka, Alan Dench and Nicholas Evans (eds.), *Catching Language: The Standing Challenge of Grammar Writing*, 1–40. Berlin/New York: Mouton de Gruyter.
Evans, Nicholas, Alice Gaby and Rachel Nordlinger. 2007. Valency mismatches and the coding of reciprocity in Australian languages. *Linguistic Typology* 11. 541–597.
Evans, Nicholas and Rhys Jones. 1997. The cradle of the Pama-Nyungans: Archaeological and linguistic speculations. In Nicholas Evans and Patrick McConvell (eds.), *Linguistics and Archaeology: Aboriginal Australia in Global Perspective*, 385–417. Oxford: Oxford University Press.
Evans, Nicholas, Stephen Levinson, Nick Enfield, Alice Gaby and Asifa Majid. 2004. Reciprocal constructions and situation type. In Asifa Majid (ed.), *Field Manual*, vol. 9, 25–30. Nijmegen: Max Planck Institute for Psycholinguistics.
Evans, Nicholas and David Wilkins. 2000. In the mind's ear: The semantic extensions of perception verbs in Australian languages. *Language* 76(3). 546–92.

Fillmore, Charles. 1975. *Santa Cruz Lectures on Deixis*. Bloomington: University of Indiana Linguistics Club.
Fillmore, Charles. 1982. Towards a descriptive framework for spatial deixis. In Robert Jarvella and Wolfgang Klein (eds.), *Speech, Place, and Action*, 31–59. Chichester: John Wiley and Sons.
Foley, William and Robert Van Valin. 1980. Role and reference grammar. In Edith Moravcsik and Jessica Wirth (eds.), *Syntax and Semantics 13: Current Approaches to Syntax*, 329–352. New York: Academic Press.
Foote, Tom and Allen Hall. 1992. *Kuuk Thaayorre Dictionary: Kuuk Thaayorre/English*. Toowong: Jollen Press.
Foote, Tom and Allen Hall. Undated manuscript. Kuuk Thaayorre readers and primers for the Pormpuraaw State School.
Gaby, Alice. 2001. A typology of the reflexoid in Australian languages. Unpublished Honours Thesis, Melbourne: University of Melbourne.
Gaby, Alice. 2005. Some participants are more equal than others: Case and the composition of arguments in Kuuk Thaayorre. In Mengistu Amberber and Helen deHoop (eds.), *Competition and Variation in Natural Languages: The Case for Case*, 9–39. Amsterdam: Elsevier.
Gaby, Alice. 2006. The Kuuk Thaayorre 'true man': Lexicon of the human body in an Australian language. *Language Sciences* 28(2/3). 201–220.
Gaby, Alice. 2008a. Pragmatically case-marked: Non-syntactic functions of the Kuuk Thaayorre ergative suffix. In Ilana Mushin and Brett Baker (eds.), *Discourse and Grammar in Australian Languages*, 11–134. Amsterdam: John Benjamins.
Gaby, Alice. 2008b. Distinguishing reciprocals from reflexives in Kuuk Thaayorre. In Ekkehard König and Volker Gast (eds.), *Reciprocals and reflexives: Cross-linguistic and Theoretical Explorations*. Berlin/New York: Mouton de Gruyter.
Gaby, Alice. 2008c. Gut feelings: Locating emotion, life force and intellect in the Kuuk Thaayorre body. In Farzad Sharifian, René Dirven and Ning Yu (eds.), *Body, culture* and *language: Conceptualizations of internal body organs across cultures* and languages. Berlin/New York: Mouton De Gruyter.
Gaby, Alice. 2010. From discourse to syntax and back: The lifecycle of Kuuk Thaayorre ergative morphology. *Lingua* 120. 1677–1692.
Gaby, Alice. 2016. Hyponymy and the structure of Kuuk Thaayorre kinship. In Jean-Christophe Verstraete and Diane Hafner (eds.), *Land and language in Cape York Peninsula and the Gulf country* (Studies in Anthropological Linguistics), 159–178. Amsterdam/Philadelphia: John Benjamins.
Gaby, Alice. 2017. Kinship semantics: Culture in the lexicon. In Farzad Sharifian (ed.), *Advances in Cultural Linguistics*. (Cultural Linguistics), 173–188. New York/London/Singapore: Springer.
Gaby, Alice. Forthcoming. Iterative conventionalization and the Kuuk Thaayorre desiderative mood.
Gaby, Alice and Sharon Inkelas. 2014. Reduplication in Kuuk Thaayorre. In René Kager, Janet Grijzenhout and Koen Sebregts (eds.). *Where the Principles Fail: A Festschrift for Wim Zonneveld on the Occasion of his 64th Birthday*, 41–52. Ridderkerk: Holland Ridderkerk.
Gaby, Alice and Ruth Singer. 2014. Semantics of Australian languages. In Harold Koch and Rachel Nordlinger (eds.), *The Languages and Linguistics of Australia: A Comprehensive Guide* (World of Languages 3), 295–327. Berlin/New York: Mouton de Gruyter.
Gaby, Alice and Clare Manning. 2013. But then again…: Temporal/adversative polysemy in Australian languages. *Australian Linguistics Society Annual Conference*, 1st–4th October, 2013. Melbourne: The University of Melbourne.
Garde, Murray. 2008. Person reference, proper names and circumspection in Bininj Kunwok conversation. In Ilana Mushin and Brett Baker (eds.), *Discourse and Grammar in Australian Languages*, 203–232. Amsterdam/Philadelphia: John Benjamins.
Garde, Murray. 2013. *Culture, Interaction and Person Reference in an Australian Language*. Amsterdam/Philadelphia: John Benjamins.

Garde, Murray. 2014. Shifting Relations: Structure and agency in the language of Bininj Gunwok kinship. In Rob Pensalfini, Myfany Turpin and Diana Guillemin (eds.), *Language Description Informed by Theory*, 361–381. Amsterdam: John Benjamins.
Gast, Volker and Florian Haas. 2008. Reflexive and reciprocal readings of anaphors in German and other European languages. In Ekkehard König and Volker Gast (eds.) *Reciprocals and Reflexives: Cross-linguistic and Theoretical Explorations*. Berlin/New York: Mouton de Gruyter.
Geniušienė, Emma. 1987. *The Typology of Reflexives*. Berlin/New York: Mouton de Gruyter
Givón, Talmy. 1984. *Syntax: A Functional-Typological Introduction*. Amsterdam: John Benjamins.
Givón, Talmy. 2001. *Syntax. An Introduction*. Amsterdam: John Benjamins.
Goddard, Cliff. 1982. Case system and case marking in Australian languages: A new interpretation. *Australian Journal of Linguistics* 2. 167–196.
Goddard, Cliff. 1985. *A grammar of Yankunytjatjara*. Alice Springs: Institute for Aboriginal Development.
Goddard, Cliff. 1996. *Pitjantjatjara/Yankunytjatjara to English Dictionary*. Alice Springs: Institute of Aboriginal Development Press.
Green, Jennifer, Anastasia Bauer, Elizabeth Ellis and Alice Gaby. In press. Pointing to the body: Kin signs in Australian Indigenous sign languages. *Gesture* 17(1).
Greenberg, Joseph. 1963. Some universals of grammar with particular reference to the order of meaningful elements. In Joseph Greenberg (ed.), *Universals of Language*. 73–113. Cambridge, MA: MIT Press.
Grimes, Barbara (ed.). 2000. *Ethnologue: Languages of the World*, 14th edition. Dallas: Summer Institute of Linguistics.
Grimshaw, Jane and Armin Mester. 1988. Light verbs and θ-marking. *Linguistic Inquiry* 19(2). 205–232.
Grimshaw, Jane. 1990. *Argument Structure*. Cambridge, MA: MIT Press.
Guerssel, Mohamed, Kenneth Hale, Mary Laughren, Beth Levin and Josie White Eagle. 1985. A Cross-linguistic Study of Transitivity Alternations. In *Causatives and agentivity. Papers from the Chicago Linguistic Society* 21(2), 48–63. Chicago: Chicago Linguistic Society.
Haiman, John. 1978. Conditionals are topics. *Language* 54. 564–589.
Haiman, John. 1980. The iconicity of grammar. *Language* 56. 515–40.
Haiman, John. 1983. Iconic and economic motivation. *Language* 59. 781–819.
Haiman, John (ed.). 1985. *Iconicity in Syntax*. Amsterdam: John Benjamins.
Haiman, John and Sandra Thompson (eds.). 1989. *Clause Combining in Grammar and Discourse*. Amsterdam: John Benjamins.
Hale, Kenneth. 1964. Classification of Northern Paman languages, Cape York Peninsula, Australia: A research report. *Oceanic Linguistics* 3. 248–265.
Hale, Kenneth. 1966a. The Paman group of the Pama-Nyungan phylic family. Appendix to XXIX. In Geoffrey O'Grady, Carl Voegelin and Frances Voegelin (eds.), *Languages of the World. Indo-Pacific Fascicle 6. Anthropological Linguistics* 8(2). 162–197.
Hale, Kenneth. 1966b. Kinship reflections in syntax: Some Australian languages. *Word* 22. 318–324.
Hale, Kenneth. 1973. Deep surface canonical disparities in relation to analysis and change: An Australian example. In Thomas Sebeok (ed.), *Current Trends in Linguistics*, 401–458. The Hague: Mouton.
Hale, Kenneth. 1976a. Phonological developments in particular Northern Paman languages. In Peter Sutton (ed.), *Languages of Cape York*, 7–40. Canberra: Australian Institute of Aboriginal Studies.
Hale, Kenneth. 1976b. The adjoined relative clause in Australia. In Robert Dixon (ed.), *Grammatical Categories in Australian Languages*, 78–105. Canberra: Australian Institute of Aboriginal Studies Press.
Hale, Kenneth. 1981. Preliminary remarks on the grammar of Part-Whole relations in Warlpiri. In James Hollyman and Andrew Pawley (eds.), *Studies in Pacific Languages and Cultures in Honor of Bruce Biggs*. Auckland: Linguistic Society of New Zealand.

Hale, Kenneth. 1983. Warlpiri and the grammar of non-configurational languages. *Natural Language and Linguistic Theory* 1. 5–59.
Hall, Allen. 1968. A depth-study of the Thaayorr language of the Edward River tribe Cape York peninsula: Being a description of the phonology with a brief grammatical outline and samples of lexicon and oral literature. Unpublished M.A. Thesis. Brisbane: University of Queensland.
Hall, Allen. 1972. A study of the Kuuk Thaayorre language of the Edward River tribe, Cape York Peninsula, Queensland: Being a description of the grammar. Unpublished PhD thesis. Brisbane: University of Queensland.
Hamilton, Philip. 1996. Constraints and markedness in the phonotactics of Australian Aboriginal languages. Unpublished Ph.D. Dissertation, Toronto: University of Toronto.
Hanks, William. 2005. Explorations in the deictic field. *Current Anthropology* 46. 191–220.
Harkins, Jean. 1990. Shame and shyness in the Aboriginal classroom: A case for practical semantics. *Australian Journal of Linguistics* 10. 293–306.
Harvey, Mark. 1996. Body parts in Warray. In Hilary Chappell and William McGregor (eds.), *The Grammar of Inalienability*, 111–154. Berlin/New York: Mouton de Gruyter.
Haspelmath, Martin. 1997. *Indefinite Pronouns*. Oxford: Oxford University Press.
Haspelmath, Martin (ed.). 2004. *Coordinating Constructions* (Typological studies in language 58). Amsterdam: John Benjamins.
Haspelmath, Martin. 2007. Coordination. In Timothy Shopen (ed.), *Language Typology and Syntactic Description, Vol. 2: Complex Constructions*, 2nd edition, 1–51. Cambridge: Cambridge University Press.
Haviland, John. 1979. Guugu Yimidhirr. In Robert Dixon and Barry Blake (eds.), *Handbook of Australian Languages, Vol. 1*, 27–180. Canberra: Australian National University Press.
Haviland, John. 1993. Anchoring, iconicity and orientation in Guugu Yimithirr pointing gestures. *Journal of Linguistic Anthropology* 3(1). 3–45.
Heath, Jeffrey. 1978. *Ngandi Grammar, Texts, and Dictionary*. Canberra: Australian Institute of Aboriginal Studies.
Heine, Bernd. 1997. *Cognitive Foundations of Grammar*. Oxford: Oxford University Press.
Hellwig, Birgit. 2003. *The Grammatical Coding of Postural Semantics in Goemai (a West Chadic language of Nigeria)*. Unpublished PhD thesis, Nijmegen: Max Planck Institut für Psycholinguistik and Katholieke Universiteit Nijmegen.
Hellwig, Birgit. and Friederike Lüpke. 2001. Caused positions. In Stephen Levinson and Nick Enfield (eds.), *Field Manual 2001*, 120–122. Nijmegen: Max Planck Institute for Psycholinguistics, Language & Cognition Group.
Himmelmann, Nikolaus. 1996. Demonstratives in narrative discourse: A taxonomy of universal uses. In Barbara Fox (ed.), *Studies in Anaphora*, 205–254. Amsterdam: John Benjamins.
Himmelmann, Nikolaus. 2001. Articles. Article 62 in Martin Haspelmath, Ekkehard König, Wulf Oesterreicher and Wolfgang Raible (eds.), *Language Typology and Language Universals*, 831–841. Berlin/New York: Mouton de Gruyter.
Hirst, Daniel and Alice Gaby. 2004. *Ngay Kuuk Thaayorre Yiik*. Language learning CD-Rom. Pormpuraaw: Pormpuraaw Community Council.
Hirst, Daniel and Alice Gaby. 2005a. *Kugu Muminh*. Language learning CD-ROM. Pormpuraaw: Pormpuraaw Community Council.
Hirst, Daniel and Alice Gaby. 2005b. *Kugu Mu'inh*. Language learning CD-ROM. Pormpuraaw: Pormpuraaw Community Council.
Hock, Hans. 1991. *Principles of Historical Linguistics*, 2nd edition. The Hague: Mouton de Gruyter.
Hoffmann, Dorothea. 2013. Mapping worlds: Frames of reference in MalakMalak. In *Proceedings of the 39th Meeting of the Berkeley Linguistic Society*, Berkeley: University of California.
Hopper, Paul. 1987. Emergent grammar. *Proceedings of the Berkeley Linguistics Society* 13. 139–157.

Hyman, Larry. 2003. Suffix ordering in Bantu: A morphocentric approach. In Geert. Booij and Jaap van Marle (eds.), *Yearbook of Morphology 2002*, 245–281. Dordrecht: Kluwer.
Inkelas, Sharon. 1998. The theoretical status of morphologically conditioned phonology: A case study of dominance effects. *Yearbook of Morphology 1997*. 121–155.
Inkelas, Sharon and Cheryl Zoll. 2005. *Reduplication: Doubling in Morphology*. Cambridge: Cambridge University Press.
Ito, Junko and Armin Mester. 1986. The phonology of voicing in Japanese, theoretical consequences for morphological accessibility. *Linguistic Inquiry* 17(1). 49–73.
Jackendoff, Ray. 1976. Toward an explanatory semantic representation. *Linguistic Inquiry* 7. 89–150.
Jakobson, Ray. 1962. Typological studies and their contribution to historical comparative linguistics: Report in the first plenary session of the Eighth International Congress of Linguists, Oslo, 5 August 1957. *Selected Writings 1: Phonological Studies*. The Hague: Mouton.
Jakobson, Roman. 1966. Quest for the essence of language. *Diogène* 51. 21–37.
Jardine, Frank, Alexander Jardine and Frederick Byerley. 1867. *Narrative of the Overland Expedition of the Messrs. Jardine from Rockhampton to Cape York, Northern Queensland, Compiled from the Journals of the Brothers, and Edited by Frederick J. Byerley*. Brisbane: J. W. Buxton. Retrived from: https://ebooks.adelaide.edu.au/j/jardine/frank/j3n/
Jones, Carolyn, Felicity Meakins and Shujau Muawiyath. 2012. Learning vowel categories from maternal speech in Gurindji Kriol. *Language Learning* 62(4). 1052–1078. doi:10.1111/j.1467-9922.2012.00725.x
Keating, Patricia, Taehong Cho, Cécile Fougeron and Chai-Shune Hsu. 1998. Domain-initial articulatory strengthening in four languages. *Laboratory Phonetics* 6. 145–163.
Kemmer, Suzanne. 1993. *The Middle Voice*. Amsterdam: John Benjamins.
Kendon, Adam. 1988. *Sign Languages of Aboriginal Australia: Cultural, Semiotic and Communicative Perspectives*. Cambridge: Cambridge University Press.
Kita, Sotaro. 2001. Semantic schism and interpretive integration in Japanese sentences with a mimetic: A reply to Tsujimura. *Linguistics* 39. 419–436.
Koch, Harold. 1984. The category of 'associated motion' in Kaytej. *Language in Central Australia* 1(1). 23–34.
Koch, Harold. 1996. Reconstruction in morphology. In M. Durie and M. Ross (eds.), *The comparative method reviewed: Regularity and irregularity in language change*, 218–263. New York: Oxford University Press.
König, Ekkehard and Shigehiro. Kokutani. 2006. Towards a typology of reciprocal constructions: Focus on German and Japanese. *Linguistics* 44(2). 271–302.
Lehmann, Christian. 1983. Directions for interlinear morphemic translations. *Folia Linguistica* 16. 193–224.
Levinson, Stephen. 2001. Motion verb stimulus, version 2. In Stephen Levinson and Nick Enfield (eds.), *Field Manual 2001*, 9–12. Nijmegen: Max Planck Institute for Psycholinguistics, Language & Cognition Group.
Levinson, Stephen. 2003. *Space in Language and Cognition: Explorations in Cognitive Diversity*. Cambridge: Cambridge University Press.
Levinson, Stephen and Sergio Meira. 2003. 'Natural concepts' in the spatial topological domain. *Language* 79(3). 485–516.
Lichtenberk, Frantisek. 2000. Inclusory pronominals. *Oceanic Linguistics* 39(1). 1–32.
Verstraete, Jean-Christophe and Dana Louagie. 2015. Personal pronouns with determining functions in Australian language. *Studies in Language* 39(1). 158–197.
Louagie, Dana and Jean-Christophe Verstraete. 2016. Noun phrase constituency in Australian languages: A typological study. *Linguistic Typology*.
Malcolm, Ian. 2002. *Aboriginal Genres in Perth*. Mt Lawley: Edith Cowan University.

Marmion, Doug, Kazuko Obata and Jakeline Troy. 2014. *Community, Identity and Wellbeing: The Report of the Second National Indigenous Languages Survey*. Canberra: Australian Institute of Aboriginal and Torres Strait Islander Studies. Retrieved from: http://www.aiatsis.gov.au/_files/research/report_of_the_2nd_national_indigenous_languages_survey.pdf.

Martinet, André. 1955. *Économie des changements phonétiques: Traité de phonologie diachronique*. Berne: A. Francke S.A.

Martinet, André. 1986. The dynamics of plurilingual situations. In Joshua Fishman, Andrée Tabouret-Keller, Michael Clyne, Bhadriraju Krishnamurti and Mohammed Abdelaziz (eds.). *The Fergusonian Impact, in Honor of Charles A. Ferguson on the Occasion of his 65th Birthday. Vol. 2, Sociolinguistics and the Sociology of Language*, 245–252. The Hague: Mouton de Gruyter.

Matthews, Peter. 1997. *The Concise Oxford Dictionary of Linguistics*. Oxford University Press.

Matisoff, James. 1973. Tonogenesis in Southeast Asia. In Larry. Hyman (ed.), *Consonant Types and Tone*, 72–95. *Southern California Papers in Linguistics* 1.

McCarthy, John and Alan Prince. 1986. Prosodic morphology. Ms., University of Massachusetts and Brandeis University.

McConnel, Ursula. 1940. Social organization of the tribes of Cape York Peninsula, North Queensland: Marriage systems – Wikmunkan. *Oceania* 10. 434–455.

McConnel, Ursula. 1953. Native Arts and industries on the Archer, Kendall and Holroyd rivers, Cape York Peninsula, North Queensland. *Records of the South Australian Museum* 11. 1–42.

McGregor, William. 1985. Body parts in Kuniyanti clause grammar. *Australian Journal of Linguistics* 5. 209–232.

McGregor, William. 1988. Mood and Subodination in Kuniyanti. In Peter Austin (ed.), *Complex Sentence Constructions in Australian Languages*, 39–68. Amsterdam: John Benjamins.

McGregor, William. 1990. *A Functional Grammar of Gooniyandi*. Amsterdam: John Benjamins.

McGregor, William. 1992. The semantics of ergative marking in Gooniyandi. *Linguistics* 30. 275–318.

McGregor, William. 1996. Dyadic and polyadic kin terms in Gooniyandi. *Anthropological Linguistics* 38(2). 216–247.

McGregor, William. 1998. 'Optional' ergative marking in Gooniyandi revisited: Implications to the theory of marking. *Leuvens Contributions in Linguistics and Philology* 87(3/4). 491–571.

McGregor, William. 2002. *Verb Classification in Australian Languages*. Berlin/New York: Mouton de Gruyter.

McGregor, William. 2006. Focal and optional ergative marking in Warrwa (Kimberley, Western Australia). *Lingua* 116. 393–423.

McKay, Graham. 1988. Figure and Ground in Rembarrnga Complex Sentences. In Peter Austin (ed.), *Complex Sentence Constructions in Australian Languages*, 7–36. Amsterdam: John Benjamins.

McKnight, David. 1999. *People, countries, and the rainbow serpent: systems of classification among the Lardil of Mornington Island*. New York: Oxford University Press.

Meakins, Felicity and Carmel O'Shannessy. 2004. Shifting functions of ergative case-marking in Light Warlpiri and Gurindji Kriol. Paper given at the *Australian Linguistics Society Conference*. Sydney: Australia, July 13–15.

Meira, Sergio and Stephen Levinson. 2001. Topological tasks. In Stephen Levinson and Nick Enfield (eds.), *Field Manual 2001*, 28–50. Nijmegen: Max Planck Institute for Psycholinguistics, Language & Cognition Group.

Merlan, Francesca and Jeffrey Heath. 1982. Dyadic kinship terms. In Jeffrey Heath, Francesca Merlan and Alan Rumsey (eds.), *The Languages of Kinship in Aboriginal Australia*, 107–124. Sydney: Oceania Linguistic Monographs.

Mayer, Mercer. 1969. *Frog, Where Are You?* New York: Dial.

Mithun, Marianne. 2001. Who shapes the record: The speaker and the linguist. In Paul Newman and Martha Ratliff (eds.), *Linguistic Fieldwork: Essays on the Practice of Empirical Linguistic Research*, 34–54. Cambridge: Cambridge University Press.

Moravcsik, Edith. 1978. Reduplicative Constructions. In Joseph Greenberg, Charles Ferguson and Edith Moravcsik (eds.), *Universals of Human Language, Vol. 3: Word Structure*, 297–334. Stanford: Stanford University Press.

Morphy, Frances. 1983. Djapu, a Yolngu dialect. In Robert Dixon and Barry Blake (eds.), *Handbook of Australian Languages, Vol. 3*, 1–188. Amsterdam: John Benjamins

Mühlhäusler, Peter. 2000. Language planning and language ecology. *Current Issues in Language Planning* 1(3). 306–367.

Mushin, Ilana. 1995. Epistememes in Australian Languages. *Australian Journal of Linguistics* 15. 1–31.

Nash, David. 1980. Topics in Warlpiri grammar. PhD dissertation. Massachusetts Institute of Technology.

Nash, David. 1982. Warlpiri verb roots and preverbs. In Stephen Swartz (ed.), *Papers in Warlpiri Grammar, in Memory of Lothar Jagst*, 165–216. Work Papers of SIL-AAB, series A, vol. 6. Berrimah, NT.

Newman, John. 2002. A cross-linguistic overview of the posture verbs 'sit', 'stand', and 'lie'. In John Newman (ed.), *The Linguistics of Sitting, Standing, and Lying*, 1–24. Amsterdam: John Benjamins.

Nichols, Johanna. 1978. Secondary predicates. *Berkeley Linguistics Society* 4. 114–127.

Nichols, Johanna. 1986. Head-marking and dependent-marking grammar. *Language* 62. 56–119.

Nordlinger, Rachel. 2006. Spearing the Emu drinking: Subordination and the adjoined relative clause in Wambaya. *Australian Journal of Linguistics* 26(1). 5–29.

Nuckolls, Janis. 1999. The case for sound symbolism. *Annual Review of Anthropology* 28. 225–252.

O'Grady, Geoffrey, Carl Voegelin and Frances Voegelin. 1966. Languages of the world: Indo-Pacific fascicle six. *Anthropological Linguistics* 8(2). Bloomington, Indiana.

Osborne, Charles. 1974. *The Tiwi language: Grammar, Myths and Dictionary of the Tiwi Language Spoken on Melville and Bathurst Islands, Northern Australia*. Canberra: Australian Institute of Aboriginal Studies.

Palmer, Frank. 2001. *Mood and Modality*, 2nd edition. Cambridge: Cambridge University Press.

Pascoe, Bruce. 2014. Dark Emu. Black seeds: Agriculture or accident? Broome, WA: Magabala Books.

Pedley, Les and Ray Isbell. 1971. Plant communities of Cape York Peninsula. *Proceedings of the Royal Society of Queensland* 82. 51–74.

Peirce, Charles. 1998 [1909]. A sketch of logical critics. In the Peirce Edition Project (ed.), *The Essential Peirce. Selected Philosophical Writings, Vol. 2*, 460–461. Bloomington, IN: Indiana University Press.

Pensalfini, Rob. 1999. The rise of case suffixes as discourse markers in Jingulu. A case study of innovation in an obsolescent language. *Australian Journal of Linguistics* 19. 225–240.

Ponsonnet, Maïa. 2014. *The language of emotions: the case of Dalabon*. Amsterdam: John Benjamins.

Radcliffe-Brown, Alfred. 1951. Murngin social organization. *American Anthropologist* 53. 37–55.

Ray, Alan. Forthcoming. *A Grammar of Wik-Mungkan*.

Reid, Nicholas. 2000. Complex Verb Collocations in Ngan'gityemerri: A non-derivational mechanisms for encoding valency alternations. In Robert Dixon and Alexandra Aikenvald (eds.), *Changing Valency: Case Studies in Transitivity* (Studies in Language Series), 333–359. Cambridge: Cambridge University Press.

Reid, Nicholas. 2002. Sit right down the back: Serialized posture verbs in Ngan'gityemerri and other Northern Australian languages. In John Newman (ed.), *The Linguistics of Sitting, Standing and Lying*, 239–267. Amsterdam: John Benjamins.

Round, Erich. 2013. Why reduplicate VC? Kuuk Thayorre answers a lingering question. Handout from *Australian Linguistics Society* 44.

Ruhl, Charles. 1989. *On Monosemy: A Study in Linguistic Semantics*. Albany: State University of New York Press.

Sands, Kristina. 1995. Nominal classification in Australia. *Anthropological Linguistics* 37. 247–346.

Sayers, Barbara. 1976. *The Sentence in Wik-Munkan: A Description of Propositional Relationships*, Series B, Vol. 44. Canberra: Pacific Linguistics.

Scancarelli, Janine. 1985. Referential strategies in Chamorro narratives: Preferred clause structure and ergativity. *Studies in Language* 9. 335–362.

Schmidt, Wilhelm. 1919. *Die Gliederung der Australischen Sprachen*. Vienna: Mechitharisten Buchdruckerei.

Schultze-Berndt, Eva. 2000. Simple and complex verbs in Jaminjung: A study of event categorisation in an Australian language. Unpublished PhD thesis. Nijmegen: Catholic University of Nijmegen.

Schultze-Berndt, Eva. 2001. Ideophone-like characteristics of uninflected predicates in Jaminjung (Australia). In F.K. Erhard Voeltz and Christa Kilian-Hatz (eds.), *Ideophones*, 355–373. Amsterdam: Benjamins.

Schultze-Berndt, Eva and Nikolaus Himmelmann. 2004. Depictive secondary predicates in crosslinguistic perspective. *Linguistic Typology* 8. 59–131.

Schwartz, Linda. 1988. Conditions for verb-coded coordinations. In Michael Hammond, Edith Moravcsik and Jessica Wirth (eds.), *Studies in Syntactic Typology*, 53–73. Amsterdam: John Benjamins.

Seifart, Frank. 2010. Nominal classification. *Language and Linguistics Compass* 4. 719–736. doi: 10.1111/j.1749-818X.2010.00194.x

Shakur, Tupac. 1991. If my homie calls. On *2Pacalypse Now*. Santa Monica, CA: Interscope Records.

Sharp, Lauriston. 1934. The social organization of the Yir-Yoront tribe, Cape York Peninsula. *Oceania* 4. 404–431.

Sharp, Lauriston. 1937. The social anthropology of a totemic system in North Queensland, Australia. Unpublished PhD dissertation. Harvard University.

Sharp, Lauriston. 1952. Steel axes for stone-age Australians. In Edward Spicer (ed.), *Human Problems in Technological Change*, 69–91. New York: Russell Sage Foundation.

Sharp, Lauriston. 1958. People without politics. In V. Ray (ed.), *Systems of Political Control and Bureaucracy in Human Societies* (Proceedings of the 1958 Annual Spring Meeting of the American Ethnological Society). Seattle: University of Washington Press.

Simmons, Roy, John Graydon and D. Carleton Gajdusek. 1958. A blood group genetical survey in Australian Aboriginal children of the Cape York Peninsula. *American Journal of Physical Anthropology* 16(1). 59–78.

Simpson, Jane. 1983. Resultatives. In Lori B. Levin, Malka Rappaport and Annie Zaenen (eds.). *Papers in Lexical-functional Grammar*, 143–157. Bloomington: Indiana University Linguistics Club.

Simpson, Jane. 1991. *Warlpiri Morpho-Syntax: A Lexicalist Approach*. Dordrecht: Kluwer.

Simpson, Jane. 2002. From common ground to syntactic construction: Associated path in Warlpiri. In Nicholas Enfield (ed.), *Ethnosyntax: Explorations in Grammar and Culture*, 287–307. Oxford: Oxford University Press.

Singer, Ruth. 2001. *The Inclusory Construction in Australian Languages*. Unpublished Honours thesis. Melbourne: University of Melbourne.

Singer, Ruth. 2006. Agreement in Mawng: Productive and lexicalised uses of agreement in an Australian language. PhD thesis. University of Melbourne.

Singer, Ruth. and Salome Harris. 2016. What practices and ideologies support small-scale multilingualism? A case study of Warruwi community, Northern Australia. *International Journal of the Sociology of Language* 241. 163–209.

Smith, Ian. 1986. Language contact and the life or death of Kugu Muminh. In Joshua Fishman, Andrée Tabouret-Keller, Michael Clyne, Bhadriraju Krishnamurti and Mohammed Abdulaziz (eds.), *Sociolinguistics and the Sociology of Language*, 513–532. Berlin: Mouton de Gruyter.

Smith, Ian and Steve Johnson. 2000. Kugu Nganhcara. In R.M.W. Dixon and Barry Blake (eds.), *The Handbook of Australian Languages, Vol. 5*, 357–489. Oxford: Oxford University Press.

Sommer, Bruce. 1969. Kunjen phonology: Synchronic and diachronic. *Pacific Linguistics* B-11. Canberra: Australian National University.

Sommer, Bruce. 1970. An Australian language without CV syllables. *International Journal of American Linguistics* 36. 57–58.
Sommer, Bruce. 1981. The shape of Kunjen syllables. In D. Goyvaerts (ed.), *Phonology in the 1980's*, 231–244. Ghent: E. Story-Scientia.
Sommer, Bruce. 1978. 'Eye' and 'no-good' in semantic extension. In Lester Hiatt (ed.), *Australian Aboriginal Concepts*, 178–181. Canberra, NJ: Australian Institute of Aboriginal Studies & Humanities Press.
Stassen, Leon. 2000. AND-languages and WITH-languages. *Linguistic Typology* 4(1). 1–54.
Stirling, Lesley. (ed.). 1993. *Switch-Reference and Discourse Representation* (Studies in Linguistics Series). Cambridge: Cambridge University Press.
Stirling, Lesley. 2001. The multifunctionality of anaphoric expressions: A typological perspective. *Australian Journal of Linguistics* 21(1). 7–23.
Stirling, Lesley. 2008. 'Double reference' in Kala Lagaw Ya narratives. In Ilana Mushin and Brett Baker (eds.), *Discourse and Grammar in Australian Languages*. Amsterdam: John Benjamins.
Stirling, Lesley and Brett Baker. 2007. Pronominal apposition and the status of 'determiner' in Australian languages. *Australian Linguistics Society Annual Conference*. Adelaide: University of Adelaide.
Sutton, Peter (ed.). 1976a. *Languages of Cape York*. Canberra: Australian Institute of Aboriginal Studies.
Sutton, Peter. 1976b. The derivational affix 'having': The 'having' affix and other morphemes in fifty Australian languages. In R.M.W. Dixon (ed.), *Grammatical Categories in Australian Languages*, 297–305. Canberra: Australian Institute of Aboriginal Studies Press.
Sutton, Peter. 1978. Wik: Aboriginal society, territory and language at Cape Keerweer, Cape York Peninsula, Australia. Unpublished PhD thesis. Brisbane: University of Queensland.
Sutton, Peter. 1991. Language in aboriginal Australia: Social dialects in a geographic idiom. In Suzanne Romaine (ed.), *Language in Australia*, 87–106. Cambridge: Cambridge University Press.
Sutton, Peter. 1995. *Wik-Ngathan dictionary*. Prospect: Caitlin Press.
Sutton, Peter and Bruce Rigsby. 1982. People with 'politicks': Management of land and personnel on Australia's Cape York peninsula. In N. Williams and E. Hunn (eds), *Resource managers: North American and Australian Hunter Gatherers*, 155–171. Boulder: Westview Press.
Tabain, Marija, Gavan Breen and Andrew Butcher. 2004. VC vs. CV syllables: A comparison of Aboriginal languages with English. *Journal of the International Phonetic Association* 34. 175–200.
Talmy, Leonard. 1978. Figure and ground in complex sentences. In Joseph Greenberg (ed.), *Universals of Human Language, Vol. 4: Syntax*, 625–49. Stanford: Stanford University Press.
Tarpencha, Mary and Alice Gaby. 2003. *Munkan Languages Picture Dictionary*. Pormpuraaw: Pormpuraaw Community Council.
Taylor, John. 1976. Mapping techniques and the reconstruction of aspects of traditional Aboriginal culture. *Australian Institute of Aboriginal Studies Newsletter* 5. 34–43.
Taylor, John. 1977. A pre-contact Aboriginal medical system on Cape York Peninsula. *Journal of Human Evolution* 6. 419–432.
Taylor, John. 1984. Of acts and axes. Unpublished PhD thesis. Townsville: James Cook University.
Timberlake, Alan. 1993. Russian. In Bernard Comrie and Greville Corbett (eds.), *The Slavonic Languages*, 827–886. London: Routledge.
Tindale, Norman. 1974. *Aboriginal Tribes of Australia: Their terrain, Environmental Controls, Distribution, Limits and Proper Names*. Canberra: Australian National University Press.
Thomson, Donald. 1935a. *Birds of Cape York Peninsula: Ecological Notes, Field Observations, and Catalogue of Specimens Collected on Three Expeditions to North Queensland*. Melbourne: Government Printer.
Thomson, Donald. 1935b. The joking relationship and organised obscenity in North Queensland. *American Anthropologist* 37. 460–490.

Thomson, Donald. 1936. *Interim General Report of Preliminary Expedition to Arnhem Land, Northern Territory of Australia 1935–36*. Typescript.

Thomson, Donald. 1955. Two devices for the avoidance of first cousin marriage among the Australian Aborigines. *Man* 55. 39–40.

Thomson, Donald. 1972. *Kinship and Behaviours in North Queensland*. Canberra: Australian Institute of Aboriginal Studies.

Thompson, Sandra and Paul Hopper. 2001. Transitivity, clause structure, and argument structure: Evidence from conversation. In Joan Bybee and Paul Hopper (eds.), *Frequency and the Emergence of Linguistic Structure*, 27–59. Amnsterdam: John Benjamins.

Traugott, Elizabeth and Bernd Heine (eds). 1991. *Approaches to Grammaticalization*. Amsterdam: John Benjamins.

Turpin, Myfany. 2002. Body part terms in Kaytetye feeling expressions. *Pragmatics and Cognition* 10(1). 271–305.

Umiker-Sebeok, D. Jean and Thomas Sebeok. 1978. *Aboriginal Sign Languages of the Americas and Australia*. New York: Plenum Press.

van Staden, Miriam, Gunter Senft, Nick Enfield and Jürgen Bohnemeyer. 2001. Staged Events. In Stephen Levinson and Nick Enfield (eds.), *Field Manual 2001*, 110–119. Nijmegen: Max Planck Institute for Psycholinguistics, Language & Cognition Group.

Van Valin, Robert and David Wilkins. 1996. The case for 'effector': Case roles, agents, and agentivity revisited. In Masayoshi Shibatani and Sandra Thompson (eds.), *Grammatical Constructions: Their Form and Meaning*, 289–322. Oxford: Clarendon Press.

Vendler, Zeno. 1967. *Linguistics in Philosophy*. Ithaca: Cornell University Press.

von Sturmer, John. 1978. The Wik region: Economy, territoriality, and totemism in western Cape York Peninsula, North Queensland. Unpublished PhD thesis. Brisbane: University of Queensland.

von Sturmer, John. 1981. *Talking with Aborigines*. Reprint from Australian Institute of Aboriginal Studies newsletter new series no. 15, March 1981. Canberra: Australian Institute of Aboriginal Studies.

Wackernagel, Jacob. 1892. Über ein Gesetz der indogermanischen Wortstellung. *Indogermanische Forschungen* 1. 333–436.

Wald, Benji. 1983. Referents and topic within and across discourse units: Observations from current vernacular English. In Flora Klein-Andreu (ed.), *Discourse perspectives on syntax*, 91–116. New York: Academic Press.

Wierzbicka, Anna. 1977. The ignorative: The semantics of speech acts. *International Review of Slavic Linguistics* 2(2/3). 251–312.

Wierzbicka, Anna. 1980. The ignorative: The semantics of speech acts. In Anna Wierzbicka, *Lingua Mentalis*, 287–345 (Chapter 8). Sydney/New York: Academic Press.

Wilkins, David. 1989. Mparntwe Arrernte (Aranda): Studies in the structure and semantics of grammar. Unpublished PhD dissertation. Australian National University.

Wilkins, David. 1992a. Linguistic research under Aboriginal control: A personal account of fieldwork in central Australia. *Australian Journal of Linguistics* 12. 171–200.

Wilkins, David. 1992b. Interjections as deictics. *Journal of Pragmatics* 18(2–3). 119–158.

Wilkins, David. 1999. Demonstrative questionnaire: 'THIS' and 'THAT' in comparative perspective. In David Wilkins (ed.), *Manual for the Field Season 1999*, 1–24. Nijmegen: Max Planck Institute for Psycholinguistics.

Wilkins, David. 2000. Ant, ancestors and medicine: A semantic and pragmatic account of classifier constructions in Arrernte (Central Australia). In Gunter Senft (ed.), *Systems of Nominal Classification* (Language, Culture and Cognition 4), 147–216. Cambridge: Cambridge University Press.

Wilkinson, Melanie. 1991. Djambarrpuyngu: A Yolngu variety of Northern Australia. Unpublished PhD thesis. Sydney: University of Sydney.

Wilson, Stephen. 1999. *Coverbs and Complex Predicates in Wagiman* (Stanford Monographs in Linguistics). Stanford: CSLI Publications.
Winkler, Susanne. 1997. *Focus and Secondary Predication*. Berlin/New York: Mouton de Gruyter.
Wittenburg, Peter, Hennie Brugman, Albert Russel, Alex Klassmann and Han Sloetjes. 2006. ELAN: A professional framework for multimodality research. In *Proceedings of LREC 2006, 5th International Conference on Language Resources and Evaluation*, 1556–1559. Genoa, Italy.
Yallop, Colin. 1977. *Alyawarra: An Aboriginal Language of Central Australia*. Canberra: Australian Institute of Aboriginal Studies.

Appendix 1: Index of tasks and narrative texts

Elicitation task	Description
AbsoluteTime	Data collected during pilot trials of a stimulus designed by the author and Lera Boroditsky. The task comprises a set of cards depicting temporally linked objects or events. Language experts are asked to place the cards in sequence.
BowPed	Unpublished booklet of picture stimuli entitled "Topological Relations Pictures Series", prepared by Melissa Bowerman and Eric Pederson.
CausedPositions	Set of video stimuli depicting caused topological relationships, published as Hellwig and Lüpke 2001.
CntSeries	Set of line drawings depicting topological relationships of containment, published as part of Meira and Levinson 2001.
Cut&Break	Set of video stimuli depicting events of material separation, published as Bohnemeyer et al. 2001.
DahlTMA	Questionnaire relating to tense, mood and aspect, included as an appendix to Dahl 1985.
Demonstratives	A questionnaire-style elicitation tool developed by Wilkins (1999) to probe the semantics and pragmatics of situational / exophoric demonstrative usage. It involves constructing a series of scenarios (e.g. an ant on the addressee's shoulder) to which the language expert is asked to respond as naturally as possible.
FigureGround	A subset of the "Moverb" video stimuli produced by Levinson (2001).
Man&Tree	Set of photographs depicting an array of topological relationships between plastic toy figures (two men, a tree, a cow, etc.). Acquired from the Max Planck Institute Nijmegen, 2002.
Moland	Set of animated video stimulus clips depicting a ball moving around a simulated landscape (Bohnemeyer 2001)
MoverbEnterExit	A subset of the "Moverb" video stimuli produced by Levinson (2001).
MoverbPath	A subset of the "Moverb" video stimuli produced by Levinson (2001).
MoverbTriads	A subset of the "Moverb" video stimuli produced by Levinson (2001).
RCP	Video stimuli used to elicit descriptions of events that fall within the broad semantic space of reciprocity (published as Evans et al. 2004).
RcpPilot	Pilot version of reciprocals video stimuli, a revised version of which was published as (Evans et al. 2004)
StagedEvents	Video stimuli of various social and other interactions between people (van Staden et al., 2001).
Sup	Set of line drawings depicting topological relationships of support, published as part of Meira and Levinson 2001.

Appendix 1: Index of tasks and narrative texts

Narrative title	Description
2Crocs	Donald William describes in prose the story behind the *wuuc* (traditional song) of the saltwater and freshwater crocodiles. This narrative – presented in **Appendix 2**–was dispersed between verses sung by the narrator and his brother, Cyril.
Adoptee	Freddy Tyore tells a traditional story of an elderly couple who find a baby in the scrub and adopt it, only to find out that it is a red-legged devil; *wang kirkunka*.
ChapmanEra	Alfred Charlie reflects on life during the mission era, and in particular under the governance of Superintendant Chapman.
Christmas	Gilbert Jack reflects on the meaning of the various activities and events in Pormpuraaw surrounding the Christmas holidays.
DarwinTrip	Gilbert Jack recounts his adventures during a trip to Darwin in 1970, just after Cyclone Tracy.
FrogStory	Myrtle Foote composes a text to accompany the wordless picture story book "Frog, where are you" (Mayer 1969).
Kanangkarr	Alfred Charlie describes life for the Kuuk Thaayorre before the Edward River mission was established.
KutaWoochorrm	Undated printed booklet containing the story of *kuta woochorrm* 'dreamtime dog', written and illustrated by †Tom Foote.
LosingIrma	Alfred Charlie tells the story of taking a white lady on a bush trip only to lose her (cf. Appendix 3).
MelbourneTrip	Gilbert Jack remembers a school trip to Melbourne he took as a child.
NewsStory	Gilbert relates a news story he had seen about a crocodile biting off the arm of a farmer who had been showing around tourists.
PlaneCrash	Alfred Charlie remembers the first time he saw a plane, when it crashed into a bog near Pormpuraaw.
PlaneSighting	Gilbert Jack recalls the first time he saw a plane, when he and his siblings were playing out in the bush on a hunting trip with their parents.
PormprRintm	Alfred Charlie tells the 'dreamtime' story of his namesake; the burning of an old man's humpy to punish him for refusing a young girl shelter.
Pormpuraaw-Kanangkarr	Ivy Conrad, Albert Jack and Gilbert Jack contrast what life was like before the establishment of the Edward River mission with life during the early mission era.
Up&Down	Wordless picture story book depicting a number of topological and other relationships between a cat, a mouse and various ground objects.
WeipaFootball	Alfred Charlie remembers taking a school group to Weipa for a football carnival.
Werngr	Alfred Charlie tells the traditional story of a man who threw a boomerang right up into the sky, where it became the moon.
Yencr	Molly Edwards (interviewed by Gilbert Jack) remembers how she first learned to make dilly bags and baskets, and provides an instructional text on how *yencr* is collected, treated, dyed and woven to make these bags and baskets.

Appendix 2: Narrative texts

Losing Irma

Author: Alfred Charlie
Recording date: 14th November 2002
Transcription collaborator: Gilbert Jack
Transcription date: 26th November 2002

Context: This story was told in Kuuk Thaayorre by Thaayorre elder Alfred Charlie, with occasional prompting, backchannelling and commentary in Kugu Muminh by Muminh elder Celia Peter. Celia's backchannelling has not been transcribed here, though the approximate content of her interjections is indicated in square brackets, thus: [CP: really?]. Alfred began to tell this story as we drove through the country it features on our way home from a fishing expedition. The story was so entertaining, we pulled off the road and asked him to tell it for the video camera. Hence Celia begins by prompting him once the camera is rolling.

Alfred tells the story of a bush trip he made with a Swiss woman, Irma, who used to work in the Housing and Aged Care Centre. They were walking together when she disappeared. Alfred was concerned for her welfare, and for his own potential legal trouble if she were not found.

[CP: Brother, whereabouts did you lose Irma?]

1. *inh=th   ii-kan   kerp-r*
   dem:sp.prx=PRAG there-at:up finish-P.PFV
   'she disappeared just up here'
   "she got lost up here"

2. *raak   inh*
   PLACE dem:sp.prx
   'this place'

[CP: Paangunth]

3. *Paangunth, angunp   kerp-r*
   Paangunth, at.that.place finish-P.PFV
   'at Paangunth, she disappeared there'
   "just here at Paangunth"

4. *ngay   inh   yuk... yuk   shovel   kal-m   man.pert-an,*
   1sg(ERG) dem:sp.prx THING   THING shovel(ACC) carry-P.IPFV shoulder-DAT
   'I was carrying a... a shovel on my shoulder'

5. | kay | axe | kal-m | ngay. |
   |---|---|---|---|
   | METAL | axe(ACC) | carry-P.IPFV | 1sg(ERG) |

   'and I was carrying an axe [too].'

6. | ngul | ulp | ngay | raak | koorre | nhaawr |
   |---|---|---|---|---|---|
   | then | dem:ad.prx | 1sg(ERG) | PLACE(ACC) | behind | see:P.PFV |

   AG: | [ngul | ulp | raak | koorre | inh | ngay | yarriy] |
   |---|---|---|---|---|---|---|
   | [then | dem:ad.prx | place(ACC) | behind | dem:sp.prx | 1sg(ERG) | thus] |

   'then I looked behind me like this'
   "then I looked back"

7. | "e'! | Paanth | ii | wanthan?" | Pokon. | "eey'!" |
   |---|---|---|---|---|---|
   | hey | woman(NOM) | there | where_TRJ | NO | hey |

   ' "hey, where's that woman gone?". Nothing [no response]. "hey [where are you?]" '
   " "where's that woman gone? No one there" "

8. | ngul | ngay | waantharr-r: | "koowe, koowe, koowe"... |
   |---|---|---|---|
   | then | 1sg(NOM) | call-P.PFV | cooee cooee cooee |

   'so I called out, "cooee, cooee, cooee"'

9. | kuuk | kaar | waantharr. |
   |---|---|---|
   | WORD(ACC) | NEG | call:NPST |

   'she doesn't say a word'
   "can't sing out"

10. | thil | waantharr-r: | "koowe, Irma, Irma!" |
    |---|---|---|
    | again | call-P.PFV | cooee Irma Irma |

    '[I] called again, "cooee, Irma, Irma!"'
    [CP: and she didn't answer you?]

11. | nhul | nganh | kaar | thaa.pirr-m |
    |---|---|---|---|
    | 3sg(ERG) | 1sgACC | NEG | reply-P.IPFV |

    "but she never answered me"

[CP: nothing!]

12. | pokon. |
    |---|
    | NO |

    'nothing.'

13. | nhul | kuuk=aar | than-m. |
    |---|---|---|
    | 3sg(NOM) | WORD=ADN.PRIV | stand-P.IPFV |

    'she kept silent'

14. | ith'tharrkoo! | paanth | wanthan | kerp-r? |
    |---|---|---|---|
    | wow | woman(NOM) | where_TRJ | finish-P.PFV |

    'Oh no! Where's this woman disappeared to?'

15. ngay   ngene=p   yithi-rr   pal?
    1sg(ERG) why=PRAG lead-P.PFV towards
    'why did I bring [her] here?'

[CP: aah]

16. trouble=okun yan   yup   paanthum   inh'nheman.
    trouble=DUB go:NPST soon woman-ABL   this.very.one:ABL
    "I might get into trouble from this woman"

[CP: yes, my word]

17. Kana. Ngul ngay   shovel=yuk   thaka-rr,   axe=yuk.
    OK   then 1sg(ERG) shovel(ACC)=STUFF   leave-P.PFV   axe(ACC)=STUFF
    'okay, so I put down the shovel thingy, and the axe'

18. ngay   ii-rr-korr   therk-r,   main road ith,   same road.
    1sg(NOM) there-towards-outside   return-P.PFV main road dem:dist same road
    'I went back that way, along that main road, the same road [I had come down]'.

19. angunp   therk-r=ay   ii-rr-korr   ii
    at.that.place   return-P.PFV=1sg(NOM) there-towards-outside   there
    'I went back over there'

20. "koowe, koowe!"   waantharr-m=ay.
    cooee   cooee   call-P.IPFV=1sg(NOM)
    ' "cooee, cooee!" I was calling'

21. "wanthan yat?   ooee!"
    where_TRJ go:P.PFV cooee
    ' "where [have you] gone? Cooee!" '

[CP: and you couldn't see her?]

22. nhul   kulam yiirr   waki-rr
    3sg(ERG) road   other(ACC)   follow-P.PFV
    'she had followed a different road'

23. thil   yoorr=p   thongk-nhat   iipal,   kuuk=aar   yancm.
    recently now=PRAG   arrive-GO&:P.PFV   from.there   word=ADN.PRIV   go:P.IPFV
    'all of a sudden she arrived from that way, coming silently'
    "then she came by"

24. nhul   yarriy kaar=p   "woy! Ngay   aw-i'i"
    3sg(NOM) thus   NEG=PRAG hey   1sg(NOM)   ATTN-here
    'she never said "hey, I'm here!"'

[CP: she didn't call out to you?]

25. *Pokon,   nhul   kuuk=aar=nhurr=p thanan-m*
    NO 3sg(NOM) WORD=ADN.PRIV=ONLY=PRAG stand:RDP-P.IPFV
    'no, she just stayed silent'

26. *ngul yuunhul nhaawr   "nge'!"*
    then that.one see:P.PFV hey
    'then I saw her in the distance, "hey!" '

27. *'"ngumpurr   ii   thongk-nhat!"*
    old.lady(NOM) there arrive-GO&:P.PFV
    'there the old lady is, just arrived!"'

28. *"Awoy, koo... ngumpurr wang   ii   thongk-nhat"*
    yes   oh   old.lady whitefella(NOM) there arrive-GO&:P.PFV
    ' "yes, aha, the white lady's just arrived over there" '
    " "this old lady here!" "

29. *"koowe, pal   kar-yup=kaar   yarr!"*
    cooee   towards like-soon=NEG go:IMP
    ' "cooee, come here immediately!" '

30. *"pam   nhunt   ngene yat?"*
    DETR 2sg(NOM) why   go:P.PFV
    ' "why on earth did you go [to my potential detriment]?" '
    " "where did you go?" "

31. *"I bin go for a walk."*
    ' "I went for a walk" [she said]'

32. *"Ngay   iirra   ritar   yat,   kumun therk,   thuuthu-n-m.*
    1sg(NOM) to.there gammon go:P.PFV thigh   return:INF pull-v^-P.IPFV
    ' "I just went for a bit over there to stretch my legs" '
    " "I was stretching my leg" "

33. *"oo, yoorrp   ongkorr!*
    oh   that.way PROHIB
    ' "oh no, don't do that!" '
    " "oh, not that way!" "

34. *"Ngay   pam   court-ak   yup   yan"*
    1sg(NOM) DETR court-DAT soon go:NPST
    " "I might go to court for that." "

35. *awoy kana=pa.*
    yes   finish=PRAG
    'yes, that's the end.'

Frog story

Author: Mrs Myrtle Foote
Recording date: 17th September 2002
Transcription collaborator: Mrs Myrtle Foote
Transcription date: 20–25th September 2002

Context: Mrs Foote composed this story in response to the picture story book "Frog, where are you?" (Mayer 1969). The first number of each line refers to the illustration described, the second number tracks sequence of clauses in the description.

Although Mrs Foote was dictating the text orally, rather than writing it down, this story has a distinctly literate flavour, and demonstrates her familiarity with and mastery of the written form. The overt realization of arguments, for example, is much more frequent than in spontaneous oral texts. Each line was repeated several times (often in different forms) while I wrote it down.

1.1 *Thatr nhul glass-ak nhiinhin.*
frog(NOM) 3sg(NOM) glass-DAT sit:RDP:NPST
'A frog is sitting in a jar.'

1.2 *Parr-an pul kuta-ku nhaanham nhunh thatr.*
child-ERG 3du(ERG) dog-ERG look.at:RDP:NPST 3sgACC frog(ACC)
'A boy and a dog are looking at the frog.'

2.3 *Parr_r nhul wut wun bed-ak.*
child(NOM) 3sg(NOM) asleep lie:NPST bed-DAT
'The boy's asleep in his bed.'

2.4 *Kuta nhangn yangk-an wun.*
dog 3sgGEN(NOM) leg-DAT lie:NPST
'His dog is lying on his legs.'

2.5 *Thatr nhul glass-nam rip-nhan.*
frog(NOM) 3sg(NOM) glass-ABL exit-GO&:NPST
'The frog is coming out of the jar.'

3.6 *Parr_r nhul glass nhaawr: thatr yuuw yat!*
child(#ERG) 3sg(ERG) glass(ACC) look.at:P.PFV frog(NOM) far.away go:P.PFV
'The boy looked at the glass: the frog's gone!'

3.7 *Kuta nhul putpun nhiinhin mut-un nhangn-mun.*
dog(NOM) 3sg(NOM) on.top sit:RDP:NPST back-DAT 3sgGEN-DAT
'The dog is sitting on top of his back.'

3.8 *Kuta   nhul   putpun yokunmanorrp nhiinhin.*
dog(NOM) 3sg(NOM) on.top same.way   sit:RDP:NPST
'The dog is also sitting down.'

3.9 *Nhul   thatr   yokunmanorrp waawath-r.*
3sg(ERG) frog(ACC) same.way   search:RDP-NPST
'The dog is also looking for the frog.'

4.10 *Parr_r   nhul   thamr puut   nhaanham.*
child(#ERG) 3sg(ERG) foot boot(ACC) look.at:RDP:NPST
'The boy is looking in a boot.'

4.11 *"Thatr   wanthan yat?"*
frog(NOM) where$_{TRJ}$ go:P.PFV
' "Where has the frog gone?" '

4.12 *Nhul   thatr   ngaathirr waawath-r.*
3sg(ERG) frog(ACC) still   search:RDP-NPST
'He's still looking for the frog'

4.13 *Kuta-ku nhul   glass   nhaanham.*
dog-ERG 3sg(ERG) glass(ACC) look.at:RDP:NPST
'The dog's looking in the jar.'

4.14 *Thatr   wanthan yat?*
frog(NOM) where$_{TRJ}$ go:P.PFV
'Where has the frog gone?'

5.15 *Pul   window   thaarawi-rr.*
3du(ERG) window(ACC) open-P.PFV
'They have opened the window.'

5.16 *Kuta   nhul   paant   glass-ak   rok-r.*
dog(NOM) 3sg(NOM) head(NOM) glass-DAT enter-P.PFV
'The dog has its head in the jar.'

5.17 *Nhul   parr_r   waawantharr   thatr-ak.*
3sg(NOM) child(NOM) call.out:RDP:NPST frog-DAT
'The boy is calling out for the frog.'

6.18 *Ngul kuta   nhul   wont-r   window-nam.*
then dog(NOM) 3sg(NOM) fall-NPST window-ABL
'Then the dog falls from the window.'

6.19 *Parr_r   nhul   kuta-kum worry rirk.*
child(NOM) 3sg(NOM) dog-ABL worry DO:NPST
'The boy is worried about the dog.'

7.20 *Nhul parr-an kuta mi'irr nhul ngamal.katpi-rr.*
3sg(ERG) child-ERG dog(ACC) pick.up:P.PFV 3sg(ERG) hug-P.PFV
'The child picked up the dog and hugged him.'

7.21 *Kuta-ku nhul thaa.put thaa+punyc-r nhunh.*
dog-ERG 3sg(ERG) cheek(ACC) mouth+suck-P.PFV 3sgACC
'The dog licked him on the cheek.'

8.22 *Nhul thatr-ak waawantharr.*
3sg(NOM) frog-DAT call.out:RDP:NPST
'He [the boy] is calling for the frog.'

9.23 *Nhul may puunh kenthentha-rr.*
3sg(ERG) VEG bee(ACC) rouse:RDP-P.PFV
'He [the dog] disturbs some bees.'

10.24 *Nhul thatr ngaathirr waawath-r.*
3sg(ERG) frog(ACC) still search.for:RDP-NPST
'He [the boy] is still searching for the frog.'

10.25 *Nhul ranth-in nhaanham.*
3sg(NOM) hole-DAT look.at:RDP:NPST
'He [the boy] is looking in a hole.'

10.26 *Nhul yik-r thatr=okun ranth-in ngaathirr wun.*
3sg(NOM) say-P.PFV frog(NOM)=DUB hole-DAT still lie:NPST
'He [the boy] thought the frog might still be in the hole.'

10.27 *Kuta-ku may puunh kookoc-r.*
dog-ERG VEG bee(ACC) bark:RDP-NPST
'The dog is barking at the bees.'

11.28 *Minh kaal rip-r ranth-im.*
MEAT rat(NOM) exit-P.PFV hole-ABL
'A rat comes out of the hole.'

11.29 *Parr_r nhul ngeengk-rithrr ranci-rr.*
child(NOM) 3sg(NOM) belly-fat jump-P.PFV
'The boy gets a fright'.

11.30 *Nhul minc thatr waath-m ngul minh kaal ripi-rr.*
3sg(ERG) UNXP frog(ACC) search.for-P.IPFV then MEAT rat(NOM) exit-P.PFV
'He [the boy] was really looking for the frog, but it was a rat that came out.'

12.31 *May puunh wont-r yuk-um.*
VEG bee(NOM) fall-NPST tree-ABL
'The bees fall from the tree'

12.32 *May puunh wont-r raak-un.*
VEG bee(NOM) fall-NPST ground-DAT
'the bees fall to the ground'

12.33 *May puunh ulp ranth-im riprip-r,*
VEG bee(NOM) dem:ad.prx hole-ABL exit:RDP-NPST
'Those bees all come out of the hole [in their hive]'

12.34 *peln yarra riiric-r.*
3pl(NOM) away run:RDP-NPST
'and they fly away.'

13.35 *Parr_r nhul yuk punth-an nhiinhin.*
child(NOM) 3sg(NOM) TREE arm-DAT sit:RDP:NPST
'The child is sitting on a tree branch.'

14.36 *Minh thaapinyc ripi-rr yuk ranth-im.*
MEAT owl(NOM) exit-P.PFV TREE hole-ABL
'An owl came out of a hole in the tree.'

14.37 *Parr_r nhul wont-r thakr nhiin.*
child(NOM) 3sg(NOM) fall-NPST front sit:NPST
'The boy falls face down.'

15.38 *May puunh-thurr kuta waawarin-r.*
VEG bee-ERG dog(ACC) chase:RDP-NPST
'The bees are chasing the dog.'

16.39 *Minh thaapinyc-in parr_r waawarin-r.*
MEAT owl-ERG child(ACC) chase:RDP-NPST
'The owl is chasing the boy.'

16.40 *Parr_r nhul weneth miinng-r minh thaapinyc-ntam.*
child(NOM) 3sg(NOM) scared take.fright-NPST MEAT owl-ABL
'The boy is frightened of the owl.'

17.41 *Parr_r nhul putpun thanan therrep-ak, waawantharr.*
child(NOM) 3sg(NOM) on.top stand:RDP:NPST rock-DAT call.out:NPST
'The boy is standing on a rock, calling out.'

17.42 *Kuta nhul pal-kop therrep-ak yan, nhuunhuth-r.*
dog(NOM) 3sg(NOM) near-at:below rock-DAT go:NPST sniff:RDP-NPST
'The dog goes just behind the rock, sniffing.'

18.43 *Nhangun minh pul ripi-rr iipal.*
3sgDAT MEAT bull(NOM) exit-P.PFV from.there
'A bull comes out towards him,'

18.44 kaal-kay ngamal-kaak.
ear-metal large-REL.PROP
'[which] has large horns.'

18.45 Kuta nhul ngaathirr=p riiric-r, pal-kop therrep-ak.
dog(NOM) 3sg(NOM) still=PRAG run:RDP-NPST near-at:below rock-DAT
'The dog is still running behind the rock.'

19.46 Parr_r nhul putpun kal-r, kaal-kay okon.
child(ACC) 3sg(ERG) on.top carry-NPST ear-metal adjacent
'He [the bull] carries the child up high, next to its horns.'

19.47 Kuta-ku nhul yokunmanorrp riiric-r,
dog-ERG^ 3sg(NOM) same.way run:RDP-NPST
'The dog's also running,'

19.48 kuta-ku nhul kookoc-r.
dog-ERG 3sg(ERG) bark-NPST
'and the dog's barking.'

20.49 Minh-al thunpi-rr parr_r ngotonyci-ntam.
MEAT-ERG throw-P.PFV child(ACC) hill-ABL
'The bull has thrown the child from the hill.'

20.50 Kuta yokunmanorrp wont-r.
dog(NOM) same.way fall-NPST
'The dog also falls.'

21.51 Parr-an pul kuta-ku ngok-eln wont-r.
child-ERG^ 3du(NOM) dog-ERG^ water-DAT fall-NPST
'The child and the dog fall into the water together.'

22–23.52 Parr_r nhul rirk-r, kuta keren kalal.
child(NOM) 3sg(NOM) arise-P.PFV dog(ACC) up.high carry:RDP:INF
'The child got up, carrying the dog up high.'

24.53 Parr_r nhul yik-r kuta-ak: "kuuk=aar!".
child(NOM) 3sg(NOM) say-P.PFV dog-DAT WORD=ADN.PRIV
'The boy says to the dog "be quiet!"'

25.54 Parr-an pul kutaku yukun man+weewerngk-r
child-ERG 3du(ERG) dog-ERG tree-DAT throat+stare:RDP-NPST
i-rr-kop nhaanham.
there-towards-below look.at:RDP:NPST
'The boy and the dog are on a log staring, looking down below them.'

26.55 *Pul   minc   nhaawr   thatr kuthirr.*
      3du(ERG) UNXP   see:P.PFV   frog two(ACC)
      'they unexpectedly saw two frogs.'

27.56 *Yoorr pul   mangmangal.*
      now   3du(NOM) happy
      'now they're happy.'

28.57 *Parr_r   nhul   thatr   mi'irr   yuur-un.*
      child(#ERG) 3sg(ERG) frog(ACC) pick.up:NPST   hand-DAT
      'the boy picks up the frog in his hand.'

28.58 *Nhul   punth   rirk   yawo.*
      3sg(NOM) arm(NOM)   rise:NPST   goodbye
      'he waves goodbye.'

29.59 *Pul   yarra therk-r,*
      3du(NOM) away   return-P.PFV
      'the two of them have headed back.'

29.60 *Peln   that-nthurr nhaanham   pulnan.*
      3pl(ERG) frog-ERG   look.at:RDP:NPST   2duACC
      'The frogs watch the two of them [leave].'

30.61 *Kana.*
      finished
      'The end.'

Two Crocs

Author:	Donald William
Recording date:	9th December, 2002
Transcription collaborator:	Gilbert Jack
Transcription date:	16th December, 2002

Context: This story was told near Yawathan outstation. Donald William and his brother Cyril William sat on the sandy bank of a dry riverbed and sang the *wuuc* of the two crocodiles. To accompany the song, Donald William told the story of the two crocodiles both in English and Kuuk Thaayorre. This song and accompanying story features on the *Wuuch / Wanum: Songs of Pormpuraaw* CD (Charlie et al. 2003).

1. *inhul   yik-nhan=ay   nhul   minh   pinc   ii-kuw*
   this.one say-GO&:NPST=1sg(NOM) 3sg(NOM) MEAT   salt.croc(NOM) there:at-west
   'This story I'm going to tell [is about] the saltwater crocodile in the west'

2. *wuurr ko'o-m*
   fish.trap(ACC) pierce-P.IPFV
   '[who was] building a fish trap'

3. *minh kanharr riica-rr ii-rr-kuw mun-ica-rr ii-rr-kaw*
   MEAT fresh.croc(NOM) run-P.PFV there-to-west summon-RUN&-P.PFV there-to-east
   'The freshwater crocodile sped to the west to summon [the saltwater croc] to the east.'

4. *kuman rica-rr nhangun*
   thigh:DAT run-P.PFV 3sgDAT
   '[to tell the saltwater croc] to speed to him [freshwater croc]'
   "tell him to come"

5. *ngul nhunh ii-rr-kaw yithi-rr Minh.Ngaankana*
   then 3sgACC there-to-east lead-P.PFV Minh.Ngaankana
   'then [the freshwater crocodile] led him east to Minh Ngaankana'

6. *ngul Minh.Ngaankana nhunh ulp pungk-pirraa-rr*
   then Minh.Ngaankana 3sgACC dem:ad.prx knee-flog-P.PFV
   'and [the freshwater crocodile] flogged him at Minh Ngaankana'

7. *kirk-unca-rr=unh*[213]
   spear-stab-P.PFV=3sgACC
   '[the freshwater crocodile] speared him.'

8. *ngul pu'am ii-rr-kuw-op therk-r*
   then wounded there-to-west-river return-P.PFV
   'then [the saltwater crocodile] went back to the west by the river, wounded.'

9. *ii-rr-kuw therk-r yuuwir-n*
   there-to-west return-P.PFV ocean-DAT
   'he went back west to the ocean.'

10. *wuurr nhangn-man nhaath-nhat*
    fishtrap 3sgGEN-DAT look-GO&P.PFV
    'and looked at his fishtrap'

11. *inthul=ay yiik kuuk inhul*
    this.one(ACC)=1sg(NOM) say:NPST WORD this.one
    'This is the story I tell, these words.'

12. *minh pinc inhul*
    MEAT salt.croc this.one
    'this one about the saltwater crocodile.'

---

213 The form *kirkuncarr* results from the apparent compounding of *kirk* 'spear' and *runcarr* 'stabbed'.

13. *theernga-rr=unh*
    kill-P.PFV=3sgACC
    '[Of how the freshwater crocodile] killed him.'

14. *nhul   ii   thono=th   thuuth-m   ii-rr-kuw   waarrwaarr-ir*
    3sg(NOM) there   one=PRAG   crawl-P.IPFV there-to-west   bad:RDP-ir
    'This one, he was crawling towards the west, sick.'

15. *may   waawath-m   pungkurthaarr*
    VEG(ACC) search.for:RDP-P.IPFV   hungry
    'he was looking for food, hungry.'

16. *ngul may pucr   katpatp-m   raak ngurnturnturr*
    then VEG nonda(ACC) grasp:RDP-P.IPFV   TIME night
    'then he was feeling around for nonda nuts at night time.'

17. *ngul ulp   yuk   ulp   mungk-m   may   kunkunk*
    then dem:ad.prx THING(ACC) dem:ad.prx eat-P.IPFV   VEG(ACC) alive:RDP
    mungk-m   manthi-th   kaar=p
    eat-P.IPFV   ripe=PRAG   NEG=PRAG
    'he ate that, you know, that food raw, not ripe.'

18. *may   ulp   mungka-rr kunk   than-r*
    VEG(ACC) dem:ad.prx eat-P.PFV alive   stand-P.PFV
    mangr   min   yancm   ii-rr-kuw
    rather   good   go:P.IPFV   there-to-west
    'he ate that fruit raw, then he was healthy, he went to the west feeling good'

19. *ii-rr-kuw-op   thuuthuth-m   ulp*
    there-to-west-river   crawl:RDP-P.IPFV   dem:ad.prx
    'he was crawling westwards to the river.'

19. *inhul   ngay   yiik   inhul=p=le*
    this.one   1sg(NOM) say:RDP:NPST   this.one=PRAG=PRAG
    'This is the one I'm telling, this [story].'

Index of subjects

abbreviations xix, 16, 73, 195
ablative, see *case*
absolute frame of reference, see *adverbs > directional*
accusative, see *case*
adjectives 79, 87, 88, 98, 99, 104, 146–148, 196, 197, 201, 203–206, 235, 307, 310–312, 361, 362, 377, 378, 386, 391, 413, 438–442, 459
    predicate ~ 73, 87, 88, 307, 377, 378
adjunct 104, 105, 117–121, 132, 209, 222, 223, 241, 294, 342, 344, 350, 351, 357, 368, 369, 371–375, 385, 393, 417
adnominal case, see *case*
adnominal demonstratives, see *demonstratives > adnominal*
adverbs
    body part prefixes to ~ 97, 363
    directional ~ 73, 94–97, 343, 363, 385
    iterative ~ 98, 356, 358, 362
    manner ~ 98, 359–363
    modal ~ 268, 434
    pal 'towards' 40, 68, 93–96, 166–170, 267, 296, 338–349
    spatial ~ 94, 95, 133, 179, 181, 188, 318, 338, 342, 343, 350
    temporal ~ 98, 103, 133, 356–358, 362
agreement 221, 233, 234, 238, 372, 442; see also *apposition*, *interjections*, *referential case*
anaphora, see *reference tracking*
ancillary languages, see *registers*
apposition 78, 80, 124, 212, 216, 217, 232, 233, 237, 241, 416, 447, 448, 456
apprehensive, see *mood > apprehensive*
articles, see *determiners*
aspect, see also *particles > kana*
    distributive 82, 276, 428
    durative 65, 276–281
    imperfective 255, 261, 266, 269–275, 299, 321
    inceptive 267, 280, 283, 303–305, 322
    iterative 98, 272, 276–279, 281, 358, 425
    perfective 64, 255–262, 266, 268, 269, 271–273, 290, 299–301, 319, 321, 450, 453
    reciprocal 82, 88, 89, 150, 160, 224, 225, 228, 231, 234, 235, 257, 259, 290, 292, 293, 298–300, 370–374, 397, 414, 415, 417, 418, 420, 422–431

associated motion 88, 174, 257, 259, 267, 268, 283, 285, 291–293, 300–305, 322, 413, 432, 437
    first associated motion morpheme 257, 259, 283, 293, 300–305, 322, 413, 437
    second associated motion morpheme 257, 283, 293, 301, 304, 305
associative plural 97, 219, 254, 352, 355
aversive, see *mood > apprehensive ~*
avoidance, see *kinship*, *registers*

bereavement terms, see *kinship*
bivalent verbs 90, 91, 256, 260, 295, 307, 369, 377, 378; see also *adjectives > predicate ~*
body part terms 78, 79, 88, 89, 97, 100, 146–150, 255, 292, 297, 307, 309, 310, 313–317, 357, 363, 417, 418
    ~ compounded with verbs 313, 314
    ~ prefixed to adverbs 363

case
    ablative ~ 46, 105–108, 111, 114–116, 122, 130, 133–140, 153, 168, 176, 180, 181, 205, 242, 247, 275, 353, 354
    accusative 81, 87, 89, 104, 105, 107, 109, 111, 114, 115, 121, 122, 124, 125, 127, 152, 153, 155, 180, 225, 368, 370, 372, 376–381, 391, 415–418, 446, 447
    adnominal ~ 144, 223–225, 233, 240
    comitative ~ 105, 106, 111, 132, 140–143, 220, 222–225, 228, 233, 234, 294–296
    dative ~ 46, 52, 81, 83, 84, 89, 92, 97, 105–108, 111, 112, 114, 115, 118, 122, 124–132, 134, 136, 137, 140, 141, 153, 162, 163, 176, 177, 180–182, 213, 218, 220, 221, 223–225, 227–229, 234, 235, 239–241, 309, 352–354, 369, 371, 373–375, 380, 381, 393, 441
    ergative ~ 63, 75, 87, 91, 105–111, 113–120, 122, 125, 129, 133, 139, 140, 152, 153, 155, 168, 176, 177, 180, 182, 187, 205, 211, 220, 225, 226, 232–234, 246, 247, 370, 371, 377, 381, 415–418, 442, 446
    nominative ~ 81, 83, 84, 89, 104–111, 113–117, 120–123, 152, 153, 155–159, 176, 180, 220, 222, 224, 225, 227–230, 232, 233, 237, 310, 368, 370–373, 376, 378, 385, 391, 393, 415, 416, 418, 447, 448

Index of subjects — **495**

privative ~ 105, 106, 111, 141, 143–145, 249, 366, 403, 409
proprietive ~ 105, 106, 111, 124, 141–144, 329, 336, 439
referential ~ 216, 217, 221, 232, 233, 237, 240
relational ~ 127, 182
cataphora, see *reference tracking*
causative, see *valence increasing suffix*
classification, see *classifying construction, nouns > generic*
clausal coordination, see *complex clauses*
clausal negation, see *negation > negative particle* kaar
clause types, see *complex clauses, construction, reciprocal clauses, reflexive clauses, transitivity, verbless clauses*
clitics
    dubitative *=okun* 63, 69, 144, 172, 236, 333–335, 406, 407, 462
    focal *=thurr* 114, 247, 248
    =nhurr 'only' 103, 358
    pragmatic enclitics 56, 59, 61, 72, 104, 117, 145, 250, 251
    privative *=(k)aar* 105, 106, 111, 141, 143–145, 249, 366, 403, 409
    pronominal ~ 63, 81, 89, 104, 154–156
    proprietive *=(k)aak* 105, 106, 111, 124, 141–144, 329, 336, 439
    =yuk 'stuff' 151, 254
completive particle 122, 310, 321, 337
complex clauses 101, 397, 444, 446, 448, 454, 455, 459
compounding 43–46, 69, 72, 77, 79, 81, 88, 95, 104, 145–149, 157, 163, 176, 178, 255, 292, 307, 312–318, 341, 365, 376, 413, 424, 492
conjugation classes 89, 256–263, 268, 297, 299–301, 304, 307, 313, 415, 445
conjunction 230–235, 458–463; see also *coordination*
    asyndetic ~ 232, 458, 459
    concessive ~ 101, 235, 458, 463
constituent negation, see *negation > consitutent negator* pokon
consultants, see *language experts*
contradiction 102, 404; see also *negation > negative interjections*
contrastive *wuump*, see *particles*
coordination
    complex clauses 458, 463
    nominal ~ 230, 458

construction
    copula ~ 88, 120, 207, 250, 257, 277, 368, 378, 379, 381–387, 389–392, 395, 396, 405, 408, 451, 452
    existential ~ 382, 395, 396
    locative ~ 342, 350, 382, 384, 385, 392–395
    postural ~ 88, 382, 385, 390–395
copula verb, see *construction > copula*
coverbs, see *light verb* rirk

deixis, see also *pronouns, temporal adverbs, tense*
    recognitional ~, see *filler terms*
    spatial ~ 94, 95, 179, 181, 188, 318, 338, 343
demonstratives 56, 63, 73, 75, 80, 81, 86, 87, 89, 94, 95, 102, 152, 154, 162, 174, 178–197, 205–216, 242, 246, 250–254, 343, 368, 480; see also *determiners*
    adnominal ~ 56, 178–181, 183, 186, 187, 189, 191, 195, 208, 211, 212, 214–216, 246
    pronominal ~ 75, 80, 81, 86, 94, 154, 162, 174, 178–183, 186, 187, 190, 191, 194, 207–209, 242, 251–254, 343, 368
derivation 77, 81, 88, 89, 95, 98, 99, 104, 145–148, 150, 151, 158, 162, 163, 178, 198, 202, 203, 224, 225, 227, 231, 255–257, 259, 260, 262, 263, 280, 283, 291–293, 295–302, 304, 306–309, 313, 314, 322, 326, 358, 361, 365, 370–372, 374, 379, 384, 407, 409, 413, 415, 417, 426, 439
desiderative, see *mood > desiderative*
determiners
    demonstrative ~ 209–215
    determiner phrase 154, 209–212, 214–216
    pronominal ~ 163, 212, 213
directed verbal prefix 97
discourse, see *clitics > pragmatic enclitics, pronouns, emphasis and focus, hedging, interjections,* kana 'well', *nouns > generic, particles > ~, pronouns > demonstrative, reference tracking*
disjunction 235, 236, 336, 458, 462–464
dual number, see *pronouns*
dubitative, see *clitics > dubitative*
dyads 142, 223, 224

emphasis and focus
    focal enclitics 248, 250

pragmatic use of ergative case 119, 227, 286, 337, 449, 490; see also *pronouns > emphatic*
thono 'ONE' 207, 231, 232, 244–246, 461, 493
enclitics, see *clitics*
epenthetic or reduced vowels 51, 52, 62, 248, 299
etiquette, speech ~ 8, 15, 18–20, 236, 339, 399, 402, 410
evidentiality, see *pronouns > ignorative ~*
evitative, see *mood > apphrehensive ~*
exclusive, see *pronouns*
existential quantification 172

fast speech 52, 63, 64, 156, 180
filler terms 174, 194, 251–254
focus, see *clitics > focal* =thurr, *emphasis and focus*
frames of reference, see *adverbs > directional, topological relations markers*
future tense, see *associated motion*, *tense > non-past*

gender, see *nouns > generic*
gesture 11, 189, 191, 327, 328, 335, 364; see also *registers > hand signs*

hand signs, see *registers > hand signs*
hedging, see *clitics* > =yuk, *demonstrative pronouns > yuunh'nhul*, *particles > kar*, *particles > =okun*

ideophones 47, 58, 62, 63, 73, 99, 100, 364, 365
imminence, see *mood > imminence*
imperative, see *mood > imperative*
imperfective aspect, see *aspect > imperfective*
inclusive, see *pronouns*
inclusory constructions 142, 219–228, 230, 233, 234, 254; see also *pronouns > inclusory ~*
indefinite, see *demonstratives, ignoratives, pronouns*
indirect object 125, 221, 224, 225, 233, 234, 380
infinitive 291, 444, 445, 453
infixation 39, 54, 56, 65, 67, 89, 276
inflection 62, 63, 73, 75, 78, 80, 84–88, 92, 98, 104–106, 109, 110, 112, 114, 117, 123, 133, 138, 139, 152, 162, 163, 168, 176, 178, 182, 187, 195, 208, 211, 241, 247, 255, 256, 262, 263, 270, 283, 287, 288, 291, 293, 301, 304, 317, 344, 353, 378, 398–400, 403, 413, 432, 433, 437, 438, 451, 453

informants, see *language experts*
interjections 47, 56, 63, 99, 100, 102, 360, 365, 366, 403, 405, 482
interrogative, see *mood > interrogative*
intrinsic frame of reference, see *topological relations markers*
iterative adverbs, see *adverbs*

jussive, see *mood > jussive*

kinship 1, 8, 10–20, 29, 55, 77, 78, 126, 142, 147, 149, 195, 203, 204, 213, 221, 252, 254, 361, 367, 411, 434

language experts vii, 4, 12, 20, 22–29, 31, 33, 44, 112, 115, 142, 156, 160, 161, 167, 180, 189, 207, 253, 267, 295, 309, 321, 322, 324, 335, 442, 446, 480
lenition 45, 46
light verb *rirk* 92, 93, 292, 308–313
loan words 40, 62, 63, 79, 82, 92, 114, 125, 140, 150, 236, 268, 308, 309, 311–313, 424, 462

manner adverbs, see *adverbs*
manual register, see *registers > hand signs*
modal adverbs, see *adverbs*
mood, see also *negation*, *potential*
    apprehensive 84, 174, 289, 307, 397, 411, 413
    counterfactual 63, 84, 174, 255, 261, 286, 287, 289, 290, 332, 337, 338, 413
    desiderative 268, 285, 304, 397, 405, 432–438
    dubitative, see *clitics > dubitative*
    imminence 255, 261, 288–290
    imperative 69, 89, 102, 116, 255, 257–259, 261–263, 283, 291, 301, 326, 397–400, 402, 445
    interrogative 84, 161, 169–172, 333, 334, 341, 397, 398, 410, 435; see also *particles > contrastive* wuump, *registers > hand signs*
    jussive 283, 397, 398, 400, 402, 403, 437
modal particles 102, 399, 405
permissive 114, 247, 399
prohibitive 102, 283, 366, 398, 399, 410
purposive 255, 261, 287–290, 433, 434, 437, 438, 444, 445, 448, 454–457
subjunctive 255, 261, 268, 284–287, 290, 301, 302, 304, 432–435, 437, 457, 458

morphophonology 40, 45, 65, 148, 276, 386, 387
multilingualism 5, 8, 11, 13, 15, 22, 28
multiple case marking 139, 213, 247

names, see *nouns > proper*
negation, see also *case > privative*
    consitutent negator *pokon* 102, 174, 366, 396, 403, 404, 407–409
    negative interjections 366, 403
    negative particle *kaar* 145, 329, 336, 400, 403, 405, 407
nomen, see *nouns*
nomina, see *nouns*
nominalizer 88, 104, 292, 302, 308, 361
non-verbal clauses, see *verbless clauses*
noun phrase 73–80, 86, 97, 102, 104, 110, 112, 120, 121, 131, 134, 138, 140, 153, 154, 170, 176, 182, 183, 187, 195–197, 199–202, 204–211, 217, 219, 221, 222, 233, 240, 243, 245, 246, 309, 338, 342, 343, 350, 369, 372, 391, 394, 407, 440, 446, 447, 452
nouns, see also *nominalizer*
    generic ~ 73, 75, 76, 78, 79, 104, 130, 148, 151, 163, 196–205, 242, 243, 357, 366
    proper ~ 76, 79, 164, 167, 250
    specific ~ 73, 75–79, 104, 196–205, 211, 243, 357
nucleus 51, 52, 55, 56, 58, 59, 62, 69
number, see *numerals and quantifiers, pronouns*
numerals and quantifiers 80, 150, 207, 358

object
    direct ~ 87, 92, 121, 122, 125, 127, 166, 176, 196, 225, 294, 296, 297, 311, 370–372, 376, 377, 379, 380, 383, 412, 415–418, 426, 427, 442, 446, 447, 457, 459
    indirect ~ 125, 221, 224, 225, 233, 234, 380
onset 37, 39, 40, 43, 46, 53–55, 58, 60, 62–65, 67, 149, 276–279
optional ergativity, see *emphasis and focus*
orthography 24, 31, 37, 43, 70, 71

particles, see also *interjections, negation > consitutent negator pokon, negation > negative particle kaar*
    ak 'optative' 56, 319, 400, 402, 437, 456
    angarr 88, 102, 284, 285, 319, 331, 362, 378, 432–434, 436, 437, 457

contrastive *wuump* 101, 102, 131, 137, 155, 238, 246, 285, 302, 332–334, 349, 377, 397, 398, 463
kana 'well' 60, 319–325
kar 'like' 101, 102, 328, 329, 331, 332, 449, 454, 455, 458
kirri 'permissive' 59, 60, 102, 114, 247, 399
minc 'against expectations' 102, 337, 338, 488, 491
ngul 'then' 48, 460, 461, 464
=*okun* 'dubitative' 63, 102, 144, 172, 235, 236, 333–336, 406, 407, 462
ongkorr 'prohibitive' 102, 229, 283, 310, 326, 366, 398–400, 410–412, 433, 485
yarriy 'thus' 117, 179, 242, 250, 299, 325–328, 359, 360, 371, 374, 388, 450, 461, 483, 484
past tense, see *tense > past*
perfective aspect, see *aspect > perfective*
permissive, see *mood > permissive*
person marking, see *pronouns*
phonotactics 51, 54–56, 58, 62, 63, 69, 99, 262, 364
plural number, see *pronouns*
politeness, see *etiquette > speech*
possession, see also *case > ablative, case > proprietive, pronouns > genitive*
    alienable ~, see *case > genitive*
    inalienable ~, see *apposition*
possessive pronouns, see *pronouns > genitive*
postpositions, see *case, topological relations markers*
postural verbs, see *postural construction*
potential 284, 285, 333, 411–413, 437, 439; see also *mood > subjunctive, particles > contrastive wuump, particles > =okun*
    ~ detriment 411–413, 485
pragmatics, see *clitics > pragmatic enclitics, discourse, etiquette > speech, registers*
prepositions, see *case, topological relations markers*
privative, see *case > privative*
prohibitive, see *mood > prohibitive*
pronouns, see also *demonstratives > pronominal, determiners*
    emphatic ~ 66, 68, 74, 80–83, 152, 158–160, 163, 180, 186, 250, 419
    enclitic ~ 63, 74, 81, 88, 89, 152, 154–156, 238, 282, 447

genitive ~ 52, 53, 73, 78, 81, 106, 110–112, 139, 196, 207, 209, 240–242
ignorative ~ 73, 74, 80, 84, 85, 152, 161–164, 171–174, 195, 205, 207–209, 253, 254, 334
inclusory ~ 80, 83, 84, 152, 160, 161, 220, 227–229
personal ~ 80, 81, 83, 101, 105, 106, 110, 122, 124, 152–154, 163, 176, 178, 179, 187, 205, 209, 215, 227, 229, 232, 370
reciprocal subject marker 82
reflexive ~ 80–82, 152, 156–158, 228, 414, 415, 418, 419, 428, 429
proprietive, see *case > proprietive*
prosody 45, 70, 99, 195, 212, 216, 218, 364–366, 397, 450, 453, 455, 459
purposive, see *mood > purposive*

questions, see *mood > interrogative*

reciprocal clauses 82, 88, 89, 150, 160, 224, 225, 228, 231, 234, 235, 257, 259, 290, 292, 293, 298–300, 370–374, 397, 414, 415, 417, 418, 420, 422–431, 480; see also *pronouns > reciprocal subject marker*
reduced vowels, see *epenthetic or reduced vowels*
reduplication 40, 41, 65–68, 79, 83, 89, 99, 146, 158, 163, 255, 256, 276–281, 357, 425, 445
reference tracking 80, 207, 237, 242
reflexive clauses 44, 63, 64, 80–82, 88, 89, 119, 152, 156–158, 228, 256, 257, 259, 292, 293, 298, 299, 370–372, 374, 383, 397, 414–424, 427–429; see also *pronouns > reflexive*
registers
    hand signs 8, 10–12, 16, 29, 78
    respect register 8, 10, 12, 13
    song language 10, 21, 28–30
respect vocabulary, see *registers > respect register*
rhyme 54, 60, 65–68, 276–281

secondary predication 237, 250, 440–443
semantic role, see *case*
singular number, see *pronouns*
speech etiquette, see *etiquette > speech*
stress 46, 68–70, 102, 103, 196, 226, 229, 245, 265, 304, 329, 389, 418, 459
    unstressed syllables 45, 46, 52, 53, 67, 69, 70, 154, 156, 329

subject
    intransitive ~ 122, 176, 226, 293–296, 371, 412, 442
    transitive ~ 117–119, 122, 138, 140, 196, 226, 293, 295, 296, 418, 442
subjunctive, see *mood > subjunctive*
subordinate clauses 172, 285, 291, 292, 305, 306, 332, 433, 434, 438, 444–459
    insubordination 285, 433
suffixaufnahme, see *multiple case marking*
syllable structure, see *phonotactics*
syntax, see *complex clauses, noun phrase*

temporal adverbs, see *adverbs*
tense, see also *adverbs > temporal*
    nonpast ~ 89, 231, 255–259, 261, 263–268, 273, 278, 282, 283, 299–301, 319, 321, 322, 400, 403, 413, 432, 435–438, 445, 450, 451, 453
    past ~ 64, 89, 255–262, 266, 268–275, 290, 299–301, 321, 450, 453
thematic role, see *case*
topic 138, 141, 185, 186, 213, 226, 244, 248, 250, 323, 325, 395, 451
topological relation markers 94, 97, 254, 351, 352, 354, 363, 385, 480, 481
transitivity, see also *valency*
    ditransitive clauses 90, 105, 117, 125, 225, 309, 368, 369, 380, 381, 456
    intransitive clauses 89–92, 118–122, 159, 176, 220, 225, 226, 237, 257, 293–296, 302, 308, 310, 312, 368–373, 376, 377, 379, 383, 385, 391, 412, 415–417, 427, 429, 430, 440, 442
    intransitive copula clauses 90, 120, 369, 373
    quasitransitive clauses 91, 120, 368–370, 376–378, 380
    semiditransitive clauses 90, 117, 120, 125, 257, 369, 370, 380, 381
    semitransitive clauses 89–91, 120, 257, 368–370, 373–375, 380, 381
    transitive clauses 89–92, 113, 117–122, 138, 140, 160, 196, 225, 226, 234, 257, 293–297, 302, 308, 312, 368–373, 375–377, 379–381, 383, 412, 415–418, 427–429, 440, 442, 446
    transitive copula clauses 90, 369, 379, 381
transitivizer, see *valence increasing suffix*
trivalent verbs 90, 368, 369, 381, 426

universal quantification 172, 359

valence increasing suffix 256, 280, 296, 371, 379
valency, see also *transitivity*
    bivalent verbs 90, 91, 256, 260, 295, 307, 369, 377, 378
    monovalent verbs 90, 257, 295, 307, 368, 369

verbalizer 257, 292, 306–308, 313, 361
verbless clauses 439
verb phrase *absent in Kuuk Thaayorre*
verbs, see *valency*
vocative kin terms, see *kinship*
voicing 38–43, 45, 67, 145

word order, see *noun phrase*

www.ingramcontent.com/pod-product-compliance
Lightning Source LLC
Chambersburg PA
CBHW081532300426
44116CB00015B/2598